DRIVER'S RECEIPT

This issue of the FMCSR Pocketbook includes all revisions issued on or before November 9, 2021.

I acknowledge receipt of this FEDERAL MOTOR CARRIER SAFETY REGULATIONS POCKETBOOK (347). In addition, I agree to familiarize myself with the Federal Motor Carrier Safety Regulations (FMCSR) of the U.S. Department of Transportation, Parts 40, 380, 382, 383, 387, 390-397, and 399 of Subchapter B, Chapter III, Title 49 of the Code of Federal Regulations, as contained therein.

D0050201

_____   _____
DRIVER'S NAME (PLEASE PRINT)   DATE

_____
DRIVER'S SIGNATURE

_____
SUPERVISOR OR CARRIER REPRESENTATIVE SIGNATURE

12/21

NOTE: This receipt shall be read and signed by the driver. A responsible company supervisor or carrier representative shall countersign the receipt and place in the driver's qualification file.

Copyright J. J. Keller & Associates, Inc.

REMOVABLE PAGE - PULL SLOWLY FROM TOP RIGHT CORNER

FEDERAL MOTOR CARRIER SAFETY REGULATIONS POCKETBOOK

This issue of the FMCSR Pocketbook includes all revisions issued on or before November 9, 2021. Featured revisions include:

PART(S) REVISED	SUBJECT	EFFECTIVE DATE
393, 396	Annual inspection of rear impact guards.	12/9/21
382, 383, 390, 392	State requirements for using drug and alcohol clearinghouse information.	11/8/21
Revisions in most parts	Technical amendments.	10/14/21
382, 383, 390, 391	Technical amendments.	7/7/21, 9/7/21
383, 391	Compliance date extended from June 22, 2021, to June 23, 2025, for certain med-exam certification provisions.	6/22/21
395	Definition of agricultural commodity.	12/9/20
395	Hours of service limits and exceptions.	9/29/20
396	DVIRs for passenger-carrying vehicles.	9/17/20
380, 383	Extended compliance date for entry-level driver training (ELDT) from February 7, 2020, to February 7, 2022.	2/4/20
382	Added note that random drug test rate increased.	1/1/20

Copyright 2021
J. J. Keller & Associates, Inc.
3003 Breezewood Lane, P.O. Box 368
Neenah,Wisconsin 54957-0368 USA
Phone 800-327-6868
JJKeller.com

Library of Congress Catalog Card Number: 7532244
ISBN: 978-1-60287-594-4

Canadian Goods and Services Tax (GST) Number: R123-317687

All rights reserved. Neither the FMCSR Pocketbook nor any part thereof may be reproduced in any manner without written permission of the Publisher.

Due to the constantly changing nature of government regulations, it is impossible to guarantee absolute accuracy of the material contained herein. The Publisher and Editors, therefore, cannot assume any responsibility for omissions, errors, misprinting, or ambiguity contained within this publication and shall not be held liable in any degree for any loss or injury caused by such omission, error, misprinting or ambiguity presented in this publication.

This publication is designed to provide reasonably accurate and authoritative information in regard to the subject matter covered. It is sold with the understanding that the Publisher is not engaged in rendering legal, accounting, or other professional service. If legal advice or other expert assistance is required, the services of a competent professional person should be sought.

CONTENTS

PART 40—PROCEDURES FOR TRANSPORTATION WORKPLACE DRUG AND ALCOHOL TESTING PROGRAMS

Subpart A—Administrative provisions

Subpart B—Employer responsibilities

Subpart C—Urine collection personnel

Subpart D—Collection sites, forms, equipment and supplies used in DOT urine collections

Subpart H—Split specimen tests

Subpart I—Problems in drug tests

AUTHORITY: 49 U.S.C. 102, 301, 322, 5331, 20140, 31306, and 54101 *et seq.*

Subpart A—Administrative Provisions

§40.1 Who does this regulation cover?

(a) This part tells all parties who conduct drug and alcohol tests required by Department of Transportation (DOT) agency regulations how to conduct these tests and what procedures to use.

(b) This part concerns the activities of transportation employers, safety-sensitive transportation employees (including self-employed individuals, contractors and volunteers as covered by DOT agency regulations), and service agents.

(c) Nothing in this part is intended to supersede or conflict with the implementation of the Federal Railroad Administration's post-accident testing program (see 49 CFR 219.200).

§40.3 What do the terms used in this part mean?

In this part, the terms listed in this section have the following meanings:

Adulterated specimen. A specimen that has been altered, as evidenced by test results showing either a substance that is not a normal constituent for that type of specimen or showing an abnormal concentration of an endogenous substance.

Affiliate. Persons are affiliates of one another if, directly or indirectly, one controls or has the power to control the other, or a third party controls or has the power to control both. Indicators of control include, but are not limited to: interlocking management or ownership; shared interest among family members; shared facilities or equipment; or common use of employees. Following the issuance of a public interest exclusion, an organization having the same or similar management, ownership, or principal employees as the service agent concerning whom a public interest exclusion is in effect is regarded as an affiliate. This definition is used in connection with the public interest exclusion procedures of Subpart R of this part.

Air blank. In evidential breath testing devices (EBTs) using gas chromatography technology, a reading of the device's internal standard. In all other EBTs, a reading of ambient air containing no alcohol.

Alcohol. The intoxicating agent in beverage alcohol, ethyl alcohol or other low molecular weight alcohols, including methyl or isopropyl alcohol.

Alcohol concentration. The alcohol in a volume of breath expressed in terms of grams of alcohol per 210 liters of breath as indicated by a breath test under this part.

Alcohol confirmation test. A subsequent test using an EBT, following a screening test with a result of 0.02 or greater, that provides quantitative data about the alcohol concentration.

Alcohol screening device (ASD). A breath or saliva device, other than an EBT, that is approved by the National Highway Traffic Safety Administration (NHTSA) and appears on ODAPC's Web page for "Approved Screening Devices to Measure Alcohol in Bodily Fluids" because it conforms to the model specifications from NHTSA.

Alcohol screening test. An analytic procedure to determine whether an employee may have a prohibited concentration of alcohol in a breath or saliva specimen.

Alcohol testing site. A place selected by the employer where employees present themselves for the purpose of providing breath or saliva for an alcohol test.

Alcohol use. The drinking or swallowing of any beverage, liquid mixture or preparation (including any medication), containing alcohol.

Aliquot. A fractional part of a specimen used for testing. It is taken as a sample representing the whole specimen.

Breath Alcohol Technician (BAT). A person who instructs and assists employees in the alcohol testing process and operates an evidential breath testing device.

Cancelled test. A drug or alcohol test that has a problem identified that cannot be or has not been corrected, or which this part otherwise requires to be cancelled. A cancelled test is neither a positive nor a negative test.

Chain of custody. The procedure used to document the handling of the urine specimen from the time the employee gives the specimen to the collector until the specimen is destroyed. This procedure uses the Federal Drug Testing Custody and Control Form (CCF) as approved by the Office of Management and Budget.

Collection container. A container into which the employee urinates to provide the specimen for a drug test.

Collection site. A place selected by the employer where employees present themselves for the purpose of providing a urine specimen for a drug test.

Collector. A person who instructs and assists employees at a collection site, who receives and makes an initial inspection of the specimen provided by those employees, and who initiates and completes the CCF.

Confirmatory drug test. A second analytical procedure performed on a different aliquot of the original specimen to identify and quantify the presence of a specific drug or drug metabolite.

Confirmatory validity test. A second test performed on a different aliquot of the original urine specimen to further support a validity test result.

Confirmed drug test. A confirmation test result received by an MRO from a laboratory.

Consortium/Third-party administrator (C/TPA). A service agent that provides or coordinates the provision of a variety of drug and alcohol testing services to employers. C/TPAs typically perform administrative tasks concerning the operation of the employers' drug and alcohol testing programs. This term includes, but is not limited to, groups of employers who join together to administer, as a single entity, the DOT drug and alcohol testing programs of its members. C/TPAs are not "employers" for purposes of this part.

Continuing education. Training for substance abuse professionals (SAPs) who have completed qualification training and are performing SAP functions, designed to keep SAPs current on changes and developments in the DOT drug and alcohol testing program.

Designated employer representative (DER). An employee authorized by the employer to take immediate action(s) to remove employees from safety-sensitive duties, or cause employees to be removed from these covered duties, and to make required decisions in the testing and evaluation processes. The DER also receives test results and other communications for the employer, consistent with the requirements of this part. Service agents cannot act as DERs.

Dilute specimen. A urine specimen with creatinine and specific gravity values that are lower than expected for human urine.

DOT, The Department, DOT agency. These terms encompass all DOT agencies, including, but not limited to, the Federal Aviation Administration (FAA), the Federal Railroad Administration (FRA), the Federal Motor Carrier Safety Administration (FMCSA), the Federal Transit Administration (FTA), the National Highway Traffic Safety Administration (NHTSA), the Pipeline and Hazardous Materials Safety Administration (PHMSA), and the Office of the Secretary (OST). For purposes of this part, the United States Coast Guard (USCG), in the Department of Homeland Security, is considered to be a DOT agency for drug testing purposes only since the USCG regulation does not incorporate Part 40 for its alcohol testing program. These terms include any designee of a DOT agency.

Drugs. The drugs for which tests are required under this part and DOT agency regulations are marijuana, cocaine, amphetamines, phencyclidine (PCP), and opioids.

Employee. Any person who is designated in a DOT agency regulation as subject to drug testing and/or alcohol testing. The term includes individuals currently performing safety-sensitive functions designated in DOT agency regulations and applicants for employment subject to pre-employment testing. For purposes of drug testing under this part, the term employee has the same meaning as the term "donor" as found on CCF and related guidance materials produced by the Department of Health and Human Services.

Employer. A person or entity employing one or more employees (including an individual who is self-employed) subject to DOT agency regulations requiring compliance with this part. The term includes an employer's officers, representatives, and management personnel. Service agents are not employers for the purposes of this part.

Error Correction Training. Training provided to BATs, collectors, and screening test technicians (STTs) following an error that resulted in the cancellation of a drug or alcohol test. Error correction training must be provided in person or by a means that provides real-time observation and interaction between the instructor and trainee.

Evidential Breath Testing Device (EBT). A device that is approved by the National Highway Traffic Safety Administration (NHTSA) for the evidential testing of breath at the .02 and .04 alcohol concentrations, and appears on ODAPC's Web page for "Approved Evidential Breath Measurement Devices" because it conforms with the model specifications available from NHTSA.

HHS. The Department of Health and Human Services or any designee of the Secretary, Department of Health and Human Services.

Initial drug test (also known as a "Screening drug test"). The test used to differentiate a negative specimen from one that requires further testing for drugs or drug metabolites.

Initial specimen validity test. The first test used to determine if a urine specimen is adulterated, diluted, substituted, or invalid.

Invalid drug test. The result reported by an HHS-certified laboratory in accordance with the criteria established by HHS Mandatory Guidelines when a positive, negative, adulterated, or substituted result cannot be established for a specific drug or specimen validity test.

Invalid result. The result reported by a laboratory for a urine specimen that contains an unidentified adulterant, contains an unidentified interfering substance, has an abnormal physical characteristic, or has an endogenous substance at an abnormal concentration that prevents the laboratory from completing testing or obtaining a valid drug test result.

Laboratory. Any U.S. laboratory certified by HHS under the National Laboratory Certification Program as meeting the minimum standards of Subpart C of the HHS Mandatory Guidelines for Federal Workplace Drug Testing Programs; or, in the case of foreign laboratories, a laboratory approved for participation by DOT under this part.

Limit of Detection (LOD). The lowest concentration at which a measurand can be identified, but (for quantitative assays) the concentration cannot be accurately calculated.

Limit of Quantitation. For quantitative assays, the lowest concentration at which the identity and concentration of the measurand can be accurately established.

Medical Review Officer (MRO). A person who is a licensed physician and who is responsible for receiving and reviewing laboratory results generated by an employer's drug testing program and evaluating medical explanations for certain drug test results.

Negative result. The result reported by an HHS-certified laboratory to an MRO when a specimen contains no drug or the concentration of the drug is less than the cutoff concentration for the drug or drug class and the specimen is a valid specimen.

Non-negative specimen. A urine specimen that is reported as adulterated, substituted, positive (for drug(s) or drug metabolite(s)), and/or invalid.

Office of Drug and Alcohol Policy and Compliance (ODAPC). The office in the Office of the Secretary, DOT, that is responsible for coordinating drug and alcohol testing program matters within the Department and providing information concerning the implementation of this part.

Oxidizing adulterant. A substance that acts alone or in combination with other substances to oxidize drugs or drug metabolites to prevent the detection of the drug or drug metabolites, or affects the reagents in either the initial or confirmatory drug test.

Positive result. The result reported by an HHS-certified laboratory when a specimen contains a drug or drug metabolite equal to or greater than the cutoff concentrations.

Primary specimen. In drug testing, the urine specimen bottle that is opened and tested by a first laboratory to determine whether the employee has a drug or drug metabolite in his or her system; and for the purpose of validity testing. The primary specimen is distinguished from the split specimen, defined in this section.

Qualification Training. The training required in order for a collector, BAT, MRO, SAP, or STT to be qualified to perform their functions in the DOT drug and alcohol testing program. Qualification training may be provided by any appropriate means (*e.g.,* classroom instruction, internet application, CD-ROM, video).

Reconfirmed. The result reported for a split specimen when the second laboratory is able to corroborate the original result reported for the primary specimen.

Refresher Training. The training required periodically for qualified collectors, BATs, and STTs to review basic requirements and provide instruction concerning changes in technology (*e.g.,* new testing methods that may be authorized) and amendments, interpretations, guidance, and issues concerning this part and DOT agency drug and alcohol testing regulations. Refresher training can be provided by any appropriate means (*e.g.,* classroom instruction, internet application, CD-ROM, video).

Rejected for testing. The result reported by an HHS-certified laboratory when no tests are performed for a specimen because of a fatal flaw or a correctable flaw that is not corrected.

Screening drug test. See Initial drug test definition above.

Screening Test Technician (STT). A person who instructs and assists employees in the alcohol testing process and operates an ASD.

Secretary. The Secretary of Transportation or the Secretary's designee.

Service agent. Any person or entity, other than an employee of the employer, who provides services to employers and/or employees in connection with DOT drug and alcohol testing requirements. This includes, but is not limited to, collectors, BATs and STTs, laboratories, MROs, substance abuse professionals, and C/TPAs. To act as service agents, persons and organizations must meet DOT qualifications, if applicable. Service agents are not employers for purposes of this part.

Shipping container. A container that is used for transporting and protecting urine specimen bottles and associated documents from the collection site to the laboratory.

Specimen bottle. The bottle that, after being sealed and labeled according to the procedures in this part, is used to hold the urine specimen during transportation to the laboratory.

Split specimen. In drug testing, a part of the urine specimen that is sent to a first laboratory and retained unopened, and which is transported to a second laboratory in the event that the employee requests that it be tested following a verified positive test of the primary specimen or a verified adulterated or substituted test result.

Split specimen collection. A collection in which the urine collected is divided into two separate specimen bottles, the primary specimen (Bottle A) and the split specimen (Bottle B).

Stand-down. The practice of temporarily removing an employee from the performance of safety-sensitive functions based only on a report from a laboratory to the MRO of a confirmed positive test for a drug or drug metabolite, an adulterated test, or a substituted test, before the MRO has completed verification of the test result.

Substance Abuse Professional (SAP). A person who evaluates employees who have violated a DOT drug and alcohol regulation and makes recommendations concerning education, treatment, follow-up testing, and aftercare.

Substituted specimen. A urine specimen with creatinine and specific gravity values that are so diminished or so divergent that they are not consistent with normal human urine.

Verified test. A drug test result or validity testing result from an HHS-certified laboratory that has undergone review and final determination by the MRO.

§40.5 Who issues authoritative interpretations of this regulation?

ODAPC and the DOT Office of General Counsel (OGC) provide written interpretations of the provisions of this part. These written DOT interpretations are the only official and authoritative interpretations concerning the provisions of this part. DOT agencies may incorporate ODAPC/OGC interpretations in written guidance they issue concerning drug and alcohol testing matters. Only Part 40 interpretations issued after August 1, 2001, are considered valid.

§40.7 How can you get an exemption from a requirement in this regulation?

(a) If you want an exemption from any provision of this part, you must request it in writing from the Office of the Secretary of Transportation, under the provisions and standards of 49 CFR part 5. You must send requests for an exemption to the following address: Department of Transportation, Deputy Assistant General Counsel for Regulation and Enforcement, 1200 New Jersey Avenue, SE., Washington, DC 20590.

(b) Under the standards of 49 CFR part 5, we will grant the request only if the request documents special or exceptional circumstances, not likely to be generally applicable and not contemplated in connection with the rulemaking that established this part, that make your compliance with a specific provision of this part impracticable.

(c) If we grant you an exemption, you must agree to take steps we specify to comply with the intent of the provision from which an exemption is granted.

(d) We will issue written responses to all exemption requests.

Subpart B—Employer Responsibilities

§40.11 What are the general responsibilities of employers under this regulation?

(a) As an employer, you are responsible for meeting all applicable requirements and procedures of this part.

(b) You are responsible for all actions of your officials, representatives, and agents (including service agents) in carrying out the requirements of the DOT agency regulations.

(c) All agreements and arrangements, written or unwritten, between and among employers and service agents concerning the implementation of DOT drug and alcohol testing requirements are deemed, as a matter of law, to require compliance with all applicable provisions of this part and DOT agency drug and alcohol testing regulations. Compliance with these provisions is a material term of all such agreements and arrangements.

§40.13 How do DOT drug and alcohol tests relate to non-DOT tests?

(a) DOT tests must be completely separate from non-DOT tests in all respects.

(b) DOT tests must take priority and must be conducted and completed before a non-DOT test is begun. For example, you must discard any excess urine left over from a DOT test and collect a separate void for the subsequent non-DOT test.

(c) Except as provided in paragraph (d) of this section, you must not perform any tests on DOT urine or breath specimens other than those specifically authorized by this part or DOT agency regulations. For example, you may not test a DOT urine specimen for additional drugs, and a laboratory is prohibited from making a DOT urine specimen available for a DNA test or other types of specimen identity testing.

(d) The single exception to paragraph (c) of this section is when a DOT drug test collection is conducted as part of a physical examination required by DOT agency regulations. It is permissible to conduct required medical tests related to this physical examination (*e.g.,* for glucose) on any urine remaining in the collection container after the drug test urine specimens have been sealed into the specimen bottles.

(e) No one is permitted to change or disregard the results of DOT tests based on the results of non-DOT tests. For example, as an employer you must not disregard a verified positive DOT drug test result because the employee presents a negative test result from a blood or urine specimen collected by the employee's physician or a DNA test result purporting to question the identity of the DOT specimen.

(f) As an employer, you must not use the CCF or the ATF in your non-DOT drug and alcohol testing programs. This prohibition includes the use of the DOT forms with references to DOT programs and agencies crossed out. You also must always use the CCF and ATF for all your DOT-mandated drug and alcohol tests.

§40.14 What collection information must employers provide to collectors?

As an employer, or an employer's service agent—for example a C/TPA, you must ensure the collector has the following information when conducting a urine specimen collection for you:

(a) Full name of the employee being tested.

(b) Employee SSN or ID number.

(c) Laboratory name and address (can be pre-printed on the CCF).

(d) Employer name, address, phone number, and fax number (can be pre-printed on the CCF at Step 1-A).

(e) DER information required at §40.35 of this part.

(f) MRO name, address, phone number, and fax number (can be pre-printed on the CCF at Step 1-B).

(g) The DOT Agency which regulates the employee's safety-sensitive duties (the checkmark can pre-printed in the appropriate box on the CCF at Step 1-D).

(h) Test reason, as appropriate: Pre-employment; Random; Reasonable Suspicion/Reasonable Cause; Post-Accident; Return-to-Duty; and Follow-up.

(i) Whether the test is to be observed or not (see §40.67 of this part).

(j) (Optional) C/TPA name, address, phone, and fax number (can be pre-printed on the CCF).

§40.15 May an employer use a service agent to meet DOT drug and alcohol testing requirements?

(a) As an employer, you may use a service agent to perform the tasks needed to comply with this part and DOT agency drug and alcohol testing regulations, consistent with the requirements of Subpart Q and other applicable provisions of this part.

(b) As an employer, you are responsible for ensuring that the service agents you use meet the qualifications set forth in this part (*e.g.,* §40.121 for MROs). You may require service agents to show you documentation that they meet the requirements of this part (*e.g.,* documentation of MRO qualifications required by §40.121(e)).

(c) You remain responsible for compliance with all applicable requirements of this part and other DOT drug and alcohol testing regulations, even when you use a service agent. If you violate this part or other DOT drug and alcohol testing regulations because a service agent has not provided services as our rules require, a DOT agency can subject you to sanctions. Your good faith use of a service agent is not a defense in an enforcement action initiated by a DOT agency in which your alleged noncompliance with this part or a DOT agency drug and alcohol regulation may have resulted from the service agent's conduct.

(d) As an employer, you must not permit a service agent to act as your DER.

§40.17 Is an employer responsible for obtaining information from its service agents?

Yes, as an employer, you are responsible for obtaining information required by this part from your service agents. This is true whether or not you choose to use a C/TPA as an intermediary in transmitting information to you. For example, suppose an applicant for a safety-sensitive job takes a pre-employment drug test, but there is a significant delay in your receipt of the test result from an MRO or C/TPA. You must not assume that "no news is good news" and permit the applicant to perform safety-sensitive duties before receiving the result. This is a violation of the Department's regulations.

§40.19 [Reserved]

§40.21 May an employer stand down an employee before the MRO has completed the verification process?

(a) As an employer, you are prohibited from standing employees down, except consistent with a waiver a DOT agency grants under this section.

(b) You may make a request to the concerned DOT agency for a waiver from the prohibition of paragraph (a) of this section. Such a waiver, if granted, permits you to stand an employee down following the MRO's receipt of a laboratory report of a confirmed positive test for a drug or drug metabolite, an adulterated test, or a substituted test pertaining to the employee.

(1) For this purpose, the concerned DOT agency is the one whose drug and alcohol testing rules apply to the majority of the covered employees in your organization. The concerned DOT agency uses its applicable procedures for considering requests for waivers.

(2) Before taking action on a waiver request, the concerned DOT agency coordinates with other DOT agencies that regulate the employer's other covered employees.

(3) The concerned DOT agency provides a written response to each employer that petitions for a waiver, setting forth the reasons for the agency's decision on the waiver request.

(c) Your request for a waiver must include, as a minimum, the following elements:

(1) Information about your organization:

(i) Your determination that standing employees down is necessary for safety in your organization and a statement of your basis for it, including any data on safety problems or incidents that could have been prevented if a stand-down procedure had been in place;

(ii) Data showing the number of confirmed laboratory positive, adulterated, and substituted test results for your employees over the two calendar years preceding your waiver request, and the number and percentage of those test results that were verified positive, adulterated, or substituted by the MRO;

(iii) Information about the work situation of the employees subject to stand-down, including a description of the size and organization of the unit(s) in which the employees work, the process through which employees will be informed of the stand-down, whether there is an in-house MRO, and whether your organization has a medical disqualification or stand-down policy for employees in situations other than drug and alcohol testing; and

(iv) A statement of which DOT agencies regulate your employees.

(2) Your proposed written company policy concerning stand-down, which must include the following elements:

(i) Your assurance that you will distribute copies of your written policy to all employees that it covers;

(ii) Your means of ensuring that no information about the confirmed positive, adulterated, or substituted test result or the reason for the employee's temporary removal from performance of safety-sensitive functions becomes available, directly or indirectly, to anyone in your organization (or subsequently to another employer) other than the employee, the MRO and the DER;

(iii) Your means of ensuring that all covered employees in a particular job category in your organization are treated the same way with respect to stand-down;

(iv) Your means of ensuring that a covered employee will be subject to stand-down only with respect to the actual performance of safety-sensitive duties;

(v) Your means of ensuring that you will not take any action adversely affecting the employee's pay and benefits pending the completion of the MRO's verification process. This includes continuing to pay the employee during the period of the stand-down in the same way you would have paid him or her had he or she not been stood down;

(vi) Your means of ensuring that the verification process will commence no later than the time an employee is temporarily removed from the performance of safety-sensitive functions and that the period of stand-down for any employee will not exceed five days, unless you are informed in writing by the MRO that a longer period is needed to complete the verification process; and

(vii) Your means of ensuring that, in the event that the MRO verifies the test negative or cancels it—

(A) You return the employee immediately to the performance of safety-sensitive duties;

(B) The employee suffers no adverse personnel or financial consequences as a result; and

(C) You maintain no individually identifiable record that the employee had a confirmed laboratory positive, adulterated, or substituted test result (*i.e.*, you maintain a record of the test only as a negative or cancelled test).

(d) The Administrator of the concerned DOT agency, or his or her designee, may grant a waiver request only if he or she determines that, in the context of your organization, there is a high probability that the procedures you propose will effectively enhance safety and protect the interests of employees in fairness and confidentiality.

(1) The Administrator, or his or her designee, may impose any conditions he or she deems appropriate on the grant of a waiver.

(2) The Administrator, or his or her designee, may immediately suspend or revoke the waiver if he or she determines that you have failed to protect effectively the interests of employees in fairness and confidentiality, that you have failed to comply with the requirements of this section, or that you have failed to comply with any other conditions the DOT agency has attached to the waiver.

(e) You must not stand employees down in the absence of a waiver, or inconsistent with the terms of your waiver. If you do, you are in violation of this part and DOT agency drug testing regulations, and you are subject to enforcement action by the DOT agency just as you are for other violations of this part and DOT agency rules.

§40.23 What actions do employers take after receiving verified test results?

(a) As an employer who receives a verified positive drug test result, you must immediately remove the employee involved from performing safety-sensitive functions. You must take this action upon receiving the initial report of the verified positive test result. Do not wait to receive the written report or the result of a split specimen test.

(b) As an employer who receives a verified adulterated or substituted drug test result, you must consider this a refusal to test and immediately remove the employee involved from performing safety-sensitive functions. You must take this action on receiving the initial report of the verified adulterated or substituted test result. Do not wait to receive the written report or the result of a split specimen test.

(c) As an employer who receives an alcohol test result of 0.04 or higher, you must immediately remove the employee involved from performing safety-sensitive functions. If you receive an alcohol test result of 0.02—0.039, you must temporarily remove the employee involved from performing safety-sensitive functions, as provided in applicable DOT agency regulations. Do not wait to receive the written report of the result of the test.

(d) As an employer, when an employee has a verified positive, adulterated, or substituted test result, or has otherwise violated a DOT agency drug and alcohol regulation, you must not return the employee to the performance of safety-sensitive functions until or unless the employee successfully completes the return-to-duty process of Subpart O of this part.

(e) As an employer who receives a drug test result indicating that the employee's specimen was dilute, take action as provided in §40.197.

(f) As an employer who receives a drug test result indicating that the employee's urine specimen test was cancelled because it was invalid and that a second collection must take place under direct observation—

(1) You must immediately direct the employee to provide a new specimen under direct observation.

(2) You must not attach consequences to the finding that the test was invalid other than collecting a new specimen under direct observation.

(3) You must not give any advance notice of this test requirement to the employee.

(4) You must instruct the collector to note on the CCF the same reason (*e.g.*, random test, post-accident test) and DOT Agency (*e.g.*, check DOT and FMCSA) as for the original collection.

(5) You must ensure that the collector conducts the collection under direct observation.

(g) As an employer who receives a cancelled test result when a negative result is required (*e.g.*, pre-employment, return-to-duty, or follow-up test), you must direct the employee to provide another specimen immediately.

(h) As an employer, you may also be required to take additional actions required by DOT agency regulations (*e.g.*, FAA rules require some positive drug tests to be reported to the Federal Air Surgeon).

(i) As an employer, you must not alter a drug or alcohol test result transmitted to you by an MRO, BAT, or C/TPA.

§40.25 Must an employer check on the drug and alcohol testing record of employees it is intending to use to perform safety-sensitive duties?

(a) Yes, as an employer, you must, after obtaining an employee's written consent, request the information about the employee listed in paragraph (b) of this section. This requirement applies only to employees seeking to begin performing safety-sensitive duties for you for the first time (*i.e.*, a new hire, an employee transfers into a safety-sensitive position). If the employee refuses to provide this written consent, you must not permit the employee to perform safety-sensitive functions.

(b) You must request the information listed in this paragraph (b) from DOT-regulated employers who have employed the employee during any period during the two years before the date of the employee's application or transfer:

(1) Alcohol tests with a result of 0.04 or higher alcohol concentration;

(2) Verified positive drug tests;

(3) Refusals to be tested (including verified adulterated or substituted drug test results);

(4) Other violations of DOT agency drug and alcohol testing regulations; and

(5) With respect to any employee who violated a DOT drug and alcohol regulation, documentation of the employee's successful completion of DOT return-to-duty requirements (including follow-up tests). If the previous employer does not have information about the return-to-duty process (*e.g.*, an employer who did not hire an employee who tested positive on a pre-employment test), you must seek to obtain this information from the employee.

(c) The information obtained from a previous employer includes any drug or alcohol test information obtained from previous employers under this section or other applicable DOT agency regulations.

(d) If feasible, you must obtain and review this information before the employee first performs safety-sensitive functions. If this is not feasible, you must obtain and review the information as soon as possible. However, you must not permit the employee to perform safety-sensitive functions after 30 days from the date on which the employee first performed safety-sensitive functions, unless you have obtained or made and documented a good faith effort to obtain this information.

(e) If you obtain information that the employee has violated a DOT agency drug and alcohol regulation, you must not use the employee to perform safety-sensitive functions unless you also obtain information that the employee has subsequently complied with the return-to-duty requirements of Subpart O of this part and DOT agency drug and alcohol regulations.

(f) You must provide to each of the employers from whom you request information under paragraph (b) of this section written consent for the release of the information cited in paragraph (a) of this section.

(g) The release of information under this section must be in any written form (*e.g.,* fax, e-mail, letter) that ensures confidentiality. As the previous employer, you must maintain a written record of the information released, including the date, the party to whom it was released, and a summary of the information provided.

(h) If you are an employer from whom information is requested under paragraph (b) of this section, you must, after reviewing the employee's specific, written consent, immediately release the requested information to the employer making the inquiry.

(i) As the employer requesting the information required under this section, you must maintain a written, confidential record of the information you obtain or of the good faith efforts you made to obtain the information. You must retain this information for three years from the date of the employee's first performance of safety-sensitive duties for you.

(j) As the employer, you must also ask the employee whether he or she has tested positive, or refused to test, on any pre-employment drug or alcohol test administered by an employer to which the employee applied for, but did not obtain, safety-sensitive transportation work covered by DOT agency drug and alcohol testing rules during the past two years. If the employee admits that he or she had a positive test or a refusal to test, you must not use the employee to perform safety-sensitive functions for you, until and unless the employee documents successful completion of the return-to-duty process (see paragraphs (b)(5) and (e) of this section).

§40.26 What form must an employer use to report Management Information System (MIS) data to a DOT agency?

As an employer, when you are required to report MIS data to a DOT agency, you must use the U.S. Department of Transportation Drug and Alcohol Testing MIS Data Collection Form to report that data. You must use the form and instructions referenced at Appendix H to part 40. You must submit the MIS report in accordance with rule requirements (*e.g.,* dates for submission; selection of companies required to submit, and method of reporting) established by the DOT agency regulating your operation.

§40.27 May an employer require an employee to sign a consent or release in connection with the DOT drug and alcohol testing program?

No, as an employer, you must not require an employee to sign a consent, release, waiver of liability, or indemnification agreement with respect to any part of the drug or alcohol testing process covered by this part (including, but not limited to, collections, laboratory testing, MRO and SAP services).

§40.29 Where is other information on employer responsibilities found in this regulation?

You can find other information on the responsibilities of employers in the following sections of this part:

§40.3—Definition.

§40.35—Information about DERs that employers must provide collectors.

§40.45—Modifying CCFs, Use of foreign-language CCFs.

§40.47—Use of non-Federal forms for DOT tests or Federal CCFs for non-DOT tests.

§40.67—Requirements for direct observation.

§40.173—Responsibility to ensure test of split specimen.

§40.193—Action in "shy bladder" situations.

§40.197—Actions following report of a dilute specimen.

§40.207—Actions following a report of a cancelled drug test.

§40.209—Actions following and consequences of non-fatal flaws in drug tests.

§40.215—Information about DERs that employers must provide BATs and STTs.

§40.225—Modifying ATFs; use of foreign-language ATFs.

§40.227—Use of non-DOT forms for DOT tests or DOT ATFs for non-DOT tests.

§40.235(c) and (d)—responsibility to follow instructions for ASDs.

§40.255(b)—receipt and storage of alcohol test information.

§40.265(c)–(e)—actions in "shy lung" situations.

§40.267—Cancellation of alcohol tests.

§40.271—Actions in "correctable flaw" situations in alcohol tests.

§40.273—Actions following cancelled tests in alcohol tests.

§40.275—Actions in "non-fatal flaw" situations in alcohol tests.

§§40.287-40.289—Responsibilities concerning SAP services.

§§40.295-40.297—Prohibition on seeking second SAP evaluation or changing SAP recommendation.

§40.303—Responsibilities concerning aftercare recommendations.

§40.305—Responsibilities concerning return-to-duty decision.

§40.309—Responsibilities concerning follow-up tests.

§40.321—General confidentiality requirement.

§40.323—Release of confidential information in litigation.

§40.331—Other circumstances for the release of confidential information.

§40.333—Record retention requirements.

§40.345—Choice of who reports drug testing information to employers.

Subpart C—Urine Collection Personnel

§40.31 Who may collect urine specimens for DOT drug testing?

(a) Collectors meeting the requirements of this subpart are the only persons authorized to collect urine specimens for DOT drug testing.

(b) A collector must meet training requirements of §40.33.

(c) As the immediate supervisor of an employee being tested, you may not act as the collector when that employee is tested, unless no other collector is available and you are permitted to do so under DOT agency drug and alcohol regulations.

(d) You must not act as the collector for the employee being tested if you work for a HHS-certified laboratory (*e.g.,* as a technician or accessioner) and could link the employee with a urine specimen, drug testing result, or laboratory report.

§40.33 What training requirements must a collector meet?

To be permitted to act as a collector in the DOT drug testing program, you must meet each of the requirements of this section:

(a) **Basic information**. You must be knowledgeable about this part, the current "DOT Urine Specimen Collection Procedures Guidelines," and DOT agency regulations applicable to the employers for whom you perform collections. DOT agency regulations, the DOT Urine Specimen Collection Procedures Guidelines, and other materials are available from ODAPC (Department of Transportation, 1200 New Jersey Avenue SE., Washington DC, 20590, 202-366-3784, or on the ODAPC Web site (*https://www.transportation.gov/odapc*). You must keep current on any changes to these materials. You must subscribe to the ODAPC list-serve at: *https://www.transportation.gov/odapc/get-odapc-email-updates*.

(b) **Qualification training**. You must receive qualification training meeting the requirements of this paragraph. Qualification training must provide instruction on the following subjects:

(1) All steps necessary to complete a collection correctly and the proper completion and transmission of the CCF;

(2) "Problem" collections (*e.g.* situations like "shy bladder" and attempts to tamper with a specimen);

(3) Fatal flaws, correctable flaws, and how to correct problems in collections; and

(4) The collector's responsibility for maintaining the integrity of the collection process, ensuring the privacy of employees being tested, ensuring the security of the specimen, and avoiding conduct or statements that could be viewed as offensive or inappropriate;

(c) **Initial Proficiency Demonstration**. Following your completion of qualification training under paragraph (b) of this section, you must demonstrate proficiency in collections under this part by completing five consecutive error-free mock collections.

(1) The five mock collections must include two uneventful collection scenarios, one insufficient quantity of urine scenario, one temperature out of range scenario, and one scenario in which the employee refuses to sign the CCF and initial the specimen bottle tamper-evident seal.

(2) Another person must monitor and evaluate your performance, in person or by a means that provides real-time observation and interaction between the instructor and trainee, and attest in writing that the mock collections are "error-free." This person must be a qualified collector who has demonstrated necessary knowledge, skills, and abilities by—

(i) Regularly conducting DOT drug test collections for a period of at least a year;

(ii) Conducting collector training under this part for a year; or

(iii) Successfully completing a "train the trainer" course.

(d) You must meet the requirements of paragraphs (b) and (c) of this section before you begin to perform collector functions.

(e) **Refresher training**. No less frequently than every five years from the date on which you satisfactorily complete the requirements of paragraphs (b) and (c) of this section, you must complete refresher training that meets all the requirements of paragraphs (b) and (c) of this section.

(f) **Error Correction Training**. If you make a mistake in the collection process that causes a test to be cancelled (*i.e.*, a fatal or uncorrected flaw), you must undergo error correction training. This training must occur within 30 days of the date you are notified of the error that led to the need for retraining.

(1) Error correction training must be provided and your proficiency documented in writing by a person who meets the requirements of paragraph (c)(2) of this section.

(2) Error correction training is required to cover only the subject matter area(s) in which the error that caused the test to be cancelled occurred.

(3) As part of the error correction training, you must demonstrate your proficiency in the collection procedures of this part by completing three consecutive error-free mock collections. The mock collections must include one uneventful scenario and two scenarios related to the area(s) in which your error(s) occurred. The person providing the training must monitor and evaluate your performance and attest in writing that the mock collections were "error-free."

(g) **Documentation**. You must maintain documentation showing that you currently meet all requirements of this section. You must provide this documentation on request to DOT agency representatives and to employers and C/TPAs who are using or negotiating to use your services.

§40.35 What information about the DER must employers provide to collectors?

As an employer, you must provide to collectors the name and telephone number of the appropriate DER (and C/TPA, where applicable) to contact about any problems or issues that may arise during the testing process.

§40.37 Where is other information on the role of collectors found in this regulation?

You can find other information on the role and functions of collectors in the following sections of this part:

§40.3—Definition.
§40.43—Steps to prepare and secure collection sites.
§§40.45-40.47—Use of CCF.
§§40.49-40.51—Use of collection kit and shipping materials.
§§40.61-40.63—Preliminary steps in collections.
§40.65—Role in checking specimens.
§40.67—Role in directly observed collections.
§40.69—Role in monitored collections.
§40.71—Role in split specimen collections.
§40.73—Chain of custody completion and finishing the collection process.
§40.191—Action in case of refusals to take test.
§40.193—Action in "shy bladder" situations.
§40.199-40.205—Collector errors in tests, effects, and means of correction.

Subpart D—Collection Sites, Forms, Equipment and Supplies Used in DOT Urine Collections

§40.41 Where does a urine collection for a DOT drug test take place?

(a) A urine collection for a DOT drug test must take place in a collection site meeting the requirements of this section.

(b) If you are operating a collection site, you must ensure that it meets the security requirements of §40.43.

(c) If you are operating a collection site, you must have all necessary personnel, materials, equipment, facilities and supervision to provide for the collection, temporary storage, and shipping of urine specimens to a laboratory, and a suitable clean surface for writing.

(d) Your collection site must include a facility for urination described in either paragraph (e) or paragraph (f) of this section.

(e) The first, and preferred, type of facility for urination that a collection site may include is a single-toilet room, having a full-length privacy door, within which urination can occur.

(1) No one but the employee may be present in the room during the collection, except for the observer in the event of a directly observed collection.

(2) You must have a source of water for washing hands, that, if practicable, should be external to the closed room where urination occurs. If an external source is not available, you may meet this requirement by securing all sources of water and other substances that could be used for adulteration and substitution (e.g., water faucets, soap dispensers) and providing moist towelettes outside the closed room.

(f) The second type of facility for urination that a collection site may include is a multistall restroom.

(1) Such a site must provide substantial visual privacy (e.g., a toilet stall with a partial-length door) and meet all other applicable requirements of this section.

(2) If you use a multi-stall restroom, you must either—

(i) Secure all sources of water and other substances that could be used for adulteration and substitution (e.g., water faucets, soap dispensers) and place bluing agent in all toilets or secure the toilets to prevent access; or

(ii) Conduct all collections in the facility as monitored collections (see §40.69 for procedures). This is the only circumstance in which you may conduct a monitored collection.

(3) No one but the employee may be present in the multistall restroom during the collection, except for the monitor in the event of a monitored collection or the observer in the event of a directly observed collection.

(g) A collection site may be in a medical facility, a mobile facility (e.g., a van), a dedicated collection facility, or any other location meeting the requirements of this section.

§40.43 What steps must operators of collection sites take to protect the security and integrity of urine collections?

(a) Collectors and operators of collection sites must take the steps listed in this section to prevent unauthorized access that could compromise the integrity of collections.

(b) As a collector, you must do the following before each collection to deter tampering with specimens:

(1) Secure any water sources or otherwise make them unavailable to employees (e.g., turn off water inlet, tape handles to prevent opening faucets);

(2) Ensure that the water in the toilet is blue;

(3) Ensure that no soap, disinfectants, cleaning agents, or other possible adulterants are present;

(4) Inspect the site to ensure that no foreign or unauthorized substances are present;

(5) Tape or otherwise secure shut any movable toilet tank top, or put bluing in the tank;

(6) Ensure that undetected access (*e.g.,* through a door not in your view) is not possible;

(7) Secure areas and items (*e.g.,* ledges, trash receptacles, paper towel holders, under-sink areas) that appear suitable for concealing contaminants; and

(8) Recheck items in paragraphs (b)(1) through (7) of this section following each collection to ensure the site's continued integrity.

(c) If the collection site uses a facility normally used for other purposes, like a public rest room or hospital examining room, you must, as a collector, also ensure before the collection that:

(1) Access to collection materials and specimens is effectively restricted; and

(2) The facility is secured against access during the procedure to ensure privacy to the employee and prevent distraction of the collector. Limited-access signs must be posted.

(d) As a collector, you must take the following additional steps to ensure security during the collection process:

(1) To avoid distraction that could compromise security, you are limited to conducting a collection for only one employee at a time. However, during the time one employee is in the period for drinking fluids in a "shy bladder" situation (see §40.193(b)), you may conduct a collection for another employee.

(2) To the greatest extent you can, keep an employee's collection container within view of both you and the employee between the time the employee has urinated and the specimen is sealed.

(3) Ensure you are the only person in addition to the employee who handles the specimen before it is poured into the bottles and sealed with tamper-evident seals.

(4) In the time between when the employee gives you the specimen and when you seal the specimen, remain within the collection site.

(5) Maintain personal control over each specimen and CCF throughout the collection process.

(e) If you are operating a collection site, you must implement a policy and procedures to prevent unauthorized personnel from entering any part of the site in which urine specimens are collected or stored.

(1) Only employees being tested, collectors and other collection site workers, DERs, employee and employer representatives authorized by the employer (*e.g.,* employer policy, collective bargaining agreement), and DOT agency representatives are authorized persons for purposes of this paragraph (e).

(2) Except for the observer in a directly observed collection or the monitor in the case of a monitored collection, you must not permit anyone to enter the urination facility in which employees provide specimens.

(3) You must ensure that all authorized persons are under the supervision of a collector at all times when permitted into the site.

(4) You or the collector may remove any person who obstructs, interferes with, or causes a delay in the collection process.

(f) If you are operating a collection site, you must minimize the number of persons handling specimens.

§40.45 What form is used to document a DOT urine collection?

(a) The Federal Drug Testing Custody and Control Form (CCF) must be used to document every urine collection required by the DOT drug testing program.

You may view this form on the Department's Web site (*http://www.transportation.gov/odapc*) or the HHS Web site (*http://www.workplace.samhsa.gov*).

(b) You must not use a non-Federal form or an expired CCF to conduct a DOT urine collection. As a laboratory, C/TPA or other party that provides CCFs to employers, collection sites, or other customers, you must not provide copies of an expired CCF to these participants. You must also affirmatively notify these participants that they must not use an expired CCF.

(c) As a participant in the DOT drug testing program, you are not permitted to modify or revise the CCF except as follows:

(1) You may include, in the area outside the border of the form, other information needed for billing or other purposes necessary to the collection process.

(2) The CCF must include the names, addresses, telephone numbers and fax numbers of the employer and the MRO, which may be preprinted, typed, or handwritten. The MRO information must include the specific physician's name and address, as opposed to only a generic clinic, health care organization, or company name. This information is required, and it is prohibited for an employer, collector, service agent or any other party to omit it. In addition, a C/TPA's name, address, fax number, and telephone number may be included, but is not required. The employer may use a C/TPA's address in place of its own, but must continue to include its name, telephone number, and fax number.

(3) As an employer, in Step 1-D of the CCF you may preprint the box for the DOT Agency under whose authority the test will occur.

(4) As a collector, you may use a CCF with your name, address, telephone number, and fax number preprinted, but under no circumstances may you sign the form before the collection event.

(5) When using an electronic CCF, you must establish adequate confidentiality and security measures to ensure that confidential employee records are not available to unauthorized persons. This includes protecting the physical security of records, access controls, and computer security measures to safeguard confidential data in electronic form.

(d) Under no circumstances may the CCF transmit personal identifying information about an employee (other than a social security number (SSN) or other employee identification (ID) number) to a laboratory.

(e) As an employer, you may use an equivalent foreign-language version of the CCF approved by ODAPC. You may use such a non-English language form only in a situation where both the employee and collector understand and can use the form in that language.

(f) An employer who uses an electronic CCF must ensure that the collection site, the primary and split laboratories, and MRO have compatible systems, and that the employee and any other program participants in the testing process will receive a legible copy of the CCF.

§40.47 May employers use the CCF for non-Federal collections or non-Federal forms for DOT collections?

(a) No, as an employer, you are prohibited from using the CCF for non-Federal urine collections. You are also prohibited from using non-Federal forms for DOT urine collections. Doing either subjects you to enforcement action under DOT agency regulations.

(b)(1) In the rare case where the collector, either by mistake or as the only means to conduct a test under difficult circumstances (*e.g.,* post-accident or reasonable suspicion test with insufficient time to obtain the CCF), uses a non-Federal form for a DOT collection, the use of a non-Federal form does not present a reason for the laboratory to reject the specimen for testing or for an MRO to cancel the result.

(2) The use of the non-Federal form is a "correctable flaw." As an MRO, to correct the problem you must follow the procedures of §40.205(b)(2).

§40.49 What materials are used to collect urine specimens?

For each DOT drug test, you must use a collection kit meeting the requirements of Appendix A of this part.

§40.51 What materials are used to send urine specimens to the laboratory?

(a) Except as provided in paragraph (b) of this section, you must use a shipping container that adequately protects the specimen bottles from shipment damage in the transport of specimens from the collection site to the laboratory.

(b) You are not required to use a shipping container if a laboratory courier hand-delivers the specimens from the collection site to the laboratory.

Subpart E—Urine Specimen Collections

§40.61 What are the preliminary steps in the collection process?

As the collector, you must take the following steps before actually beginning a collection:

(a) When a specific time for an employee's test has been scheduled, or the collection site is at the employee's work site, and the employee does not appear at the collection site at the scheduled time, contact the DER to determine the appropriate interval within which the DER has determined the employee is authorized to arrive. If the employee's arrival is delayed beyond that time, you must notify the DER that the employee has not reported for testing. In a situation where a C/TPA has notified an owner/operator or other individual employee to report for testing and the employee does not appear, the C/TPA must notify the employee that he or she has refused to test (see §40.191(a)(1)).

(b) Ensure that, when the employee enters the collection site, you begin the testing process without undue delay. For example, you must not wait because the employee says he or she is not ready or is unable to urinate or because an authorized employer or employee representative is delayed in arriving.

(1) If the employee is also going to take a DOT alcohol test, you must, to the greatest extent practicable, ensure that the alcohol test is completed before the urine collection process begins.

Example to Paragraph (b)(1): An employee enters the test site for both a drug and an alcohol test. Normally, the collector would wait until the BAT had completed the alcohol test process before beginning the drug test process. However, there are some situations in which an exception to this normal practice would be reasonable. One such situation might be if several people were waiting for the BAT to conduct alcohol tests, but a drug testing collector in the same facility were free. Someone waiting might be able to complete a drug test without unduly delaying his or her alcohol test. Collectors and BATs should work together, however, to ensure that post-accident and reasonable suspicion alcohol tests happen as soon as possible (*e.g.,* by moving the employee to the head of the line for alcohol tests).

(2) If the employee needs medical attention (*e.g.,* an injured employee in an emergency medical facility who is required to have a post-accident test), do not delay this treatment to collect a specimen.

(3) You must not collect, by catheterization or other means, urine from an unconscious employee to conduct a drug test under this part. Nor may you catheterize a conscious employee. However, you must inform an employee who normally voids through self-catheterization that the employee is required to provide a specimen in that manner.

(4) If, as an employee, you normally void through self-catheterization, and decline to do so, this constitutes a refusal to test.

(c) Require the employee to provide positive identification. You must see a photo ID issued by the employer (other than in the case of an owner-operator or other self-employed individual) or a Federal, state, or local government (*e.g.,* a driver's license). You may not accept faxes or photocopies of identification. Positive identification by an employer representative (not a co-worker or another employee being tested) is also acceptable. If the employee cannot produce positive identification, you must contact a DER to verify the identity of the employee.

(d) If the employee asks, provide your identification to the employee. Your identification must include your name and your employer's name, but does not have to include your picture, address, or telephone number.

(e) Explain the basic collection procedure to the employee, including showing the employee the instructions on the back of the CCF.

(f) Direct the employee to remove outer clothing (*e.g.,* coveralls, jacket, coat, hat) that could be used to conceal items or substances that could be used to tamper with a specimen. You must also direct the employee to leave these garments and any briefcase, purse, or other personal belongings with you or in a mutually agreeable location. You must advise the employee that failure to comply with your directions constitutes a refusal to test.

(1) If the employee asks for a receipt for any belongings left with you, you must provide one.

(2) You must allow the employee to keep his or her wallet.

(3) You must not ask the employee to remove other clothing (*e.g.,* shirts, pants, dresses, underwear), to remove all clothing, or to change into a hospital or examination gown (unless the urine collection is being accomplished simultaneously with a DOT agency-authorized medical examination).

(4) You must direct the employee to empty his or her pockets and display the items in them to ensure that no items are present which could be used to adulterate the specimen. If nothing is there that can be used to adulterate a specimen, the employee can place the items back into his or her pockets. As the employee, you must allow the collector to make this observation.

(5) If, in your duties under paragraph (f)(4) of this section, you find any material that could be used to tamper with a specimen, you must:

(i) Determine if the material appears to be brought to the collection site with the intent to alter the specimen, and, if it is, conduct a directly observed collection using direct observation procedures (see §40.67); or

(ii) Determine if the material appears to be inadvertently brought to the collection site (*e.g.,* eye drops), secure and maintain it until the collection process is completed and conduct a normal (*i.e.,* unobserved) collection.

(g) You must instruct the employee not to list medications that he or she is currently taking on the CCF. (The employee may make notes of medications on the back of the employee copy of the form for his or her own convenience, but these notes must not be transmitted to anyone else.)

§40.63 What steps does the collector take in the collection process before the employee provides a urine specimen?

As the collector, you must take the following steps before the employee provides the urine specimen:

(a) Complete Step 1 of the CCF.

(b) Instruct the employee to wash and dry his or her hands at this time. You must tell the employee not to wash his or her hands again until after delivering the specimen to you. You must not give the employee any further access to water or other materials that could be used to adulterate or dilute a specimen.

(c) Select, or allow the employee to select, an individually wrapped or sealed collection container from collection kit materials. Either you or the employee, with both of you present, must unwrap or break the seal of the collection container. You must not unwrap or break the seal on any specimen bottle at this time. You must not allow the employee to take anything from the collection kit into the room used for urination except the collection container.

(d) Direct the employee to go into the room used for urination, provide a specimen of at least 45 mL, not flush the toilet, and return to you with the specimen as soon as the employee has completed the void.

(1) Except in the case of an observed or a monitored collection (see §§40.67 and 40.69), neither you nor anyone else may go into the room with the employee.

(2) As the collector, you may set a reasonable time limit for voiding.

(e) You must pay careful attention to the employee during the entire collection process to note any conduct that clearly indicates an attempt to tamper with a specimen (e.g., substitute urine in plain view or an attempt to bring into the collection site an adulterant or urine substitute). If you detect such conduct, you must require that a collection take place immediately under direct observation (see §40.67) and complete Step 2 by noting the conduct in the "Remarks" line of the CCF and the fact that the collection was observed by checking the "Observed" box. You must also, as soon as possible, inform the DER and collection site supervisor that a collection took place under direct observation and the reason for doing so.

§40.65 What does the collector check for when the employee presents a specimen?

As a collector, you must check the following when the employee gives the collection container to you:

(a) **Sufficiency of specimen.** You must check to ensure that the specimen contains at least 45 mL of urine.

(1) If it does not, you must follow "shy bladder" procedures (see §40.193(b)).

(2) When you follow "shy bladder" procedures, you must discard the original specimen, unless another problem (i.e., temperature out of range, signs of tampering) also exists.

(3) You are never permitted to combine urine collected from separate voids to create a specimen.

(4) You must discard any excess urine.

(b) **Temperature.** You must check the temperature of the specimen no later than four minutes after the employee has given you the specimen.

(1) The acceptable temperature range is 32–38° C/90–100° F.

(2) You must determine the temperature of the specimen by reading the temperature strip attached to the collection container.

(3) If the specimen temperature is within the acceptable range, you must mark the "Yes" box on the CCF (Step 2).

(4) If the specimen temperature is outside the acceptable range, you must mark the "No" box and enter in the "Remarks" line (Step 2) your findings about the temperature.

(5) If the specimen temperature is outside the acceptable range, you must immediately conduct a new collection using direct observation procedures (see §40.67).

(6) In a case where a specimen is collected under direct observation because of the temperature being out of range, you must process both the original specimen and the specimen collected using direct observation and send the two sets of specimens to the laboratory. This is true even in a case in which the original specimen has insufficient volume but the temperature is out of range. You must also, as soon as possible, inform the DER and collection site supervisor that a collection took place under direct observation and the reason for doing so.

(7) In a case where the employee refuses to provide another specimen (see §40.191(a)(3)) or refuses to provide another specimen under direct observation (see §40.191(a)(4)), you must notify the DER. As soon as you have notified the DER, you must discard any specimen the employee has provided previously during the collection procedure.

(c) **Signs of tampering.** You must inspect the specimen for unusual color, presence of foreign objects or material, or other signs of tampering (*e.g.,* if you notice any unusual odor).

(1) If it is apparent from this inspection that the employee has tampered with the specimen (*e.g.,* blue dye in the specimen, excessive foaming when shaken, smell of bleach), you must immediately conduct a new collection using direct observation procedures (see §40.67).

(2) In a case where a specimen is collected under direct observation because of showing signs of tampering, you must process both the original specimen and the specimen collected using direct observation and send the two sets of specimens to the laboratory. This is true even in a case in which the original specimen has insufficient volume but it shows signs of tampering. You must also, as soon as possible, inform the DER and collection site supervisor that a collection took place under direct observation and the reason for doing so.

(3) In a case where the employee refuses to provide a specimen under direct observation (see §40.191(a)(4)), you must discard any specimen the employee provided previously during the collection procedure. Then you must notify the DER as soon as practicable.

§40.67 When and how is a directly observed collection conducted?

(a) As an employer, you must direct an immediate collection under direct observation with no advance notice to the employee, if:

(1) The laboratory reported to the MRO that a specimen is invalid, and the MRO reported to you that there was not an adequate medical explanation for the result;

(2) The MRO reported to you that the original positive, adulterated, or substituted test result had to be cancelled because the test of the split specimen could not be performed; or

(3) The laboratory reported to the MRO that the specimen was negative-dilute with a creatinine concentration greater than or equal to 2 mg/dL but less than or equal to 5 mg/dL, and the MRO reported the specimen to you as negative-dilute and that a second collection must take place under direct observation (see §40.197(b)(1)).

(b) As an employer, you must direct a collection under direct observation of an employee if the drug test is a return-to-duty test or a follow-up test.

(c) As a collector, you must immediately conduct a collection under direct observation if:

(1) You are directed by the DER to do so (see paragraphs (a) and (b) of this section); or

(2) You observed materials brought to the collection site or the employee's conduct clearly indicates an attempt to tamper with a specimen (see §§40.61(f)(5)(i) and 40.63(e)); or

(3) The temperature on the original specimen was out of range (see §40.65(b)(5)); or

(4) The original specimen appeared to have been tampered with (see §40.65(c)(1)).

(d)(1) As the employer, you must explain to the employee the reason for a directly observed collection under paragraph (a) or (b) of this section.

(2) As the collector, you must explain to the employee the reason, if known, under this part for a directly observed collection under paragraphs (c)(1) through (3) of this section.

(e) As the collector, you must complete a new CCF for the directly observed collection.

(1) You must mark the "reason for test" block (Step 1) the same as for the first collection.

(2) You must check the "Observed, (Enter Remark)" box and enter the reason (see §40.67(b)) in the "Remarks" line (Step 2).

(f) In a case where two sets of specimens are being sent to the laboratory because of suspected tampering with the specimen at the collection site, enter on the "Remarks" line of the CCF (Step 2) for each specimen a notation to this effect (e.g., collection 1 of 2, or 2 of 2) and the specimen ID number of the other specimen.

(g) As the collector, you must ensure that the observer is the same gender as the employee. You must never permit an opposite gender person to act as the observer. The observer can be a different person from the collector and need not be a qualified collector.

(h) As the collector, if someone else is to observe the collection (e.g., in order to ensure a same gender observer), you must verbally instruct that person to follow procedures at paragraphs (i) and (j) of this section. If you, the collector, are the observer, you too must follow these procedures.

(i) As the observer, you must request the employee to raise his or her shirt, blouse, or dress/skirt, as appropriate, above the waist; and lower clothing and underpants to show you, by turning around, that they do not have a prosthetic device. After you have determined that the employee does not have such a device, you may permit the employee to return clothing to its proper position for observed urination.

(j) As the observer, you must watch the employee urinate into the collection container. Specifically, you are to watch the urine go from the employee's body into the collection container.

(k) As the observer but not the collector, you must not take the collection container from the employee, but you must observe the specimen as the employee takes it to the collector.

(l) As the collector, when someone else has acted as the observer, you must include the observer's name in the "Remarks" line of the CCF (Step 2).

(m) As the employee, if you decline to allow a directly observed collection required or permitted under this section to occur, this is a refusal to test.

(n) As a service agent, when you learn that a directly observed collection should have been collected but was not, you must inform the employer that it must direct the employee to have an immediate recollection under direct observation.

§40.69 How is a monitored collection conducted?

(a) As the collector, you must secure the room being used for the monitored collection so that no one except the employee and the monitor can enter it until after the collection has been completed.

(b) As the collector, you must ensure that the monitor is the same gender as the employee, unless the monitor is a medical professional (e.g., nurse, doctor, physician's assistant, technologist, or technician licensed or certified to practice in the jurisdiction in which the collection takes place). The monitor can be a different person from the collector and need not be a qualified collector.

(c) As the collector, if someone else is to monitor the collection (e.g., in order to ensure a same gender monitor), you must verbally instruct that person to follow the procedures of paragraphs (d) and (e) of this section. If you, the collector, are the monitor, you must follow these procedures.

(d) As the monitor, you must not watch the employee urinate into the collection container. If you hear sounds or make other observations indicating an attempt to tamper with a specimen, there must be an additional collection under direct observation (see §§40.63(e), 40.65(c), and 40.67(b)).

(e) As the monitor, you must ensure that the employee takes the collection container directly to the collector as soon as the employee has exited the enclosure.

(f) As the collector, when someone else has acted as the monitor, you must note that person's name in the "Remarks" line of the CCF (Step 2).

(g) As the employee being tested, if you decline to permit a collection authorized under this section to be monitored, it is a refusal to test.

§40.71 How does the collector prepare the specimens?

(a) All collections under DOT agency drug testing regulations must be split specimen collections.

(b) As the collector, you must take the following steps, in order, after the employee brings the urine specimen to you. You must take these steps in the presence of the employee.

(1) Check the box on the CCF (Step 2) indicating that this was a split specimen collection.

(2) You, not the employee, must first pour at least 30 mL of urine from the collection container into one specimen bottle, to be used for the primary specimen.

(3) You, not the employee, must then pour at least 15 mL of urine from the collection container into the second specimen bottle to be used for the split specimen.

(4) You, not the employee, must place and secure (i.e., tighten or snap) the lids/caps on the bottles.

(5) You, not the employee, must seal the bottles by placing the tamper-evident bottle seals over the bottle caps/lids and down the sides of the bottles.

(6) You, not the employee, must then write the date on the tamper-evident bottle seals.

(7) You must then ensure that the employee initials the tamper-evident bottle seals for the purpose of certifying that the bottles contain the specimens he or she provided. If the employee fails or refuses to do so, you must note this in the "Remarks" line of the CCF (Step 2) and complete the collection process.

(8) You must discard any urine left over in the collection container after both specimen bottles have been appropriately filled and sealed. There is one exception to this requirement: you may use excess urine to conduct clinical tests (*e.g.*, protein, glucose) if the collection was conducted in conjunction with a physical examination required by a DOT agency regulation. Neither you nor anyone else may conduct further testing (such as adulteration testing) on this excess urine and the employee has no legal right to demand that the excess urine be turned over to the employee.

§40.73 How is the collection process completed?

(a) As the collector, when using the paper CCF, you must do the following things to complete the collection process. You must complete the steps called for in paragraphs (a)(1) through (7) of this section in the employee's presence.

(1) Direct the employee to read and sign the certification statement on Copy 2 (Step 5) of the CCF and provide date of birth, printed name, and day and evening contact telephone numbers. If the employee refuses to sign the CCF or to provide date of birth, printed name, or telephone numbers, you must note this in the "Remarks" line (Step 2) of the CCF, and complete the collection. If the employee refuses to fill out any information, you must, as a minimum, print the employee's name in the appropriate place.

(2) Complete the chain of custody on the CCF (Step 4) by printing your name (note: you may pre-print your name), recording the time and date of the collection, signing the statement, and entering the name of the delivery service transferring the specimen to the laboratory.

(3) Ensure that all copies of the CCF are legible and complete.

(4) Remove Copy 5 of the CCF and give it to the employee.

(5) Place the specimen bottles and Copy 1 of the CCF in the appropriate pouches of the plastic bag.

(6) Secure both pouches of the plastic bag.

(7) Advise the employee that he or she may leave the collection site.

(8) To prepare the sealed plastic bag containing the specimens and CCF for shipment you must:

(i) Place the sealed plastic bag in a shipping container (*e.g.*, standard courier box) designed to minimize the possibility of damage during shipment. (More than one sealed plastic bag can be placed into a single shipping container if you are doing multiple collections.)

(ii) Seal the container as appropriate.

(iii) If a laboratory courier hand-delivers the specimens from the collection site to the laboratory, prepare the sealed plastic bag for shipment as directed by the courier service.

(9) Send Copy 2 of the CCF to the MRO and Copy 4 to the DER. You must fax or otherwise transmit these copies to the MRO and DER within 24 hours or

during the next business day. Keep Copy 3 for at least 30 days, unless otherwise specified by applicable DOT agency regulations.

(b) As a collector, when using other forms of the CCF as approved by the Office of Management and Budget, you must follow the procedures approved for that form.

(c) As a collector or collection site, you must ensure that each specimen you collect is shipped to a laboratory as quickly as possible, but in any case, within 24 hours or during the next business day.

Subpart F—Drug Testing Laboratories

§40.81 What laboratories may be used for DOT drug testing?

(a) As a drug testing laboratory located in the U.S., you are permitted to participate in DOT drug testing only if you are certified by HHS under the National Laboratory Certification Program (NLCP) for all testing required under this part.

(b) As a drug testing laboratory located in Canada or Mexico which is not certified by HHS under the NLCP, you are permitted to participate in DOT drug testing only if:

(1) The DOT, based on a written recommendation from HHS, has approved your laboratory as meeting HHS laboratory certification standards or deemed your laboratory fully equivalent to a laboratory meeting HHS laboratory certification standards for all testing required under this part; or

(2) The DOT, based on a written recommendation from HHS, has recognized a Canadian or Mexican certifying organization as having equivalent laboratory certification standards and procedures to those of HHS, and the Canadian or Mexican certifying organization has certified your laboratory under those equivalent standards and procedures.

(c) As a laboratory participating in the DOT drug testing program, you must comply with the requirements of this part. You must also comply with all applicable requirements of HHS in testing DOT specimens, whether or not the HHS requirements are explicitly stated in this part.

(d) If DOT determines that you are in noncompliance with this part, you could be subject to PIE proceedings under Subpart R of this part. If the Department issues a PIE with respect to you, you are ineligible to participate in the DOT drug testing program even if you continue to meet the requirements of paragraph (a) or (b) of this section.

§40.83 How do laboratories process incoming specimens?

As the laboratory, you must do the following when you receive a DOT specimen:

(a) You are authorized to receive only Copy 1 of the CCF. You are not authorized to receive other copies of the CCF or any copies of the alcohol testing form.

(b) You must comply with applicable provisions of the HHS Guidelines concerning accessioning and processing urine drug specimens.

(c) You must inspect each specimen and CCF for the following "fatal flaws:"

(1) There is no CCF;

(2) In cases where a specimen has been collected, there is no specimen submitted with the CCF;

(3) There is no printed collector's name and no collector's signature;

(4) Two separate collections are performed using one CCF;

(5) The specimen ID numbers on the specimen bottle and the CCF do not match;

(6) The specimen bottle seal is broken or shows evidence of tampering, unless a split specimen can be redesignated (see paragraph (h) of this section);

(7) There is an insufficient amount of urine in the primary bottle for analysis, unless the specimens can be redesignated (see paragraph (h) of this section).

(d) When you find a specimen meeting the criteria of paragraph (c) of this section, you must document your findings and stop the testing process. Report the result in accordance with §40.97(a)(3).

(e) You must inspect each CCF for the presence of the collector's signature on the certification statement in Step 4 of the CCF. Upon finding that the signature is omitted, document the flaw and continue the testing process.

(1) In such a case, you must retain the specimen for a minimum of 5 business days from the date on which you initiated action to correct the flaw.

(2) You must then attempt to correct the flaw by following the procedures of §40.205(b)(1).

(3) If the flaw is not corrected, report the result as rejected for testing in accordance with §40.97(a)(3).

(f) If you determine that the specimen temperature was not checked and the "Remarks" line did not contain an entry regarding the temperature being outside of range, you must then attempt to correct the problem by following the procedures of §40.208.

(1) In such a case, you must continue your efforts to correct the problem for five business days, before you report the result.

(2) When you have obtained the correction, or five business days have elapsed, report the result in accordance with §40.97(a).

(g) If you determine that a CCF that fails to meet the requirements of §40.45(a) (e.g., a non-Federal form or an expired Federal form was used for the collection), you must attempt to correct the use of the improper form by following the procedures of §40.205(b)(2).

(1) In such a case, you must retain the specimen for a minimum of 5 business days from the date on which you initiated action to correct the problem.

(2) If the problem(s) is not corrected, you must reject the test and report the result in accordance with §40.97(a)(3).

(h) If the CCF is marked indicating that a split specimen collection was collected and if the split specimen does not accompany the primary, has leaked, or is otherwise unavailable for testing, you must still test the primary specimen and follow appropriate procedures outlined in §40.175(b) regarding the unavailability of the split specimen for testing.

(1) The primary specimen and the split specimen can be redesignated (i.e., Bottle B is redesignated as Bottle A, and vice-versa) if:

(i) The primary specimen appears to have leaked out of its sealed bottle and the laboratory believes a sufficient amount of urine exists in the split specimen to conduct all appropriate primary laboratory testing; or

(ii) The primary specimen is labeled as Bottle B, and the split specimen as Bottle A; or

(iii) The laboratory opens the split specimen instead of the primary specimen, the primary specimen remains sealed, and the laboratory believes a sufficient amount of urine exists in the split specimen to conduct all appropriate primary laboratory testing; or

(iv) The primary specimen seal is broken but the split specimen remains sealed and the laboratory believes a sufficient amount of urine exists in the split specimen to conduct all appropriate primary laboratory testing.

(2) In situations outlined in paragraph (g)(1) of this section, the laboratory shall mark through the "A" and write "B," then initial and date the change. A corresponding change shall be made to the other bottle by marking through the "B" and writing "A," and initialing and dating the change.

(i) A notation shall be made on Copy 1 of the CCF (Step 5a) and on any laboratory internal chain of custody documents, as appropriate, for any fatal or correctable flaw.

§40.85 What drugs do laboratories test for?

As a laboratory, you must test for the following five drugs or classes of drugs in a DOT drug test. You must not test "DOT specimens" for any other drugs.

(a) Marijuana metabolites.

(b) Cocaine metabolites.

(c) Amphetamines.

(d) Opioids.

(e) Phencyclidine (PCP).

§40.87 What are the cutoff concentrations for drug tests?

(a) As a laboratory, you must use the cutoff concentrations displayed in the following table for initial and confirmatory drug tests. All cutoff concentrations are expressed in nanograms per milliliter (ng/mL). The table follows:

Initial test analyte	Initial test cutoff [1]	Confirmatory test analyte	Confirmatory test cutoff concentration
Marijuana metabolites (THCA) [2]	50 ng/mL[3]	THCA	15 ng/mL.
Cocaine metabolite (Benzoylecgonine)	150 ng/mL [3]	Benzoylecgonine	100 ng/mL.
Codeine/	2000 ng/mL	Codeine	2000 ng/mL.
Morphine		Morphine	2000 ng/mL.
Hydrocodone/	300 ng/mL	Hydrocodone	100 ng/mL.
Hydromorphone		Hydromorphone	100 ng/mL.
Oxycodone/	100 ng/mL	Oxycodone	100 ng/mL.
Oxymorphone		Oxymorphone	100 ng/mL.
6-Acetylmorphine	10 ng/mL	6-Acetylmorphine	10 ng/mL.
Phencyclidine	25 ng/mL	Phencyclidine	25 ng/mL.
Amphetamine/	500 ng/mL	Amphetamine	250 ng/mL.
Methamphetamine		Methamphetamine	250 ng/mL.
MDMA[4]/MDA[5]	500 ng/mL	MDMA	250 ng/mL.
		MDA	250 ng/mL.

[1] For grouped analytes (i.e., two or more analytes that are in the same drug class and have the same initial test cutoff):

Immunoassay: The test must be calibrated with one analyte from the group identified as the target analyte. The cross-reactivity of the immunoassay to the other analyte(s) within the group must be 80 percent or greater; if not, separate immunoassays must be used for the analytes within the group.

Alternate technology: Either one analyte or all analytes from the group must be used for calibration, depending on the technology. At least one analyte within the group must have a concentration equal to or greater than the initial test cutoff or, alternatively, the sum of the analytes present (i.e., equal to or greater than the laboratory's validated limit of quantification) must be equal to or greater than the initial test cutoff.

[2] An immunoassay must be calibrated with the target analyte, Δ-9-tetrahydrocannabinol-9-carboxylic acid (THCA).

[3] *Alternate technology (THCA and Benzoylecgonine):* When using an alternate technology initial test for the specific target analytes of THCA and Benzoylecgonine, the laboratory must use the same cutoff for the initial and confirmatory tests (i.e., 15 ng/mL for THCA and 100ng/mL for Benzoylecgonine).

[4] Methylenedioxymethamphetamine (MDMA).

[5] Methylenedioxyamphetamine (MDA).

(b) On an initial drug test, you must report a result below the cutoff concentration as negative. If the result is at or above the cutoff concentration, you must conduct a confirmation test.

(c) On a confirmation drug test, you must report a result below the cutoff concentration as negative and a result at or above the cutoff concentration as confirmed positive.

(d) You must report quantitative values for morphine or codeine at 15,000 ng/mL or above.

§40.89 What is validity testing, and are laboratories required to conduct it?

(a) Specimen validity testing is the evaluation of the specimen to determine if it is consistent with normal human urine. The purpose of validity testing is to determine whether certain adulterants or foreign substances were added to the urine, if the urine was diluted, or if the specimen was substituted.

(b) As a laboratory, you must conduct validity testing.

§40.91 What validity tests must laboratories conduct on primary specimens?

As a laboratory, when you conduct validity testing under §40.89, you must conduct it in accordance with the requirements of this section.

(a) You must determine the creatinine concentration on each primary specimen. You must also determine its specific gravity if you find the creatinine concentration to be less than 20 mg/dL.

(b) You must determine the pH of each primary specimen.

(c) You must perform one or more validity tests for oxidizing adulterants on each primary specimen.

(d) You must perform additional validity tests on the primary specimen when the following conditions are observed:

(1) Abnormal physical characteristics;

(2) Reactions or responses characteristic of an adulterant obtained during initial or confirmatory drug tests (*e.g.,* non-recovery of internal standards, unusual response); or

(3) Possible unidentified interfering substance or adulterant.

(e) If you determine that the specimen is invalid and HHS guidelines direct you to contact the MRO, you must contact the MRO and together decide if testing the primary specimen by another HHS certified laboratory would be useful in being able to report a positive or adulterated test result.

§40.93 What criteria do laboratories use to establish that a specimen is dilute or substituted?

(a) As a laboratory, you must consider the primary specimen to be dilute when:

(1) The creatinine concentration is greater than or equal to 2 mg/dL but less than 20 mg/dL, and

(2) The specific gravity is greater than 1.0010 but less than 1.0030 on a single aliquot.

(b) As a laboratory, you must consider the primary specimen to be substituted when the creatinine concentration is less than 2 mg/dL and the specific gravity is less than or equal to 1.0010 or greater than or equal to 1.0200 on both the initial and confirmatory creatinine tests and on both the initial and confirmatory specific gravity tests on two separate aliquots.

§40.95 What are adulterant cutoff concentrations for initial and confirmation tests?

(a) As a laboratory, you must use the cutoff concentrations for the initial and confirmation adulterant testing as required by the HHS Mandatory Guidelines and you must use two separate aliquots—one for the initial test and another for the confirmation test.

(b) As a laboratory, you must report results at or above the cutoffs (or for pH, at or above or below the values, as appropriate) as adulterated and provide the numerical value that supports the adulterated result.

§40.96 What criteria do laboratories use to establish that a specimen is invalid?

(a) As a laboratory, you must use the invalid test result criteria for the initial and confirmation testing as required by the HHS Mandatory Guidelines, and you must use two separate aliquots— one for the initial test and another for the confirmation test.

(b) As a laboratory, for a specimen having an invalid result for one of the reasons outlined in the HHS Mandatory Guidelines, you must contact the MRO to discuss whether sending the specimen to another HHS certified laboratory for testing would be useful in being able to report a positive or adulterated result.

(c) As a laboratory, you must report invalid results in accordance with the invalid test result criteria as required by the HHS Guidelines and provide the numerical value that supports the invalid result, where appropriate, such as pH.

(d) As a laboratory, you must report the reason a test result is invalid.

§40.97 What do laboratories report and how do they report it?

(a) As a laboratory, you must report the results for each primary specimen. The result of a primary specimen will fall into one of the following three categories. However, as a laboratory, you must report the actual results (and not the categories):

(1) Category 1: Negative Results. As a laboratory, when you find a specimen to be negative, you must report the test result as being one of the following, as appropriate:

(i) Negative, or

(ii) Negative-dilute, with numerical values for creatinine and specific gravity.

(2) Category 2: Non-negative Results. As a laboratory, when you find a specimen to be non-negative, you must report the test result as being one or more of the following, as appropriate:

(i) Positive, with drug(s)/metabolite(s) noted, with numerical values for the drug(s) or drug metabolite(s).

(ii) Positive-dilute, with drug(s)/metabolite(s) noted, with numerical values for the drug(s) or drug metabolite(s) and with numerical values for creatinine and specific gravity;

(iii) Adulterated, with adulterant(s) noted, with confirmatory test values (when applicable), and with remark(s);

(iv) Substituted, with confirmatory test values for creatinine and specific gravity; or

(v) Invalid result, with remark(s). Laboratories will report actual values for pH results.

(3) Category 3: Rejected for Testing. As a laboratory, when you reject a specimen for testing, you must report the result as being Rejected for Testing, with remark(s).

(b) As a laboratory, you must report laboratory results directly, and only, to the MRO at his or her place of business. You must not report results to or through the DER or a service agent (e.g., C/TPA).

(1) Negative results: You must fax, courier, mail, or electronically transmit a legible image or copy of the fully-completed Copy 1 of the CCF which has been signed by the certifying scientist, or you may provide the laboratory results report electronically (i.e., computer data file).

(i) If you elect to provide the laboratory results report, you must include the following elements, as a minimum, in the report format:

(A) Laboratory name and address;

(B) Employer's name (you may include I.D. or account number);

(C) Medical review officer's name;

(D) Specimen I.D. number;

(E) Donor's SSN or employee I.D. number, if provided;

(F) Reason for test, if provided;

(G) Collector's name and telephone number;

(H) Date of the collection;

(I) Date received at the laboratory;

(J) Date certifying scientist released the results;

(K) Certifying scientist's name;

(L) Results (e.g., positive, adulterated) as listed in paragraph (a) of this section; and

(M) Remarks section, with an explanation of any situation in which a correctable flaw has been corrected.

(ii) You may release the laboratory results report only after review and approval by the certifying scientist. It must reflect the same test result information as contained on the CCF signed by the certifying scientist. The information contained in the laboratory results report may not contain information that does not appear on the CCF.

(iii) The results report may be transmitted through any means that ensures accuracy and confidentiality. You, as the laboratory, together with the MRO, must ensure that the information is adequately protected from unauthorized access or release, both during transmission and in storage.

(2) Non-negative and Rejected for Testing results: You must fax, courier, mail, or electronically transmit a legible image or copy of the fully-completed Copy 1 of the CCF that has been signed by the certifying scientist. In addition, you may provide the electronic laboratory results report following the format and procedures set forth in paragraphs (b)(1)(i) and (ii) of this section.

(c) In transmitting laboratory results to the MRO, you, as the laboratory, together with the MRO, must ensure that the information is adequately protected from unauthorized access or release, both during transmission and in storage. If the results are provided by fax, the fax connection must have a fixed telephone number accessible only to authorized individuals.

(d) You must transmit test results to the MRO in a timely manner, preferably the same day that review by the certifying scientist is completed.

(e)(1) You must provide quantitative values for confirmed positive drug test results to the MRO.

(2) You must provide the numerical values that support the adulterated (when applicable) or substituted result, without a request from the MRO.

(3) You must also provide to the MRO numerical values for creatinine and specific gravity for the negative-dilute test result, without a request from the MRO.

(f) You must provide quantitative values for confirmed opiate results for morphine or codeine at 15,000 ng/mL or above, even if the MRO has not requested quantitative values for the test result.

§40.99 How long does the laboratory retain specimens after testing?

(a) As a laboratory testing the primary specimen, you must retain a specimen that was reported with positive, adulterated, substituted, or invalid results for a minimum of one year.

(b) You must keep such a specimen in secure, long-term, frozen storage in accordance with HHS requirements.

(c) Within the one-year period, the MRO, the employee, the employer, or a DOT agency may request in writing that you retain a specimen for an additional period of time (e.g., for the purpose of preserving evidence for litigation or a safety investigation). If you receive such a request, you must comply with it. If you do not receive such a request, you may discard the specimen at the end of the year.

(d) If you have not sent the split specimen to another laboratory for testing, you must retain the split specimen for an employee's test for the same period of time that you retain the primary specimen and under the same storage conditions.

(e) As the laboratory testing the split specimen, you must meet the requirements of paragraphs (a) through (d) of this section with respect to the split specimen.

§40.101 What relationship may a laboratory have with an MRO?

(a) As a laboratory, you may not enter into any relationship with an MRO that creates a conflict of interest or the appearance of a conflict of interest with the MRO's responsibilities for the employer. You may not derive any financial benefit by having an employer use a specific MRO.

(b) The following are examples of relationships between laboratories and MROs that the Department regards as creating conflicts of interest, or the appearance of such conflicts. This following list of examples is not intended to be exclusive or exhaustive:

(1) The laboratory employs an MRO who reviews test results produced by the laboratory;

(2) The laboratory has a contract or retainer with the MRO for the review of test results produced by the laboratory;

(3) The laboratory designates which MRO the employer is to use, gives the employer a slate of MROs from which to choose, or recommends certain MROs;

(4) The laboratory gives the employer a discount or other incentive to use a particular MRO;

(5) The laboratory has its place of business co-located with that of an MRO or MRO staff who review test results produced by the laboratory; or

(6) The laboratory permits an MRO, or an MRO's organization, to have a financial interest in the laboratory.

§40.107 Who may inspect laboratories?

As a laboratory, you must permit an inspection, with or without prior notice, by ODAPC, a DOT agency, or a DOT-regulated employer that contracts with the laboratory for drug testing under the DOT drug testing program, or the designee of such an employer.

§40.109 What documentation must the laboratory keep, and for how long?

(a) As a laboratory, you must retain all records pertaining to each employee urine specimen for a minimum of two years.

(b) As a laboratory, you must also keep for two years employer-specific data required in §40.111.

(c) Within the two-year period, the MRO, the employee, the employer, or a DOT agency may request in writing that you retain the records for an additional period of time (*e.g.,* for the purpose of preserving evidence for litigation or a safety investigation). If you receive such a request, you must comply with it. If you do not receive such a request, you may discard the records at the end of the two-year period.

§40.111 When and how must a laboratory disclose statistical summaries and other information it maintains?

(a) As a laboratory, you must transmit an aggregate statistical summary, by employer, of the data listed in Appendix B to this part to the employer on a semi-annual basis.

(1) The summary must not reveal the identity of any employee.

(2) In order to avoid sending data from which it is likely that information about an employee's test result can be readily inferred, you must not send a summary if the employer has fewer than five aggregate tests results.

(3) The summary must be sent by January 20 of each year for July 1 through December 31 of the prior year.

(4) The summary must also be sent by July 20 of each year for January 1 through June 30 of the current year.

(b) When the employer requests a summary in response to an inspection, audit, or review by a DOT agency, you must provide it unless the employer had fewer than five aggregate test results. In that case, you must send the employer a report indicating that not enough testing was conducted to warrant a summary. You may transmit the summary or report by hard copy, fax, or other electronic means.

(c) You must also release information to appropriate parties as provided in §§40.329 and 40.331.

(d) As a laboratory, you must transmit an aggregate statistical summary of the data listed in Appendix C to this part to DOT on a semi-annual basis. The summary must be sent by January 31 of each year for July 1 through December 31 of the prior year; it must be sent by July 31 of each year for January 1 through June 30 of the current year.

§40.113 Where is other information concerning laboratories found in this regulation?

You can find more information concerning laboratories in several sections of this part:

Subpart G—Medical Review Officers and the Verification Process

§40.121 Who is qualified to act as an MRO?

To be qualified to act as an MRO in the DOT drug testing program, you must meet each of the requirements of this section:

(a) **Credentials.** You must be a licensed physician (Doctor of Medicine or Osteopathy). If you are a licensed physician in any U.S., Canadian, or Mexican jurisdiction and meet the other requirements of this section, you are authorized to perform MRO services with respect to all covered employees, wherever they are located. For example, if you are licensed as an M.D. in one state or province in the U.S., Canada, or Mexico, you are not limited to performing MRO functions in that state or province, and you may perform MRO functions for employees in other states or provinces without becoming licensed to practice medicine in the other jurisdictions.

(b) **Basic knowledge.** You must be knowledgeable in the following areas:

(1) You must be knowledgeable about and have clinical experience in controlled substances abuse disorders, including detailed knowledge of alternative medical explanations for laboratory confirmed drug test results.

(2) You must be knowledgeable about issues relating to adulterated and substituted specimens as well as the possible medical causes of specimens having an invalid result.

(3) You must be knowledgeable about this part, the DOT MRO Guidelines, and the DOT agency regulations applicable to the employers for whom you evaluate drug test results, and you must keep current on any changes to these materials. You must subscribe to the ODAPC list-serve at *https://www.transportation.gov/odapc/get-odapc-email-updates.* DOT agency regulations, DOT MRO Guidelines, and other materials are available from ODAPC (Department of Transportation, 1200 New Jersey Avenue SE, Washington, DC 20590, 202-366-3784), or on the ODAPC Web site (*http://www.transportation.gov/odapc*).

(c) **Qualification training.** You must receive qualification training meeting the requirements of this paragraph (c).

(1) Qualification training must provide instruction on the following subjects:

(i) Collection procedures for urine specimens;

(ii) Chain of custody, reporting, and recordkeeping;

(iii) Interpretation of drug and validity tests results;

(iv) The role and responsibilities of the MRO in the DOT drug testing program;

(v) The interaction with other participants in the program (*e.g.*, DERs, SAPs); and

(vi) Provisions of this part and DOT agency rules applying to employers for whom you review test results, including changes and updates to this part and DOT agency rules, guidance, interpretations, and policies affecting the performance of MRO functions, as well as issues that MROs confront in carrying out their duties under this part and DOT agency rules.

(2) Following your completion of qualification training under paragraph (c)(1) of this section, you must satisfactorily complete an examination administered by a nationally-recognized MRO certification board or subspecialty board for medical practitioners in the field of medical review of DOT-mandated drug tests. The examination must comprehensively cover all the elements of qualification training listed in paragraph (c)(1) of this section.

(3) You must meet the requirements of paragraphs (a), (b), and (c) of this section before you begin to perform MRO functions.

(d) **Requalification training**. During each five-year period from the date on which you satisfactorily completed the examination under paragraph (c)(2) of this section, you must complete requalification training.

(1) This requalification training must meet the requirements of the qualification training under paragraph (c)(1) of this section.

(2) Following your completion of requalification training, you must satisfactorily complete an examination administered by a nationally-recognized MRO certification board or subspecialty board for medical practitioners in the field of medical review of DOT-mandated drug tests. The examination must comprehensively cover all the elements of qualification training listed in paragraph (c)(1) of this section.

(e) **Documentation.** You must maintain documentation showing that you currently meet all requirements of this section. You must provide this documentation on request to DOT agency representatives and to employers and C/TPAs who are using or negotiating to use your services.

§40.123 What are the MRO's responsibilities in the DOT drug testing program?

As an MRO, you have the following basic responsibilities:

(a) Acting as an independent and impartial "gatekeeper" and advocate for the accuracy and integrity of the drug testing process.

(b) Providing a quality assurance review of the drug testing process for the specimens under your purview. This includes, but is not limited to:

(1) Ensuring the review of the CCF on all specimen collections for the purposes of determining whether there is a problem that may cause a test to be cancelled (see §§40.199–40.203). As an MRO, you are not required to review laboratory internal chain of custody documentation. No one is permitted to cancel a test because you have not reviewed this documentation;

(2) Providing feedback to employers, collection sites and laboratories regarding performance issues where necessary; and

(3) Reporting to and consulting with the ODAPC or a relevant DOT agency when you wish DOT assistance in resolving any program issue. As an employer or service agent, you are prohibited from limiting or attempting to limit the

MRO's access to DOT for this purpose and from retaliating in any way against an MRO for discussing drug testing issues with DOT.

(c) You must determine whether there is a legitimate medical explanation for confirmed positive, adulterated, substituted, and invalid drug tests results from the laboratory.

(d) While you provide medical review of employees' test results, this part does not deem that you have established a doctor-patient relationship with the employees whose tests you review.

(e) You must act to investigate and correct problems where possible and notify appropriate parties (*e.g.,* HHS, DOT, employers, service agents) where assistance is needed, (*e.g.,* cancelled or problematic tests, incorrect results).

(f) You must ensure the timely flow of test results and other information to employers.

(g) You must protect the confidentiality of the drug testing information.

(h) You must perform all your functions in compliance with this part and other DOT agency regulations.

§40.125 What relationship may an MRO have with a laboratory?

As an MRO, you may not enter into any relationship with an employer's laboratory that creates a conflict of interest or the appearance of a conflict of interest with your responsibilities to that employer. You may not derive any financial benefit by having an employer use a specific laboratory. For examples of relationships between laboratories and MROs that the Department views as creating a conflict of interest or the appearance of such a conflict, see §40.101(b).

§40.127 What are the MRO's functions in reviewing negative test results?

As the MRO, you must do the following with respect to negative drug test results you receive from a laboratory, prior to verifying the result and releasing it to the DER:

(a) Review Copy 2 of the CCF to determine if there are any fatal or correctable errors that may require you to initiate corrective action or to cancel the test (see §§40.199 and 40.203).

(b) Review the negative laboratory test result and ensure that it is consistent with the information contained on the CCF.

(c) Before you report a negative test result, you must have in your possession the following documents:

(1) Copy 2 of the CCF, a legible copy of it, or any other CCF copy containing the employee's signature; and

(2) A legible copy (fax, photocopy, image) of Copy 1 of the CCF or the electronic laboratory results report that conveys the negative laboratory test result.

(d) If the copy of the documentation provided to you by the collector or laboratory appears unclear, you must request that the collector or laboratory send you a legible copy.

(e) On Copy 2 of the CCF, place a check mark in the "Negative" box (Step 6), provide your name, and sign, initial, or stamp and date the verification statement.

(f) Report the result in a confidential manner (see §§40.163–40.167).

(g) Staff under your direct, personal supervision may perform the administrative functions of this section for you, but only you can cancel a test. If you cancel a laboratory-confirmed negative result, check the "Test Cancelled" box

(Step 6) on Copy 2 of the CCF, make appropriate annotation in the "Remarks" line, provide your name, and sign, initial or stamp and date the verification statement.

(1) On specimen results that are reviewed by your staff, you are responsible for assuring the quality of their work.

(2) You are required to personally review at least 5 percent of all CCFs reviewed by your staff on a quarterly basis, including all results that required a corrective action. However, you need not review more than 500 negative results in any quarter.

(3) Your review must, as a minimum, include the CCF, negative laboratory test result, any accompanying corrective documents, and the report sent to the employer. You must correct any errors that you discover. You must take action as necessary to ensure compliance by your staff with this part and document your corrective action. You must attest to the quality assurance review by initialing the CCFs that you review.

(4) You must make these CCFs easily identifiable and retrievable by you for review by DOT agencies.

§40.129 What are the MRO's functions in reviewing laboratory confirmed non-negative drug test results?

(a) As the MRO, you must do the following with respect to confirmed positive, adulterated, substituted, or invalid drug tests you receive from a laboratory, before you verify the result and release it to the DER:

(1) Review Copy 2 of the CCF to determine if there are any fatal or correctable errors that may require you to cancel the test (see §§40.199 and 40.203). Staff under your direct, personal supervision may conduct this administrative review for you, but only you may verify or cancel a test.

(2) Review Copy 1 of the CCF and ensure that it is consistent with the information contained on Copy 2, that the test result is legible, and that the certifying scientist signed the form. You are not required to review any other documentation generated by the laboratory during their analysis or handling of the specimen (e.g., the laboratory internal chain of custody).

(3) If the copy of the documentation provided to you by the collector or laboratory appears unclear, you must request that the collector or laboratory send you a legible copy.

(4) Except in the circumstances spelled out in §40.133, conduct a verification interview. This interview must include direct contact in person or by telephone between you and the employee. You may initiate the verification process based on the laboratory results report.

(5) Verify the test result, consistent with the requirements of §§40.135 through 40.145, 40.159, and 40.160, as:

(i) Negative; or

(ii) Cancelled; or

(iii) Positive, and/or refusal to test because of adulteration or substitution.

(b) Before you report a verified negative, positive, test cancelled, refusal to test because of adulteration or substitution, you must have in your possession the following documents:

(1) Copy 2 of the CCF, a legible copy of it, or any other CCF copy containing the employee's signature; and

(2) A legible copy (fax, photocopy, image) of Copy 1 of the CCF, containing the certifying scientist's signature.

(c) With respect to verified positive test results, place a checkmark in the "Positive" box in Step 6 on Copy 2 of the CCF, indicate the drug(s)/metabolite(s) verified positive, and sign and date the verification statement.

(d) If you cancel a laboratory confirmed positive, adulterated, substituted, or invalid drug test report, check the "test cancelled" box (Step 6) on Copy 2 of the CCF, make appropriate annotation in the "Remarks" line, sign, provide your name, and date the verification statement.

(e) Report the result in a confidential manner (see §§40.163–40.167).

(f) With respect to adulteration or substitution test results, check the "refusal to test because:" box (Step 6) on Copy 2 of the CCF, check the "Adulterated" or "Substituted" box, as appropriate, make appropriate annotation in the "Remarks" line, sign and date the verification statement.

(g) As the MRO, your actions concerning reporting confirmed positive, adulterated, or substituted results to the employer before you have completed the verification process are also governed by the stand-down provisions of §40.21.

(1) If an employer has a stand-down policy that meets the requirements of §40.21, you may report to the DER that you have received an employee's laboratory confirmed positive, adulterated, or substituted test result, consistent with the terms of the waiver the employer received. You must not provide any further details about the test result (*e.g.,* the name of the drug involved).

(2) If the employer does not have a stand-down policy that meets the requirements of §40.21, you must not inform the employer that you have received an employee's laboratory confirmed positive, adulterated, or substituted test result until you verify the test result. For example, as an MRO employed directly by a company, you must not tell anyone on the company's staff or management that you have received an employee's laboratory confirmed test result.

§40.131 How does the MRO or DER notify an employee of the verification process after receiving laboratory confirmed non-negative drug test results?

(a) When, as the MRO, you receive a confirmed positive, adulterated, substituted, or invalid test result from the laboratory, you must contact the employee directly (*i.e.,* actually talk to the employee), on a confidential basis, to determine whether the employee wants to discuss the test result. In making this contact, you must explain to the employee that, if he or she declines to discuss the result, you will verify the test as positive or as a refusal to test because of adulteration or substitution, as applicable.

(b) As the MRO, staff under your personal supervision may conduct this initial contact for you.

(1) This staff contact must be limited to scheduling the discussion between you and the employee and explaining the consequences of the employee's declining to speak with you (*i.e.,* that the MRO will verify the test without input from the employee). If the employee declines to speak with you, the staff person must document the employee's decision, including the date and time.

(2) A staff person must not gather any medical information or information concerning possible explanations for the test result.

(3) A staff person may advise an employee to have medical information (*e.g.,* prescriptions, information forming the basis of a legitimate medical explanation for a confirmed positive test result) ready to present at the interview with the MRO.

(4) Since you are required to speak personally with the employee, face-to-face or on the phone, your staff must not inquire if the employee wishes to speak with you.

(c) As the MRO, you or your staff must make reasonable efforts to reach the employee at the day and evening telephone numbers listed on the CCF. Reasonable efforts include, as a minimum, three attempts, spaced reasonably over a 24-hour period, to reach the employee at the day and evening telephone numbers listed on the CCF. If you or your staff cannot reach the employee directly after making these efforts, you or your staff must take the following steps:

(1) Document the efforts you made to contact the employee, including dates and times. If both phone numbers are incorrect (*e.g.,* disconnected, wrong number), you may take the actions listed in paragraph (c)(2) of this section without waiting the full 24-hour period.

(2) Contact the DER, instructing the DER to contact the employee.

(i) You must simply direct the DER to inform the employee to contact you.

(ii) You must not inform the DER that the employee has a confirmed positive, adulterated, substituted, or invalid test result.

(iii) You must document the dates and times of your attempts to contact the DER, and you must document the name of the DER you contacted and the date and time of the contact.

(d) As the DER, you must attempt to contact the employee immediately, using procedures that protect, as much as possible, the confidentiality of the MRO's request that the employee contact the MRO. If you successfully contact the employee (*i.e.,* actually talk to the employee), you must document the date and time of the contact, and inform the MRO. You must inform the employee that he or she should contact the MRO immediately. You must also inform the employee of the consequences of failing to contact the MRO within the next 72 hours (see §40.133(a)(2)).

(1) As the DER, you must not inform anyone else working for the employer that you are seeking to contact the employee on behalf of the MRO.

(2) If, as the DER, you have made all reasonable efforts to contact the employee but failed to do so, you may place the employee on temporary medically unqualified status or medical leave. Reasonable efforts include, as a minimum, three attempts, spaced reasonably over a 24-hour period, to reach the employee at the day and evening telephone numbers listed on the CCF.

(i) As the DER, you must document the dates and times of these efforts.

(ii) If, as the DER, you are unable to contact the employee within this 24-hour period, you must leave a message for the employee by any practicable means (*e.g.,* voice mail, e-mail, letter) to contact the MRO and inform the MRO of the date and time of this attempted contact.

§40.133 Without interviewing the employee, under what circumstances may the MRO verify a test result as positive, or as a refusal to test because of adulteration or substitution, or as cancelled because the test was invalid?

(a) As the MRO, you normally may verify a confirmed positive test (for any drug or drug metabolite, including opiates), or as a refusal to test because of adulteration or substitution, only after interviewing the employee as provided in §§40.135–40.145. However, there are three circumstances in which you may verify such a result without an interview:

(1) You may verify a test result as a positive or refusal to test, as applicable, if the employee expressly declines the opportunity to discuss the test with you. You must maintain complete documentation of this occurrence, including notation of informing, or attempting to inform, the employee of the consequences of not exercising the option to speak with you.

(2) You may verify a test result as a positive or refusal to test, as applicable, if the DER has successfully made and documented a contact with the employee and instructed the employee to contact you and more than 72 hours have passed since the time the DER contacted the employee.

(3) You may verify a test result as a positive or refusal to test, as applicable, if neither you nor the DER, after making and documenting all reasonable efforts, has been able to contact the employee within ten days of the date on which the MRO receives the confirmed test result from the laboratory.

(b) As the MRO, you may verify an invalid test result as cancelled (with instructions to recollect immediately under direct observation) without interviewing the employee, as provided at §40.159 :

(1) If the employee expressly declines the opportunity to discuss the test with you;

(2) If the DER has successfully made and documented a contact with the employee and instructed the employee to contact you and more than 72 hours have passed since the time the DER contacted the employee; or

(3) If neither you nor the DER, after making and documenting all reasonable efforts, has been able to contact the employee within ten days of the date on which you received the confirmed invalid test result from the laboratory.

(c) As the MRO, after you verify a test result as a positive or as a refusal to test under this section, you must document the date and time and reason, following the instructions in §40.163. For a cancelled test due to an invalid result under this section, you must follow the instructions in §40.159(a)(5).

(d) As the MRO, after you have verified a test result under this section and reported the result to the DER, you must allow the employee to present information to you within 60 days of the verification to document that serious illness, injury, or other circumstances unavoidably precluded contact with the MRO and/or DER in the times provided. On the basis of such information, you may reopen the verification, allowing the employee to present information concerning whether there is a legitimate medical explanation of the confirmed test result.

§40.135 What does the MRO tell the employee at the beginning of the verification interview?

(a) As the MRO, you must tell the employee that the laboratory has determined that the employee's test result was positive, adulterated, substituted, or invalid, as applicable. You must also tell the employee of the drugs for which his or her specimen tested positive, or the basis for the finding of adulteration or substitution.

(b) You must explain the verification interview process to the employee and inform the employee that your decision will be based on information the employee provides in the interview.

(c) You must explain that, if further medical evaluation is needed for the verification process, the employee must comply with your request for this evaluation and that failure to do so is equivalent of expressly declining to discuss the test result.

(d) As the MRO, you must warn an employee who has a confirmed positive, adulterated, substituted or invalid test that you are required to provide to third parties drug test result information and medical information affecting the performance of safety-sensitive duties that the employee gives you in the verification process without the employee's consent (see §40.327).

(1) You must give this warning to the employee before obtaining any medical information as part of the verification process.

(2) For purposes of this paragraph (d), medical information includes information on medications or other substances affecting the performance of safety-sensitive duties that the employee reports using or medical conditions the employee reports having.

(3) For purposes of this paragraph (d), the persons to whom this information may be provided include the employer, a SAP evaluating the employee as part of the return to duty process (see §40.293(g)), DOT, another Federal safety agency (e.g., the NTSB), or any state safety agency as required by state law.

(e) You must also advise the employee that, before informing any third party about any medication the employee is using pursuant to a legally valid prescription consistent with the Controlled Substances Act, you will allow 5 business days from the date you report the verified negative result for the employee to have the prescribing physician contact you to determine if the medication can be changed to one that does not make the employee medically unqualified or does not pose a significant safety risk. If, in your reasonable medical judgment, a medical qualification issue or a significant safety risk remains after you communicate with the employee's prescribing physician or after 5 business days, whichever is shorter, you must follow §40.327. If, as the MRO, you receive information that eliminates the medical qualification issue or significant safety risk, you must transmit this information to any third party to whom you previously provided information under §40.327.

§40.137 On what basis does the MRO verify test results involving marijuana, cocaine, amphetamines, semi-synthetic opioids, or PCP?

(a) As the MRO, you must verify a confirmed positive test result for marijuana, cocaine, amphetamines, semi-synthetic opioids (i.e., hydrocodone, hydromorphone, oxycodone, and oxymorphone), and/or PCP unless the employee presents a legitimate medical explanation for the presence of the drug(s)/ metabolite(s) in his or her system. In determining whether an employee's legally valid prescription consistent with the Controlled Substances Act for a substance in these categories constitutes a legitimate medical explanation, you must not question whether the prescribing physician should have prescribed the substance.

(b) You must offer the employee an opportunity to present a legitimate medical explanation in all cases.

(c) The employee has the burden of proof that a legitimate medical explanation exists. The employee must present information meeting this burden at the time of the verification interview. As the MRO, you have discretion to extend the time available to the employee for this purpose for up to five days before verifying the test result, if you determine that there is a reasonable basis to believe that the employee will be able to produce relevant evidence concerning a legitimate medical explanation within that time.

(d) If you determine that there is a legitimate medical explanation, you must verify the test result as negative. Otherwise, you must verify the test result as positive.

(e) In determining whether a legitimate medical explanation exists, you may consider the employee's use of a medication from a foreign country. You must exercise your professional judgment consistently with the following principles:

(1) There can be a legitimate medical explanation only with respect to a substance that is obtained legally in a foreign country.

(2) There can be a legitimate medical explanation only with respect to a substance that has a legitimate medical use. Use of a drug of abuse (*e.g.,* heroin, PCP, marijuana) or any other substance (see §40.151(f) and (g)) that cannot be viewed as having a legitimate medical use can never be the basis for a legitimate medical explanation, even if the substance is obtained legally in a foreign country.

(3) Use of the substance can form the basis of a legitimate medical explanation only if it is used consistently with its proper and intended medical purpose.

(4) Even if you find that there is a legitimate medical explanation under this paragraph (e) and verify a test negative, you may have a responsibility to raise fitness-for-duty considerations with the employer (see §40.327).

§40.139 On what basis does the MRO verify test results involving 6-acetylmorphine, codeine, and morphine?

As the MRO, you must proceed as follows when you receive a laboratory confirmed positive opiate result:

(a) If the laboratory confirms the presence of 6-acetylmorphine (6-AM) in the specimen, you must verify the test result positive.

(b) In the absence of 6-AM, if the laboratory confirms the presence of either morphine or codeine at 15,000 ng/mL or above, you must verify the test result positive unless the employee presents a legitimate medical explanation for the presence of the drug or drug metabolite in his or her system, as in the case of other drugs (see §40.137). Consumption of food products (e.g., poppy seeds) must not be considered a legitimate medical explanation for the employee having morphine or codeine at these concentrations.

(c) For all other codeine and morphine positive results, you must verify a confirmed positive test result only if you determine that there is clinical evidence, in addition to the urine test, of unauthorized use of any opium, opiate, or opium derivative (*i.e.,* morphine, codeine, or heroin).

(1) As an MRO, it is your responsibility to use your best professional and ethical judgement and discretion to determine whether there is clinical evidence of unauthorized use of opiates. Examples of information that you may consider in making this judgement include, but are not limited to, the following:

(i) Recent needle tracks;

(ii) Behavioral and psychological signs of acute opiate intoxication or withdrawal;

(iii) Clinical history of unauthorized use recent enough to have produced the laboratory test result;

(iv) Use of a medication from a foreign country. See §40.137(e) for guidance on how to make this determination.

(2) In order to establish the clinical evidence referenced in paragraphs (c)(1)(i) and (ii) of this section, personal observation of the employee is essential.

(i) Therefore, you, as the MRO, must conduct, or cause another physician to conduct, a face-to-face examination of the employee.

(ii) No face-to-face examination is needed in establishing the clinical evidence referenced in paragraph (c)(1)(iii) or (iv) of this section.

(3) To be the basis of a verified positive result for codeine or morphine, the clinical evidence you find must concern a drug that the laboratory found in the specimen. (For example, if the test confirmed the presence of codeine, and the employee admits to unauthorized use of hydrocodone, you must not verify the test positive for codeine. The admission must be for the substance that was found through the actual drug test.)

(4) As the MRO, you have the burden of establishing that there is clinical evidence of unauthorized use of opiates referenced in this paragraph (c). If you cannot make this determination (e.g., there is not sufficient clinical evidence or history), you must verify the test as negative. The employee does not need to show you that a legitimate medical explanation exists if no clinical evidence is established.

§40.141 How does the MRO obtain information for the verification decision?

As the MRO, you must do the following as you make the determinations needed for a verification decision:

(a) You must conduct a medical interview. You must review the employee's medical history and any other relevant biomedical factors presented to you by the employee. You may direct the employee to undergo further medical evaluation by you or another physician.

(b) If the employee asserts that the presence of a drug or drug metabolite in his or her specimen results from taking prescription medication (*i.e.,* a legally valid prescription consistent with the Controlled Substances Act), you must review and take all reasonable and necessary steps to verify the authenticity of all medical records the employee provides. You may contact the employee's physician or other relevant medical personnel for further information. You may request an HHS-certified laboratory with validated protocols (see §40.81(c)) to conduct testing for D,L stereoisomers of amphetamine and methamphetamine or testing for tetrahydrocannabivarin (THC- V) when verifying lab results, as you determine necessary.

§40.143 [Reserved]

§40.145 On what basis does the MRO verify test results involving adulteration or substitution?

(a) As an MRO, when you receive a laboratory report that a specimen is adulterated or substituted, you must treat that report in the same way you treat the laboratory's report of a confirmed positive for a drug or drug metabolite.

(b) You must follow the same procedures used for verification of a confirmed positive test for a drug or drug metabolite (see §§40.129–40.135, 40.141, 40.151), except as otherwise provided in this section.

(c) In the verification interview, you must explain the laboratory findings to the employee and address technical questions or issues the employee may raise.

(d) You must offer the employee the opportunity to present a legitimate medical explanation for the laboratory findings with respect to presence of the adulterant in, or the creatinine and specific gravity findings for, the specimen.

(e) The employee has the burden of proof that there is a legitimate medical explanation.

(1) To meet this burden in the case of an adulterated specimen, the employee must demonstrate that the adulterant found by the laboratory entered the specimen through physiological means.

(2) To meet this burden in the case of a substituted specimen, the employee must demonstrate that he or she did produce or could have produced urine through physiological means, meeting the creatinine concentration criterion of less than 2 mg/dL and the specific gravity criteria of less than or equal to 1.0010 or greater than or equal to 1.0200 (see §40.93(b)).

(3) The employee must present information meeting this burden at the time of the verification interview. As the MRO, you have discretion to extend the time available to the employee for this purpose for up to five days before verifying the specimen, if you determine that there is a reasonable basis to believe that the employee will be able to produce relevant evidence supporting a legitimate medical explanation within that time.

(f) As the MRO or the employer, you are not responsible for arranging, conducting, or paying for any studies, examinations or analyses to determine whether a legitimate medical explanation exists.

(g) As the MRO, you must exercise your best professional judgment in deciding whether the employee has established a legitimate medical explanation.

(1) If you determine that the employee's explanation does not present a reasonable basis for concluding that there may be a legitimate medical explanation, you must report the test to the DER as a verified refusal to test because of adulteration or substitution, as applicable.

(2) If you believe that the employee's explanation may present a reasonable basis for concluding that there is a legitimate medical explanation, you must direct the employee to obtain, within the five-day period set forth in paragraph (e)(3) of this section, a further medical evaluation. This evaluation must be performed by a licensed physician (the "referral physician"), acceptable to you, with expertise in the medical issues raised by the employee's explanation. (The MRO may perform this evaluation if the MRO has appropriate expertise.)

(i) As the MRO or employer, you are not responsible for finding or paying a referral physician. However, on request of the employee, you must provide reasonable assistance to the employee's efforts to find such a physician. The final choice of the referral physician is the employee's, as long as the physician is acceptable to you.

(ii) As the MRO, you must consult with the referral physician, providing guidance to him or her concerning his or her responsibilities under this section. As part of this consultation, you must provide the following information to the referral physician:

(A) That the employee was required to take a DOT drug test, but the laboratory reported that the specimen was adulterated or substituted, which is treated as a refusal to test;

(B) The consequences of the appropriate DOT agency regulation for refusing to take the required drug test;

(C) That the referral physician must agree to follow the requirements of paragraphs (g)(3) through (g)(4) of this section; and

(D) That the referral physician must provide you with a signed statement of his or her recommendations.

(3) As the referral physician, you must evaluate the employee and consider any evidence the employee presents concerning the employee's medical explanation. You may conduct additional tests to determine whether there is a legitimate medical explanation. Any additional urine tests must be performed in an HHS-certified laboratory.

(4) As the referral physician, you must then make a written recommendation to the MRO about whether the MRO should determine that there is a legitimate medical explanation. As the MRO, you must seriously consider and assess the referral physician's recommendation in deciding whether there is a legitimate medical explanation.

(5) As the MRO, if you determine that there is a legitimate medical explanation, you must cancel the test and inform ODAPC in writing of the determination and the basis for it (e.g., referral physician's findings, evidence produced by the employee).

(6) As the MRO, if you determine that there is not a legitimate medical explanation, you must report the test to the DER as a verified refusal to test because of adulteration or substitution.

(h) The following are examples of types of evidence an employee could present to support an assertion of a legitimate medical explanation for a substituted result.

(1) Medically valid evidence demonstrating that the employee is capable of physiologically producing urine meeting the creatinine and specific gravity criteria of §40.93(b).

(i) To be regarded as medically valid, the evidence must have been gathered using appropriate methodology and controls to ensure its accuracy and reliability.

(ii) Assertion by the employee that his or her personal characteristics (e.g., with respect to race, gender, weight, diet, working conditions) are responsible for the substituted result does not, in itself, constitute a legitimate medical explanation. To make a case that there is a legitimate medical explanation, the employee must present evidence showing that the cited personal characteristics actually result in the physiological production of urine meeting the creatinine and specific gravity criteria of §40.93(b).

(2) Information from a medical evaluation under paragraph (g) of this section that the individual has a medical condition that has been demonstrated to cause the employee to physiologically produce urine meeting the creatinine and specific gravity criteria of §40.93(b).

(i) A finding or diagnosis by the physician that an employee has a medical condition, in itself, does not constitute a legitimate medical explanation.

(ii) To establish there is a legitimate medical explanation, the employee must demonstrate that the cited medical condition actually results in the physiological production of urine meeting the creatinine and specific gravity criteria of §40.93(b).

§40.147 [Reserved]

§40.149 May the MRO change a verified drug test result?

(a) As the MRO, you may change a verified test result only in the following situations:

(1) When you have reopened a verification that was done without an interview with an employee (see §40.133(d)).

(2) If you receive information, not available to you at the time of the original verification, demonstrating that the laboratory made an error in identifying (e.g., a paperwork mistake) or testing (e.g., a false positive or negative) the employee's primary or split specimen. For example, suppose the laboratory originally reported a positive test result for Employee X and a negative result for Employee Y. You verified the test results as reported to you. Then the laboratory notifies

you that it mixed up the two test results, and X was really negative and Y was really positive. You would change X's test result from positive to negative and contact Y to conduct a verification interview.

(3) If, within 60 days of the original verification decision—

(i) You receive information that could not reasonably have been provided to you at the time of the decision demonstrating that there is a legitimate medical explanation for the presence of drug(s)/metabolite(s) in the employee's specimen; or

(ii) You receive credible new or additional evidence that a legitimate medical explanation for an adulterated or substituted result exists.

Example to Paragraph (a)(3): If the employee's physician provides you a valid prescription that he or she failed to find at the time of the original verification, you may change the test result from positive to negative if you conclude that the prescription provides a legitimate medical explanation for the drug(s)/metabolite(s) in the employee's specimen.

(4) If you receive the information in paragraph (a)(3) of this section after the 60-day period, you must consult with ODAPC prior to changing the result.

(5) When you have made an administrative error and reported an incorrect result.

(b) If you change the result, you must immediately notify the DER in writing, as provided in §§40.163–40.165.

(c) You are the only person permitted to change a verified test result, such as a verified positive test result or a determination that an individual has refused to test because of adulteration or substitution. This is because, as the MRO, you have the sole authority under this part to make medical determinations leading to a verified test (*e.g.,* a determination that there was or was not a legitimate medical explanation for a laboratory test result). For example, an arbitrator is not permitted to overturn the medical judgment of the MRO that the employee failed to present a legitimate medical explanation for a positive, adulterated, or substituted test result of his or her specimen.

§40.151 What are MROs prohibited from doing as part of the verification process?

As an MRO, you are prohibited from doing the following as part of the verification process:

(a) You must not consider any evidence from tests of urine samples or other body fluids or tissues (*e.g.,* blood or hair samples) that are not collected or tested in accordance with this part. For example, if an employee tells you he went to his own physician, provided a urine specimen, sent it to a laboratory, and received a negative test result or a DNA test result questioning the identity of his DOT specimen, you are required to ignore this test result.

(b) It is not your function to make decisions about factual disputes between the employee and the collector concerning matters occurring at the collection site that are not reflected on the CCF (*e.g.,* concerning allegations that the collector left the area or left open urine containers where other people could access them).

(c) It is not your function to determine whether the employer should have directed that a test occur. For example, if an employee tells you that the employer misidentified her as the subject of a random test, or directed her to take a reasonable suspicion or post-accident test without proper grounds under a DOT agency drug or alcohol regulation, you must inform the employee that you cannot play a role in deciding these issues.

(d) It is not your function to consider explanations of confirmed positive, adulterated, or substituted test results that would not, even if true, constitute a legitimate medical explanation. For example, an employee may tell you that someone slipped amphetamines into her drink at a party, that she unknowingly ingested a marijuana brownie, or that she traveled in a closed car with several people smoking crack. MROs are unlikely to be able to verify the facts of such passive or unknowing ingestion stories. Even if true, such stories do not present a legitimate medical explanation. Consequently, you must not declare a test as negative based on an explanation of this kind.

(e) You must not verify a test negative based on information that a physician recommended that the employee use a drug listed in Schedule I of the Controlled Substances Act. (*e.g.,* under a state law that purports to authorize such recommendations, such as the "medical marijuana" laws that some states have adopted).

(f) You must not accept an assertion of consumption or other use of a hemp or other non-prescription marijuana-related product as a basis for verifying a marijuana test negative. You also must not accept such an explanation related to consumption of coca teas as a basis for verifying a cocaine test result as negative. Consuming or using such a product is not a legitimate medical explanation.

(g) You must not accept an assertion that there is a legitimate medical explanation for the presence of PCP, 6–AM, MDMA, MDA, or MDEA in a specimen.

(h) You must not accept, as a legitimate medical explanation for an adulterated specimen, an assertion that soap, bleach, or glutaraldehyde entered a specimen through physiological means. There are no physiological means through which these substances can enter a specimen.

(i) You must not accept, as a legitimate medical explanation for a substituted specimen, an assertion that an employee can produce urine with no detectable creatinine. There are no physiological means through which a person can produce a urine specimen having this characteristic.

§40.153 How does the MRO notify employees of their right to a test of the split specimen?

(a) As the MRO, when you have verified a drug test as positive for a drug or drug metabolite, or as a refusal to test because of adulteration or substitution, you must notify the employee of his or her right to have the split specimen tested. You must also notify the employee of the procedures for requesting a test of the split specimen.

(b) You must inform the employee that he or she has 72 hours from the time you provide this notification to him or her to request a test of the split specimen.

(c) You must tell the employee how to contact you to make this request. You must provide telephone numbers or other information that will allow the employee to make this request. As the MRO, you must have the ability to receive the employee's calls at all times during the 72 hour period (*e.g.,* by use of an answering machine with a "time stamp" feature when there is no one in your office to answer the phone).

(d) You must tell the employee that if he or she makes this request within 72 hours, the employer must ensure that the test takes place, and that the employee is not required to pay for the test from his or her own funds before the test takes place. You must also tell the employee that the employer may seek reimbursement for the cost of the test (see §40.173).

(e) You must tell the employee that additional tests of the specimen *e.g.,* (DNA tests) are not authorized.

§40.155 What does the MRO do when a negative or positive test result is also dilute?

(a) When the laboratory reports that a specimen is dilute, you must, as the MRO, report to the DER that the specimen, in addition to being negative or positive, is dilute.

(b) You must check the "dilute" box (Step 6) on Copy 2 of the CCF.

(c) When you report a dilute specimen to the DER, you must explain to the DER the employer's obligations and choices under §40.197, to include the requirement for an immediate recollection under direct observation if the creatinine concentration of a negative-dilute specimen was greater than or equal to 2mg/dL but less than or equal to 5mg/dL.

(d) If the employee's recollection under direct observation, in paragraph (c) of this section, results in another negative-dilute, as the MRO, you must:

(1) Review the CCF to ensure that there is documentation that the recollection was directly observed.

(2) If the CCF documentation shows that the recollection was directly observed as required, report this result to the DER as a negative-dilute result.

(3) If CCF documentation indicates that the recollection was not directly observed as required, do not report a result but again explain to the DER that there must be an immediate recollection under direct observation.

§40.157 [Reserved]

§40.159 What does the MRO do when a drug test is invalid?

(a) As the MRO, when the laboratory reports that the test result is an invalid result, you must do the following:

(1) Discuss the laboratory results with a certifying scientist to determine if the primary specimen should be tested at another HHS certified laboratory. If the laboratory did not contact you as required by §§40.91(e) and 40.96(c), you must contact the laboratory.

(2) If you and the laboratory have determined that no further testing is necessary, contact the employee and inform the employee that the specimen was invalid. In contacting the employee, use the procedures set forth in §40.131.

(3) After explaining the limits of disclosure (see §§40.135(d) and 40.327), you must determine if the employee has a medical explanation for the invalid result. You must inquire about the medications the employee may have taken.

(4) If the employee gives an explanation that is acceptable, you must:

(i) Place a check mark in the "Test Cancelled" box (Step 6) on Copy 2 of the CCF and enter "Invalid Result" and "direct observation collection not required" on the "Remarks" line.

(ii) Report to the DER that the test is cancelled, the reason for cancellation, and that no further action is required unless a negative test result is required (i.e., pre-employment, return-to-duty, or follow-up tests).

(iii) If a negative test result is required and the medical explanation concerns a situation in which the employee has a permanent or long-term medical condition that precludes him or her from providing a valid specimen, as the MRO, you must follow the procedures outlined at §40.160 for determining if there is clinical evidence that the individual is an illicit drug user.

(5) If the employee is unable to provide an explanation and/or a valid prescription for a medication that interfered with the immunoassay test but denies having adulterated the specimen, you must:

(i) Place a check mark in the "Test Cancelled" box (Step 6) on Copy 2 of the CCF and enter "Invalid Result" and "direct observation collection required" on the "Remarks" line.

(ii) Report to the DER that the test is cancelled, the reason for cancellation, and that a second collection must take place immediately under direct observation.

(iii) Instruct the employer to ensure that the employee has the minimum possible advance notice that he or she must go to the collection site.

(6) When the test result is invalid because pH is greater than or equal to 9.0 but less than or equal to 9.5 and the employee has no other medical explanation for the pH, you should consider whether there is evidence of elapsed time and increased temperature that could account for the pH value.

(i) You are authorized to consider the temperature conditions that were likely to have existed between the time of collection and transportation of the specimen to the laboratory, and the length of time between the specimen collection and arrival at the laboratory.

(ii) You may talk with the collection site and laboratory to discuss time and temperature issues, including any pertinent information regarding specimen storage.

(iii) If you determine that time and temperature account for the pH value, you must cancel the test and take no further action, as provided at paragraph (a)(4) of this section.

(iv) If you determine that time and temperature fail to account for the pH value, you must cancel the test and direct another collection under direct observation, as provided at paragraph (a)(5) of this section.

(b) You may only report an invalid test result when you are in possession of a legible copy of Copy 1 of the CCF. In addition, you must have Copy 2 of the CCF, a legible copy of it, or any other copy of the CCF containing the employee's signature.

(c) If the employee admits to having adulterated or substituted the specimen, you must, on the same day, write and sign your own statement of what the employee told you. You must then report a refusal to test in accordance with §40.163.

(d) If the employee admits to using a drug, you must, on the same day, write and sign your own statement of what the employee told you. You must then report that admission to the DER for appropriate action under DOT Agency regulations. This test will be reported as cancelled with the reason noted.

(e) If the employee's recollection (required at paragraph (a)(5) of this section) results in another invalid result for the same reason as reported for the first specimen, as the MRO, you must:

(1) Review the CCF to ensure that there is documentation that the recollection was directly observed.

(2) If the CCF review indicates that the recollection was directly observed as required, document that the employee had another specimen with an invalid result for the same reason.

(3) Follow the recording and reporting procedures at (a)(4)(i) and (ii) of this section.

(4) If a negative result is required (*i.e.,* pre-employment, return-to-duty, or follow-up tests), follow the procedures at §40.160 for determining if there is clinical evidence that the individual is an illicit drug user.

(5) If the recollection was not directly observed as required, do not report a result but again explain to the DER that there must be an immediate recollection under direct observation.

(f) If the employee's recollection (required at paragraph (a)(5) of this section) results in another invalid result for a different reason than that reported for the first specimen, as the MRO, you must:

(1) Review the CCF to ensure that there is documentation that the recollection was directly observed.

(2) If the CCF review indicates that the recollection was directly observed as required, document that the employee had another specimen with an invalid result for a different reason.

(3) As the MRO, you should not contact the employee to discuss the result, but rather direct the DER to conduct an immediate recollection under direct observation without prior notification to the employee.

(4) If the CCF documentation indicates that the recollection was not directly observed as required, do not report a result but again explain to the DER that there must be an immediate recollection under direct observation.

(g) If, as the MRO, you receive a laboratory invalid result in conjunction with a positive, adulterated, and/or substituted result and you verify any of those results as being a positive and/or refusal to test, you do not report the invalid result unless the split specimen fails to reconfirm the result(s) of the primary specimen.

§40.160 What does the MRO do when a valid test result cannot be produced and a negative result is required?

(a) If a valid test result cannot be produced and a negative result is required, (under § 40.159 (a)(5)(iii) and (e)(4)), as the MRO, you must determine if there is clinical evidence that the individual is currently an illicit drug user. You must make this determination by personally conducting, or causing to be conducted, a medical evaluation. In addition, if appropriate, you may also consult with the employee's physician to gather information you need to reach this determination.

(b) If you do not personally conduct the medical evaluation, as the MRO, you must ensure that one is conducted by a licensed physician acceptable to you.

(c) For purposes of this section, the MRO or the physician conducting the evaluation may conduct an alternative test (e.g., blood) as part of the medically appropriate procedures in determining clinical evidence of drug use.

(d) If the medical evaluation reveals no clinical evidence of drug use, as the MRO, you must report this to the employer as a negative test result with written notations regarding the medical examination. The report must also state why the medical examination was required (i.e., either the basis for the determination that a permanent or long-term medical condition exists or because the recollection under direct observation resulted in another invalid result for the same reason, as appropriate) and for the determination that no signs and symptoms of drug use exist.

(1) Check "Negative" (Step 6) on the CCF.

(2) Sign and date the CCF.

(e) If the medical evaluation reveals clinical evidence of drug use, as the MRO, you must report the result to the employer as a cancelled test with written notations regarding the results of the medical examination. The report must also state why the medical examination was required (i.e., either the basis for the determination that a permanent or long-term medical condition exists or because the recollection under direct observation resulted in another invalid result for the same reason, as appropriate) and state the reason for the determination that signs and symptoms of drug use exist. Because this is a cancelled test, it does not serve the purpose of an actual negative test result (*i.e.*, the employer is not authorized to allow the employee to begin or resume performing safety-sensitive functions, because a negative test result is needed for that purpose).

§40.161 What does the MRO do when a drug test specimen is rejected for testing?

As the MRO, when the laboratory reports that the specimen is rejected for testing (*e.g.*, because of a fatal or uncorrected flaw), you must do the following:

(a) Place a check mark in the "Test Cancelled" box (Step 6) on Copy 2 of the CCF and enter the reason on the "Remarks" line.

(b) Report to the DER that the test is cancelled and the reason for cancellation, and that no further action is required unless a negative test is required (*e.g.*, in the case of a pre-employment, return-to-duty, or follow-up test).

(c) You may only report a test cancelled because of a rejected for testing test result when you are in possession of a legible copy of Copy 1 of the CCF. In addition, you must have Copy 2 of the CCF, a legible copy of it, or any other copy of the CCF containing the employee's signature.

§40.162 What must MROs do with multiple verified results for the same testing event?

(a) If the testing event is one in which there was one specimen collection with multiple verified non-negative results, as the MRO, you must report them all to the DER. For example, if you verified the specimen as being positive for marijuana and cocaine and as being a refusal to test because the specimen was also adulterated, as the MRO, you should report the positives and the refusal to the DER.

(b) If the testing event was one in which two separate specimen collections (*e.g.*, a specimen out of temperature range and the subsequent observed collection) were sent to the laboratory, as the MRO, you must:

(1) If both specimens were verified negative, report the result as negative.

(2) If either of the specimens was verified negative and the other was verified as one or more non-negative(s), report the non-negative result(s) only. For example, if you verified one specimen as negative and the other as a refusal to test because the second specimen was substituted, as the MRO you should report only the refusal to the DER.

(i) If the first specimen is reported as negative, but the result of the second specimen has not been reported by the laboratory, as the MRO, you should hold—not report—the result of the first specimen until the result of the second specimen is received.

(ii) If the first specimen is reported as non-negative, as the MRO, you should report the result immediately and not wait to receive the result of the second specimen.

(3) If both specimens were verified non-negative, report all of the non-negative results. For example, if you verified one specimen as positive and the other as a refusal to test because the specimen was adulterated, as the MRO, you should report the positive and the refusal results to the DER.

(c) As an exception to paragraphs (a) and (b) of this section, as the MRO, you must follow procedures at §40.159(g) when any verified non-negative result is also invalid.

§40.163 How does the MRO report drug test results?

(a) As the MRO, it is your responsibility to report all drug test results to the employer.

(b) You may use a signed or stamped and dated legible photocopy of Copy 2 of the CCF to report test results.

(c) If you do not report test results using Copy 2 of the CCF for this purpose, you must provide a written report (*e.g.,* a letter) for each test result. This report must, as a minimum, include the following information:

(1) Full name, as indicated on the CCF, of the employee tested;

(2) Specimen ID number from the CCF and the donor SSN or employee ID number;

(3) Reason for the test, if indicated on the CCF (*e.g.,* random, post-accident);

(4) Date of the collection;

(5) Date you received Copy 2 of the CCF;

(6) Result of the test (*i.e.,* positive, negative, dilute, refusal to test, test cancelled) and the date the result was verified by the MRO;

(7) For verified positive tests, the drug(s)/metabolite(s) for which the test was positive;

(8) For cancelled tests, the reason for cancellation; and

(9) For refusals to test, the reason for the refusal determination (*e.g.,* in the case of an adulterated test result, the name of the adulterant).

(d) As an exception to the reporting requirements of paragraph (b) and (c) of this section, the MRO may report negative results using an electronic data file.

(1) If you report negatives using an electronic data file, the report must contain, as a minimum, the information specified in paragraph (c) of this section, as applicable for negative test results.

(2) In addition, the report must contain your name, address, and phone number, the name of any person other than you reporting the results, and the date the electronic results report is released.

(e) You must retain a signed or stamped and dated copy of Copy 2 of the CCF in your records. If you do not use Copy 2 for reporting results, you must maintain a copy of the signed or stamped and dated letter in addition to the signed or stamped and dated Copy 2. If you use the electronic data file to report negatives, you must maintain a retrievable copy of that report in a format suitable for inspection and auditing by a DOT representative.

(f) You must not use Copy 1 of the CCF to report drug test results.

(g) You must not provide quantitative values to the DER or C/TPA for drug or validity test results. However, you must provide the test information in your possession to a SAP who consults with you (see §40.293(g)).

(h) You must maintain reports and records related to negatives and cancelled results for one year; you must maintain reports and records related to positives and refusals for five years, unless otherwise specified by applicable DOT agency regulations.

§40.165 To whom does the MRO transmit reports of drug test results?

(a) As the MRO, you must report all drug test results to the DER, except in the circumstances provided for in §40.345.

(b) If the employer elects to receive reports of results through a C/TPA, acting as an intermediary as provided in §40.345, you must report the results through the designated C/TPA.

§40.167 How are MRO reports of drug results transmitted to the employer?

As the MRO or C/TPA who transmits drug test results to the employer, you must comply with the following requirements:

(a) You must report the results in a confidential manner.

(b) You must transmit to the DER on the same day the MRO verifies the result or the next business day all verified positive test results, results requiring an immediate collection under direct observation, adulterated or substituted specimen results, and other refusals to test.

(1) Direct telephone contact with the DER is the preferred method of immediate reporting. Follow up your phone call with appropriate documentation (see §40.163).

(2) You are responsible for identifying yourself to the DER, and the DER must have a means to confirm your identification.

(3) The MRO's report that you transmit to the employer must contain all of the information required by §40.163.

(c) You must transmit the MRO's report(s) of verified tests to the DER so that the DER receives it within two days of verification by the MRO.

(1) You must fax, courier, mail, or electronically transmit a legible image or copy of either the signed or stamped and dated Copy 2 or the written report (see§40.163(b) and (c)).

(2) Negative results reported electronically (*i.e.,* computer data file) do not require an image of Copy 2 or the written report.

(d) In transmitting test results, you or the C/TPA and the employer must ensure the security of the transmission and limit access to any transmission, storage, or retrieval systems.

(e) MRO reports are not subject to modification or change by anyone other than the MRO, as provided in §40.149(c).

§40.169 Where is other information concerning the role of MROs and the verification process found in this regulation?

You can find more information concerning the role of MROs in several sections of this part:

§40.3—Definition.

§§40.47-40.49—Correction of form and kit errors.

§40.67—Role in direct observation and other atypical test situations.

§40.83—Laboratory handling of fatal and correctable flaws.

§40.97—Laboratory handling of test results and quantitative values.

§40.99—Authorization of longer laboratory retention of specimens.

§40.101—Relationship with laboratories; avoidance of conflicts of interest.

§40.171—Request for test of split specimen.

§40.187—Action concerning split specimen test results.

§40.193—Role in "shy bladder" situations.

§40.195—Role in cancelling tests.

§§40.199-40.203—Documenting errors in tests.

§40.327—Confidentiality and release of information.

§40.347—Transfer of records.

§40.353—Relationships with service agents.

Subpart H—Split Specimen Tests

§40.171 How does an employee request a test of a split specimen?

(a) As an employee, when the MRO has notified you that you have a verified positive drug test and/or refusal to test because of adulteration or substitution, you have 72 hours from the time of notification to request a test of the split specimen. The request may be verbal or in writing. If you make this request to the MRO within 72 hours, you trigger the requirements of this section for a test of the split specimen. There is no split specimen testing for an invalid result.

(b)(1) If, as an employee, you have not requested a test of the split specimen within 72 hours, you may present to the MRO information documenting that serious injury, illness, lack of actual notice of the verified test result, inability to contact the MRO (*e.g.,* there was no one in the MRO's office and the answering machine was not working), or other circumstances unavoidably prevented you from making a timely request.

(2) As the MRO, if you conclude from the employee's information that there was a legitimate reason for the employee's failure to contact you within 72 hours, you must direct that the test of the split specimen take place, just as you would when there is a timely request.

(c) When the employee makes a timely request for a test of the split specimen under paragraphs (a) and (b) of this section, you must, as the MRO, immediately provide written notice to the laboratory that tested the primary specimen, directing the laboratory to forward the split specimen to a second HHS-certified laboratory. You must also document the date and time of the employee's request.

§40.173 Who is responsible for paying for the test of a split specimen?

(a) As the employer, you are responsible for making sure (*e.g.,* by establishing appropriate accounts with laboratories for testing split specimens) that the MRO, first laboratory, and second laboratory perform the functions noted in §§40.175-40.185 in a timely manner, once the employee has made a timely request for a test of the split specimen.

(b) As the employer, you must not condition your compliance with these requirements on the employee's direct payment to the MRO or laboratory or the employee's agreement to reimburse you for the costs of testing. For example, if you ask the employee to pay for some or all of the cost of testing the split specimen, and the employee is unwilling or unable to do so, you must ensure that the test takes place in a timely manner, even though this means that you pay for it.

(c) As the employer, you may seek payment or reimbursement of all or part of the cost of the split specimen from the employee (*e.g.,* through your written company policy or a collective bargaining agreement). This part takes no position on who ultimately pays the cost of the test, so long as the employer ensures that the testing is conducted as required and the results released appropriately.

§40.175 What steps does the first laboratory take with a split specimen?

(a) As the laboratory at which the primary and split specimen first arrive, you must check to see whether the split specimen is available for testing.

(b) If the split specimen is unavailable or appears insufficient, you must then do the following:

(1) Continue the testing process for the primary specimen as you would normally. Report the results for the primary specimen without providing the MRO information regarding the unavailable split specimen.

(2) Upon receiving a letter from the MRO instructing you to forward the split specimen to another laboratory for testing, report to the MRO that the split specimen is unavailable for testing. Provide as much information as you can about the cause of the unavailability.

(c) As the laboratory that tested the primary specimen, you are not authorized to open the split specimen under any circumstances (except when the split specimen is redesignated as provided in §40.83).

(d) When you receive written notice from the MRO instructing you to send the split specimen to another HHS-certified laboratory, you must forward the following items to the second laboratory:

(1) The split specimen in its original specimen bottle, with the seal intact;

(2) A copy of the MRO's written request; and

(3) A copy of Copy 1 of the CCF, which identifies the drug(s)/metabolite(s) or the validity criteria to be tested for.

(e) You must not send to the second laboratory any information about the identity of the employee. Inadvertent disclosure does not, however, cause a fatal flaw.

(f) This subpart does not prescribe who gets to decide which HHS-certified laboratory is used to test the split specimen. That decision is left to the parties involved.

§40.177 What does the second laboratory do with the split specimen when it is tested to reconfirm the presence of a drug or drug metabolite?

(a) As the laboratory testing the split specimen, you must test the split specimen for the drug(s)/drug metabolite(s) detected in the primary specimen.

(b) You must conduct this test without regard to the cutoff concentrations of §40.87.

(c) If the test fails to reconfirm the presence of the drug(s)/drug metabolite(s) that were reported positive in the primary specimen, you must conduct validity tests in an attempt to determine the reason for being unable to reconfirm the presence of the drug(s)/metabolite(s). You should conduct the same validity tests as you would conduct on a primary specimen set forth in §40.91.

(d) In addition, if the test fails to reconfirm the presence of the drug(s)/drug metabolite(s) reported in the primary specimen, you may send the specimen or an aliquot of it for testing at another HHS-certified laboratory that has the capability to conduct another reconfirmation test.

§40.179 What does the second laboratory do with the split specimen when it is tested to reconfirm an adulterated test result?

(a) As the laboratory testing the split specimen, you must test the split specimen for the adulterant detected in the primary specimen, using the confirmatory test for the adulterant and using criteria in §40.95 and confirmatory cutoff levels required by the HHS Mandatory Guidelines.

(b) In addition, if the test fails to reconfirm the adulterant result reported in the primary specimen, you may send the specimen or an aliquot of it for testing at another HHS-certified laboratory that has the capability to conduct another reconfirmation test.

§40.181 What does the second laboratory do with the split specimen when it is tested to reconfirm a substituted test result?

As the laboratory testing the split specimen, you must test the split specimen using the confirmatory tests for creatinine and specific gravity, and using the confirmatory criteria set forth in §40.93(b).

§40.183 What information do laboratories report to MROs regarding split specimen results?

(a) As the laboratory responsible for testing the split specimen, you must report split specimen test results by checking the "Reconfirmed" box and/or the "Failed to Reconfirm" box (Step 5(b)) on Copy 1 of the CCF, as appropriate, and by providing clarifying remarks using current HHS Mandatory Guidelines requirements.

(b) As the laboratory certifying scientist, enter your name, sign, and date the CCF.

§40.185 Through what methods and to whom must a laboratory report split specimen results?

(a) As the laboratory testing the split specimen, you must report laboratory results directly, and only, to the MRO at his or her place of business. You must not report results to or through the DER or another service agent (e.g., a C/TPA).

(b) You must fax, courier, mail, or electronically transmit a legible image or copy of the fully-completed Copy 1 of the CCF, which has been signed by the certifying scientist.

(c) You must transmit the laboratory result to the MRO immediately, preferably on the same day or next business day as the result is signed and released.

§40.187 What does the MRO do with split specimen laboratory results?

As the MRO, the split specimen laboratory results you receive will fall into five categories. You must take the following action, as appropriate, when a laboratory reports split specimen results to you.

(a) **Category 1**: The laboratory reconfirmed one or more of the primary specimen results. As the MRO, you must report to the DER and the employee the result(s) that was/were reconfirmed.

(1) In the case of a reconfirmed positive test(s) for drug(s) or drug metabolite(s), the positive is the final result.

(2) In the case of a reconfirmed adulterated or substituted result, the refusal to test is the final result.

(3) In the case of a combination positive and refusal to test results, the final result is both positive and refusal to test.

(b) **Category 2**: The laboratory failed to reconfirm all of the primary specimen results because, as appropriate, drug(s)/drug metabolite(s) were not detected; adulteration criteria were not met; and/or substitution criteria were not met. As the MRO, you must report to the DER and the employee that the test must be cancelled.

(1) As the MRO, you must inform ODAPC of the failure to reconfirm using the format in Appendix D to this part.

(2) In a case where the split failed to reconfirm because the substitution criteria were not met and the split specimen creatinine concentration was equal to or greater than 2mg/dL but less than or equal to 5mg/dL, as the MRO, you must, in addition to step (b)(1) of this paragraph, direct the DER to ensure the immediate collection of another specimen from the employee under direct observation, with no notice given to the employee of this collection requirement until immediately before the collection.

(3) In a case where the split failed to reconfirm and the primary specimen's result was also invalid, direct the DER to ensure the immediate collection of

another specimen from the employee under direct observation, with no notice given to the employee of this collection requirement until immediately before the collection.

(c) **Category 3**: The laboratory failed to reconfirm all of the primary specimen results, and also reported that the split specimen was invalid, adulterated, and/or substituted.

(1) In the case where the laboratory failed to reconfirm all of the primary specimen results and the split was reported as invalid, as the MRO, you must:

(i) Report to the DER and the employee that the test must be cancelled and the reason for the cancellation.

(ii) Direct the DER to ensure the immediate collection of another specimen from the employee under direct observation, with no notice given to the employee of this collection requirement until immediately before the collection.

(iii) Inform ODAPC of the failure to reconfirm using the format in Appendix D to this part.

(2) In the case where the laboratory failed to reconfirm any of the primary specimen results, and the split was reported as adulterated and/or substituted, as the MRO, you must:

(i) Contact the employee and inform the employee that the laboratory has determined that his or her split specimen is adulterated and/or substituted, as appropriate.

(ii) Follow the procedures of §40.145 to determine if there is a legitimate medical explanation for the laboratory finding of adulteration and/or substitution, as appropriate.

(iii) If you determine that there is a legitimate medical explanation for the adulterated and/or substituted test result, report to the DER and the employee that the test must be cancelled; and inform ODAPC of the failure to reconfirm using the format in Appendix D to this part.

(iv) If you determine that there is not a legitimate medical explanation for the adulterated and/or substituted test result, you must take the following steps:

(A) Report the test to the DER and the employee as a verified refusal to test. Inform the employee that he or she has 72 hours to request a test of the primary specimen to determine if the adulterant found in the split specimen is also present in the primary specimen and/or to determine if the primary specimen meets appropriate substitution criteria.

(B) Except when the request is for a test of the primary specimen and is being made to the laboratory that tested the primary specimen, follow the procedures of §§40.153, 40.171, 40.173, 40.179, 40.181, and 40.185, as appropriate.

(C) As the laboratory that tests the primary specimen to reconfirm the presence of the adulterant found in the split specimen and/or to determine that the primary specimen meets appropriate substitution criteria, report your result to the MRO on a photocopy (faxed, mailed, scanned, couriered) of Copy 1 of the CCF.

(D) If the test of the primary specimen reconfirms the adulteration and/or substitution finding of the split specimen, as the MRO you must report the result as a refusal to test as provided in paragraph (a)(2) of this section.

(E) If the test of the primary specimen fails to reconfirm the adulteration and/or substitution finding of the split specimen, as the MRO you must cancel the test, following procedures in paragraph (b) of this section.

(d) **Category 4**: The laboratory failed to reconfirm one or more but not all of the primary specimen results, and also reported that the split specimen was invalid, adulterated, and/or substituted. As the MRO, in the case where the laboratory reconfirmed one or more of the primary specimen result(s), you must follow procedures in paragraph (a) of this section and:

(1) Report that the split was also reported as being invalid, adulterated, and/or substituted (as appropriate).

(2) Inform the DER to take action only on the reconfirmed result(s).

(e) **Category 5**: The split specimen was not available for testing or there was no split laboratory available to test the specimen. As the MRO, you must:

(1) Report to the DER and the employee that the test must be cancelled and the reason for the cancellation;

(2) Direct the DER to ensure the immediate recollection of another specimen from the employee under direct observation, with no notice given to the employee of this collection requirement until immediately before the collection; and

(3) Notify ODAPC of the failure to reconfirm using the format in Appendix D to this part.

(f) For all split specimen results, as the MRO you must in Step 7 of Copy 2 of the CCF:

(1) Report split specimen test results by checking the "Reconfirmed" box and/or the "Failed to Reconfirm" box, or the "Test Cancelled" box, as appropriate.

(2) Enter your name, sign, and date.

(3) Send a legible copy of Copy 2 of the CCF (or a signed and dated letter, see§40.163) to the employer and keep a copy for your records. Transmit the document as provided in §40.167.

§40.189 Where is other information concerning split specimens found in this regulation?

You can find more information concerning split specimens in several sections of this part:

§40.3—Definition.

§40.65—Quantity of split specimen.

§40.67—Directly observed test when split specimen is unavailable.

§§40.71-40.73—Collection process for split specimens.

§40.83—Laboratory accessioning of split specimens.

§40.99—Laboratory retention of split specimens.

§40.153—MRO notice to employees on tests of split specimen.

§§40.193 and 40.201—MRO actions on insufficient or unavailable split specimens.

Appendix D to Part 40—Report format for split specimen failure to reconfirm.

Subpart I—Problems in Drug Tests

§40.191 What is a refusal to take a DOT drug test, and what are the consequences?

(a) As an employee, you have refused to take a drug test if you:

(1) Fail to appear for any test (except a pre-employment test) within a reasonable time, as determined by the employer, consistent with applicable DOT agency regulations, after being directed to do so by the employer. This includes the failure of an employee (including an owner-operator) to appear for a test when called by a C/TPA (see §40.61(a));

(2) *Fail to remain at the testing site until the testing process is complete; Provided,* That an employee who leaves the testing site before the testing process commences (see §40.63 (c)) for a pre-employment test is not deemed to have refused to test;

(3) Fail to provide a urine specimen for any drug test required by this part or DOT agency regulations; *Provided,* That an employee who does not provide a urine specimen because he or she has left the testing site before the testing process commences (see §40.63 (c)) for a pre-employment test is not deemed to have refused to test;

(4) In the case of a directly observed or monitored collection in a drug test, fail to permit the observation or monitoring of your provision of a specimen (see §§40.67(l) and 40.69(g));

(5) Fail to provide a sufficient amount of urine when directed, and it has been determined, through a required medical evaluation, that there was no adequate medical explanation for the failure (see §40.193(d)(2));

(6) Fail or decline to take an additional drug test the employer or collector has directed you to take (see, for instance, §40.197(b));

(7) Fail to undergo a medical examination or evaluation, as directed by the MRO as part of the verification process, or as directed by the DER under §40.193(d). In the case of a pre-employment drug test, the employee is deemed to have refused to test on this basis only if the pre-employment test is conducted following a contingent offer of employment. If there was no contingent offer of employment, the MRO will cancel the test; or

(8) Fail to cooperate with any part of the testing process (*e.g.*, refuse to empty pockets when directed by the collector, behave in a confrontational way that disrupts the collection process, fail to wash hands after being directed to do so by the collector).

(9) For an observed collection, fail to follow the observer's instructions to raise your clothing above the waist, lower clothing and underpants, and to turn around to permit the observer to determine if you have any type of prosthetic or other device that could be used to interfere with the collection process.

(10) Possess or wear a prosthetic or other device that could be used to interfere with the collection process.

(11) Admit to the collector or MRO that you adulterated or substituted the specimen.

(b) As an employee, if the MRO reports that you have a verified adulterated or substituted test result, you have refused to take a drug test.

(c) As an employee, if you refuse to take a drug test, you incur the consequences specified under DOT agency regulations for a violation of those DOT agency regulations.

(d) As a collector or an MRO, when an employee refuses to participate in the part of the testing process in which you are involved, you must terminate the portion of the testing process in which you are involved, document the refusal on the CCF (including, in the case of the collector, printing the employee's name on Copy 2 of the CCF), immediately notify the DER by any means (*e.g.*, telephone or secure fax machine) that ensures that the refusal notification is immediately received. As a referral physician (*e.g.*, physician evaluating a "shy bladder" condition or a claim of a legitimate medical explanation in a validity testing situation), you must notify the MRO, who in turn will notify the DER.

(1) As the collector, you must note the refusal in the "Remarks" line (Step 2), and sign and date the CCF.

(2) As the MRO, you must note the refusal by checking the "Refusal to Test" box in Step 6 on Copy 2 of the CCF, checking whether the specimen was adulterated or substituted and, if adulterated, noting the adulterant/reason. If there was another reason for the refusal, check "Other" in Step 6 on Copy 2 of the CCF,

and note the reason next to the "Other" box and on the "Remarks" lines, as needed. You must then sign and date the CCF.

(e) As an employee, when you refuse to take a non-DOT test or to sign a non-DOT form, you have not refused to take a DOT test. There are no consequences under DOT agency regulations for refusing to take a non-DOT test.

§40.193 What happens when an employee does not provide a sufficient amount of urine for a drug test?

(a) This section prescribes procedures for situations in which an employee does not provide a sufficient amount of urine to permit a drug test (*i.e.,* 45 mL of urine).

(b) As the collector, you must do the following:

(1) Discard the insufficient specimen, except where the insufficient specimen was out of temperature range or showed evidence of adulteration or tampering (see §40.65(b) and (c)).

(2) Urge the employee to drink up to 40 ounces of fluid, distributed reasonably through a period of up to three hours, or until the individual has provided a sufficient urine specimen, whichever occurs first. It is not a refusal to test if the employee declines to drink. Document on the Remarks line of the CCF (Step 2), and inform the employee of, the time at which the three-hour period begins and ends.

(3) If the employee refuses to make the attempt to provide a new urine specimen or leaves the collection site before the collection process is complete, you must discontinue the collection, note the fact on the "Remarks" line of the CCF (Step 2), and immediately notify the DER. This is a refusal to test.

(4) If the employee has not provided a sufficient specimen within three hours of the first unsuccessful attempt to provide the specimen, you must discontinue the collection, note the fact on the "Remarks" line of the CCF (Step 2), and immediately notify the DER. You must also discard any specimen the employee previously provided to include any specimen that is "out of temperature range" or shows signs of tampering. In the remarks section of the CCF that you will distribute to the MRO and DER, note the fact that the employee provided an "out of temperature range specimen" or "specimen that shows signs of tampering" and that it was discarded because the employee did not provide a second sufficient specimen.

(5) Send Copy 2 of the CCF to the MRO and Copy 4 to the DER. You must send or fax these copies to the MRO and DER within 24 hours or the next business day.

(c) As the DER, when the collector informs you that the employee has not provided a sufficient amount of urine (see paragraph (b)(4) of this section), you must, after consulting with the MRO, direct the employee to obtain, within five days, an evaluation from a licensed physician, acceptable to the MRO, who has expertise in the medical issues raised by the employee's failure to provide a sufficient specimen. (The MRO may perform this evaluation if the MRO has appropriate expertise.)

(1) As the MRO, if another physician will perform the evaluation, you must provide the other physician with the following information and instructions:

(i) That the employee was required to take a DOT drug test, but was unable to provide a sufficient amount of urine to complete the test;

(ii) The consequences of the appropriate DOT agency regulation for refusing to take the required drug test;

(iii) That the referral physician must agree to follow the requirements of paragraphs (d) through (g) of this section.

(2) [Reserved.]

(d) As the referral physician conducting this evaluation, you must recommend that the MRO make one of the following determinations:

(1) A medical condition has, or with a high degree of probability could have, precluded the employee from providing a sufficient amount of urine. As the MRO, if you accept this recommendation, you must:

(i) Check "Test Cancelled" (Step 6) on the CCF; and

(ii) Sign and date the CCF.

(2) There is not an adequate basis for determining that a medical condition has, or with a high degree of probability could have, precluded the employee from providing a sufficient amount of urine. As the MRO, if you accept this recommendation, you must:

(i) Check the "Refusal to Test" box and "Other" box in Step 6 on Copy 2 of the CCF and note the reason next to the "Other" box and on the "Remarks" lines, as needed.

(ii) Sign and date the CCF.

(e) For purposes of this paragraph, a medical condition includes an ascertainable physiological condition (e.g., a urinary system dysfunction) or a medically documented pre-existing psychological disorder, but does not include unsupported assertions of "situational anxiety" or dehydration.

(f) As the referral physician making the evaluation, after completing your evaluation, you must provide a written statement of your recommendations and the basis for them to the MRO. You must not include in this statement detailed information on the employee's medical condition beyond what is necessary to explain your conclusion.

(g) If, as the referral physician making this evaluation in the case of a pre-employment test, you determine that the employee's medical condition is a serious and permanent or long-term disability that is highly likely to prevent the employee from providing a sufficient amount of urine for a very long or indefinite period of time, you must set forth your determination and the reasons for it in your written statement to the MRO. As the MRO, upon receiving such a report, you must follow the requirements of §40.195, where applicable.

(h) As the MRO, you must seriously consider and assess the referral physician's recommendations in making your determination about whether the employee has a medical condition that has, or with a high degree of probability could have, precluded the employee from providing a sufficient amount of urine. You must report your determination to the DER in writing as soon as you make it.

(i) As the employer, when you receive a report from the MRO indicating that a test is cancelled as provided in paragraph (d)(1) of this section, you take no further action with respect to the employee. The employee remains in the random testing pool.

§40.195 What happens when an individual is unable to provide a sufficient amount of urine for a pre-employment, follow-up, or return-to-duty test because of a permanent or long-term medical condition?

(a) This section concerns a situation in which an employee has a medical condition that precludes him or her from providing a sufficient specimen for a pre-employment, follow-up, or return-to-duty test and the condition involves a permanent or long-term disability. As the MRO in this situation, you must do the following:

(1) You must determine if there is clinical evidence that the individual is an illicit drug user. You must make this determination by personally conducting, or causing to be conducted, a medical evaluation and through consultation with the employee's physician and/or the physician who conducted the evaluation under §40.193(d).

(2) If you do not personally conduct the medical evaluation, you must ensure that one is conducted by a licensed physician acceptable to you.

(3) For purposes of this section, the MRO or the physician conducting the evaluation may conduct an alternative test (*e.g.,* blood) as part of the medically appropriate procedures in determining clinical evidence of drug use.

(b) If the medical evaluation reveals no clinical evidence of drug use, as the MRO, you must report the result to the employer as a negative test with written notations regarding results of both the evaluation conducted under §40.193(d) and any further medical examination. This report must state the basis for the determination that a permanent or long-term medical condition exists, making provision of a sufficient urine specimen impossible, and for the determination that no signs and symptoms of drug use exist.

(1) Check "Negative" (Step 6) on the CCF.

(2) Sign and date the CCF.

(c) If the medical evaluation reveals clinical evidence of drug use, as the MRO, you must report the result to the employer as a cancelled test with written notations regarding results of both the evaluation conducted under §40.193(d) and any further medical examination. This report must state that a permanent or long-term medical condition exists, making provision of a sufficient urine specimen impossible, and state the reason for the determination that signs and symptoms of drug use exist. Because this is a cancelled test, it does not serve the purposes of a negative test (*i.e.,* the employer is not authorized to allow the employee to begin or resume performing safety-sensitive functions, because a negative test is needed for that purpose).

(d) For purposes of this section, permanent or long-term medical conditions are those physiological, anatomic, or psychological abnormalities documented as being present prior to the attempted collection, and considered not amenable to correction or cure for an extended period of time, if ever.

(1) Examples would include destruction (any cause) of the glomerular filtration system leading to renal failure; unrepaired traumatic disruption of the urinary tract; or a severe psychiatric disorder focused on genito-urinary matters.

(2) Acute or temporary medical conditions, such as cystitis, urethritis or prostatitis, though they might interfere with collection for a limited period of time, cannot receive the same exceptional consideration as the permanent or long-term conditions discussed in paragraph (d)(1) of this section.

§40.197 What happens when an employer receives a report of a dilute specimen?

(a) As the employer, if the MRO informs you that a positive drug test was dilute, you simply treat the test as a verified positive test. You must not direct the employee to take another test based on the fact that the specimen was dilute.

(b) As an employer, if the MRO informs you that a negative test was dilute, take the following action:

(1) If the MRO directs you to conduct a recollection under direct observation (*i.e.*, because the creatinine concentration of the specimen was equal to or greater than 2mg/dL, but less than or equal to 5 mg/dL (*see* §40.155(c)), you must do so immediately.

(2) Otherwise (*i.e.*, if the creatinine concentration of the dilute specimen is greater than 5 mg/dL), you may, but are not required to, direct the employee to take another test immediately.

(i) Such recollections must not be collected under direct observation, unless there is another basis for use of direct observation (see§40.67 (b) and (c)).

(ii) You must treat all employees the same for this purpose. For example, you must not retest some employees and not others. You may, however, establish different policies for different types of tests (*e.g.*, conduct retests in pre-employment situations, but not in random test situations). You must inform your employees in advance of your decisions on these matters.

(c) The following provisions apply to all tests you direct an employee to take under paragraph (b) of this section:

(1) You must ensure that the employee is given the minimum possible advance notice that he or she must go to the collection site;

(2) You must treat the result of the test you directed the employee to take under paragraph (b) of this section—and not a prior test—as the test result of record, on which you rely for purposes of this part;

(3) If the result of the test you directed the employee to take under paragraph (b)(1) of this section is also negative and dilute, you are not permitted to make the employee take an additional test because the result was dilute.

(4) If the result of the test you directed the employee to take under paragraph (b)(2) of this section is also negative and dilute, you are not permitted to make the employee take an additional test because the result was dilute. Provided, however, that if the MRO directs you to conduct a recollection under direct observation under paragraph (b)(1) of this section, you must immediately do so.

(5) If the employee declines to take a test you directed him or her to take under paragraph (b) of this section, the employee has refused the test for purposes of this part and DOT agency regulations.

§40.199 What problems always cause a drug test to be cancelled?

(a) As the MRO, when the laboratory discovers a "fatal flaw" during its processing of incoming specimens (see §40.83), the laboratory will report to you that the specimen has been "Rejected for Testing" (with the reason stated). You must always cancel such a test.

(b) The following are "fatal flaws":

(1) There is no CCF;

(2) In cases where a specimen has been collected, there is no specimen submitted with the CCF;

(3) There is no printed collector's name and no collector's signature;

(4) Two separate collections are performed using one CCF;

(5) The specimen ID numbers on the specimen bottle and the CCF do not match;

(6) The specimen bottle seal is broken or shows evidence of tampering (and a split specimen cannot be re-designated, see §40.83(h)); or

(7) Because of leakage or other causes, there is an insufficient amount of urine in the primary specimen bottle for analysis and the specimens cannot be re-designated (see §40.83(h)).

(c) You must report the result as provided in §40.161.

§40.201 What problems always cause a drug test to be cancelled and may result in a requirement for another collection?

As the MRO, you must cancel a drug test when a laboratory reports that any of the following problems have occurred. You must inform the DER that the test was cancelled. You must also direct the DER to ensure that an additional collection occurs immediately, if required by the applicable procedures specified in paragraphs (a) through (e) of this section.

(a) The laboratory reports an "Invalid Result." You must follow applicable procedures in §40.159 (recollection under direct observation may be required).

(b) The laboratory reports the result as "Rejected for Testing." You must follow applicable procedures in §40.161 (a recollection may be required).

(c) The laboratory reports that the split specimen failed to reconfirm all of the primary specimen results because the drug(s)/drug metabolite(s) were not detected; adulteration criteria were not met; and/or substitution criteria were not met. You must follow the applicable procedures in §40.187(b)—no recollection is required in this case, unless the split specimen creatinine concentration for a substituted primary specimen was greater than or equal to 2mg/dL but less than or equal to 5mg/dL, or the primary specimen had an invalid result which was not reported to the DER. Both these cases require recollection under direct observation.

(d) The laboratory reports that the split specimen failed to reconfirm all of the primary specimen results, and that the split specimen was invalid. You must follow the procedures in §40.187(c)(1)—recollection under direct observation is required in this case.

(e) The laboratory reports that the split specimen failed to reconfirm all of the primary specimen results because the split specimen was not available for testing or there was no split laboratory available to test the specimen. You must follow the applicable procedures in §40.187(e)—recollection under direct observation is required in this case.

(f) The examining physician has determined that there is an acceptable medical explanation of the employee's failure to provide a sufficient amount of urine. You must follow applicable procedures in §40.193(d)(1) (no recollection is required in this case).

§40.203 What problems cause a drug test to be cancelled unless they are corrected?

(a) As the MRO, when a laboratory discovers a "correctable flaw" during its processing of incoming specimens (see §40.83), the laboratory will attempt to correct it. If the laboratory is unsuccessful in this attempt, it will report to you that the specimen has been "Rejected for Testing" (with the reason stated).

(b) The following is a "correctable flaw" that laboratories must attempt to correct: The collector's signature is omitted on the certification statement on the CCF.

(c) As the MRO, when you discover a "correctable flaw" during your review of the CCF, you must cancel the test unless the flaw is corrected.

(d) The following are correctable flaws that you must attempt to correct:

(1) The employee's signature is omitted from the certification statement, unless the employee's failure or refusal to sign is noted on the "Remarks" line of the CCF.

(2) The certifying scientist's signature is omitted on Copy 1 of the CCF for a positive, adulterated, substituted, or invalid test result.

(3) The collector uses a non-Federal form or an expired CCF for the test. This flaw may be corrected through the procedure set forth in §40.205(b)(2), provided that the collection testing process has been conducted in accordance with the procedures in this part in an HHS-certified laboratory.

§40.205 How are drug test problems corrected?

(a) As a collector, you have the responsibility of trying to successfully complete a collection procedure for each employee.

(1) If, during or shortly after the collection process, you become aware of any event that prevents the completion of a valid test or collection (*e.g.*, a procedural or paperwork error), you must try to correct the problem promptly, if doing so is practicable. You may conduct another collection as part of this effort.

(2) If another collection is necessary, you must begin the new collection procedure as soon as possible, using a new CCF and a new collection kit.

(b) If, as a collector, laboratory, MRO, employer, or other person implementing these drug testing regulations, you become aware of a problem that can be corrected (see §40.203), but which has not already been corrected under paragraph (a) of this section, you must take all practicable action to correct the problem so that the test is not cancelled.

(1) If the problem resulted from the omission of required information, you must, as the person responsible for providing that information, supply in writing the missing information and a statement that it is true and accurate. For example, suppose you are a collector, and you forgot to make a notation on the "Remarks" line of the CCF that the employee did not sign the certification. You would, when the problem is called to your attention, supply a signed statement that the employee failed or refused to sign the certification and that your statement is true and accurate. You must supply this information on the same business day on which you are notified of the problem, transmitting it by fax or courier.

(2) If the problem is the use of a non-Federal form or an expired Federal form, you must provide a signed statement (*i.e.*, a memorandum for the record). It must state that the incorrect form contains all the information needed for a valid DOT drug test, and that the incorrect form was used inadvertently or as the only means of conducting a test, in circumstances beyond your control. The statement must also list the steps you have taken to prevent future use of non-Federal forms or expired Federal forms for DOT tests. For this flaw to be corrected, the test of the specimen must have occurred at a HHS-certified laboratory where it was tested consistent with the requirements of this part. You must supply this information on the same business day on which you are notified of the problem, transmitting it by fax or courier.

(3) You must maintain the written documentation of a correction with the CCF.

(4) You must mark the CCF in such a way (*e.g.*, stamp noting correction) as to make it obvious on the face of the CCF that you corrected the flaw.

(c) If the correction does not take place, as the MRO you must cancel the test.

§40.207 What is the effect of a cancelled drug test?

(a) A cancelled drug test is neither positive nor negative.

(1) As an employer, you must not attach to a cancelled test the consequences of a positive test or other violation of a DOT drug testing regulation (*e.g.*, removal from a safety-sensitive position).

(2) As an employer, you must not use a cancelled test for the purposes of a negative test to authorize the employee to perform safety-sensitive functions (*i.e.*, in the case of a pre-employment, return-to-duty, or follow-up test).

(3) However, as an employer, you must not direct a recollection for an employee because a test has been cancelled, except in the situations cited in paragraph (a)(2) of this section or other provisions of this part that require another test to be conducted (*e.g.*, §§40.159(a)(5) and 40.187(b)(2), (c)(1), and (e)).

(b) A cancelled test does not count toward compliance with DOT requirements (*e.g.*, being applied toward the number of tests needed to meet the employer's minimum random testing rate).

(c) A cancelled DOT test does not provide a valid basis for an employer to conduct a non-DOT test (*i.e.*, a test under company authority).

§40.208 What problem requires corrective action but does not result in the cancellation of a test?

(a) If, as a laboratory, collector, employer, or other person implementing the DOT drug testing program, you become aware that the specimen temperature on the CCF was not checked and the "Remarks" line did not contain an entry regarding the temperature being out of range, you must take corrective action, including securing a memorandum for the record explaining the problem and taking appropriate action to ensure that the problem does not recur.

(b) This error does not result in the cancellation of the test.

(c) As an employer or service agent, this error, even though not sufficient to cancel a drug test result, may subject you to enforcement action under DOT agency regulations or Subpart R of this part.

§40.209 What procedural problems do not result in the cancellation of a test and do not require corrective action?

(a) As a collector, laboratory, MRO, employer or other person administering the drug testing process, you must document any errors in the testing process of which you become aware, even if they are not considered problems that will cause a test to be cancelled as listed in this subpart. Decisions about the ultimate impact of these errors will be determined by other administrative or legal proceedings, subject to the limitations of paragraph (b) of this section.

(b) No person concerned with the testing process may declare a test cancelled based on an error that does not have a significant adverse effect on the right of the employee to have a fair and accurate test. Matters that do not result in the cancellation of a test include, but are not limited to, the following:

(1) A minor administrative mistake (*e.g.*, the omission of the employee's middle initial, a transposition of numbers in the employee's social security number, the omission of the DOT Agency in Step 1–D of the CCF.)

(2) An error that does not affect employee protections under this part (*e.g.*, the collector's failure to add bluing agent to the toilet bowl, which adversely affects only the ability of the collector to detect tampering with the specimen by the employee);

(3) The collection of a specimen by a collector who is required to have been trained (see §40.33), but who has not met this requirement;

(4) A delay in the collection process (see §40.61(a));

(5) Verification of a test result by an MRO who has the basic credentials to be qualified as an MRO (see §40.121(a) through (b)) but who has not met training and/or documentation requirements (see §40.121(c) through (e));

(6) The failure to directly observe or monitor a collection that the rule requires or permits to be directly observed or monitored, or the unauthorized use of direct observation or monitoring for a collection;

(7) The fact that a test was conducted in a facility that does not meet the requirements of §40.41;

(8) If the specific name of the courier on the CCF is omitted or erroneous;

(9) Personal identifying information is inadvertently contained on the CCF (e.g., the employee signs his or her name on Copy 1); or

(10) Claims that the employee was improperly selected for testing.

(c) As an employer or service agent, these types of errors, even though not sufficient to cancel a drug test result, may subject you to enforcement action under DOT agency regulations or action under Subpart R of this part.

§40.210 Are drug tests other than urine permitted under the regulations?

No. Drug tests other than on urine specimens are not authorized for testing under this part. Only urine specimens screened and confirmed at HHS certified laboratories (see §40.81) are allowed for drug testing under this part. Point-of-collection urine testing or instant tests are not authorized.

Subpart J—Alcohol Testing Personnel

§40.211 Who conducts DOT alcohol tests?

(a) Screening test technicians (STTs) and breath alcohol technicians (BATs) meeting their respective requirements of this subpart are the only people authorized to conduct DOT alcohol tests.

(b) An STT can conduct only alcohol screening tests, but a BAT can conduct alcohol screening and confirmation tests.

(c) As a BAT- or STT-qualified immediate supervisor of a particular employee, you may not act as the STT or BAT when that employee is tested, unless no other STT or BAT is available and DOT agency regulations do not prohibit you from doing so.

§40.213 What training requirements must STTs and BATs meet?

To be permitted to act as a BAT or STT in the DOT alcohol testing program, you must meet each of the requirements of this section:

(a) You must be knowledgeable about the alcohol testing procedures in this part and the current DOT guidance. Procedures and guidance are available from ODAPC (Department of Transportation, 1200 New Jersey Avenue SE., Washington, DC 20590, 202-366-3784, or on the ODAPC Web site, *http://www.transportation.gov/odapc*). You must keep current on any changes to these materials. You must subscribe to the ODAPC list-serve at (*https://www.transportation.gov/odapc/get-odapc-email-updates*).

(b) **Qualification training**. You must receive qualification training meeting the requirements of this paragraph (b).

(1) Qualification training must be in accordance with the DOT Model BAT or STT Course, as applicable. The DOT Model Courses are available from ODAPC (Department of Transportation, 1200 New Jersey Avenue, SE., Washington DC, 20590, 202-366-3784, or on the ODAPC web site, http://www.dot.gov/ost/dapc). The training can also be provided using a course of instruction equivalent to the DOT Model Courses. On request, ODAPC will review BAT and STT instruction courses for equivalency.

(2) Qualification training must include training to proficiency in using the alcohol testing procedures of this part and in the operation of the particular alcohol testing device(s) (*i.e.*, the ASD(s) or EBT(s)) you will be using.

(3) The training must emphasize that you are responsible for maintaining the integrity of the testing process, ensuring the privacy of employees being tested, and avoiding conduct or statements that could be viewed as offensive or inappropriate.

(4) The instructor must be an individual who has demonstrated necessary knowledge, skills, and abilities by regularly conducting DOT alcohol tests as an STT or BAT, as applicable, for a period of at least a year, who has conducted STT or BAT training, as applicable, under this part for a year, or who has successfully completed a "train the trainer" course.

(c) **Initial Proficiency Demonstration**. Following your completion of qualification training under paragraph (b) of this section, you must demonstrate proficiency in alcohol testing under this part by completing seven consecutive error-free mock tests (BATs) or five consecutive error-free tests (STTs).

(1) Another person must monitor and evaluate your performance, in person or by a means that provides real-time observation and interaction between the instructor and trainee, and attest in writing that the mock collections are "error-free." This person must be an individual who meets the requirements of paragraph (b)(4) of this section.

(2) These tests must use the alcohol testing devices (*e.g.*, EBT(s) or ASD(s)) that you will use as a BAT or STT.

(3) If you are an STT who will be using an ASD that indicates readings by changes, contrasts, or other readings in color, you must demonstrate as part of the mock test that you are able to discern changes, contrasts, or readings correctly.

(d) You must meet the requirements of paragraphs (b) and (c) of this section before you begin to perform STT or BAT functions.

(e) **Refresher training**. No less frequently than every five years from the date on which you satisfactorily complete the requirements of paragraphs (b) and (c) of this section, you must complete refresher training that meets all the requirements of paragraphs (b) and (c) of this section.

(f) **Error Correction Training**. If you make a mistake in the alcohol testing process that causes a test to be cancelled (*i.e.*, a fatal or uncorrected flaw), you must undergo error correction training. This training must occur within 30 days of the date you are notified of the error that led to the need for retraining.

(1) Error correction training must be provided and your proficiency documented in writing by a person who meets the requirements of paragraph (b)(4) of this section.

(2) Error correction training is required to cover only the subject matter area(s) in which the error that caused the test to be cancelled occurred.

(3) As part of the error correction training, you must demonstrate your proficiency in the alcohol testing procedures of this part by completing three consecutive error-free mock tests. The mock tests must include one uneventful scenario and two scenarios related to the area(s) in which your error(s) occurred. The person providing the training must monitor and evaluate your performance and attest in writing that the mock tests were error-free.

(g) **Documentation**. You must maintain documentation showing that you currently meet all requirements of this section. You must provide this documentation on request to DOT agency representatives and to employers and C/TPAs who are negotiating to use your services.

(h) **Other persons who may serve as BATs or STTs**. (1) Anyone meeting the requirements of this section to be a BAT may act as an STT, provided that the individual has demonstrated initial proficiency in the operation of the ASD that he or she is using, as provided in paragraph (c) of this section.

(2) Law enforcement officers who have been certified by state or local governments to conduct breath alcohol testing are deemed to be qualified as BATs. They are not required to also complete the training requirements of this section in order to act as BATs. In order for a test conducted by such an officer to be accepted under DOT alcohol testing requirements, the officer must have been certified by a state or local government to use the EBT or ASD that was used for the test.

§40.215 What information about the DER do employers have to provide to BATs and STTs?

As an employer, you must provide to the STTs and BATs the name and telephone number of the appropriate DER (and C/TPA, where applicable) to contact about any problems or issues that may arise during the testing process.

§40.217 Where is other information on the role of STTs and BATs found in this regulation?

You can find other information on the role and functions of STTs and BATs in the following sections of this part:

§40.3—Definitions.

§40.223—Responsibility for supervising employees being tested.

§§40.225-40.227—Use of the alcohol testing form.

§§40.241-40.245—Screening test procedures with ASDs and EBTs.

§§40.251-40.255—Confirmation test procedures.

§40.261—Refusals to test.

§§40.263-40.265—Insufficient saliva or breath.

§40.267—Problems requiring cancellation of tests.

§§40.269-40.271—Correcting problems in tests.

Subpart K—Testing Sites, Forms, Equipment and Supplies Used in Alcohol Testing

§40.221 Where does an alcohol test take place?

(a) A DOT alcohol test must take place at an alcohol testing site meeting the requirements of this section.

(b) If you are operating an alcohol testing site, you must ensure that it meets the security requirements of §40.223.

(c) If you are operating an alcohol testing site, you must ensure that it provides visual and aural privacy to the employee being tested, sufficient to prevent unauthorized persons from seeing or hearing test results.

(d) If you are operating an alcohol testing site, you must ensure that it has all needed personnel, materials, equipment, and facilities to provide for the collection and analysis of breath and/or saliva samples, and a suitable clean surface for writing.

(e) If an alcohol testing site fully meeting all the visual and aural privacy requirements of paragraph (c) is not readily available, this part allows a reasonable suspicion or post-accident test to be conducted at a site that partially meets these requirements. In this case, the site must afford visual and aural privacy to the employee to the greatest extent practicable.

(f) An alcohol testing site can be in a medical facility, a mobile facility (*e.g.,* a van), a dedicated collection facility, or any other location meeting the requirements of this section.

§40.223 What steps must be taken to protect the security of alcohol testing sites?

(a) If you are a BAT, STT, or other person operating an alcohol testing site, you must prevent unauthorized personnel from entering the testing site.

(1) The only people you are to treat as authorized persons are employees being tested, BATs, STTs, and other alcohol testing site workers, DERs, employee representatives authorized by the employer (*e.g.,* on the basis of employer policy or labor-management agreement), and DOT agency representatives.

(2) You must ensure that all persons are under the supervision of a BAT or STT at all times when permitted into the site.

(3) You may remove any person who obstructs, interferes with, or causes unnecessary delay in the testing process.

(b) As the BAT or STT, you must not allow any person other than you, the employee, or a DOT agency representative to actually witness the testing process (see §§40.241-40.255).

(c) If you are operating an alcohol testing site, you must ensure that when an EBT or ASD is not being used for testing, you store it in a secure place.

(d) If you are operating an alcohol testing site, you must ensure that no one other than BATs or other employees of the site have access to the site when an EBT is unsecured.

(e) As a BAT or STT, to avoid distraction that could compromise security, you are limited to conducting an alcohol test for only one employee at a time.

(1) When an EBT screening test on an employee indicates an alcohol concentration of 0.02 or higher, and the same EBT will be used for the confirmation test, you are not allowed to use the EBT for a test on another employee before completing the confirmation test on the first employee.

(2) As a BAT who will conduct both the screening and the confirmation test, you are to complete the entire screening and confirmation process on one employee before starting the screening process on another employee.

(3) You are not allowed to leave the alcohol testing site while the testing process for a given employee is in progress, except to notify a supervisor or contact a DER for assistance in the case an employee or other person who obstructs, interferes with, or unnecessarily delays the testing process.

§40.225 What form is used for an alcohol test?

(a) The DOT Alcohol Testing Form (ATF) must be used for every DOT alcohol test. The ATF must be a three-part carbonless manifold form. The ATF is found in Appendix G to this part. You may view this form on the ODAPC web site (*http://www.transportation.gov/odapc*).

(b) As an employer in the DOT alcohol testing program, you are not permitted to modify or revise the ATF except as follows:

(1) You may include other information needed for billing purposes, outside the boundaries of the form.

(2) You may use a ATF directly generated by an EBT which omits the space for affixing a separate printed result to the ATF, provided the EBT prints the result directly on the ATF.

(3) You may use an ATF that has the employer's name, address, and telephone number preprinted. In addition, a C/TPA's name, address, and telephone number may be included, to assist with negative results.

(4) You may use an ATF in which all pages are printed on white paper. You may modify the ATF by using colored paper, or have clearly discernable borders or designation statements on Copy 2 and Copy 3. When colors are used, they must be green for Copy 2 and blue for Copy 3.

(5) As a BAT or STT, you may add, on the "Remarks" line of the ATF, the name of the DOT agency under whose authority the test occurred.

(6) As a BAT or STT, you may use a ATF that has your name, address, and telephone number preprinted, but under no circumstances can your signature be preprinted.

(c) As an employer, you may use an equivalent foreign-language version of the ATF approved by ODAPC. You may use such a non-English language form only in a situation where both the employee and BAT/STT understand and can use the form in that language.

§40.227 May employers use the ATF for non-DOT tests, or non-DOT forms for DOT tests?

(a) No, as an employer, BAT, or STT, you are prohibited from using the ATF for non-DOT alcohol tests. You are also prohibited from using non-DOT forms for DOT alcohol tests. Doing either subjects you to enforcement action under DOT agency regulations.

(b) If the STT or BAT, either by mistake, or as the only means to conduct a test under difficult circumstances (e.g., post-accident test with insufficient time to obtain the ATF), uses a non-DOT form for a DOT test, the use of a non-DOT form does not, in and of itself, require the employer or service agent to cancel the test. However, in order for the test to be considered valid, a signed statement must be obtained from the STT or BAT in accordance with §40.271(b).

§40.229 What devices are used to conduct alcohol screening tests?

ASDs listed on ODAPC's Web page for "Approved Screening Devices to Measure Alcohol in Bodily Fluids" and EBTs listed on ODAPC's Web page for "Approved Evidential Breath Measurement Devices" are the only devices you are allowed to use to conduct alcohol screening tests under this part. You may use an ASD for DOT alcohol tests only if there are instructions for its use in this part. An ASD can be used only for screening tests for alcohol, and must not be used for confirmation tests.

§40.231 What devices are used to conduct alcohol confirmation tests?

(a) EBTs on ODAPC's Web page for "Approved Evidential Breath Measurement Devices" that meet the requirements of paragraph (b) of this section are the only devices you may use to conduct alcohol confirmation tests under this part.

(b) To conduct a confirmation test, you must use an EBT that has the following capabilities:

(1) Provides a printed triplicate result (or three consecutive identical copies of a result) of each breath test;

(2) Assigns a unique number to each completed test, which the BAT and employee can read before each test and which is printed on each copy of the result;

(3) Prints, on each copy of the result, the manufacturer's name for the device, its serial number, and the time of the test;

(4) Distinguishes alcohol from acetone at the 0.02 alcohol concentration level;

(5) Tests an air blank; and

(6) Performs an external calibration check.

§40.233 What are the requirements for proper use and care of EBTs?

(a) As an EBT manufacturer, you must submit, for NHTSA approval, a quality assurance plan (QAP) for your EBT before ODAPC places the EBT on its Web page for "Approved Evidential Breath Measurement Devices."

(1) Your QAP must specify the methods used to perform external calibration checks on the EBT, the tolerances within which the EBT is regarded as being in proper calibration, and the intervals at which these checks must be performed. In designating these intervals, your QAP must take into account factors like frequency of use, environmental conditions (*e.g.,* temperature, humidity, altitude) and type of operation (*e.g.*, stationary or mobile).

(2) Your QAP must also specify the inspection, maintenance, and calibration requirements and intervals for the EBT.

(b) As the manufacturer, you must include, with each EBT, instructions for its use and care consistent with the QAP.

(c) As the user of the EBT (*e.g.,* employer, service agent), you must do the following:

(1) You must follow the manufacturer's instructions (see paragraph (b) of this section), including performance of external calibration checks at the intervals the instructions specify.

(2) In conducting external calibration checks, you must use only calibration devices appearing on NHTSA's CPL for "Calibrating Units for Breath Alcohol Tests."

(3) If an EBT fails an external check of calibration, you must take the EBT out of service. You may not use the EBT again for DOT alcohol testing until it is repaired and passes an external calibration check.

(4) You must maintain records of the inspection, maintenance, and calibration of EBTs as provided in §40.333(a)(3).

(5) You must ensure that inspection, maintenance, and calibration of the EBT are performed by its manufacturer or a maintenance representative certified either by the manufacturer or by a state health agency or other appropriate state agency.

§40.235 What are the requirements for proper use and care of ASDs?

(a) As an ASD manufacturer, you must submit, for NHTSA approval, a QAP for your ASD before NHTSA approves it and ODAPC places the device on its Web page for "Approved Screening Devices to Measure Alcohol in Bodily Fluids". Your QAP must specify the methods used for quality control checks, temperatures at which the ASD must be stored and used, the shelf life of the device, and environmental conditions (*e.g.,* temperature, altitude, humidity) that may affect the ASD's performance.

(b) As a manufacturer, you must include with each ASD instructions for its use and care consistent with the QAP. The instructions must include directions on the proper use of the ASD, and, where applicable the time within which the device must be read, and the manner in which the reading is made.

(c) As the user of the ASD (*e.g.,* employer, STT), you must follow the QAP instructions.

(d) You are not permitted to use an ASD that does not pass the specified quality control checks or that has passed its expiration date.

(e) As an employer, with respect to breath ASDs, you must also follow the device use and care requirements of §40.233.

Subpart L—Alcohol Screening Tests

§40.241 What are the first steps in any alcohol screening test?

As the BAT or STT you will take the following steps to begin all alcohol screening tests, regardless of the type of testing device you are using:

(a) When a specific time for an employee's test has been scheduled, or the collection site is at the employee's worksite, and the employee does not appear at the collection site at the scheduled time, contact the DER to determine the appropriate interval within which the DER has determined the employee is authorized to arrive. If the employee's arrival is delayed beyond that time, you must notify the DER that the employee has not reported for testing. In a situation where a C/TPA has notified an owner/operator or other individual employee to report for testing and the employee does not appear, the C/TPA must notify the employee that he or she has refused to test.

(b) Ensure that, when the employee enters the alcohol testing site, you begin the alcohol testing process without undue delay. For example, you must not wait because the employee says he or she is not ready or because an authorized employer or employee representative is delayed in arriving.

(1) If the employee is also going to take a DOT drug test, you must, to the greatest extent practicable, ensure that the alcohol test is completed before the urine collection process begins.

(2) If the employee needs medical attention (*e.g.,* an injured employee in an emergency medical facility who is required to have a post-accident test), do not delay this treatment to conduct a test.

(c) Require the employee to provide positive identification. You must see a photo ID issued by the employer (other than in the case of an owner-operator or other self-employer individual) or a Federal, state, or local government (*e.g.,* a driver's license). You may not accept faxes or photocopies of identification. Positive identification by an employer representative (not a co-worker or another employee being tested) is also acceptable. If the employee cannot produce positive identification, you must contact a DER to verify the identity of the employee.

(d) If the employee asks, provide your identification to the employee. Your identification must include your name and your employer's name but is not required to include your picture, address, or telephone number.

(e) Explain the testing procedure to the employee, including showing the employee the instructions on the back of the ATF.

(f) Complete Step 1 of the ATF.

(g) Direct the employee to complete Step 2 on the ATF and sign the certification. If the employee refuses to sign this certification, you must document this refusal on the "Remarks" line of the ATF and immediately notify the DER. This is a refusal to test.

§40.243 What is the procedure for an alcohol screening test using an EBT or non-evidential breath ASD?

As the BAT or STT, you must take the following steps:

(a) Select, or allow the employee to select, an individually wrapped or sealed mouthpiece from the testing materials.

(b) Open the individually wrapped or sealed mouthpiece in view of the employee and insert it into the device in accordance with the manufacturer's instructions.

(c) Instruct the employee to blow steadily and forcefully into the mouthpiece for at least six seconds or until the device indicates that an adequate amount of breath has been obtained.

(d) Show the employee the displayed test result.

(e) If the device is one that prints the test number, testing device name and serial number, time, and result directly onto the ATF, you must check to ensure that the information has been printed correctly onto the ATF.

(f) If the device is one that prints the test number, testing device name and serial number, time and result, but on a separate printout rather than directly onto the ATF, you must affix the printout of the information to the designated space on the ATF with tamper-evident tape or use a self-adhesive label that is tamper-evident.

(g) If the device is one that does not print the test number, testing device name and serial number, time, and result, or it is a device not being used with a printer, you must record this information in Step 3 of the ATF.

§40.245 What is the procedure for an alcohol screening test using a saliva ASD or a breath tube ASD?

(a) As the STT or BAT, you must take the following steps when using the saliva ASD:

(1) Check the expiration date on the device or on the package containing the device and show it to the employee. You may not use the device after its expiration date.

(2) Open an individually wrapped or sealed package containing the device in the presence of the employee.

(3) Offer the employee the opportunity to use the device. If the employee uses it, you must instruct the employee to insert it into his or her mouth and use it in a manner described by the device's manufacturer.

(4) If the employee chooses not to use the device, or in all cases in which a new test is necessary because the device did not activate (see paragraph (a)(7) of this section), you must insert the device into the employee's mouth and gather saliva in the manner described by the device's manufacturer. You must wear single-use examination or similar gloves while doing so and change them following each test.

(5) When the device is removed from the employee's mouth, you must follow the manufacturer's instructions regarding necessary next steps in ensuring that the device has activated.

(6)(i) If you were unable to successfully follow the procedures of paragraphs (a)(3) through (a)(5) of this section (*e.g.*, the device breaks, you drop the device on the floor), you must discard the device and conduct a new test using a new device.

(ii) The new device you use must be one that has been under your control or that of the employee before the test.

(iii) You must note on the "Remarks" line of the ATF the reason for the new test. (**Note**: You may continue using the same ATF with which you began the test.)

(iv) You must offer the employee the choice of using the device or having you use it unless the employee, in the opinion of the STT or BAT, was responsible (*e.g.,*the employee dropped the device) for the new test needing to be conducted.

(v) If you are unable to successfully follow the procedures of paragraphs (a)(3) through (a)(5) of this section on the new test, you must end the collection and put an explanation on the "Remarks" line of the ATF.

(vi) You must then direct the employee to take a new test immediately, using an EBT for the screening test.

(7) If you are able to successfully follow the procedures of paragraphs (a)(3)-(a)(5) of this section, but the device does not activate, you must discard the device and conduct a new test, in the same manner as provided in paragraph (a)(6) of this section. In this case, you must place the device into the employee's mouth to collect saliva for the new test.

(8) You must read the result displayed on the device no sooner than the device's manufacturer instructs. In all cases the result displayed must be read within 15 minutes of the test. You must then show the device and it's reading to the employee and enter the result on the ATF.

(9) You must never re-use devices, swabs, gloves or other materials used in saliva testing.

(10) You must note the fact that you used a saliva ASD in Step 3 of the ATF.

(b) As the STT or BAT, you must take the following steps when using the breath tube ASD:

(1) Check the expiration date on the detector device and the electronic analyzer or on the package containing the device and the analyzer and show it to the employee. You must not use the device or the analyzer after their expiration date. You must not use an analyzer which is not specifically pre-calibrated for the device being used in the collection.

(2) Remove the device from the package and secure an inflation bag onto the appropriate end of the device, as directed by the manufacturer on the device's instructions.

(3) Break the tube's ampoule in the presence of the employee.

(4) Offer the employee the opportunity to use the device. If the employee chooses to use (*e.g.* hold) the device, instruct the employee to blow forcefully and steadily into the blowing end of device until the inflation bag fills with air (approximately 12 seconds).

(5) If the employee chooses not to hold the device, you must hold it and provide the use instructions in paragraph (b)(4) of this section.

(6) When the employee completes the breath process, take the device from the employee (or if you were holding it, remove it from the employee's mouth), remove the inflation bag, and prepare the device to be read by the analyzer in accordance with the manufacturer's directions.

(7)(i) If you were unable to successfully follow the procedures of paragraphs (b)(4) through (b)(6) of this section (*e.g.*, the device breaks apart, the employee did not fill the inflation bag), you must discard the device and conduct a new test using a new one.

(ii) The new device you use must be one that has been under your control or that of the employer before the test.

(iii) You must note on the "Remarks" line of the ATF the reason for the new test. (**Note**: You may continue using the same ATF with which you began the test.)

(iv) You must offer the employee the choice of holding the device or having you hold it unless the employee, in the your opinion, was responsible (*e.g.,* the employee failed to fill the inflation bag) for the new test needing to be conducted.

(v) If you are unable to successfully follow the procedures of paragraphs (b)(4) through (b)(6) of this section on the new test, you must end the collection and put an explanation on the "Remarks" line of the ATF.

(vi) You must then direct the employee to take a new test immediately, using another type of ASD (*e.g.,* saliva device) or an EBT.

(8) If you were able to successfully follow the procedures of paragraphs (b)(4) through (b)(6) of this section and after having waited the required amount of time directed by the manufacturer for the detector device to incubate, you must place the device in the analyzer in accordance with the manufacturer's directions. The result must be read from the analyzer no earlier then the required incubation time of the device. In all cases, the result must be read within 15 minutes of the test.

(9) You must follow the manufacturer's instructions for determining the result of the test. You must show the analyzer result to the employee and record the result on Step 3 of the ATF.

(10) You must never re-use detector devices or any gloves used in breath tube testing. The inflation bag must be voided of air following removal from a device. Inflation bags and electronic analyzers may be re-used but only in accordance with the manufacturer's directions.

(11) You must note the fact that you used a breath tube device in Step 3 of the ATF.

§40.247 What procedures does the BAT or STT follow after a screening test result?

(a) If the test result is an alcohol concentration of less than 0.02, as the BAT or STT, you must do the following:

(1) Sign and date Step 3 of the ATF; and

(2) Transmit the result to the DER in a confidential manner, as provided in §40.255.

(b) If the test result is an alcohol concentration of 0.02 or higher, as the BAT or STT, you must direct the employee to take a confirmation test.

(1) If you are the BAT who will conduct the confirmation test, you must then conduct the test using the procedures beginning at §40.251.

(2) If you are not the BAT who will conduct the confirmation test, direct the employee to take a confirmation test, sign and date Step 3 of the ATF, and give the employee Copy 2 of the ATF.

(3) If the confirmation test will be performed at a different site from the screening test, you must take the following additional steps:

(i) Advise the employee not to eat, drink, put anything (*e.g.,* cigarette, chewing gum) into his or her mouth, or belch;

(ii) Tell the employee the reason for the waiting period required by §40.251(a) (*i.e.,* to prevent an accumulation of mouth alcohol from leading to an artificially high reading);

(iii) Explain that following your instructions concerning the waiting period is to the employee's benefit;

(iv) Explain that the confirmation test will be conducted at the end of the waiting period, even if the instructions have not been followed;

(v) Note on the "Remarks" line of the ATF that the waiting period instructions were provided;

(vi) Instruct the person accompanying the employee to carry a copy of the ATF to the BAT who will perform the confirmation test; and

(vii) Ensure that you or another BAT, STT, or employer representative observe the employee as he or she is transported to the confirmation testing site. You must direct the employee not to attempt to drive a motor vehicle to the confirmation testing site.

(c) If the screening test is invalid, you must, as the BAT or STT, tell the employee the test is cancelled and note the problem on the "Remarks" line of the ATF. If practicable, repeat the testing process (see §40.271).

Subpart M—Alcohol Confirmation Tests

§40.251 What are the first steps in an alcohol confirmation test?

As the BAT for an alcohol confirmation test, you must follow these steps to begin the confirmation test process:

(a) You must carry out a requirement for a waiting period before the confirmation test, by taking the following steps:

(1) You must ensure that the waiting period lasts at least 15 minutes, starting with the completion of the screening test. After the waiting period has elapsed, you should begin the confirmation test as soon as possible, but not more than 30 minutes after the completion of the screening test.

(i) If the confirmation test is taking place at a different location from the screening test (see §40.247(b)(3)) the time of transit between sites counts toward the waiting period if the STT or BAT who conducted the screening test provided the waiting period instructions.

(ii) If you cannot verify, through review of the ATF, that waiting period instructions were provided, then you must carry out the waiting period requirement.

(iii) You or another BAT or STT, or an employer representative, must observe the employee during the waiting period.

(2) Concerning the waiting period, you must tell the employee:

(i) Not to eat, drink, put anything (e.g., cigarette, chewing gum) into his or her mouth, or belch;

(ii) The reason for the waiting period (i.e., to prevent an accumulation of mouth alcohol from leading to an artificially high reading);

(iii) That following your instructions concerning the waiting period is to the employee's benefit; and

(iv) That the confirmation test will be conducted at the end of the waiting period, even if the instructions have not been followed.

(3) If you become aware that the employee has not followed the instructions, you must note this on the "Remarks" line of the ATF.

(b) If you did not conduct the screening test for the employee, you must require positive identification of the employee, explain the confirmation procedures, and use a new ATF. You must note on the "Remarks" line of the ATF that a different BAT or STT conducted the screening test.

(c) Complete Step 1 of the ATF.

(d) Direct the employee to complete Step 2 on the ATF and sign the certification. If the employee refuses to sign this certification, you must document this refusal on the "Remarks" line of the ATF and immediately notify the DER. This is a refusal to test.

(e) Even if more than 30 minutes have passed since the screening test result was obtained, you must begin the confirmation test procedures in §40.253, not another screening test.

(f) You must note on the "Remarks" line of the ATF the time that elapsed between the two events, and if the confirmation test could not begin within 30 minutes of the screening test, the reason why.

(g) Beginning the confirmation test procedures after the 30 minutes have elapsed does not invalidate the screening or confirmation tests, but it may constitute a regulatory violation subject to DOT agency sanction.

§40.253 What are the procedures for conducting an alcohol confirmation test?

As the BAT conducting an alcohol confirmation test, you must follow these steps in order to complete the confirmation test process:

(a) In the presence of the employee, you must conduct an air blank on the EBT you are using before beginning the confirmation test and show the reading to the employee.

(1) If the reading is 0.00, the test may proceed. If the reading is greater than 0.00, you must conduct another air blank.

(2) If the reading on the second air blank is 0.00, the test may proceed. If the reading is greater than 0.00, you must take the EBT out of service.

(3) If you take an EBT out of service for this reason, no one may use it for testing until the EBT is found to be within tolerance limits on an external check of calibration.

(4) You must proceed with the test of the employee using another EBT, if one is available.

(b) You must open a new individually wrapped or sealed mouthpiece in view of the employee and insert it into the device in accordance with the manufacturer's instructions.

(c) You must ensure that you and the employee read the unique test number displayed on the EBT.

(d) You must instruct the employee to blow steadily and forcefully into the mouthpiece for at least six seconds or until the device indicates that an adequate amount of breath has been obtained.

(e) You must show the employee the result displayed on the EBT.

(f) You must show the employee the result and unique test number that the EBT prints out either directly onto the ATF or onto a separate printout.

(g) If the EBT provides a separate printout of the result, you must attach the printout to the designated space on the ATF with tamper-evident tape, or use a self-adhesive label that is tamper-evident.

§40.255 What happens next after the alcohol confirmation test result?

(a) After the EBT has printed the result of an alcohol confirmation test, you must, as the BAT, take the following additional steps:

(1) Sign and date Step 3 of the ATF.

(2) If the alcohol confirmation test result is lower than 0.02, nothing further is required of the employee. As the BAT, you must sign and date Step 3 of the ATF.

(3) If the alcohol confirmation test result is 0.02 or higher, direct the employee to sign and date Step 4 of the ATF. If the employee does not do so, you must note this on the "Remarks" line of the ATF. However, this is not considered a refusal to test.

(4) If the test is invalid, tell the employee the test is cancelled and note the problem on the "Remarks" line of the ATF. If practicable, conduct a re-test. (see §40.271).

(5) Immediately transmit the result directly to the DER in a confidential manner.

(i) You may transmit the results using Copy 1 of the ATF, in person, by telephone, or by electronic means. In any case, you must immediately notify the DER of any result of 0.02 or greater by any means (*e.g.,* telephone or secure fax machine) that ensures the result is immediately received by the DER. You must not transmit these results through C/TPAs or other service agents.

(ii) If you do not make the initial transmission in writing, you must follow up the initial transmission with Copy 1 of the ATF.

(b) As an employer, you must take the following steps with respect to the receipt and storage of alcohol test result information:

(1) If you receive any test results that are not in writing (*e.g.,* by telephone or electronic means), you must establish a mechanism to establish the identity of the BAT sending you the results.

(2) You must store all test result information in a way that protects confidentiality.

Subpart N—Problems in Alcohol Testing

§40.261 What is a refusal to take an alcohol test, and what are the consequences?

(a) As an employee, you are considered to have refused to take an alcohol test if you:

(1) Fail to appear for any test (except a pre-employment test) within a reasonable time, as determined by the employer, consistent with applicable DOT agency regulations, after being directed to do so by the employer. This includes the failure of an employee (including an owner-operator) to appear for a test when called by a C/TPA (see §40.241(a));

(2) Fail to remain at the testing site until the testing process is complete; *Provided,* That an employee who leaves the testing site before the testing process commences (see §40.243(a)) for a pre-employment test is not deemed to have refused to test;

(3) Fail to provide an adequate amount of saliva or breath for any alcohol test required by this part or DOT agency regulations; *Provided,* That an employee who does not provide an adequate amount of breath or saliva because he or she has left the testing site before the testing process commences (see §40.243(a)) for a pre-employment test is not deemed to have refused to test;

(4) Fail to provide a sufficient breath specimen, and the physician has determined, through a required medical evaluation, that there was no adequate medical explanation for the failure (see §40.265(c));

(5) Fail to undergo a medical examination or evaluation, as directed by the employer as part of the insufficient breath procedures outlined at §40.265(c);

(6) Fail to sign the certification at Step 2 of the ATF (see §§40.241(g) and 40.251(d)); or

(7) Fail to cooperate with any part of the testing process.

(b) As an employee, if you refuse to take an alcohol test, you incur the same consequences specified under DOT agency regulations for a violation of those DOT agency regulations.

(c) As a BAT or an STT, or as the physician evaluating a "shy lung" situation, when an employee refuses to test as provided in paragraph (a) of this section, you must terminate the portion of the testing process in which you are involved, document the refusal on the ATF (or in a separate document which you cause to be attached to the form), immediately notify the DER by any means (*e.g.,* telephone or secure fax machine) that ensures the refusal notification is immediately received. You must make this notification directly to the DER (not using a C/TPA as an intermediary).

(d) As an employee, when you refuse to take a non-DOT test or to sign a non-DOT form, you have not refused to take a DOT test. There are no consequences under DOT agency regulations for such a refusal.

§40.263 What happens when an employee is unable to provide a sufficient amount of saliva for an alcohol screening test?

(a) As the STT, you must take the following steps if an employee is unable to provide sufficient saliva to complete a test on a saliva screening device (*e.g.,* the employee does not provide sufficient saliva to activate the device).

(1) You must conduct a new screening test using a new screening device.

(2) If the employee refuses to make the attempt to complete the new test, you must discontinue testing, note the fact on the "Remarks" line of the ATF, and immediately notify the DER. This is a refusal to test.

(3) If the employee has not provided a sufficient amount of saliva to complete the new test, you must note the fact on the "Remarks" line of the ATF and immediately notify the DER.

(b) As the DER, when the STT informs you that the employee has not provided a sufficient amount of saliva (see paragraph (a)(3) of this section), you must immediately arrange to administer an alcohol test to the employee using an EBT or other breath testing device.

§40.265 What happens when an employee is unable to provide a sufficient amount of breath for an alcohol test?

(a) If an employee does not provide a sufficient amount of breath to permit a valid breath test, you must take the steps listed in this section.

(b) As the BAT or STT, you must instruct the employee to attempt again to provide a sufficient amount of breath and about the proper way to do so.

(1) If the employee refuses to make the attempt, you must discontinue the test, note the fact on the "Remarks" line of the ATF, and immediately notify the DER. This is a refusal to test.

(2) If the employee again attempts and fails to provide a sufficient amount of breath, you may provide another opportunity to the employee to do so if you believe that there is a strong likelihood that it could result in providing a sufficient amount of breath.

(3) When the employee's attempts under paragraph (b)(2) of this section have failed to produce a sufficient amount of breath, you must note the fact on the "Remarks" line of the ATF and immediately notify the DER.

(4) If you are using an EBT that has the capability of operating manually, you may attempt to conduct the test in manual mode.

(5) If you are qualified to use a saliva ASD and you are in the screening test stage, you may change to a saliva ASD only to complete the screening test.

(c) As the employer, when the BAT or STT informs you that the employee has not provided a sufficient amount of breath, you must direct the employee to obtain, within five days, an evaluation from a licensed physician who is acceptable to you and who has expertise in the medical issues raised by the employee's failure to provide a sufficient specimen.

(1) You are required to provide the physician who will conduct the evaluation with the following information and instructions:

(i) That the employee was required to take a DOT breath alcohol test, but was unable to provide a sufficient amount of breath to complete the test;

(ii) The consequences of the appropriate DOT agency regulation for refusing to take the required alcohol test;

(iii) That the physician must provide you with a signed statement of his or her conclusions; and

(iv) That the physician, in his or her reasonable medical judgment, must base those conclusions on one of the following determinations:

(A) A medical condition has, or with a high degree of probability could have, precluded the employee from providing a sufficient amount of breath. The physician must not include in the signed statement detailed information on the employee's medical condition. In this case, the test is cancelled.

(B) There is not an adequate basis for determining that a medical condition has, or with a high degree of probability could have, precluded the employee from providing a sufficient amount of breath. This constitutes a refusal to test.

(C) For purposes of paragraphs (c)(1)(iv)(A) and (B) of this section, a medical condition includes an ascertainable physiological condition (*e.g.,* a respiratory system dysfunction) or a medically documented pre-existing psychological disorder, but does not include unsupported assertions of "situational anxiety" or hyperventilation.

(2) As the physician making the evaluation, after making your determination, you must provide a written statement of your conclusions and the basis for them to the DER directly (and not through a C/TPA acting as an itermediary). You must not include in this statement detailed information on the employee's medical condition beyond what is necessary to explain your conclusion.

(3) Upon receipt of the report from the examining physician, as the DER you must immediately inform the employee and take appropriate action based upon your DOT agency regulations.

§40.267 What problems always cause an alcohol test to be cancelled?

As an employer, a BAT, or an STT, you must cancel an alcohol test if any of the following problems occur. These are "fatal flaws." You must inform the DER that the test was cancelled and must be treated as if the test never occurred. These problems are:

(a) In the case of a screening test conducted on a saliva ASD or a breath tube ASD:

(1) The STT or BAT reads the result either sooner than or later than the time allotted by the manufacturer and this Part (see §40.245(a)(8) for the saliva ASD and §40.245(b)(8) for the breath tube ASD).

(2) The saliva ASD does not activate (see §40.245(a)(7); or

(3) The device is used for a test after the expiration date printed on the device or on its package (see §40.245(a)(1) for the saliva ASD and §40.245(b)(1) for the breath tube ASD).

(4) The breath tube ASD is tested with an analyzer which has not been pre-calibrated for that device's specific lot (see Sec. 40.245(b)(1)).

(b) In the case of a screening or confirmation test conducted on an EBT, the sequential test number or alcohol concentration displayed on the EBT is not the same as the sequential test number or alcohol concentration on the printed result (see §40.253(c), (e) and (f)).

(c) In the case of a confirmation test:

(1) The BAT conducts the confirmation test before the end of the minimum 15-minute waiting period (see §40.251(a)(1));

(2) The BAT does not conduct an air blank before the confirmation test (see §40.253(a));

(3) There is not a 0.00 result on the air blank conducted before the confirmation test (see §40.253(a)(1) and (2));

(4) The EBT does not print the result (see §40.253(f)); or

(5) The next external calibration check of the EBT produces a result that differs by more than the tolerance stated in the QAP from the known value of the test standard. In this case, every result of 0.02 or above obtained on the EBT since the last valid external calibration check is cancelled (see §40.233(a)(1) and (c)(3)).

§40.269 What problems cause an alcohol test to be cancelled unless they are corrected?

As a BAT or STT, or employer, you must cancel an alcohol test if any of the following problems occur, unless they are corrected. These are "correctable flaws." These problems are:

(a) The BAT or STT does not sign the ATF (see §§40.247(a)(1) and 40.255(a)(1)).

(b) The BAT or STT fails to note on the "Remarks" line of the ATF that the employee has not signed the ATF after the result is obtained (see §40.255(a)(3)).

(c) The BAT or STT uses a non-DOT form for the test (see §40.225(a)).

§40.271 How are alcohol testing problems corrected?

(a) As a BAT or STT, you have the responsibility of trying to complete successfully an alcohol test for each employee.

(1) If, during or shortly after the testing process, you become aware of any event that will cause the test to be cancelled (see §40.267), you must try to correct the problem promptly, if practicable. You may repeat the testing process as part of this effort.

(2) If repeating the testing process is necessary, you must begin a new test as soon as possible. You must use a new ATF, a new sequential test number, and, if needed, a new ASD and/or a new EBT. It is permissible to use additional technical capabilities of the EBT (*e.g.,* manual operation) if you have been trained to do so in accordance with §40.213(c) .

(3) If repeating the testing process is necessary, you are not limited in the number of attempts to complete the test, provided that the employee is making a good faith effort to comply with the testing process.

(4) If another testing device is not available for the new test at the testing site, you must immediately notify the DER and advise the DER that the test could not be completed. As the DER who receives this information, you must make all reasonable efforts to ensure that the test is conducted at another testing site as soon as possible.

(b) If, as an STT, BAT, employer or other service agent administering the testing process, you become aware of a "correctable flaw" (see §40.269) that has not already been corrected, you must take all practicable action to correct the problem so that the test is not cancelled.

(1) If the problem resulted from the omission of required information, you must, as the person responsible for providing that information, supply in writing

the missing information and a signed statement that it is true and accurate. For example, suppose you are a BAT and you forgot to make a notation on the "Remarks" line of the ATF that the employee did not sign the certification. You would, when the problem is called to your attention, supply a signed statement that the employee failed or refused to sign the certification after the result was obtained, and that your signed statement is true and accurate.

(2) If the problem is the use of a non-DOT form, you must, as the person responsible for the use of the incorrect form, certify in writing that the incorrect form contains all the information needed for a valid DOT alcohol test. You must also provide a signed statement that the incorrect form was used inadvertently or as the only means of conducting a test, in circumstances beyond your control, and the steps you have taken to prevent future use of non-DOT forms for DOT tests. You must supply this information on the same business day on which you are notified of the problem, transmitting it by fax or courier.

(c) If you cannot correct the problem, you must cancel the test.

§40.273 What is the effect of a cancelled alcohol test?

(a) A cancelled alcohol test is neither positive nor negative.

(1) As an employer, you must not attach to a cancelled test the consequences of a test result that is 0.02 or greater (*e.g.,* removal from a safety-sensitive position).

(2) As an employer, you must not use a cancelled test in a situation where an employee needs a test result that is below 0.02 (*e.g.,* in the case of a return-to-duty or follow-up test to authorize the employee to perform safety-sensitive functions).

(3) As an employer, you must not direct a recollection for an employee because a test has been cancelled, except in the situations cited in paragraph (a)(2) of this section or other provisions of this part.

(b) A cancelled test does not count toward compliance with DOT requirements, such as a minimum random testing rate.

(c) When a test must be cancelled, if you are the BAT, STT, or other person who determines that the cancellation is necessary, you must inform the affected DER within 48 hours of the cancellation.

(d) A cancelled DOT test does not provide a valid basis for an employer to conduct a non-DOT test (*i.e.,* a test under company authority).

§40.275 What is the effect of procedural problems that are not sufficient to cancel an alcohol test?

(a) As an STT, BAT, employer, or a service agent administering the testing process, you must document any errors in the testing process of which you become aware, even if they are not "fatal flaws" or "correctable flaws" listed in this subpart. Decisions about the ultimate impact of these errors will be determined by administrative or legal proceedings, subject to the limitation of paragraph (b) of this section.

(b) No person concerned with the testing process may declare a test cancelled based on a mistake in the process that does not have a significant adverse effect on the right of the employee to a fair and accurate test. For example, it is inconsistent with this part to cancel a test based on a minor administrative mistake (*e.g.,* the omission of the employee's middle initial) or an error that does not affect employee protections under this part. Nor does the failure of an employee to sign in Step 4 of the ATF result in the cancellation of the test. Nor is a test to be cancelled on the basis of a claim by an employee that he or she was improperly selected for testing.

(c) As an employer, these errors, even though not sufficient to cancel an alcohol test result, may subject you to enforcement action under DOT agency regulations.

§40.277 Are alcohol tests other than saliva or breath permitted under these regulations?

No, other types of alcohol tests (*e.g.,* blood and urine) are not authorized for testing done under this part. Only saliva or breath for screening tests and breath for confirmation tests using approved devices are permitted.

Subpart O—Substance Abuse Professionals and the Return-to-Duty Process

§40.281 Who is qualified to act as a SAP?

To be permitted to act as a SAP in the DOT drug and alcohol testing program, you must meet each of the requirements of this section:

(a) **Credentials**. You must have one of the following credentials:

(1) You are a licensed physician (Doctor of Medicine or Osteopathy);

(2) You are a licensed or certified social worker;

(3) You are a licensed or certified psychologist;

(4) You are a licensed or certified employee assistance professional;

(5) You are a state-licensed or certified marriage and family therapist; or

(6) You are a drug and alcohol counselor certified by an organization listed at *https://www.transportation.gov/odapc/sap*.

(b) **Basic knowledge**. You must be knowledgeable in the following areas:

(1) You must be knowledgeable about and have clinical experience in the diagnosis and treatment of alcohol and controlled substances-related disorders.

(2) You must be knowledgeable about the SAP function as it relates to employer interests in safety-sensitive duties.

(3) You must be knowledgeable about this part, the DOT agency regulations applicable to the employers for whom you evaluate employees, and the DOT SAP Guidelines. You must keep current on any changes to these materials. You must subscribe to the ODAPC list-serve at *https://www.transportation.gov/odapc/get-odapc-email-updates*. DOT agency regulations, DOT SAP Guidelines, and other materials are available from ODAPC (Department of Transportation, 1200 New Jersey Avenue SE., Washington DC, 20590 (202-366-3784), or on the ODAPC Web site (*http://www.transportation.gov/odapc*).

(c) **Qualification training**. You must receive qualification training meeting the requirements of this paragraph (c).

(1) Qualification training must provide instruction on the following subjects:

(i) Background, rationale, and coverage of the Department's drug and alcohol testing program;

(ii) 49 CFR Part 40 and DOT agency drug and alcohol testing rules;

(iii) Key DOT drug testing requirements, including collections, laboratory testing, MRO review, and problems in drug testing;

(iv) Key DOT alcohol testing requirements, including the testing process, the role of BATs and STTs, and problems in alcohol tests;

(v) SAP qualifications and prohibitions;

(vi) The role of the SAP in the return-to-duty process, including the initial employee evaluation, referrals for education and/or treatment, the follow-up evaluation, continuing treatment recommendations, and the follow-up testing plan;

(vii) SAP consultation and communication with employers, MROs, and treatment providers;

(viii) Reporting and recordkeeping requirements;

(ix) Issues that SAPs confront in carrying out their duties under the program.

(2) Following your completion of qualification training under paragraph (c)(1) of this section, you must satisfactorily complete an examination administered by a nationally-recognized professional or training organization. The examination must comprehensively cover all the elements of qualification training listed in paragraph (c)(1) of this section.

(3) You must meet the requirements of paragraphs (a), (b), and (c) of this section before you begin to perform SAP functions.

(d) **Continuing education**. During each three-year period from the date on which you satisfactorily complete the examination under paragraph (c)(2) of this section, you must complete continuing education consisting of at least 12 professional development hours (*e.g.,* CEUs) relevant to performing SAP functions.

(1) This continuing education must include material concerning new technologies, interpretations, recent guidance, rule changes, and other information about developments in SAP practice, pertaining to the DOT program, since the time you met the qualification training requirements of this section.

(2) Your continuing education activities must include documentable assessment tools to assist you in determining whether you have adequately learned the material.

(e) **Documentation**. You must maintain documentation showing that you currently meet all requirements of this section. You must provide this documentation on request to DOT agency representatives and to employers and C/TPAs who are using or contemplating using your services.

§40.283 How does a certification organization obtain recognition for its members as SAPs?

(a) If you represent a certification organization that wants DOT to authorize its certified drug and alcohol counselors to be added to §40.281(a)(6), you may submit a written petition to DOT requesting a review of your petition for inclusion.

(b) You must obtain the National Commission for Certifying Agencies (NCCA) accreditation before DOT will act on your petition.

(c) You must also meet the minimum requirements of Appendix E to this part before DOT will act on your petition.

§40.285 When is a SAP evaluation required?

(a) As an employee, when you have violated DOT drug and alcohol regulations, you cannot again perform any DOT safety-sensitive duties for any employer until and unless you complete the SAP evaluation, referral, and education /treatment process set forth in this subpart and in applicable DOT agency regulations. The first step in this process is a SAP evaluation.

(b) For purposes of this subpart, a verified positive DOT drug test result, a DOT alcohol test with a result indicating an alcohol concentration of 0.04 or greater, a refusal to test (including by adulterating or substituting a urine specimen) or any other violation of the prohibition on the use of alcohol or drugs under a DOT agency regulation constitutes a DOT drug and alcohol regulation violation.

§40.287 What information is an employer required to provide concerning SAP services to an employee who has a DOT drug and alcohol regulation violation?

As an employer, you must provide to each employee (including an applicant or new employee) who violates a DOT drug and alcohol regulation a listing of SAPs readily available to the employee and acceptable to you, with names, addresses, and telephone numbers. You cannot charge the employee any fee for compiling or providing this list. You may provide this list yourself or through a C/TPA or other service agent.

§40.289 Are employers required to provide SAP and treatment services to employees?

(a) As an employer, you are not required to provide a SAP evaluation or any subsequent recommended education or treatment for an employee who has violated a DOT drug and alcohol regulation.

(b) However, if you offer that employee an opportunity to return to a DOT safety-sensitive duty following a violation, you must, before the employee again performs that duty, ensure that the employee receives an evaluation by a SAP meeting the requirements of §40.281 and that the employee successfully complies with the SAP's evaluation recommendations.

(c) Payment for SAP evaluations and services is left for employers and employees to decide and may be governed by existing management-labor agreements and health care benefits.

§40.291 What is the role of the SAP in the evaluation, referral, and treatment process of an employee who has violated DOT agency drug and alcohol testing regulations?

(a) As a SAP, you are charged with:

(1) Making a face-to-face clinical assessment and evaluation to determine what assistance is needed by the employee to resolve problems associated with alcohol and/or drug use;

(2) Referring the employee to an appropriate education and/or treatment program;

(3) Conducting a face-to-face follow-up evaluation to determine if the employee has actively participated in the education and/or treatment program and has demonstrated successful compliance with the initial assessment and evaluation recommendations;

(4) Providing the DER with a follow-up drug and/or alcohol testing plan for the employee; and

(5) Providing the employee and employer with recommendations for continuing education and/or treatment.

(b) As a SAP, you are not an advocate for the employer or employee. Your function is to protect the public interest in safety by professionally evaluating the employee and recommending appropriate education/treatment, follow-up tests, and aftercare.

§40.293 What is the SAP's function in conducting the initial evaluation of an employee?

As a SAP, for every employee who comes to you following a DOT drug and alcohol regulation violation, you must accomplish the following:

(a) Provide a comprehensive face-to-face assessment and clinical evaluation.

(b) Recommend a course of education and/or treatment with which the employee must demonstrate successful compliance prior to returning to DOT safety-sensitive duty.

(1) You must make such a recommendation for every individual who has violated a DOT drug and alcohol regulation.

(2) You must make a recommendation for education and/or treatment that will, to the greatest extent possible, protect public safety in the event that the employee returns to the performance of safety-sensitive functions.

(c) Appropriate education may include, but is not limited to, self-help groups (*e.g.,* Alcoholics Anonymous) and community lectures, where attendance can be independently verified, and bona fide drug and alcohol education courses.

(d) Appropriate treatment may include, but is not limited to, in-patient hospitalization, partial in-patient treatment, out-patient counseling programs, and aftercare.

(e) You must provide a written report directly to the DER highlighting your specific recommendations for assistance (see §40.311(c)).

(f) For purposes of your role in the evaluation process, you must assume that a verified positive test result has conclusively established that the employee committed a DOT drug and alcohol regulation violation. You must not take into consideration in any way, as a factor in determining what your recommendation will be, any of the following:

(1) A claim by the employee that the test was unjustified or inaccurate;

(2) Statements by the employee that attempt to mitigate the seriousness of a violation of a DOT drug or alcohol regulation (*e.g.,* related to assertions of use of hemp oil, "medical marijuana" use, "contact positives," poppy seed ingestion, job stress); or

(3) Personal opinions you may have about the justification or rationale for drug and alcohol testing.

(g) In the course of gathering information for purposes of your evaluation in the case of a drug-related violation, you may consult with the MRO. As the MRO, you are required to cooperate with the SAP and provide available information the SAP requests. It is not necessary to obtain the consent of the employee to provide this information.

§40.295 May employees or employers seek a second SAP evaluation if they disagree with the first SAP's recommendations?

(a) As an employee with a DOT drug and alcohol regulation violation, when you have been evaluated by a SAP, you must not seek a second SAP's evaluation in order to obtain another recommendation.

(b) As an employer, you must not seek a second SAP's evaluation if the employee has already been evaluated by a qualified SAP. If the employee, contrary to paragraph (a) of this section, has obtained a second SAP evaluation, as an employer you may not rely on it for any purpose under this part.

§40.297 Does anyone have the authority to change a SAP's initial evaluation?

(a) Except as provided in paragraph (b) of this section, no one (*e.g.,* an employer, employee, a managed-care provider, any service agent) may change in any way the SAP's evaluation or recommendations for assistance. For example, a third party is not permitted to make more or less stringent a SAP's recommendation by changing the SAP's evaluation or seeking another SAP's evaluation.

(b) The SAP who made the initial evaluation may modify his or her initial evaluation and recommendations based on new or additional information (*e.g.,* from an education or treatment program).

§40.299 What is the SAP's role and what are the limits on a SAP's discretion in referring employees for education and treatment?

(a) As a SAP, upon your determination of the best recommendation for assistance, you will serve as a referral source to assist the employee's entry into a education and/or treatment program.

(b) To prevent the appearance of a conflict of interest, you must not refer an employee requiring assistance to your private practice or to a person or organization from which you receive payment or to a person or organization in which you have a financial interest. You are precluded from making referrals to entities with which you are financially associated.

(c) There are four exceptions to the prohibitions contained in paragraph (b) of this section. You may refer an employee to any of the following providers of assistance, regardless of your relationship with them:

(1) A public agency (*e.g.,* treatment facility) operated by a state, county, or municipality;

(2) The employer or a person or organization under contract to the employer to provide alcohol or drug treatment and/or education services (*e.g.,* the employer's contracted treatment provider);

(3) The sole source of therapeutically appropriate treatment under the employee's health insurance program (*e.g.,* the single substance abuse in-patient treatment program made available by the employee's insurance coverage plan); or

(4) The sole source of therapeutically appropriate treatment reasonably available to the employee (*e.g.,* the only treatment facility or education program reasonably located within the general commuting area).

§40.301 What is the SAP's function in the follow-up evaluation of an employee?

(a) As a SAP, after you have prescribed assistance under §40.293, you must re-evaluate the employee to determine if the employee has successfully carried out your education and/or treatment recommendations.

(1) This is your way to gauge for the employer the employee's ability to demonstrate successful compliance with the education and/or treatment plan.

(2) Your evaluation may serve as one of the reasons the employer decides to return the employee to safety-sensitive duty.

(b) As the SAP making the follow-up evaluation determination, you must:

(1) Confer with or obtain appropriate documentation from the appropriate education and/or treatment program professionals where the employee was referred; and

(2) Conduct a face-to-face clinical interview with the employee to determine if the employee demonstrates successful compliance with your initial evaluation recommendations.

(c)(1) If the employee has demonstrated successful compliance, you must provide a written report directly to the DER highlighting your clinical determination that the employee has done so with your initial evaluation recommendation (see §40.311(d)).

(2) You may determine that an employee has successfully demonstrated compliance even though the employee has not yet completed the full regimen of education and/or treatment you recommended or needs additional assistance. For example, if the employee has successfully completed the 30-day in-patient program you prescribed, you may make a "successful compliance" determination even though you conclude that the employee has not yet completed the out-patient counseling you recommended or should continue in an aftercare program.

(d)(1) As the SAP, if you believe, as a result of the follow-up evaluation, that the employee has not demonstrated successful compliance with your recommendations, you must provide written notice directly to the DER (see §40.311(e)).

(2) As an employer who receives the SAP's written notice that the employee has not successfully complied with the SAP's recommendations, you must not return the employee to the performance of safety-sensitive duties.

(3) As the SAP, you may conduct additional follow-up evaluation(s) if the employer determines that doing so is consistent with the employee's progress as you have reported it and with the employer's policy and/or labor-management agreements.

(4) As the employer, following a SAP report that the employee has not demonstrated successful compliance, you may take personnel action consistent with your policy and/or labor-management agreements.

§40.303 What happens if the SAP believes the employee needs additional treatment, aftercare, or support group services even after the employee returns to safety-sensitive duties?

(a) As a SAP, if you believe that ongoing services (in addition to follow-up tests) are needed to assist an employee to maintain sobriety or abstinence from drug use after the employee resumes the performance of safety-sensitive duties, you must provide recommendations for these services in your follow-up evaluation report (see §40.311(d)(10)).

(b) As an employer receiving a recommendation for these services from a SAP, you may, as part of a return-to-duty agreement with the employee, require the employee to participate in the recommended services. You may monitor and document the employee's participation in the recommended services. You may also make use of SAP and employee assistance program (EAP) services in assisting and monitoring employees' compliance with SAP recommendations. Nothing in this section permits an employer to fail to carry out its obligations with respect to follow-up testing (see §40.309).

(c) As an employee, you are obligated to comply with the SAP's recommendations for these services. If you fail or refuse to do so, you may be subject to disciplinary action by your employer.

§40.305 How does the return-to-duty process conclude?

(a) As the employer, if you decide that you want to permit the employee to return to the performance of safety-sensitive functions, you must ensure that the employee takes a return-to-duty test. This test cannot occur until after the SAP has determined that the employee has successfully complied with prescribed education and/or treatment. The employee must have a negative drug test result and/or an alcohol test with an alcohol concentration of less than 0.02 before resuming performance of safety-sensitive duties.

(b) As an employer, you must not return an employee to safety-sensitive duties until the employee meets the conditions of paragraph (a) of this section. However, you are not required to return an employee to safety-sensitive duties because the employee has met these conditions. That is a personnel decision that you have the discretion to make, subject to collective bargaining agreements or other legal requirements.

(c) As a SAP or MRO, you must not make a "fitness for duty" determination as part of this re-evaluation unless required to do so under an applicable DOT agency regulation. It is the employer, rather than you, who must decide whether to put the employee back to work in a safety-sensitive position.

§40.307 What is the SAP's function in prescribing the employee's follow-up tests?

(a) As a SAP, for each employee who has committed a DOT drug or alcohol regulation violation, and who seeks to resume the performance of safety-sensitive functions, you must establish a written follow-up testing plan. You do not establish this plan until after you determine that the employee has successfully complied with your recommendations for education and/or treatment.

(b) You must present a copy of this plan directly to the DER (see §40.311(d)(9)).

(c) You are the sole determiner of the number and frequency of follow-up tests and whether these tests will be for drugs, alcohol, or both, unless otherwise directed by the appropriate DOT agency regulation. For example, if the employee had a positive drug test, but your evaluation or the treatment program professionals determined that the employee had an alcohol problem as well, you should require that the employee have follow-up tests for both drugs and alcohol.

(d) However, you must, at a minimum, direct that the employee be subject to six unannounced follow-up tests in the first 12 months of safety-sensitive duty following the employee's return to safety-sensitive functions.

(1) You may require a greater number of follow-up tests during the first 12-month period of safety-sensitive duty (e.g., you may require one test a month during the 12-month period; you may require two tests per month during the first 6-month period and one test per month during the final 6-month period).

(2) You may also require follow-up tests during the 48 months of safety-sensitive duty following this first 12-month period.

(3) You are not to establish the actual dates for the follow-up tests you prescribe. The decision on specific dates to test is the employer's.

(4) As the employer, you must not impose additional testing requirements (e.g., under company authority) on the employee that go beyond the SAP's follow-up testing plan.

(e) The requirements of the SAP's follow-up testing plan "follow the employee" to subsequent employers or through breaks in service.

Example 1 to Paragraph (e): The employee returns to duty with Employer A. Two months afterward, after completing the first two of six follow-up tests required by the SAP's plan, the employee quits his job with Employer A and begins to work in a similar position for Employer B. The employee remains obligated to complete the four additional tests during the next 10 months of safety-sensitive duty, and Employer B is responsible for ensuring that the employee does so. Employer B learns of this obligation through the inquiry it makes under §40.25.

Example 2 to Paragraph (e): The employee returns to duty with Employer A. Three months later, after the employee completes the first two of six follow-up tests required by the SAP's plan, Employer A lays the employee off for economic or seasonal employment reasons. Four months later, Employer A recalls the employee. Employer A must ensure that the employee completes the remaining four follow-up tests during the next nine months.

(f) As the SAP, you may modify the determinations you have made concerning follow-up tests. For example, even if you recommended follow-up testing beyond the first 12-months, you can terminate the testing requirement at any time after the first year of testing. You must not, however, modify the requirement that the employee take at least six follow-up tests within the first 12 months after returning to the performance of safety-sensitive functions.

§40.309 What are the employer's responsibilities with respect to the SAP's directions for follow-up tests?

(a) As the employer, you must carry out the SAP's follow-up testing requirements. You may not allow the employee to continue to perform safety-sensitive functions unless follow-up testing is conducted as directed by the SAP.

(b) You should schedule follow-up tests on dates of your own choosing, but you must ensure that the tests are unannounced with no discernable pattern as to their timing, and that the employee is given no advance notice.

(c) You cannot substitute any other tests (*e.g.,* those carried out under the random testing program) conducted on the employee for this follow-up testing requirement.

(d) You cannot count a follow-up test that has been cancelled as a completed test. A cancelled follow-up test must be recollected.

§40.311 What are the requirements concerning SAP reports?

(a) As the SAP conducting the required evaluations, you must send the written reports required by this section in writing directly to the DER and not to a third party or entity for forwarding to the DER (except as provided in §40.355(e)). You may, however, forward the document simultaneously to the DER and to a C/TPA.

(b) As an employer, you must ensure that you receive SAP written reports directly from the SAP performing the evaluation and that no third party or entity changed the SAP's report in any way.

(c) The SAP's written report, following an initial evaluation that determines what level of assistance is needed to address the employee's drug and/or alcohol problems, must be on the SAP's own letterhead (and not the letterhead of another service agent) signed and dated by the SAP, and must contain the following delineated items:

(1) Employee's name and SSN;

(2) Employer's name and address;

(3) Reason for the assessment (specific violation of DOT regulations and violation date);

(4) Date(s) of the assessment;

(5) SAP's education and/or treatment recommendation; and

(6) SAP's telephone number.

(d) The SAP's written report concerning a follow-up evaluation that determines the employee has demonstrated successful compliance must be on the

SAP's own letterhead (and not the letterhead of another service agent), signed by the SAP and dated, and must contain the following items:

(1) Employee's name and SSN;

(2) Employer's name and address;

(3) Reason for the initial assessment (specific violation of DOT regulations and violation date);

(4) Date(s) of the initial assessment and synopsis of the treatment plan;

(5) Name of practice(s) or service(s) providing the recommended education and/or treatment;

(6) Inclusive dates of employee's program participation;

(7) Clinical characterization of employee's program participation;

(8) SAP's clinical determination as to whether the employee has demonstrated successful compliance;

(9) Follow-up testing plan;

(10) Employee's continuing care needs with specific treatment, aftercare, and/or support group services recommendations; and

(11) SAP's telephone number.

(e) The SAP's written report concerning a follow-up evaluation that determines the employee has not demonstrated successful compliance must be on the SAP's own letterhead (and not the letterhead of another service agent), signed by the SAP and dated, and must contain the following items:

(1) Employee's name and SSN;

(2) Employer's name and address;

(3) Reason for the initial assessment (specific DOT violation and date);

(4) Date(s) of initial assessment and synopsis of treatment plan;

(5) Name of practice(s) or service(s) providing the recommended education and/or treatment;

(6) Inclusive dates of employee's program participation;

(7) Clinical characterization of employee's program participation;

(8) Date(s) of the first follow-up evaluation;

(9) Date(s) of any further follow-up evaluation the SAP has scheduled;

(10) SAP's clinical reasons for determining that the employee has not demonstrated successful compliance; and

(11) SAP's telephone number.

(f) As a SAP, you must also provide these written reports directly to the employee if the employee has no current employer and to the gaining DOT regulated employer in the event the employee obtains another transportation industry safety-sensitive position.

(g) As a SAP, you are to maintain copies of your reports to employers for 5 years, and your employee clinical records in accordance with Federal, state, and local laws regarding record maintenance, confidentiality, and release of information. You must make these records available, on request, to DOT agency representatives (*e.g.*, inspectors conducting an audit or safety investigation) and representatives of the NTSB in an accident investigation.

(h) As an employer, you must maintain your reports from SAPs for 5 years from the date you received them.

§40.313 Where is other information on SAP functions and the return-to-duty process found in this regulation?

You can find other information on the role and functions of SAPs in the following sections of this part:

§40.3—Definition.

§40.347—Service agent assistance with SAP-required follow-up testing.

§40.355—Transmission of SAP reports.

§40.329(c)—Making SAP reports available to employees on request.

Appendix E to Part 40—SAP Equivalency Requirements for Certification Organizations.

Subpart P—Confidentiality and Release of Information

§40.321 What is the general confidentiality rule for drug and alcohol test information?

Except as otherwise provided in this subpart, as a service agent or employer participating in the DOT drug or alcohol testing process, you are prohibited from releasing individual test results or medical information about an employee to third parties without the employee's specific written consent.

(a) A "third party" is any person or organization to whom other subparts of this regulation do not explicitly authorize or require the transmission of information in the course of the drug or alcohol testing process.

(b) "Specific written consent" means a statement signed by the employee that he or she agrees to the release of a particular piece of information to a particular, explicitly identified, person or organization at a particular time. "Blanket releases," in which an employee agrees to a release of a category of information (e.g., all test results) or to release information to a category of parties (e.g., other employers who are members of a C/TPA, companies to which the employee may apply for employment), are prohibited under this part.

§40.323 May program participants release drug or alcohol test information in connection with legal proceedings?

(a) As an employer, you may release information pertaining to an employee's drug or alcohol test without the employee's consent in certain legal proceedings.

(1) These proceedings include a lawsuit (e.g., a wrongful discharge action), grievance (e.g., an arbitration concerning disciplinary action taken by the employer), or administrative proceeding (e.g., an unemployment compensation hearing) brought by, or on behalf of, an employee and resulting from a positive DOT drug or alcohol test or a refusal to test (including, but not limited to, adulterated or substituted test results).

(2) These proceedings also include a criminal or civil action resulting from an employee's performance of safety-sensitive duties, in which a court of competent jurisdiction determines that the drug or alcohol test information sought is relevant to the case and issues an order directing the employer to produce the information. For example, in personal injury litigation following a truck or bus collision, the court could determine that a post-accident drug test result of an employee is relevant to determining whether the driver or the driver's employer was negligent. The employer is authorized to respond to the court's order to produce the records.

(b) In such a proceeding, you may release the information to the decision-maker in the proceeding (e.g., the court in a lawsuit). You may release the information only with a binding stipulation that the decisionmaker to whom it is released will make it available only to parties to the proceeding.

(c) If you are a service agent, and the employer requests its employee's drug or alcohol testing information from you to use in a legal proceeding as authorized in paragraph (a) of this section (*e.g.*, the laboratory's data package), you must provide the requested information to the employer.

(d) As an employer or service agent, you must immediately notify the employee in writing of any information you release under this section.

§40.325 [Reserved]

§40.327 When must the MRO report medical information gathered in the verification process?

(a) As the MRO, you must, except as provided in paragraph (c) of this section, report drug test results and medical information you learned as part of the verification process to third parties without the employee's consent if you determine, in your reasonable medical judgment, that:

(1) The information is likely to result in the employee being determined to be medically unqualified under an applicable DOT agency regulation; or

(2) The information indicates that continued performance by the employee of his or her safety-sensitive function is likely to pose a significant safety risk.

(b) The third parties to whom you are authorized to provide information by this section include the employer, a physician or other health care provider responsible for determining the medical qualifications of the employee under an applicable DOT agency safety regulation, a SAP evaluating the employee as part of the return to duty process (see §40.293(g)), a DOT agency, or the National Transportation Safety Board in the course of an accident investigation.

(c) If the law of a foreign country (*e.g.*, Canada) prohibits you from providing medical information to the employer, you may comply with that prohibition.

§40.329 What information must laboratories, MROs, and other service agents release to employees?

(a) As an MRO or service agent you must provide, within 10 business days of receiving a written request from an employee, copies of any records pertaining to the employee's use of alcohol and/or drugs, including records of the employee's DOT-mandated drug and/or alcohol tests. You may charge no more than the cost of preparation and reproduction for copies of these records.

(b) As a laboratory, you must provide, within 10 business days of receiving a written request from an employee, and made through the MRO, the records relating to the results of the employee's drug test (*i.e.*, laboratory report and data package). You may charge no more than the cost of preparation and reproduction for copies of these records.

(c) As a SAP, you must make available to an employee, on request, a copy of all SAP reports (see §40.311). However, you must redact follow-up testing information from the report before providing it to the employee.

§40.331 To what additional parties must employers and service agents release information?

As an employer or service agent you must release information under the following circumstances:

(a) If you receive a specific, written consent from an employee authorizing the release of information about that employee's drug or alcohol tests to an identified person, you must provide the information to the identified person. For example, as an employer, when you receive a written request from a former employee to provide information to a subsequent employer, you must do so. In providing the information, you must comply with the terms of the employee's consent.

(b) If you are an employer, you must, upon request of DOT agency representatives, provide the following:

(1) Access to your facilities used for this part and DOT agency drug and alcohol program functions.

(2) All written, printed, and computer-based drug and alcohol program records and reports (including copies of name-specific records or reports), files, materials, data, documents/documentation, agreements, contracts, policies, and statements that are required by this part and DOT agency regulations. You must provide this information at your principal place of business in the time required by the DOT agency.

(3) All items in paragraph (b)(2) of this section must be easily accessible, legible, and provided in an organized manner. If electronic records do not meet these standards, they must be converted to printed documentation that meets these standards.

(c) If you are a service agent, you must, upon request of DOT agency representatives, provide the following:

(1) Access to your facilities used for this part and DOT agency drug and alcohol program functions.

(2) All written, printed, and computer-based drug and alcohol program records and reports (including copies of name-specific records or reports), files, materials, data, documents/documentation, agreements, contracts, policies, and statements that are required by this part and DOT agency regulations. You must provide this information at your principal place of business in the time required by the DOT agency.

(3) All items in paragraph (c)(2) of this section must be easily accessible, legible, and provided in an organized manner. If electronic records do not meet these standards, they must be converted to printed documentation that meets these standards.

(d) If requested by the National Transportation Safety Board as part of an accident investigation, you must provide information concerning post-accident tests administered after the accident.

(e) If requested by a Federal, state or local safety agency with regulatory authority over you or the employee, you must provide drug and alcohol test records concerning the employee.

(f) Except as otherwise provided in this part, as a laboratory you must not release or provide a specimen or a part of a specimen to a requesting party, without first obtaining written consent from ODAPC. DNA testing and other types of identity testing are not authorized and ODAPC will not give permission for such testing. If a party seeks a court order directing you to release a specimen or part of a specimen contrary to any provision of this part, you must take necessary legal steps to contest the issuance of the order (*e.g.,* seek to quash a subpoena, citing the requirements of §40.13). This part does not require you to disobey a court order, however.

(g) Notwithstanding any other provision of this Part, as an employer of Commercial Motor Vehicle (CMV) drivers holding commercial driving licenses (CDLs) or as a third party administrator for owner-operator CMV drivers with CDLs, you are authorized to comply with State laws requiring you to provide to State CDL licensing authorities information about all violations of DOT drug and alcohol testing rules (including positive tests and refusals) by any CMV driver holding a CDL.

§40.333 What records must employers keep?

(a) As an employer, you must keep the following records for the following periods of time:

(1) You must keep the following records for five years:

(i) Records of alcohol test results indicating an alcohol concentration of 0.02 or greater;

(ii) Records of verified positive drug test results;

(iii) Documentation of refusals to take required alcohol and/or drug tests (including substituted or adulterated drug test results);

(iv) SAP reports; and

(v) All follow-up tests and schedules for follow-up tests.

(2) You must keep records for three years of information obtained from previous employers under §40.25 concerning drug and alcohol test results of employees.

(3) You must keep records of the inspection, maintenance, and calibration of EBTs, for two years.

(4) You must keep records of negative and cancelled drug test results and alcohol test results with a concentration of less than 0.02 for one year.

(b) You do not have to keep records related to a program requirement that does not apply to you (e.g., a maritime employer who does not have a DOT-mandated random alcohol testing program need not maintain random alcohol testing records).

(c) You must maintain the records in a location with controlled access.

(d) A service agent may maintain these records for you. However, you must ensure that you can produce these records at your principal place of business in the time required by the DOT agency. For example, as a motor carrier, when an FMCSA inspector requests your records, you must ensure that you can provide them within two business days.

(e) If you store records electronically, where permitted by this part, you must ensure that the records are easily accessible, legible, and formatted and stored in an organized manner. If electronic records do not meet these criteria, you must convert them to printed documentation in a rapid and readily auditable manner, at the request of DOT agency personnel.

Subpart Q—Roles and Responsibilities of Service Agents

§40.341 Must service agents comply with DOT drug and alcohol testing requirements?

(a) As a service agent, the services you provide to transportation employers must meet the requirements of this part and the DOT agency drug and alcohol testing regulations.

(b) If you do not comply, DOT may take action under the Public Interest Exclusions procedures of this part (see Subpart R of this part) or applicable provisions of other DOT agency regulations.

§40.343 What tasks may a service agent perform for an employer?

As a service agent, you may perform for employers the tasks needed to comply with DOT agency drug and alcohol testing regulations, subject to the requirements and limitations of this part.

§40.345 In what circumstances may a C/TPA act as an intermediary in the transmission of drug and alcohol testing information to employers?

(a) As a C/TPA or other service agent, you may act as an intermediary in the transmission of drug and alcohol testing information in the circumstances specified in this section only if the employer chooses to have you do so. Each employer makes the decision about whether to receive some or all of this information from you, acting as an intermediary, rather than directly from the service agent who originates the information (*e.g.,* an MRO or BAT).

(b) The specific provisions of this part concerning which you may act as an intermediary are listed in Appendix F to this part. These are the only situations in which you may act as an intermediary. You are prohibited from doing so in all other situations.

(c) In every case, you must ensure that, in transmitting information to employers, you meet all requirements (*e.g.,* concerning confidentiality and timing) that would apply if the service agent originating the information (*e.g.,* an MRO or collector) sent the information directly to the employer. For example, if you transmit drug testing results from MROs to DERs, you must transmit each drug test result to the DER in compliance with the MRO requirements set forth in §40.167.

§40.347 What functions may C/TPAs perform with respect to administering testing?

As a C/TPA, except as otherwise specified in this part, you may perform the following functions for employers concerning random selection and other selections for testing.

(a) You may operate random testing programs for employers and may assist (*i.e.,* through contracting with laboratories or collection sites, conducting collections) employers with other types of testing (*e.g.,* pre-employment, post-accident, reasonable suspicion, return-to-duty, and follow-up).

(b) You may combine employees from more than one employer or one transportation industry in a random pool if permitted by all the DOT agency drug and alcohol testing regulations involved.

(1) If you combine employees from more than one transportation industry, you must ensure that the random testing rate is at least equal to the highest rate required by each DOT agency.

(2) Employees not covered by DOT agency regulations may not be part of the same random pool with DOT covered employees.

(c) You may assist employers in ensuring that follow-up testing is conducted in accordance with the plan established by the SAP. However, neither you nor the employer are permitted to randomly select employees from a "follow-up pool" for follow-up testing.

§40.349 What records may a service agent receive and maintain?

(a) Except where otherwise specified in this part, as a service agent you may receive and maintain all records concerning DOT drug and alcohol testing programs, including positive, negative, and refusal to test individual test results. You do not need the employee's consent to receive and maintain these records.

(b) You may maintain all information needed for operating a drug/alcohol program (*e.g.,* CCFs, ATFs, names of employees in random pools, random selection lists, copies of notices to employers of selected employees) on behalf of an employer.

(c) If a service agent originating drug or alcohol testing information, such as an MRO or BAT, sends the information directly to the DER, he or she may also provide the information simultaneously to you, as a C/TPA or other service agent who maintains this information for the employer.

(d) If you are serving as an intermediary in transmitting information that is required to be provided to the employer, you must ensure that it reaches the employer in the same time periods required elsewhere in this part.

(e) You must ensure that you can make available to the employer within two business days any information the employer is asked to produce by a DOT agency representative.

(f) On request of an employer, you must, at any time on the request of an employer, transfer immediately all records pertaining to the employer and its employees to the employer or to any other service agent the employer designates. You must carry out this transfer as soon as the employer requests it. You are not required to obtain employee consent for this transfer. You must not charge more than your reasonable administrative costs for conducting this transfer. You may not charge a fee for the release of these records.

(g) If you are planning to go out of business or your organization will be bought by or merged with another organization, you must immediately notify all employers and offer to transfer all records pertaining to the employer and its employees to the employer or to any other service agent the employer designates. You must carry out this transfer as soon as the employer requests it. You are not required to obtain employee consent for this transfer. You must not charge more than your reasonable administrative costs for conducting this transfer. You may not charge a fee for the release of these records.

§40.351 What confidentiality requirements apply to service agents?

Except where otherwise specified in this part, as a service agent the following confidentiality requirements apply to you:

(a) When you receive or maintain confidential information about employees (*e.g.,* individual test results), you must follow the same confidentiality regulations as the employer with respect to the use and release of this information.

(b) You must follow all confidentiality and records retention requirements applicable to employers.

(c) You may not provide individual test results or other confidential information to another employer without a specific, written consent from the employee. For example, suppose you are a C/TPA that has employers X and Y as clients. Employee Jones works for X, and you maintain Jones' drug and alcohol test for X. Jones wants to change jobs and work for Y. You may not inform Y of the result of a test conducted for X without having a specific, written consent from Jones. Likewise, you may not provide this information to employer Z, who is not a C/TPA member, without this consent.

(d) You must not use blanket consent forms authorizing the release of employee testing information.

(e) You must establish adequate confidentiality and security measures to ensure that confidential employee records are not available to unauthorized persons. This includes protecting the physical security of records, access controls, and computer security measures to safeguard confidential data in electronic data bases.

§40.353 What principles govern the interaction between MROs and other service agents?

As a service agent other than an MRO (*e.g.*, a C/TPA), the following principles govern your interaction with MROs:

(a) You may provide MRO services to employers, directly or through contract, if you meet all applicable provisions of this part.

(b) If you employ or contract for an MRO, the MRO must perform duties independently and confidentially. When you have a relationship with an MRO, you must structure the relationship to ensure that this independence and confidentiality are not compromised. Specific means (including both physical and operational measures, as appropriate) to separate MRO functions and other service agent functions are essential.

(c) Only your staff who are actually under the day-to-day supervision and control of an MRO with respect to MRO functions may perform these functions. This does not mean that those staff may not perform other functions at other times. However, the designation of your staff to perform MRO functions under MRO supervision must be limited and not used as a subterfuge to circumvent confidentiality and other requirements of this part and DOT agency regulations. You must ensure that MRO staff operate under controls sufficient to ensure that the independence and confidentiality of the MRO process are not compromised.

(d) Like other MROs, an MRO you employ or contract with must personally conduct verification interviews with employees and must personally make all verification decisions. Consequently, your staff cannot perform these functions.

§40.355 What limitations apply to the activities of service agents?

As a service agent, you are subject to the following limitations concerning your activities in the DOT drug and alcohol testing program.

(a) You must not require an employee to sign a consent, release, waiver of liability, or indemnification agreement with respect to any part of the drug or alcohol testing process covered by this part (including, but not limited to, collections, laboratory testing, MRO, and SAP services). No one may do so on behalf of a service agent.

(b) You must not act as an intermediary in the transmission of drug test results from the laboratory to the MRO. That is, the laboratory may not send results to you, with you in turn sending them to the MRO for verification. For example, a practice in which the laboratory transmits results to your computer system, and you then assign the results to a particular MRO, is not permitted.

(c) You must not transmit drug test results directly from the laboratory to the employer (by electronic or other means) or to a service agent who forwards them to the employer. All confirmed laboratory results must be processed by the MRO before they are released to any other party.

(d) You must not act as an intermediary in the transmission of alcohol test results of 0.02 or higher from the STT or BAT to the DER.

(e) Except as provided in paragraph (f) of this section, you must not act as an intermediary in the transmission of individual SAP reports to the actual employer. That is, the SAP may not send such reports to you, with you in turn sending them to the actual employer. However, you may maintain individual SAP summary reports and follow-up testing plans after they are sent to the DER, and the SAP may transmit such reports to you simultaneously with sending them to the DER.

(f) As an exception to paragraph (e) of this section, you may act as an intermediary in the transmission of SAP report from the SAP to an owner-operator or other self-employed individual.

(g) Except as provided in paragraph (h) of this section, you must not make decisions to test an employee based upon reasonable suspicion, post-accident, return-to-duty, and follow-up determination criteria. These are duties the actual employer cannot delegate to a C/TPA. You may, however, provide advice and information to employers regarding these testing issues and how the employer should schedule required testing.

(h) As an exception to paragraph (g) of this section, you may make decisions to test an employee based upon reasonable suspicion, post-accident, return-to-duty, and follow-up determination criteria with respect to an owner-operator or other self-employed individual.

(i) Except as provided in paragraph (j) of this section, you must not make a determination that an employee has refused a drug or alcohol test. This is a non-delegable duty of the actual employer. You may, however, provide advice and information to employers regarding refusal-to-test issues.

(j) As an exception to paragraph (i) of this section, you may make a determination that an employee has refused a drug or alcohol test, if:

(1) You schedule a required test for an owner-operator or other self-employed individual, and the individual fails to appear for the test without a legitimate reason; or

(2) As an MRO, you determine that an individual has refused to test on the basis of adulteration or substitution.

(k) You must not act as a DER. For example, while you may be responsible for transmitting information to the employer about test results, you must not act on behalf of the employer in actions to remove employees from safety-sensitive duties.

(l) In transmitting documents to laboratories, you must ensure that you send to the laboratory that conducts testing only Copy 1 of the CCF. You must not transmit other copies of the CCF or any ATFs to the laboratory.

(m) You must not impose conditions or requirements on employers that DOT regulations do not authorize. For example, as a C/TPA serving employers in the pipeline or motor carrier industry, you must not require employers to have provisions in their DOT plans that PHMSA or FMCSA regulations do not require.

(n) You must not intentionally delay the transmission of drug or alcohol testing-related documents concerning actions you have performed, because of a payment dispute or other reasons.

Example 1 to Paragraph (n): A laboratory that has tested a specimen must not delay transmitting the documentation of the test result to an MRO because of a billing or payment dispute with the MRO or a C/TPA.

Example 2 to Paragraph (n): An MRO or SAP who has interviewed an employee must not delay sending a verified test result or SAP report to the employer because of such a dispute with the employer or employee.

Example 3 to Paragraph (n): A collector who has performed a urine specimen collection must not delay sending the drug specimen and CCF to the laboratory because of a payment or other dispute with the laboratory or a C/TPA.

Example 4 to Paragraph (n): A BAT who has conducted an alcohol test must not delay sending test result information to an employer or C/TPA because of a payment or other dispute with the employer or C/TPA.

(o) While you must follow the DOT agency regulations, the actual employer remains accountable to DOT for compliance, and your failure to implement any aspect of the program as required in this part and other applicable DOT agency regulations makes the employer subject to enforcement action by the Department.

Subpart R—Public Interest Exclusions

§40.361 What is the purpose of a public interest exclusion (PIE)?

(a) To protect the public interest, including protecting transportation employers and employees from serious noncompliance with DOT drug and alcohol testing rules, the Department's policy is to ensure that employers conduct business only with responsible service agents.

(b) The Department therefore uses PIEs to exclude from participation in DOT's drug and alcohol testing program any service agent who, by serious noncompliance with this part or other DOT agency drug and alcohol testing regulations, has shown that it is not currently acting in a responsible manner.

(c) A PIE is a serious action that the Department takes only to protect the public interest. We intend to use PIEs only to remedy situations of serious noncompliance. PIEs are not used for the purpose of punishment.

(d) Nothing in this subpart precludes a DOT agency or the Inspector General from taking other action authorized by its regulations with respect to service agents or employers that violate its regulations.

§40.363 On what basis may the Department issue a PIE?

(a) If you are a service agent, the Department may issue a PIE concerning you if we determine that you have failed or refused to provide drug or alcohol testing services consistent with the requirements of this part or a DOT agency drug and alcohol regulation.

(b) The Department also may issue a PIE if you have failed to cooperate with DOT agency representatives concerning inspections, complaint investigations, compliance and enforcement reviews, or requests for documents and other information about compliance with this part or DOT agency drug and alcohol regulations.

§40.365 What is the Department's policy concerning starting a PIE proceeding?

(a) It is the Department's policy to start a PIE proceeding only in cases of serious, uncorrected noncompliance with the provisions of this part, affecting such matters as safety, the outcomes of test results, privacy and confidentiality, due process and fairness for employees, the honesty and integrity of the testing program, and cooperation with or provision of information to DOT agency representatives.

(b) The following are examples of the kinds of serious noncompliance that, as a matter of policy, the Department views as appropriate grounds for starting a PIE proceeding. These examples are not intended to be an exhaustive or exclusive list of the grounds for starting a PIE proceeding. We intend them to illustrate the level of seriousness that the Department believes supports starting a PIE proceeding. The examples follow:

(1) For an MRO, verifying tests positive without interviewing the employees as required by this part or providing MRO services without meeting the qualifications for an MRO required by this part;

(2) For a laboratory, refusing to provide information to the Department, an employer, or an employee as required by this part; failing or refusing to conduct a validity testing program when required by this part; or a pattern or practice of testing errors that result in the cancellation of tests. (As a general matter of policy, the Department does not intend to initiate a PIE proceeding concerning a laboratory with respect to matters on which HHS initiates certification actions under its laboratory guidelines.);

(3) For a collector, a pattern or practice of directly observing collections when doing so is unauthorized, or failing or refusing to directly observe collections when doing so is mandatory;

(4) For collectors, BATs, or STTs, a pattern or practice of using forms, testing equipment, or collection kits that do not meet the standards in this part;

(5) For a collector, BAT, or STT, a pattern or practice of "fatal flaws" or other significant uncorrected errors in the collection process;

(6) For a laboratory, MRO or C/TPA, failing or refusing to report tests results as required by this part or DOT agency regulations;

(7) For a laboratory, falsifying, concealing, or destroying documentation concerning any part of the drug testing process, including, but not limited to, documents in a "litigation package";

(8) For SAPs, providing SAP services while not meeting SAP qualifications required by this part or performing evaluations without face-to-face interviews;

(9) For any service agent, maintaining a relationship with another party that constitutes a conflict of interest under this part (*e.g.,* a laboratory that derives a financial benefit from having an employer use a specific MRO);

(10) For any service agent, falsely representing that the service agent or its activities is approved or certified by the Department or a DOT agency (such representation includes, but is not limited to, the use of a Department or DOT agency logo, title, or emblem).

(11) For any service agent, disclosing an employee's test result information to any party this part or a DOT agency regulation does not authorize, including by obtaining a "blanket" consent from employees or by creating a data base from which employers or others can retrieve an employee's DOT test results without the specific consent of the employee;

(12) For any service agent, interfering or attempting to interfere with the ability of an MRO to communicate with the Department, or retaliating against an MRO for communicating with the Department;

(13) For any service agent, directing or recommending that an employer fail or refuse to implement any provision of this part; or

(14) With respect to noncompliance with a DOT agency regulation, conduct that affects important provisions of Department-wide concern (*e.g.,* failure to properly conduct the selection process for random testing).

§40.367 Who initiates a PIE proceeding?

The following DOT officials may initiate a PIE proceeding:

(a) The drug and alcohol program manager of a DOT agency;

(b) An official of ODAPC, other than the Director; or

(c) The designee of any of these officials.

§40.369 What is the discretion of an initiating official in starting a PIE proceeding?

(a) Initiating officials have broad discretion in deciding whether to start a PIE proceeding.

(b) In exercising this discretion, the initiating official must consider the Department's policy regarding the seriousness of the service agent's conduct (see §40.365) and all information he or she has obtained to this point concerning the facts of the case. The initiating official may also consider the availability of the resources needed to pursue a PIE proceeding.

(c) A decision not to initiate a PIE proceeding does not necessarily mean that the Department regards a service agent as being in compliance or that the Department may not use other applicable remedies in a situation of noncompliance.

§40.371 On what information does an initiating official rely in deciding whether to start a PIE proceeding?

(a) An initiating official may rely on credible information from any source as the basis for starting a PIE proceeding.

(b) Before sending a correction notice (see §40.373), the initiating official informally contacts the service agent to determine if there is any information that may affect the initiating official's determination about whether it is necessary to send a correction notice. The initiating official may take any information resulting from this contact into account in determining whether to proceed under this subpart.

§40.373 Before starting a PIE proceeding, does the initiating official give the service agent an opportunity to correct problems?

(a) If you are a service agent, the initiating official must send you a correction notice before starting a PIE proceeding.

(b) The correction notice identifies the specific areas in which you must come into compliance in order to avoid being subject to a PIE proceeding.

(c) If you make and document changes needed to come into compliance in the areas listed in the correction notice to the satisfaction of the initiating official within 60 days of the date you receive the notice, the initiating official does not start a PIE proceeding. The initiating official may conduct appropriate fact finding to verify that you have made and maintained satisfactory corrections. When he or she is satisfied that you are in compliance, the initiating official sends you a notice that the matter is concluded.

§40.375 How does the initiating official start a PIE proceeding?

(a) As a service agent, if your compliance matter is not correctable (see §40.373(a)), or if have not resolved compliance matters as provided in §40.373(c), the initiating official starts a PIE proceeding by sending you a notice of proposed exclusion (NOPE). The NOPE contains the initiating official's recommendations concerning the issuance of a PIE, but it is not a decision by the Department to issue a PIE.

(b) The NOPE includes the following information:

(1) A statement that the initiating official is recommending that the Department issue a PIE concerning you;

(2) The factual basis for the initiating official's belief that you are not providing drug and/or alcohol testing services to DOT-regulated employers consistent with the requirements of this part or are in serious noncompliance with a DOT agency drug and alcohol regulation;

(3) The factual basis for the initiating official's belief that your noncompliance has not been or cannot be corrected;

(4) The initiating official's recommendation for the scope of the PIE;

(5) The initiating official's recommendation for the duration of the PIE; and

(6) A statement that you may contest the issuance of the proposed PIE, as provided in §40.379.

(c) The initiating official sends a copy of the NOPE to the ODAPC Director at the same time he or she sends the NOPE to you.

§40.377 Who decides whether to issue a PIE?

(a) The ODAPC Director, or his or her designee, decides whether to issue a PIE. If a designee is acting as the decisionmaker, all references in this subpart to the Director refer to the designee.

(b) To ensure his or her impartiality, the Director plays no role in the initiating official's determination about whether to start a PIE proceeding.

(c) There is a "firewall" between the initiating official and the Director. This means that the initiating official and the Director are prohibited from having any discussion, contact, or exchange of information with one another about the matter, except for documents and discussions that are part of the record of the proceeding.

§40.379 How do you contest the issuance of a PIE?

(a) If you receive a NOPE, you may contest the issuance of the PIE.

(b) If you want to contest the proposed PIE, you must provide the Director information and argument in opposition to the proposed PIE in writing, in person, and/or through a representative. To contest the proposed PIE, you must take one or more of the steps listed in this paragraph (b) within 30 days after you receive the NOPE.

(1) You may request that the Director dismiss the proposed PIE without further proceedings, on the basis that it does not concern serious noncompliance with this part or DOT agency regulations, consistent with the Department's policy as stated in §40.365.

(2) You may present written information and arguments, consistent with the provisions of §40.381, contesting the proposed PIE.

(3) You may arrange with the Director for an informal meeting to present your information and arguments.

(c) If you do not take any of the actions listed in paragraph (b) of this section within 30 days after you receive the NOPE, the matter proceeds as an uncontested case. In this event, the Director makes his or her decision based on the record provided by the initiating official (*i.e.,* the NOPE and any supporting information or testimony) and any additional information the Director obtains.

§40.381 What information do you present to contest the proposed issuance of a PIE?

(a) As a service agent who wants to contest a proposed PIE, you must present at least the following information to the Director:

(1) Specific facts that contradict the statements contained in the NOPE (see §40.375(b)(2) and (3)). A general denial is insufficient to raise a genuine dispute over facts material to the issuance of a PIE;

(2) Identification of any existing, proposed or prior PIE; and

(3) Identification of your affiliates, if any.

(b) You may provide any information and arguments you wish concerning the proposed issuance, scope and duration of the PIE (see §40.375(b)(4) and (5)).

(c) You may provide any additional relevant information or arguments concerning any of the issues in the matter.

§40.383 What procedures apply if you contest the issuance of a PIE?

(a) DOT conducts PIE proceedings in a fair and informal manner. The Director may use flexible procedures to allow you to present matters in opposition. The Director is not required to follow formal rules of evidence or procedure in creating the record of the proceeding.

(b) The Director will consider any information or argument he or she determines to be relevant to the decision on the matter.

(c) You may submit any documentary evidence you want the Director to consider. In addition, if you have arranged an informal meeting with the Director, you may present witnesses and confront any person the initiating official presents as a witness against you.

(d) In cases where there are material factual issues in dispute, the Director or his or her designee may conduct additional fact-finding.

(e) If you have arranged a meeting with the Director, the Director will make a transcribed record of the meeting available to you on your request. You must pay the cost of transcribing and copying the meeting record.

§40.385 Who bears the burden of proof in a PIE proceeding?

(a) As the proponent of issuing a PIE, the initiating official bears the burden of proof.

(b) This burden is to demonstrate, by a preponderance of the evidence, that the service agent was in serious noncompliance with the requirements of this part for drug and/or alcohol testing-related services or with the requirements of another DOT agency drug and alcohol testing regulation.

§40.387 What matters does the Director decide concerning a proposed PIE?

(a) Following the service agent's response (see §40.379(b)) or, if no response is received, after 30 days have passed from the date on which the service agent received the NOPE, the Director may take one of the following steps:

(1) In response to a request from the service agent (see §40.379(b)(1)) or on his or her own motion, the Director may dismiss a PIE proceeding if he or she determines that it does not concern serious noncompliance with this part or DOT agency regulations, consistent with the Department's policy as stated in §40.365.

(i) If the Director dismisses a proposed PIE under this paragraph (a), the action is closed with respect to the noncompliance alleged in the NOPE.

(ii) The Department may initiate a new PIE proceeding against you on the basis of different or subsequent conduct that is in noncompliance with this part or other DOT drug and alcohol testing rules.

(2) If the Director determines that the initiating official's submission does not have complete information needed for a decision, the Director may remand the matter to the initiating official. The initiating official may resubmit the matter to the Director when the needed information is complete. If the basis for the proposed PIE has changed, the initiating official must send an amended NOPE to the service agent.

(b) The Director makes determinations concerning the following matters in any PIE proceeding that he or she decides on the merits:

(1) Any material facts that are in dispute;

(2) Whether the facts support issuing a PIE;

(3) The scope of any PIE that is issued; and

(4) The duration of any PIE that is issued.

§40.389 What factors may the Director consider?

This section lists examples of the kind of mitigating and aggravating factors that the Director may consider in determining whether to issue a PIE concerning you, as well as the scope and duration of a PIE. This list is not exhaustive or exclusive. The Director may consider other factors if appropriate in the circumstances of a particular case. The list of examples follows:

(a) The actual or potential harm that results or may result from your noncompliance;

(b) The frequency of incidents and/or duration of the noncompliance;

(c) Whether there is a pattern or prior history of noncompliance;

(d) Whether the noncompliance was pervasive within your organization, including such factors as the following:

(1) Whether and to what extent your organization planned, initiated, or carried out the noncompliance;

(2) The positions held by individuals involved in the noncompliance, and whether your principals tolerated their noncompliance; and

(3) Whether you had effective standards of conduct and control systems (both with respect to your own organization and any contractors or affiliates) at the time the noncompliance occurred;

(e) Whether you have demonstrated an appropriate compliance disposition, including such factors as the following:

(1) Whether you have accepted responsibility for the noncompliance and recognize the seriousness of the conduct that led to the cause for issuance of the PIE;

(2) Whether you have cooperated fully with the Department during the investigation. The Director may consider when the cooperation began and whether you disclosed all pertinent information known to you;

(3) Whether you have fully investigated the circumstances of the noncompliance forming the basis for the PIE and, if so, have made the result of the investigation available to the Director;

(4) Whether you have taken appropriate disciplinary action against the individuals responsible for the activity that constitutes the grounds for issuance of the PIE; and

(5) Whether your organization has taken appropriate corrective actions or remedial measures, including implementing actions to prevent recurrence;

(f) With respect to noncompliance with a DOT agency regulation, the degree to which the noncompliance affects matters common to the DOT drug and alcohol testing program;

(g) Other factors appropriate to the circumstances of the case.

§40.391 What is the scope of a PIE?

(a) The scope of a PIE is the Department's determination about the divisions, organizational elements, types of services, affiliates, and/or individuals (including direct employees of a service agent and its contractors) to which a PIE applies.

(b) If, as a service agent, the Department issues a PIE concerning you, the PIE applies to all your divisions, organizational elements, and types of services that are involved with or affected by the noncompliance that forms the factual basis for issuing the PIE.

(c) In the NOPE (see §40.375(b)(4)), the initiating official sets forth his or her recommendation for the scope of the PIE. The proposed scope of the PIE is one of the elements of the proceeding that the service agent may contest (see §40.381(b)) and about which the Director makes a decision (see §40.387(b)(3)).

(d) In recommending and deciding the scope of the PIE, the initiating official and Director, respectively, must take into account the provisions of paragraphs (e) through (j) of this section.

(e) The pervasiveness of the noncompliance within a service agent's organization (see §40.389(d)) is an important consideration in determining the scope of a PIE. The appropriate scope of a PIE grows broader as the pervasiveness of the noncompliance increases.

(f) The application of a PIE is not limited to the specific location or employer at which the conduct that forms the factual basis for issuing the PIE was discovered.

(g) A PIE applies to your affiliates, if the affiliate is involved with or affected by the conduct that forms the factual basis for issuing the PIE.

(h) A PIE applies to individuals who are officers, employees, directors, shareholders, partners, or other individuals associated with your organization in the following circumstances:

(1) Conduct forming any part of the factual basis of the PIE occurred in connection with the individual's performance of duties by or on behalf of your organization; or

(2) The individual knew of, had reason to know of, approved, or acquiesced in such conduct. The individual's acceptance of benefits derived from such conduct is evidence of such knowledge, acquiescence, or approval.

(i) If a contractor to your organization is solely responsible for the conduct that forms the factual basis for a PIE, the PIE does not apply to the service agent itself unless the service agent knew or should have known about the conduct and did not take action to correct it.

(j) PIEs do not apply to drug and alcohol testing that DOT does not regulate.

(k) The following examples illustrate how the Department intends the provisions of this section to work:

Example 1 to §40.391. Service Agent P provides a variety of drug testing services. P's SAP services are involved in a serious violation of this Part 40. However, P's other services fully comply with this part, and P's overall management did not plan or concur in the noncompliance, which in fact was contrary to P's articulated standards. Because the noncompliance was isolated in one area of the organization's activities, and did not pervade the entire organization, the scope of the PIE could be limited to SAP services.

Example 2 to §40.391. Service Agent Q provides a similar variety of services. The conduct forming the factual basis for a PIE concerns collections for a transit authority. As in Example 1, the noncompliance is not pervasive throughout Q's organization. The PIE would apply to collections at all locations served by Q, not just the particular transit authority or not just in the state in which the transit authority is located.

Example 3 to §40.391. Service Agent R provides a similar array of services. One or more of the following problems exists: R's activities in several areas— collections, MROs, SAPs, protecting the confidentiality of information—are involved in serious noncompliance; DOT determines that R's management knew or should have known about serious noncompliance in one or more areas, but management did not take timely corrective action; or, in response to an inquiry from

DOT personnel, R's management refuses to provide information about its operations. In each of these three cases, the scope of the PIE would include all aspects of R's services.

Example 4 to §40.391. Service Agent W provides only one kind of service (*e.g.,* laboratory or MRO services). The Department issues a PIE concerning these services. Because W only provides this one kind of service, the PIE necessarily applies to all its operations.

Example 5 to §40.391. Service Agent X, by exercising reasonably prudent oversight of its collection contractor, should have known that the contractor was making numerous "fatal flaws" in tests. Alternatively, X received a correction notice pointing out these problems in its contractor's collections. In neither case did X take action to correct the problem. X, as well as the contractor, would be subject to a PIE with respect to collections.

Example 6 to §40.391. Service Agent Y could not reasonably have known that one of its MROs was regularly failing to interview employees before verifying tests positive. When it received a correction notice, Y immediately dismissed the erring MRO. In this case, the MRO would be subject to a PIE but Y would not.

Example 7 to §40.391. The Department issues a PIE with respect to Service Agent Z. Z provides services for DOT-regulated transportation employers, a Federal agency under the HHS-regulated Federal employee testing program, and various private businesses and public agencies that DOT does not regulate. The PIE applies only to the DOT-regulated transportation employers with respect to their DOT-mandated testing, not to the Federal agency or the other public agencies and private businesses. The PIE does not prevent the non-DOT regulated entities from continuing to use Z's services.

§40.393 How long does a PIE stay in effect?

(a) In the NOPE (see §40.375(b)(5)), the initiating official proposes the duration of the PIE. The duration of the PIE is one of the elements of the proceeding that the service agent may contest (see §40.381(b)) and about which the Director makes a decision (see §40.387(b)(4)).

(b) In deciding upon the duration of the PIE, the Director considers the seriousness of the conduct on which the PIE is based and the continued need to protect employers and employees from the service agent's noncompliance. The Director considers factors such as those listed in §40.389 in making this decision.

(c) The duration of a PIE will be between one and five years, unless the Director reduces its duration under §40.407.

§40.395 Can you settle a PIE proceeding?

At any time before the Director's decision, you and the initiating official can, with the Director's concurrence, settle a PIE proceeding.

§40.397 When does the Director make a PIE decision?

The Director makes his or her decision within 60 days of the date when the record of a PIE proceeding is complete (including any meeting with the Director and any additional fact-finding that is necessary). The Director may extend this period for good cause for additional periods of up to 30 days.

§40.399 How does the Department notify service agents of its decision?

If you are a service agent involved in a PIE proceeding, the Director provides you written notice as soon as he or she makes a PIE decision. The notice includes the following elements:

(a) If the decision is not to issue a PIE, a statement of the reasons for the decision, including findings of fact with respect to any material factual issues that were in dispute.

(b) If the decision is to issue a PIE—

(1) A reference to the NOPE;

(2) A statement of the reasons for the decision, including findings of fact with respect to any material factual issues that were in dispute;

(3) A statement of the scope of the PIE; and

(4) A statement of the duration of the PIE.

§40.401 How does the Department notify employers and the public about a PIE?

(a) The Department maintains a document called the "List of Excluded Drug and Alcohol Service Agents." This document may be found on the Department's web site (*http://www.transportation.gov/odapc*). You may also request a copy of the document from ODAPC.

(b) When the Director issues a PIE, he or she adds to the List the name and address of the service agent, and any other persons or organizations, to whom the PIE applies and information about the scope and duration of the PIE.

(c) When a service agent ceases to be subject to a PIE, the Director removes this information from the List.

(d) The Department also publishes a *Federal Register* notice to inform the public on any occasion on which a service agent is added to or taken off the List.

§40.403 Must a service agent notify its clients when the Department issues a PIE?

(a) As a service agent, if the Department issues a PIE concerning you, you must notify each of your DOT-regulated employer clients, in writing, about the issuance, scope, duration, and effect of the PIE. You may meet this requirement by sending a copy of the Director's PIE decision or by a separate notice. You must send this notice to each client within three business days of receiving from the Department the notice provided for in §40.399(b).

(b) As part of the notice you send under paragraph (a) of this section, you must offer to transfer immediately all records pertaining to the employer and its employees to the employer or to any other service agent the employer designates. You must carry out this transfer as soon as the employer requests it.

§40.405 May the Federal courts review PIE decisions?

The Director's decision is a final administrative action of the Department. Like all final administrative actions of Federal agencies, the Director's decision is subject to judicial review under the Administrative Procedure Act (5 U.S.C. 551 *et. seq*).

§40.407 May a service agent ask to have a PIE reduced or terminated?

(a) Yes, as a service agent concerning whom the Department has issued a PIE, you may request that the Director terminate a PIE or reduce its duration and/or scope. This process is limited to the issues of duration and scope. It is not an appeal or reconsideration of the decision to issue the PIE.

(b) Your request must be in writing and supported with documentation.

(c) You must wait at least nine months from the date on which the Director issued the PIE to make this request.

(d) The initiating official who was the proponent of the PIE may provide information and arguments concerning your request to the Director.

(e) If the Director verifies that the sources of your noncompliance have been eliminated and that all drug or alcohol testing-related services you would provide to DOT-regulated employers will be consistent with the requirements of this part, the Director may issue a notice terminating or reducing the PIE.

§40.409 What does the issuance of a PIE mean to transportation employers?

(a) As an employer, you are deemed to have notice of the issuance of a PIE when it appears on the List mentioned in §40.401(a) or the notice of the PIE appears in the *Federal Register* as provided in §40.401(d). You should check this List to ensure that any service agents you are using or planning to use are not subject to a PIE.

(b) As an employer who is using a service agent concerning whom a PIE is issued, you must stop using the services of the service agent no later than 90 days after the Department has published the decision in the *Federal Register* or posted it on its web site. You may apply to the ODAPC Director for an extension of 30 days if you demonstrate that you cannot find a substitute service agent within 90 days.

(c) Except during the period provided in paragraph (b) of this section, you must not, as an employer, use the services of a service agent that are covered by a PIE that the Director has issued under this subpart. If you do so, you are in violation of the Department's regulations and subject to applicable DOT agency sanctions (*e.g.,* civil penalties, withholding of Federal financial assistance).

(d) You also must not obtain drug or alcohol testing services through a contractor or affiliate of the service agent to whom the PIE applies.

Example to Paragraph (d): Service Agent R was subject to a PIE with respect to SAP services. As an employer, not only must you not use R's own SAP services, but you also must not use SAP services you arrange through R, such as services provided by a subcontractor or affiliate of R or a person or organization that receives financial gain from its relationship with R.

(e) This section's prohibition on using the services of a service agent concerning which the Director has issued a PIE applies to employers in all industries subject to DOT drug and alcohol testing regulations.

Example to Paragraph (e): The initiating official for a PIE was the FAA drug and alcohol program manager, and the conduct forming the basis of the PIE pertained to the aviation industry. As a motor carrier, transit authority, pipeline, railroad, or maritime employer, you are also prohibited from using the services of the service agent involved in connection with the DOT drug and alcohol testing program.

(f) The issuance of a PIE does not result in the cancellation of drug or alcohol tests conducted using the service agent involved before the issuance of the Director's decision or up to 90 days following its publication in the *Federal Register* or posting on the Department's web site, unless otherwise specified in the Director's PIE decision or the Director grants an extension as provided in paragraph (b) of this section.

Example to Paragraph (f): The Department issues a PIE concerning Service Agent N on September 1. All tests conducted using N's services before September

1, and through November 30, are valid for all purposes under DOT drug and alcohol testing regulations, assuming they meet all other regulatory requirements.

§40.411 What is the role of the DOT Inspector General's office?

(a) Any person may bring concerns about waste, fraud, or abuse on the part of a service agent to the attention of the DOT Office of Inspector General.

(b) In appropriate cases, the Office of Inspector General may pursue criminal or civil remedies against a service agent.

(c) The Office of Inspector General may provide factual information to other DOT officials for use in a PIE proceeding.

§40.413 How are notices sent to service agents?

(a) If you are a service agent, DOT sends notices to you, including correction notices, notices of proposed exclusion, decision notices, and other notices, in any of the ways mentioned in paragraph (b) or (c) of this section.

(b) DOT may send a notice to you, your identified counsel, your agent for service of process, or any of your partners, officers, directors, owners, or joint venturers to the last known street address, fax number, or e-mail address. DOT deems the notice to have been received by you if sent to any of these persons.

(c) DOT considers notices to be received by you—

(1) When delivered, if DOT mails the notice to the last known street address, or five days after we send it if the letter is undeliverable;

(2) When sent, if DOT sends the notice by fax or five days after we send it if the fax is undeliverable; or

(3) When delivered, if DOT sends the notice by e-mail or five days after DOT sends it if the e-mail is undeliverable.

Appendix A to Part 40—DOT Standards for Urine Collection Kits

The Collection Kit Contents

1. *Collection Container*

a. Single-use container, made of plastic, large enough to easily catch and hold at least 55 mL of urine voided from the body.

b. Must have graduated volume markings clearly noting levels of 45 mL and above.

c. Must have a temperature strip providing graduated temperature readings 32–38°C/90–100°F, that is affixed or can be affixed at a proper level on the outside of the collection container. Other methodologies (*e.g.,* temperature device built into the wall of the container) are acceptable provided the temperature measurement is accurate and such that there is no potential for contamination of the specimen.

d. Must be individually wrapped in a sealed plastic bag or shrink wrapping; or must have a peelable, sealed lid or other easily visible tamper-evident system.

e. May be made available separately at collection sites to address shy bladder situations when several voids may be required to complete the testing process.

2. *Plastic Specimen Bottles*

a. Each bottle must be large enough to hold at least 35 mL; or alternatively, they may be two distinct sizes of specimen bottles provided that the bottle designed to hold the primary specimen holds at least 35 mL of urine and the bottle designed to hold the split specimen holds at least 20 mL.

b. Must have screw-on or snap-on caps that prevent seepage of the urine from the bottles during shipment.

c. Must have markings clearly indicating the appropriate levels (30 mL for the primary specimen and 15 mL for the split) of urine that must be poured into the bottles.

d. Must be designed so that the required tamper-evident bottle seals made available on the CCF fit with no damage to the seal when the employee initials it nor with the chance that the seal overlap would conceal printed information.

e. Must be wrapped (with caps) together in a sealed plastic bag or shrink wrapping separate from the collection container; or must be wrapped (with cap) individually in sealed plastic bags or shrink wrapping; or must have peelable, sealed lid or other easily visible tamper-evident system.

f. Plastic material must be leach resistant.

3. *Leak-Resistant Plastic Bag*

a. Must have two sealable compartments or pouches which are leak-resistant; one large enough to hold two specimen bottles and the other large enough to hold the CCF paperwork.

b. The sealing methodology must be such that once the compartments are sealed, any tampering or attempts to open either compartment will be evident.

4. *Absorbent material*

Each kit must contain enough absorbent material to absorb the entire contents of both specimen bottles. Absorbent material must be designed to fit inside the leak-resistant plastic bag pouch into which the specimen bottles are placed.

5. *Shipping Container*

a. Must be designed to adequately protect the specimen bottles from shipment damage in the transport of specimens from the collection site to the laboratory (*e.g.,* standard courier box, small cardboard box, plastic container).

b. May be made available separately at collection sites rather than being part of an actual kit sent to collection sites.

c. A shipping container is not necessary if a laboratory courier hand-delivers the specimen bottles in the plastic leak-proof bags from the collection site to the laboratory.

Appendix B to Part 40—DOT Drug Testing Semi-Annual Laboratory Report to Employers

The following items are required on each laboratory report:

Reporting Period: (inclusive dates)

Laboratory Identification: (name and address)

Employer Identification: (name; may include Billing Code or ID code)

C/TPA Identification: (where applicable; name and address)

1. Specimen Results Reported (total number)

By Test Reason

(a) Pre-employment (number)

(b) Post-Accident (number)

(c) Random (number)
(d) Reasonable Suspicion/Cause (number)
(e) Return-to-Duty (number)
(f) Follow-up (number)
(g) Type of Test Not Noted on CCF (number)
2. Specimens Reported
(a) Negative (number)
(b) Negative and Dilute (number)
3. Specimens Reported as Rejected for Testing (total number)
By Reason
(a) Fatal flaw (number)
(b) Uncorrected Flaw (number)
4. Specimens Reported as Positive (total number) By Drug
(a) Marijuana Metabolite (number)
(b) Cocaine Metabolite (number)
(c) Opioids (number)
(1) Codeine (number)
(2) Morphine (number)
(3) 6-AM (number)
(4) Hydrocodone (number)
(5) Hydromorphone (number)
(6) Oxycodone (number)
(7) Oxymorphone (number)
(d) Phencyclidine (number)
(e) Amphetamines (number)
(1) Amphetamine (number)
(2) Methamphetamine (number)
(3) MDMA (number)
(4) MDA (number)
5. Adulterated (number)
6. Substituted (number)
7. Invalid Result (number)

Appendix C to Part 40—DOT Drug Testing Semi-Annual Laboratory Report to DOT

Mail, fax, or email to:
U.S. Department of Transportation, Office of Drug and Alcohol Policy and Compliance, W62-300, 1200 New Jersey Avenue SE., Washington, DC 20590, *Fax:* (202) 366-3897, *Email: ODAPCWebMail@dot.gov.*
The following items are required on each report:
Reporting Period: (inclusive dates)
Laboratory Identification: (name and address)
1. DOT Specimen Results Reported (total number)
2. Negative Results Reported (total number)
    Negative (number)
    Negative-Dilute (number)
3. Rejected for Testing Results Reported (total number)
    By Reason
(a) Fatal flaw (number)
(b) Uncorrected Flaw (number)

4. Positive Results Reported (total number)
   By Drug
(a) Marijuana Metabolite (number)
(b) Cocaine Metabolite (number)
(c) Opioids (number)
(1) Codeine (number)
(2) Morphine (number)
(3) 6-AM (number)
(4) Hydrocodone (number)
(5) Hydromorphone (number)
(6) Oxycodone (number)
(7) Oxymorphone (number)
(d) Phencyclidine (number)
(e) Amphetamines (number)
(1) Amphetamine (number)
(2) Methamphetamine (number)
(3) MDMA (number)
(4) MDA (number)
5. Adulterated Results Reported (total number)
   By Reason (number)
6. Substituted Results Reported (total number)
7. Invalid Results Reported (total number)
   By Reason (number)

Appendix D to Part 40—Report Format: Split Specimen Failure to Reconfirm

Mail, fax, or submit electronically to:

U.S. Department of Transportation, Office of Drug and Alcohol Policy and Compliance, W62-300, 1200 New Jersey Avenue SE., Washington, DC 20590, *Fax: (202) 366-3897*. Submit Electronically: *https://www.transportation.gov/content/split-specimen-cancellation-notification-49-cfr-part-40187-appendix-d*

The following items are required on each report:

1. MRO name, address, phone number, and fax number.

2. Collection site name, address, and phone number.

3. Date of collection.

4. Specimen I.D. number.

5. Laboratory accession number.

6. Primary specimen laboratory name, address, and phone number.

7. Date result reported or certified by primary laboratory.

8. Split specimen laboratory name, address, and phone number.

9. Date split specimen result reported or certified by split specimen laboratory.

10. Primary specimen results (*e.g.*, name of drug, adulterant) in the primary specimen.

11. Reason for split specimen failure-to-reconfirm result (*e.g.*, drug or adulterant not present, specimen invalid, split not collected, insufficient volume).

12. Actions taken by the MRO (*e.g.*, notified employer of failure to reconfirm and requirement for recollection).

13. Additional information explaining the reason for cancellation.

14. Name of individual submitting the report (if not the MRO)

Appendix E to Part 40—SAP Equivalency Requirements for Certification Organizations

1. *Experience:* Minimum requirements are for three years of full-time supervised experience or 6,000 hours of supervised experience as an alcoholism and/or drug abuse counselor. The supervision must be provided by a licensed or certified practitioner. Supervised experience is important if the individual is to be considered a professional in the field of alcohol and drug abuse evaluation and counseling.

2. *Education:* There exists a requirement of 270 contact hours of education and training in alcoholism and/or drug abuse or related training. These hours can take the form of formal education, in-service training, and professional development courses. Part of any professional counselor's development is participation in formal and non-formal education opportunities within the field.

3. *Continuing Education:* The certified counselor must receive at least 40–60 hours of continuing education units (CEU) during each two year period. These CEUs are important to the counselor's keeping abreast of changes and improvements in the field.

4. *Testing:* A passing score on a national test is a requirement. The test must accurately measure the application of the knowledge, skills, and abilities possessed by the counselor. The test establishes a national standard that must be met to practice.

5. *Testing Validity:* The certification examination must be reviewed by an independent authority for validity (examination reliability and relationship to the knowledge, skills, and abilities required by the counseling field). The reliability of the exam is paramount if counselor attributes are to be accurately measured. The examination passing score point must be placed at an appropriate minimal level score as gauged by statistically reliable methodology.

6. *Measurable Knowledge Base:* The certification process must be based upon measurable knowledge possessed by the applicant and verified through collateral data and testing. That level of knowledge must be of sufficient quantity to ensure a high quality of SAP evaluation and referral services.

7. *Measurable Skills Base:* The certification process must be based upon measurable skills possessed by the applicant and verified through collateral data and testing. That level of skills must be of sufficient quality to ensure a high quality of SAP evaluation and referral services.

8. *Quality Assurance Plan:* The certification agency must ensure that a means exists to determine that applicant records are verified as being true by the certification staff. This is an important check to ensure that true information is being accepted by the certifying agency.

9. *Code of Ethics:* Certified counselors must pledge to adhere to an ethical standard for practice. It must be understood that code violations could result in de-certification. These standards are vital in maintaining the integrity of practitioners. High ethical standards are required to ensure quality of client care and confidentiality of client information as well as to guard against inappropriate referral practices.

10. *Re-certification Program:* Certification is not just a one-time event. It is a continuing privilege with continuing requirements. Among these are continuing education, continuing state certification, and concomitant adherence to the code of ethics. Re-certification serves as a protector of client interests by removing poor performers from the certified practice.

11. *Fifty State Coverage:* Certification must be available to qualified counselors in all 50 states and, therefore, the test must be available to qualified applicants in all 50 states. Because many companies are multi-state operators, consistency in SAP evaluation quality and opportunities is paramount. The test need not be given in all 50 states but should be accessible to candidates from all states.

12. *National Commission for Certifying Agencies (NCCA) Accreditation:* Having NCCA accreditation is a means of demonstrating to the Department of Transportation that your certification has been reviewed by a panel of impartial experts that have determined that your examination(s) has met stringent and appropriate testing standards.

Appendix F to Part 40—Drug and Alcohol Testing Information That C/TPAs May Transmit to Employers

1. If you are a C/TPA, you may, acting as an intermediary, transmit the information in the following sections of this part to the DER for an employer, if the employer chooses to have you do so. These are the only items that you are permitted to transmit to the employer as an intermediary. The use of C/TPA intermediaries is prohibited in all other cases, such as transmission of laboratory drug test results to MROs, the transmission of medical information from MROs to employers, the transmission of SAP reports to employers, the transmission of positive alcohol test results, and the transmission of medical information from MROs to employers.

2. In every case, you must ensure that, in transmitting the information, you meet all requirements (*e.g.,* concerning confidentiality and timing) that would apply if the party originating the information (*e.g.,* an MRO or collector) sent the information directly to the employer. For example, if you transmit MROs' drug testing results to DERs, you must transmit each drug test result to the DER in compliance with the requirements for MROs set forth in §40.167.

Drug Testing Information

§40.25: Previous two years' test results

§40.35: Notice to collectors of contact information for DER

§40.61(a): Notification to DER that an employee is a "no show" for a drug test

§40.63(e): Notification to DER of a collection under direct observation

§40.65(b)(6) and (7) and (c)(2) and (3): Notification to DER of a refusal to provide a specimen or an insufficient specimen

§40.73(a)(9): Transmission of CCF copies to DER (However, MRO copy of CCF must be sent by collector directly to the MRO, not through the C/TPA.)

§40.111(a): Transmission of laboratory statistical report to employer

§40.127(f): Report of test results to DER

§§40.127(g), 40.129(d), 40.159(a)(4)(ii); 40.161(b): Reports to DER that test is cancelled

§40.129 (d): Report of test results to DER

§40.129(g)(1): Report to DER of confirmed positive test in stand-down situation

§§40.149(b): Report to DER of changed test result

§40.155(a): Report to DER of dilute specimen

§40.167(b) and (c): Reports of test results to DER

§40.187(a) through (e) Reports to DER concerning the reconfirmation of tests

§40.191(d): Notice to DER concerning refusals to test

§40.193(b)(3): Notification to DER of refusal in shy bladder situation

§40.193(b)(4): Notification to DER of insufficient specimen

§40.193(b)(5): Transmission of CCF copies to DER (not to MRO)

§40.199: Report to DER of cancelled test and direction to DER for additional collection

§40.201: Report to DER of cancelled test

Alcohol Testing Information

§40.215: Notice to BATs and STTs of contact information for DER

§40.241(b)(1): Notification to DER that an employee is a "no show" for an alcohol test

§40.247(a)(2): Transmission of alcohol screening test results only when the test result is less than 0.02

§40.255(a)(4): Transmission of alcohol confirmation test results only when the test result is less than 0.02

§40.263(a)(3) and 263(b)(3): Notification of insufficient saliva and failure to provide sufficient amount of breath

Appendix G to Part 40—Alcohol Testing Form

The following form is the alcohol testing form required for use in the DOT alcohol testing program beginning January 1, 2011. Employers are authorized to use the form effective February 25, 2010.

U.S. Department of Transportation (DOT)
Alcohol Testing Form
(The instructions for completing this form are on the back of Copy 3)

Print Screening Results Here or Affix with Tamper Evident Tape

Step 1: TO BE COMPLETED BY ALCOHOL TECHNICIAN

A: Employee Name _____
(Print)   (First, M.I., Last)

B: SSN or Employee ID No. _____

C: Employer Name _____
   Street
   City, State, Zip

DER Name and
Telephone No. _____   ( )_____
            DER Name   DER Phone Number

D: Reason for Test: ☐ Random ☐ Reasonable Susp ☐ Post-Accident ☐ Return to Duty ☐ Follow-up ☐ Pre-employment

STEP 2: TO BE COMPLETED BY EMPLOYEE

I certify that I am about to submit to alcohol testing required by US Department of Transportation regulations and that the identifying information provided on the form is true and correct.

Print Confirmation Results Here or Affix with Tamper Evident Tape

_____   ___/___/___
Signature of Employee   Date Month Day Year

STEP 3: TO BE COMPLETED BY ALCOHOL TECHNICIAN

(If the technician conducting the screening test is not the same technician who will be conducting the confirmation test, each technician must complete their own form.) I certify that I have conducted alcohol testing on the above named individual in accordance with the procedures established in the US Department of Transportation regulation, 49 CFR Part 40, that I am qualified to operate the testing device(s) identified, and that the results are as recorded.

TECHNICIAN: ☐ BAT ☐ STT   DEVICE: ☐ SALIVA ☐ BREATH*   15-Minute Wait: ☐ Yes ☐ No

SCREENING TEST: *(For BREATH DEVICE* write in the space below only if the testing device is not designed to print.)*

Test #	Testing Device Name	Device Serial # OR Lot # & Exp Date	Activation Time	Reading Time	Result

CONFIRMATION TEST: *Results MUST be affixed to each copy of this form or printed directly onto the form.*

REMARKS:

Print Additional Results Here or Affix With Tamper Evident Tape

_____   _____
Alcohol Technician's Company   Company Street Address

_____   ( )_____
(PRINT) Alcohol Technician's Name (First, M.I., Last)   Company City, State, Zip   Phone Number

_____   ___/___/___
Signature of Alcohol Technician   Date Month Day Year

STEP 4: TO BE COMPLETED BY EMPLOYEE IF TEST RESULT IS 0.02 OR HIGHER

I certify that I have submitted to the alcohol test, the results of which are accurately recorded on this form. I understand that I must not drive, perform safety-sensitive duties, or operate heavy equipment because the results are 0.02 or greater.

_____   ___/___/___
Signature of Employee   Date Month Day Year

Form DOT F 1380 (Rev. 5/2008)   OMB No. 2105-0529

COPY 1 – ORIGINAL – FORWARD TO THE EMPLOYER

U.S. Department of Transportation (DOT)
Alcohol Testing Form
(The instructions for completing this form are on the back of Copy 3)

Print Screening Results Here or Affix with Tamper Evident Tape

Step 1: TO BE COMPLETED BY ALCOHOL TECHNICIAN

A: Employee Name _____
             (Print)   (First, M.I., Last)

B: SSN or Employee ID No. _____

C: Employer Name _____
   Street
   City, State, Zip _____

   DER Name and
   Telephone No.   ( )
                DER Name   DER Phone Number

D: Reason for Test: ☐ Random ☐ Reasonable Susp ☐ Post-Accident ☐ Return to Duty ☐ Follow-up ☐ Pre-employment

STEP 2: TO BE COMPLETED BY EMPLOYEE

I certify that I am about to submit to alcohol testing required by US Department of Transportation regulations and that the identifying information provided on the form is true and correct.

                                                  / /
Signature of Employee   Date Month Day Year

Print Confirmation Results Here or Affix with Tamper Evident Tape

STEP 3: TO BE COMPLETED BY ALCOHOL TECHNICIAN

(If the technician conducting the screening test is not the same technician who will be conducting the confirmation test, each technician must complete their own form.) I certify that I have conducted alcohol testing on the above named individual in accordance with the procedures established in the US Department of Transportation regulation, 49 CFR Part 40, that I am qualified to operate the testing device(s) identified, and that the results are as recorded.

TECHNICIAN: ☐ BAT ☐ STT   DEVICE: ☐ SALIVA ☐ BREATH*   15-Minute Wait: ☐ Yes ☐ No

SCREENING TEST: *(For BREATH DEVICE* write in the space below only if the testing device is not designed to print.)*

_____

Test #   Testing Device Name   Device Serial # *OR* Lot # & Exp Date   Activation Time   Reading Time   Result

CONFIRMATION TEST: Results *MUST* be affixed to each copy of this form or printed directly onto the form.

REMARKS:

_____
_____
_____

Print Additional Results Here or Affix With Tamper Evident Tape

Alcohol Technician's Company   Company Street Address

                                     ( )
(PRINT) Alcohol Technician's Name (First, M.I., Last)   Company City, State, Zip   Phone Number

                                        / /
Signature of Alcohol Technician   Date Month Day Year

STEP 4: TO BE COMPLETED BY EMPLOYEE IF TEST RESULT IS 0.02 OR HIGHER

I certify that I have submitted to the alcohol test, the results of which are accurately recorded on this form. I understand that I must not drive, perform safety-sensitive duties, or operate heavy equipment because the results are 0.02 or greater.

                                          / /
Signature of Employee   Date Month Day Year

Form DOT F 1380 (Rev. 5/2008)   OMB No. 2105-0529

COPY 2 – EMPLOYEE RETAINS

U.S. Department of Transportation (DOT)
Alcohol Testing Form
(The instructions for completing this form are on the back of Copy 3)

Print Screening Results Here or Affix with Tamper Evident Tape

Step 1: TO BE COMPLETED BY ALCOHOL TECHNICIAN

A: Employee Name _____
           (Print)   (First, M.I., Last)

B: SSN or Employee ID No. _____

C: Employer Name _____
    Street
    City, State, Zip _____

DER Name and
Telephone No. _____
    DER Name   ( )   DER Phone Number

D: Reason for Test: ☐ Random ☐ Reasonable Susp ☐ Post-Accident ☐ Return to Duty ☐ Follow-up ☐ Pre-employment

STEP 2: TO BE COMPLETED BY EMPLOYEE

I certify that I am about to submit to alcohol testing required by US Department of Transportation regulations and that the identifying information provided on the form is true and correct.

_____   / /
Signature of Employee   Date Month Day Year

Print Confirmation Results Here or Affix with Tamper Evident Tape

STEP 3: TO BE COMPLETED BY ALCOHOL TECHNICIAN

(If the technician conducting the screening test is not the same technician who will be conducting the confirmation test, each technician must complete their own form.) I certify that I have conducted alcohol testing on the above named individual in accordance with the procedures established in the US Department of Transportation regulation, 49 CFR Part 40, that I am qualified to operate the testing device(s) identified, and that the results are as recorded.

TECHNICIAN: ☐ BAT ☐ STT   DEVICE: ☐ SALIVA ☐ BREATH* 15-Minute Wait: ☐ Yes ☐ No

SCREENING TEST: *(For BREATH DEVICE* write in the space below only if the testing device is not designed to print.)*

_____

Test # Testing Device Name Device Serial # *OR* Lot # & Exp Date Activation Time Reading Time Result

CONFIRMATION TEST: *Results MUST be affixed to each copy of this form or printed directly onto the form.*

REMARKS: _____
_____
_____

Print Additional Results Here or Affix With Tamper Evident Tape

Alcohol Technician's Company _____ Company Street Address _____
                                      ( )
(PRINT) Alcohol Technician's Name (First, M.I., Last) Company City, State, Zip Phone Number

_____   / /
Signature of Alcohol Technician   Date Month Day Year

STEP 4: TO BE COMPLETED BY EMPLOYEE IF TEST RESULT IS 0.02 OR HIGHER

I certify that I have submitted to the alcohol test, the results of which are accurately recorded on this form. I understand that I must not drive, perform safety-sensitive duties, or operate heavy equipment because the results are 0.02 or greater.

_____   / /
Signature of Employee   Date Month Day Year

Form DOT F 1380 (Rev. 5/2008)   OMB No. 2105-0529

COPY 3 – ALCOHOL TECHNICIAN RETAINS

PAPERWORK REDUCTION ACT NOTICE (as required by 5 CFR 1320.21)

A federal agency may not conduct or sponsor, and a person is not required to respond to, nor shall a person be subject to a penalty for failure to comply with a collection of information subject to the requirements of the Paperwork Reduction Act unless that collection of information displays a current valid OMB Control Number. The OMB Control Number for this information collection is 2105-0529. Public reporting for this collection of information is estimated to be approximately 8 minutes per response, including the time for reviewing instructions, completing and reviewing the collection of information. All responses to this collection of information are mandatory. Send comments regarding this burden estimate or any other aspect of this collection of information, including suggestions for reducing this burden to: Information Collection Clearance Officer, U.S. Department of Transportation, Office of Drug and Alcohol Policy and Compliance, 1200 New Jersey Avenue, SE, Suite W62-300, Washington, D.C. 20590.

BACK OF PAGES 1 and 2

INSTRUCTIONS FOR COMPLETING THE U.S. DEPARTMENT OF TRANSPORTATION ALCOHOL TESTING FORM

NOTE: Use a ballpoint pen, press hard, and check all copies for legibility.

STEP 1 The Breath Alcohol Technician (BAT) or Screening Test Technician (STT) completes the information required in this step. Be sure to print the employee's name and check the box identifying the reason for the test.

NOTE: If the employee refuses to provide SSN or I.D. number, be sure to indicate this in the remarks section in STEP 3. Proceed with STEP 2.

STEP 2 Instruct the employee to read, sign, and date the employee certification statement in STEP 2.

NOTE: If the employee refuses to sign the certification statement, do not proceed with the alcohol test. Contact the designated employer representative.

STEP 3 The BAT or STT completes the information required in this step and checks the type of device (saliva or breath) being used. After conducting the alcohol screening test, do the following (as appropriate):

Enter the information for the screening test (test number, testing device name, testing device serial number or lot number and expiration date, time of test with any device-dependent activation times, and the results), on the front of the AFT. For a breath testing device capable of printing, the information may be part of the printed record.

NOTE: Be sure to enter the result of the test exactly as it is indicated on the breath testing device, e.g., 0.00, 0.02, 0.04, etc.

Affix the printed information to the front of the form in the space provided, or to the back of the form, in a tamper-evident manner (e.g., tape) such that it does not obscure the original printed information, or the device may print the results directly on the ATF. If the results of the screening test are less than 0.02, print, sign your name, and enter today's date in the space provided. The test process is complete.

If the results of the screening test are 0.02 or greater, a confirmation test must be administered in accordance with DOT regulations. An EVIDENTIAL BREATH TESTING device that is capable of printing confirmation test information must be used in conducting this test.

Ensure that a waiting period of at least 15 minutes occurs before the confirmation test begins. Check the box indicating that the waiting period lasted at least 15 minutes.

After conducting the alcohol confirmation test, affix the printed information to the front of the form in the space provided, or to the back of the form, in a tamper-evident manner (e.g., tape) such that it does not obscure the original information, or the device may print the results directly on the ATF. Print, sign your name, and enter the date in the space provided. Go to STEP 4.

STEP 4 If the employee has a breath alcohol confirmation test result of 0.02 or higher, instruct the employee to read, sign, and date the employee certification statement in STEP 4.

NOTE: If the employee refuses to sign the certification statement in STEP 4, be sure to indicate this in the remarks line in STEP 3.

Immediately notify the DER if the employee has a breath alcohol confirmation test result of 0.02 or higher.

Forward **Copy 1** to the employer. Give **Copy 2** to the employee. Retain **Copy 3** for BAT/STT records.

BACK OF PAGE 3

Editor's Note: Appendix H to Part 40, which contains a Management Information System form, is not included in this pocketbook due to space considerations.

PART 380—SPECIAL TRAINING REQUIREMENTS

Subpart A—Longer Combination Vehicle (LCV) Driver-Training and Driver-Instructor Requirements—General

Subpart B—LCV Driver-Training Program

Subpart C—LCV Driver-Instructor Requirements

Subpart D—Driver-Training Certification

Subpart E—Entry-Level Driver Training Requirements Before February 7, 2022

Subpart F—Entry-Level Driver Training Requirements On and After February 7, 2022

Subpart G—Registry of Entry-Level Driver Training Providers On and After February 7, 2022

Authority: 49 U.S.C. 31133, 31136, 31305, 31307, 31308, 31502; sec. 4007(a) and (b), Pub. L. 102-240, 105 Stat. 1914, 2151-2152; sec. 32304, Pub. L. 112-141, 126 Stat. 405, 791; and 49 CFR 1.87.

Subpart A—Longer Combination Vehicle (LCV) Driver-Training and Driver-Instructor Requirements—General

§380.101 Purpose and scope.

(a) **Purpose** . The purpose of this part is to establish minimum requirements for operators of longer combination vehicles (LCVs) and LCV driver-instructors.

(b) **Scope** . This part establishes:

(1) Minimum training requirements for operators of LCVs;

(2) Minimum qualification requirements for LCV driver-instructors; and

(3) Procedures for determining compliance with this part by operators, instructors, training institutions, and employers.

§380.103 Applicability.

The rules in this part apply to all operators of LCVs in interstate commerce, employers of such persons, and LCV driver-instructors.

§380.105 Definitions.

(a) The definitions in part 383 of this subchapter apply to this part, except where otherwise specifically noted.

(b) As used in this part:

Classroom instructor means a qualified LCV driver-instructor who provides knowledge instruction that does not involve the actual operation of a longer combination vehicle or its components. Instruction may take place in a parking lot, garage, or any other facility suitable for instruction.

Longer combination vehicle (LCV) means any combination of a truck-tractor and two or more trailers or semi-trailers, which operate on the National System of Interstate and Defense Highways with a gross vehicle weight (GVW) greater than 36,288 kilograms (80,000 pounds).

LCV Double means an LCV consisting of a truck-tractor in combination with two trailers and/or semi-trailers.

LCV Triple means an LCV consisting of a truck-tractor in combination with three trailers and/or semi-trailers.

Qualified LCV driver-instructor means an instructor meeting the requirements contained in subpart C of this part. There are two types of qualified LCV driver-instructors: (1) classroom instructor and (2) skills instructor.

Skills instructor means a qualified LCV driver-instructor who provides behind-the-wheel instruction involving the actual operation of a longer combination vehicle or its components outside a classroom.

Training institution means any technical or vocational school accredited by an accrediting institution recognized by the U.S. Department of Education. A motor carrier's training program for its drivers or an entity that exclusively offers services to a single motor carrier is not a training institution.

§380.107 General requirements.

(a) Except as provided in §380.111, a driver who wishes to operate an LCV shall first take and successfully complete an LCV driver-training program that provides the knowledge and skills necessary to operate an LCV. The specific types of knowledge and skills that a training program shall include are outlined in Appendix F to this part.

(b) Before a person receives training:

(1) That person shall present evidence to the LCV driver-instructor showing that he/she meets the general requirements set forth in subpart B of this part for the specific type of LCV training to be taken.

(2) The LCV driver-instructor shall verify that each trainee applicant meets the general requirements for the specific type of LCV training to be taken.

(c) Upon successful completion of the training requirement, the driver-student shall be issued an LCV Driver Training Certificate by a certifying official of the training entity in accordance with the requirements specified in subpart D of this part.

§380.109 Driver testing.

(a) **Testing methods**. The driver-student must pass knowledge and skills tests in accordance with the following requirements, to determine whether a driver-student has successfully completed an LCV driver-training program as specified in subpart B of this part. The written knowledge test may be administered by any qualified driver-instructor. The skills tests, based on actual operation of an LCV, must be administered by a qualified LCV skills instructor.

(1) All tests shall be constructed to determine if the driver-student possesses the required knowledge and skills set forth in Appendix F to this part for the specific type of LCV training program being taught.

(2) Instructors shall develop their own tests for the specific type of LCV-training program being taught, but those tests must be at least as stringent as the requirements set forth in paragraph (b) of this section.

(3) LCV driver-instructors shall establish specific methods for scoring the knowledge and skills tests.

(4) Passing scores must meet the requirements of paragraph (b) of this section.

(5) Knowledge and skills tests shall be based upon the information taught in the LCV training programs as set forth in Appendix F to this part.

(6) Each knowledge test shall address the training provided during both theoretical and behind-the-wheel instruction, and include at least one question from

each of the units listed in the table to Appendix F to this part, for the specific type of LCV training program being taught.

(7) Each skills test shall include all the maneuvers and operations practiced during the Proficiency Development unit of instruction (behind-the-wheel instruction), as described in Appendix F to this part, for the specific type of LCV training program being taught.

(b) **Proficiency determinations**. The driver-student must meet the following conditions to be certified as an LCV driver:

(1) Answer correctly at least 80 percent of the questions on each knowledge test; and

(2) Demonstrate that he/she can successfully perform all of the skills addressed in paragraph (a)(7) of this section.

(c) **Automatic test failure**. Failure to obey traffic laws or involvement in a preventable crash during the skills portion of the test will result in automatic failure. Automatic test failure determinations are made at the sole discretion of the qualified LCV driver-instructor.

§380.111 Substitute for driver training.

(a) **Grandfather clause**. The LCV driver-training requirements specified in subpart B of this part do not apply to an individual who meets the conditions set forth in paragraphs (b), (c), and (d) of this section. A motor carrier must ensure that an individual claiming eligibility to operate an LCV on the basis of this section meets these conditions before allowing him/her to operate an LCV.

(b) An individual must certify that, during the 2-year period immediately preceding the date of application for a Certificate of Grandfathering, he/she had:

(1) A valid Class A CDL with a "double/triple trailers" endorsement;

(2) No more than one driver's license;

(3) No suspension, revocation, or cancellation of his/her CDL;

(4) No convictions for a major offense while operating a CMV as defined in §383.51(b) of this subchapter;

(5) No convictions for a railroad-highway grade crossing offense while operating a CMV as defined in §383.51(d) of this subchapter;

(6) No convictions for violating an out-of-service order as defined in §383.51(e) of this subchapter;

(7) No more than one conviction for a serious traffic violation, as defined in §383.5 of this subchapter, while operating a CMV; and

(8) No convictions for a violation of State or local law relating to motor vehicle traffic control arising in connection with any traffic crash while operating a CMV.

(c) An individual must certify and provide evidence that he/she:

(1) Is regularly employed in a job requiring the operation of a CMV that requires a CDL with a double/triple trailers endorsement; and

(2) Has operated, during the 2 years immediately preceding the date of application for a Certificate of Grandfathering, vehicles representative of the type of LCV that he/she seeks to continue operating.

(d) A motor carrier must issue a Certificate of Grandfathering to a person who meets the requirements of this section and must maintain a copy of the certificate in the individual's Driver Qualification file.

Longer Combination Vehicle (LCV) Driver-Training Certificate of Grandfathering

I certify that _____ has presented evidence of meeting the prerequisites set forth in the Federal Motor Carrier Safety Regulations (49 CFR § 380.111) for the substitute for LCV driver-training and is qualified to operate the LCVs indicated below:

YES	NO	
☐	☐	LCV Doubles
☐	☐	LCV Triples

DRIVER NAME (Firstname, MI, Lastname)	
Commercial Driver's License Number	STATE
ADDRESS OF DRIVER (Street Address, City, State and Zip Code)	
FULL NAME OF MOTOR CARRIER	Telephone Number
ADDRESS OF PRINCIPAL PLACE OF BUSINESS (Street Address, City, State, and Zip Code)	
SIGNATURE OF MOTOR CARRIER OFFICIAL	DATE ISSUED

(e) An applicant may be grandfathered under this section only during the year following June 1, 2004.

§380.113 Employer responsibilities.

(a) No motor carrier shall:

(1) Allow, require, permit or authorize an individual to operate an LCV unless he/she meets the requirements in §§380.203 or 380.205 and has been issued the LCV driver-training certificate described in §380.401. This provision does not apply to individuals who are eligible for the substitute for driver training provision in §380.111.

(2) Allow, require, permit, or authorize an individual to operate an LCV which the LCV driver-training certificate, CDL, and CDL endorsement(s) do not authorize the driver to operate. This provision applies to individuals employed by or under contract to the motor carrier.

(b) A motor carrier that employs or has under contract LCV drivers shall provide evidence of the certifications required by §380.401 or §380.111 of this part when requested by an authorized FMCSA, State, or local official in the course of a compliance review.

Subpart B—LCV Driver-Training Program

§380.201 General requirements.

(a) The LCV Driver-Training Program that is described in Appendix F to this part requires training using an LCV Double or LCV Triple and must include the following general categories of instruction:

(1) Orientation;

(2) Basic operation;

(3) Safe operating practices;

(4) Advanced operations; and

(5) Non driving activities.

(b) The LCV Driver-Training Program must include the minimum topics of training set forth in Appendix F to this part and behind-the-wheel instruction that is designed to provide an opportunity to develop the skills outlined under the Proficiency Development unit of the training program.

§380.203 LCV Doubles.

(a) To qualify for the training necessary to operate an LCV Double, a driver-student shall, during the 6 months immediately preceding application for training, have:

(1) A valid Class A CDL with a double/triple trailer endorsement;

(2) Driving experience in a Group A vehicle as described in §383.91 of this subchapter. Evidence of driving experience shall be an employer's written statement that the driver has, for at least 6 months immediately preceding application, operated a Group A vehicle while under his/her employ;

(3) No more than one driver's license;

(4) No suspension, revocation, or cancellation of his/her CDL;

(5) No convictions for a major offense, as defined in §383.51(b) of this subchapter, while operating a CMV;

(6) No convictions for a railroad-highway grade crossing offense, as defined in §383.51(d) of this subchapter, while operating a CMV;

(7) No convictions for violating an out-of-service order as defined in §383.51(e) of this subchapter;

(8) No more than one conviction for a serious traffic violation, as defined in §383.5 of this subchapter, while operating a CMV; and

(9) No convictions for a violation of State or local law relating to motor vehicle traffic control arising in connection with any traffic crash while operating a CMV.

(b) Driver-students meeting the preliminary requirements in paragraph (a) of this section shall successfully complete a training program that meets the minimum unit requirements for LCV Doubles as set forth in Appendix F to this part.

(c) Driver-students who successfully complete the Driver Training Program for LCV Doubles shall be issued a certificate, in accordance with subpart D of this part, indicating the driver is qualified to operate an LCV Double.

§380.205 LCV Triples.

(a) To qualify for the training necessary to operate an LCV Triple, a driver-student shall, during the 6 months immediately preceding application for training, have:

(1) A valid Class A CDL with a double/triple trailer endorsement;

(2) Experience operating the vehicle listed under paragraph (a)(2)(i) or (a)(2)(ii) of this section. Evidence of driving experience shall be an employer's written statement that the driver has, during the 6 months immediately preceding application, operated the applicable vehicle(s):

(i) Group A truck-tractor/semi-trailer combination as described in §383.91 of this subchapter; or

(ii) Group A truck-tractor/semi-trailer/trailer combination that operates at a gross vehicle weight of 80,000 pounds or less;

(3) No more than one driver's license;

(4) No suspension, revocation, or cancellation of his/her CDL;

(5) No convictions for a major offense, as defined in §383.51(b) of this subchapter, while operating a CMV;

(6) No convictions for a railroad-highway grade crossing offense, as defined in §383.51(d) of this subchapter, while operating a CMV;

(7) No convictions for violating an out-of-service order, as defined in §383.51(e) of this subchapter;

(8) No more than one conviction for a serious traffic violation, as defined in §383.5 of this subchapter, while operating a CMV; and

(9) No convictions for a violation of State or local law relating to motor vehicle traffic control arising in connection with any traffic crash, while operating a CMV.

(b) Driver-students meeting the preliminary requirements in paragraph (a) of this section shall successfully complete a training program that meets the minimum unit requirements for LCV Triples as set forth in Appendix F to this part.

(c) Driver-students who successfully complete the Driver Training Program for LCV Triples shall be issued a certificate, in accordance with subpart D of this part, indicating the driver is qualified to operate an LCV Triple.

Subpart C—LCV Driver-Instructor Requirements

§380.301 General requirements.

There are two types of LCV driver-instructors: Classroom instructors and Skills instructors. Except as provided in §380.303, you must meet the conditions under paragraph (a) or paragraph (b) of this section to qualify as an LCV driver-instructor.

(a) **Classroom instructor**. To qualify as an LCV Classroom instructor, a person shall:

(1) Have audited the driver-training course that he/she intends to instruct.

(2) If employed by a training institution, meet all State requirements for a vocational instructor.

(b) **Skills instructor**. To qualify as an LCV skills instructor, a person shall:

(1) Provide evidence of successful completion of the Driver-Training Program requirements, as set forth in subpart B of this part, when requested by employers and/or an authorized FMCSA, State, or local official in the course of a compliance review. The Driver-Training Program must be for the operation of CMVs representative of the subject matter that he/she will teach.

(2) If employed by a training institution, meet all State requirements for a vocational instructor;

(3) Possess a valid Class A CDL with all endorsements necessary to operate the CMVs applicable to the subject matter being taught (LCV Doubles and/or LCV Triples, including any specialized variation thereof, such as a tank vehicle, that requires an additional endorsement); and

(4) Have at least 2 years' CMV driving experience in a vehicle representative of the type of driver training to be provided (LCV Doubles or LCV Triples).

§380.303 Substitute for instructor requirements.

(a) **Classroom instructor**. The requirements specified under §380.301(a) of this part for a qualified LCV driver-instructor are waived for a classroom instructor-candidate who has 2 years of recent satisfactory experience teaching the classroom portion of a program similar in content to that set forth in Appendix F to this part.

(b) **Skills instructor**. The requirements specified under §380.301(b) of this part for a qualified LCV driver-instructor are waived for a skills instructor-candidate who:

(1) Meets the conditions of §380.111(b);

(2) Has CMV driving experience during the previous 2 years in a vehicle representative of the type of LCV that is the subject of the training course to be provided;

(3) Has experience during the previous 2 years in teaching the operation of the type of LCV that is the subject of the training course to be provided; and

(4) If employed by a training institution, meets all State requirements for a vocational instructor.

§380.305 Employer responsibilities.

(a) No motor carrier shall: (1) Knowingly allow, require, permit or authorize a driver-instructor in its employ, or under contract to the motor carrier, to provide LCV driver training unless such person is a qualified LCV driver-instructor under the requirements of this subpart; or

(2) Contract with a training institution to provide LCV driver training unless the institution:

(i) Uses instructors who are qualified LCV driver-instructors under the requirements of this subpart;

(ii) Is accredited by an accrediting institution recognized by the U.S. Department of Education;

(iii) Is in compliance with all applicable State training school requirements; and

(iv) Identifies drivers certified under §380.401 of this part, when requested by employers and/or an authorized FMCSA, State, or local official in the course of a compliance review.

(b) A motor carrier that employs or has under contract qualified LCV driver-instructors shall provide evidence of the certifications required by §380.301 or §380.303 of this part, when requested by an authorized FMCSA, State, or local official in the course of a compliance review.

Subpart D—Driver-Training Certification

§380.401 Certification document.

(a) A student who successfully completes LCV driver training shall be issued a Driver-Training Certificate that is substantially in accordance with the following form.

Longer Combination Vehicle (LCV) Driver-Training Certificate

I certify that _____ has presented evidence of meeting the training prerequisites set forth in the Federal Motor Carrier Safety Regulations (49 CFR §§ 380.203(a) and 380.205(a)) for LCV training, and has successfully completed the LCV Driver-Training Course(s) indicated below:

YES NO
☐ ☐   LCV Doubles _____
                    Date Training Completed

☐ ☐   LCV Triples _____
                    Date Training Completed

I certify that the indicated LCV Driver-Training course(s) was provided by a qualified LCV driver-instructor as defined under 49 CFR § 380.105 and meet(s) the minimum requirements set forth in 49 CFR part 380, subparts A and B.

DRIVER NAME (First Name, MI, Last Name)	
Commercial Driver's License Number	STATE
ADDRESS OF DRIVER (Street Address, City, State and Zip Code)	
FULL NAME OF TRAINING ENTITY	Telephone Number
BUSINESS ADDRESS (Street Address, City, State, and Zip Code)	
SIGNATURE OF TRAINING CERTIFYING OFFICIAL	DATE ISSUED

(b) An LCV driver must provide a copy of the Driver-Training Certificate to his/her employer to be filed in the Driver Qualification File.

Subpart E—Entry-Level Driver Training Requirements Before February 7, 2022

§380.501 Applicability.

All entry-level drivers who drive in interstate commerce and are subject to the CDL requirements of part 383 of this chapter must comply with the rules of this subpart, except drivers who are subject to the jurisdiction of the Federal Transit Administration or who are otherwise exempt under §390.3(f) of this subchapter.

§380.502 Definitions.

(a) The definitions in part 383 of this chapter apply to this part, except where otherwise specifically noted.

(b) As used in this subpart:

Entry-level driver is a driver with less than one year of experience operating a CMV with a CDL in interstate commerce.

Entry-level driver training is training the CDL driver receives in driver qualification requirements, hours of service of drivers, driver wellness, and whistle-blower protection as appropriate to the entry-level driver's current position in addition to passing the CDL test.

§380.503 Entry-level driver training requirements.

Entry-level driver training must include instruction addressing the following four areas:

(a) **Driver qualification requirements**. The Federal rules on medical certification, medical examination procedures, general qualifications, responsibilities, and disqualifications based on various offenses, orders, and loss of driving privileges (part 391, subparts B and E of this subchapter).

(b) **Hours of service of drivers**. The limitations on driving hours, the requirement to be off-duty for certain periods of time, record of duty status preparation, and exceptions (part 395 of this subchapter). Fatigue countermeasures as a means to avoid crashes.

(c) **Driver wellness**. Basic health maintenance including diet and exercise. The importance of avoiding excessive use of alcohol.

(d) **Whistleblower protection**. The right of an employee to question the safety practices of an employer without the employee's risk of losing a job or being subject to reprisals simply for stating a safety concern (29 CFR part 1978).

§380.505 Proof of training.

An employer who uses an entry-level driver must ensure the driver has received a training certificate containing all the information contained in §380.513 from the training provider.

§380.507 Driver responsibilities.

Each entry-level driver must receive training required by §380.503.

§380.509 Employer responsibilities.

(a) Each employer must ensure each entry-level driver who first began operating a CMV requiring a CDL in interstate commerce after July 20, 2003, receives training required by §380.503.

(b) Each employer must place a copy of the driver's training certificate in the driver's personnel or qualification file.

(c) All records required by this subpart shall be maintained as required by §390.31 of this subchapter and shall be made available for inspection at the employer's principal place of business within two business days after a request has been made by an authorized representative of the Federal Motor Carrier Safety Administration.

§380.511 Employer recordkeeping responsibilities

The employer must keep the records specified in §380.505 for as long as the employer employs the driver and for one year thereafter.

§380.513 Required information on the training certificate.

The training provider must provide a training certificate or diploma to the entry-level driver. If an employer is the training provider, the employer must provide a training certificate or diploma to the entry-level driver. The certificate or diploma must contain the following seven items of information:

(a) Date of certificate issuance.

(b) Name of training provider.

(c) Mailing address of training provider.

(d) Name of driver.

(e) A statement that the driver has completed training in driver qualification requirements, hours of service of drivers, driver wellness, and whistleblower protection requirements substantially in accordance with the following sentence:

I certify _____ has completed training requirements set forth in the Federal Motor Carrier Safety Regulations for entry-level driver training in accordance with 49 CFR 380.503.

(f) The printed name of the person attesting that the driver has received the required training.

(g) The signature of the person attesting that the driver has received the required training.

Subpart F—Entry-Level Driver Training Requirements On and After February 7, 2022

§380.600 Compliance date for training requirements for entry-level drivers.

Compliance with the provisions of this subpart is required on or after February 7, 2022.

§380.601 Purpose and scope.

This subpart establishes training requirements for entry-level drivers, as defined in this subpart, and minimum content for theory and Behind-the-Wheel (BTW) training curricula. Entry-level driver training, as defined in this subpart, applies only to those individuals who apply for a commercial driver's license (CDL) or a CDL upgrade or endorsement and does not otherwise amend substantive CDL requirements in part 383 of this chapter.

§380.603 Applicability.

(a) The rules in this subpart apply to all entry-level drivers, as defined in this subpart, who intend to drive CMVs as defined in §383.5 of this chapter in interstate and/or intrastate commerce, except:

(1) Drivers excepted from the CDL requirements under §383.3(c), (d), and (h) of this chapter;

(2) Drivers applying for a restricted CDL under §383.3(e) through (g) of this chapter;

(3) Military personnel with military CMV experience who meet all the requirements and conditions of §383.77 of this chapter; and

(4) Drivers applying for a removal of a restriction in accordance with §383.135(b)(7).

(b) Drivers issued a Class A CDL, Class B CDL, or a passenger (P), school bus (S), or hazardous materials (H) endorsement before February 7, 2022, are not required to comply with this subpart pertaining to that CDL or endorsement.

(c)(1) Individuals who obtain a CLP before February 7, 2022, are not required to comply with this subpart if they obtain a CDL before the CLP or renewed CLP expires.

(2) Individuals who obtain a CLP on or after February 7, 2022, are required to comply with this subpart.

(3) Except for individuals seeking the H endorsement, individuals must complete the theory and BTW (range and public road) portions of entry-level driver training within one year of completing the first portion.

§380.605 Definitions.

The definitions in parts 383 and 384 of this subchapter apply to this subpart, except as stated below. As used in this subpart:

Behind-the-wheel (BTW) instructor means an individual who provides BTW training involving the actual operation of a CMV by an entry-level driver on a range or a public road and meets one of these qualifications:

(1) Holds a CDL of the same (or higher) class and with all endorsements necessary to operate the CMV for which training is to be provided and has at least 2 years of experience driving a CMV requiring a CDL of the same or higher class and/or the same endorsement and meets all applicable State qualification requirements for CMV instructors; or

(2) Holds a CDL of the same (or higher) class and with all endorsements necessary to operate the CMV for which training is to be provided and has at least 2 years of experience as a BTW CMV instructor and meets all applicable State qualification requirements for CMV instructors.

Exception applicable to paragraphs (1) and (2) of this definition: A BTW instructor who provides training solely on a range which is not a public road is not required to hold a CDL of the same (or higher) class and with all endorsements necessary to operate the CMV for which training is to be provided, as long as the instructor previously held a CDL of the same (or higher) class and with all endorsements necessary to operate the CMV for which training is to be provided, and complies with the other requirements set forth in paragraphs (1) or (2) of this definition.

(3) If an instructor's CDL has been cancelled, suspended, or revoked due to any of the disqualifying offenses identified in §383.51 of this subchapter, the instructor is prohibited from engaging in BTW instruction for 2 years following the date his or her CDL is reinstated.

Behind-the-wheel (BTW) public road training means training provided by a BTW instructor when an entry-level driver has actual control of the power unit during a driving lesson conducted on a public road. BTW public road training does not include the time that an entry-level driver spends observing the operation of a CMV when he or she is not in control of the vehicle.

Behind-the-wheel (BTW) range training means training provided by a BTW instructor when an entry-level driver has actual control of the power unit during a driving lesson conducted on a range. BTW range training does not include time an entry-level driver spends observing the operation of a CMV when he or she is not in control of the vehicle.

Entry-level driver means an individual who must complete the CDL skills test requirements under §383.71 of this subchapter prior to receiving a CDL for the first time, upgrading to a Class A or Class B CDL, or obtaining a hazardous materials, passenger, or school bus endorsement for the first time. This definition does not include individuals for whom States waive the CDL skills test under §383.77 or individuals seeking to remove a restriction in accordance with §383.135(b)(7) of this subchapter.

Entry-level driver training means training an entry-level driver receives from an entity listed on FMCSA's Training Provider Registry prior to:

(1) Taking the CDL skills test required to receive the Class A or Class B CDL for the first time;

(2) Taking the CDL skills test required to upgrade to a Class A or Class B CDL; or

(3) Taking the CDL skills test required to obtain a passenger and/or school bus endorsement for the first time or the CDL knowledge test required to obtain a hazardous materials endorsement for the first time.

Range means an area that must be free of obstructions, enables the driver to maneuver safely and free from interference from other vehicles and hazards, and has adequate sight lines.

Theory instruction means knowledge instruction on the operation of a CMV and related matters provided by a theory instructor through lectures, demonstrations, audio-visual presentations, computer-based instruction, driving simulation devices, online training, or similar means.

Theory instructor means an individual who provides knowledge instruction on the operation of a CMV and meets one of these qualifications:

(1) Holds a CDL of the same (or higher) class and with all endorsements necessary to operate the CMV for which training is to be provided and has at least 2 years of experience driving a CMV requiring a CDL of the same (or higher) class and/or the same endorsement and meets all applicable State qualification requirements for CMV instructors; or

(2) Holds a CDL of the same (or higher) class and with all endorsements necessary to operate the CMV for which training is to be provided and has at least 2 years of experience as a BTW CMV instructor and meets all applicable State qualification requirements for CMV instructors.

Exceptions applicable to paragraphs (1) and (2) of this definition:

1. An instructor is not required to hold a CDL of the same (or higher) class and with all endorsements necessary to operate the CMV for which training is to be provided, if the instructor previously held a CDL of the same (or higher) class and complies with the other requirements set forth in paragraphs (1) or (2) of this definition.

2. Training providers offering online content exclusively are not required to meet State qualification requirements for theory instructors.

(3) If an instructor's CDL has been cancelled, suspended, or revoked due to any of the disqualifying offenses identified in §383.51 of this subchapter, the instructor is prohibited from engaging in theory instruction for 2 years following the date his or her CDL is reinstated.

Training provider means an entity that is listed on the FMCSA Training Provider Registry, as required by subpart G of this part. Training providers include, but are not limited to, training schools, educational institutions, rural electric cooperatives, motor carriers, State/local governments, school districts, joint labor management programs, owner-operators, and individuals.

§380.609 General entry-level driver training requirements.

(a) An individual who applies, for the first time, for a Class A or Class B CDL, or who upgrades to a Class A or B CDL, must complete driver training from a provider listed on the Training Provider Registry (TPR), as set forth in subpart G.

(b) An individual seeking to obtain a passenger (P), school bus (S), or hazardous materials (H) endorsement for the first time, must complete the training related to that endorsement from a training provider listed on the TPR, as set forth in subpart G.

Subpart G—Registry of Entry-Level Driver Training Providers On and After February 7, 2022

§380.700 Scope.

The rules in this subpart establish the eligibility requirements for listing on FMCSA's Training Provider Registry (TPR). In order to provide entry-level driver training in compliance with this part, training providers must be listed on the TPR.

§380.703 Requirements for listing on the training provider registry (TPR)

(a) To be eligible for listing on the TPR, an entity must:

(1) Follow a curriculum that meets the applicable criteria set forth in appendices A through E of part 380,

(2) Utilize facilities that meet the criteria set forth in §380.709;

(3) Utilize vehicles that meet the criteria set forth in §380.711;

(4) Utilize driver training instructors that meet the criteria set forth in §380.713;

(5)(i) Be licensed, certified, registered, or authorized to provide training in accordance with the applicable laws and regulations of any State where in-person training is conducted.

(ii) **Exception:** State qualification requirements otherwise applicable to theory instruction do not apply to providers offering such instruction only online.

(6) Allow FMCSA or its authorized representative to audit or investigate the training provider's operations to ensure that the provider meets the criteria set forth in this section.

(7) Electronically transmit an Entry-Level Driver Training Provider Registration Form through the TPR Web site maintained by FMCSA, which attests that the training provider meets all the applicable requirements of this section, to obtain a unique TPR number. If a training provider has more than one campus or training location, the training provider must electronically transmit an Entry-Level Driver Training Provider Registration Form for each campus or training location in order to obtain a unique TPR number for each location.

(b) When a provider meets the requirements of §§380.703 and 380.707, FMCSA will issue the provider a unique TPR number and, as applicable, add the provider's name and/or contact information to the TPR Web site.

§380.707 Entry-level training provider.

(a) Training providers must require all accepted applicants for behind-the-wheel (BTW) training to certify that they will comply with U.S. Department of Transportation regulations in parts 40, 382, 383, and 391, as well as State and/or local laws, related to controlled substances testing, age, medical certification, licensing, and driving record. Training providers must verify that all accepted BTW applicants or Class A theory instruction upgrade curriculum applicants hold a valid commercial learner's permit or commercial driver's license, as applicable.

(b) Training providers offering online training must ensure that the content is prepared and/or delivered by a theory instructor, as defined in §380.605.

(c) Separate training providers may deliver the theory and BTW portions of the training, but both portions (range and public road) of the BTW training must be delivered by the same training provider.

§380.709 Facilities.

The training provider's classroom and range facilities must comply with all applicable Federal, State, and/or local statutes and regulations.

§380.711 Equipment.

(a) All vehicles used in the behind-the-wheel training must comply with applicable Federal and State safety requirements.

(b) Training vehicles must be in the same group and type that driver-trainees intend to operate for their CDL skills test.

§380.713 Instructor requirements.

(a) Theory training providers must utilize instructors who are theory instructors as defined in §380.605.

(b) BTW training providers must utilize instructors who are BTW instructors as defined in §380.605.

§380.715 Assessments.

(a) Training providers must use written assessments to determine driver-trainees' proficiency in the knowledge objectives in the theory portion of each unit of instruction in appendices A through E of part 380, as applicable. The driver-trainee must receive an overall minimum score of 80 percent on the theory assessment.

(b) Training instructors must evaluate and document a driver-trainee's proficiency in BTW skills in accordance with the curricula in appendices A through D of part 380, as applicable.

§380.717 Training certification.

After an individual completes training administered by a provider listed on the TPR, that provider must, by midnight of the second business day after the driver-trainee completes the training, electronically transmit training certification information through the TPR Web site including the following:

(a) Driver-trainee name, number of driver's license/commercial learner's permit /commercial driver's license, as applicable, and State of licensure;

(b) Commercial driver's license class and/or endorsement and type of training (theory and/or BTW) the driver-trainee completed;

(c) Total number of clock hours the driver-trainee spent to complete BTW training, as applicable;

(d) Name of the training provider and its unique TPR identification number; and

(e) Date(s) of successful training completion.

§380.719 Requirements for continued listing on the training provider registry (TPR).

(a) To be eligible for continued listing on the TPR, a provider must:

(1) Meet the requirements of this subpart and the applicable requirements of §380.703.

(2) Biennially update the Entry-Level Driver Training Provider Registration Form.

(3) Report to FMCSA changes to key information, as identified in paragraph (a)(3)(i) of this section, within 30 days of the change.

(i) Key information is defined as training provider name, address, phone number, type(s) of training offered, training provider status, and, if applicable, any change in State licensure, certification, or accreditation status.

(ii) Changes must be reported by electronically transmitting an updated Entry-Level Driver Training Provider Registration Form.

(4) Maintain documentation of State licensure, registration, or certification verifying that the provider is authorized to provide training in that State, if applicable.

(5) Allow an audit or investigation of the training provider to be completed by FMCSA or its authorized representative, if requested.

(6) Ensure that all required documentation, as set forth in §380.725, is available to FMCSA or its authorized representative, upon request. The provider must submit this documentation within 48 hours of the request.

(b) [Reserved]

§380.721 Removal from training provider registry: factors considered.

FMCSA may remove a provider from the TPR when a provider fails to meet or maintain any of the qualifications established by this subpart or the requirements of other State and Federal regulations applicable to the provider. If FMCSA removes a provider from the TPR, any training conducted after the removal date will be considered invalid.

(a) The factors FMCSA may consider for removing a provider from the TPR include, but are not limited to, the following:

(1) The provider fails to comply with the requirements for continued listing on the TPR, as described in §380.719.

(2) The provider denies FMCSA or its authorized representatives the opportunity to conduct an audit or investigation of its training operations.

(3) The audit or investigation conducted by FMCSA or its authorized representatives identifies material deficiencies, pertaining to the training provider's program, operations, or eligibility.

(4) The provider falsely claims to be licensed, certified, registered, or authorized to provide training in accordance with the applicable laws and regulations in any State where in-person training is provided.

(5) The State-administered CDL skills examination passage rate for applicants for the Class A CDL, Class B CDL, passenger endorsement, and/or school bus endorsement who complete the provider's training and the CDL knowledge test passage rate for applicants for the hazardous materials endorsement who complete the provider's training.

(b) In instances of fraud or other criminal behavior by a training provider in which driver-trainees have knowingly participated, FMCSA reserves the right, on a case-by-case basis, to retroactively invalidate training conducted under this subpart.

§380.723 Removal from training provider registry: procedure.

(a) **Voluntary removal**. To be voluntarily removed from the Training Provider Registry (TPR), a provider must submit written notice to FMCSA, ATTN: Training Provider Registry Removal, 1200 New Jersey Avenue SE, Washington, DC 20590. Upon receiving the written notice, FMCSA will remove the training provider from the TPR. On and after the date of issuance of a notice of proposed removal from the TPR issued in accordance with paragraph (b) of this section, such a voluntary removal notice will not be effective.

(b) **Involuntary removal; Notice of proposed removal**. Except as provided by paragraphs (a) and (e) of this section, FMCSA initiates the process for involuntary removal of a provider from the TPR by issuing a written notice to the provider, stating the reasons for the proposed removal and setting forth any corrective actions necessary for the provider to remain listed on the TPR. If a notice of proposed removal is issued, the provider must notify current driver-trainees and driver-trainees scheduled for future training of the proposed removal. If a notice of proposed removal is issued to a training provider listed on the TPR Web site, FMCSA will note on the TPR Web site that such notice has been issued. FMCSA will remove the notation if the notice is withdrawn.

(c) **Response to notice of proposed removal and corrective action**. A training provider that has received a notice of proposed removal and wishes to remain on the TPR must submit a written response to FMCSA no later than 30 days after the date of issuance of the notice explaining why it believes that decision is not proper, as described in paragraph (c)(1) of this section. Alternatively, the provider will set forth corrective actions taken in response to FMCSA's notice of proposed removal, as described in paragraph (c)(2) of this section.

(1) **Opposing a notice of proposed removal**. If the provider believes FMCSA has relied on erroneous information in proposing removal from the TPR, the provider must explain the basis for that belief and provide supporting documentation. The FMCSA will review the explanation.

(i) If FMCSA finds that FMCSA has relied on erroneous information to propose removal of a training provider from the TPR, FMCSA will withdraw the notice of proposed removal and notify the provider of the withdrawal in writing.

(ii) If FMCSA finds that FMCSA has not relied on erroneous information in proposing removal, FMCSA will affirm the notice of proposed removal and notify the provider in writing of the determination. No later than 60 days after the date FMCSA affirms the notice of proposed removal, or as otherwise agreed to by the provider and FMCSA, the provider must comply with this subpart and correct the deficiencies identified in the notice of proposed removal as described in paragraph (c)(2) of this section.

(iii) If the provider does not respond in writing within 30 days of the date of issuance of a notice of proposed removal, the removal becomes effective immediately and the provider will be removed from the TPR. Any training conducted after the removal date is invalid.

(2) **Corrective action**. (i) The provider must comply with this subpart and complete the corrective actions specified in the notice of proposed removal no

later than 60 days after either the date of issuance of the notice of proposed removal or the date FMCSA subsequently affirms or modifies the notice of proposed removal. The provider must provide documentation of completion of the corrective action(s) to FMCSA. FMCSA may conduct an investigation and request any documentation necessary to verify that the provider has complied with this subpart and completed the required corrective action(s). FMCSA will notify the provider in writing whether it has met the requirements for continued listing on the TPR.

(ii) If the provider fails to complete the proposed corrective action(s) within the 60-day period, the provider will be removed from the TPR. FMCSA will notify the provider in writing of the removal.

(d) **Request for administrative review**. If a provider has been removed from the TPR under paragraph (c)(1)(iii), (c)(2)(ii), or (e) of this section, the provider may request an administrative review. The request must be submitted in writing to FMCSA, ATTN: §380.723 Training Provider Registry Removal Proceedings, 1200 New Jersey Avenue SE, Washington, DC 20590 no later than 30 days after the effective date of the removal. The request must explain the alleged error(s) committed in removing the provider from the TPR, and include all factual, legal, and procedural issues in dispute, as well as any supporting documentation.

(1) **Additional procedures for administrative review**. FMCSA may ask the provider to submit additional information or attend a conference to discuss the removal. If the provider does not provide the information requested, or does not attend the scheduled conference, FMCSA may dismiss the request for administrative review.

(2) **Decision on administrative review**. FMCSA will complete the administrative review and notify the provider in writing of the decision. The decision constitutes final Agency action. If FMCSA deems the removal to be invalid, FMCSA will reinstate the provider's listing on the TPR.

(e) **Emergency removal**. In cases of fraud, criminal behavior, or willful disregard of the regulations in this subpart or in which public health, interest, or safety requires, the provisions of paragraph (b) of this section are not applicable. In these cases, FMCSA may immediately remove a provider from the TPR. In instances of fraud or other criminal behavior by a training provider in which driver-trainees have knowingly participated, FMCSA reserves the right to retroactively invalidate training conducted under this subpart. A provider who has been removed under the provisions of this paragraph may request an administrative review of that decision as described under paragraph (d) of this section.

(f) **Reinstatement to the Training Provider Registry**. (1) Any time after a training provider's voluntary removal from the TPR, the provider may apply to FMCSA to be reinstated.

(2) No sooner than 30 days after the date of a provider's involuntary removal from the TPR, the provider may apply to FMCSA to be reinstated. The provider must submit documentation showing completion of any corrective action(s) identified in the notice of proposed removal or final notice of removal, as applicable.

§380.725 Documentation and record retention.

(a) **Applicability**. The documentation and retention of records required by this subpart apply to entities that meet the requirements of subpart G of this part and are eligible for listing on the Training Provider Registry (TPR).

(b) **Document retention**. All training providers on the TPR must retain the following:

(1) Self-certifications by all accepted applicants for behind-the-wheel (BTW) training attesting that they will comply with U.S. Department of Transportation regulations in parts 40, 382, 383 and 391, as well as State and/or local laws, related to alcohol and controlled substances testing, age, medical certification, licensing, and driver records, as required in 380.707(a).

(2) A copy of the driver-trainee's commercial learner's permit(s) or commercial driver's license, as applicable, as required in 380.707(a).

(3) Instructor qualification documentation indicating driving and/or training experience, as applicable, for each instructor and copies of commercial driver's licenses and applicable endorsements held by BTW instructors or theory instructors, as applicable.

(4) The lesson plans for theory and BTW (range and public road) training curricula, as applicable.

(5) Records of individual entry-level driver training assessments as described in §380.715.

(c) **Retention of records**. Training providers listed on the TPR must retain the records identified in paragraph (b) of this section for a minimum of three years from the date each required record is generated or received, unless a record, such as a BTW instructor's CDL, has expired or been canceled, in which case the most recent, valid CDL should be retained, if applicable. The provisions of this part do not affect a training provider's obligation to comply with any other local, State, or Federal requirements prescribing longer retention periods for any category of records described herein.

Appendix A to Part 380—Class A—CDL Training Curriculum

Editor's Note: This Appendix has a compliance date of February 7, 2022.

Class A CDL applicants must complete the Class A CDL curriculum outlined in this Appendix. The curriculum for Class A applicants pertains to combination vehicles (Group A) as defined in 49 CFR 383.91(a)(1) . Class A CDL applicants who possess a valid Class B CDL may complete the Theory Instruction Upgrade Curriculum in lieu of the Theory Instruction Standard Curriculum. There is no required minimum number of instruction hours for theory training, but the training instructor must cover all topics set forth in the curriculum. There is no required minimum number of instruction hours for BTW (range and public road) training, but the training instructor must cover all topics set forth in the BTW curriculum. BTW training must be conducted in a CMV for which a Class A CDL is required. The instructor must determine and document that each driver-trainee has demonstrated proficiency in all elements of the BTW curriculum, unless otherwise noted. Consistent with the definitions of BTW range training and BTW public road training in §380.605 , a simulation device cannot be used to conduct such training or to demonstrate proficiency. Training instructors must document the total number of clock hours each driver-trainee spends to complete the BTW curriculum. The Class A curriculum must, at a minimum, include the following:

Theory Instruction Standard Curriculum

Section A1.1 Basic Operation

This section must cover the interaction between driver-trainees and the CMV. Driver-trainees will receive instruction in the Federal Motor Carrier

Safety Regulations (FMCSRs) and will be introduced to the basic CMV instruments and controls. Training providers will teach driver-trainees the basic operating characteristics of a CMV. This section must also teach driver-trainees how to properly perform vehicle inspections, control the motion of CMVs under various road and traffic conditions, employ shifting and backing techniques, and properly couple and uncouple combination vehicles. Driver-trainees must familiarize themselves with the basic operating characteristics of a CMV.

Unit A1.1.1 Orientation

This unit must introduce driver-trainees to the combination vehicle driver training curriculum and the components of a combination vehicle. The training providers must teach the safety fundamentals, essential regulatory requirements (*e.g.,* overview of FMCSRs and Hazardous Materials Regulations), and driver-trainees' responsibilities not directly related to CMV driving, such as proper cargo securement. This unit must also cover the ramifications, including driver disqualification provisions and fines, for non-compliance with parts 380, 382, 383, and 390 through 399 of the FMCSRs. This unit must also include an overview of the applicability of State and local laws relating to the safe operation of the CMV, stopping at weigh stations/scales, hazard awareness of vehicle size and weight limitations, low clearance areas (*e.g.,* CMV height restrictions), and bridge formulas.

Unit A1.1.2 Control Systems/Dashboard

This unit must introduce driver-trainees to vehicle instruments, controls, and safety components. The training providers must teach driver-trainees to read gauges and instruments correctly and the proper use of vehicle safety components, including safety belts and mirrors. The training providers must teach driver-trainees to identify, locate, and explain the function of each of the primary and secondary controls including those required for steering, accelerating, shifting, braking systems (*e.g.,* ABS, hydraulic, air), as applicable, and parking.

Unit A1.1.3 Pre- and Post-Trip Inspections

This unit must teach the driver-trainees to conduct pre-trip and post-trip inspections as specified in §§392.7 and 396.11, including appropriate inspection locations. Instruction must also be provided on enroute vehicle inspections.

Unit A1.1.4 Basic Control

This unit must introduce basic vehicular control and handling as it applies to combination vehicles. This unit must include instruction addressing basic combination vehicle controls in areas such as executing sharp left and right turns, centering the vehicle, maneuvering in restricted areas, and entering and exiting the interstate or controlled access highway.

Unit A1.1.5 Shifting/Operating Transmissions

This unit must introduce shifting patterns and procedures to driver-trainees to prepare them to safely and competently perform basic shifting maneuvers. This unit must include training driver-trainees to execute up and down shifting techniques on multi-speed dual range transmissions, if appropriate. The training providers must teach the importance of increased vehicle control and improved fuel economy achieved by utilizing proper shifting techniques.

Unit A1.1.6 Backing and Docking

This unit must teach driver-trainees to back and dock the combination vehicle safely. This unit must cover "Get Out and Look" (GOAL), evaluation of backing/loading facilities, knowledge of backing set ups, as well as instruction in how to back with the use of spotters.

Unit A1.1.7 Coupling and Uncoupling

This unit must provide instruction for driver-trainees to develop the skills necessary to conduct the procedures for safe coupling and uncoupling of combination vehicle units, as applicable.

Section A1.2 Safe Operating Procedures

This section must teach the practices required for safe operation of the combination vehicle on the highway under various road, weather, and traffic conditions. The training providers must teach driver-trainees the Federal rules governing the proper use of seat belt assemblies (§392.16).

Unit A1.2.1 Visual Search

This unit must teach driver-trainees to visually search the road for potential hazards and critical objects, including instruction on recognizing distracted pedestrians or distracted drivers.

Unit A1.2.2 Communication

This unit must instruct driver-trainees on how to communicate their intentions to other road users. Driver-trainees must be instructed in techniques for different types of communication on the road, including proper use of headlights, turn signals, four-way flashers, and horns. This unit must cover instruction in proper utilization of eye contact techniques with other drivers, bicyclists, and pedestrians.

Unit A1.2.3 Distracted Driving

This unit must instruct driver-trainees in FMCSRs related to distracted driving and other key driver distraction driving issues, including improper cell phone use, texting, and use of in-cab technology (*e.g.,* §§392.80 and 392.82). This instruction will include training in the following aspects: visual attention (keeping eyes on the road); manual control (keeping hands on the wheel); and cognitive awareness (keeping mind on the task and safe operation of the CMV).

Unit A1.2.4 Speed Management

This unit must teach driver-trainees how to manage speed effectively in response to various road, weather, and traffic conditions. The instruction must include methods for calibrating safe following distances taking into account CMV braking distances under an array of conditions including traffic, weather, and CMV weight and length.

Unit A1.2.5 Space Management

This unit must teach driver-trainees about the importance of managing the space surrounding the vehicle under various traffic and road conditions.

Unit A1.2.6 Night Operation

This unit must instruct driver-trainees in the factors affecting the safe operation of CMVs at night and in darkness. Additionally, driver-trainees must be instructed in changes in vision, communications, speed space management, and proper use of lights, as needed, to deal with the special problems night driving presents.

Unit A1.2.7 Extreme Driving Conditions

This unit must teach driver-trainees about the specific problems presented by extreme driving conditions. The training provider will emphasize the factors affecting the operation of CMVs in cold, hot, and inclement weather and on steep grades and sharp curves. The training provider must teach proper tire chaining procedures.

Section A1.3 Advanced Operating Practices

This section must introduce higher-level skills that can be acquired only after the more fundamental skills and knowledge taught in the prior two sections have been mastered. The training providers must teach driver-trainees about the advanced skills necessary to recognize potential hazards and must teach the driver-trainees the procedures needed to handle a CMV when faced with a hazard.

Unit A1.3.1 Hazard Perception

The unit must teach driver-trainees to recognize potential hazards in the driving environment in order to reduce the severity of the hazard and neutralize possible emergency situations. The training providers must teach driver-trainees to identify road conditions and other road users that are a potential threat to the safety of the combination vehicle and suggest appropriate adjustments. The instruction must emphasize hazard recognition, visual search, adequate surveillance, and response to possible emergency-producing situations encountered by CMV drivers in various traffic situations. The training providers must teach driver-trainees to recognize potential dangers and the safety procedures that must be utilized while driving in construction/work zones.

Unit A1.3.2 Skid Control/Recovery, Jackknifing, and Other Emergencies

This unit must teach the causes of skidding and jackknifing and techniques for avoiding and recovering from them. The training providers must teach the importance of maintaining directional control and bringing the CMV to a stop in the shortest possible distance while operating over a slippery surface. This unit must provide instruction in appropriate responses when faced with CMV emergencies. This instruction must include evasive steering, emergency braking, and off-road recovery, as well as the proper response to brake failures, tire blowouts, hydroplaning, and rollovers. The instruction must include a review of unsafe acts and the role the acts play in producing or worsening hazardous situations.

Unit A1.3.3 Railroad-Highway Grade Crossings

This unit must teach driver-trainees to recognize potential dangers and the appropriate safety procedures to utilize at railroad (RR)-highway grade crossings. This instruction must include an overview of various Federal/State RR grade crossing regulations, RR grade crossing environments, obstructed view conditions, clearance around the tracks, and rail signs and signals. The training providers must instruct driver-trainees that railroads have personnel available ("Emergency Notification Systems") to receive notification of any information relating to an unsafe condition at the RR-highway grade crossing or a disabled vehicle or other obstruction blocking a railroad track at the RR-highway grade crossing.

Section A1.4 Vehicle Systems and Reporting Malfunctions

This section must provide entry-level driver-trainees with sufficient knowledge of the combination vehicle and its systems and subsystems to ensure that they understand and respect their role in vehicle inspection, operation, and maintenance and the impact of those factors upon highway safety and operational efficiency.

Unit A1.4.1 Identification and Diagnosis of Malfunctions

This unit must teach driver-trainees to identify major combination vehicle systems. The goal is to explain their function and how to check all key vehicle systems, (*e.g.,* engine, engine exhaust auxiliary systems, brakes, drive train, coupling systems, and suspension) to ensure their safe operation. Driver-trainees must be provided with a detailed description of each system, its importance to safe and efficient operation, and what is needed to keep the system in good operating condition.

Unit A1.4.2 Roadside Inspections

This unit must instruct driver-trainees on what to expect during a standard roadside inspection conducted by authorized personnel. The training providers must teach driver-trainees on what vehicle and driver violations are classified as out-of-service (OOS), including the ramifications and penalties for operating a CMV when subject to an OOS order as defined in section 390.5.

Unit A1.4.3 Maintenance

This unit must introduce driver-trainees to the basic servicing and checking procedures for various engine and vehicle components and to help develop their ability to perform preventive maintenance and simple emergency repairs.

Section A1.5 Non-Driving Activities

This section must teach driver-trainees the activities that do not involve actually operating the CMV.

Unit A1.5.1 Handling and Documenting Cargo

This unit must teach the basic theory of cargo weight distribution, cargo securement on the vehicle, cargo covering, and techniques for safe and efficient loading/unloading. The training providers must teach driver-trainees the basic cargo security/cargo theft prevention procedures. The training provider must teach driver-trainees the basic information regarding the proper handling and documentation of HM cargo.

Unit A1.5.2 Environmental Compliance Issues

This unit must teach driver-trainees to recognize environmental hazards and issues related to the CMV and load, and also make the driver-trainee aware that city, county, State, and Federal requirements may apply to such circumstances.

Unit A1.5.3 Hours of Service Requirements

This unit must teach driver-trainees to understand that there are different hours-of-service (HOS) requirements applicable to different industries. The training providers must teach driver-trainees all applicable HOS regulatory requirements. The training providers must teach driver-trainees to complete a Driver's Daily Log (electronic and paper), timesheet, and logbook recap, as appropriate. The training providers must teach driver-trainees the consequences (safety, legal, and personal) of violating the HOS regulations, including the fines and penalties imposed for these types of violations.

Unit A1.5.4 Fatigue and Wellness Awareness

This unit must teach driver-trainees about the issues and consequences of chronic and acute driver fatigue and the importance of staying alert. The training providers must teach driver-trainees wellness and basic health maintenance information that affect a driver's ability to safely operate a CMV.

Unit A1.5.5 Post-Crash Procedures

This unit must teach driver-trainees appropriate post-crash procedures, including the requirement that the driver, if possible, assess his or her physical condition immediately after the crash and notify authorities or assign the task to other individuals at the crash scene. The training providers must teach driver-trainees how to protect the area; obtain emergency medical assistance; move on-road vehicles off the road in minor crashes so as to avoid subsequent crashes or injuries; engage flashers; place reflective triangles and other warning devices for stopped vehicles; and properly use a fire extinguisher, if necessary. The training providers must instruct driver-trainees in post-crash testing requirements related to controlled substances and alcohol.

Unit A1.5.6 External Communications

This unit must teach driver-trainees the value of effective interpersonal communication techniques/skills to interact with enforcement officials. The training providers must teach driver-trainees the specifics of the roadside vehicle inspection process, and what to expect during this activity. Driver-trainees who are not English speakers must be instructed in FMCSA English language proficiency requirements. The training providers must teach driver-trainees the impact that violating Federal and state regulations has on their driving records and their employing motor carrier's records.

Unit A1.5.7 Whistleblower/Coercion

This unit must teach the driver-trainees about the right of an employee to question the safety practices of an employer without incurring the risk of losing a job or being subject to reprisals simply for stating a safety concern. The training providers must instruct driver-trainees in the whistleblower protection regulations in 29 CFR part 1978. The training providers must teach the procedures for reporting to FMCSA incidents of coercion from motor carriers, shippers, receivers, or transportation intermediaries.

Unit A1.5.8 Trip Planning

This unit must address the importance of and requirements for planning routes and trips. This instruction must address planning the safest route, planning for rest stops, heavy traffic areas, railroad-highway grade crossing safe clearance and ground clearance (*i.e.,* "high center"), the importance of Federal and State requirements on the need for permits, and vehicle size and weight limitations. The training providers must teach driver-trainees in the correct identification of restricted routes, the pros and cons of Global Positioning System (GPS)/trip routing software, and the importance of selecting fuel-efficient routes.

Unit A1.5.9 Drugs/Alcohol

This unit must teach driver-trainees the rules applicable to controlled substances (including prescription drugs) and alcohol use and testing related to the operation of a CMV.

Unit A1.5.10 Medical Requirements

This unit must teach driver-trainees the Federal rules on medical certification, medical examination procedures, general qualifications, responsibilities, and disqualifications based on various offenses, orders, and loss of driving privileges (49 CFR part 391, subparts B and E).

Behind-the-Wheel—Range

BTW range training must teach driving exercises related to basic vehicle control skills and mastery of basic maneuvers, as covered in §§383.111 and 383.113 of this chapter, necessary to operate the vehicle safely. The training providers will teach activities in this unit on a driving range as defined in §380.605. The training provider must teach "Get Out and Look" (GOAL) to the driver-trainee as it applies to units A2.2-2.6.

Unit A2.1 Vehicle Inspection Pre-Trip/Enroute/Post-Trip

Driver-trainees must demonstrate proficiency in conducting pre-trip and post-trip inspections as specified in §§392.7 and 396.11, including appropriate inspection locations. Instruction must also be provided on enroute vehicle inspections.

Unit A2.2 Straight Line Backing

Driver-trainees must demonstrate proficiency in proper techniques for performing various straight line backing maneuvers to appropriate criteria/acceptable tolerances.

Unit A2.3 Alley Dock Backing (45/90 Degree)

Driver-trainees must demonstrate proficiency in proper techniques for performing 45/90 degree alley dock maneuvers to appropriate criteria/acceptable tolerances.

Unit A2.4 Off-Set Backing

Driver-trainees must demonstrate proficiency in proper techniques for performing off-set right and left backing maneuvers to appropriate criteria/acceptable tolerances.

Unit A2.5 Parallel Parking Blind Side

Driver-trainees must demonstrate proficiency in proper techniques for performing parallel parking blind side positions/maneuvers to appropriate criteria/acceptable tolerances.

Unit A2.6 Parallel Parking Sight Side

Driver-trainees must demonstrate proficiency in proper techniques for performing sight side parallel parking maneuvers to appropriate criteria/acceptable tolerances.

Unit A2.7 Coupling and Uncoupling

Driver-trainees must demonstrate proficiency in proper techniques for coupling, inspecting, and uncoupling combination vehicle units, as applicable.

Behind-the-Wheel—Public Road

The instructor must engage in active two-way communication with the driver-trainees during all active BTW public road training sessions. Skills described in paragraphs A3.8 through 3.12 of this section must be discussed during public road training, but not necessarily performed. Driver-trainees are not required to demonstrate proficiency in the skills described in paragraphs A3.8 through 3.12.

Unit A3.1 Vehicle Controls Including: Left Turn, Right Turns, Lane Changes, Curves at Highway Speeds, and Entry and Exit on the Interstate or Controlled Access Highway

Driver-trainees must demonstrate proficiency in proper techniques for initiating vehicle movement, executing left and right turns, changing lanes, navigating curves at speed, entry and exit on the interstate or controlled access highway, and stopping the vehicle in a controlled manner.

Unit A3.2 Shifting/Transmission

Driver-trainees must demonstrate proficiency in proper techniques for performing safe and fuel-efficient shifting.

Unit A3.3 Communications/Signaling

Driver-trainees must demonstrate proficiency in proper techniques for signaling intentions and effectively communicating with other drivers.

Unit A3.4 Visual Search

Driver-trainees must demonstrate proficiency in proper techniques for visually searching the road for potential hazards and critical objects.

Unit A3.5 Speed and Space Management

Driver-trainees must demonstrate proficiency in proper habits and techniques for adjusting and maintaining vehicle speed, taking into consideration various factors such as traffic and road conditions. Driver-trainees must demonstrate proficiency in maintaining proper speed to keep appropriate spacing between the driver-trainee's CMV and other vehicles. Instruction must include methods for calibrating safe following distances under an array of conditions including traffic, weather, and CMV weight and length.

Unit A3.6 Safe Driver Behavior

Driver-trainees must demonstrate proficiency in safe driver behavior during their operation of the CMV.

Unit A3.7 Hours of Service (HOS) Requirements

Driver-trainees must demonstrate proficiency in the basic activities required by the HOS regulations, such as completing a Driver's Daily Log (electronic and paper), timesheet, and logbook recap, as appropriate.

Unit A3.8 Hazard Perception

Driver-trainees must demonstrate their ability to recognize potential hazards in the driving environment in time to reduce the severity of the hazard and neutralize possible emergency situations. Driver-trainees must demonstrate the ability to identify road conditions and other road users that are a potential threat to the safety of the combination vehicle and suggest appropriate adjustments.

Unit A3.9 Railroad (RR)-Highway Grade Crossing

Driver-trainees must demonstrate the ability to recognize potential dangers and to demonstrate appropriate safety procedures when RR-highway grade crossings are reasonably available.

Unit A3.10 Night Operation

Driver-trainees must be familiar with how to operate a CMV safely at night. Training providers must teach driver-trainees that night driving presents specific circumstances that require heightened attention on the part of the driver. Driver-trainees must be taught special requirements for night vision, communications, speed, space management, and proper use of lights.

Unit A3.11 Extreme Driving Conditions

Driver-trainees must be familiar with the special risks created by, and the heightened precautions required by, driving CMVs under extreme driving conditions, such as heavy rain, high wind, high heat, fog, snow, ice, steep grades, and sharp curves. Driver-trainees must demonstrate their ability to recognize the changes in basic driving habits needed to deal with the specific challenges presented by these extreme driving conditions.

Unit A3.12 Skid Control/Recovery, Jackknifing, and Other Emergencies

Driver-trainees must know the causes of skidding and jackknifing and techniques for avoiding and recovering from them. Driver-trainees must know how to maintain directional control and bring the CMV to a stop in the shortest possible distance while operating over a slippery surface. Driver-trainees must be familiar with proper techniques for responding to CMV emergencies, such as evasive steering, emergency braking, and off-road recovery. They must also know how to prevent or respond to brake failures, tire blowouts, hydroplaning, and rollovers.

Theory Instruction Upgrade Curriculum

Section BA1.1 Basic Operation

This section must cover the interaction between driver-trainees and the CMV. Driver-trainees will receive instruction in the Federal Motor Carrier Safety Regulations (FMCSRs) and will be introduced to the basic CMV instruments and controls. Training providers will teach driver-trainees the basic operating characteristics of a CMV. This section must also teach driver-trainees how to properly perform vehicle inspections, control the motion of CMVs under various road and traffic conditions, employ shifting and backing techniques, and properly couple and uncouple combination vehicles. Driver-trainees must familiarize themselves with the basic operating characteristics of a CMV.

Unit BA1.1.1 Orientation

This unit must introduce driver-trainees to the combination vehicle driver training curriculum and the components of a combination vehicle. The training providers must teach the safety fundamentals, essential regulatory requirements (*e.g.,* overview of FMCSRs and Hazardous Materials Regulations), and driver-trainees' responsibilities not directly related to CMV driving, such as proper cargo securement. This unit must also cover the ramifications, including driver disqualification provisions and fines, for non-compliance with parts 380, 382, 383, and 390 through 399 of the FMCSRs. This unit must also include an overview of the applicability of State and local laws relating to the safe operation of the CMV, stopping at weigh stations/scales, hazard awareness of vehicle size and weight limitations, low clearance areas (*e.g.,* CMV height restrictions), and bridge formulas.

Unit BA1.1.2 Control Systems/Dashboard

This unit must introduce driver-trainees to vehicle instruments, controls, and safety components. The training providers must teach driver-trainees to read gauges and instruments correctly and the proper use of vehicle safety components, including safety belts and mirrors. The training providers must teach driver-trainees to identify, locate, and explain the function of each of the primary and secondary controls including those required for steering, accelerating, shifting, braking systems (*e.g.,* ABS, hydraulic, air), as applicable, and parking.

Unit BA1.1.3 Pre- and Post-Trip Inspections

This unit must teach the driver-trainees to conduct pre-trip and post-trip inspections as specified in §§392.7 and 396.11, including appropriate inspection locations. Instruction must also be provided on en route vehicle inspections.

Unit BA1.1.4 Basic Control

This unit must introduce basic vehicular control and handling as it applies to combination vehicles. This unit must include instruction addressing basic combination vehicle controls in areas such as executing sharp left and right turns, centering the vehicle, maneuvering in restricted areas, and entering and exiting the interstate or controlled access highway.

Unit BA1.1.5 Shifting/Operating Transmissions

This unit must introduce shifting patterns and procedures to driver-trainees to prepare them to safely and competently perform basic shifting maneuvers. This unit must include training driver-trainees to execute up and down shifting techniques on multi-speed dual range transmissions, if appropriate. The training providers must teach the importance of increased vehicle control and improved fuel economy achieved by utilizing proper shifting techniques.

Unit BA1.1.6 Backing and Docking

This unit must teach driver-trainees to back and dock the combination vehicle safely. This unit must cover "Get Out and Look" (GOAL), evaluation of backing/loading facilities, knowledge of backing set ups, as well as instruction in how to back with the use of spotters.

Unit BA1.1.7 Coupling and Uncoupling

This unit must provide instruction for driver-trainees to develop the skills necessary to conduct the procedures for safe coupling and uncoupling of combination vehicle units, as applicable.

Section BA1.2 Safe Operating Procedures

This section must teach the practices required for safe operation of the combination vehicle on the highway under various road, weather, and traffic conditions. The training providers must teach driver-trainees the Federal rules governing the proper use of seat belt assemblies (§392.16).

Unit BA1.2.1 Visual Search

This unit must teach driver-trainees to visually search the road for potential hazards and critical objects, including instruction on recognizing distracted pedestrians or distracted drivers.

Unit BA1.2.2 Communication

This unit must instruct driver-trainees on how to communicate their intentions to other road users. Driver-trainees must be instructed in techniques for different types of communication on the road, including proper use of headlights, turn signals, four-way flashers, and horns. This unit must cover instruction in proper utilization of eye contact techniques with other drivers, bicyclists, and pedestrians.

Unit BA1.2.3 Distracted Driving

This unit must instruct driver-trainees in FMCSRs related to distracted driving and other key driver distraction driving issues, including improper cell phone use, texting, and use of in-cab technology (*e.g.,* §§392.80 and 392.82). This instruction will include training in the following aspects: visual attention (keeping eyes on the road); manual control (keeping hands on the wheel); and cognitive awareness (keeping mind on the task and safe operation of the CMV).

Unit BA1.2.4 Speed Management

This unit must teach driver-trainees how to manage speed effectively in response to various road, weather, and traffic conditions. The instruction must include methods for calibrating safe following distances taking into account CMV braking distances under an array of conditions including traffic, weather, and CMV weight and length.

Unit BA1.2.5 Space Management

This unit must teach driver-trainees about the importance of managing the space surrounding the vehicle under various traffic and road conditions.

Unit BA1.2.6 Night Operation

This unit must instruct driver-trainees in the factors affecting the safe operation of CMVs at night and in darkness. Additionally, driver-trainees must be instructed in changes in vision, communications, speed space management, and proper use of lights, as needed, to deal with the special problems night driving presents.

Unit BA1.2.7 Extreme Driving Conditions

This unit must teach driver-trainees about the specific problems presented by extreme driving conditions. The training provider will emphasize the factors affecting the operation of CMVs in cold, hot, and inclement weather and on steep grades and sharp curves. The training provider must teach proper tire chaining procedures.

Section BA1.3 Advanced Operating Practices

This section must introduce higher-level skills that can be acquired only after the more fundamental skills and knowledge taught in the prior two sections have been mastered. The training providers must teach driver-trainees about the advanced skills necessary to recognize potential hazards and must teach the driver-trainees the procedures needed to handle a CMV when faced with a hazard.

Unit BA1.3.1 Hazard Perception

The unit must teach driver-trainees to recognize potential hazards in the driving environment in order to reduce the severity of the hazard and neutralize possible emergency situations. The training providers must teach driver-trainees to identify road conditions and other road users that are a potential threat to the safety of the combination vehicle and suggest appropriate adjustments. The instruction must emphasize hazard recognition, visual search, adequate surveillance, and response to possible emergency-producing situations encountered by CMV drivers in various traffic situations. The training providers must teach driver-trainees to recognize potential dangers and the safety procedures that must be utilized while driving in construction/work zones.

Unit BA1.3.2 Skid Control/Recovery, Jackknifing, and Other Emergencies

This unit must teach the causes of skidding and jackknifing and techniques for avoiding and recovering from them. The training providers must teach the importance of maintaining directional control and bringing the CMV to a stop in the shortest possible distance while operating over a slippery surface. This unit must provide instruction in appropriate responses when faced with CMV emergencies. This instruction must include evasive steering, emergency braking, and off-road recovery, as well as the proper response to brake failures, tire blowouts, hydroplaning, and rollovers. The instruction must include a review of unsafe acts and the role the acts play in producing or worsening hazardous situations.

Unit BA1.3.3 Railroad-Highway Grade Crossings

This unit must teach driver-trainees to recognize potential dangers and the appropriate safety procedures to utilize at railroad (RR)-highway grade crossings. This instruction must include an overview of various Federal/State RR grade crossing regulations, RR grade crossing environments, obstructed view conditions, clearance around the tracks, and rail signs and signals. The training providers must instruct driver-trainees that railroads have personnel available ("Emergency Notification Systems") to receive notification of any information relating to an unsafe condition at the RR-highway grade crossing or a disabled vehicle or other obstruction blocking a railroad track at the RR-highway grade crossing.

Section BA1.4 Vehicle Systems and Reporting Malfunctions

This section must provide entry-level driver-trainees with sufficient knowledge of the combination vehicle and its systems and subsystems to ensure that they understand and respect their role in vehicle inspection, operation, and maintenance and the impact of those factors upon highway safety and operational efficiency.

Unit BA1.4.1 Identification and Diagnosis of Malfunctions

This unit must teach driver-trainees to identify major combination vehicle systems. The goal is to explain their function and how to check all key vehicle systems, (*e.g.,* engine, engine exhaust auxiliary systems, brakes, drive train, coupling systems, and suspension) to ensure their safe operation. Driver-trainees must be provided with a detailed description of each system, its importance to safe and efficient operation, and what is needed to keep the system in good operating condition.

Unit BA1.4.2 Roadside Inspections

This unit must instruct driver-trainees on what to expect during a standard roadside inspection conducted by authorized personnel. The training providers must teach driver-trainees on what vehicle and driver violations are classified as out-of-service (OOS), including the ramifications and penalties for operating a CMV when subject to an OOS order as defined in section 390.5.

Unit BA1.4.3 Maintenance

This unit must introduce driver-trainees to the basic servicing and checking procedures for various engine and vehicle components and to help develop their ability to perform preventive maintenance and simple emergency repairs.

Section BA1.5 Non-Driving Activities

This section must teach driver-trainees the activities that do not involve actually operating the CMV.

Unit BA1.5.1 Hours of Service Requirements

This unit must teach driver-trainees to understand that there are different hours-of-service (HOS) requirements applicable to different industries. The training providers must teach driver-trainees all applicable HOS regulatory requirements. The training providers must teach driver-trainees to complete a Driver's Daily Log (electronic and paper), timesheet, and logbook recap, as appropriate. The training providers must teach driver-trainees the consequences (safety, legal, and personal) of violating the HOS regulations, including the fines and penalties imposed for these types of violations.

Unit BA1.5.2 Fatigue and Wellness Awareness

This unit must teach driver-trainees about the issues and consequences of chronic and acute driver fatigue and the importance of staying alert. The training providers must teach driver-trainees wellness and basic health maintenance information that affect a driver's ability to safely operate a CMV.

Appendix B to Part 380—Class B—CDL Training Curriculum

Editor's Note: This Appendix has a compliance date of February 7, 2022.

Class B CDL applicants must complete the Class B CDL curriculum outlined in this Appendix. The curriculum for Class B applicants pertains to heavy straight vehicles (Group B) as defined in 49 CFR 383.91(a)(2). There is no required minimum number of instruction hours for theory training, but the training instructor must cover all the topics in curriculum. There is no required minimum number of instruction hours required for BTW (range and public road) training, but the training instructor must cover all topics set forth in the BTW curriculum. BTW training must be conducted in a CMV for which a Class B CDL is required. The instructor must determine and document that each driver-trainee has demonstrated proficiency in all elements of the BTW curriculum unless otherwise noted. Consistent with the definitions of BTW range training and BTW public road training in §380.605, a simulation device cannot be used to conduct such training or to demonstrate proficiency. Training instructors must document the total number of clock hours each driver-trainee spends to complete the BTW curriculum. The Class B curriculum must, at a minimum, include the following:

Theory Instruction

Section B1.1 Basic Operation

This section must cover the interaction between driver-trainees and the CMV. Driver-trainees will receive instruction in the Federal Motor Carrier Safety Regulations (FMCSRs) and will be introduced to the basic CMV instruments and controls. This section must also teach driver-trainees how to perform vehicle inspections, control the CMVs under various road and traffic conditions, employ shifting and backing techniques, and couple and uncouple, as applicable. Driver-trainees must familiarize themselves with the basic operating characteristics of a CMV.

Unit B1.1.1 Orientation

This unit must introduce driver-trainees to the commercial motor vehicle driver training curriculum and the components of a commercial motor vehicle. The training providers must teach driver-trainees the safety fundamentals, essential regulatory requirements (*i.e.,* overview of FMCSRs/hazardous materials (HM) regulations), and driver-trainees' responsibilities not directly related to driving. This unit must also cover the ramifications and driver disqualification provisions and fines for non-compliance with parts 380, 382, 383, and 390 through 399 of the FMCSRs. This unit must also include an overview of the applicability of State and local laws relating to the safe operation of the CMV, stopping at weigh stations/scales, hazard awareness of vehicle size and weight limitations, low clearance areas (*e.g.,* CMV height restrictions), and bridge formulas.

Unit B1.1.2 Control Systems/Dashboard

This unit must introduce driver-trainees to vehicle instruments, controls, and safety components. The training providers must teach driver-trainees to read gauges and instruments correctly and the proper use of vehicle safety components, including safety belts and mirrors. The training providers must teach driver-trainees to identify, locate, and explain the function of each of the primary and secondary controls including those required for steering, accelerating, shifting, braking systems (*e.g.,* ABS, hydraulic, air), as applicable, and parking.

Unit B1.1.3 Pre- and Post-Trip Inspections

The training provider must teach the driver-trainees to conduct pre-trip and post-trip inspections as specified in §§392.7 and 396.11, including appropriate inspection locations. Instruction must also be provided on enroute vehicle inspections.

Unit B1.1.4 Basic Control

This unit must introduce basic vehicular control and handling as it applies to commercial motor vehicles. This unit must include instruction addressing basic CMV controls in areas such as executing sharp left and right turns, centering the vehicle, maneuvering in restricted areas, and entering and exiting the interstate or controlled access highway.

Unit B1.1.5 Shifting/Operating Transmissions

This unit must introduce shifting patterns and procedures to driver-trainees to prepare them to safely and competently perform basic shifting maneuvers. This unit must teach driver-trainees to execute up and down shifting techniques on multi-speed dual range transmissions, if appropriate. The training providers must teach driver-trainees the importance of increased fuel economy achieved by utilizing proper shifting techniques.

Unit B1.1.6 Backing and Docking

This unit must teach driver-trainees to back and dock the vehicle safely. This unit must cover "Get Out and Look" (GOAL), evaluation of backing/loading facilities, knowledge of backing set ups, as well as instruction in how to back with use of spotters.

Section B1.2 Safe Operating Procedures

This section must teach the practices required for safe operation of the CMV on the highway under various road, weather, and traffic conditions. The training providers must teach driver-trainees the Federal rules governing the proper use of seat belt assemblies (§392.16).

Unit B1.2.1 Visual Search

This unit must teach driver-trainees to visually search the road for potential hazards and critical objects, including instruction on recognizing distracted pedestrians or distracted drivers. This unit must include instruction in how to ensure a driver-trainee's personal security/general awareness in common surroundings such as truck stops and/or rest areas and at shipper/receiver locations.

Unit B1.2.2 Communication

This unit must teach driver-trainees how to communicate their intentions to other road users. Driver-trainees must be instructed in techniques for different types of communication on the road, including proper use of headlights, turn signals, four-way flashers, and horns. This unit must cover instruction in proper utilization of eye contact techniques with other drivers, bicyclists, and pedestrians.

Unit B1.2.3 Distracted Driving

This unit must instruct driver-trainees in FMCSRs related to distracted driving and other key driver distraction driving issues, including improper cell phone use, texting, and use of in-cab technology (e.g., §§392.80 and 392.82). This instruction will include training in the following aspects: Visual attention (keeping eyes on the road); manual control (keeping hands on the wheel); and cognitive awareness (keeping mind on the task and safe operation of the CMV).

Unit B1.2.4 Speed Management

This unit must teach driver-trainees how to manage speed effectively in response to various road, weather, and traffic conditions. The instruction must include methods for calibrating safe following distances under an array of conditions including traffic, weather and CMV weight and length.

Unit B1.2.5 Space Management

This unit must teach driver-trainees about the importance of managing the space surrounding the vehicle under various traffic and road conditions.

Unit B1.2.6 Night Operation

This unit must instruct driver-trainees in the factors affecting the safe operation of CMVs at night and in darkness. Additionally, driver-trainees must be instructed in changes in vision, communications, speed, space management, and proper use of lights, as needed, to deal with the special problems night driving presents.

Unit B1.2.7 Extreme Driving Conditions

This unit must teach driver-trainees the specific problems presented by extreme driving conditions. The training will emphasize the factors affecting the operation of CMVs in cold, hot, and inclement weather and on steep grades and sharp curves. The training providers must teach driver-trainees the proper tire chaining procedures in this unit.

Section B1.3 Advanced Operating Practices

This section must introduce higher-level skills that can be acquired only after the more fundamental skills and knowledge taught in the prior two sections have been mastered. The training providers must teach driver-trainees the advanced skills necessary to recognize potential hazards and must teach driver-trainees the procedures needed to handle a CMV when faced with a hazard.

Unit B1.3.1 Hazard Perception

The unit must provide instruction for recognizing potential hazards in the driving environment in order to reduce the severity of the hazard and neutralize possible emergency situations. The training providers must teach driver-trainees to identify road conditions and other road users that are a potential threat to the safety of the CMV and suggest appropriate adjustments. The instruction must emphasize hazard recognition, visual search, adequate surveillance, and response to possible emergency-producing situations encountered by CMV drivers in various traffic situations. The training providers must also teach driver-trainees to recognize potential dangers and the safety procedures that must be utilized while driving in construction/work zones.

Unit B1.3.2 Skid Control/Recovery, Jackknifing, and Other Emergencies

This unit must teach the causes of skidding and jackknifing and techniques for avoiding and recovering from them. The training providers must teach the importance of maintaining directional control and bringing the CMV to a stop in the shortest possible distance while operating over a slippery surface. This unit must provide instruction in appropriate responses when faced with CMV emergencies. This instruction must include evasive steering, emergency braking, and off-road recovery, as well as the proper response to brake failures, tire blowouts, hydroplaning, and rollovers. The instruction must include a review of unsafe acts and the role the acts play in producing or worsening hazardous situations.

Unit B1.3.3 Railroad-Highway Grade Crossings

This unit must teach driver-trainees to recognize potential dangers and appropriate safety procedures to utilize at railroad (RR)-highway grade crossings. This instruction must include an overview of various Federal/State RR grade crossing regulations, RR grade crossing environments, obstructed view conditions, clearance around the tracks, and rail signs and signals. The training providers must instruct driver-trainees that railroads have personnel available ("Emergency Notification Systems") to receive notification of any information relating to an unsafe condition at the RR-highway grade crossing or a disabled vehicle or other obstruction blocking a railroad track at the RR-highway grade crossing.

Section B1.4 Vehicle Systems and Reporting Malfunctions

This unit must provide entry-level driver-trainees with sufficient knowledge of the CMV and its systems and subsystems to ensure that they understand and respect their role in vehicle inspection, operation, and maintenance and the impact of those factors upon highway safety and operational efficiency.

Unit B1.4.1 Identification and Diagnosis of Malfunctions

This unit must teach driver-trainees to identify major vehicle systems. The goal is to explain their function and how to check all key vehicle systems, as appropriate (*e.g.*, engine, engine exhaust auxiliary systems, brakes, drive train, coupling systems, and suspension) to ensure their safe operation. Driver-trainees must be provided with a detailed description of each system, its importance to safe and efficient operation, and what is needed to keep the system in good operating condition.

Unit B1.4.2 Roadside Inspections

This unit must instruct driver-trainees on what to expect during a standard roadside inspection conducted by authorized personnel. The training providers must teach driver-trainees on what vehicle and driver violations are classified as out-of-service (OOS), including the ramifications and penalties for operating a CMV when subject to an OOS order as defined in section 390.5.

Unit B1.4.3 Maintenance

This unit must introduce driver-trainees to the basic servicing and checking procedures for various engine and vehicle components and to help develop their ability to perform preventive maintenance and simple emergency repairs.

Section B1.5 Non-Driving Activities

This section must teach driver-trainees activities that do not involve actually operating the CMV, *e.g.,* proper cargo securement.

Unit B1.5.1 Handling and Documenting Cargo

This unit must teach driver-trainees the basic theory of cargo weight distribution, cargo securement on the vehicle, cargo covering, and techniques for safe and efficient loading/unloading. The training providers must also teach driver-trainees the basic cargo security/cargo theft prevention procedures. The training providers must teach driver-trainees the basic information regarding the proper handling and documentation of HM cargo.

Unit B1.5.2 Environmental Compliance Issues

This unit must teach driver-trainees to recognize environmental hazards and issues related to the CMV and load, and also make aware that city, county, State, and Federal requirements may apply to such circumstances.

Unit B1.5.3 Hours of Service Requirements

This unit must teach driver-trainees to understand that there are different hours-of-service (HOS) requirements applicable to different industries. The training providers must teach driver-trainees all applicable HOS regulatory requirements. The training providers must teach driver-trainees to complete a Driver's Daily Log (electronic and paper), timesheet, and logbook recap, as appropriate. The training providers must teach driver-trainees the consequences (safety, legal, and personal) of violating the HOS regulations, including the fines and penalties imposed for these types of violations.

Unit B1.5.4 Fatigue and Wellness Awareness

The issues and consequences of chronic and acute driver fatigue and the importance of staying alert will be covered in this unit. The training providers must teach driver-trainees about wellness and basic health maintenance information that affect a driver's ability to safely operate a CMV.

Unit B1.5.5 Post-Crash Procedures

This unit must teach driver-trainees the appropriate post-crash procedures, including the requirement that the driver, if possible, assess his or her physical condition immediately after the crash and notify authorities, or assign the task to other individuals at the crash scene. The training providers must teach driver-trainees how to protect the area; obtain emergency medical assistance; move on-road vehicles off the road in minor crashes so as to avoid subsequent crashes or injuries; engage flashers; place reflective triangles and other warning devices for stopped vehicles; and properly use a fire extinguisher, if necessary. The training providers must instruct driver-trainees in post-crash testing requirements related to controlled substances and alcohol.

Unit B1.5.6 External Communications

This unit must instruct driver-trainees in the value of effective interpersonal communication techniques/skills to interact with enforcement officials. The training providers must teach driver-trainees the specifics of the roadside vehicle inspection process, and what to expect during this activity. Driver-trainees who are not native English speakers must be instructed in FMCSA English language proficiency requirements and the consequences for violations. The training providers must teach driver-trainees the implications of violating Federal and state regulations will have on their driving records and their employing motor carrier's records.

Unit B1.5.7 Whistleblower/Coercion

This unit must teach the driver-trainees about the right of an employee to question the safety practices of an employer without incurring the risk of losing a job or being subject to reprisals simply for stating a safety concern. The training providers must instruct driver-trainees in the whistleblower protection regulations in 29 CFR part 1978. The training providers must teach driver-trainees the procedures for reporting to FMCSA incidents of coercion from motor carriers, shippers, receivers, or transportation intermediaries.

Unit B1.5.8 Trip Planning

This unit must address the importance of and requirements for planning routes and trips. This instruction must address planning the safest route, planning for rest stops, heavy traffic areas, railroad-highway grade crossing safe clearance and ground clearance (*i.e.,* "high center"), the importance of Federal and State requirements on the need for permits, and vehicle size and weight limitations. The training providers must teach driver-trainees the correct identification of restricted routes, the pros and cons of Global Positioning System (GPS)/trip routing software, and the importance of selecting fuel-efficient routes.

Unit B1.5.9 Drugs/Alcohol

This unit must teach driver-trainees the rules applicable to controlled substances (including prescription drugs) and alcohol use and testing related to the operation of a CMV.

Unit B1.5.10 Medical Requirements

This unit must teach driver-trainees the Federal rules on medical certification, medical examination procedures, general qualifications, responsibilities, and disqualifications based on various offenses, orders, and loss of driving privileges (49 CFR part 391, subparts B and E).

Behind-the-Wheel Range

This unit must teach driving exercises related to basic vehicle control skills and mastery of basic maneuvers, as covered in §§383.111 and 383.113 of this chapter necessary to operate the vehicle safely. The training providers must teach driver-trainees activities in this unit on a driving range as defined in §380.605. The training provider must teach "Get Out and Look" (GOAL) to the driver-trainee as it applies to units B2.2-2.6.

Unit B2.1 Vehicle Inspection Pre-Trip/Enroute/Post-Trip

Driver-trainees must demonstrate proficiency in conducting pre-trip and post-trip inspections as specified in §§392.7 and 396.11, including appropriate inspection locations. Instruction must also be provided on enroute vehicle inspections.

Unit B2.2 Straight Line Backing

Driver-trainees must demonstrate proficiency in proper techniques for performing various straight line backing maneuvers to appropriate criteria/acceptable tolerances.

Unit B2.3 Alley Dock Backing (45/90 Degree)

Driver-trainees must demonstrate proficiency in proper techniques for performing 45/90 degree alley dock maneuvers to appropriate criteria/acceptable tolerances.

Unit B2.4 Off-Set Backing

Driver-trainees must demonstrate proficiency in proper techniques for performing off-set backing maneuvers to appropriate criteria/acceptable tolerances.

Unit B2.5 Parallel Parking Blind Side

Driver-trainees must demonstrate proficiency in proper techniques for performing parallel parking blind side positions/maneuvers to appropriate criteria/acceptable tolerances.

Unit B2.6 Parallel Parking Sight Side

Driver-trainees must demonstrate proficiency in proper techniques for performing sight side parallel parking maneuvers to appropriate criteria/acceptable tolerances.

Behind-the-Wheel Public Road

The instructor must engage in active two-way communication with the driver-trainees during all active BTW public road training sessions. Skills described in paragraphs B3.8 through 3.12 of this section must be discussed during public road training, but not necessarily performed. Driver-trainees are not required to demonstrate proficiency in the skills described in paragraphs B3.8 through 3.12.

Unit B3.1 Vehicle Controls Including: Left Turns, Right Turns, Lane Changes, Curves at Highway Speeds, and Entry and Exit on the Interstate or Controlled Access Highway

Driver-trainees must demonstrate proficiency in proper techniques for initiating vehicle movement, executing left and right turns, changing lanes, navigating curves at speed, exiting and entering the interstate, and stopping the vehicle in a controlled manner.

Unit B3.2 Shifting/Transmission

Driver-trainees must demonstrate proficiency in proper techniques for performing safe and fuel-efficient shifting.

Unit B3.3 Communications/Signaling

Driver-trainees must demonstrate proficiency in proper techniques for signaling intentions and effectively communicating with other drivers.

Unit B3.4 Visual Search

Driver-trainees must demonstrate proficiency in proper techniques for visually searching the road for potential hazards and critical objects.

Unit B3.5 Speed and Space Management

Driver-trainees must demonstrate proficiency in proper habits and techniques for adjusting and maintaining vehicle speed, taking into consideration various factors such as traffic and road conditions. Driver-trainees must demonstrate proficiency in maintaining proper speed to keep appropriate spacing between the driver-trainee's CMV and other vehicles. Instruction must include methods for calibrating safe following distances under an array of conditions including traffic, weather, and CMV weight and length.

Unit B3.6 Safe Driver Behavior

Driver-trainees must demonstrate proficiency in safe driver behavior during their operation of the CMV.

Unit B3.7 Hours of Service (HOS) Requirements

Driver-trainees must demonstrate proficiency in the basic activities required by the HOS regulations, such as completing a Driver's Daily Log (electronic and paper), timesheet, and logbook recap, as appropriate.

Unit B3.8 Hazard Perception

Driver-trainees must demonstrate their ability to recognize potential hazards in the driving environment in time to reduce the severity of the hazard and neutralize possible emergency situations. Driver-trainees must demonstrate the ability to identify road conditions and other road users that are a potential threat to vehicle safety and suggest appropriate adjustments.

Unit B3.9 Railroad (RR)-Highway Grade Crossing

Driver-trainees must demonstrate the ability to recognize potential dangers and to demonstrate appropriate safety procedures when RR-highway grade crossings are reasonably available.

Unit B3.10 Night Operation

Driver-trainees must be familiar with how to operate a CMV safely at night. Training providers must teach driver-trainees that night driving presents specific circumstances that require heightened attention on the part of the driver. Driver-trainees must be taught special requirements for night vision, communications, speed, space management, and proper use of lights.

Unit B3.11 Extreme Driving Conditions

Driver-trainees must be familiar with the special risks created by, and the heightened precautions required by, driving CMVs under extreme driving conditions, such as heavy rain, high wind, high heat, fog, snow, ice, steep grades, and curves. Training providers must teach driver-trainees the basic driving habits needed to deal with the specific challenges presented by these extreme driving conditions.

Unit B3.12 Skid Control/Recovery, Jackknifing, and Other Emergencies

Driver-trainees must know the causes of skidding and jackknifing and techniques for avoiding and recovering from them. Driver-trainees must know how to maintain directional control and bring the CMV to a stop in the shortest possible distance while operating over a slippery surface. Driver-trainees must be familiar with proper techniques for responding to CMV emergencies, such as evasive steering, emergency braking, and off-road recovery. They must also know how to prevent or respond to brake failures, tire blowouts, hydroplaning, and rollovers.

Appendix C to Part 380—Passenger Endorsement Training Curriculum

Editor's Note: This Appendix has a compliance date of February 7, 2022.

Passenger (P) endorsement applicants must complete the curriculum outlined in this section, which applies to driver-trainees who expect to operate CMVs in the any of the vehicle groups defined in §383.91(a)(1)-(3) for which a P endorsement is required.

There is no required minimum number of instruction hours for theory training, but the training provider must cover all the topics set forth in the curriculum. There is no required minimum number of instruction hours for BTW training, but training providers must determine whether driver-trainees have demonstrated proficiency in all elements of the BTW curriculum. Training instructors must document the total number of clock hours each driver-trainee spends to complete the BTW curriculum. The training must be conducted in a passenger vehicle of the same vehicle group as the applicant intends to drive. The passenger endorsement training must, at a minimum, contain the following:

Theory Instruction

Unit C1.1 Post-Crash Procedures

This unit must teach driver-trainees appropriate post-crash procedures, including the requirement that the driver, if possible, assess his or her physical condition immediately after the crash and notify authorities, or assign the task to a passenger or other individuals at the crash scene. Also, training providers must teach driver-trainees how to obtain emergency medical assistance; move on-road vehicles off the road in minor crashes so as to avoid subsequent crashes or injuries; engage flashers, reflective triangles and other warning devices for stopped vehicles; and properly use a fire extinguisher if necessary.

Unit C1.2 Other Emergency Procedures

This unit must instruct driver-trainees in managing security breaches, onboard fires, emergency exit and passenger evacuation training, medical emergencies, and emergency stopping procedures including the deployment of various emergency hazard signals. Instruction must also include procedures for dealing with mechanical breakdowns and vehicle defects while enroute.

Unit C1.3 Vehicle Orientation

This unit must teach driver-trainees the basic physical and operational characteristics of passenger-carrying CMV (*e.g.* bus and motor coach), including overall height, length, width, ground clearances, rear overhang, Gross Vehicle Weight and Gross Vehicle Weight Rating, axle weights, wheels and rims, tires, tire ratings, mirrors, steer wheels, lighting, windshield, windshield wipers, engine compartments, basic electrical system, brake systems, as applicable, and spare tire storage. Additionally, training providers must instruct driver-trainees in techniques for proper driver seat and mirror adjustments.

Unit C1.4 Pre-Trip, Enroute, and Post-Trip Inspection

This unit must teach the driver-trainee the importance of pre-trip, enroute, and post-trip inspections; and provide instruction in techniques for conducting such inspections as stated in §§392.7 and 396.11, and demonstrate their ability to inspect the following:

(1) Emergency exits;

(2) Passenger-carrying CMV interiors (including passenger seats as applicable);

(3) Restrooms and associated environmental requirements;

(4) Temperature controls (for maintaining passenger comfort);

(5) Driver and passenger seat belts.

Additionally, training providers must instruct driver-trainees in procedures, as applicable, in security-related inspections, including inspections for unusual wires or other abnormal visible materials, interior and exterior luggage compartments, packages or luggage left behind, and signs of cargo or vehicle tampering. Finally, training providers must instruct driver-trainees in cycling-accessible lifts and procedures for inspecting them for functionality and defects.

Unit C1.5 Fueling

This unit must instruct driver-trainees on the significance of avoiding refueling a bus while passengers are onboard and the imperative of avoiding refueling in an enclosed space.

Unit C1.6 Idling

This unit must teach driver-trainees the importance of compliance with State and local laws and regulations, including for example, idling limits, fuel savings; and the consequences of non-compliance, including adverse health effects and penalties.

Unit C1.7 Baggage and/or Cargo Management

In this unit, training providers must teach driver-trainees:

(1) Proper methods for handling and securing passenger baggage and containers, as applicable.

(2) Procedures for identifying and inspecting baggage and containers for prohibited items, such as hazardous materials.

(3) Proper handling and securement of devices associated with the Americans with Disabilities Act (ADA) compliance, including oxygen, wheeled mobility devices, and other associated apparatuses.

Unit C1.8 Passenger Safety Awareness Briefing

This unit must teach driver-trainees how to brief passengers on safety topics including fastening seat belts, emergency exits, emergency phone contact information, fire extinguisher location, safely walking in the aisle when the bus is moving, and restroom emergency push button or switch.

Unit C1.9 Passenger Management

In this unit, training providers must teach driver-trainees:

(1) Proper procedures for safe loading and unloading of passengers prior to departure, including rules concerning standing passengers and the standee line.

(2) Procedures for dealing with disruptive passengers.

Unit C1.10 Americans With Disabilities Act (ADA) Compliance

Along with addressing the proper operation of accessibility equipment (*e.g.*, lifts), this must teach driver-trainees the applicable regulations and proper procedures for engaging persons with disabilities or special needs under the ADA. Training must cover passengers with mobility issues, engaging passengers with sight, hearing, or cognitive impairments, and recognizing the permitted use of service animals.

Unit C1.11 Hours of Service (HOS) Requirements

This unit must teach driver-trainees the HOS regulations that apply to drivers for interstate passenger carriers. Training providers must teach driver-trainees the basic activities required by the HOS regulations, such as completing a Driver's Daily Log (electronic and paper), timesheet, and logbook recap, as appropriate. Training providers must teach driver-trainees how to recognize the signs of fatigue and basic fatigue countermeasures as a means to avoid crashes.

Unit C1.12 Safety Belt Safety

This unit must teach driver-trainees the Federal rules governing the proper use of safety restraint systems by CMV drivers, as set forth in §392.16.

Unit C1.13 Distracted Driving

This unit must teach driver-trainees FMCSA regulations that prohibit drivers from texting or using hand-held mobile phones while operating their vehicles (*e.g.*, §§392.80 and 392.82); and must teach the serious consequences of violations, including crashes, heavy fines, and impacts on a motor carrier's and/or driver's safety records, such as driver disqualification.

Unit C1.14 Railroad (RR)-Highway Grade Crossings and Drawbridges

This unit must instruct driver-trainees in applicable regulations, techniques, and procedures for navigating RR-highway grade crossings and drawbridges appropriate to passenger buses.

Unit C1.15 Weigh Stations

This unit must teach driver-trainees the weigh-station regulations that apply to buses.

Unit C1.16 Security and Crime

This unit must teach driver-trainees the basic techniques for recognizing and minimizing physical risks from criminal activities.

Unit C1.17 Roadside Inspections

This unit must teach driver-trainees what to expect during a standard roadside inspection conducted by authorized personnel. Training providers must teach driver-trainees what passenger-carrying vehicle and driver violations are classified as out-of-service (OOS), including the ramifications and penalties for operating a CMV when subject to an OOS order as defined in §390.5.

Unit C1.18 Penalties and Fines

This unit must teach driver-trainees the potential consequences of violating driver-related regulations, including impacts on driver and motor carrier safety records, adverse impacts on the driver's Pre-employment Screening Program record; financial penalties for both the driver and carrier; and possible loss of CMV driving privileges.

Behind the Wheel—Range and Public Road

This BTW training consists of exercises related to basic vehicle control skills and mastery of basic maneuvers necessary to operate the vehicle safely. Activities in this unit will take place on a driving range or a public road as defined in §380.605. The instructor must engage in active communication with the driver-trainees during all BTW training sessions.

Unit C2.1 Vehicle Orientation

Driver-trainees must demonstrate their familiarity with basic passenger-carrying CMV physical and operational characteristics including overall height, length, width, ground clearances, rear overhang, gross vehicle weight and gross vehicle weight rating, axle weights, wheels and rims, tires, tire ratings, mirrors, steer wheels, lighting, windshield, windshield wipers, engine compartments, basic electric system, and spare tire storage. Additionally, driver-trainees must demonstrate techniques for proper driver's seat and mirror adjustments.

Unit C2.2 Pre-Trip, Enroute, and Post-Trip Inspection

Driver-trainees must demonstrate proficiency in conducting such pre-trip, enroute and post-trip inspections of buses and key components of §§392.7 and 396.11, and demonstrate their ability to inspect the following:

(1) Emergency exits;

(2) Passenger-carrying CMV interiors (including passenger seats as applicable);

(3) Restrooms and associated environmental requirements;

(4) Temperature controls (for maintaining passenger comfort); and

(5) Driver and passenger seat belts.

Additionally, driver-trainees must demonstrate their knowledge of procedures, as applicable, in security-related inspections, including inspections for unusual wires or other abnormal visible materials, interior and exterior luggage compartments, packages or luggage left behind, and signs of cargo or vehicle tampering. Driver-trainees must be familiar with the operation of cycling-accessible lifts and the procedures for inspecting them for functionality and defects. For passenger-carrying vehicles equipped with said lifts and tie-down positions, trainee must demonstrate their ability to operate the cycling-accessible lifts.

Unit C2.3 Baggage and/or Cargo Management

In this unit, driver-trainees must demonstrate their ability to:

(1) Properly handle passenger baggage and containers to avoid worker, passenger, and non-passenger related injuries and property damage;

(2) Visually inspect baggage and containers for prohibited items, such as hazardous materials and identify such items;

(3) Properly handle and secure devices associated with ADA compliance including oxygen, wheeled mobility devices, and other associated apparatuses.

Unit C2.4 Passenger Safety Awareness Briefing

Driver-trainees must demonstrate their ability to brief passengers on safety on topics including: Fastening seat belts, emergency exits, emergency phone contact information, fire extinguisher location, safely walking in the aisle when the bus is moving, and restroom emergency push button or switch.

Unit C2.5 Passenger Management

In this unit, driver-trainees must demonstrate their ability to safely load and unload passengers prior to departure and to deal with disruptive passengers.

Unit C2.6 Railroad-Highway Grade Crossings

Driver-trainees must demonstrate proper procedures for safely navigating railroad-highway grade crossings in a passenger-carrying CMV.

Appendix D to Part 380—School Bus Endorsement Training Curriculum

Editor's Note: This Appendix has a compliance date of February 7, 2022.

School bus (S) endorsement applicants must complete the curriculum outlined in this section, which applies to driver-trainees who expect to operate a "school bus" as defined in §383.5. There is no required minimum number of instruction hours for theory training, but the training provider must cover all the topics set forth in the curriculum. There is no required minimum number of instruction hours for BTW training, but the training provider must determine whether driver-trainees have demonstrated proficiency in all elements of the BTW curriculum. Training instructors must document the total number of clock hours each driver-trainee spends to complete the BTW curriculum. The training must be conducted in a school bus of the same vehicle group as the applicant intends to drive. The school bus endorsement training must, at a minimum, include the following:

Theory Instruction

Unit D1.1 Danger Zones and Use of Mirrors

This unit must teach driver-trainees the danger zones that exist around the school bus and the techniques to ensure the safety of those around the bus. These techniques include correct mirror adjustment and usage. The types of mirrors and their use must be discussed, as well as the requirements found in Federal Motor Vehicle Safety Standard (FMVSS) 111 (49 CFR 571.111). Training providers must teach driver-trainees the dangers of "dart-outs." Training providers must teach driver-trainees the importance of training students how to keep out of the danger zone when around school buses and the techniques for doing so.

Unit D1.2 Loading and Unloading

This unit must be instruct driver-trainees on the laws and regulations for loading and unloading, as well as the required procedures for students waiting at a bus stop and crossing the roadway at a bus stop. Special dangers involved in loading and unloading must be specifically discussed, including procedures to ensure the danger zone is clear and that no student has been caught in the doorway prior to moving the vehicle. Instruction also must be included on the proper use of lights, stop arms, crossing gates, and safe operation of the door during loading and unloading; the risks involved with leaving students unattended on a school bus; and the proper techniques for checking the bus for sleeping children and lost items at the end of each route.

Unit D1.3 Vehicle Orientation

This unit must teach driver-trainees the basic physical and operational characteristics of school buses, including overall height, length, width, ground clearances, rear overhang, Gross Vehicle Weight and Gross Vehicle Weight Rating, axle weights, wheels and rims, tires, tire ratings, mirrors, steer wheels, lighting, windshield, windshield wipers, engine compartments, basic electrical system, brake systems, as applicable, and spare tire storage. Additionally, the training providers must instruct driver-trainees in techniques for proper driver seat and mirror adjustments.

Unit D1.4 Post-Crash Procedures

This unit must instruct driver-trainees on the proper procedures following a school bus crash. The instruction must include use of fire extinguisher(s), first aid kit(s), tending to injured passengers, post-crash vehicle securement, notification procedures, deciding whether to evacuate the bus, data gathering, and interaction with law enforcement officials.

Unit D1.5 Emergency Exit and Evacuation

This unit must teach driver-trainees their role in safely evacuating the bus in an emergency and planning for an emergency in advance. Training must include proper evacuation methods and procedures, such as the safe evacuation of students on field and activity trips who only occasionally ride school buses and thus may not be familiar with the procedures.

Unit D1.6 Railroad-Highway Grade Crossings

This unit must teach driver-trainees the dangers trains present and the importance of the school bus driver and students strictly following railroad crossing procedures. Instruction must be given on the types of crossings, warning signs and devices, and State and local procedures and regulations for school buses when crossing railroad-highway grade crossings.

Unit D1.7 Student Management

This unit must teach driver-trainees how to manage student behavior on the bus to ensure that safety is maintained and the rights of others are respected. Specific student management techniques must be discussed, including warning signs of bullying and the techniques for managing student behavior and administering discipline. Training providers must teach driver-trainees to avoid becoming distracted by student behavior while driving, especially when crossing railroad tracks and during loading and unloading.

Unit D1.8 Special Safety Considerations

This unit must teach the driver-trainees the special safety considerations and equipment in school bus operations. Topics discussed must include use of strobe lights, driving in high winds, safe backing techniques, and preventing tail swing crashes.

Unit D1.9 Pre- and Post-Trip Inspections

This unit must teach the driver-trainees the importance of pre-trip, enroute, and post-trip inspections; and provide instruction in techniques for conducting

PART 380

such inspections of buses as stated in §§392.7 and 396.11, and additionally demonstrate their ability to inspect the following:

(1) Stop arms,

(2) Crossing arms,

(3) Emergency exits,

(4) Fire extinguishers,

(5) Passenger seats,

(6) First aid kits,

(7) Interior lights, and

(8) Temperature control (for maintaining passenger comfort).

Training providers must instruct driver-trainees in State and local requirements, as applicable, for inspection of school bus equipment.

Unit D1.10 School Bus Security

This unit must teach driver-trainees the security issues facing school bus drivers. Training providers must also teach driver-trainees potential security threats, techniques for preventing and responding to security threats, how to recognize and report suspicious behavior, and what to do in the event of a hijacking or attack on a school bus.

Unit D1.11 Route and Stop Reviews

This unit must teach driver-trainees the importance of planning their routes prior to beginning driving in order to avoid distraction while on the road. The training provider must also teach driver-trainees the techniques for reviewing routes and stops, as well as State and local procedures for reporting hazards along the route and at bus stops.

Behind the Wheel—Range and Public Road

This unit must consist of exercises related to basic vehicle control skills and mastery of basic maneuvers. Activities in this unit will take place on a driving range or a public road as defined in §380.605. The instructor must engage in active communication with the driver-trainees during all active training sessions.

Unit D2.1 Danger Zones and Use of Mirrors

Driver-trainees must demonstrate the techniques necessary to ensure the safety of persons in the danger zone around the bus. Driver-trainees must practice mirror adjustment and usage. The types of mirrors and their use are shown, and cones used to demonstrate the requirements of 49 CFR 571.111.

Unit D2.2 Loading and Unloading

Driver-trainees must demonstrate the loading and unloading techniques learned in the theory portion of the training. Driver-trainees must demonstrate checking the vehicle for sleeping children and lost items at the end of the route.

Unit D2.3 Emergency Exit and Evacuation

Driver-trainees must demonstrate their role in safely evacuating the bus in an emergency.

Unit D2.4 Special Safety Considerations

Driver-trainees must demonstrate safe backing techniques and demonstrate their ability to avoid tail swing crashes by using reference points when making turns.

Unit D2.5 Pre- and Post-Trip Inspections

Driver-trainees must demonstrate proficiency in conducting pre-and post-trip inspections, as stated in §§392.7 and 396.11, and of school bus-specific equipment, such as mirrors, stop arms, crossing arms, emergency exits, fire extinguishers, passenger seats, first aid kits, interior lights, and temperature control.

Unit D2.6 Railroad-Highway Grade Crossings

Driver-trainees must demonstrate proper procedures for safely navigating railroad-highway grade crossings in a school bus.

Appendix E to Part 380—Hazardous Materials Endorsement Training Curriculum

Editor's Note: This Appendix has a compliance date of February 7, 2022.

Hazardous materials (H) endorsement applicants must complete the Hazardous materials curriculum, which apply to driver-trainees who intend to operate CMVs used in the transportation of hazardous materials (HM) as defined in §383.5. Driver-trainees seeking an H endorsement, as defined in §383.93(c)(4), must complete this curriculum in order to take the State-administered knowledge test for the H endorsement. There is no required minimum number of instruction hours for theory training, but the training provider must cover all the topics in the curriculum. The HM curriculum must, at a minimum, include the following:

Theory Instruction

Unit E1.1 Basic Introductory HM Requirements

This unit must teach driver-trainees the basic HM competencies, including applicable FMCSR requirements when HM is being transported. The training provider must also teach driver-trainees HM communication requirements including: Shipping paper requirements, marking, labeling, placarding, emergency response information, and shipper's responsibilities.

Unit E1.2 Operational HM Requirements

This unit must teach driver-trainees the basic competencies for transportation of HM.

Unit E1.3 Reporting HM Crashes and Releases

The unit must teach driver-trainees the proper procedures and contacts for the immediate notification related to certain HM incidents, including instruction in the proper completion and submission of HM Incident Reports.

Unit E.4 Tunnels and Railroad (RR)-Highway Grade Crossing Requirements

This unit must teach driver-trainees the proper operation of an HM vehicle at RR-highway grade crossings and in vehicular tunnels.

Unit E1.5 Loading and Unloading HM

This unit must teach driver-trainees the proper loading and unloading procedures for hazardous material cargo. Training providers must also teach driver-trainees the requirements for proper segregation and securement of HM, and the prohibitions on transporting certain solid and liquid poisons with foodstuffs.

Unit E1.6 HM on Passenger Vehicles

This unit must teach driver-trainees the various requirements for vehicles transporting passengers and property, and the types and quantities of HM that can and cannot be transported in these vehicles/situations.

Unit E1.7 Bulk Packages

This unit must teach driver-trainees the specialized requirements for transportation of cargo in bulk packages, including cargo tanks, intermediate bulk containers, bulk cylinders and portable tanks. The unit must include training in the operation of emergency control features, special vehicle handling characteristics, rollover prevention, and the properties and hazards of the HM transported. Training providers must teach driver-trainees methods specifically designed to reduce cargo tank rollovers including, but not limited to, vehicle design and performance, load effects, highway factors, and driver factors.

Unit E1.8 Operating Emergency Equipment

This unit must teach driver-trainees the applicable requirements of the FMCSRs and the procedures necessary for the safe operation of the motor vehicle. This includes training in special precautions for fires, loading and unloading, operation of cargo tank motor vehicle equipment, and shut-off/shutdown equipment.

Unit E1.9 Emergency Response Procedures

This unit must teach driver-trainees the proper procedures and best practices for handling an emergency response and post-response operations, including what to do in the event of an unintended release of an HM. All training, preparation, and response efforts must focus on the hazards of the materials that have been released and the protection of people, property, and the environment.

Unit E1.10 Engine (Fueling)

This unit must teach driver-trainees the procedures for fueling a vehicle that contains HM.

Unit E1.11 Tire Check

This unit must teach driver-trainees the proper procedures for checking the vehicle tires at the start of a trip and each time the vehicle is parked.

Unit E1.12 Routes and Route Planning

This unit must teach driver-trainees the proper routing procedures that they are required to follow for the transportation of radioactive and non-radioactive HM.

Unit E1.13 Hazardous Materials Safety Permits (HMSP)

This unit must teach driver-trainees the proper procedures and operational requirements including communications, constant attendance, and parking that apply to the transportation of HM for which an HMSP is required.

Appendix F to Part 380—LCV Driver Training Programs, Required Knowledge and Skills

The following table lists topics of instruction required for drivers of longer combination vehicles pursuant to 49 CFR part 380, subpart B. The training courses for operators of LCV Doubles and LCV Triples must be distinct and tailored to address their unique operating and handling characteristics. Each course must include the minimum topics of instruction, including behind-the-wheel training designed to provide an opportunity to develop the skills outlined under the Proficiency Development unit of the training program. Only a skills instructor may administer behind-the-wheel training involving the operation of an LCV or one of its components. A classroom instructor may administer only instruction that does not involve the operation of an LCV or one of its components.

Table to the Appendix—Course topics for LCV drivers

Section 1: Orientation	
1.1	LCVs in Trucking
1.2	Regulatory Factors
1.3	Driver Qualifications
1.4	Vehicle Configuration Factors

Section 2: Basic Operation	
2.1	Coupling and Uncoupling
2.2	Basic Control and Handling
2.3	Basic Maneuvers
2.4	Turning, Steering and Tracking
2.5	Proficiency Development

Section 3: Safe Operating Practices	
3.1	Interacting with Traffic
3.2	Speed and Space Management
3.3	Night Operations
3.4	Extreme Driving Conditions
3.5	Security Issues
3.6	Proficiency Development

Section 4: Advanced Operations	
4.1	Hazard Perception
4.2	Hazardous Situations
4.3	Maintenance and Troubleshooting

Section 5: Non-Driving Activities	
5.1	Routes and Trip Planning
5.2	Cargo and Weight Considerations

Section 1—Orientation

The units in this section must provide an orientation to the training curriculum and must cover the role LCVs play within the motor carrier industry, the factors that affect their operations, and the role that drivers play in the safe operation of LCVs.

Unit 1.1—LCVs in Trucking. This unit must provide an introduction to the emergence of LCVs in trucking and must serve as an orientation to the course content. Emphasis must be placed upon the role the driver plays in transportation.

Unit 1.2—Regulatory factors. This unit must provide instruction addressing the Federal, State, and local governmental bodies that propose, enact, and implement the laws, rules, and regulations that affect the trucking industry. Emphasis must be placed on those regulatory factors that affect LCVs, including 23 CFR 658.23 and Appendix C to part 658.

Unit 1.3—Driver qualifications. This unit must provide classroom instruction addressing the Federal and State laws, rules, and regulations that define LCV driver qualifications. It also must include a discussion on medical examinations, drug and alcohol tests, certification, and basic health and wellness issues. Emphasis must be placed upon topics essential to physical and mental health maintenance, including (1) diet, (2) exercise, (3) avoidance of alcohol and drug abuse, and caution in the use of prescription and nonprescription drugs, (4) the adverse effects of driver fatigue, and (5) effective fatigue countermeasures. Driver-trainees who have successfully completed the Entry-level training segments at §380.503(a) and (c) are considered to have satisfied the requirements of Unit 1.3.

Unit 1.4—Vehicle configuration factors. This unit must provide classroom instruction addressing the key vehicle components used in the configuration of longer combination vehicles. It also must familiarize the driver-trainee with various vehicle combinations, as well as provide instruction about unique characteristics and factors associated with LCV configurations.

Section 2—Basic Operation

The units in this section must cover the interaction between the driver and the vehicle. They must teach driver-trainees how to couple and uncouple LCVs, ensure the vehicles are in proper operating condition, and control the motion of LCVs under various road and traffic conditions.

During the driving exercises at off-highway locations required by this section, the driver-trainee must first familiarize himself/herself with basic operating characteristics of an LCV. Utilizing an LCV, students must be able to perform the skills learned in each unit to a level of proficiency required to permit safe transition to on-street driving.

Unit 2.1—Coupling and uncoupling. This unit must provide instruction addressing the procedures for coupling and uncoupling LCVs. While vehicle coupling and uncoupling procedures are common to all truck-tractor/semi-trailer operations, some factors are peculiar to LCVs. Emphasis must be placed upon pre-planning and safe operating procedures.

Unit 2.2—Basic control and handling. This unit must provide an introduction to basic vehicular control and handling as it applies to LCVs. This must include instruction addressing brake performance, handling characteristics and factors affecting LCV stability while braking, turning, and cornering. Emphasis must be placed upon safe operating procedures.

Unit 2.3—Basic maneuvers. This unit must provide instruction addressing the basic vehicular maneuvers that will be encountered by LCV drivers. This must include instruction relative to backing, lane positioning and path selection, merging situations, and parking LCVs. Emphasis must be placed upon safe operating procedures as they apply to brake performance and directional stability while accelerating, braking, merging, cornering, turning, and parking.

Unit 2.4—Turning, steering, and tracking. This unit must provide instruction addressing turning situations, steering maneuvers, and the tracking of LCV trailers. This must include instruction related to trailer sway and off-tracking. Emphasis must be placed on maintaining directional stability.

Unit 2.5—Proficiency development: basic operations. The purpose of this unit is to enable driver-students to gain the proficiency in basic operation needed to safely undertake on-street instruction in the Safe Operations Practices section of the curriculum.

The activities of this unit must consist of driving exercises that provide practice for the development of basic control skills and mastery of basic maneuvers. Driver-students practice skills and maneuvers learned in the Basic Control and Handling; Basic Maneuvers; and Turning, Steering and Tracking units. A series of basic exercises is practiced at off-highway locations until students develop sufficient proficiency for transition to on-street driving.

Once the driver-student's skills have been measured and found adequate, the driver-student must be allowed to move to on-the-street driving.

Nearly all activity in this unit will take place on the driving range or on streets or roads that have low-density traffic conditions.

Section 3—Safe Operating Practices

The units in this section must cover the interaction between student drivers, the vehicle, and the traffic environment. They must teach driver-students how to apply their basic operating skills in a way that ensures their safety and that of other road users under various road, weather, and traffic conditions.

Unit 3.1—Interacting with traffic. This unit must provide instruction addressing the principles of visual search, communication, and sharing the road with other traffic. Emphasis must be placed upon visual search, mirror usage, signaling and/or positioning the vehicle to communicate, and understanding the special situations encountered by LCV drivers in various traffic situations.

Unit 3.2—Speed and space management. This unit must provide instruction addressing the principles of speed and space management. Emphasis must be placed upon maintaining safe vehicular speed and appropriate space surrounding the vehicle under various traffic and road conditions. Particular attention must be placed upon understanding the special situations encountered by LCVs in various traffic situations.

Unit 3.3—Night operations. This unit must provide instruction addressing the principles of Night Operations. Emphasis must be placed upon the factors affecting operation of LCVs at night. Night driving presents specific factors that require special attention on the part of the driver. Changes in vehicle safety inspection, vision, communications, speed management, and space management are needed to deal with the special problems night driving presents.

Unit 3.4—Extreme driving conditions. This unit must provide instruction addressing the driving of LCVs under extreme driving conditions. Emphasis must be placed upon the factors affecting the operation of LCVs in cold, hot, and inclement weather and in the mountains and desert. Changes in basic driving habits are needed to deal with the specific problems presented by these extreme driving conditions.

Unit 3.5—Security issues. This unit must include a discussion of security requirements imposed by the Department of Homeland Security, Transportation Security Administration; the U.S. Department of Transportation, Pipeline and Hazardous Materials Safety Administration; and any other State or Federal agency with responsibility for highway or motor carrier security.

Unit 3.6—Proficiency development. This unit must provide driver-students an opportunity to refine, within the on-street traffic environment, their vehicle handling skills learned in the first three sections. Driver-student performance progress must be closely monitored to determine when the level of proficiency required for carrying out the basic traffic maneuvers of stopping, turning, merging, straight driving, curves, lane changing, passing, driving on hills, driving through traffic restrictions, and parking has been attained. The driver-student must also be assessed for regulatory compliance with all traffic laws.

Nearly all activity in this unit will take place on public roadways in a full range of traffic environments applicable to this vehicle configuration. This must include urban and rural uncontrolled roadways, expressways or freeways, under light, moderate, and heavy traffic conditions. There must be a brief classroom session to familiarize driver-students with the type of on-street maneuvers they will perform and how their performance will be rated.

The instructor must assess the level of skill development of the driver-student and must increase in difficulty, based upon the level of skill attained, the types of maneuvers, roadways and traffic conditions to which the driver-student is exposed.

Section 4—Advanced Operations

The units in this section must introduce higher level skills that can be acquired only after the more fundamental skills and knowledge taught in sections two and three have been mastered. They must teach the perceptual skills necessary to recognize potential hazards, and must demonstrate the procedures needed to handle an LCV when faced with a hazard.

The Maintenance and Trouble-shooting Unit must provide instruction that addresses how to keep the vehicle in safe and efficient operating condition. The purpose of this unit is to teach the correct way to perform simple maintenance tasks, and how to troubleshoot and report those vehicle discrepancies or deficiencies that must be repaired by a qualified mechanic.

Unit 4.1—Hazard perception. This unit must provide instruction addressing the principles of recognizing hazards in sufficient time to reduce the severity of the hazard and neutralize a possible emergency situation. While hazards are present in all motor vehicle traffic operations, some are peculiar to LCV operations. Emphasis must be placed upon hazard recognition, visual search, and response to possible emergency-producing situations encountered by LCV drivers in various traffic situations.

Unit 4.2—Hazardous situations. This unit must address dealing with specific procedures appropriate for LCV emergencies. These must include evasive steering, emergency braking, off-road recovery, brake failures, tire blowouts, rearward amplification, hydroplaning, skidding, jackknifing and the rollover phenomenon. The discussion must include a review of unsafe acts and the role they play in producing hazardous situations.

Unit 4.3—Maintenance and trouble-shooting. This unit must introduce driver-students to the basic servicing and checking procedures for the various vehicle components and provide knowledge of conducting preventive maintenance functions, making simple emergency repairs, and diagnosing and reporting vehicle malfunctions.

Section 5—Non-Driving Activities

The units in this section must cover activities that are not directly related to the vehicle itself but must be performed by an LCV driver. The units in this section must ensure these activities are performed in a manner that ensures the safety of the driver, vehicle, cargo, and other road users.

Unit 5.1—Routes and trip planning. This unit must address the importance of and requirements for planning routes and trips. This must include classroom discussion of Federal and State requirements for a number of topics including permits, vehicle size and weight limitations, designated highways, local access, the reasonable access rule, staging areas, and access zones.

Unit 5.2—Cargo and weight considerations. This unit must address the importance of proper cargo documentation, loading, securing and unloading cargo, weight distribution, load sequencing and trailer placement. Emphasis must be placed on the importance of axle weight distribution, as well as on trailer placement and its effect on vehicle handling.

PART 382—CONTROLLED SUBSTANCES AND ALCOHOL USE AND TESTING

Subpart A—General

Subpart B—Prohibitions

Subpart C—Tests Required

Subpart D—Handling of Test Results, Record Retention, and Confidentiality

Subpart E—Consequences for Drivers Engaging in Substance Use-Related Conduct

Authority: 49 U.S.C. 31133, 31136, 31301 *et seq.*, 31502; sec. 32934 of Pub. L. 112-141, 126 Stat. 405, 830; and 49 CFR 1.87.

Subpart A—General

§382.101 Purpose.

The purpose of this part is to establish programs designed to help prevent accidents and injuries resulting from the misuse of alcohol or use of controlled substances by drivers of commercial motor vehicles.

§382.103 Applicability.

(a) This part applies to service agents and to every person and to all employers of such persons who operate a commercial motor vehicle in commerce in any State and are subject to:

(1) The commercial driver's license requirements of part 383 of this subchapter;

(2) The Licencia Federal de Conductor (Mexico) requirements; or

(3) The commercial drivers license requirements of the Canadian National Safety Code.

(b) An employer who employs himself/herself as a driver must comply with both the requirements in this part that apply to employers and the requirements in this part that apply to drivers. An employer who employs only himself/herself as a driver shall implement a random alcohol and controlled substances testing program of two or more covered employees in the random testing selection pool.

(c) The exceptions contained in §390.3(f) of this subchapter do not apply to this part. The employers and drivers identified in §390.3(f) of this subchapter must comply with the requirements of this part, unless otherwise specifically provided in paragraph (d) of this section.

(d) **Exceptions.** This part shall not apply to employers and their drivers:

(1) Required to comply only with the alcohol and/or controlled substances testing requirements of part 655 of this title (Federal Transit Administration alcohol and controlled substances testing regulations); or

(2) Who a State must waive from the requirements of part 383 of this subchapter. These individuals include active duty military personnel; members of the reserves; and members of the national guard on active duty, including personnel on full-time national guard duty, personnel on part-time national guard training and national guard military technicians (civilians who are required to wear military uniforms), and active duty U.S. Coast Guard personnel; or

(3) Who a State has, at its discretion, exempted from the requirements of part 383 of this subchapter. These individuals may be:

(i) Operators of a farm vehicle which is:

(A) Controlled and operated by a farmer;

(B) Used to transport either agricultural products, farm machinery, farm supplies, or both to or from a farm;

(C) Not used in the operations of a for-hire motor carrier, except for an exempt motor carrier as defined in §390.5 of this subchapter; and

(D) Used within 241 kilometers (150 miles) of the farmer's farm.

(ii) Firefighters or other persons who operate commercial motor vehicles which are necessary for the preservation of life or property or the execution of emergency governmental functions, are equipped with audible and visual signals, and are not subject to normal traffic regulation.

(4) Who operate "covered farm vehicles," as defined in 49 CFR 390.5.

§382.105 Testing procedures.

Each employer shall ensure that all alcohol or controlled substances testing conducted under this part complies with the procedures set forth in part 40 of this title. The provisions of part 40 of this title that address alcohol or controlled substances testing are made applicable to employers by this part.

§382.107 Definitions.

Words or phrases used in this part are defined in §§386.2 and 390.5 of this subchapter, and §40.3 of this title, except as provided in this section—

Actual knowledge for the purpose of subpart B of this part, means actual knowledge by an employer that a driver has used alcohol or controlled substances based on the employer's direct observation of the employee, information provided by the driver's previous employer(s), a traffic citation for driving a CMV while under the influence of alcohol or controlled substances or an employee's admission of alcohol or controlled substance use, except as provided in §382.121. Direct observation as used in this definition means observation of alcohol or controlled substances use and does not include observation of employee behavior or physical characteristics sufficient to warrant reasonable suspicion testing under §382.307. As used in this section, "traffic citation" means a ticket, complaint, or other document charging driving a CMV while under the influence of alcohol or controlled substances.

Alcohol means the intoxicating agent in beverage alcohol, ethyl alcohol, or other low molecular weight alcohols including methyl and isopropyl alcohol.

Alcohol concentration (or content) means the alcohol in a volume of breath expressed in terms of grams of alcohol per 210 liters of breath as indicated by an evidential breath test under this part.

Alcohol use means the drinking or swallowing of any beverage, liquid mixture or preparation (including any medication), containing alcohol.

Commerce means:

(1) Any trade, traffic or transportation within the jurisdiction of the United States between a place in a State and a place outside of such State, including a place outside of the United States; or

(2) Trade, traffic, and transportation in the United States which affects any trade, traffic, and transportation described in paragraph (1) of this definition.

Commercial Driver's License Drug and Alcohol Clearinghouse (Clearinghouse) means the FMCSA database that subpart G of this part requires employers and service agents to report information to and to query regarding drivers who are subject to the DOT controlled substance and alcohol testing regulations.

Commercial motor vehicle means a motor vehicle or combination of motor vehicles used in commerce to transport passengers or property if the vehicle

(1) Has a gross combination weight rating or gross combination weight of 11,794 kilograms or more (26,001 pounds or more), whichever is greater, inclusive of a towed unit(s) with a gross vehicle weight rating or gross vehicle weight of more than 4,536 kilograms (10,000 pounds), whichever is greater; or

(2) Has a gross vehicle weight rating or gross vehicle weight of 11,794 or more kilograms (26,001 or more pounds), whichever is greater; or

(3) Is designed to transport 16 or more passengers, including the driver; or

(4) Is of any size and is used in the transportation of materials found to be hazardous for the purposes of the Hazardous Materials Transportation Act (49 U.S.C. 5103(b)) and which require the motor vehicle to be placarded under the Hazardous Materials Regulations (49 CFR part 172, subpart F).

Confirmation (or confirmatory) drug test means a second analytical procedure performed on a urine specimen to identify and quantify the presence of a specific drug or drug metabolite.

Confirmation (or confirmatory) validity test means a second test performed on a urine specimen to further support a validity test result.

Confirmed drug test means a confirmation test result received by an MRO from a laboratory.

Consortium/Third party administrator (C/TPA) means a service agent that provides or coordinates one or more drug and/or alcohol testing services to DOT-regulated employers. C/TPAs typically provide or coordinate the provision of a number of such services and perform administrative tasks concerning the operation of the employers' drug and alcohol testing programs. This term includes, but is not limited to, groups of employers who join together to administer, as a single entity, the DOT drug and alcohol testing programs of its members (*e.g.,* having a combined random testing pool). C/TPAs are not "employers" for purposes of this part, except as provided in §382.705(c).

Controlled substances mean those substances identified in §40.85 of this title.

Designated employer representative (DER) is an individual identified by the employer as able to receive communications and test results from service agents and who is authorized to take immediate actions to remove employees from safety-sensitive duties and to make required decisions in the testing and evaluation processes. The individual must be an employee of the company. Service agents cannot serve as DERs.

Disabling damage means damage which precludes departure of a motor vehicle from the scene of the accident in its usual manner in daylight after simple repairs.

(1) **Inclusions.** Damage to motor vehicles that could have been driven, but would have been further damaged if so driven.

(2) **Exclusions.**

(i) Damage which can be remedied temporarily at the scene of the accident without special tools or parts.

(ii) Tire disablement without other damage even if no spare tire is available.

(iii) Headlight or taillight damage.

(iv) Damage to turn signals, horn, or windshield wipers which make them inoperative.

DOT Agency means an agency (or "operating administration") of the United States Department of Transportation administering regulations requiring alcohol and/or drug testing (14 CFR parts 61, 63, 65, 121, and 135; 49 CFR parts 199, 219, 382, and 655), in accordance with part 40 of this title.

Driver means any person who operates a commercial motor vehicle. This includes, but is not limited to: Full time, regularly employed drivers; casual, intermittent or occasional drivers; leased drivers and independent owner-operator contractors.

Employer means a person or entity employing one or more employees (including an individual who is self-employed) that is subject to DOT agency regulations requiring compliance with this part. The term, as used in this part, means the entity responsible for overall implementation of DOT drug and alcohol program requirements, including individuals employed by the entity who take personnel actions resulting from violations of this part and any applicable DOT agency regulations. Service agents are not employers for the purposes of this part.

Licensed medical practitioner means a person who is licensed, certified, and/or registered, in accordance with applicable Federal, State, local, or foreign laws and regulations, to prescribe controlled substances and other drugs.

Negative return-to-duty test result means a return-to-duty test with a negative drug result and/or an alcohol test with an alcohol concentration of less than 0.02, as described in §40.305 of this title.

Performing (a safety-sensitive function) means a driver is considered to be performing a safety-sensitive function during any period in which he or she is actually performing, ready to perform, or immediately available to perform any safety-sensitive functions.

Positive rate for random drug testing means the number of verified positive results for random drug tests conducted under this part plus the number of refusals of random drug tests required by this part, divided by the total number of random drug tests results (*i.e.*, positives, negatives, and refusals) under this part.

PART 382

Refuse to submit (to an alcohol or controlled substances test) means that a driver:

(1) Fail to appear for any test (except a pre-employment test) within a reasonable time, as determined by the employer, consistent with applicable DOT agency regulations, after being directed to do so by the employer. This includes the failure of an employee (including an owner-operator) to appear for a test when called by a C/TPA (see §40.61(a) of this title);

(2) Fail to remain at the testing site until the testing process is complete. Provided, that an employee who leaves the testing site before the testing process commences (see §40.63(c) of this title) a pre-employment test is not deemed to have refused to test;

(3) Fail to provide a urine specimen for any drug test required by this part or DOT agency regulations. Provided, that an employee who does not provide a urine specimen because he or she has left the testing site before the testing process commences (see §40.63(c) of this title) for a pre-employment test is not deemed to have refused to test;

(4) In the case of a directly observed or monitored collection in a drug test, fails to permit the observation or monitoring of the driver's provision of a specimen (see §§40.67(l) and 40.69(g) of this title);

(5) Fail to provide a sufficient amount of urine when directed, and it has been determined, through a required medical evaluation, that there was no adequate medical explanation for the failure (see §40.193(d)(2) of this title);

(6) Fail or declines to take a second test the employer or collector has directed the driver to take;

(7) Fail to undergo a medical examination or evaluation, as directed by the MRO as part of the verification process, or as directed by the DER under §40.193(d) of this title. In the case of a pre-employment drug test, the employee is deemed to have refused to test on this basis only if the pre-employment test is conducted following a contingent offer of employment;

(8) Fail to cooperate with any part of the testing process (e.g., refuse to empty pockets when so directed by the collector, behave in a confrontational way that disrupts the collection process); or

(9) Is reported by the MRO as having a verified adulterated or substituted test result.

Safety-sensitive function means all time from the time a driver begins to work or is required to be in readiness to work until the time he/she is relieved from work and all responsibility for performing work. Safety-sensitive functions shall include:

(1) All time at an employer or shipper plant, terminal, facility, or other property, or on any public property, waiting to be dispatched, unless the driver has been relieved from duty by the employer;

(2) All time inspecting equipment as required by §§392.7 and 392.8 of this subchapter or otherwise inspecting, servicing, or conditioning any commercial motor vehicle at any time;

(3) All time spent at the driving controls of a commercial motor vehicle in operation;

(4) All time, other than driving time, in or upon any commercial motor vehicle except time spent resting in a sleeper berth (a berth conforming to the requirements of §393.76 of this sub-chapter);

(5) All time loading or unloading a vehicle, supervising, or assisting in the loading or unloading, attending a vehicle being loaded or unloaded, remaining in readiness to operate the vehicle, or in giving or receiving receipts for shipments loaded or unloaded; and

(6) All time repairing, obtaining assistance, or remaining in attendance upon a disabled vehicle.

Screening test (or initial test) means:

(1) In drug testing, a test to eliminate "negative" urine specimens from further analysis or to identify a specimen that requires additional testing for the presence of drugs.

(2) In alcohol testing, an analytical procedure to determine whether an employee may have a prohibited concentration of alcohol in a breath or saliva specimen.

Stand-down means the practice of temporarily removing an employee from the performance of safety-sensitive functions based only on a report from a laboratory to the MRO of a confirmed positive test for a drug or drug metabolite, an adulterated test, or a substituted test, before the MRO has completed verification of the test results.

Violation rate for random alcohol testing means the number of 0.04 and above random alcohol confirmation test results conducted under this part plus the number of refusals of random alcohol tests required by this part, divided by the total number of random alcohol screening tests (including refusals) conducted under this part.

§382.109 Preemption of State and local laws.

(a) Except as provided in paragraph (b) of this section, this part preempts any State or local law, rule, regulation, or order to the extent that:

(1) Compliance with both the State or local requirement in this part is not possible; or

(2) Compliance with the State or local requirement is an obstacle to the accomplishment and execution of any requirement in this part.

(b) This part shall not be construed to preempt provisions of State criminal law that impose sanctions for reckless conduct leading to actual loss of life, injury, or damage to property, whether the provisions apply specifically to transportation employees, employers, or the general public.

§382.111 Other requirements imposed by employers.

Except as expressly provided in this part, nothing in this part shall be construed to affect the authority of employers, or the rights of drivers, with respect to the use of alcohol, or the use of controlled substances, including authority and rights with respect to testing and rehabilitation.

§382.113 Requirement for notice.

Before performing each alcohol or controlled substances test under this part, each employer shall notify a driver that the alcohol or controlled substances test is required by this part. No employer shall falsely represent that a test is administered under this part.

§382.115 Starting date for testing programs.

(a) All domestic-domiciled employers must implement the requirements of this part on the date the employer begins commercial motor vehicle operations.

(b) All foreign-domiciled employers must implement the requirements of this part on the date the employer begins commercial motor vehicle operations in the United States.

§382.117 Public interest exclusion.

No employer shall use the services of a service agent who is subject to public interest exclusion in accordance with 49 CFR part 40, Subpart R.

§382.119 Stand-down waiver provision.

(a) Employers are prohibited from standing employees down, except consistent with a waiver from the Federal Motor Carrier Safety Administration as required under this section.

(b) An employer subject to this part who seeks a waiver from the prohibition against standing down an employee before the MRO has completed the verification process shall follow the procedures in 49 CFR 40.21. The employer must send a written request, which includes all of the information required by that section to the Administrator, Federal Motor Carrier Safety Administration, 1200 New Jersey Ave., SE., Washington, DC 20590-0001.

(c) The final decision whether to grant or deny the application for a waiver will be made by the Administrator or the Administrator's designee.

(d) After a decision is signed by the Administrator or the Administrator's designee, the employer will be sent a copy of the decision, which will include the terms and conditions for the waiver or the reason for denying the application for a waiver.

(e) Questions regarding waiver applications should be directed to the Federal Motor Carrier Safety Administration, Office of Enforcement and Compliance (MC-EC), 1200 New Jersey Ave., SE., Washington, DC 20590-0001.

§382.121 Employee admission of alcohol and controlled substances use.

(a) Employees who admit to alcohol misuse or controlled substances use are not subject to the referral, evaluation and treatment requirements of this part and part 40 of this title, provided that:

(1) The admission is in accordance with a written employer-established voluntary self-identification program or policy that meets the requirements of paragraph (b) of this section;

(2) The driver does not self-identify in order to avoid testing under the requirements of this part;

(3) The driver makes the admission of alcohol misuse or controlled substances use prior to performing a safety sensitive function (i.e., prior to reporting for duty); and

(4) The driver does not perform a safety sensitive function until the employer is satisfied that the employee has been evaluated and has successfully completed education or treatment requirements in accordance with the self-identification program guidelines.

(b) A qualified voluntary self-identification program or policy must contain the following elements:

(1) It must prohibit the employer from taking adverse action against an employee making a voluntary admission of alcohol misuse or controlled substances use within the parameters of the program or policy and paragraph (a) of this section;

(2) It must allow the employee sufficient opportunity to seek evaluation, education or treatment to establish control over the employee's drug or alcohol problem;

(3) It must permit the employee to return to safety sensitive duties only upon successful completion of an educational or treatment program, as determined by a drug and alcohol abuse evaluation expert, i.e., employee assistance professional, substance abuse professional, or qualified drug and alcohol counselor;

(4) It must ensure that:

(i) Prior to the employee participating in a safety sensitive function, the employee shall undergo a non-DOT return to duty test with a result indicating an alcohol concentration of less than 0.02; and/or

(ii) Prior to the employee participating in a safety sensitive function, the employee shall undergo a non-DOT return to duty controlled substance test with a verified negative test result for controlled substances use; and

(5) It may incorporate employee monitoring and include non-DOT follow-up testing.

§382.123 Driver identification.

(a) **Identification information on the Alcohol Testing Form (ATF)**. For each alcohol test performed under this part, the employer shall provide the driver's commercial driver's license number and State of issuance in Step 1, Section B of the ATF.

(b) **Identification information on the Federal Drug Testing Custody and Control Form (CCF)**. For each controlled substance test performed under this part, the employer shall provide the following information, which must be recorded as follows:

(1) The driver's commercial driver's license number and State of issuance in Step 1, section C of the CCF.

(2) The employer's name and other identifying information required in Step 1, section A of the CCF.

Subpart B—Prohibitions

§382.201 Alcohol concentration.

No driver shall report for duty or remain on duty requiring the performance of safety-sensitive functions while having an alcohol concentration of 0.04 or greater. No employer having knowledge that a driver has an alcohol concentration of 0.04 or greater shall permit the driver to perform or continue to perform safety-sensitive functions.

§382.205 On-duty use.

No driver shall use alcohol while performing safety-sensitive functions. No employer having actual knowledge that a driver is using alcohol while performing safety-sensitive functions shall permit the driver to perform or continue to perform safety-sensitive functions.

§382.207 Pre-duty use.

No driver shall perform safety-sensitive functions within four hours after using alcohol. No employer having actual knowledge that a driver has used alcohol within four hours shall permit a driver to perform or continue to perform safety-sensitive functions.

§382.209 Use following an accident.

No driver required to take a post-accident alcohol test under §382.303 shall use alcohol for eight hours following the accident, or until he/she undergoes a post-accident alcohol test, whichever occurs first.

§382.211 Refusal to submit to a required alcohol or controlled substances test.

No driver shall refuse to submit to a pre-employment controlled substance test required under §382.301, a post-accident alcohol or controlled substance test required under §382.303, a random alcohol or controlled substances test required under §382.305, a reasonable suspicion alcohol or controlled substance test required under §382.307, a return-to-duty alcohol or controlled substances test required under §382.309, or a follow-up alcohol or controlled substance test required under §382.311. No employer shall permit a driver who refuses to submit to such tests to perform or continue to perform safety-sensitive functions.

§382.213 Controlled substance use.

(a) No driver shall report for duty or remain on duty requiring the performance of safety sensitive functions when the driver uses any drug or substance identified in 21 CFR 1308.11 Schedule I.

(b) No driver shall report for duty or remain on duty requiring the performance of safety-sensitive functions when the driver uses any non-Schedule I drug or substance that is identified in the other Schedules in 21 CFR part 1308 except when the use is pursuant to the instructions of a licensed medical practitioner, as defined in §382.107, who is familiar with the driver's medical history and has advised the driver that the substance will not adversely affect the driver's ability to safely operate a commercial motor vehicle.

(c) No employer having actual knowledge that a driver has used a controlled substance shall permit the driver to perform or continue to perform a safety-sensitive function.

(d) An employer may require a driver to inform the employer of any therapeutic drug use.

§382.215 Controlled substances testing.

No driver shall report for duty, remain on duty or perform a safety-sensitive function, if the driver tests positive or has adulterated or substituted a test specimen for controlled substances. No employer having knowledge that a driver has tested positive or has adulterated or substituted a test specimen for controlled substances shall permit the driver to perform or continue to perform safety-sensitive functions.

§382.217 Employer responsibilities.

No employer may allow, require, permit or authorize a driver to operate a commercial motor vehicle during any period in which an employer determines that a driver is not in compliance with the return-to-duty requirements in 49 CFR part 40, subpart O, after the occurrence of any of the following events:

(a) The driver receives a positive, adulterated, or substituted drug test result conducted under part 40 of this title.

(b) The driver receives an alcohol confirmation test result of 0.04 or higher alcohol concentration conducted under part 40 of this title.

(c) The driver refused to submit to a test for drugs or alcohol required under this part.

(d) The driver used alcohol prior to a post-accident alcohol test in violation of §382.209.

(e) An employer has actual knowledge, as defined at §382.107, that a driver has:

(1) Used alcohol while performing safety-sensitive functions in violation of §382.205;

(2) Used alcohol within four hours of performing safety-sensitive functions in violation of §382.207; or

(3) Used a controlled substance.

Subpart C—Tests Required

§382.301 Pre-employment testing.

(a) Prior to the first time a driver performs safety-sensitive functions for an employer, the driver shall undergo testing for controlled substances as a condition prior to being used, unless the employer uses the exception in paragraph (b) of this section. No employer shall allow a driver, who the employer intends to hire or use, to perform safety-sensitive functions unless the employer has received a controlled substances test result from the MRO or C/TPA indicating a verified negative test result for that driver.

(b) An employer is not required to administer a controlled substances test required by paragraph (a) of this section if:

(1) The driver has participated in a controlled substances testing program that meets the requirements of this part within the previous 30 days; and

(2) While participating in that program, either:

(i) Was tested for controlled substances within the past 6 months (from the date of application with the employer), or

(ii) Participated in the random controlled substances testing program for the previous 12 months (from the date of application with the employer); and

(3) The employer ensures that no prior employer of the driver of whom the employer has knowledge has records of a violation of this part or the controlled substances use rule of another DOT agency within the previous six months.

(c)(1) An employer who exercises the exception in paragraph (b) of this section shall contact the controlled substances testing program(s) in which the driver participates or participated and shall obtain and retain from the testing program(s) the following information:

(i) Name(s) and address(es) of the program(s).

(ii) Verification that the driver participates or participated in the program(s).

(iii) Verification that the program(s) conforms to part 40 of this title.

(iv) Verification that the driver is qualified under the rules of this part, including that the driver has not refused to be tested for controlled substances.

(v) The date the driver was last tested for controlled substances.

(vi) The results of any tests taken within the previous six months and any other violations of subpart B of this part.

(2) An employer who uses, but does not employ a driver more than once a year to operate commercial motor vehicles must obtain the information in paragraph (c)(1) of this section at least once every six months. The records prepared under this paragraph shall be maintained in accordance with §382.401. If the employer cannot verify that the driver is participating in a controlled substances testing program in accordance with this part and part 40 of this title, the employer shall conduct a pre-employment controlled substances test.

(d) An employer may, but is not required to, conduct pre-employment alcohol testing under this part. If an employer chooses to conduct pre-employment alcohol testing, it must comply with the following requirements:

(1) It must conduct a pre-employment alcohol test before the first performance of safety-sensitive functions by every covered employee (whether a new employee or someone who has transferred to a position involving the performance of safety-sensitive functions).

(2) It must treat all safety-sensitive employees performing safety-sensitive functions the same for the purpose of pre-employment alcohol testing (i.e., it must not test some covered employees and not others).

(3) It must conduct the pre-employment tests after making a contingent offer of employment or transfer, subject to the employee passing the pre-employment alcohol test.

(4) It must conduct all pre-employment alcohol tests using the alcohol testing procedures of 49 CFR part 40 of this title.

(5) It must not allow a covered employee to begin performing safety-sensitive functions unless the result of the employee's test indicates an alcohol concentration of less than 0.04.

§382.303 Post-accident testing.

(a) As soon as practicable following an occurrence involving a commercial motor vehicle operating on a public road in commerce, each employer shall test for alcohol for each of its surviving drivers:

(1) Who was performing safety-sensitive functions with respect to the vehicle, if the accident involved the loss of human life; or

(2) Who receives a citation within 8 hours of the occurrence under State or local law for a moving traffic violation arising from the accident, if the accident involved:

(i) Bodily injury to any person who, as a result of the injury, immediately receives medical treatment away from the scene of the accident; or

(ii) One or more motor vehicles incurring disabling damage as a result of the accident, requiring the motor vehicle to be transported away from the scene by a tow truck or other motor vehicle.

(b) As soon as practicable following an occurrence involving a commercial motor vehicle operating on a public road in commerce, each employer shall test for controlled substances for each of its surviving drivers:

(1) Who was performing safety-sensitive functions with respect to the vehicle, if the accident involved the loss of human life; or

(2) Who receives a citation within thirty-two hours of the occurrence under State or local law for a moving traffic violation arising from the accident, if the accident involved:

(i) Bodily injury to any person who, as a result of the injury, immediately receives medical treatment away from the scene of the accident; or

(ii) One or more motor vehicles incurring disabling damage as a result of the accident, requiring the motor vehicle to be transported away from the scene by a tow truck or other motor vehicle.

(c) The following table notes when a post-accident test is required to be conducted by paragraphs (a)(1), (a)(2), (b)(1), and (b)(2) of this section:

Table for §382.303 (A) and (B)

Type of accident involved	Citation issued to the CMV driver	Test must be performed by employer
i. Human fatality	YES NO	YES YES
ii. Bodily injury with immediate medical treatment away from the scene	YES NO	YES NO
iii. Disabling damage to any motor vehicle requiring tow away	YES NO	YES NO

(d)(1) **Alcohol tests**. If a test required by this section is not administered within two hours following the accident, the employer shall prepare and maintain on file a record stating the reasons the test was not promptly administered. If a test required by this section is not administered within eight hours following the accident, the employer shall cease attempts to administer an alcohol test and shall prepare and maintain the same record. Records shall be submitted to the FMCSA upon request.

(2) **Controlled substance tests**. If a test required by this section is not administered within 32 hours following the accident, the employer shall cease attempts to administer a controlled substances test, and prepare and maintain on file a record stating the reasons the test was not promptly administered. Records shall be submitted to the FMCSA upon request.

(e) A driver who is subject to post-accident testing shall remain readily available for such testing or may be deemed by the employer to have refused to submit to testing. Nothing in this section shall be construed to require the delay of necessary medical attention for injured people following an accident or to prohibit a driver from leaving the scene of an accident for the period necessary to obtain assistance in responding to the accident, or to obtain necessary emergency medical care.

(f) An employer shall provide drivers with necessary post-accident information, procedures and instructions, prior to the driver operating a commercial motor vehicle, so that drivers will be able to comply with the requirements of this section.

(g)(1) The results of a breath or blood test for the use of alcohol, conducted by Federal, State, or local officials having independent authority for the test, shall be considered to meet the requirements of this section, provided such tests conform to the applicable Federal, State or local alcohol testing requirements, and that the results of the tests are obtained by the employer.

(2) The results of a urine test for the use of controlled substances, conducted by Federal, State, or local officials having independent authority for the test, shall be considered to meet the requirements of this section, provided such tests conform to the applicable Federal, State or local controlled substances testing requirements, and that the results of the tests are obtained by the employer.

(h) **Exception**. This section does not apply to:

(1) An occurrence involving only boarding or alighting from a stationary motor vehicle; or

(2) An occurrence involving only the loading or unloading of cargo; or

(3) An occurrence in the course of the operation of a passenger car or a multipurpose passenger vehicle (as defined in §571.3 of this title) by an employer

unless the motor vehicle is transporting passengers for hire or hazardous materials of a type and quantity that require the motor vehicle to be marked or placarded in accordance with §177.823 of this title.

§382.305 Random testing.

(a) Every employer shall comply with the requirements of this section. Every driver shall submit to random alcohol and controlled substance testing as required in this section.

(b)(1) Except as provided in paragraphs (c) through (e) of this section, the minimum annual percentage rate for random alcohol testing shall be 10 percent of the average number of driver positions.

(2) Except as provided in paragraphs (f) through (h) of this section, the minimum annual percentage rate for random controlled substances testing shall be 50 percent of the average number of driver positions.

(c) The FMCSA Administrator's decision to increase or decrease the minimum annual percentage rate for alcohol testing is based on the reported violation rate for the entire industry. All information used for this determination is drawn from the alcohol management information system reports required by §382.403. In order to ensure reliability of the data, the FMCSA Administrator considers the quality and completeness of the reported data, may obtain additional information or reports from employers, and may make appropriate modifications in calculating the industry violation rate. In the event of a change in the annual percentage rate, the FMCSA Administrator will publish in the *Federal Register* the new minimum annual percentage rate for random alcohol testing of drivers. The new minimum annual percentage rate for random alcohol testing will be applicable starting January 1 of the calendar year following publication in the *Federal Register*.

(d)(1) When the minimum annual percentage rate for random alcohol testing is 25 percent or more, the FMCSA Administrator may lower this rate to 10 percent of all driver positions if the FMCSA Administrator determines that the data received under the reporting requirements of §382.403 for two consecutive calendar years indicate that the violation rate is less than 0.5 percent.

(2) When the minimum annual percentage rate for random alcohol testing is 50 percent, the FMCSA Administrator may lower this rate to 25 percent of all driver positions if the FMCSA Administrator determines that the data received under the reporting requirements of §382.403 for two consecutive calendar years indicate that the violation rate is less than 1.0 percent but equal to or greater than 0.5 percent.

(e)(1) When the minimum annual percentage rate for random alcohol testing is 10 percent, and the data received under the reporting requirements of §382.403 for that calendar year indicate that the violation rate is equal to or greater than 0.5 percent, but less than 1.0 percent, the FMCSA Administrator will increase the minimum annual percentage rate for random alcohol testing to 25 percent for all driver positions.

(2) When the minimum annual percentage rate for random alcohol testing is 25 percent or less, and the data received under the reporting requirements of §382.403 for that calendar year indicate that the violation rate is equal to or greater than 1.0 percent, the FMCSA Administrator will increase the minimum annual percentage rate for random alcohol testing to 50 percent for all driver positions.

(f) The FMCSA Administrator's decision to increase or decrease the minimum annual percentage rate for controlled substances testing is based on the reported positive rate for the entire industry. All information used for this determination is drawn from the controlled substances management information system reports required by §382.403. In order to ensure reliability of the data, the FMCSA Administrator considers the quality and completeness of the reported data, may obtain additional information or reports from employers, and may make appropriate modifications in calculating the industry positive rate. In the event of a change in the annual percentage rate, the FMCSA Administrator will publish in the *Federal Register* the new minimum annual percentage rate for controlled substances testing of drivers. The new minimum annual percentage rate for random controlled substances testing will be applicable starting January 1 of the calendar year following publication in the *Federal Register*.

(g) When the minimum annual percentage rate for random controlled substances testing is 50 percent, the FMCSA Administrator may lower this rate to 25 percent of all driver positions if the FMCSA Administrator determines that the data received under the reporting requirements of §382.403 for two consecutive calendar years indicate that the positive rate is less than 1.0 percent.

(h) When the minimum annual percentage rate for random controlled substances testing is 25 percent, and the data received under the reporting requirements of §382.403 for any calendar year indicate that the reported positive rate is equal to or greater than 1.0 percent, the FMCSA Administrator will increase the minimum annual percentage rate for random controlled substances testing to 50 percent of all driver positions.

(i)(1) The selection of drivers for random alcohol and controlled substances testing shall be made by a scientifically valid method, such as a random number table or a computer-based random number generator that is matched with drivers' Social Security numbers, payroll identification numbers, or other comparable identifying numbers.

(2) Each driver selected for random alcohol and controlled substances testing under the selection process used, shall have an equal chance of being tested each time selections are made.

(3) Each driver selected for testing shall be tested during the selection period.

(j)(1) To calculate the total number of covered drivers eligible for random testing throughout the year, as an employer, you must add the total number of covered drivers eligible for testing during each random testing period for the year and divide that total by the number of random testing periods. Covered employees, and only covered employees, are to be in an employer's random testing pool, and all covered drivers must be in the random pool. If you are an employer conducting random testing more often than once per month (*e.g.*, daily, weekly, bi-weekly) you do not need to compute this total number of covered drivers rate more than on a once per month basis.

(2) As an employer, you may use a service agent (*e.g.*, a C/TPA) to perform random selections for you, and your covered drivers may be part of a larger random testing pool of covered employees. However, you must ensure that the service agent you use is testing at the appropriate percentage established for your industry and that only covered employees are in the random testing pool.

(k)(1) Each employer shall ensure that random alcohol and controlled substances tests conducted under this part are unannounced.

(2) Each employer shall ensure that the dates for administering random alcohol and controlled substances tests conducted under this part are spread reasonably throughout the calendar year.

(l) Each employer shall require that each driver who is notified of selection for random alcohol and/or controlled substances testing proceeds to the test site immediately; provided, however, that if the driver is performing a safety-sensitive function, other than driving a commercial motor vehicle, at the time of notification, the employer shall instead ensure that the driver ceases to perform the safety-sensitive function and proceeds to the testing site as soon as possible.

(m) A driver shall only be tested for alcohol while the driver is performing safety-sensitive functions, just before the driver is to perform safety-sensitive functions, or just after the driver has ceased performing such functions.

(n) If a given driver is subject to random alcohol or controlled substances testing under the random alcohol or controlled substances testing rules of more than one DOT agency for the same employer, the driver shall be subject to random alcohol and/or controlled substances testing at the annual percentage rate established for the calendar year by the DOT agency regulating more than 50 percent of the driver's function.

(o) If an employer is required to conduct random alcohol or controlled substances testing under the alcohol or controlled substances testing rules of more than one DOT agency, the employer may—

(1) Establish separate pools for random selection, with each pool containing the DOT-covered employees who are subject to testing at the same required minimum annual percentage rate; or

(2) Randomly select such employees for testing at the highest minimum annual percentage rate established for the calendar year by any DOT agency to which the employer is subject.

§382.307 Reasonable suspicion testing.

(a) An employer shall require a driver to submit to an alcohol test when the employer has reasonable suspicion to believe that the driver has violated the prohibitions of subpart B of this part concerning alcohol. The employer's determination that reasonable suspicion exists to require the driver to undergo an alcohol test must be based on specific, contemporaneous, articulable observations concerning the appearance, behavior, speech or body odors of the driver.

(b) An employer shall require a driver to submit to a controlled substances test when the employer has reasonable suspicion to believe that the driver has violated the prohibitions of subpart B of this part concerning controlled substances. The employer's determination that reasonable suspicion exists to require the driver to undergo a controlled substances test must be based on specific, contemporaneous, articulable observations concerning the appearance, behavior, speech or body odors of the driver. The observations may include indications of the chronic and withdrawal effects of controlled substances.

(c) The required observations for alcohol and/or controlled substances reasonable suspicion testing shall be made by a supervisor or company official who is trained in accordance with §382.603. The person who makes the determination that reasonable suspicion exists to conduct an alcohol test shall not conduct the alcohol test of the driver.

(d) Alcohol testing is authorized by this section only if the observations required by paragraph (a) of this section are made during, just preceding, or just after the period of the work day that the driver is required to be in compliance with this part. A driver may be directed by the employer to only undergo reasonable suspicion testing while the driver is performing safety-sensitive functions, just before the driver is to perform safety-sensitive functions, or just after the driver has ceased performing such functions.

(e)(1) If an alcohol test required by this section is not administered within two hours following the determination under paragraph (a) of this section, the employer shall prepare and maintain on file a record stating the reasons the alcohol test was not promptly administered. If an alcohol test required by this section is not administered within eight hours following the determination under paragraph (a) of this section, the employer shall cease attempts to administer an alcohol test and shall state in the record the reasons for not administering the test.

(2) Notwithstanding the absence of a reasonable suspicion alcohol test under this section, no driver shall report for duty or remain on duty requiring the performance of safety-sensitive functions while the driver is under the influence of or impaired by alcohol, as shown by the behavioral, speech, and performance indicators of alcohol misuse, nor shall an employer permit the driver to perform or continue to perform safety-sensitive functions, until:

(i) An alcohol test is administered and the driver's alcohol concentration measures less than 0.02; or

(ii) Twenty four hours have elapsed following the determination under paragraph (a) of this section that there is reasonable suspicion to believe that the driver has violated the prohibitions in this part concerning the use of alcohol.

(3) Except as provided in paragraph (e)(2) of this section, no employer shall take any action under this part against a driver based solely on the driver's behavior and appearance, with respect to alcohol use, in the absence of an alcohol test. This does not prohibit an employer with independent authority of this part from taking any action otherwise consistent with law.

(f) A written record shall be made of the observations leading to an alcohol or controlled substances reasonable suspicion test, and signed by the supervisor or company official who made the observations, within 24 hours of the observed behavior or before the results of the alcohol or controlled substances tests are released, whichever is earlier.

§382.309 Return-to-duty testing.
The requirements for return-to-duty testing must be performed in accordance with 49 CFR part 40, Subpart O.

§382.311 Follow-up testing.
The requirements for follow-up testing must be performed in accordance with 49 CFR part 40, Subpart O.

Subpart D—Handling of Test Results, Record Retention and Confidentiality

§382.401 Retention of records.
(a) **General requirement**. Each employer shall maintain records of its alcohol misuse and controlled substances use prevention programs as provided in this section. The records shall be maintained in a secure location with controlled access.

(b) **Period of retention**. Each employer shall maintain the records in accordance with the following schedule:

(1) **Five years**. The following records shall be maintained for a minimum of five years:

(i) Records of driver alcohol test results indicating an alcohol concentration of 0.02 or greater,

(ii) Records of driver verified positive controlled substances test results,

(iii) Documentation of refusals to take required alcohol and/or controlled substances tests,

(iv) Driver evaluation and referrals,

(v) Calibration documentation,

(vi) Records related to the administration of the alcohol and controlled substances testing program, including records of all driver violations, and

(vii) A copy of each annual calendar year summary required by §382.403.

(2) **Two years**. Records related to the alcohol and controlled substances collection process (except calibration of evidential breath testing devices) shall be maintained for a minimum of 2 years.

(3) **One year**. Records of negative and canceled controlled substances test results (as defined in part 40 of this title) and alcohol test results with a concentration of less than 0.02 shall be maintained for a minimum of one year.

(4) **Indefinite period**. Records related to the education and training of breath alcohol technicians, screening test technicians, supervisors, and drivers shall be maintained by the employer while the individual performs the functions which require the training and for two years after ceasing to perform those functions.

(c) **Types of records**. The following specific types of records shall be maintained. "Documents generated" are documents that may have to be prepared under a requirement of this part. If the record is required to be prepared, it must be maintained.

(1) Records related to the collection process:

(i) Collection logbooks, if used;

(ii) Documents relating to the random selection process;

(iii) Calibration documentation for evidential breath testing devices;

(iv) Documentation of breath alcohol technician training;

(v) Documents generated in connection with decisions to administer reasonable suspicion alcohol or controlled substances tests;

(vi) Documents generated in connection with decisions on post-accident tests;

(vii) Documents verifying existence of a medical explanation of the inability of a driver to provide adequate breath or to provide a urine specimen for testing; and

(viii) A copy of each annual calendar year summary as required by §382.403.

(2) Records related to a driver's test results:

(i) The employer's copy of the alcohol test form, including the results of the test;

(ii) The employer's copy of the controlled substances test chain of custody and control form;

(iii) Documents sent by the MRO to the employer, including those required by part 40, subpart G, of this title;

(iv) Documents related to the refusal of any driver to submit to an alcohol or controlled substances test required by this part;

(v) Documents presented by a driver to dispute the result of an alcohol or controlled substances test administered under this part; and

(vi) Documents generated in connection with verifications of prior employers' alcohol or controlled substances test results that the employer:

(A) Must obtain in connection with the exception contained in §382.301, and

(B) Must obtain as required by §382.413.

(3) Records related to other violations of this part.

(4) Records related to evaluations:

(i) Records pertaining to a determination by a substance abuse professional concerning a driver's need for assistance; and

(ii) Records concerning a driver's compliance with recommendations of the substance abuse professional.

(5) Records related to education and training:

(i) Materials on alcohol misuse and controlled substance use awareness, including a copy of the employer's policy on alcohol misuse and controlled substance use;

(ii) Documentation of compliance with the requirements of §382.601, including the driver's signed receipt of education materials;

(iii) Documentation of training provided to supervisors for the purpose of qualifying the supervisors to make a determination concerning the need for alcohol and/or controlled substances testing based on reasonable suspicion;

(iv) Documentation of training for breath alcohol technicians as required by §40.213(g) of this title; and

(v) Certification that any training conducted under this part complies with the requirements for such training.

(6) Administrative records related to alcohol and controlled substances testing:

(i) Agreements with collection site facilities, laboratories, breath alcohol technicians, screening test technicians, medical review officers, consortia, and third party service providers;

(ii) Names and positions of officials and their role in the employer's alcohol and controlled substances testing program(s);

(iii) Semi-annual laboratory statistical summaries of urinalysis required by §40.111(a) of this title; and

(iv) The employer's alcohol and controlled substances testing policy and procedures.

(d) **Location of records**. All records required by this part shall be maintained as required by §390.29 of this subchapter and shall be made available for inspection at the employer's principal place of business within two business days after a request has been made by an authorized representative of the Federal Motor Carrier Safety Administration.

(e) **OMB control number**.

(1) The information collection requirements of this part have been reviewed by the Office of Management and Budget pursuant to the Paperwork Reduction Act of 1995 (44 U.S.C. 3501 et seq.) and have been assigned OMB control number 2126-0012.

(2) The information collection requirements of this part are found in the following sections: Sections 382.105, 382.113, 382.301, 382.303, 382.305, 382.307, 382.401, 382.403, 382.405, 382.409, 382.411, 382.601, 382.603.

§382.403 Reporting of results in a management information system.

(a) An employer shall prepare and maintain a summary of the results of its alcohol and controlled substances testing programs performed under this part during the previous calendar year, when requested by the Secretary of Transportation, any DOT agency, or any State or local officials with regulatory authority over the employer or any of its drivers.

(b) If an employer is notified, during the month of January, of a request by the Federal Motor Carrier Safety Administration to report the employer's annual calendar year summary information, the employer shall prepare and submit the report to the FMCSA by March 15 of that year. The employer shall ensure that the annual summary report is accurate and received by March 15 at the location that the FMCSA specifies in its request. The employer must use the Management Information System (MIS) form and instructions as required by 49 CFR part 40 (at §40.26 and appendix H to part 40). The employer may also use the electronic version of the MIS form provided by the DOT. The Administrator may designate means (*e.g.*, electronic program transmitted via the Internet), other than hard-copy, for MIS form submission. For information on the electronic version of the form, see: *http://www.fmcsa.dot.gov/safetyprogs/drugs/engtesting.htm*.

(c) When the report is submitted to the FMCSA by mail or electronic transmission, the information requested shall be typed, except for the signature of the certifying official. Each employer shall ensure the accuracy and timeliness of each report submitted by the employer or a consortium.

(d) If you have a covered employee who performs multi-DOT agency functions (*e.g.*, an employee drives a commercial motor vehicle and performs pipeline maintenance duties for the same employer), count the employee only on the MIS report for the DOT agency under which he or she is randomly tested. Normally, this will be the DOT agency under which the employee performs more than 50% of his or her duties. Employers may have to explain the testing data for these employees in the event of a DOT agency inspection or audit.

(e) A service agent (*e.g.*, *Consortium/Third party administrator* as defined in 49 CFR 382.107) may prepare the MIS report on behalf of an employer. However, a company official (*e.g.*, *Designated employer representative* as defined in §382.107) must certify the accuracy and completeness of the MIS report, no matter who prepares it.

§382.405 Access to facilities and records.

(a) Except as required by law or expressly authorized or required in this section, no employer shall release driver information that is contained in records required to be maintained under §382.401.

(b) A driver is entitled, upon written request, to obtain copies of any records pertaining to the driver's use of alcohol or controlled substances, including any records pertaining to his or her alcohol or controlled substances tests. The employer shall promptly provide the records requested by the driver. Access to a driver's records shall not be contingent upon payment for records other than those specifically requested.

(c) Each employer shall permit access to all facilities utilized in complying with the requirements of this part to the Secretary of Transportation, any DOT agency, or any State or local officials with regulatory authority over the employer or any of its drivers.

(d) Each employer, and each service agent who maintains records for an employer, must make available copies of all results for DOT alcohol and/or controlled substances testing conducted by the employer under this part and any other information pertaining to the employer's alcohol misuse and/or controlled substances use prevention program when requested by the Secretary of Transportation, any DOT agency, or any State or local officials with regulatory authority over the employer or any of its drivers.

(e) When requested by the National Transportation Safety Board as a part of a crash investigation:

(1) Employers must disclose information related to the employer's administration of a post-accident alcohol and/or a controlled substances test administered following the crash under investigation; and

(2) FMCSA will provide access to information in the Clearinghouse concerning drivers who are involved with the crash under investigation.

(f) Records shall be made available to a subsequent employer upon receipt of a written request from a driver. Disclosure by the subsequent employer is permitted only as expressly authorized by the terms of the driver's request.

(g) An employer may disclose information required to be maintained under this part pertaining to a driver to the decision maker in a lawsuit, grievance, or administrative proceeding initiated by or on behalf of the individual, and arising from a positive DOT drug or alcohol test or a refusal to test (including, but not limited to, adulterated or substituted test results) of this part (including, but not limited to, a worker's compensation, unemployment compensation, or other proceeding relating to a benefit sought by the driver). Additionally, an employer may disclose information in criminal or civil actions in accordance with §40.323(a)(2) of this title.

(h) An employer shall release information regarding a driver's records as directed by the specific written consent of the driver authorizing release of the information to an identified person. Release of such information by the person receiving the information is permitted only in accordance with the terms of the employee's specific written consent as outlined in §40.321(b) of this title.

§382.407 Medical review officer notifications to the employer.

Medical review officers shall report the results of controlled substances tests to employers in accordance with the requirements of part 40, Subpart G, of this title.

§382.409 Medical review officer or consortium/third party administrator record retention for controlled substances.

(a) A medical review officer or third party administrator shall maintain all dated records and notifications, identified by individual, for a minimum of five years for verified positive controlled substances test results.

(b) A medical review officer or third party administrator shall maintain all dated records and notifications, identified by individual, for a minimum of one year for negative and canceled controlled substances test results.

(c) No person may obtain the individual controlled substances test results retained by a medical review officer (MRO as defined in §40.3 of this title) or a consortium/third party administrator (C/TPA as defined in §382.107), and no MRO or C/TPA may release the individual controlled substances test results of any driver to any person, without first obtaining a specific, written authorization from the tested driver. Nothing in this paragraph (c) shall prohibit a MRO or a C/TPA from releasing to the employer, the Clearinghouse, or to the Secretary of Transportation, any DOT agency, or any State or local officials with regulatory authority over the controlled substances and alcohol testing program under this part, the information delineated in part 40, subpart G, of this title.

§382.411 Employer notifications.

(a) An employer shall notify a driver of the results of a pre-employment controlled substances test conducted under this part, if the driver requests such results within 60 calendar days of being notified of the disposition of the employment application. An employer shall notify a driver of the results of random, reasonable suspicion and post-accident tests for controlled substances conducted under this part if the test results are verified positive. The employer shall also inform the driver which controlled substance or substances were verified as positive.

(b) The designated employer representative shall make reasonable efforts to contact and request each driver who submitted a specimen under the employer's program, regardless of the driver's employment status, to contact and discuss the results of the controlled substances test with a medical review officer who has been unable to contact the driver.

(c) The designated employer representative shall immediately notify the medical review officer that the driver has been notified to contact the medical review officer within 72 hours.

§382.413 Inquiries for alcohol and controlled substances information from previous employers.

(a) Employers must request alcohol and controlled substances information from previous employers in accordance with the requirements of §40.25 of this title, except that the employer must request information from all DOT-regulated employers that employed the driver within the previous 3 years and the scope of the information requested must date back 3 years.

(b) As of January 6, 2023, employers must use the Drug and Alcohol Clearinghouse in accordance with §382.701(a) to comply with the requirements of §40.25 of this title with respect to FMCSA-regulated employers. Exception: When an employee who is subject to follow-up testing has not successfully completed all follow-up tests, employers must request the employee's follow-up testing plan directly from the previous employer in accordance with §40.25(b)(5) of this title.

(c) If an applicant was subject to an alcohol and controlled substance testing program under the requirements of a DOT Agency other than FMCSA, the employer must request the alcohol and controlled substances information required under this section and §40.25 of this title directly from those employers regulated by a DOT Agency other than FMCSA.

§382.415 Notification to employers of a controlled substances or alcohol testing program violation.

Each person holding a commercial driver's license and subject to the DOT controlled substances and alcohol testing requirements in this part who has violated the alcohol and controlled substances prohibitions under part 40 of this title or this part without complying with the requirements of part 40, subpart O, must notify in writing all current employers of such violation(s). The driver is not required to provide notification to the employer that administered the test or documented the circumstances that gave rise to the violation. The notification must be made before the end of the business day following the day the employee received notice of the violation, or prior to performing any safety-sensitive function, whichever comes first.

Subpart E—Consequences for Drivers Engaging in Substance Use-Related Conduct

§382.501 Removal from safety-sensitive function.

(a) Except as provided in subpart F of this part, no driver shall perform safety-sensitive functions, including driving a commercial motor vehicle, if the driver has engaged in conduct prohibited by subpart B of this part or an alcohol or controlled substances rule of another DOT agency.

(b) No employer shall permit any driver to perform safety-sensitive functions; including driving a commercial motor vehicle, if the employer has determined that the driver has violated this section.

(c) For purposes of this subpart, commercial motor vehicle means a commercial motor vehicle in commerce as defined in §382.107, and a commercial motor vehicle in interstate commerce as defined in Part 390 of this subchapter.

§382.503 Required evaluation and testing, reinstatement of commercial driving privilege.

(a) No driver who has engaged in conduct prohibited by subpart B of this part shall perform safety-sensitive functions, including driving a commercial motor vehicle, unless the driver has met the requirements of part 40, subpart O, of this title. No employer shall permit a driver who has engaged in conduct prohibited by subpart B of this part to perform safety-sensitive functions, including driving a commercial motor vehicle, unless the driver has met the requirements of part 40, subpart O, of this title.

(b) No driver whose commercial driving privilege has been removed from the driver's license, pursuant to §382.501(a), shall drive a commercial motor vehicle until the State Driver Licensing Agency reinstates the CLP or CDL privilege to the driver's license.

§382.505 Other alcohol-related conduct.

(a) No driver tested under the provisions of subpart C of this part who is found to have an alcohol concentration of 0.02 or greater but less than 0.04 shall perform or continue to perform safety-sensitive functions for an employer, including driving a commercial motor vehicle, nor shall an employer permit the driver to perform or continue to perform safety-sensitive functions, until the start of the driver's next regularly scheduled duty period, but not less than 24 hours following administration of the test.

(b) Except as provided in paragraph (a) of this section, no employer shall take any action under this part against a driver based solely on test results showing an alcohol concentration less than 0.04. This does not prohibit an employer with authority independent of this part from taking any action otherwise consistent with law.

§382.507 Penalties.

Any employer or driver who violates the requirements of this part shall be subject to the civil and/or criminal penalty provisions of 49 U.S.C. 521(b). In addition, any employer or driver who violates the requirements of 49 CFR part 40 shall be subject to the civil and/or criminal penalty provisions of 49 U.S.C. 521(b).

Subpart F—Alcohol Misuse and Controlled Substances Use Information, Training, and Referral

§382.601 Employer obligation to promulgate a policy on the misuse of alcohol and use of controlled substances.

(a) **General requirements**. Each employer shall provide educational materials that explain the requirements of this part and the employer's policies and procedures with respect to meeting these requirements.

(1) The employer shall ensure that a copy of these materials is distributed to each driver prior to the start of alcohol and controlled substances testing under this part and to each driver subsequently hired or transferred into a position requiring driving a commercial motor vehicle.

(2) Each employer shall provide written notice to representatives of employee organizations of the availability of this information.

(b) **Required content**. The materials to be made available to drivers shall include detailed discussion of at least the following:

(1) The identity of the person designated by the employer to answer driver questions about the materials;

(2) The categories of drivers who are subject to the provisions of this part;

(3) Sufficient information about the safety-sensitive functions performed by those drivers to make clear what period of the work day the driver is required to be in compliance with this part;

(4) Specific information concerning driver conduct that is prohibited by this part;

(5) The circumstances under which a driver will be tested for alcohol and/or controlled substances under this part, including post-accident testing under §382.303(d);

(6) The procedures that will be used to test for the presence of alcohol and controlled substances, protect the driver and the integrity of the testing processes, safeguard the validity of the test results, and ensure that those results are attributed to the correct driver, including post-accident information, procedures and instructions required by §382.303(d);

(7) The requirement that a driver submit to alcohol and controlled substances tests administered in accordance with this part;

(8) An explanation of what constitutes a refusal to submit to an alcohol or controlled substances test and the attendant consequences;

(9) The consequences for drivers found to have violated subpart B of this part, including the requirement that the driver be removed immediately from safety-sensitive functions, and the procedures under part 40, subpart O, of this title;

(10) The consequences for drivers found to have an alcohol concentration of 0.02 or greater but less than 0.04;

(11) Information concerning the effects of alcohol and controlled substances use on an individual's health, work, and personal life; signs and symptoms of an alcohol or a controlled substances problem (the driver's or a co-worker's); and available methods of intervening when an alcohol or a controlled substances problem is suspected, including confrontation, referral to any employee assistance program and/or referral to management; and

(12) The requirement that the following personal information collected and maintained under this part shall be reported to the Clearinghouse:

(i) A verified positive, adulterated, or substituted drug test result;

(ii) An alcohol confirmation test with a concentration of 0.04 or higher;

(iii) A refusal to submit to any test required by subpart C of this part;

(iv) An employer's report of actual knowledge, as defined at §382.107:

(A) On duty alcohol use pursuant to §382.205;

(B) Pre-duty alcohol use pursuant to §382.207;

(C) Alcohol use following an accident pursuant to §382.209; and

(D) Controlled substance use pursuant to §382.213;

(v) A substance abuse professional (SAP as defined in §40.3 of this title) report of the successful completion of the return-to-duty process;

(vi) A negative return-to-duty test; and

(vii) An employer's report of completion of follow-up testing.

(c) **Optional provision**. The materials supplied to drivers may also include information on additional employer policies with respect to the use of alcohol or controlled substances, including any consequences for a driver found to have a specified alcohol or controlled substances level, that are based on the employer's authority independent of this part. Any such additional policies or consequences must be clearly and obviously described as being based on independent authority.

(d) **Certificate of receipt**. Each employer shall ensure that each driver is required to sign a statement certifying that he or she has received a copy of these materials described in this section. Each employer shall maintain the signed certificate and may provide a copy of the certificate to the driver.

§382.603 Training for supervisors.

Each employer shall ensure that all persons designated to supervise drivers receive at least 60 minutes of training on alcohol misuse and receive at least an additional 60 minutes of training on controlled substances use. The training will be used by the supervisors to determine whether reasonable suspicion exists to require a driver to undergo testing under §382.307. The training shall include the physical, behavioral, speech, and performance indicators of probable alcohol misuse and use of controlled substances. Recurrent training for supervisory personnel is not required.

§382.605 Referral, evaluation, and treatment.

The requirements for referral, evaluation, and treatment must be performed in accordance with 49 CFR part 40, Subpart O.

Subpart G—Requirements and Procedures for Implementation of the Commercial Driver's License Drug and Alcohol Clearinghouse

§382.701 Drug and Alcohol Clearinghouse.

(a) **Pre-employment query required**. (1) Employers must not employ a driver subject to controlled substances and alcohol testing under this part to perform a safety-sensitive function without first conducting a pre-employment query of the Clearinghouse to obtain information about whether the driver has a verified positive, adulterated, or substituted controlled substances test result; has an alcohol confirmation test with a concentration of 0.04 or higher; has refused to submit to a test in violation of §382.211; or that an employer has reported actual knowledge, as defined at §382.107, that the driver used alcohol on duty in violation of §382.205, used alcohol before duty in violation of

PART 382

§382.207, used alcohol following an accident in violation of §382.209, or used a controlled substance, in violation of §382.213.

(2) The employer must conduct a full query under this section, which releases information in the Clearinghouse to an employer and requires that the individual driver give specific consent.

(b) **Annual query required.** (1) Employers must conduct a query of the Clearinghouse at least once per year for information for all employees subject to controlled substance and alcohol testing under this part to determine whether information exists in the Clearinghouse about those employees.

(2) In lieu of a full query, as described in paragraph (a)(2) of this section, an employer may obtain the individual driver's consent to conduct a limited query to satisfy the annual query requirement in paragraph (b)(1) of this section. The limited query will tell the employer whether there is information about the individual driver in the Clearinghouse, but will not release that information to the employer. The individual driver may give consent to conduct limited queries that is effective for more than one year.

(3) If the limited query shows that information exists in the Clearinghouse about the individual driver, the employer must conduct a full query, in accordance with paragraph (a)(2) of this section, within 24 hours of conducting the limited query. If the employer fails to conduct a full query within 24 hours, the employer must not allow the driver to continue to perform any safety-sensitive function until the employer conducts the full query and the results confirm that the driver's Clearinghouse record contains no prohibitions as defined in paragraph (d) of this section.

(c) **Employer notification.** If any information described in paragraph (a) of this section is entered into the Clearinghouse about a driver during the 30-day period immediately following an employer conducting a query of that driver's records, FMCSA will notify the employer.

(d) **Prohibition.** No employer may allow a driver the employer employs or intends to hire or use to perform any safety-sensitive function if the results of a Clearinghouse query demonstrate that the driver has a verified positive, adulterated, or substituted controlled substances test result; has an alcohol confirmation test with a concentration of 0.04 or higher; has refused to submit to a test in violation of §382.211; or that an employer has reported actual knowledge, as defined at §382.107, that the driver used alcohol on duty in violation of §382.205, used alcohol before duty in violation of §382.207, used alcohol following an accident in violation of §382.209, or used a controlled substance in violation of §382.213, except where a query of the Clearinghouse demonstrates:

(1) That the driver has successfully completed the SAP evaluation, referral, and education/treatment process set forth in part 40, subpart O, of this title; achieves a negative return-to-duty test result; and completes the follow-up testing plan prescribed by the SAP.

(2) That, if the driver has not completed all follow-up tests as prescribed by the SAP in accordance with §40.307 of this title and specified in the SAP report required by §40.311 of this title, the driver has completed the SAP evaluation, referral, and education/treatment process set forth in part 40, subpart O, of this title and achieves a negative return-to-duty test result, and the employer assumes the responsibility for managing the follow-up testing process associated with the testing violation.

(e) **Recordkeeping required**. Employers must retain for 3 years a record of each query and all information received in response to each query made under this section. As of January 6, 2023, an employer who maintains a valid registration fulfills this requirement.

§382.703 Driver consent to permit access to information in the Clearinghouse.

(a) No employer may query the Clearinghouse to determine whether a record exists for any particular driver without first obtaining that driver's written or electronic consent. The employer conducting the search must retain the consent for 3 years from the date of the last query.

(b) Before the employer may access information contained in the driver's Clearinghouse record, the driver must submit electronic consent through the Clearinghouse granting the employer access to the following specific records:

(1) A verified positive, adulterated, or substituted controlled substances test result;

(2) An alcohol confirmation test with a concentration of 0.04 or higher;

(3) A refusal to submit to a test in violation of §382.211;

(4) An employer's report of actual knowledge, as defined at §382.107, of:

(i) On duty alcohol use pursuant to §382.205;

(ii) Pre-duty alcohol use pursuant to §382.207;

(iii) Alcohol use following an accident pursuant to §382.209; and

(iv) Controlled substance use pursuant to §382.213;

(5) A SAP report of the successful completion of the return-to-duty process;

(6) A negative return-to-duty test; and

(7) An employer's report of completion of follow-up testing.

(c) No employer may permit a driver to perform a safety-sensitive function if the driver refuses to grant the consent required by paragraph (a) or (b) of this section.

(d) A driver granting consent under this section must provide consent electronically to the Agency through the Clearinghouse prior to release of information to an employer in accordance with §382.701(a)(2) or (b)(3).

(e) A driver granting consent under this section grants consent for the Agency to release information to an employer in accordance with §382.701(c).

§382.705 Reporting to the Clearinghouse.

(a) **MROs**. (1) Within 2 business days of making a determination or verification, MROs must report the following information about a driver to the Clearinghouse:

(i) Verified positive, adulterated, or substituted controlled substances test results;

(ii) Refusal-to-test determination by the MRO in accordance with 49 CFR 40.191(a)(5), (7), and (11), (b), and (d)(2).

(2) MROs must provide the following information for each controlled substances test result specified in paragraph (a)(1) of this section:

(i) Reason for the test;

(ii) Federal Drug Testing Custody and Control Form specimen ID number;

(iii) Driver's name, date of birth, and CDL number and State of issuance;

(iv) Employer's name, address, and USDOT number, if applicable;

(v) Date of the test;

(vi) Date of the verified result; and

(vii) Test result. The test result must be one of the following:

(A) Positive (including the controlled substance(s) identified);

(B) Refusal to test: Adulterated;

(C) Refusal to test: Substituted; or

(D) Refusal to provide a sufficient specimen after the MRO makes a determination, in accordance with §40.193 of this title, that the employee does not have a medical condition that has, or with a high degree of probability could have, precluded the employee from providing a sufficient amount of urine. Under this subpart a refusal would also include a refusal to undergo a medical examination or evaluation to substantiate a qualifying medical condition.

(3) Within 1 business day of making any change to the results report in accordance with paragraph (a)(1) of this section, a MRO must report that changed result to the Clearinghouse.

(b) **Employers**. (1) Employers must report the following information about a driver to the Clearinghouse by the close of the third business day following the date on which they obtained that information:

(i) An alcohol confirmation test result with an alcohol concentration of 0.04 or greater;

(ii) A negative return-to-duty test result;

(iii) A refusal to take an alcohol test pursuant to 49 CFR 40.261;

(iv) A refusal to test determination made in accordance with 49 CFR 40.191(a)(1) through (4), (a)(6), (a)(8) through (11), or (d)(1), but in the case of a refusal to test under (a)(11), the employer may report only those admissions made to the specimen collector; and

(v) A report that the driver has successfully completed all follow-up tests as prescribed in the SAP report in accordance with §§40.307, 40.309, and 40.311 of this title.

(2) The information required to be reported under paragraph (b)(1) of this section must include, as applicable:

(i) Reason for the test;

(ii) Driver's name, date of birth, and CDL number and State of issuance;

(iii) Employer name, address, and USDOT number;

(iv) Date of the test;

(v) Date the result was reported; and

(vi) Test result. The test result must be one of the following:

(A) Negative (only required for return-to-duty tests administered in accordance with §382.309);

(B) Positive; or

(C) Refusal to take a test.

(3) For each report of a violation of 49 CFR 40.261(a)(1) or 40.191(a)(1), the employer must report the following information:

(i) Documentation, including, but not limited to, electronic mail or other contemporaneous record of the time and date the driver was notified to appear at a testing site; and the time, date and testing site location at which the employee was directed to appear, or an affidavit providing evidence of such notification;

(ii) Documentation, including, but not limited to, electronic mail or other correspondence, or an affidavit, indicating the date the employee was terminated or resigned (if applicable);

(iii) Documentation, including, but not limited to, electronic mail or other correspondence, or an affidavit, showing that the C/TPA reporting the violation was authorized to act as a service agent for an employer who employs himself

/herself as a driver pursuant to paragraph (b)(6) of this section when the reported refusal occurred (if applicable); and

(iv) Documentation, including a certificate of service or other evidence, showing that the employer provided the employee with all documentation reported under paragraph (b)(3) of this section (if applicable).

(4) Employers must report the following violations by the close of the third business day following the date on which the employer obtains actual knowledge, as defined at §382.107, of:

(i) On-duty alcohol use pursuant to §382.205;

(ii) Pre-duty alcohol use pursuant to §382.207;

(iii) Alcohol use following an accident pursuant to §382.209; and

(iv) Controlled substance use pursuant to §382.213.

(5) For each violation in paragraph (b)(4) of this section, the employer must report the following information:

(i) Driver's name, date of birth, CDL number and State of issuance;

(ii) Employer name, address, and USDOT number, if applicable;

(iii) Date the employer obtained actual knowledge of the violation;

(iv) Witnesses to the violation, if any, including contact information;

(v) Description of the violation;

(vi) Evidence supporting each fact alleged in the description of the violation required under paragraph (b)(4) of this section, which may include, but is not limited to, affidavits, photographs, video or audio recordings, employee statements (other than admissions pursuant to §382.121), correspondence, or other documentation; and

(vii) A certificate of service or other evidence showing that the employer provided the employee with all information reported under paragraph (b)(4) of this section (if applicable).

(6) An employer who employs himself/herself as a driver must designate a C/TPA to comply with the employer requirements in paragraph (b) of this section related to his or her own alcohol and controlled substances use.

(c) **C/TPAs.** Any employer may designate a C/TPA to perform the employer requirements in paragraph (b) of this section. Regardless of whether it uses a C/TPA to perform its requirements, the employer retains ultimate responsibility for compliance with this section. Exception: An employer does not retain responsibility where the C/TPA is designated to comply with employer requirements as described in paragraph (b)(6) of this section.

(d) **SAPs.** (1) SAPs must report to the Clearinghouse for each driver who has completed the return-to-duty process in accordance with 49 CFR part 40, subpart O, the following information:

(i) SAPs name, address, and telephone number;

(ii) Driver's name, date of birth, and CDL number and State of issuance;

(iii) Date of the initial substance-abuse-professional assessment; and

(iv) Date the SAP determined that the driver demonstrated successful compliance as defined in 49 CFR part 40, subpart O, and was eligible for return-to-duty testing under this part.

(2) SAP must report the information required by paragraphs (d)(1)(i) through (iii) of this section by the close of the business day following the date of the initial substance abuse assessment, and must report the information required by paragraph (d)(1)(iv) of this section by the close of the business day following the determination that the driver has completed the return-to-duty process.

PART 382

(e) **Reporting truthfully and accurately**. Every person or entity with access must report truthfully and accurately to the Clearinghouse and is expressly prohibited from reporting information he or she knows or should know is false or inaccurate.

Reporting Entities and Circumstances

Reporting entity	When information will be reported to clearinghouse
Prospective/Current Employer of CDL Driver	—An alcohol confirmation test with a concentration of 0.04 or higher. —Refusal to test (alcohol) as specified in 49 CFR 40.261. —Refusal to test (drug) not requiring a determination by the MRO as specified in 49 CFR 40.191. —Actual knowledge, as defined in 49 CFR 382.107, that a driver has used alcohol on duty, used alcohol within four hours of coming on duty, used alcohol prior to post-accident testing, or has used a controlled substance. —Negative return-to-duty test results (drug and alcohol testing, as applicable) —Completion of follow-up testing.
Service Agent acting on behalf of Current Employer of CDL Driver...................................	—An alcohol confirmation test with a concentration of 0.04 or higher. —Refusal to test (alcohol) as specified in 49 CFR 40.261. —Refusal to test (drug) not requiring a determination by the MRO as specified in 49 CFR 40.191. —Actual knowledge, as defined in 49 CFR 382.107, that a driver has used alcohol on duty, used alcohol within four hours of coming on duty, used alcohol prior to post-accident testing, or has used a controlled substance. —Negative return-to-duty test results (drug and alcohol testing, as applicable) —Completion of follow-up testing.
MRO	—Verified positive, adulterated, or substituted drug test result. —Refusal to test (drug) requiring a determination by the MRO as specified in 49 CFR 40.191.
SAP..	—Identification of driver and date the initial assessment was initiated. —Successful completion of treatment and/or education and the determination of eligibility for return-to-duty testing.

§382.707 Notice to drivers of entry, revision, removal, or release of information.

(a) FMCSA must notify a driver when information concerning that driver has been added to, revised, or removed from the Clearinghouse.

(b) FMCSA must notify a driver when information concerning that driver has been released from the Clearinghouse to an employer and specify the reason for the release.

(c) Drivers will be notified by letter sent by U.S. Mail to the address on record with the State Driver Licensing Agency that issued the driver's commercial driver's license. Exception: A driver may provide the Clearinghouse with an alternative means or address for notification, including electronic mail.

§382.709 Drivers' access to information in the Clearinghouse.

A driver may review information in the Clearinghouse about himself or herself, except as otherwise restricted by law or regulation. A driver must register with the Clearinghouse before accessing his or her information.

§382.711 Clearinghouse registration.

(a) **Clearinghouse registration required**. Each employer and service agent must register with the Clearinghouse before accessing or reporting information in the Clearinghouse.

(b) **Employers**. (1) Employer Clearinghouse registration must include:

(i) Name, address, and telephone number;

(ii) USDOT number, except if the registrant does not have a USDOT Number, it may be requested to provide other information to verify identity; and

(iii) Name of the person(s) the employer authorizes to report information to or obtain information from the Clearinghouse and any additional information FMCSA needs to validate his or her identity.

(2) Employers must verify the names of the person(s) authorized under paragraph (b)(1)(iii) of this section annually.

(3) Identification of the C/TPA or other service agent used to comply with the requirements of this part, if applicable, and authorization for the C/TPA to query or report information to the Clearinghouse. Employers must update any changes to this information within 10 days.

(c) **MROs and SAPs**. Each MRO or SAP must provide the following to apply for Clearinghouse registration:

(1) Name, address, telephone number, and any additional information FMCSA needs to validate the applicant's identity;

(2) A certification that the applicant's access to the Clearinghouse is conditioned on his or her compliance with the applicable qualification and/or training requirements in 49 CFR part 40; and

(3) Evidence of required professional credentials to verify that the applicant currently meets the applicable qualification and/or training requirements in 49 CFR part 40.

(d) **C/TPAs and other service agents**. Each consortium/third party administrator or other service agent must provide the following to apply for Clearinghouse registration:

(1) Name, address, telephone number, and any additional information FMCSA needs to validate the applicant's identity; and

(2) Name, title, and telephone number of the person(s) authorized to report information to and obtain information from the Clearinghouse.

(3) Each C/TPA or other service agent must verify the names of the person(s) authorized under paragraph (d)(2) of this section annually.

§382.713 Duration, cancellation, and revocation of access.

(a) **Term**. Clearinghouse registration is valid for 5 years, unless cancelled or revoked.

(b) **Cancellation**. FMCSA will cancel Clearinghouse registrations for anyone who has not queried or reported to the Clearinghouse for 2 years.

(c) **Revocation**. FMCSA has the right to revoke the Clearinghouse registration of anyone who fails to comply with any of the prescribed rights and restrictions on access to the Clearinghouse, including but not limited to, submission of inaccurate or false information and misuse or misappropriation of access

PART 382

rights or protected information from the Clearinghouse and failure to maintain the requisite qualifications, certifications and/or training requirements as set forth in part 40 of this title.

§382.715 Authorization to enter information into the Clearinghouse.

(a) **C/TPAs**. No C/TPA or other service agent may enter information into the Clearinghouse on an employer's behalf unless the employer designates the C/TPA or other service agent.

(b) **SAPs**. A driver must designate a SAP before that SAP can enter any information about the driver's return-to-duty process into the Clearinghouse.

§382.717 Procedures for correcting certain information in the database.

(a) **Petitions limited to incorrectly reported information**. (1) Under this section, petitioners may request only that administrative errors be corrected (*e.g.*, errors in data entry or a duplicate report of a positive test result); petitioners may not contest the accuracy of test results, test refusals, or other violation information, under this section.

(2) **Exceptions**. (i) Petitioners may request that FMCSA add documentary evidence of a non-conviction to an employer's report of actual knowledge that the driver received a traffic citation for driving a commercial motor vehicle while under the influence of alcohol or controlled substances if the citation did not result in a conviction. For the purposes of this section, conviction has the same meaning as used in 49 CFR part 383.

(ii) Petitioners may request that FMCSA remove from the Clearinghouse an employer's report of actual knowledge (other than as provided for in paragraph (a)(2)(i) of this section) if that report does not comply with the reporting requirements in §382.705(b)(5).

(iii) Petitioners may request that FMCSA remove from the Clearinghouse an employer's report of a violation under 49 CFR 40.261(a)(1) or 40.191(a)(1) if that report does not comply with the reporting requirements in §382.705(b)(3).

(b) **Petition**. Any driver or authorized representative of the driver may submit a petition to the FMCSA contesting the accuracy of information in the Clearinghouse. The petition must include:

(1) The petitioner's name, address, telephone number, and CDL number and State of issuance;

(2) Detailed description of the basis for the allegation that the information is not accurate; and

(3) Evidence supporting the allegation that the information is not accurate. Failure to submit evidence is cause for dismissing the petition.

(c) **Submission of petition**. The petitioner may submit his/her petition electronically through the Clearinghouse or in writing to: Federal Motor Carrier Safety Administration, ATTN: Drug and Alcohol Clearinghouse Petition for Review, 1200 New Jersey Avenue SE., Washington, DC 20590.

(d) **Notice of decision**. Within 45 days of receiving a complete petition, FMCSA will inform the driver in writing of its decision to remove, retain, or correct the information in the database and provide the basis for the decision.

(e) **Request for expedited treatment**. (1) A driver may request expedited treatment to correct inaccurate information in his or her Clearinghouse record under paragraph (a)(1) of this section if the inaccuracy is currently preventing him or her from performing safety-sensitive functions, or to remove employer reports under paragraph (a)(2) of this section if such reports are currently preventing him or her from performing safety-sensitive functions. This request may be included in the original petition or as a separate document.

(2) If FMCSA grants expedited treatment, it will subsequently inform the driver of its decision in writing within 14 days of receipt of a complete petition.

(f) **Administrative review**. (1) A driver may request FMCSA to conduct an administrative review if he or she believes that a decision made in accordance with paragraph (d) or (e) of this section was in error.

(2) The request must prominently state at the top of the document: "Administrative Review of Drug and Alcohol Clearinghouse Decision" and the driver may submit his/her request electronically through the Clearinghouse or in writing to FMCSA, ATTN: Drug and Alcohol Clearinghouse Administrative Review, Federal Motor Carrier Safety Administration, 1200 New Jersey Ave. SE., Washington, DC 20590.

(3) The driver's request must explain the error he or she believes FMCSA committed and provide information and/or documents to support his or her argument.

(4) FMCSA will complete its administrative review no later than 30 days after receiving the driver's request for review. FMCSA's decision will constitute the final Agency action.

(g) **Subsequent notification to employers**. When information is corrected or removed in accordance with this section, or in accordance with 49 CFR part 10, FMCSA will notify any employer that accessed the incorrect information that a correction or removal was made.

§382.719 Availability and removal of information.

(a) **Driver information not available**. Information about a driver's drug or alcohol violation will not be available to an employer conducting a query of the Clearinghouse after all of the following conditions relating to the violation are satisfied:

(1) The SAP reports to the Clearinghouse the information required in §382.705(d);

(2) The employer reports to the Clearinghouse that the driver's return-to-duty test results are negative;

(3) The driver's current employer reports that the driver has successfully completed all follow-up tests as prescribed in the SAP report in accordance with §§40.307, 40.309, and 40.311 of this title; and

(4) Five years have passed since the date of the violation determination.

(b) **Driver information remains available**. Information about a particular driver's drug or alcohol violation will remain available to employers conducting a query until all requirements in paragraph (a) of this section have been met.

(c) **Exceptions**. (1) Within 2 business days of granting a request for removal pursuant to §382.717(a)(2)(i), FMCSA will remove information from the Clearinghouse.

(2) Information about a particular driver's drug or alcohol violation may be removed in accordance with §382.717(a)(2)(ii) and (iii) or in accordance with 49 CFR part 10.

(d) **Driver information remains available**. Nothing in this part shall prevent FMCSA from using information removed under this section for research, auditing, or enforcement purposes.

§382.721 Fees.

FMCSA may collect a reasonable fee from entities required to query the Clearinghouse. Exception: No driver may be required to pay a fee to access his or her own information in the Clearinghouse.

§382.723 Unauthorized access or use prohibited.

(a) Except as expressly authorized in this subpart, no person or entity may access the Clearinghouse. No person or entity may share, distribute, publish, or otherwise release any information in the Clearinghouse except as specifically authorized by law. No person may report inaccurate or misleading information to the Clearinghouse.

(b) An employer's use of information received from the Clearinghouse is limited to determining whether a prohibition applies to a driver performing a safety-sensitive function with respect to a commercial motor vehicle. No employer may divulge or permit any other person or entity to divulge any information from the Clearinghouse to any person or entity not directly involved in determining whether a prohibition applies to a driver performing a safety-sensitive function with respect to a commercial motor vehicle.

(c) Violations of this section are subject to civil and criminal penalties in accordance with applicable law, including those set forth at §382.507.

(d) Nothing in this part shall prohibit FMCSA from accessing information about individual drivers in the Clearinghouse for research, auditing, or enforcement purposes.

§382.725 Access by State licensing authorities.

(a)(1) Before November 18, 2024, in order to determine whether a driver is qualified to operate a commercial motor vehicle, the chief commercial driver's licensing official of a State may obtain the driver's record from the Clearinghouse if the driver has applied for a commercial driver's license or commercial learner's permit from that State.

(2) On or after November 18, 2024, in order to determine whether a driver is qualified to operate a commercial motor vehicle, the chief commercial driver's licensing official of a State must obtain the driver's record from the Clearinghouse if the driver has applied for a commercial driver's license or commercial learner's permit from that State.

(b) By applying for a commercial driver's license or a commercial learner's permit, a driver is deemed to have consented to the release of information from the Clearinghouse in accordance with this section.

(c) The chief commercial driver's licensing official's use of information received from the Clearinghouse is limited to determining an individual's qualifications to operate a commercial motor vehicle. No chief commercial driver's licensing official may divulge or permit any other person or entity to divulge any information from the Clearinghouse to any person or entity not directly involved in determining an individual's qualifications to operate a commercial motor vehicle.

(d) A chief commercial driver's licensing official who does not take appropriate safeguards to protect the privacy and confidentiality of information obtained under this section is subject to revocation of his or her right of access under this section.

§382.727 Penalties.

An employer, employee, MRO, or service agent who violates any provision of this subpart shall be subject to the civil and/or criminal penalty provisions of 49 U.S.C. 521(b)(2)(C).

PART 383—COMMERCIAL DRIVER'S LICENSE STANDARDS; REQUIREMENTS AND PENALTIES

Subpart A—General

Subpart B—Single License Requirement

Subpart C—Notification Requirements and Employer Responsibilities

Subpart D—Driver Disqualifications and Penalties

Subpart E—Testing and Licensing Procedures

Subpart F—Vehicle Groups and Endorsements

Subpart G—Required Knowledge and Skills

Subpart H—Tests

Subpart I—Requirement for Transportation Security Administration Approval of Hazardous Materials Endorsement Issuances

Subpart J—Commercial Learner's Permit and Commercial Driver's License Documents

Authority: 49 U.S.C. 521, 31136, 31301 *et seq.*, and 31502; secs. 214 and 215 of Pub. L. 106-159, 113 Stat. 1748, 1766, 1767; sec. 1012(b) of Pub. L. 107-56, 115 Stat. 272, 297, sec. 4140 of Pub. L. 109-59, 119 Stat. 1144, 1746; sec. 32934 of Pub. L. 112-141, 126 Stat. 405, 830; and 49 CFR 1.87.

Subpart A—General

§383.1 Purpose and scope.

(a) The purpose of this part is to help reduce or prevent truck and bus accidents, fatalities, and injuries by requiring drivers to have a single commercial motor vehicle driver's license and by disqualifying drivers who operate commercial motor vehicles in an unsafe manner.

(b) This part:

(1) Prohibits a commercial motor vehicle driver from having more than one commercial motor vehicle driver's license;

(2) Requires a driver to notify the driver's current employer and the driver's State of domicile of certain convictions;

(3) Requires that a driver provide previous employment information when applying for employment as an operator of a commercial motor vehicle;

(4) Prohibits an employer from allowing a person with a suspended license to operate a commercial motor vehicle;

(5) Establishes periods of disqualification and penalties for those persons convicted of certain criminal and other offenses and serious traffic violations, or subject to any suspensions, revocations, or cancellations of certain driving privileges;

(6) Establishes testing and licensing requirements for commercial motor vehicle operators;

(7) Requires States to give knowledge and skills tests to all qualified applicants for commercial drivers' licenses which meet the Federal standard;

(8) Sets forth commercial motor vehicle groups and endorsements;

(9) Sets forth the knowledge and skills test requirements for the motor vehicle groups and endorsements;

(10) Sets forth the Federal standards for procedures, methods, and minimum passing scores for States and others to use in testing and licensing commercial motor vehicle operators; and

PART 383

(11) Establishes requirements for the State issued commercial license documentation.

§383.3 Applicability.

(a) The rules in this part apply to every person who operates a commercial motor vehicle (CMV) in interstate, foreign, or intrastate commerce, to all employers of such persons, and to all States.

(b) The exceptions contained in §390.3(f) of this subchapter do not apply to this part. The employers and drivers identified in §390.3(f) must comply with the requirements of this part, unless otherwise provided in this section.

(c) **Exception for certain military drivers.** Each State must exempt from the requirements of this part individuals who operate CMVs for military purposes. This exception is applicable to active duty military personnel; members of the military reserves; members of the national guard on active duty, including personnel on full-time national guard duty, personnel on part-time national guard training, and national guard military technicians (civilians who are required to wear military uniforms); and active duty U.S. Coast Guard personnel. This exception is not applicable to U.S. Reserve technicians.

(d) **Exception for farmers, firefighters, emergency response vehicle drivers; and drivers removing snow and ice.** A State may, at its discretion, exempt individuals identified in paragraphs (d)(1), (d)(2), and (d)(3) of this section from the requirements of this part. The use of this waiver is limited to the driver's home State unless there is a reciprocity agreement with adjoining States.

(1) Operators of a farm vehicle which is:

(i) Controlled and operated by a farmer, including operation by employees or family members;

(ii) Used to transport either agricultural products, farm machinery, farm supplies, or both to or from a farm;

(iii) Not used in the operations of a for-hire motor carrier, except for an exempt motor carrier as defined in §390.5 of this subchapter; and

(iv) Used within 241 kilometers (150 miles) of the farmer's farm.

(2) Firefighters and other persons who operate CMVs which are necessary to the preservation of life or property or the execution of emergency governmental functions, are equipped with audible and visual signals and are not subject to normal traffic regulation. These vehicles include fire trucks, hook and ladder trucks, foam or water transport trucks, police SWAT team vehicles, ambulances, or other vehicles that are used in response to emergencies.

(3)(i) A driver, employed by an eligible unit of local government, operating a commercial motor vehicle within the boundaries of that unit for the purpose of removing snow or ice from a roadway by plowing, sanding, or salting, if

(A) The properly licensed employee who ordinarily operates a commercial motor vehicle for these purposes is unable to operate the vehicle; or

(B) The employing governmental entity determines that a snow or ice emergency exists that requires additional assistance.

(ii) This exemption shall not preempt State laws and regulations concerning the safe operation of commercial motor vehicles.

(e) **Restricted commercial drivers license (CDL) for certain drivers in the State of Alaska**. (1) The State of Alaska may, at its discretion, waive only the following requirements of this part and issue a CDL to each driver that meets the conditions set forth in paragraphs (e) (2) and (3) of this section:

(i) The knowledge tests standards for testing procedures and methods of subpart H, but must continue to administer knowledge tests that fulfill the content requirements of subpart G for *all* applicants;

(ii) All the skills test requirements; and

(iii) The requirement under §383.153(a)(4) to have a photograph on the license document.

(2) Drivers of CMVs in the State of Alaska must operate exclusively over roads that meet *both* of the following criteria to be eligible for the exception in paragraph (e)(1) of this section:

(i) Such roads are not connected by land highway or vehicular way to the land-connected State highway system; and

(ii) Such roads are not connected to any highway or vehicular way with an average daily traffic volume greater than 499.

(3) Any CDL issued under the terms of this paragraph must carry two restrictions:

(i) Holders may not operate CMVs over roads other than those specified in paragraph (e)(2) of this section; and

(ii) The license is not valid for CMV operation outside the State of Alaska.

(f) **Restricted CDL for certain drivers in farm-related service industries**. (1) A State may, at its discretion, waive the required knowledge and skills tests of subpart H of this part and issue restricted CDLs to employees of these designated farm-related service industries:

(i) Agri-chemical businesses;

(ii) Custom harvesters;

(iii) Farm retail outlets and suppliers;

(iv) Livestock feeders.

(2) A restricted CDL issued pursuant to this paragraph shall meet all the requirements of this part, except subpart H of this part. A restricted CDL issued pursuant to this paragraph shall be accorded the same reciprocity as a CDL meeting all of the requirements of this part. The restrictions imposed upon the issuance of this restricted CDL shall not limit a person's use of the CDL in a non-CMV during either validated or non-validated periods, nor shall the CDL affect a State's power to administer its driver licensing program for operators of vehicles other than CMVs.

(3) A State issuing a CDL under the terms of this paragraph must restrict issuance as follows:

(i) Applicants must have a good driving record as defined in this paragraph. Drivers who have not held any motor vehicle operator's license for at least one year shall not be eligible for this CDL. Drivers who have between one and two years of driving experience must demonstrate a good driving record for their entire driving history. Drivers with more than two years of driving experience must have a good driving record for the two most recent years. For the purposes of this paragraph, the term *good driving record* means that an applicant:

(A) Has not had more than one license;

(B) Has not had *any* license suspended, revoked, or canceled;

(C) Has not had *any* conviction for any type of motor vehicle for the disqualifying offenses contained in §383.51(b);

(D) Has not had *any* conviction for any type of motor vehicle for serious traffic violations; and

(E) Has not had *any* conviction for a violation of State or local law relating to motor vehicle traffic control (other than a parking violation) arising in connection with any traffic accident, and has no record of an accident in which he/she was at fault.

(ii) Restricted CDLs shall have the same renewal cycle as unrestricted CDLs, but shall be limited to the seasonal period or periods as defined by the State of licensure, provided that the total number of calendar days in any 12-month period for which the restricted CDL is valid does not exceed 180. If a State elects to provide for more than one seasonal period, the restricted CDL is valid for commercial motor vehicle operation only during the currently approved season, and must be revalidated for each successive season. Only one seasonal period of validity may appear on the license document at a time. The good driving record must be confirmed prior to any renewal or revalidation.

(iii) Restricted CDL holders are limited to operating Group B and C vehicles, as described in subpart F of this part.

(iv) Restricted CDLs shall not be issued with *any* endorsements on the license document. Only the limited tank vehicle and hazardous materials endorsement privileges that the restricted CDL automatically confers and are described in paragraph (f)(3)(v) of this section are permitted.

(v) Restricted CDL holders may not drive vehicles carrying any placardable quantities of hazardous materials, except for diesel fuel in quantities of 3,785 liters (1,000 gallons) or less; liquid fertilizers (i.e., plant nutrients) in vehicles or implements of husbandry in total quantities of 11,355 liters (3,000 gallons) or less; and solid fertilizers (i.e., solid plant nutrients) that are not transported with any organic substance.

(vi) Restricted CDL holders may not hold an unrestricted CDL at the same time.

(vii) Restricted CDL holders may not operate a commercial motor vehicle beyond 241 kilometers (150 miles) from the place of business or the farm currently being served.

(g) **Restricted CDL for certain drivers in the pyrotechnic industry**. (1) A State may, at its discretion, waive the required hazardous materials knowledge tests of subpart H of this part and issue restricted CDLs to part-time drivers operating commercial motor vehicles transporting less than 227 kilograms (500 pounds) of fireworks classified as DOT Class 1.3G explosives.

(2) A State issuing a CDL under the terms of this paragraph must restrict issuance as follows:

(i) The GVWR of the vehicle to be operated must be less than 4,537 kilograms (10,001 pounds);

(ii) If a State believes, at its discretion, that the training required by §172.704 of this title adequately prepares part-time drivers meeting the other requirements of this paragraph to deal with fireworks and the other potential dangers posed by fireworks transportation and use, the State may waive the hazardous materials knowledge tests of subpart H of this part. The State may impose any requirements it believes is necessary to ensure itself that a driver is properly trained pursuant to §172.704 of this title.

(iii) A restricted CDL document issued pursuant to this paragraph shall have a statement clearly imprinted on the face of the document that is substantially similar as follows: "For use as a CDL only during the period from June 30 through

July 6 for purposes of transporting less than 227 kilograms (500 pounds) of fireworks classified as DOT Class 1.3G explosives in a vehicle with a GVWR of less than 4,537 kilograms (10,001 pounds).

(3) A restricted CDL issued pursuant to this paragraph shall meet all the requirements of this part, except those specifically identified. A restricted CDL issued pursuant to this paragraph shall be accorded the same reciprocity as a CDL meeting all of the requirements of this part. The restrictions imposed upon the issuance of this restricted CDL shall not limit a person's use of the CDL in a non-CMV during either validated or non-validated periods, nor shall the CDL affect a State's power to administer its driver licensing program for operators of vehicles other than CMVs.

(4) Restricted CDLs shall have the same renewal cycle as unrestricted CDLs, but shall be limited to the seasonal period of June 30 through July 6 of each year or a lesser period as defined by the State of licensure.

(5) Persons who operate commercial motor vehicles during the period from July 7 through June 29 for purposes of transporting less than 227 kilograms (500 pounds) of fireworks classified as DOT Class 1.3G explosives in a vehicle with a GVWR of less than 4,537 kilograms (10,001 pounds) and who also operate such vehicles for the same purposes during the period June 30 through July 6 shall not be issued a restricted CDL pursuant to this paragraph.

(h) **Exception for drivers of "covered farm vehicles."** The rules in this part do not apply to a driver of a "covered farm vehicle," as defined in §390.5 of this chapter.

(i) **Hazardous materials endorsement exemption for certain drivers transporting diesel**. A State may waive the requirement for a holder of a Class A commercial driver's license to obtain a hazardous materials endorsement under this part, if the license holder is:

(1) Acting within the scope of the license holder's employment, and within the State of domicile (or another State with a hazardous materials endorsement exemption) as an employee of a custom harvester operation, agrichemical business, farm retail outlet and supplier, or livestock feeder; and

(2) Operating a service vehicle that is:

(i) Transporting diesel in a quantity of 3,785 liters (1,000 gallons) or less; and

(ii) Clearly marked with a "flammable" or "combustible" placard, as appropriate.

§383.5 Definitions.

As used in this part:

Administrator means the Federal Motor Carrier Safety Administrator, the chief executive of the Federal Motor Carrier Safety Administration, an agency within the Department of Transportation.

Alcohol or alcoholic beverage means:

(1) Beer as defined in 26 U.S.C. 5052(a), of the Internal Revenue Code of 1954,

(2) wine of not less than one-half of one per centum of alcohol by volume, or

(3) distilled spirits as defined in section 5002(a)(8), of such Code.

Alcohol concentration (AC) means the concentration of alcohol in a person's blood or breath. When expressed as a percentage it means grams of alcohol per 100 milliliters of blood or grams of alcohol per 210 liters of breath.

Alien means any person not a citizen or national of the United States.

CDL downgrade means either:

(1) A State allows the driver to change his or her self-certification to interstate, but operating exclusively in transportation or operation excepted from part 391, as provided in §390.3(f), 391.2, 391.68 or 398.3 of this chapter;

(2) A State allows the driver to change his or her self-certification to intrastate only, if the driver qualifies under that State's physical qualification requirements for intrastate only;

(3) A State allows the driver to change his or her certification to intrastate, but operating exclusively in transportation or operations excepted from all or part of the State driver qualification requirements, or

(4) A State removes the CLP or CDL privilege from the driver's license.

CDL driver means a person holding a CDL or a person required to hold a CDL.

CDLIS driver record means the electronic record of the individual CDL driver's status and history stored by the State-of-Record as part of the Commercial Driver's License Information System (CDLIS) established under 49 U.S.C. 31309.

Commerce means

(1) Any trade, traffic, or transportation within the jurisdiction of the United States between a place in a State and a place outside of such State, including a place outside of the United States; or

(2) Trade, traffic, and transportation in the United States that affects any trade, traffic, and transportation described in paragraph (1) of this definition.

Commercial driver's license (CDL) means a license issued to an individual by a State or other jurisdiction of domicile, in accordance with the standards contained in this part, which authorizes the individual to operate a class of a commercial motor vehicle.

Commercial driver's license information system (CDLIS) means the CDLIS established by FMCSA pursuant to section 12007 of the Commercial Motor Vehicle Safety Act of 1986.

Commercial learner's permit (CLP) means a permit issued to an individual by a State or other jurisdiction of domicile, in accordance with the standards contained in this part, which, when carried with a valid driver's license issued by the same State or jurisdiction, authorizes the individual to operate a class of a commercial motor vehicle when accompanied by a holder of a valid CDL for purposes of behind-the-wheel training. When issued to a CDL holder, a CLP serves as authorization for accompanied behind-the-wheel training in a CMV for which the holder's current CDL is not valid.

Commercial motor vehicle (CMV) means a motor vehicle or combination of motor vehicles used in commerce to transport passengers or property if the motor vehicle is a—

(1) Combination Vehicle (Group A)—having a gross combination weight rating or gross combination weight of 11,794 kilograms or more (26,001 pounds or more), whichever is greater, inclusive of a towed unit(s) with a gross vehicle weight rating or gross vehicle weight of more than 4,536 kilograms (10,000 pounds), whichever is greater; or

(2) Heavy Straight Vehicle (Group B)—having a gross vehicle weight rating or gross vehicle weight of 11,794 or more kilograms (26,001 pounds or more), whichever is greater; or

(3) Small Vehicle (Group C) that does not meet Group A or B requirements but that either—

(i) Is designed to transport 16 or more passengers, including the driver; or

(ii) Is of any size and is used in the transportation of hazardous materials as defined in this section.

Controlled substance has the meaning such term has under 21 U.S.C. 802(6) and includes all substances listed on schedules I through V of 21 CFR 1308, (§§1308.11 through 1308.15) as they may be amended by the United States Department of Justice.

Conviction means an unvacated adjudication of guilt, or a determination that a person has violated or failed to comply with the law in a court of original jurisdiction or by an authorized administrative tribunal, an unvacated forfeiture of bail or collateral deposited to secure the person's appearance in court, a plea of guilty or nolo contendere accepted by the court, the payment of a fine or court cost, or violation of a condition of release without bail, regardless of whether or not the penalty is rebated, suspended, or probated.

Disqualification means any of the following three actions:

(1) The suspension, revocation, or cancellation of a CLP or CDL by the State or jurisdiction of issuance.

(2) Any withdrawal of a person's privileges to drive a CMV by a State or other jurisdiction as the result of a violation of State or local law relating to motor vehicle traffic control (other than parking, vehicle weight or vehicle defect violations).

(3) A determination by the FMCSA that a person is not qualified to operate a commercial motor vehicle under part 391 of this subchapter.

Driver applicant means an individual who applies to a State or other jurisdiction to obtain, transfer, upgrade, or renew a CDL or to obtain or renew a CLP.

Driver's license means a license issued by a State or other jurisdiction, to an individual which authorizes the individual to operate a motor vehicle on the highways.

Driving a commercial motor vehicle while under the influence of alcohol means committing any one or more of the following acts in a CMV—

(1) Driving a CMV while the person's alcohol concentration is 0.04 or more;

(2) Driving under the influence of alcohol, as prescribed by State law; or

(3) Refusal to undergo such testing as is required by any State or jurisdiction in the enforcement of §383.51(b) or §392.5(a)(2) of this subchapter.

Electronic device includes, but is not limited to, a cellular telephone; personal digital assistant; pager; computer; or any other device used to input, write, send, receive, or read text.

Eligible unit of local government means a city, town, borough, county, parish, district, or other public body created by or pursuant to State law which has a total population of 3,000 individuals or less.

Employee means any operator of a commercial motor vehicle, including full time, regularly employed drivers; casual, intermittent or occasional drivers; leased drivers and independent, owner-operator contractors (while in the course of operating a commercial motor vehicle) who are either directly employed by or under lease to an employer.

Employer means any person (including the United States, a State, District of Columbia or a political subdivision of a State) who owns or leases a commercial motor vehicle or assigns employees to operate such a vehicle.

Endorsement means an authorization to an individual's CLP or CDL required to permit the individual to operate certain types of commercial motor vehicles.

Fatality means the death of a person as a result of a motor vehicle accident.

Felony means an offense under State or Federal law that is punishable by death or imprisonment for a term exceeding 1 year.

Foreign means outside the fifty United States and the District of Columbia.

Foreign commercial driver means an individual licensed to operate a commercial motor vehicle by an authority outside the United States, or a citizen of a foreign country who operates a commercial motor vehicle in the United States.

Gross combination weight rating (GCWR) is the greater of:

(1) A value specified by the manufacturer of the power unit, if such value is displayed on the Federal Motor Vehicle Safety Standard (FMVSS) certification label required by the National Highway Traffic Safety Administration, or

(2) The sum of the gross vehicle weight ratings (GVWRs) or the gross vehicle weights (GVWs) of the power unit and the towed unit(s), or any combination thereof, that produces the highest value. Exception: The GCWR of the power unit will not be used to define a commercial motor vehicle when the power unit is not towing another vehicle.

Gross vehicle weight rating (GVWR) means the value specified by the manufacturer as the loaded weight of a single vehicle.

Hazardous materials means any material that has been designated as hazardous under 49 U.S.C. 5103 and is required to be placarded under subpart F of 49 CFR part 172 or any quantity of a material listed as a select agent or toxin in 42 CFR part 73.

Imminent hazard means the existence of any condition of vehicle, employee, or commercial motor vehicle operations that substantially increases the likelihood of serious injury or death if not discontinued immediately; or a condition relating to hazardous material that presents a substantial likelihood that death, serious illness, severe personal injury, or a substantial endangerment to health, property, or the environment may occur before the reasonably foreseeable completion date of a formal proceeding begun to lessen the risk of that death, illness, injury or endangerment.

Manual transmission (also known as a stick shift, stick, straight drive or standard transmission) means a transmission utilizing a driver-operated clutch that is activated by a pedal or lever and a gear-shift mechanism operated either by hand or foot. All other transmissions, whether semi-automatic or automatic, will be considered automatic for the purposes of the standardized restriction code.

Military service member means a member of the United States Army, Navy, Marine Corps, Air Force, and Coast Guard, and their associated reserve, and National Guard units.

Military services means the United States Army, Navy, Marine Corps, Air Force, and Coast Guard, and their associated reserve and National Guard units.

Mobile telephone means a mobile communication device that falls under or uses any commercial mobile radio service, as defined in regulations of the Federal Communications Commission, 47 CFR 20.3. It does not include two-way or Citizens Band Radio services.

Motor vehicle means a vehicle, machine, tractor, trailer, or semitrailer propelled or drawn by mechanical power used on highways, except that such term does not include a vehicle, machine, tractor, trailer, semitrailer operated exclusively on a rail.

Non-CDL means any other type of motor vehicle license, such as an automobile driver's license, a chauffeur's license, or a motorcycle license.

Non-domiciled CLP or Non-domiciled CDL means a CLP or CDL, respectively, issued by a State or other jurisdiction under either of the following two conditions:

(1) To an individual domiciled in a foreign country meeting the requirements of §383.23(b)(1).

(2) To an individual domiciled in another State meeting the requirements of §383.23(b)(2).

Non-CMV means a motor vehicle or combination of motor vehicles not defined by the term "commercial motor vehicle (CMV)" in this section.

Out-of-service order means a declaration by an authorized enforcement officer of a Federal, State, Canadian, Mexican, or local jurisdiction that a driver, a commercial motor vehicle, or a motor carrier operation, is out-of-service pursuant to §§386.72, 392.5, 395.13, 396.9, or compatible laws, or the North American Uniform Out-of-Service Criteria.

Representative vehicle means a motor vehicle which represents the type of motor vehicle that a driver applicant operates or expects to operate.

School bus means a CMV used to transport pre-primary, primary, or secondary school students from home to school, from school to home, or to and from school-sponsored events. School bus does not include operations of a for-hire motor carrier.

State means a State of the United States and the District of Columbia.

State of domicile means that State where a person has his/her true, fixed, and permanent home and principal residence and to which he/she has the intention of returning whenever he/she is absent.

Tank vehicle means any commercial motor vehicle that is designed to transport any liquid or gaseous materials within a tank or tanks having an individual rated capacity of more than 119 gallons and an aggregate rated capacity of 1,000 gallons or more that is either permanently or temporarily attached to the vehicle or the chassis. A commercial motor vehicle transporting an empty storage container tank, not designed for transportation, with a rated capacity of 1,000 gallons or more that is temporarily attached to a flatbed trailer is not considered a tank vehicle.

Texting means manually entering alphanumeric text into, or reading text from, an electronic device.

(1) This action includes, but is not limited to, short message service, emailing, instant messaging, a command or request to access a World Wide Web page, pressing more than a single button to initiate or terminate a voice communication using a mobile telephone, or engaging in any other form of electronic text retrieval or entry, for present or future communication.

(2) Texting does not include:

(i) Inputting, selecting, or reading information on a global positioning system or navigation system; or

(ii) Pressing a single button to initiate or terminate a voice communication using a mobile telephone; or

(iii) Using a device capable of performing multiple functions (*e.g.*, fleet management systems, dispatching devices, smart phones, citizens band radios, music players, *etc.*) for a purpose that is not otherwise prohibited in this part.

Third party skills test examiner means a person employed by a third party tester who is authorized by the State to administer the CDL skills tests specified in subparts G and H of this part.

Third party tester means a person (including, but not limited to, another State, a motor carrier, a private driver training facility or other private institution, or a department, agency or instrumentality of a local government) authorized by the State to employ skills test examiners to administer the CDL skills tests specified in subparts G and H of this part.

TWIC means Transportation Worker Identification Credential as that term is defined in 49 CFR 1570.3, which is the transportation security card issued by TSA under the authority of 46 U.S.C. 70105.

United States means the 50 States and the District of Columbia.

Vehicle means a motor vehicle unless otherwise specified.

Vehicle group means a class or type of vehicle with certain operating characteristics.

§383.7 Validity of CDL issued by decertified State.

A CDL issued by a State prior to the date the State is notified by the Administrator, in accordance with the provisions of §384.405 of this subchapter, that the State is prohibited from issuing CDLs, will remain valid until its stated expiration date.

Subpart B—Single License Requirement

§383.21 Number of drivers' licenses.

No person who operates a commercial motor vehicle shall at any time have more than one driver's license.

§383.23 Commercial driver's license.

(a) **General rule.** (1) No person shall operate a CMV unless such person has taken and passed knowledge and driving skills tests for a CLP or CDL that meet the Federal standards contained in subparts F, G, and H of this part for the CMV that person operates or expects to operate.

(2) Except as provided in paragraph (b) of this section, no person may legally operate a CMV unless such person possesses a CDL which meets the standards contained in subpart J of this part, issued by his/her State or jurisdiction of domicile.

(b) **Exception.** (1) If a CMV operator is not domiciled in a foreign jurisdiction that the Administrator has determined tests drivers and issues CDLs in accordance with, or under standards similar to, the standards contained in subparts F, G, and H of this part, [1] the person may obtain a Non-domiciled CLP or Non-domiciled CDL from a State that does comply with the testing and licensing standards contained in such subparts F, G, and H of this part, so long as that person meets the requirements of §383.71(f).

---

[1] Effective December 29, 1988, the Administrator determined that commercial driver's licenses issued by Canadian Provinces and Territories in conformity with the Canadian National Safety Code are in accordance with the standards of this part. Effective November 21, 1991, and as amended on January 19, 2017, the Administrator determined that the new Licencias Federales de Conductor issued by the United Mexican States are in accordance with the standards of this part. Therefore, under the single license provision of §383.21, a driver

(2) If an individual is domiciled in a State while that State is prohibited from issuing CDLs in accordance with §384.405 of this subchapter, that individual is eligible to obtain a Non-domiciled CLP or Non-domiciled CDL from any State that elects to issue a Non-domiciled CDL and which complies with the testing and licensing standards contained in subparts F, G, and H of this part, so long as that person meets the requirements of §383.71(f).

(3) If an individual possesses a CLP, as defined in §383.5, the individual is authorized to operate a class of CMV as provided by the CLP in accordance with §383.25.

§383.25 Commercial learner's permit (CLP).

(a) A CLP is considered a valid CDL for purposes of behind-the-wheel training on public roads or highways, if all of the following minimum conditions are met:

(1) The CLP holder is at all times accompanied by the holder of a valid CDL who has the proper CDL group and endorsement(s) necessary to operate the CMV. The CDL holder must at all times be physically present in the front seat of the vehicle next to the CLP holder or, in the case of a passenger vehicle, directly behind or in the first row behind the driver and must have the CLP holder under observation and direct supervision.

(2) The CLP holder holds a valid driver's license issued by the same jurisdiction that issued the CLP.

(3) The CLP holder must have taken and passed a general knowledge test that meets the Federal standards contained in subparts F, G, and H of this part for the commercial motor vehicle that person operates or expects to operate.

(4) The CLP holder must be 18 years of age or older.

(5) Endorsements:

(i) A CLP holder with a passenger (P) endorsement must have taken and passed the P endorsement knowledge test. A CLP holder with a P endorsement is prohibited from operating a CMV carrying passengers, other than Federal /State auditors and inspectors, test examiners, other trainees, and the CDL holder accompanying the CLP holder as prescribed by paragraph (a)(1) of this section. The P endorsement must be class specific.

(ii) A CLP holder with a school bus (S) endorsement must have taken and passed the S endorsement knowledge test. A CLP holder with an S endorsement is prohibited from operating a school bus with passengers other than Federal /State auditors and inspectors, test examiners, other trainees, and the CDL holder accompanying the CLP holder as prescribed by paragraph (a)(1) of this section.

(iii) A CLP holder with a tank vehicle (N) endorsement must have taken and passed the N endorsement knowledge test. A CLP holder with an N endorsement may only operate an empty tank vehicle and is prohibited from operating any tank vehicle that previously contained hazardous materials that has not been purged of any residue.

(iv) All other Federal endorsements are prohibited on a CLP.

(6) The CLP holder does not operate a commercial motor vehicle transporting hazardous materials as defined in §383.5.

(b) The CLP must be a separate document from the CDL or non-CDL.

holding a commercial driver's license issued under the Canadian National Safety Code or a new Licencia Federal de Conductor issued by Mexico is prohibited from obtaining a non-domiciled CDL, or any other type of driver's license, from a State or other jurisdiction in the United States.

(c) The CLP must be valid for no more than one year from the initial date of issuance without requiring the CLP holder to retake the general and endorsement knowledge tests. CLPs issued for a period of less than one year may be renewed provided the CLP is not valid for more than one year from the date of initial issuance.

(d) The issuance of a CLP is a precondition to the initial issuance of a CDL. The issuance of a CLP is also a precondition to the upgrade of a CDL if the upgrade requires a skills test.

(e) The CLP holder is not eligible to take the CDL skills test in the first 14 days after initial issuance of the CLP.

Subpart C—Notification Requirements and Employer Responsibilities

§383.31 Notification of convictions for driver violations.

(a) Except as provided in paragraph (d) of this section, each person who operates a commercial motor vehicle, who has a commercial learner's permit or commercial driver's license issued by a State or jurisdiction, and who is convicted of violating, in any type of motor vehicle, a State or local law relating to motor vehicle traffic control (other than a parking violation) in a State or jurisdiction other than the one which issued his/her permit or license, shall notify an official designated by the State or jurisdiction which issued such permit or license, of such conviction. The notification must be made within 30 days after the date that the person has been convicted.

(b) Each person who operates a commercial motor vehicle, who has a commercial driver's license issued by a State or jurisdiction, and who is convicted of violating, in any type of motor vehicle, a State or local law relating to motor vehicle traffic control (other than a parking violation), shall notify his/her current employer of such conviction. The notification must be made within 30 days after the date that the person has been convicted. If the driver is not currently employed, he/she must notify the State or jurisdiction which issued the license according to §383.31(a).

(c) **Notification**. The notification to the State official and employer must be made in writing and contain the following information:

(1) Driver's full name;

(2) Driver's license number;

(3) Date of conviction;

(4) The specific criminal or other offense(s), serious traffic violation(s), and other violation(s) of State or local law relating to motor vehicle traffic control, for which the person was convicted and any suspension, revocation, or cancellation of certain driving privileges which resulted from such conviction(s);

(5) Indication whether the violation was in a commercial motor vehicle;

(6) Location of offense; and

(7) Driver's signature.

(d) A person is considered to be in compliance with the requirements of paragraph (a) of this section if the conviction occurs in a State or jurisdiction that is in substantial compliance with 49 CFR 384.209 and has not been de-certified in accordance with 49 CFR 384.405.

§383.33 Notification of driver's license suspensions.

Each employee who has a driver's license suspended, revoked, or canceled by a State or jurisdiction, who loses the right to operate a commercial motor vehicle in a State or jurisdiction for any period, or who is disqualified from operating a commercial motor vehicle for any period, shall notify his/her current employer of such suspension, revocation, cancellation, lost privilege, or disqualification. The notification must be made before the end of the business day following the day the employee received notice of suspension, revocation, cancellation, lost privilege, or disqualification.

§383.35 Notification of previous employment.

(a) Any person applying for employment as an operator of a commercial motor vehicle shall provide at the time of application for employment, the information specified in paragraph (c) of this section.

(b) All employers shall request the information specified in paragraph (c) of this section from all persons applying for employment as a commercial motor vehicle operator. The request shall be made at the time of application for employment.

(c) The following employment history information for the 10 years preceding the date the application is submitted shall be presented to the prospective employer by the applicant:

(1) A list of the names and addresses of the applicant's previous employers for which the applicant was an operator of a commercial motor vehicle;

(2) The dates the applicant was employed by these employers; and

(3) The reason for leaving such employment.

(d) The applicant shall certify that all information furnished is true and complete.

(e) An employer may require an applicant to provide additional information.

(f) Before an application is submitted, the employer shall inform the applicant that the information he/she provides in accordance with paragraph (c) of this section may be used, and the applicant's previous employers may be contacted for the purpose of investigating the applicant's work history.

§383.37 Employer responsibilities.

No employer may allow, require, permit, or authorize a driver to operate a CMV in the United States if he or she knows or should reasonably know that any of the following circumstances exist:

(a) During any period in which the driver does not have a current CLP or CDL or does not have a CLP or CDL with the proper class or endorsements. An employer may not use a driver to operate a CMV who violates any restriction on the driver's CLP or CDL.

(b) During any period in which the driver has a CLP or CDL disqualified by a State, has lost the right to operate a CMV in a State, or has been disqualified from operating a CMV.

(c) During any period in which the driver has more than one CLP or CDL.

(d) During any period in which the driver, or the CMV he/she is driving, or the motor carrier operation, is subject to an out-of-service order.

(e) In violation of a Federal, State, or local law or regulation pertaining to railroad-highway grade crossings.

PART 383

Subpart D—Driver Disqualifications and Penalties

§383.51 Disqualification of drivers.

(a) **General**. (1) A person required to have a CLP or CDL who is disqualified must not drive a CMV.

(2) An employer must not knowingly allow, require, permit, or authorize a driver who is disqualified to drive a CMV.

(3) A holder of a CLP or CDL is subject to disqualification sanctions designated in paragraphs (b) and (c) of this section, if the holder drives a CMV or non-CMV and is convicted of the violations listed in those paragraphs.

(4) Determining first and subsequent violations. For purposes of determining first and subsequent violations of the offenses specified in this subpart, each conviction for any offense listed in Tables 1 through 4 to this section resulting from a separate incident, whether committed in a CMV or non-CMV, must be counted.

(5) The disqualification period must be in addition to any other previous periods of disqualification.

(6) Reinstatement after lifetime disqualification. A State may reinstate any driver disqualified for life for offenses described in paragraphs (b)(1) through (8) of this section (Table 1 to §383.51) after 10 years, if that person has voluntarily entered and successfully completed an appropriate rehabilitation program approved by the State. Any person who has been reinstated in accordance with this provision and who is subsequently convicted of a disqualifying offense described in paragraphs (b)(1) through (8) of this section (Table 1 to §383.51) must not be reinstated.

(7) A foreign commercial driver is subject to disqualification under this subpart.

(b) **Disqualification for major offenses**. Table 1 to §383.51 contains a list of the offenses and periods for which a person who is required to have a CLP or CDL is disqualified, depending upon the type of vehicle the driver is operating at the time of the violation, as follows:

Table 1 to §383.51

If a driver operates a motor vehicle and is convicted of:	For a first conviction or refusal to be tested while operating a CMV, a person required to have a CLP or CDL and a CLP or CDL holder must be disqualified from operating a CMV for	For a first conviction or refusal to be tested while operating a non-CMV, a CLP or CDL holder must be disqualified from operating a CMV for	For a first conviction or refusal to be tested while operating a CMV transporting hazardous materials as defined in §383.5, a person required to have a CLP or CDL and a CLP or CDL holder must be disqualified from operating a CMV for	For a second conviction or refusal to be tested in a separate incident of any combination of offenses in this Table while operating a CMV, a person required to have a CLP or CDL and a CLP or CDL holder must be disqualified from operating a CMV for	For a second conviction or refusal to be tested in a separate incident of any combination of offenses in this Table while operating a non-CMV, a CLP or CDL holder must be disqualified from operating a CMV for ....
(1) Being under the influence of alcohol as prescribed by State law.	1 year	1 year	3 years	Life	Life
(2) Being under the influence of a controlled substance.	1 year	1 year	3 years	Life	Life
(3) Having an alcohol concentration of 0.04 or greater while operating a CMV	1 year	Not applicable	3 years	Life	Not applicable
(4) Refusing to take an alcohol test as required by a State or jurisdiction under its implied consent laws or regulations as defined in §383.72 of this part.	1 year	1 year	3 years	Life	Life
(5) Leaving the scene of an accident.	1 year	1 year	3 years	Life	Life
(6) Using the vehicle to commit a felony, other than a felony described in paragraph (b)(9) or (10) of this table.	1 year	1 year	3 years	Life	Life

Table 1 to §383.51, Continued

(7) Driving a CMV when, as a result of prior violations committed operating a CMV, the driver's CLP or CDL is revoked, suspended, or canceled, or the driver is disqualified from operating a CMV.	1 year	Not applicable	3 years	Life	Not applicable
(8) Causing a fatality through the negligent operation of a CMV, including but not limited to the crimes of motor vehicle manslaughter, homicide by motor vehicle and negligent homicide.	1 year	Not applicable	3 years	Life	Not applicable
(9) Using the vehicle in the commission of a felony involving manufacturing, distributing, or dispensing a controlled substance.	Life-not eligible for 10-year reinstatement.	Life-not eligible for 10-year reinstatement.	Life-not eligible for 10-year reinstatement.	Life-not eligible for 10-year reinstatement.	Life-not eligible for 10-year reinstatement.
(10) Using a CMV in the commission of a felony involving an act or practice of severe forms of trafficking in persons, as defined and described in 22 U.S.C. 7102(11).	Life—not eligible for 10-year reinstatement.	Not applicable	Life—not eligible for 10-year reinstatement.	Life—not eligible for 10-year reinstatement.	Not applicable.

(c) **Disqualification for serious traffic violations.** Table 2 to §383.51 contains a list of the offenses and the periods for which a person who is required to have a CLP or CDL is disqualified, depending upon the type of vehicle the driver is operating at the time of the violation, as follows:

Table 2 to §383.51

If the driver operates a motor vehicle and is convicted of:	For a second conviction of any combination of offenses in this Table in a separate incident within a 3-year period while operating a CMV, a person required to have a CLP or CDL and a CLP or CDL holder must be disqualified from operating a CMV for .	For a second conviction of any combination of offenses in this Table in a separate incident within a 3-year period while operating a non-CMV, a CLP or CDL holder must be disqualified from operating a CMV, if the conviction results in the revocation, cancellation, or suspension of the CLP or CDL holder's license or non-CMV driving privileges, for .	For a third or subsequent conviction of any combination of offenses in this Table in a separate incident within a 3-year period while operating a CMV, a person required to have a CLP or CDL and a CLP or CDL holder must be disqualified from operating a CMV for .	For a third or subsequent conviction of any combination of offenses in this Table in a separate incident within a 3-year period while operating a non-CMV, a CLP or CDL holder must be disqualified from operating a CMV, if the conviction results in the revocation, cancellation, or suspension of the CLP or CDL holder's license or non-CMV driving privileges, for .
(1) Speeding excessively, involving any speed of 24.1 kmph (15 mph) or more above the regulated or posted speed limit.	60 days	60 days	120 days	120 days
(2) Driving recklessly, as defined by State or local law or regulation, including but, not limited to, offenses of driving a motor vehicle in willful or wanton disregard for the safety of persons or property.	60 days	60 days	120 days	120 days
(3) Making improper or erratic traffic lane changes.	60 days	60 days	120 days	120 days
(4) Following the vehicle ahead too closely.	60 days	60 days	120 days	120 days

Table 2 to §383.51, Continued

(5) Violating State or local law relating to motor vehicle traffic control (other than a parking violation) arising in connection with a fatal accident.	60 days	60 days	120 days	120 days	120 days
(6) Driving a CMV without obtaining a CLP or CDL.	60 days	Not applicable	120 days	120 days	Not applicable
(7) Driving a CMV without a CLP or CDL in the driver's possession[1].	60 days	Not applicable	120 days	120 days	Not applicable
(8) Driving a CMV without the proper class of CLP or CDL and/or endorsements for the specific vehicle group being operated or for the passengers or type of cargo being transported.	60 days	Not applicable	120 days	120 days	Not applicable
(9) Violating a State or local law or ordinance on motor vehicle traffic control prohibiting texting while driving a CMV.[2]	60 days	Not applicable	120 days	120 days	Not applicable.
(10) Violating a State or local law or ordinance on motor vehicle traffic control restricting or prohibiting the use of a hand-held mobile telephone while driving a CMV.[2]	60 days	Not applicable	120 days	120 days	Not applicable.

[1]Any individual who provides proof to the enforcement authority that issued the citation, by the date the individual must appear in court or pay any fine for such a violation, that the individual held a valid CLP or CDL on the date the citation was issued, shall not be guilty of this offense.

[2]*Driving, for the purpose of this disqualification*, means operating a commercial motor vehicle on a highway, including while temporarily stationary because of traffic, a traffic control device, or other momentary delays. Driving does not include operating a commercial motor vehicle when the driver has moved the vehicle to the side of, or off, a highway and has halted in a location where the vehicle can safely remain stationary.

(d) **Disqualification for railroad-highway grade crossing offenses.** Table 3 to §383.51 contains a list of the offenses and the periods for which a person who is required to have a CLP or CDL is disqualified, when the driver is operating a CMV at the time of the violation, as follows:

Table 3 to §383.51

If the driver is convicted of operating a CMV in violation of a Federal, State or local law because	For a first conviction a person required to have a CLP or CDL and a CLP or CDL holder must be disqualified from operating a CMV for	For a second conviction of any combination of offenses in this Table in a separate incident within a 3-year period, a person required to have a CLP or CDL and a CLP or CDL holder must be disqualified from operating a CMV for .	For a third or subsequent conviction of any combination of offenses in this Table in a separate incident within a 3-year period, a person required to have a CLP or CDL and a CLP or CDL holder must be disqualified from operating a CMV for ....
(1) The driver is not required to always stop, but fails to slow down and check that tracks are clear of an approaching train.	No less than 60 days	No less than 120 days	No less than 1 year.
(2) The driver is not required to always stop, but fails to stop before reaching the crossing, if the tracks are not clear.	No less than 60 days	No less than 120 days	No less than 1 year.
(3) The driver is always required to stop, but fails to stop before driving onto the crossing.	No less than 60 days	No less than 120 days	No less than 1 year.
(4) The driver fails to have sufficient space to drive completely through the crossing without stopping.	No less than 60 days	No less than 120 days	No less than 1 year.
(5) The driver fails to obey a traffic control device or the directions of an enforcement official at the crossing.	No less than 60 days	No less than 120 days	No less than 1 year.
(6) The driver fails to negotiate a crossing because of insufficient undercarriage clearance.	No less than 60 days	No less than 120 days	No less than 1 year.

(e) **Disqualification for violating out-of-service orders.** Table 4 to §383.51 contains a list of the offenses and periods for which a person who is required to have a CLP or CDL is disqualified when the driver is operating a CMV at the time of the violation, as follows:

Table 4 to §383.51

If the driver operates a CMV and is convicted of	For a first conviction while operating a CMV, a person required to have a CLP or CDL and a CLP or CDL holder must be disqualified from operating a CMV for	For a second conviction in a separate incident within a 10-year period while operating a CMV, a person required to have a CLP or CDL and a CLP or CDL holder must be disqualified from operating a CMV for ...	For a third or subsequent conviction in a separate incident within a 10-year period while operating a CMV, a person required to have a CLP or CDL and a CLP or CDL holder must be disqualified from operating a CMV for ...
(1) Violating a driver or vehicle out-of-service order while transporting nonhazardous materials.	No less than 180 days or more than 1 year.	No less than 2 years or more than 5 years.	No less than 3 years or more than 5 years.
(2) Violating a driver or vehicle out-of-service order while transporting hazardous materials as defined in §383.5 of this title, or while operating a vehicle designed to transport 16 or more passengers, including the driver.	No less than 180 days or more than 2 years.	No less than 3 years or more than 5 years.	No less than 3 years or more than 5 years.

§383.52 Disqualification of drivers determined to constitute an imminent hazard.

(a) The Assistant Administrator or his/her designee must disqualify from operating a CMV any driver whose driving is determined to constitute an imminent hazard, as defined in §383.5.

(b) The period of the disqualification may not exceed 30 days unless the FMCSA complies with the provisions of paragraph (c) of this section.

(c) The Assistant Administrator or his/her delegate may provide the driver an opportunity for a hearing after issuing a disqualification for a period of 30 days or less. The Assistant Administrator or his/her delegate must provide the driver notice of a proposed disqualification period of more than 30 days and an opportunity for a hearing to present a defense to the proposed disqualification. A disqualification imposed under this paragraph may not exceed one year in duration. The driver, or a representative on his/her behalf, may file an appeal of the disqualification issued by the Assistant Administrator's delegate with the Assistant Administrator, Adjudications Counsel (MC-CC), Federal Motor Carrier Safety Administration, 1200 New Jersey Ave., SE., Washington, DC 20590-0001.

(d) Any disqualification imposed in accordance with the provisions of this section must be transmitted by the FMCSA to the jurisdiction where the driver is licensed and must become a part of the driver's record maintained by that jurisdiction.

(e) A driver who is simultaneously disqualified under this section and under other provisions of this subpart, or under State law or regulation, shall serve those disqualification periods concurrently.

§383.53 Penalties.

(a) **General rule**. Any person who violates the rules set forth in subparts B and C of this part may be subject to civil or criminal penalties under 49 U.S.C. 521(b), as provided in part 386, Appendix B, of this chapter.

(b) **Special penalties pertaining to violation of out-of-service orders** — (1) **Driver violations**. A driver who is convicted of violating an out-of-service order shall be subject to a civil penalty as stated in part 386 Appendix B, in addition to disqualification under §383.51(e).

(2) **Employer violations**. An employer who is convicted of a violation of §383.37(d) shall be subject to a civil penalty as stated in part 386, appendix B, of this chapter.

(c) **Special penalties pertaining to railroad-highway grade crossing violations**. An employer who is convicted of a violation of §383.37(e) shall be subject to a civil penalty stated in part 386, appendix B, of this chapter.

Subpart E—Testing and Licensing Procedures

§383.71 Driver application and certification procedures.

(a) **Commercial Learner's Permit**. Prior to obtaining a CLP, a person must meet the following requirements:

(1) The person must be 18 years of age or older and provide proof of his/her age.

(2) The person must have taken and passed a general knowledge test that meets the Federal standards contained in subparts F, G, and H of this part for the commercial motor vehicle group that person operates or expects to operate.

(3) The person must certify that he/she is not subject to any disqualification under §383.51, or any license disqualification under State law, and that he/she does not have a driver's license from more than one State or jurisdiction.

(4) The person must provide to the State of issuance the information required to be included on the CLP as specified in subpart J of this part.

(5) The person must provide to the State proof of citizenship or lawful permanent residency as specified in Table 1 of this section or obtain a Non-domiciled CLP as specified in paragraph (f) of this section.

(6) The person must provide proof that the State to which application is made is his/her State of domicile, as the term is defined in §383.5. Acceptable proof of domicile is a document with the person's name and residential address within the State, such as a government issued tax form.

(7) The person must provide the names of all States where the applicant has been licensed to drive any type of motor vehicle during the previous 10 years.

(8) A person seeking a passenger (P), school bus (S) or tank vehicle (N) endorsement must have taken and passed the endorsement knowledge test for the specific endorsement.

(9) The person must provide the State the certification contained in paragraph (b)(1) of this section.

(10) Beginning on February 7, 2022, a person must complete the training prescribed in subpart F of part 380 of this chapter before taking the skills test for a Class A or B CDL for the first time, or a skills test for a passenger (P) or school bus (S) endorsement for the first time, or the knowledge test for a hazardous materials (H) endorsement for the first time. The training must be administered by a provider listed on the Training Provider Registry.

(b) **Initial Commercial Driver's License**. Prior to obtaining a CDL, a person must meet all of the following requirements:

(1) **Initial Commercial Driver's License applications submitted on or after January 30, 2012**. Any person applying for a CDL on or after January 30, 2012, must meet the requirements set forth in paragraphs (b)(2) through (10), and (h) of this section, and make one of the following applicable certifications in paragraph (b)(1)(i), (ii), (iii), or (iv) of this section:

(i) **Non-excepted interstate**. A person must certify that he/she operates or expects to operate in interstate commerce, is both subject to and meets the qualification requirements under 49 CFR part 391, and is required to obtain a medical examiner's certificate by §391.45 of this chapter;

(ii) **Excepted interstate**. A person must certify that he/she operates or expects to operate in interstate commerce, but engages exclusively in transportation or operations excepted under 49 CFR 390.3(f), 391.2, 391.68, or 398.3 from all or parts of the qualification requirements of 49 CFR part 391, and is therefore not required to obtain a medical examiner's certificate by 49 CFR 391.45 of this chapter;

(iii) **Non-excepted intrastate**. A person must certify that he/she operates only in intrastate commerce and therefore is subject to State driver qualification requirements; or

(iv) **Excepted intrastate**. A person must certify that he/she operates in intrastate commerce, but engages exclusively in transportation or operations excepted from all or parts of the State driver qualification requirements.

(2) The person must pass a driving or skills test in accordance with the standards contained in subparts F, G, and H of this part taken in a motor vehicle that is representative of the type of motor vehicle the person operates or expects to

operate; or provide evidence that he/she has successfully passed a driving test administered by an authorized third party.

(3) The person must certify that the motor vehicle in which the person takes the driving skills test is representative of the type of motor vehicle that person operates or expects to operate.

(4) The person must provide the State the information required to be included on the CDL as specified in subpart J of this part.

(5) The person must certify that he/she is not subject to any disqualification under §383.51, or any license disqualification under State law, and that he/she does not have a driver's license from more than one State or jurisdiction.

(6) The person must surrender his/her non-CDL driver's licenses and CLP to the State.

(7) The person must provide the names of all States where he/she has previously been licensed to drive any type of motor vehicle during the previous 10 years.

(8) If the person is applying for a hazardous materials endorsement, he/she must comply with Transportation Security Administration requirements codified in 49 CFR part 1572. A lawful permanent resident of the United States requesting a hazardous materials endorsement must additionally provide his /her U.S. Citizenship and Immigration Services (USCIS) Alien registration number.

(9) The person must provide proof of citizenship or lawful permanent residency as specified in Table 1 of this section, or be registered under paragraph (f) of this section.

Table 1 to §383.71—List of Acceptable Proofs of Citizenship or Lawful Permanent Residency

Status	Proof of status
U.S. Citizen	• Valid, unexpired U.S. Passport.
	• Certified copy of a birth certificate filed with a State Office of Vital Statistics or equivalent agency in the individual's State of birth, Puerto Rico, the Virgin Islands, Guam, American Samoa or the Commonwealth of the Northern Mariana Islands.
	• Consular Report of Birth Abroad (CRBA) issued by the U.S. Department of State.
	• Certificate of Naturalization issued by the U.S. Department of Homeland Security (DHS).
	• Certificate of Citizenship issued by DHS.
Lawful Permanent Resident	• Valid, unexpired Permanent Resident Card, issued by USCIS or INS.

(10) The person must provide proof that the State to which application is made is his/her State of domicile, as the term is defined in §383.5. Acceptable proof of domicile is a document with the person's name and residential address within the State, such as a government issued tax form.

(11) Beginning on February 7, 2022, a person must complete the training prescribed in subpart F of part 380 of this chapter before taking the skills test for a Class A or B CDL, a passenger (P) or school bus (S) endorsement for the first

time or the knowledge test for a hazardous materials (H) endorsement for the first time. The training must be administered by a provider listed on the Training Provider Registry.

(c) **License transfer**. When applying to transfer a CDL from one State of domicile to a new State of domicile, an applicant must apply for a CDL from the new State of domicile within no more than 30 days after establishing his/her new domicile. The applicant must:

(1) Provide to the new State of domicile the certifications contained in paragraphs (b)(1) and (5) of this section;

(2) Provide to the new State of domicile updated information as specified in subpart J of this part;

(3) If the applicant wishes to retain a hazardous materials endorsement, he/she must comply with the requirements specified in paragraph (b)(8) of this section and State requirements as specified in §383.73(c)(4);

(4) Surrender the CDL from the old State of domicile to the new State of domicile; and

(5) Provide the names of all States where the applicant has previously been licensed to drive any type of motor vehicle during the previous 10 years.

(6) Provide to the State proof of citizenship or lawful permanent residency as specified in Table 1 of this section, or be registered under paragraph (f) of this section.

(7) Provide proof to the State that this is his/her State of domicile, as the term is defined in §383.5. Acceptable proof of domicile is a document with the person's name and residential address within the State, such as a government issued tax form.

(d) **License renewal**. When applying for a renewal of a CDL, all applicants must:

(1) Provide to the State certifications contained in paragraphs (b)(1) and (5) of this section;

(2) Provide to the State updated information as specified in subpart J of this part; and

(3) If a person wishes to retain a hazardous materials endorsement, he/she must comply with the requirements specified in paragraph (b)(8) of this section and pass the test specified in §383.121 for such endorsement.

(4) Provide the names of all States where the applicant has previously been licensed to drive any type of motor vehicle during the previous 10 years.

(5) Provide to the State proof of citizenship or lawful permanent residency as specified in Table 1 of this section, or be registered under paragraph (f) of this section.

(6) Provide proof to the State that this is his/her State of domicile, as the term is defined in §383.5. Acceptable proof of domicile is a document, such as a government issued tax form, with the person's name and residential address within the State.

(e) **License upgrades**. When applying for a CDL or an endorsement authorizing the operation of a CMV not covered by the current CDL, all applicants must:

(1) Provide the certifications specified in paragraph (b) of this section;

(2) Pass all the knowledge tests in accordance with the standards contained in subparts F, G, and H of this part and all the skills tests specified in paragraph (b)(2) of this section for the new vehicle group and/or different endorsements;

(3) Comply with the requirements specified in paragraph (b)(8) of this section to obtain a hazardous materials endorsement;

(4) Surrender the previous CDL; and

(5) Beginning on February 7, 2022, a person must complete the training prescribed in subpart F of part 380 of this chapter before taking the skills test for upgrading to a Class A or B for the first time; or adding a passenger or school bus endorsement to a CDL for the first time; or knowledge test for hazardous materials endorsement for the first time. The training must be administered by a provider on the Training Provider Registry.

(f) **Non-domiciled CLP and CDL.** (1) A person must obtain a Non-domiciled CLP or CDL:

(i) If the applicant is domiciled in a foreign jurisdiction, as defined in §383.5, and the Administrator has not determined that the commercial motor vehicle operator testing and licensing standards of that jurisdiction meet the standards contained in subparts G and H of this part.

(ii) If the applicant is domiciled in a State that is prohibited from issuing CLPs and CDLs in accordance with §384.405 of this subchapter. That person is eligible to obtain a Non-domiciled CLP or CDL from any State that elects to issue a Non-domiciled CLP or CDL and that complies with the testing and licensing standards contained in subparts F, G, and H of this part.

(2) An applicant for a Non-domiciled CLP and CDL must do both of the following:

(i) Complete the requirements to obtain a CLP contained in paragraph (a) of this section or a CDL contained in paragraph (b) of this section. *Exception*: An applicant domiciled in a foreign jurisdiction must provide an unexpired employment authorization document (EAD) issued by USCIS or an unexpired foreign passport accompanied by an approved I-94 form documenting the applicant's most recent admittance into the United States. No proof of domicile is required.

(ii) After receipt of the Non-domiciled CLP or CDL, and for as long as it is valid, notify the State which issued the Non-domiciled CLP or CDL of any adverse action taken by any jurisdiction or governmental agency, foreign or domestic, against his/her driving privileges. Such adverse actions include, but are not limited to, license disqualification or disqualification from operating a commercial motor vehicle for the convictions described in §383.51. Notifications must be made within the time periods specified in §383.33.

(3) An applicant for a Non-domiciled CLP or CDL is not required to surrender his/her foreign license.

(g) **Existing CLP and CDL Holder's Self-Certification**. Every person who holds a CLP or CDL must provide to the State the certification contained in §383.71(b)(1) of this subpart.

(h) **Medical Certification Documentation Required by the State.** An applicant or CLP or CDL holder who certifies to non-excepted, interstate driving operations according to §383.71(b)(1)(i) must comply with applicable requirements in paragraphs (h)(1) through (3) of this section:

(1) **New CLP and CDL applicants**. (i) Before June 23, 2025, a new CLP or CDL applicant who certifies that he/she will operate CMVs in non-excepted, interstate commerce must provide the State with an original or copy (as required by the State) of a medical examiner's certificate prepared by a medical examiner, as defined in 49 CFR 390.5, and the State will post a medical qualification status of "certified" on the CDLIS driver record for the driver;

(ii) On or after June 23, 2025, a new CLP or CDL applicant who certifies that he/she will operate CMVs in non-excepted, interstate commerce must be medically examined and certified in accordance with 49 CFR 391.43 as medically qualified to operate a CMV by a medical examiner, as defined in 49 CFR 390.5. Upon receiving an electronic copy of the medical examiner's certificate from FMCSA, the State will post a medical qualifications status of "certified" on the CDLIS driver record for the driver;

(2) Existing CLP and CDL holders. By January 30, 2014, provide the State with an original or copy (as required by the State) of a current medical examiner's certificate prepared by a medical examiner, as defined in 49 CFR 390.5, and the State will post a certification status of "certified" on CDLIS driver record for the driver. If the non-excepted, interstate CLP or CDL holder fails to provide the State with a current medical examiner's certificate, the State will post a certification status of "not-certified" in the CDLIS driver record for the driver, and initiate a CLP or CDL downgrade following State procedures in accordance with §383.73(o)(4); and

(3) **Maintaining the medical certification status of "certified."** (i) Before June 23, 2025, in order to maintain a medical certification status of "certified," a CLP or CDL holder who certifies that he/she will operate CMVs in non-excepted, interstate commerce must provide the State with an original or copy (as required by the State) of each subsequently issued medical examiner's certificate;

(ii) On or after June 23, 2025, in order to maintain a medical certification status of "certified," a CLP or CDL holder who certifies that he/she will operate CMVs in non-excepted, interstate commerce must continue to be medically examined and certified in accordance with 49 CFR 391.43 as physically qualified to operate a commercial motor vehicle by a medical examiner, as defined in 49 CFR 390.5. FMCSA will provide the State with an electronic copy of the medical examiner's certificate information for all subsequent medical examinations in which the driver has been deemed qualified.

(4) In the event of a conflict between the medical certification information provided electronically by FMCSA and a paper copy of the medical examiner's certificate, the medical certification information provided electronically by FMCSA shall control.

§383.72 Implied consent to alcohol testing.

Any person who holds a CLP or CDL or is required to hold a CLP or CDL is considered to have consented to such testing as is required by any State or jurisdiction in the enforcement of item (4) of Table 1 to §383.51 of this subpart and §392.5(a)(2) of this subchapter. Consent is implied by driving a commercial motor vehicle.

§383.73 State procedures.

(a) **Commercial Learner's Permit**. Prior to issuing a CLP to a person, a State must:

(1) Require the applicant to make the certifications, pass the tests, and provide the information as described in §383.71(a).

(2) Initiate and complete a check of the applicant's driving record as described in paragraph (b)(3) of this section.

(3) Make the CLP valid for no more than one year from the date of issuance without requiring the CLP holder to retake the general and endorsement knowledge tests. CLPs issued for a period of less than one year may be renewed provided the CLP is not valid for more than one year from the date of initial issuance.

(4) Allow only a group-specific passenger (P) and school bus (S) endorsement and tank vehicle (N) endorsement on a CLP, provided the applicant has taken and passed the knowledge test for the specified endorsement. All other Federal endorsements are prohibited on a CLP; and

(5) Complete the Social Security Number verification required by paragraph (g) of this section.

(6) Require compliance with the standards for providing proof of citizenship or lawful permanent residency specified in *§383.71(a)(5)* and proof of State of domicile specified in *§383.71(a)(6)*. *Exception:* A State is required to check the proof of citizenship or legal presence specified in this paragraph only for initial issuance, renewal or upgrade of a CLP or Non-domiciled CLP and for initial issuance, renewal, upgrade or transfer of a CDL or Non-domiciled CDL for the first time after July 8, 2011, provided a notation is made on the driver's record confirming that the proof of citizenship or legal presence check required by this paragraph has been made and noting the date it was done.

(7)(i) Before June 23, 2025, for drivers who certified their type of driving according to §383.71(b)(1)(i) (non-excepted interstate) and, if the CLP applicant submits a current medical examiner's certificate, date-stamp the medical examiner's certificate, and post all required information from the medical examiner's certificate to the CDLIS driver record in accordance with paragraph (o) of this section.

(ii) On or after June 23, 2025, for drivers who certified their type of driving according to §383.71(b)(1)(i) (non-excepted interstate) and, if FMCSA provides current medical examiner's certificate information electronically, post all required information matching the medical examiner's certificate to the CDLIS driver record in accordance with paragraph (o) of this section.

(8) Beginning November 18, 2024, the State must request information from the Drug and Alcohol Clearinghouse, and if, in response to the request, the State receives notification that pursuant to § 382.501(a) of this chapter the applicant is prohibited from operating a commercial motor vehicle, the State must not issue, renew, or upgrade the CLP. If the applicant currently holds a CLP issued by the State, the State must also comply with the procedures set forth in paragraph (q) of this section.

(b) **Initial CDL**. Prior to issuing a CDL to a person, a State must:

(1) Require the driver applicant to certify, pass tests, and provide information as described in §383.71(b);

(2) Check that the vehicle in which the applicant takes his/her test is representative of the vehicle group the applicant has certified that he/she operates or expects to operate;

(3) Initiate and complete a check of the applicant's driving record to ensure that the person is not subject to any disqualification under §383.51, or any license disqualification under State law, and does not have a driver's license from more than one State or jurisdiction. The record check must include, but is not limited to, the following:

(i) A check of the applicant's driving record as maintained by his/her current State of licensure, if any;

(ii) A check with the CDLIS to determine whether the driver applicant already has been issued a CDL, whether the applicant's license has been disqualified, or if the applicant has been disqualified from operating a commercial motor vehicle;

(iii) A check with the Problem Driver Pointer System (PDPS) to determine whether the driver applicant has:

(A) Been disqualified from operating a motor vehicle (other than a commercial motor vehicle);

(B) Had a license (other than CDL) disqualified for cause in the 3-year period ending on the date of application; or

(C) Been convicted of any offenses contained in 49 U.S.C. 30304(a)(3);

(iv) A request for the applicant's complete driving record from all States where the applicant was previously licensed over the last 10 years to drive any type of motor vehicle. *Exception:* A State is only required to make the request for the complete driving record specified in this paragraph for initial issuance of a CLP, transfer of CDL from another State or for drivers renewing a CDL for the first time after September 30, 2002, provided a notation is made on the driver's record confirming that the driver record check required by this paragraph has been made and noting the date it was done;

(v) Beginning January 30, 2012, a check that the medical certification status of a driver that self-certified according to §383.71(b)(1)(i) of this chapter (non-excepted interstate) is "certified;"

(4) Require the driver applicant to surrender his/her non-CDL driver's license and CLP;

(5)(i) Before June 23, 2025, for drivers who certified their type of driving according to §383.71(b)(1)(i) (non-excepted interstate) and, if the CDL holder submits a current medical examiner's certificate, date-stamp the medical examiner's certificate and post all required information from the medical examiner's certificate to the CDLIS driver record in accordance with paragraph (o) of this section.

(ii) On or after June 23, 2025, for drivers who certified their type of driving according to §383.71(b)(1)(i) (non-excepted interstate) and, if FMCSA provides current medical examiner's certificate information electronically, post all required information matching the medical examiner's certificate to the CDLIS driver record in accordance with paragraph (o) of this section.

(6) Require compliance with the standards for providing proof of citizenship or lawful permanent residency specified in §383.71(b)(9) and proof of State of domicile specified in §383.71(b)(10). *Exception:* A State is required to check the proof of citizenship or legal presence specified in this paragraph only for initial issuance, renewal or upgrade of a CLP or Non-domiciled CLP and for initial issuance, renewal, upgrade or transfer of a CDL or Non-domiciled CDL for the first time after July 8, 2011, provided a notation is made on the driver's record confirming that the proof of citizenship or legal presence check required by this paragraph has been made and noting the date it was done;

(7) If not previously done, complete the Social Security Number verification required by paragraph (g) of this section;

(8) For persons applying for a hazardous materials endorsement, require compliance with the standards for such endorsement specified in §§383.71(b)(8) and 383.141;

(9) Make the CDL valid for no more than 8 years from the date of issuance; and

(10) Beginning November 18, 2024, the State must request information from the Drug and Alcohol Clearinghouse. If, in response to that request, the State

receives notification that pursuant to §382.501(a) of this chapter the applicant is prohibited from operating a commercial motor vehicle, the State must not issue the CDL.

(11) Beginning on February 7, 2022, not conduct a skills test of an applicant for a Class A or Class B CDL, or a passenger (P) or school bus (S) endorsement until the State verifies electronically that the applicant completed the training prescribed in subpart F of part 380 of this subchapter.

(c) **License transfers**. Prior to issuing a CDL to a person who has a CDL from another State, a State must:

(1) Require the driver applicant to make the certifications contained in §383.71(b)(1) and (5);

(2) Complete a check of the driver applicant's record as contained in paragraph (b)(3) of this section;

(3) Request and receive updates of information specified in subpart J of this part;

(4) If such applicant wishes to retain a hazardous materials endorsement, require compliance with standards for such endorsement specified in §§383.71(b)(8) and 383.141 and ensure that the driver has, within the 2 years preceding the transfer, either:

(i) Passed the test for such endorsement specified in §383.121; or

(ii) Successfully completed a hazardous materials test or training that is given by a third party and that is deemed by the State to substantially cover the same knowledge base as that described in §383.121;

(5) If not previously done, complete the Social Security Number verification required by paragraph (g) of this section;

(6) Require the applicant to surrender the CDL issued by the applicant's previous State of domicile;

(7) Require compliance with the standards for providing proof of citizenship or lawful permanent residency specified in §383.71(b)(9) and proof of State of domicile specified in §383.71(b)(10). *Exception:* A State is required to check the proof of citizenship or legal presence specified in this paragraph only for initial issuance, renewal or upgrade of a CLP or Non-domiciled CLP and for initial issuance, renewal, upgrade or transfer of a CDL or Non-domiciled CDL for the first time after July 8, 2011, provided a notation is made on the driver's record confirming that the proof of citizenship or legal presence check required by this paragraph has been made and noting the date it was done;

(8) Beginning January 30, 2012, verify from the CDLIS driver record that the medical certification status of driver is "certified" for those who certified according to §383.71(b)(1)(i). *Exception :* A driver who certified according to §383.71(b)(1)(i) that he/she plans to operate in non-excepted interstate commerce may present a current medical examiner's certificate issued prior to January 30, 2012. The medical examiner's certificate provided by the driver must be posted to the CDLIS driver record in accordance with paragraph (o) of this section;

(9) Make the CDL valid for no more than 8 years from the date of issuance; and

(10) Beginning November 18, 2024, the State must request information from the Drug and Alcohol Clearinghouse. If, in response to that request, the State receives notification that pursuant to §382.501(a) of this chapter the applicant is prohibited from operating a commercial motor vehicle, the State must not transfer the CDL.

(d) **License Renewals**. Prior to renewing any CDL a State must:

(1) Require the driver applicant to make the certifications contained in §383.71(b);

(2) Complete a check of the driver applicant's record as contained in paragraph (b)(3) of this section;

(3) Request and receive updates of information specified in subpart J of this part;

(4) If such applicant wishes to retain a hazardous materials endorsement, require the driver to pass the test specified in §383.121 and comply with the standards specified in §§383.71(b)(8) and 383.141 for such endorsement;

(5) If not previously done, complete the Social Security Number verification required by paragraph (g) of this section;

(6) Make the renewal of the CDL valid for no more than 8 years from the date of issuance;

(7) Require compliance with the standards for providing proof of citizenship or lawful permanent residency specified in §383.71(b)(9) and proof of State of domicile specified in §383.71(b)(10). *Exception:* A State is required to check the proof of citizenship or legal presence specified in this paragraph only for initial issuance, renewal or upgrade of a CLP or Non-domiciled CLP and for initial issuance, renewal, upgrade or transfer of a CDL or Non-domiciled CDL for the first time after July 8, 2011, provided a notation is made on the driver's record confirming that the proof of citizenship or legal presence check required by this paragraph has been made and noting the date it was done;

(8) Beginning January 30, 2012, verify from the CDLIS driver record that the medical certification status is "certified" for drivers who self-certified according to §383.71(b)(1)(i). *Exception:* A driver who certified according to §383.71(b)(1)(i) may present a current medical examiner's certificate issued prior to January 30, 2012. The medical examiner's certificate provided by the driver must be posted to the CDLIS driver record in accordance with paragraph (o) of this section; and

(9) Beginning November 18, 2024, the State must request information from the Drug and Alcohol Clearinghouse. If, in response to that request, the State receives notification that pursuant to §382.501(a) of this chapter the applicant is prohibited from operating a commercial motor vehicle, the State must not renew the CDL or H endorsement and must comply with the procedures set forth in paragraph (q) of this section.

(e) **License upgrades**. Prior to issuing an upgrade of a CDL, a State must:

(1) Require such driver applicant to provide certifications, pass tests, and meet applicable hazardous materials standards specified in §383.71(e);

(2) Complete a check of the driver applicant's record as described in paragraph (b)(3) of this section;

(3) If not previously done, complete the Social Security Number verification required by paragraph (g) of this section;

(4) Require the driver applicant to surrender his/her previous CDL;

(5) Require compliance with the standards for providing proof of citizenship or lawful permanent residency specified in §383.71(b)(9) and proof of State of domicile specified in §383.71(b)(10). *Exception:* A State is required to check the proof of citizenship or legal presence specified in this paragraph only for initial issuance, renewal or upgrade of a CLP or Non-domiciled CLP and for initial issuance, renewal, upgrade, or transfer of a CDL or Non-domiciled CDL, for the first time after July 8, 2011, provided a notation is made on the driver's record confirming that the proof of citizenship or legal presence check required by this paragraph has been made and noting the date it was done;

(6) Beginning January 30, 2012, verify from the CDLIS driver record that the medical certification status is "certified" for drivers who self-certified according to §383.71(b)(1)(i). *Exception:* A driver who certified according to §383.71(b)(1)(i) may present a current medical examiner's certificate issued prior to January 30, 2012. The medical examiner's certificate provided by the driver must be posted to the CDLIS driver record in accordance with paragraph (o) of this section;

(7) Make the CDL valid for no more than 8 years from the date of issuance; and

(8) Beginning November 18, 2024, the State must request information from the Drug and Alcohol Clearinghouse. If, in response to that request, the State receives notification that pursuant to §382.501(a) of this chapter the applicant is prohibited from operating a commercial motor vehicle, the State must not issue an upgrade of the CDL and must comply with the procedures set forth in paragraph (q) of this section.

(9) Beginning on February 7, 2022, not conduct a skills test of an applicant for an upgrade to a Class A or Class B CDL, or a passenger (P), school bus (S) endorsement, or administer the knowledge test to an applicant for the hazardous materials (H) endorsement, unless the applicant has completed the training required by subpart F of part 380 of this subchapter.

(f) **Non-domiciled CLP and CDL**. (1) A State may only issue a Non-domiciled CLP or CDL to a person who meets one of the circumstances described in §383.71(f)(1).

(2) State procedures for the issuance of a non-domiciled CLP and CDL, for any modifications thereto, and for notifications to the CDLIS must at a minimum be identical to those pertaining to any other CLP or CDL, with the following exceptions:

(i) If the applicant is requesting a transfer of his/her Non-domiciled CDL, the State must obtain the Non-domiciled CDL currently held by the applicant and issued by another State;

(ii) The State must add the word "non-domiciled" to the face of the CLP or CDL, in accordance with §383.153(c); and

(iii) The State must have established, prior to issuing any Non-domiciled CLP or CDL, the practical capability of disqualifying the holder of any Non-domiciled CLP or CDL, by withdrawing or disqualifying his/her Non-domiciled CLP or CDL as if the Non-domiciled CLP or CDL were a CLP or CDL issued to a person domiciled in the State.

(3) The State must require compliance with the standards for providing proof of legal presence specified in §383.71(b)(9) and §383.71(f)(2)(i).

(4) Beginning November 18, 2024, the State must request information from the Drug and Alcohol Clearinghouse. If, in response to that request, the State receives notification that pursuant to §382.501(a) of this chapter the applicant is prohibited from operating a commercial motor vehicle, the State must not issue, renew, transfer or upgrade a non-domiciled CLP or CDL and must comply with the procedures set forth in paragraph (q) of this section, as applicable.

(g) **Social Security Number verification**. (1) Prior to issuing a CLP or a CDL to a person the State must verify the name, date of birth, and Social Security Number provided by the applicant with the information on file with the Social Security Administration. The State is prohibited from issuing, renewing, upgrading, or transferring a CLP or CDL if the Social Security Administration database does not match the applicant-provided data.

(2) *Exception*. A State is only required to perform the Social Security Number verification specified in this paragraph for initial issuance of a CLP, transfer of CDL from another State or for drivers renewing a CDL for the first time after July 8, 2011 who have not previously had their Social Security Number information verified, provided a notation is made on the driver's record confirming that the verification required by this paragraph has been made and noting the date it was done.

(h) **License issuance**. After the State has completed the procedures described in paragraphs (a) through (g) of this section, as applicable, it may issue a CLP or CDL to the driver applicant. The State must notify the operator of the CDLIS of such issuance, transfer, renewal, or upgrade within the 10-day period beginning on the date of license issuance.

(i) **Surrender procedure**. A State may return a surrendered license to a driver after physically marking it so that it cannot be mistaken for a valid document. Simply punching a hole in the expiration date of the document is insufficient. A document perforated with the word "VOID" is considered invalidated.

(j) **Penalties for false information**. If a State determines, in its check of an applicant's license status and record prior to issuing a CLP or CDL, or at any time after the CLP or CDL is issued, that the applicant has falsified information contained in subpart J of this part, in any of the certifications required in §383.71(b) or (g), or in any of the documents required to be submitted by §383.71(h), the State must at a minimum disqualify the person's CLP or CDL or his/her pending application, or disqualify the person from operating a commercial motor vehicle for a period of at least 60 consecutive days.

(k) **Drivers convicted of fraud related to the testing and issuance of a CLP or CDL**. (1) The State must have policies in effect that result, at a minimum, in the disqualification of the CLP or CDL of a person who has been convicted of fraud related to the issuance of that CLP or CDL. The application of a person so convicted who seeks to renew, transfer, or upgrade the fraudulently obtained CLP or CDL must also, at a minimum, be disqualified. The State must record any such withdrawal in the person's driving record. The person may not reapply for a new CDL for at least 1 year.

(2) If a State receives credible information that a CLP- or CDL-holder is suspected, but has not been convicted, of fraud related to the issuance of his/her CLP or CDL, the State must require the driver to re-take the skills and/or knowledge tests. Within 30 days of receiving notification from the State that re-testing is necessary, the affected CLP- or CDL-holder must make an appointment or otherwise schedule to take the next available test. If the CLP- or CDL-holder fails to make an appointment within 30 days, the State must disqualify his/her CLP or CDL. If the driver fails either the knowledge or skills test or does not take the test, the State must disqualify his/her CLP or CDL. Once a CLP- or CDL-holder's CLP or CDL has been disqualified, he/she must reapply for a CLP or CDL under State procedures applicable to all CLP and CDL applicants.

(l) **Reciprocity**. A State must allow any person who has a valid CLP, CDL, Non-domiciled CLP, or Non-domiciled CDL and who is not disqualified from operating a CMV, to operate a CMV in the State.

(m) **Document verification**. The State must require at least two persons within the driver licensing agency to participate substantively in the processing and verification of the documents involved in the licensing process for initial issuance, renewal or upgrade of a CLP or Non-domiciled CLP and for initial issuance, renewal, upgrade or transfer of a CDL or Non-domiciled CDL. The documents being processed and verified must include, at a minimum, those provided by the applicant to prove legal presence and domicile, the information filled out on the application form, and knowledge and skills test scores. This section does not require two people to process or verify each document involved in the licensing process. *Exception:* For offices with only one staff member, at least some of the documents must be processed or verified by a supervisor before issuance or, when a supervisor is not available, copies must be made of some of the documents involved in the licensing process and a supervisor must verify them within one business day of issuance of the CLP, Non-domiciled CLP, CDL or Non-domiciled CDL.

(n) **Computer system controls**. The State must establish computer system controls that will:

(1) Prevent the issuance of an initial, renewed or upgraded CLP or an initial, renewed, upgraded, or transferred CDL when the results of transactions indicate the applicant is unqualified. These controls, at a minimum, must be established for the following transactions: State, CDLIS, and PDPS driver record checks; and Social Security Number verification. Knowledge and skills test scores verification controls must be established for an initial, renewed, or upgraded CDL.

(2) Suspend the issuance process whenever State, CDLIS, and/or PDPS driver record checks return suspect results. The State must demonstrate that it has a system to detect and prevent fraud when a driver record check returns suspect results. At a minimum, the system must ensure that:

(i) The results are not connected to a violation of any State or local law relating to motor vehicle traffic control (other than parking, vehicle weight, or vehicle defect violations);

(ii) The name of the persons performing the record check and authorizing the issuance, and the justification for the authorization are documented by the State; and

(iii) The person performing the record check and the person authorizing the issuance are not the same.

(o) **Medical recordkeeping** — (1)(i) **Status of CLP or CDL holder**. Before June 23, 2025, for each operator of a commercial motor vehicle required to have a CLP or CDL, the current licensing State must:

(A) Post the driver's self-certification of type of driving under §383.71(b)(1) to the CDLIS driver record;

(B) Post the information from the medical examiner's certificate within 10 calendar days to the CDLIS driver record, including:

(1) Medical examiner's name;

(2) Medical examiner's telephone number;

(3) Date of medical examiner's certificate issuance;

(4) Medical examiner's license number and the State that issued it;

(5) Medical examiner's National Registry identification number;

(6) The indicator of medical certification status, *i.e.,* "certified" or "not-certified";

(7) Expiration date of the medical examiner's certificate;

(8) Existence of any medical variance on the medical examiner's certificate, such as an exemption, SPE certification, or grandfather provisions;

(9) Any restrictions (*e.g.,* corrective lenses, hearing aid, required to have possession of an exemption letter or SPE certificate while on-duty, etc.); and

(10) Date the medical examiner's certificate information was posted to the CDLIS driver record; and

(C) Post the medical variance information within 10 calendar days to the CDLIS driver record, including:

(1) Date of medical variance issuance; and

(2) Expiration date of medical variance;

(D) Retain the original or a copy of the medical examiner's certificate of any driver required to provide documentation of physical qualification for 3 years beyond the date the certificate was issued.

(ii) **Status of CLP or CDL holder**. On or after June 23, 2025, for each operator of a commercial motor vehicle required to have a CLP or CDL, the current licensing State must:

(A) Post the driver's self-certification of type of driving under §383.71(b)(1) to the CDLIS driver record;

(B) Post the information from the medical examiner's certificate received from FMCSA to the CDLIS driver record, including:

(1) Medical examiner's name;

(2) Medical examiner's telephone number;

(3) Date of medical examiner's certificate issuance;

(4) Medical examiner's license number and the State that issued it;

(5) Medical examiner's National Registry identification number;

(6) The indicator of medical certification status, *i.e.,* "certified" or "not-certified";

(7) Expiration date of the medical examiner's certificate;

(8) Existence of any medical variance on the medical examiner's certificate, such as an exemption, Skill Performance Evaluation (SPE) certification, or grandfather provisions;

(9) Any restrictions (*e.g.,* corrective lenses, hearing aid, required to have possession of an exemption letter or SPE certificate while on-duty, etc.); and

(10) Date the medical examiner's certificate information was posted to the CDLIS driver record;

(C) Post the medical variance information received from FMCSA within 1 business day to the CDLIS driver record, including:

(1) Date of medical variance issuance; and

(2) Expiration date of medical variance;

(D) Retain the electronic record of the medical examiner's certificate information for any driver required to have documentation of physical qualification for 3 years beyond the date the certificate was issued.

(2) **Status update**. (i) Before June 23, 2025, the State must, within 10 calendar days of the driver's medical examiner's certificate or medical variance expiring, the medical variance being rescinded or the medical examiner's certificate being voided by FMCSA, update the medical certification status of that driver as "not certified."

(ii) On or after June 23, 2025, the State must, within 10 calendar days of the driver's medical examiner's certificate or medical variance expiring, the medical examiner's certificate becoming invalid, the medical variance being rescinded, or the medical examiner's certificate being voided by FMCSA, update the medical certification status of that driver as "not certified."

(3) **Variance update**. (i) Before June 23, 2025, within 10 calendar days of receiving information from FMCSA regarding issuance or renewal of a medical variance for a driver, the State must update the CDLIS driver record to include the medical variance information provided by FMCSA.

(ii) On or after June 23, 2025, within 1 business day of electronically receiving medical variance information from FMCSA regarding the issuance or renewal of a medical variance for a driver, the State must update the CDLIS driver record to include the medical variance information provided by FMCSA.

(4) **Downgrade**. (i) If a driver's medical certification or medical variance expires, or FMCSA notifies the State that a medical certification was invalidated or voided or a medical variance was removed or rescinded, the State must:

(A)*(1)* Before June 23, 2025, notify the CLP or CDL holder of his/her CLP or CDL "not-certified" medical certification status and that the CDL privileges will be removed from the CLP or CDL unless the driver submits a current medical examiner's certificate and/or medical variance, or changes his/her self-certification to driving only in excepted or intrastate commerce (if permitted by the State).

(2) On or after June 23, 2025, notify the CLP or CDL holder of his/her CLP or CDL "not-certified" medical certification status and that the CDL privileges will be removed from the CLP or CDL unless the driver has been medically examined and certified in accordance with 49 CFR 391.43 as physically qualified to operate a commercial motor vehicle by a medical examiner, as defined in 49 CFR 390.5, or the driver changes his/her self-certification to driving only in excepted or intrastate commerce (if permitted by the State).

(B) Initiate established State procedures for downgrading the CLP or CDL. The CLP or CDL downgrade must be completed and recorded within 60 days of the driver's medical certification status becoming "not-certified" to operate a CMV.

(ii)(A) Before June 23, 2025, if a driver fails to provide the State with the certification contained in §383.71(b)(1), or a current medical examiner's certificate if the driver self-certifies according to §383.71(b)(1)(i) that he/she is operating in non-excepted interstate commerce as required by §383.71(h), the State must mark that CDLIS driver record as "not-certified" and initiate a CLP or CDL downgrade following State procedures in accordance with paragraph (o)(4)(i)(B) of this section.

(B) On or after June 23, 2025, if a driver fails to provide the State with the certification contained in §383.71(b)(1), or, if the driver self-certifies according to §383.71(b)(1)(i) that he/she is operating in non-excepted interstate commerce as required by §383.71(h) and the information required by paragraph (o)(2)(ii) of this section is not received and posted, the State must mark that CDLIS driver record as "not-certified" and initiate a CLP or CDL downgrade following State procedures in accordance with paragraph (o)(4)(i)(B) of this section.

(5) **State contacts for medical variances.** FMCSA Medical Programs is designated as the keeper of the list of State contacts for receiving medical variance information from FMCSA. Beginning January 30, 2012, States are responsible for ensuring their medical variance contact information is always up-to-date with FMCSA's Medical Programs.

(6) **Conflicting medical certification information.** In the event of a conflict between the medical certification information provided electronically by FMCSA and a paper copy of the medical examiner's certificate, the medical certification information provided electronically by FMCSA shall control.

(p) After February 7, 2022, the State must notify FMCSA that a training provider in the State does not meet applicable State requirements for CMV instruction.

(q) **Drug and Alcohol Clearinghouse.** Beginning November 18, 2024, the State must, upon receiving notification that pursuant to §382.501(a) of this chapter, the CLP or CDL holder is prohibited from operating a commercial motor vehicle, initiate established State procedures for downgrading the CLP or

CDL. The downgrade must be completed and recorded on the CDLIS driver record within 60 days of the State's receipt of such notification.

(1) Termination of downgrade process when the driver is no longer prohibited. If, before the State completes and records the downgrade on the CDLIS driver record, the State receives notification that pursuant to §382.501(a) of this chapter the CLP or CDL holder is no longer prohibited from operating a commercial motor vehicle, the State must, if permitted by State law, terminate the downgrade process without removing the CLP or CDL privilege from the driver's license.

(2) Reinstatement after FMCSA notification that the driver is no longer prohibited. If, after the State completes and records the downgrade on the CDLIS driver record, FMCSA notifies the State that pursuant to §382.501(a) of this chapter a driver is no longer prohibited from operating a commercial motor vehicle, the State must make the driver eligible for reinstatement of the Start Printed Page 55743 CLP or CDL privilege to the driver's license, if permitted by State law.

(3) Reinstatement after Clearinghouse error correction. If, after the State completes and records the downgrade on the CDLIS driver record, FMCSA notifies the State that the driver was erroneously identified as prohibited from operating a commercial motor vehicle, the State shall:

(i) Reinstate the CLP or CDL privilege to the driver's license as expeditiously as possible; and

(ii) Expunge from the CDLIS driver record and, if applicable, the motor vehicle record, as defined in §390.5T of this chapter, any reference related to the driver's erroneous prohibited status.

§383.75 Third party testing.

(a) **Third party tests**. A State may authorize a third party tester to administer the skills tests as specified in subparts G and H of this part, if the following conditions are met:

(1) The skills tests given by the third party are the same as those that would otherwise be given by the State using the same version of the skills tests, the same written instructions for test applicants, and the same scoring sheets as those prescribed in subparts G and H of this part;

(2) The State must conduct an on-site inspection of each third party tester at least once every 2 years, with a focus on examiners with irregular results such as unusually high or low pass/fail rates;

(3) The State must issue the third party tester a CDL skills testing certificate upon the execution of a third party skills testing agreement.

(4) The State must issue each third party CDL skills test examiner a skills testing certificate upon successful completion of a formal skills test examiner training course prescribed in §384.228.

(5) The State must, at least once every 2 years, do one of the following for each third party examiner:

(i) Have State employees covertly take the tests administered by the third party as if the State employee were a test applicant;

(ii) Have State employees co-score along with the third party examiner during CDL skills tests to compare pass/fail results; or

(iii) Re-test a sample of drivers who were examined by the third party to compare pass/fail results;

(6) The State must take prompt and appropriate remedial action against a third party tester that fails to comply with State or Federal standards for the CDL testing program, or with any other terms of the third party contract;

(7) A skills test examiner who is also a skills instructor either as a part of a school, training program or otherwise is prohibited from administering a skills test to an applicant who received skills training by that skills test examiner; and

(8) The State has an agreement with the third party containing, at a minimum, provisions that:

(i) Allow the FMCSA, or its representative, and the State to conduct random examinations, inspections, and audits of its records, facilities, and operations without prior notice;

(ii) Require that all third party skills test examiners meet the qualification and training standards of §384.228;

(iii) Allow the State to do any of the following:

(A) Have State employees covertly take the tests administered by the third party as if the State employee were a test applicant;

(B) Have State employees co-score along with the third party examiner during CDL skills tests to compare pass/fail results; or

(C) Have the State re-test a sample of drivers who were examined by the third party;

(iv) Reserve unto the State the right to take prompt and appropriate remedial action against a third party tester that fails to comply with State or Federal standards for the CDL testing program, or with any other terms of the third party contract;

(v) Require the third party tester to initiate and maintain a bond in an amount determined by the State to be sufficient to pay for re-testing drivers in the event that the third party or one or more of its examiners is involved in fraudulent activities related to conducting skills testing of applicants for a CDL. *Exception:* A third party tester that is a government entity is not required to maintain a bond.

(vi) Require the third party tester to use only CDL skills examiners who have successfully completed a formal CDL skills test examiner training course as prescribed by the State and have been certified by the State as a CDL skills examiner qualified to administer CDL skills tests;

(vii) Require the third party tester to use designated road test routes that have been approved by the State;

(viii) Require the third party tester to submit a schedule of CDL skills testing appointments to the State no later than two business days prior to each test; and

(ix) Require the third party tester to maintain copies of the following records at its principal place of business:

(A) A copy of the State certificate authorizing the third party tester to administer a CDL skills testing program for the classes and types of commercial motor vehicles listed;

(B) A copy of each third party examiner's State certificate authorizing the third party examiner to administer CDL skills tests for the classes and types of commercial motor vehicles listed;

(C) A copy of the current third party agreement;

(D) A copy of each completed CDL skills test scoring sheet for the current year and the past two calendar years;

(E) A copy of the third party tester's State-approved road test route(s); and

(F) A copy of each third party examiner's training record.

(b) **Proof of testing by a third party**. The third party tester must notify the State driver licensing agency through secure electronic means when a driver applicant passes skills tests administered by the third party tester.

(c) **Minimum number of tests conducted**.

The State must revoke the skills testing certification of any examiner who does not conduct skills test examinations of at least 10 different applicants per calendar year. *Exception*: Examiners who do not meet the 10-test minimum must either take the refresher training specified in §384.228 of this chapter or have a State examiner ride along to observe the third party examiner successfully administer at least one skills test.

§383.77 Substitute for knowledge and driving skills tests for drivers with military CMV experience.

(a) **Knowledge test waivers for certain current or former military service members applying for a CLP or CDL**—(1) **In general.** For current or former military service members, as defined in §383.5, who meet the conditions and limitations set forth in paragraph (a)(2) of this section, a State may waive the requirements in §§383.23(a)(1) and 383.25(a)(3) that a person must pass a knowledge test for a CLP or CDL.

(2) **Conditions and limitations.** A current or former military service member applying for waiver of the knowledge test described in paragraph (a)(1) of this section must certify and provide evidence that, during the 1-year period immediately prior to the application, he/she:

(i) Is or was regularly employed and designated as a:

(A) Motor Transport Operator—88M (Army);

(B) PATRIOT Launching Station Operator—14T (Army);

(C) Fueler—92F (Army);

(D) Vehicle Operator—2T1 (Air Force);

(E) Fueler—2F0 (Air Force);

(F) Pavement and Construction Equipment Operator—3E2 (Air Force);

(G) Motor Vehicle Operator—3531 (Marine Corps); or

(H) Equipment Operator—E.O. (Navy).

(ii) Is operating a vehicle representative of the CMV type the driver applicant expects to operate upon separation from the military, or operated such a vehicle type immediately preceding separation from the military;

(iii) Has not simultaneously held more than one civilian license (in addition to a military license);

(iv) Has not had any license suspended, revoked, or cancelled;

(v) Has not had any convictions for any type of motor vehicle for the disqualifying offenses contained in §383.51(b);

(vi) Has not had more than one conviction for any type of motor vehicle for serious traffic violations contained in §383.51(c); and

(vii) Has not had any conviction for a violation of military, State, or local law relating to motor vehicle traffic control (other than a parking violation) arising in connection with any traffic accident, and has no record of an accident in which he/she was at fault.

(b) **Driving skills test waivers for certain current or former military service members applying for a CDL**—(1) **In general.** At the discretion of a State, the driving skills test required by §383.23(a)(1), and as specified in §383.113, may be waived for a CMV driver with military CMV experience who is currently licensed at the time of his/her application for a CDL and substituted with an applicant's driving record in combination with certain driving experience.

(2) **Conditions and limitations.** The State shall impose conditions and limitations to restrict the applicants from whom a State may accept alternative requirements for the driving skills test described in §383.113. Such conditions must require at least the following:

(i) An applicant must provide evidence and certify that he/she:

(A) Is regularly employed or was regularly employed within the last year in a military position requiring operation of a CMV;

(B) Was exempted from the CDL requirements in §383.3(c); and

(C) Was operating a vehicle representative of the CMV type the driver applicant operates or expects to operate, for at least the 2 years immediately preceding separation from the military.

(ii) An applicant must certify that, during the 2-year period immediately prior to applying for a CDL, he/she:

(A) Has not simultaneously held more than one civilian license (in addition to a military license);

(B) Has not had any license suspended, revoked, or cancelled;

(C) Has not had any convictions for any type of motor vehicle for the disqualifying offenses contained in §383.51(b);

(D) Has not had more than one conviction for any type of motor vehicle for serious traffic violations contained in §383.51(c); and

(E) Has not had any conviction for a violation of military, State or local law relating to motor vehicle traffic control (other than a parking violation) arising in connection with any traffic crash, and has no record of a crash in which he/she was at fault.

(c) **Endorsement waivers for certain current or former military service members applying for a CLP or a CDL**—(1) **Passenger.** For current or former military service members, as defined in §383.5, who meet the conditions and limitations set forth in paragraph (c)(4) of this section, a State may waive the requirements in §383.25(a)(5)(i), §383.93(a) and (c)(2) that an applicant must pass a driving skills test and a specialized knowledge test, described in §383.117, for a passenger (P) endorsement.

(2) **Tank vehicle.** For current or former military service members, as defined in §383.5, who meet the conditions and limitations set forth in paragraph (c)(4) of this section, a State may waive the requirements in §§383.25(a)(5)(iii) and §383.93(a) and (c)(3) that an applicant must pass a specialized knowledge test, described in §383.119, for a tank vehicle (N) endorsement.

(3) **Hazardous materials.** For current or former military service members, as defined in §383.5, who meet the conditions and limitations set forth in paragraph (c)(4) of this section, a State may waive the requirements in §383.93(a)(1) and (c)(4) that an applicant must pass a specialized knowledge test, described in §383.121, for a hazardous materials (H) endorsement. States must continue to meet the requirements for a hazardous materials endorsement in subpart I of this part.

(4) **Conditions and limitations.** A current or former military service member applying for waiver of the driving skills test or the specialized knowledge test for a passenger carrier endorsement, the knowledge test for the tank vehicle endorsement, or the knowledge test for the hazardous materials endorsement,

must certify and provide evidence that, during the 1-year period immediately prior to the application, he/she:

(i) Is or was regularly employed in a military position requiring operation of a passenger CMV, if the applicant is requesting a waiver of the knowledge and driving skills test for a passenger endorsement; operation of a tank vehicle, if the applicant is requesting a waiver of the knowledge test for a tank vehicle endorsement; or transportation of hazardous materials, if the applicant is requesting a waiver of the knowledge test for a hazardous materials endorsement;

(ii) Has not simultaneously held more than one civilian license (in addition to a military license);

(iii) Has not had any license suspended, revoked, or cancelled;

(iv) Has not had any convictions for any type of motor vehicle for the disqualifying offenses contained in §383.51(b);

(v) Has not had more than one conviction for any type of motor vehicle for serious traffic violations contained in §383.51(c); and

(vi) Has not had any conviction for a violation of military, State or local law relating to motor vehicle traffic control (other than a parking violation) arising in connection with any traffic crash, and has no record of a crash in which he/she was at fault.

§383.79 Driving skills testing of out-of-State students; knowledge and driving skills testing of military personnel.

(a) **CDL applicants trained out-of-State**—(1) **State that administers the driving skills test.** A State may administer its driving skills test, in accordance with subparts F, G, and H of this part, to a person who has taken training in that State and is to be licensed in another United States jurisdiction (*i.e.,* his or her State of domicile). Such test results must be transmitted electronically directly from the testing State to the licensing State in a direct, efficient and secure manner.

(2) **The State of domicile.** The State of domicile of a CDL applicant must accept the results of a driving skills test administered to the applicant by any other State, in accordance with subparts F, G, and H of this part, in fulfillment of the applicant's testing requirements under §383.71, and the State's test administration requirements under §383.73.

(b) **Active duty military service members.** An active-duty military service member may apply for a CLP or a CDL in the State where the individual is stationed but not domiciled if the requirements of this section are met.

(1) **Role of State of duty station**. (i) Upon prior agreement with the State of domicile, a State where active-duty military service members are stationed, but not domiciled, may accept an application for a CLP or CDL, including an application for waiver of the knowledge test or driving skills test prescribed in §§383.23(a)(1) and 383.25(a)(3), from such a military service member who:

(A) Is regularly employed or was regularly employed within the last year in a military position requiring operation of a CMV;

(B) Has a valid driver's license from his or her State of domicile;

(C) Has a valid active-duty military identification card; and

(D) Has a current copy of either the service member's military leave and earnings statement, or his or her orders.

(ii) A State where active-duty military service members are stationed, but not domiciled, may:

(A) Administer the knowledge and driving skills tests to the military service member, as appropriate, in accordance with subparts F, G, and H of this part, if the State of domicile requires those tests; or

(B) Waive the knowledge and driving skills tests in accordance with §383.77, if the State of domicile has exercised the option to waive those tests; and

(C) Destroy the military service member's civilian driver's license on behalf of the State of domicile, unless the latter requires the driver's license to be surrendered to its own driver licensing agency.

(iii) The State of duty station must transmit to the State of domicile by a direct, secure, and efficient electronic system the completed application, any supporting documents, and—if the State of domicile has not exercised its waiver option—the results of any knowledge and driving skills administered.

(2) **Role of State of domicile.** Upon completion of the applicant's application pursuant to §383.71 and any testing administered by the State of duty station pursuant to §§383.71 and 383.73, the State of domicile of the military service member applying for a CLP or CDL may:

(i) Accept the completed application, any supporting documents, and the results of the knowledge and driving skills tests administered by the State of duty station (unless waived at the discretion of the State of domicile); and

(ii) Issue the applicant a CLP or CDL.

Subpart F—Vehicle Groups and Endorsements

§383.91 Commercial motor vehicle groups.

(a) **Vehicle group descriptions**. Each driver applicant must possess and be tested on his/her knowledge and skills, described in subpart G of this part, for the commercial motor vehicle group(s) for which he/she desires a CDL. The commercial motor vehicle groups are as follows:

(1) Combination vehicle (Group A)—Any combination of vehicles with a gross combination weight rating (GCWR) of 11,794 kilograms or more (26,001 pounds or more) provided the GVWR of the vehicle(s) being towed is in excess of 4,536 kilograms (10,000 pounds).

(2) Heavy Straight Vehicle (Group B)—Any single vehicle with a GVWR of 11,794 kilograms or more (26,001 pounds or more), or any such vehicle towing a vehicle not in excess of 4,536 kilograms (10,000 pounds) GVWR.

(3) Small Vehicle (Group C)—Any single vehicle, or combination of vehicles, that meets neither the definition of Group A nor that of Group B as contained in this section, but that either is designed to transport 16 or more passengers including the driver, or is used in the transportation of hazardous materials as defined in §383.5.

(b) **Representative vehicle**. For purposes of taking the driving test in accordance with §383.113, a representative vehicle for a given vehicle group contained in §383.91(a), is any commercial motor vehicle which meets the definition of that vehicle group.

(c) **Relation between vehicle groups**. Each driver applicant who desires to operate in a different commercial motor vehicle group from the one which his/her CDL authorizes shall be required to retake and pass all related tests, except the following:

(1) A driver who has passed the knowledge and skills tests for a combination vehicle (Group A) may operate a heavy straight vehicle (Group B) or a small vehicle (Group C), provided that he/she possesses the requisite endorsement(s); and

(2) A driver who has passed the knowledge and skills tests for a heavy straight vehicle (Group B) may operate any small vehicle (Group C), provided that he/she possesses the requisite endorsement(s).

(d) **Vehicle group illustration**. Figure 1 illustrates typical vehicles within each of the vehicle groups defined in this section.

Figure 1
VEHICLE GROUPS (SECTION 383.91)

[Note: Certain types of vehicles, such as passenger and doubles/triples, will require an endorsement. Please consult text for particulars.]

Group: *Description:

A   Any combination of vehicles with a GCWR of 26,001 or more pounds provided the GVWR of the vehicle(s) being towed is in excess of 10,000 pounds. (Holders of a Group A license may, with any appropriate endorsements, operate all vehicles within Groups B and C.)

         Examples include but are not limited to:

B   Any single vehicle with a GVWR of 26,001 or more pounds, or any such vehicle towing a vehicle not in excess of 10,000 pounds GVWR. (Holders of a Group B license may, with any appropriate endorsements, operate all vehicles within Group C.)

         Examples include but are not limited to:

C   Any single vehicle, or combination of vehicles, that does not meet the definition of Group A or Group B as contained herein, but that either is designed to transport 16 or more passengers including the driver, or is placarded for hazardous materials.

         Examples include but are not limited to:

*
The representative vehicle for the skills test must meet the written description for that group. The silhouettes typify, but do not fully cover, the types of vehicles falling within each group.

PART 383

§383.93 Endorsements.

(a) **General**. (1) In addition to passing the knowledge and skills tests described in subpart G of this part, all persons who operate or expect to operate the type(s) of motor vehicles described in paragraph (b) of this section must pass specialized tests to obtain each endorsement. The State shall issue CDL endorsements only to drivers who successfully complete the tests.

(2) The only endorsements allowed on a CLP are the following:

(i) Passenger (P);

(ii) School bus (S); and

(iii) Tank vehicle (N).

(3) The State must use the codes listed in §383.153 when placing endorsements on a CLP or CDL.

(b) **Endorsement descriptions**. An operator must obtain State-issued endorsements to his/her CDL to operate commercial motor vehicles which are:

(1) Double/triple trailers;

(2) Passenger vehicles;

(3) Tank vehicles;

(4) Used to transport hazardous materials as defined in §383.5; or

(5) School buses.

(c) **Endorsement testing requirements**. The following tests are required for the endorsements contained in paragraph (b) of this section:

(1) **Double/Triple Trailers** — a knowledge test;

(2) **Passenger** — a knowledge and a skills test;

(3) **Tank vehicle** — a knowledge test;

(4) **Hazardous Materials** —a knowledge test; and

(5) **School bus** — a knowledge and a skills test.

§383.95 Restrictions.

(a) **Air brake**. (1) If an applicant either fails the air brake component of the knowledge test, or performs the skills test in a vehicle not equipped with air brakes, the State must indicate on the CLP or CDL, if issued, that the person is restricted from operating a CMV equipped with any type of air brakes.

(2) For the purposes of the skills test and the restriction, air brakes include any braking system operating fully or partially on the air brake principle.

(b) **Full air brake**. (1) If an applicant performs the skills test in a vehicle equipped with air over hydraulic brakes, the State must indicate on the CDL, if issued, that the person is restricted from operating a CMV equipped with any braking system operating fully on the air brake principle.

(2) For the purposes of the skills test and the restriction, air over hydraulic brakes includes any braking system operating partially on the air brake and partially on the hydraulic brake principle.

(c) **Manual transmission**. (1) If an applicant performs the skills test in a vehicle equipped with an automatic transmission, the State must indicate on the CDL, if issued, that the person is restricted from operating a CMV equipped with a manual transmission.

(2) For the purposes of the skills test and the restriction, an automatic transmission includes any transmission other than a manual transmission as defined in §383.5.

(d) **Tractor-trailer**. If an applicant performs the skills test in a combination vehicle for a Group A CDL with the power unit and towed unit connected with a pintle hook or other non-fifth wheel connection, the State must indicate on the CDL, if issued, that the person is restricted from operating a tractor-trailer combination connected by a fifth wheel that requires a Group A CDL.

(e) **Group A passenger vehicle**. If an applicant applying for a passenger endorsement performs the skills test in a passenger vehicle requiring a Group B CDL, the State must indicate on the CDL, if issued, that the person is restricted from operating a passenger vehicle requiring a Group A CDL.

(f) **Group A and B passenger vehicle**. If an applicant applying for a passenger endorsement performs the skills test in a passenger vehicle requiring a Group C CDL, the State must indicate on the CDL, if issued, that the person is restricted from operating a passenger vehicle requiring a Group A or B CDL.

(g) **Medical Variance Restrictions**. If the State is notified according to §383.73(o)(3) that the driver has been issued a medical variance, the State must indicate the existence of such a medical variance on the CDLIS driver record and the CDL document, if issued, using the restriction code "V" to indicate there is information about a medical variance on the CDLIS driver record. **Note:** In accordance with the agreement between Canada and the United States (see footnote to §391.41 of this chapter), drivers with a medical variance restriction code on their CDL are restricted from operating a CMV in the other country.

Subpart G—Required Knowledge and Skills

§383.110 General requirement.

All drivers of CMVs must have the knowledge and skills necessary to operate a CMV safely as contained in this subpart. The specific types of items that a State must include in the knowledge and skills tests that it administers to CDL applicants are included in this subpart.

§383.111 Required knowledge.

(a) All CMV operators must have knowledge of the following 20 general areas:

(1) **Safe operations regulations**. Driver-related elements of the regulations contained in parts 391, 392, 393, 395, 396, and 397 of this subchapter, such as:

(i) Motor vehicle inspection, repair, and maintenance requirements;

(ii) Procedures for safe vehicle operations;

(iii) The effects of fatigue, poor vision, hearing impairment, and general health upon safe commercial motor vehicle operation;

(iv) The types of motor vehicles and cargoes subject to the requirements contained in part 397 of this subchapter; and

(v) The effects of alcohol and drug use upon safe commercial motor vehicle operations.

(2) **Safe vehicle control systems**. The purpose and function of the controls and instruments commonly found on CMVs.

(3) **CMV safety control systems**.

(i) Proper use of the motor vehicle's safety system, including lights, horns, side and rear-view mirrors, proper mirror adjustments, fire extinguishers, symptoms of improper operation revealed through instruments, motor vehicle operation characteristics, and diagnosing malfunctions.

(ii) CMV drivers must have knowledge of the correct procedures needed to use these safety systems in an emergency situation, e.g., skids and loss of brakes.

(4) **Basic control**. The proper procedures for performing various basic maneuvers, including:

PART 383

(i) Starting, warming up, and shutting down the engine;

(ii) Putting the vehicle in motion and stopping;

(iii) Backing in a straight line; and

(iv) Turning the vehicle, e.g., basic rules, off tracking, right/left turns and right curves.

(5) **Shifting**. The basic shifting rules and terms for common transmissions, including:

(i) Key elements of shifting, e.g., controls, when to shift, and double clutching;

(ii) Shift patterns and procedures; and

(iii) Consequences of improper shifting.

(6) **Backing**. The procedures and rules for various backing maneuvers, including:

(i) Backing principles and rules; and

(ii) Basic backing maneuvers, e.g., straight-line backing, and backing on a curved path.

(7) **Visual search**. The importance of proper visual search, and proper visual search methods, including:

(i) Seeing ahead and to the sides;

(ii) Use of mirrors; and

(iii) Seeing to the rear.

(8) **Communication**. The principles and procedures for proper communications and the hazards of failure to signal properly, including:

(i) Signaling intent, e.g., signaling when changing direction in traffic;

(ii) Communicating presence, e.g., using horn or lights to signal presence; and

(iii) Misuse of communications.

(9) **Speed management**. The importance of understanding the effects of speed, including:

(i) Speed and stopping distance;

(ii) Speed and surface conditions;

(iii) Speed and the shape of the road;

(iv) Speed and visibility; and

(v) Speed and traffic flow.

(10) **Space management**. The procedures and techniques for controlling the space around the vehicle, including:

(i) The importance of space management;

(ii) Space cushions, e.g., controlling space ahead/to the rear;

(iii) Space to the sides; and

(iv) Space for traffic gaps.

(11) **Night operation**. Preparations and procedures for night driving, including:

(i) Night driving factors, e.g., driver factors (vision, glare, fatigue, inexperience);

(ii) Roadway factors (low illumination, variation in illumination, unfamiliarity with roads, other road users, especially drivers exhibiting erratic or improper driving); and

(iii) Vehicle factors (headlights, auxiliary lights, turn signals, windshields and mirrors).

(12) **Extreme driving conditions**. The basic information on operating in extreme driving conditions and the hazards encountered in such conditions, including:

(i) Bad weather, e.g., snow, ice, sleet, high wind;

(ii) Hot weather; and

(iii) Mountain driving.

(13) **Hazard perceptions**. The basic information on hazard perception and clues for recognition of hazards, including:

(i) Road characteristics; and

(ii) Road user activities.

(14) **Emergency maneuvers**. The basic information concerning when and how to make emergency maneuvers, including:

(i) Evasive steering;

(ii) Emergency stop;

(iii) Off road recovery;

(iv) Brake failure; and

(v) Blowouts.

(15) **Skid control and recovery**. The information on the causes and major types of skids, as well as the procedures for recovering from skids.

(16) **Relationship of cargo to vehicle control**. The principles and procedures for the proper handling of cargo, including:

(i) Consequences of improperly secured cargo, drivers' responsibilities, and Federal/State and local regulations;

(ii) Principles of weight distribution; and

(iii) Principles and methods of cargo securement.

(17) **Vehicle inspections**. The objectives and proper procedures for performing vehicle safety inspections, as follows:

(i) The importance of periodic inspection and repair to vehicle safety.

(ii) The effect of undiscovered malfunctions upon safety.

(iii) What safety-related parts to look for when inspecting vehicles, e.g., fluid leaks, interference with visibility, bad tires, wheel and rim defects, braking system defects, steering system defects, suspension system defects, exhaust system defects, coupling system defects, and cargo problems.

(iv) Pre-trip/enroute/post-trip inspection procedures.

(v) Reporting findings.

(18) **Hazardous materials**. Knowledge of the following:

(i) What constitutes hazardous material requiring an endorsement to transport;

(ii) Classes of hazardous materials;

(iii) Labeling/placarding requirements; and

(iv) Need for specialized training as a prerequisite to receiving the endorsement and transporting hazardous cargoes.

(19) **Mountain driving**. Practices that are important when driving upgrade and downgrade, including:

(i) Selecting a safe speed;

(ii) Selecting the right gear; and

(iii) Proper braking techniques.

(20) **Fatigue and awareness**. Practices that are important to staying alert and safe while driving, including;

(i) Being prepared to drive;

(ii) What to do when driving to avoid fatigue;

(iii) What to do when sleepy while driving; and

(iv) What to do when becoming ill while driving.

(b) **Air brakes**. All CMV drivers operating vehicles equipped with air brakes must have knowledge of the following 7 areas:

(1) General air brake system nomenclature;

(2) The dangers of contaminated air supply (dirt, moisture, and oil);

(3) Implications of severed or disconnected air lines between the power unit and the trailer(s);

(4) Implications of low air pressure readings;

(5) Procedures to conduct safe and accurate pre-trip inspections, including knowledge about:

(i) Automatic fail-safe devices;

(ii) System monitoring devices; and

(iii) Low pressure warning alarms.

(6) Procedures for conducting en route and post-trip inspections of air-actuated brake systems, including:

(i) Ability to detect defects that may cause the system to fail;

(ii) Tests that indicate the amount of air loss from the braking system within a specified period, with and without the engine running; and

(iii) Tests that indicate the pressure levels at which the low air pressure warning devices and the tractor protection valve should activate.

(7) General operating practices and procedures, including:

(i) Proper braking techniques;

(ii) Antilock brakes;

(iii) Emergency stops; and

(iv) Parking brake.

(c) **Combination vehicles**. All CMV drivers operating combination vehicles must have knowledge of the following 3 areas:

(1) Coupling and uncoupling—The procedures for proper coupling and uncoupling a tractor to a semi-trailer;

(2) Vehicle inspection—The objectives and proper procedures that are unique for performing vehicle safety inspections on combination vehicles; and

(3) General operating practices and procedures, including:

(i) Safely operating combination vehicles; and

(ii) Air brakes.

§383.113 Required skills.

(a) **Pre-trip vehicle inspection skills**. Applicants for a CDL must possess the following basic pre-trip vehicle inspection skills for the vehicle class that the driver operates or expects to operate:

(1) **All test vehicles**. Applicants must be able to identify each safety-related part on the vehicle and explain what needs to be inspected to ensure a safe operating condition of each part, including:

(i) Engine compartment;

(ii) Cab/engine start;

(iii) Steering;

(iv) Suspension;

(v) Brakes;

(vi) Wheels;

(vii) Side of vehicle;

(viii) Rear of vehicle; and

(ix) Special features of tractor trailer, school bus, or coach/transit bus, if this type of vehicle is being used for the test.

(2) **Air brake equipped test vehicles**. Applicants must demonstrate the following skills with respect to inspection and operation of air brakes:

(i) Locate and verbally identify air brake operating controls and monitoring devices;

(ii) Determine the motor vehicle's brake system condition for proper adjustments and that air system connections between motor vehicles have been properly made and secured;

(iii) Inspect the low pressure warning device(s) to ensure that they will activate in emergency situations;

(iv) With the engine running, make sure that the system maintains an adequate supply of compressed air;

(v) Determine that required minimum air pressure build up time is within acceptable limits and that required alarms and emergency devices automatically deactivate at the proper pressure level; and

(vi) Operationally check the brake system for proper performance.

(b) **Basic vehicle control skills**. All applicants for a CDL must possess and demonstrate the following basic motor vehicle control skills for the vehicle class that the driver operates or expects to operate:

(1) Ability to start, warm up, and shut down the engine;

(2) Ability to put the motor vehicle in motion and accelerate smoothly, forward and backward;

(3) Ability to bring the motor vehicle to a smooth stop;

(4) Ability to back the motor vehicle in a straight line, and check path and clearance while backing;

(5) Ability to position the motor vehicle to negotiate safely and then make left and right turns;

(6) Ability to shift as required and select appropriate gear for speed and highway conditions; and

(7) Ability to back along a curved path.

(c) **Safe on-road driving skills**. All applicants for a CDL must possess and demonstrate the following safe on-road driving skills for their vehicle class:

(1) Ability to use proper visual search methods;

(2) Ability to signal appropriately when changing direction in traffic;

(3) Ability to adjust speed to the configuration and condition of the roadway, weather and visibility conditions, traffic conditions, and motor vehicle, cargo and driver conditions;

(4) Ability to choose a safe gap for changing lanes, passing other vehicles, as well as for crossing or entering traffic;

(5) Ability to position the motor vehicle correctly before and during a turn to prevent other vehicles from passing on the wrong side, as well as to prevent problems caused by off-tracking;

(6) Ability to maintain a safe following distance depending on the condition of the road, visibility, and vehicle weight;

(7) Ability to adjust operation of the motor vehicle to prevailing weather conditions including speed selection, braking, direction changes, and following distance to maintain control; and

(8) Ability to observe the road and the behavior of other motor vehicles, particularly before changing speed and direction.

(d) **Test area**. Skills tests shall be conducted in on-street conditions or under a combination of on-street and off-street conditions.

(e) **Simulation technology**. A State may utilize simulators to perform skills testing, but under no circumstances as a substitute for the required testing in on-street conditions.

§383.115 Requirements for double/triple trailers endorsement.

In order to obtain a double/triple trailers endorsement each applicant must have knowledge covering:

(a) Procedures for assembly and hookup of the units;

(b) Proper placement of heaviest trailer;

(c) Handling and stability characteristics including off-tracking, response to steering, sensory feedback, braking, oscillatory sway, rollover in steady turns, and yaw stability in steady turns;

(d) Potential problems in traffic operations, including problems the motor vehicle creates for other motorists due to slower speeds on steep grades, longer passing times, possibility for blocking entry of other motor vehicles on freeways, splash and spray impacts, aerodynamic buffeting, view blockages, and lateral placement; and

(e) Operating practices and procedures not otherwise specified.

§383.117 Requirements for passenger endorsement.

An applicant for the passenger endorsement must satisfy both of the following additional knowledge and skills test requirements.

(a) **Knowledge test**. All applicants for the passenger endorsement must have knowledge covering the following topics:

(1) Proper procedures for loading/unloading passengers;

(2) Proper use of emergency exits, including push-out windows;

(3) Proper responses to such emergency situations as fires and unruly passengers;

(4) Proper procedures at railroad-highway grade crossings and drawbridges;

(5) Proper braking procedures; and

(6) Operating practices and procedures not otherwise specified.

(b) **Skills test**. To obtain a passenger endorsement applicable to a specific vehicle class, an applicant must take his/her skills test in a passenger vehicle satisfying the requirements of that vehicle group as defined in §383.91.

§383.119 Requirements for tank vehicle endorsement.

In order to obtain a tank vehicle endorsement, each applicant must have knowledge covering the following:

(a) Causes, prevention, and effects of cargo surge on motor vehicle handling;

(b) Proper braking procedures for the motor vehicle when it is empty, full, and partially full;

(c) Differences in handling of baffled/compartmented tank interiors versus non-baffled motor vehicles;

(d) Differences in tank vehicle type and construction;

(e) Differences in cargo surge for liquids of varying product densities;

(f) Effects of road grade and curvature on motor vehicle handling with filled, half-filled, and empty tanks;

(g) Proper use of emergency systems;

(h) For drivers of DOT specification tank vehicles, retest and marking requirements; and

(i) Operating practices and procedures not otherwise specified.

§383.121 Requirements for hazardous materials endorsement.

In order to obtain a hazardous materials endorsement, each applicant must have such knowledge as is required of a driver of a hazardous materials laden vehicle, from information contained in 49 CFR parts 171, 172, 173, 177, 178, and 397, on the following:

(a) Hazardous materials regulations including:

(1) Hazardous materials table;

(2) Shipping paper requirements;

(3) Marking;

(4) Labeling;

(5) Placarding requirements;

(6) Hazardous materials packaging;

(7) Hazardous materials definitions and preparation;

(8) Other regulated material (e.g., ORM-D);

(9) Reporting hazardous materials accidents; and

(10) Tunnels and railroad crossings.

(b) Hazardous materials handling including:

(1) Forbidden materials and packages;

(2) Loading and unloading materials;

(3) Cargo segregation;

(4) Passenger carrying buses and hazardous materials;

(5) Attendance of motor vehicles;

(6) Parking;

(7) Routes;

(8) Cargo tanks; and

(9) "Safe havens."

(c) Operation of emergency equipment including:

(1) Use of equipment to protect the public;

(2) Special precautions for equipment to be used in fires;

(3) Special precautions for use of emergency equipment when loading or unloading a hazardous materials laden motor vehicle; and

(4) Use of emergency equipment for tank vehicles.

(d) Emergency response procedures including:

(1) Special care and precautions for different types of accidents;

(2) Special precautions for driving near a fire and carrying hazardous materials, and smoking and carrying hazardous materials;

(3) Emergency procedures; and

(4) Existence of special requirements for transporting Class 1.1 and 1.2 explosives.

(e) Operating practices and procedures not otherwise specified.

§383.123 Requirements for a school bus endorsement.

(a) An applicant for the school bus endorsement must satisfy the following three requirements:

(1) **Qualify for passenger vehicle endorsement**. Pass the knowledge and skills test for obtaining a passenger vehicle endorsement.

(2) **Knowledge test**. Must have knowledge covering the following topics:

(i) Loading and unloading children, including the safe operation of stop signal devices, external mirror systems, flashing lights, and other warning and passenger safety devices required for school buses by State or Federal law or regulation.

(ii) Emergency exits and procedures for safely evacuating passengers in an emergency.

(iii) State and Federal laws and regulations related to safely traversing railroad-highway grade crossings; and

(iv) Operating practices and procedures not otherwise specified.

PART 383

(3) **Skills test**. Must take a driving skills test in a school bus of the same vehicle group (see §383.91(a)) as the school bus applicant will drive.

(b) **Exception**. Knowledge and skills tests administered before September 30, 2002 and approved by FMCSA as meeting the requirements of this section, meet the requirements of paragraphs (a)(2) and (3) of this section.

Subpart H—Tests

§383.131 Test manuals.

(a) **Driver information manual**. (1) A State must provide an FMCSA pre-approved driver information manual to a CLP or CDL applicant. The manual must be comparable to the American Association of Motor Vehicle Administrators' (AAMVA's) "2005 CDL Test System (July 2010 or newer Version) Model Commercial Driver Manual", which FMCSA has approved and provides to all State Driver Licensing Agencies. The driver information manual must include:

(i) Information on how to obtain a CDL and endorsements;

(ii) Information on the requirements described in §383.71, the implied consent to alcohol testing described in §383.72, the procedures and penalties contained in §383.51(b) to which a CLP or CDL holder is exposed for refusal to comply with such alcohol testing, State procedures described in §383.73, and other appropriate driver information contained in subpart E of this part;

(iii) Information on vehicle groups and endorsements as specified in subpart F of this part;

(iv) The substance of the knowledge and skills that drivers must have, as outlined in subpart G of this part for the different vehicle groups and endorsements; and

(v) Details of testing procedures, including the purpose of the tests, how to respond, and directions for taking the tests.

(2) A State may include any additional State-specific information related to the CDL testing and licensing process.

(b) **Examiner information manual**. (1) A State must provide an FMCSA pre-approved examiner information manual that conforms to model requirements in paragraphs (b)(1)(i-xi) of this section to all knowledge and skills test examiners. To be pre-approved by FMCSA, the examiner information manual must be comparable to AAMVA's "2005 CDL Test System (July 2010 or newer Version) Model CDL Examiner's Manual," which FMCSA has approved and provides to all State Driver Licensing Agencies. The examiner information manual must include:

(i) Information on driver application procedures contained in §383.71, State procedures described in §383.73, and other appropriate driver information contained in subpart E of this part;

(ii) Details on information that must be given to the applicant;

(iii) Details on how to conduct the knowledge and skills tests;

(iv) Scoring procedures and minimum passing scores for the knowledge and skills tests;

(v) Information for selecting driving test routes for the skills tests;

(vi) List of the skills to be tested;

(vii) Instructions on where and how the skills will be tested;

(viii) How performance of the skills will be scored;

(ix) Causes for automatic failure of skills tests;

(x) Standardized scoring sheets for the skills tests; and

(xi) Standardized driving instructions for the applicants.

(2) A State may include any additional State-specific information related to the CDL testing process.

§383.133 Test methods.

(a) All tests must be constructed in such a way as to determine if the applicant possesses the required knowledge and skills contained in subpart G of this part for the type of motor vehicle or endorsement the applicant wishes to obtain.

(b) Knowledge tests:

(1) States must use the FMCSA pre-approved pool of test questions to develop knowledge tests for each vehicle group and endorsement. The pool of questions must be comparable to those in AAMVA's "2005 CDL Test System (July 2010 or newer Version) 2005 Test Item Summary Forms," which FMCSA has approved and provides to all State Driver Licensing Agencies.

(2) The State method of generating knowledge tests must conform to the requirements in paragraphs (b)(2)(i) through (iv) of this section and be pre-approved by FMCSA. The State method of generating knowledge tests must be comparable to the requirements outlined in AAMVA's "2005 CDL Test System (July 2010 or newer Version) 2005 Requirements Document For Use In Developing Computer-Generated Multiple-Choice CDL Knowledge Tests", which FMCSA has approved and provides to all State Driver Licensing Agencies to develop knowledge tests for each vehicle group and endorsement. These requirements include:

(i) The total difficulty level of the questions used in each version of a test must fall within a set range;

(ii) Twenty-five percent of the questions on a test must be new questions that were not contained in the previous version of the test;

(iii) Identical questions from the previous version of the test must be in a different location on the test and the three possible responses to the questions must be in a different order; and

(iv) Each test must contain a set number of questions with a prescribed number of questions from each of the knowledge areas.

(3) Each knowledge test must be valid and reliable so as to ensure that driver applicants possess the knowledge required under §383.111. The knowledge tests may be administered in written form, verbally, or in automated format and can be administered in a foreign language, provided no interpreter is used in administering the test.

(4) A State must use a different version of the test when an applicant retakes a previously failed test.

(c) Skills tests:

(1) A State must develop, administer and score the skills tests based solely on the information and standards contained in the driver and examiner manuals referred to in §383.131(a) and (b).

(2) A State must use the standardized scores and instructions for administering the tests contained in the examiner manual referred to in §383.131(b).

(3) An applicant must complete the skills tests in a representative vehicle to ensure that the applicant possess the skills required under §383.113. In determining whether the vehicle is a representative vehicle for the skills test and the group of CDL for which the applicant is applying, the vehicle's gross vehicle weight rating or gross combination weight rating must be used, not the vehicle's actual gross vehicle weight or gross combination weight.

(4) Skills tests must be conducted in on-street conditions or under a combination of on-street and off-street conditions.

(5) Interpreters are prohibited during the administration of skills tests. Applicants must be able to understand and respond to verbal commands and instructions in English by a skills test examiner. Neither the applicant nor the examiner may communicate in a language other than English during the skills test.

(6) The skills test must be administered and successfully completed in the following order: Pre-trip inspection, basic vehicle control skills, on-road skills. If an applicant fails one segment of the skills test:

(i) The applicant cannot continue to the next segment of the test; and

(ii) Scores for the passed segments of the test are only valid during initial issuance of the CLP. If the CLP is renewed, all three segments of the skills test must be retaken.

(d) Passing scores for the knowledge and skills tests must meet the standards contained in §383.135.

§383.135 Passing knowledge and skills tests.

(a) **Knowledge tests**. (1) To achieve a passing score on each of the knowledge tests, a driver applicant must correctly answer at least 80 percent of the questions.

(2) If a driver applicant who fails the air brake portion of the knowledge test (scores less than 80 percent correct) is issued a CLP or CDL, an air brake restriction must be indicated on the CLP or CDL as required in §383.95(a).

(3) A driver applicant who fails the combination vehicle portion of the knowledge test (scores less than 80 percent correct) must not be issued a Group A CLP or CDL.

(b) **Skills Tests**. (1) To achieve a passing score on each segment of the skills test, the driver applicant must demonstrate that he/she can successfully perform all of the skills listed in §383.113 and attain the scores listed in Appendix A of the examiner manual referred to in §383.131(b) for the type of vehicle being used in the test.

(2) A driver applicant who does not obey traffic laws, causes an accident during the test, or commits any other offense listed as a reason for automatic failure in the standards contained in the driver and examiner manuals referred to in §§383.131(a) and (b), must automatically fail the test.

(3) If a driver applicant who performs the skills test in a vehicle not equipped with any type of air brake system is issued a CDL, an air brake restriction must be indicated on the license as required in §383.95(a).

(4) If a driver applicant who performs the skills test in a vehicle equipped with air over hydraulic brakes is issued a CDL, a full air brake restriction must be indicated on the license as required in §383.95(b).

(5) If a driver applicant who performs the skills test in a vehicle equipped with an automatic transmission is issued a CDL, a manual transmission restriction must be indicated on the license as required in §383.95(c).

(6) If a driver applicant who performs the skills test in a combination vehicle requiring a Group A CDL equipped with any non-fifth wheel connection is issued a CDL, a tractor-trailer restriction must be indicated on the license as required in §383.95(d).

(7) If a driver applicant wants to remove any of the restrictions in paragraphs (b)(3) through (5) of this section, the applicant does not have to retake the complete skills test. The State may administer a modified skills test that demonstrates that the applicant can safely and effectively operate the vehicle's full air brakes, air over hydraulic brakes, and/or manual transmission. In addition, to

remove the air brake or full air brake restriction, the applicant must successfully perform the air brake pre-trip inspection and pass the air brake knowledge test.

(8) If a driver applicant wants to remove the tractor-trailer restriction in paragraph (b)(6) of this section, the applicant must retake all three skills tests in a representative tractor-trailer.

(c) **State recordkeeping**. States must record and retain the knowledge and skills test scores of tests taken by driver applicants. The test scores must either be made part of the driver history record or be linked to the driver history record in a separate file.

Subpart I—Requirement for Transportation Security Administration Approval of Hazardous Materials Endorsement Issuances

§383.141 General.

(a) **Applicability**. This section applies to State agencies responsible for issuing hazardous materials endorsements for a CDL, and applicants for such endorsements.

(b) **Prohibition.** A state may not issue, renew, upgrade, or transfer a hazardous material endorsement for a CDL to any individual authorizing that individual to operate a commercial motor vehicle transporting a hazardous material in commerce unless—

(1) The Transportation Security Administration has determined that the individual does not pose a security risk warranting denial of the endorsement; or

(2) The individual holds a valid TWIC.

(c) **Individual notification**. At least 60 days prior to the expiration date of the CDL or hazardous materials endorsement, a State must notify the holder of a hazardous materials endorsement that the individual must pass a Transportation Security Administration security threat assessment process as part of any application for renewal of the hazardous materials endorsement. The notice must advise a driver that, in order to expedite the security screening process, he or she should file a renewal application as soon as possible, but not later than 30 days before the date of expiration of the endorsement. An individual who does not successfully complete the Transportation Security Administration security threat assessment process referenced in paragraph (b) of this section may not be issued a hazardous materials endorsement.

(d) **Hazardous materials endorsement renewal cycle**. Each State must require that hazardous materials endorsements be renewed every 5 years or less so that individuals are subject to a Transportation Security Administration security screening requirement referenced in paragraph (b) of this section at least every 5 years.

Subpart J—Commercial Learner's Permit and Commercial Driver's License Documents

§383.151 General.

(a) The CDL must be a document that is easy to recognize as a CDL.

(b) The CLP must be a separate document from the CDL or non-CDL.

(c) At a minimum, the CDL and the CLP must contain the information specified in §383.153.

PART 383

§383.153 Information on the CLP and CDL documents and applications.

(a) **Commercial Driver's License**. All CDLs must contain all of the following information:

(1) The prominent statement that the license is a "Commercial Driver's License" or "CDL," except as specified in paragraph (c) of this section.

(2) The full name, signature, and mailing or residential address in the licensing State of the person to whom such license is issued.

(3) Physical and other information to identify and describe such person including date of birth (month, day, and year), sex, and height.

(4) Color photograph, digitized color image, or black and white laser engraved photograph of the driver. The State may issue a temporary CDL without a photo or image, if it is valid for no more than 60 days.

(5) The driver's State license number.

(6) The name of the State which issued the license.

(7) The date of issuance and the date of expiration of the license.

(8) The group or groups of commercial motor vehicle(s) that the driver is authorized to operate, indicated as follows:

(i) A for Combination Vehicle;

(ii) B for Heavy Straight Vehicle; and

(iii) C for Small Vehicle.

(9) The endorsement(s) for which the driver has qualified, if any, indicated as follows:

(i) T for double/triple trailers;

(ii) P for passenger;

(iii) N for tank vehicle;

(iv) H for hazardous materials;

(v) X for a combination of tank vehicle and hazardous materials endorsements;

(vi) S for school bus; and

(vii) At the discretion of the State, additional codes for additional groupings of endorsements, as long as each such discretionary code is fully explained on the front or back of the CDL document.

(10) The restriction(s) placed on the driver from operating certain equipment or vehicles, if any, indicated as follows:

(i) L for No Air brake equipped CMV;

(ii) Z for No Full air brake equipped CMV;

(iii) E for No Manual transmission equipped CMV;

(iv) O for No Tractor-trailer CMV;

(v) M for No Class A passenger vehicle;

(vi) N for No Class A and B passenger vehicle;

(vii) K for Intrastate only;

(viii) V for medical variance; and

(ix) At the discretion of the State, additional codes for additional restrictions, as long as each such restriction code is fully explained on the front or back of the CDL document.

(b) **Commercial Learner's Permit**. (1) A CLP may, but is not required to, contain a digital color image or photograph or black and white laser engraved photograph.

(2) All CLPs must contain all of the following information:

(i) The prominent statement that the permit is a "Commercial Learner's Permit" or "CLP," except as specified in paragraph (c) of this section, and that it is invalid unless accompanied by the underlying driver's license issued by the same jurisdiction.

(ii) The full name, signature, and mailing or residential address in the permitting State of the person to whom the permit is issued.

(iii) Physical and other information to identify and describe such person including date of birth (month, day, and year), sex, and height.

(iv) The driver's State license number.

(v) The name of the State which issued the permit.

(vi) The date of issuance and the date of expiration of the permit.

(vii) The group or groups of commercial motor vehicle(s) that the driver is authorized to operate, indicated as follows:

(A) A for Combination Vehicle;

(B) B for Heavy Straight Vehicle; and

(C) C for Small Vehicle.

(viii) The endorsement(s) for which the driver has qualified, if any, indicated as follows:

(A) **P for passenger endorsement.** A CLP holder with a P endorsement is prohibited from operating a CMV carrying passengers, other than Federal/State auditors and inspectors, test examiners, other trainees, and the CDL holder accompanying the CLP holder as prescribed by §383.25(a)(1) of this part;

(B) **S for school bus endorsement.** A CLP holder with an S endorsement is prohibited from operating a school bus with passengers other than Federal /State auditors and inspectors, test examiners, other trainees, and the CDL holder accompanying the CLP holder as prescribed by §383.25(a)(1) of this part; and

(C) **N for tank vehicle endorsement.** A CLP holder with an N endorsement may only operate an empty tank vehicle and is prohibited from operating any tank vehicle that previously contained hazardous materials that has not been purged of any residue.

(ix) The restriction(s) placed on the driver, if any, indicated as follows:

(A) P for No passengers in CMV bus;

(B) X for No cargo in CMV tank vehicle;

(C) L for No Air brake equipped CMV;

(D) V for medical variance;

(E) M for No Class A passenger vehicle;

(F) N for No Class A and B passenger vehicle;

(G) K for Intrastate only.

(H) Any additional jurisdictional restrictions that apply to the CLP driving privilege.

(c) If the CLP or CDL is a Non-domiciled CLP or CDL, it must contain the prominent statement that the license or permit is a "Non-domiciled Commercial Driver's License," "Non-domiciled CDL," "Non-domiciled Commercial Learner's Permit," or "Non-domiciled CLP," as appropriate. The word "Non-domiciled" must be conspicuously and unmistakably displayed, but may be noncontiguous with the words "Commercial Driver's License," "CDL," "Commercial Learner's Permit," or "CLP."

(d) If the State has issued the applicant an air brake restriction as specified in §383.95, that restriction must be indicated on the CLP or CDL.

(e) Except in the case of a Non-domiciled CLP or CDL holder who is domiciled in a foreign jurisdiction:

(1) A driver applicant must provide his/her Social Security Number on the application of a CLP or CDL.

(2) The State must provide the Social Security Number to the CDLIS.

(3) The State must not display the Social Security Number on the CLP or CDL.

(f) The State may issue a multipart CDL provided that:

(1) Each document is explicitly tied to the other document(s) and to a single driver's record.

(2) The multipart license document includes all of the data elements specified in this section.

(g) Current CDL holders are not required to be retested to determine whether they need any of the new restrictions for no full air brakes, no manual transmission and no tractor-trailer. These new restrictions only apply to CDL applicants who take skills tests on or after July 8, 2015 (including those applicants who previously held a CDL before the new restrictions went into effect).

(h) On or after July 8, 2015 current CLP and CDL holders who do not have the standardized endorsement and restriction codes and applicants for a CLP or CDL are to be issued CLPs with the standardized codes upon initial issuance, renewal or upgrade and CDLs with the standardized codes upon initial issuance, renewal, upgrade or transfer.

§383.155 Tamperproofing requirements.

States must make the CLP and CDL tamperproof to the maximum extent practicable. At a minimum, a State must use the same tamperproof method used for noncommercial drivers' licenses.

PART 387—MINIMUM LEVELS OF FINANCIAL RESPONSIBILITY FOR MOTOR CARRIERS

Subpart A—Motor Carriers of Property

Subpart B—Motor Carriers of Passengers

Subpart C—Surety Bonds and Policies of Insurance for Motor Carriers and Property Brokers

§387.1

Authority: 49 U.S.C. 13101, 13301, 13906, 13908, 14701, 31138, 31139; sec. 204(a), Pub. L. 104-88, 109 Stat. 803, 941; and 49 CFR 1.87.

Editorial Note: Nomenclature changes to Part 387 appear at 67 FR 61821-61824, Oct. 2, 2002.

Subpart A—Motor Carriers of Property

§387.1 Purpose and scope.

This subpart prescribes the minimum levels of financial responsibility required to be maintained by motor carriers of property operating motor vehicles in interstate, foreign, or intrastate commerce. The purpose of these regulations is to create additional incentives to motor carriers to maintain and operate their vehicles in a safe manner and to assure that motor carriers maintain an appropriate level of financial responsibility for motor vehicles operated on public highways.

§387.3 Applicability.

(a) This subpart applies to for-hire motor carriers operating motor vehicles transporting property in interstate or foreign commerce.

(b) This subpart applies to motor carriers operating motor vehicles transporting hazardous materials, hazardous substances, or hazardous wastes in interstate, foreign, or intrastate commerce.

(c) **Exception.** (1) The rules in this subpart do not apply to a motor vehicle that has a gross vehicle weight rating (GVWR) of less than 10,001 pounds. This exception does not apply if the vehicle is used to transport any quantity of a Division 1.1, 1.2, or 1.3 material, any quantity of a Division 2.3, Hazard Zone A, or Division 6.1, Packing Group I, Hazard Zone A, or to a highway route controlled quantity of a Class 7 material as it is defined in 49 CFR 173.403, in interstate or foreign commerce.

(2) The rules in this subpart do not apply to the transportation of nonbulk oil, nonbulk hazardous materials, substances, or wastes in intrastate commerce, except that the rules in this subpart do apply to the transportation of a highway route controlled quantity of a Class 7 material as defined in 49 CFR 173.403, in intrastate commerce.

§387.5 Definitions.

As used in this subpart—

Accident includes continuous or repeated exposure to the same conditions resulting in public liability which the insured neither expected nor intended.

Bodily injury means injury to the body, sickness, or disease including death resulting from any of these.

Cancellation of insurance means the withdrawal of insurance coverage by either the insurer or the insured.

Endorsement means an amendment to an insurance policy.

Environmental restoration means restitution for the loss, damage, or destruction of natural resources arising out of the accidental discharge, dispersal, release or escape into or upon the land, atmosphere, watercourse, or body of water of any commodity transported by a motor carrier. This shall include the cost of removal and the cost of necessary measure taken to minimize or mitigate damage to human health, the natural environment, fish, shellfish, and wildlife.

Evidence of security means a surety bond or a policy of insurance with the appropriate endorsement attached.

Financial responsibility means the financial reserves (e.g., insurance policies or surety bonds) sufficient to satisfy liability amounts set forth in this part covering public liability.

For-hire carriage means the business of transporting, for compensation, the goods or property of another.

In bulk means the transportation, as cargo, of property, except Division 1.1, 1.2, or 1.3 materials, and Division 2.3, Hazard Zone A gases, in containment systems with capacities in excess of 3,500 water gallons.

In bulk (Division 1.1, 1.2, and 1.3 explosives) means the transportation, as cargo, of any Division 1.1, 1.2, or 1.3 materials in any quantity.

In bulk (Division 2.3, Hazard Zone A or Division 6.1, Packing Group I, Hazard Zone A materials) means the transportation, as cargo, of any Division 2.3, Hazard Zone A, or Division 6.1, Packing Group I, Hazard Zone A material, in any quantity.

Insured and principal means the motor carrier named in the policy of insurance, surety bond, endorsement, or notice of cancellation, and also the fiduciary of such motor carrier.

Insurance premium means the monetary sum an insured pays an insurer for acceptance of liability for public liability claims made against the insured.

Motor carrier means a for-hire motor carrier or a private motor carrier. The term includes, but is not limited to, a motor carrier's agent, officer, or representative; an employee responsible for hiring, supervising, training, assigning, or dispatching a driver; or an employee concerned with the installation, inspection, and maintenance of motor vehicle equipment and/or accessories.

Property damage means damage to or loss of use of tangible property.

Public liability means liability for bodily injury or property damage and includes liability for environmental restoration.

State means a State of the United States, the District of Columbia, Puerto Rico, the Virgin Islands, American Samoa, Guam, and the Northern Mariana Islands.

§387.7 Financial responsibility required.

(a) No motor carrier shall operate a motor vehicle until the motor carrier has obtained and has in effect the minimum levels of financial responsibility as set forth in §387.9 of this subpart.

(b)(1) Policies of insurance, surety bonds, and endorsements required under this section shall remain in effect continuously until terminated. Cancellation may be effected by the insurer or the insured motor carrier giving 35 days' notice in writing to the other. The 35 days' notice shall commence to run from the date the notice is transmitted. Proof of transmission shall be sufficient proof of notice.

(2) **Exception**. Policies of insurance and surety bonds may be obtained for a finite period of time to cover any lapse in continuous compliance.

(3) **Exception**. (i) A Mexico-domiciled motor carrier operating solely in municipalities in the United States on the U.S.-Mexico international border or within the commercial zones of such municipalities with a Certificate of Registration issued under part 368 may meet the minimum financial responsibility requirements of this subpart by obtaining insurance coverage, in the required amounts, for periods of 24 hours or longer, from insurers that meet the requirements of §387.11.

(ii) A Mexican motor carrier so insured must have available for inspection in each of its vehicles copies of the following documents:

(A) The Certificate of Registration;

(B) The required insurance endorsement (Form MCS-90); and

(C) An insurance identification card, binder, or other document issued by an authorized insurer which specifies both the effective date and the expiration date of the temporary insurance coverage authorized by this exception.

(iii) Mexican motor carriers insured under this exception are also exempt from the notice of cancellation requirements stated on Form MCS-90.

(c) Policies of insurance and surety bonds required under this section may be replaced by other policies of insurance or surety bonds. The liability of the retiring insurer or surety, as to events after the termination date, shall be considered as having terminated on the effective date of the replacement policy of insurance or surety bond or at the end of the 35 day cancellation period required in paragraph (b) of this section, whichever is sooner.

(d) Proof of the required financial responsibility shall be maintained at the motor carrier's principal place of business. The proof shall consist of:

(1) "Endorsement(s) for Motor Carrier Policies of Insurance for Public Liability Under Sections 29 and 30 of the Motor Carrier Act of 1980" (Form MCS-90) issued by an insurer(s);

(2) A "Motor Carrier Surety Bond for Public Liability Under Section 30 of the Motor Carrier Act of 1980" (Form MCS-82) issued by a surety; or

(3) A written decision, order, or authorization of the Federal Motor Carrier Safety Administration authorizing a motor carrier to self-insure under §387.309, provided the motor carrier maintains a satisfactory safety rating as determined by the Federal Motor Carrier Safety Administration under part 385 of this chapter.

(e)(1) The proof of minimum levels of financial responsibility required by this section shall be considered public information and be produced for review upon reasonable request by a member of the public.

(2) In addition to maintaining proof of financial responsibility as required by paragraph (d) of this section, non-North America-domiciled private and for-hire

motor carriers shall file evidence of financial responsibility with FMCSA in accordance with the requirements of subpart C of this part.

(f) All vehicles operated within the United States by motor carriers domiciled in a contiguous foreign country, shall have on board the vehicle a legible copy, in English, of the proof of the required financial responsibility (Forms MCS-90 or MCS-82) used by the motor carrier to comply with paragraph (d) of this section.

(g) Any motor vehicle in which there is no evidence of financial responsibility required by paragraph (f) of this section shall be denied entry into the United States.

§387.9 Financial responsibility, minimum levels.

The minimum levels of financial responsibility referred to in §387.7 are hereby prescribed as follows:

Table 1 to §387.9—Schedule of Limits—Public Liability

Type of carriage	Commodity transported	January 1, 1985
(1) For-hire (In interstate or foreign commerce, with a gross vehicle weight rating of 10,001 or more pounds).	Property (nonhazardous)	$750,000
(2) For-hire and Private (In interstate, foreign, or intrastate commerce, with a gross vehicle weight rating of 10,001 or more pounds).	Hazardous substances, as defined in 49 CFR 171.8, transported in bulk in cargo tanks, portable tanks, or hopper-type vehicles with capacities in bulk Division 1.1, 1.2 or 1.3 materials; Division 2.3, Hazard Zone A material; in bulk Division 6.1, Packing Group I, Hazard Zone A material; in bulk Division 2.1 or 2.2 material; or highway route controlled quantities of a Class 7 material, as defined in 49 CFR 173.403	5,000,000
(3) For-hire and Private (In interstate or foreign commerce, in any quantity; or in intrastate commerce, in bulk only; with a gross vehicle weight rating of 10,001 or more pounds).	Oil listed in 49 CFR 172.101; hazardous waste, hazardous materials, or hazardous substances defined in 49 CFR 171.8 and listed in 49 CFR 172.101, but not mentioned in entry (2) or (4) of this table	1,000,000
(4) For-hire and Private (In interstate or foreign commerce, with a gross vehicle weight rating of less than 10,001 pounds).	In bulk Division 1.1, 1.2, or 1.3 material; in bulk Division 2.3, Hazard Zone A material; in bulk Division 6.1, Packing Group I, Hazard Zone A material; or highway route controlled quantities of a Class 7 material as defined in 49 CFR 173.403	5,000,000

§387.11 State authority and designation of agent.

A policy of insurance or surety bond does not satisfy the financial responsibility requirements of this subpart unless the insurer or surety furnishing the policy or bond is—

(a) Legally authorized to issue such policies or bonds in each State in which the motor carrier operates; or

(b) Legally authorized to issue such policies or bonds in the State in which the motor carrier has its principal place of business or domicile, and is willing to designate a person upon whom process, issued by or under the authority of any court having jurisdiction of the subject matter, may be served in any proceeding at law or equity brought in any State in which the motor carrier operates; or

(c) Legally authorized to issue such policies or bonds in any State of the United States and eligible as an excess or surplus lines insurer in any State in which business is written, and is willing to designate a person upon whom process, issued by or under the authority of any court having jurisdiction of the subject matter, may be served in any proceeding at law or equity brought in any State in which the motor carrier operates.

(d) A Canadian insurance company legally authorized to issue a policy of insurance in the Province or Territory of Canada in which the Canadian motor carrier has its principal place of business or domicile, and that is willing to designate a person upon whom process, issued by or under the authority of any court having jurisdiction over the subject matter, may be served in any proceeding at law or equity brought in any State in which the motor carrier operates.

§387.13 Fiduciaries.

The coverage of fiduciaries shall attach at the moment of succession of such fiduciaries.

§387.15 Forms.

Endorsements for policies of insurance (Form MCS-90) and surety bonds (Form MCS-82) must be in the form prescribed by the FMCSA and approved by the OMB. Endorsements to policies of insurance and surety bonds shall specify that coverage thereunder will remain in effect continuously until terminated, as required in §387.7 of this subpart. The continuous coverage requirement does not apply to Mexican motor carriers insured under §387.7(b)(3) of this subpart. The endorsement and surety bond shall be issued in the exact name of the motor carrier. The Forms MCS-82 and MCS-90 are available from the FMCSA website at *http://www.fmcsa.dot.gov/mission/forms*.

§387.17 Violation and penalty.

Any person (except an employee who acts without knowledge) who knowingly violates the rules of this subpart shall be liable to the United States for a civil penalty as stated in part 386, appendix B, of this chapter, and if any such violation is a continuing one, each day of violation will constitute a separate offense. The amount of any such penalty shall be assessed by FMCSA's Administrator, by written notice. In determining the amount of such penalty, the Administrator, or his/her authorized delegate shall take into account the nature, circumstances, extent, the gravity of the violation committed and, with respect to the person found to have committed such violation, the degree of culpability, any history of prior violations, ability to pay, and any effect on ability to continue to do business, and such other matters as justice may require.

Subpart B—Motor Carriers of Passengers

§387.25 Purpose and scope.

This subpart prescribes the minimum levels of financial responsibility required to be maintained by for-hire motor carriers of passengers operating motor vehicles in interstate or foreign commerce. The purpose of these regulations is to create additional incentives to carriers to operate their vehicles in a safe manner and to assure that they maintain adequate levels of financial responsibility.

§387.27 Applicability.

(a) This subpart applies to for-hire motor carriers transporting passengers in interstate or foreign commerce.

(b) **Exception**. The rules in this subpart do not apply to—

(1) A motor vehicle transporting only school children and teachers to or from school;

(2) A motor vehicle providing taxicab service and having a seating capacity of less than 7 passengers and not operated on a regular route or between specified points;

(3) A motor vehicle carrying less than 16 individuals in a single daily round trip to commute to and from work; and

(4) A motor vehicle operated by a motor carrier under contract providing transportation of preprimary, primary, and secondary students for extracurricular trips organized, sponsored, and paid by a school district.

§387.29 Definitions.

As used in this subpart—

Accident includes continuous or repeated exposure to the same conditions resulting in public liability which the insured neither expected nor intended.

Bodily injury means injury to the body, sickness, or disease including death resulting from any of these.

Endorsement means an amendment to an insurance policy.

Financial responsibility means the financial reserves (e.g., insurance policies or surety bonds) sufficient to satisfy liability amounts set forth in this subpart covering public liability.

For hire carriage means the business of transporting, for compensation, passengers and their property, including any compensated transportation of the goods or property or another.

Insured and principal means the motor carrier named in the policy of insurance, surety bond, endorsement, or notice of cancellation, and also the fiduciary of such motor carrier.

Insurance premium means the monetary sum an insured pays an insurer for acceptance of liability for public liability claims made against the insured.

Motor carrier means a for-hire motor carrier. The term includes, but is not limited to, a motor carrier's agent, officer, or representative; an employee responsible for hiring, supervising, training, assigning, or dispatching a driver; or an employee concerned with the installation, inspection, and maintenance of motor vehicle equipment and/or accessories.

Property damage means damage to or loss of use of tangible property.

Public liability means liability for bodily injury or property damage.

Seating capacity means any plan view location capable of accommodating a person at least as large as a 5th percentile adult female, if the overall seat configuration and design and vehicle design is such that the position is likely to be used as a seating position while the vehicle is in motion, except for auxiliary seating accommodations such as temporary or folding jump seats. Any bench or split bench seat in a passenger car, truck or multipurpose passenger vehicle with a gross vehicle weight rating less than 10,000 pounds, having greater than 50 inches of hip room (measured in accordance with SEA Standards

J1100(a)) shall have not less than three designated seating positions, unless the seat design or vehicle design is such that the center position cannot be used for seating.

§387.31 Financial responsibility required.

(a) No motor carrier shall operate a motor vehicle transporting passengers until the motor carrier has obtained and has in effect the minimum levels of financial responsibility as set forth in §387.33 of this subpart.

(b) Policies of insurance, surety bonds, and endorsements required under this section shall remain in effect continuously until terminated.

(1) Cancellation may be effected by the insurer or the insured motor carrier giving 35 days' notice in writing to the other. The 35 days' notice shall commence to run from the date the notice is transmitted. Proof of transmission shall be sufficient proof of notice.

(2) **Exception**. Policies of insurance and surety bonds may be obtained for a finite period of time to cover any lapse in continuous compliance.

(3) **Exception**. Mexican motor carriers may meet the minimum financial responsibility requirements of this subpart by obtaining insurance coverage, in the required amounts, for periods of 24 hours or longer, from insurers that meet the requirements of §387.35 of this subpart. A Mexican motor carrier so insured must have available for inspection in each of its vehicles copies of the following documents:

(i) The required insurance endorsement (Form MCS-90B); and

(ii) An insurance identification card, binder, or other document issued by an authorized insurer which specifies both the effective date and the expiration date of the temporary insurance coverage authorized by this exception.

Mexican motor carriers insured under this exception are also exempt from the notice of cancellation requirements stated on Form MCS-90B.

(c) Policies of insurance and surety bonds required under this section may be replaced by other policies of insurance or surety bonds. The liability of retiring insurer or surety, as to events after the termination date, shall be considered as having terminated on the effective date of the replacement policy of insurance or surety bond or at the end or the 35 day cancellation period required in paragraph (b) of this section, whichever is sooner.

(d) Proof of the required financial responsibility shall be maintained at the motor carrier's principal place of business. The proof shall consist of—

(1) "Endorsement(s) for Motor Carriers of Passengers Policies of Insurance for Public Liability Under Section 18 of the Bus Regulatory Reform Act of 1982" (Form MCS-90B) issued by an insurer(s); or

(2) A "Motor Carrier of Passengers Surety Bond for Public Liability Under Section 18 of the Bus Regulatory Reform Act of 1982" (Form MCS-82B) issued by a surety.

(e)(1) The proof of minimum levels of financial responsibility required by this section shall be considered public information and be produced for review upon reasonable request by a member of the public.

(2) In addition to maintaining proof of financial responsibility as required by paragraph (d) of this section, non-North America-domiciled private and for-hire motor carriers shall file evidence of financial responsibility with FMCSA in accordance with the requirements of subpart C of this part.

(f) All passenger carrying vehicles operated within the United States by motor carriers domiciled in a contiguous foreign country, shall have on board the vehicle a legible copy, in English, of the proof of the required financial responsibility (Forms MCS-90B or MCS-82B) used by the motor carrier to comply with paragraph (d) of this section.

(g) Any motor vehicle in which there is no evidence of financial responsibility required by paragraph (f) of this section shall be denied entry into the United States.

§387.33T Financial responsibility, minimum levels.

Except as provided in §387.27(b), the minimum levels of financial responsibility referred to in §387.31 are hereby prescribed as follows:

SCHEDULE OF LIMITS

Public Liability

For-hire motor carriers of passengers operating in interstate or foreign commerce.

Vehicle seating capacity	Minimum limits
(a) Any vehicle with a seating capacity of 16 passengers or more, including the driver......................................	$5,000,000
(b) Any vehicle with a seating capacity of 15 passengers or less, including the driver......................................	1,500,000

§387.33 Financial responsibility, minimum levels. [Suspended]

(a) **General limits**. Except as provided in §387.27(b), the minimum levels of financial responsibility referred to in §387.31 are prescribed as follows:

SCHEDULE OF LIMITS

Public Liability

For-hire motor carriers of passengers operating in interstate or foreign commerce.

Vehicle seating capacity	Minimum limits
(1) Any vehicle with a seating capacity of 16 passengers or more, including the driver......................................	$5,000,000
(2) Any vehicle with a seating capacity of 15 passengers or less, including the driver......................................	1,500,000

(b) **Limits applicable to transit service providers**. Notwithstanding the provisions of paragraph (a) of this section, the minimum level of financial responsibility for a motor vehicle used to provide transportation services within a transit service area located in more than one State under an agreement with a Federal, State, or local government funded, in whole or in part, with a grant under 49 U.S.C. 5307, 5310 or 5311, including transportation designed and carried out to meet the special needs of elderly individuals and individuals with disabilities, will be the highest level required for any of the States in which it operates. This paragraph applies to transit service providers that operate in more than one State, as well as transit service providers that operate in only one State but interline with other motor carriers that provide interstate transportation within or outside the transit service area. Transit service providers conducting such operations must register as for-hire passenger carriers under part 365, subpart A and part 390, subpart E, of this subchapter, identify the State(s) in which they operate under the applicable grants, and certify on their registration documents that they have in effect financial responsibility levels in an amount equal to or greater than the highest level required by any of the States in which they are operating under a qualifying grant.

§387.35 State authority and designation of agent.

A policy of insurance or surety bond does not satisfy the financial responsibility requirements of this subpart unless the insurer or surety furnishing the policy or bond is—

(a) Legally authorized to issue such policies or bonds in each State in which the motor carrier operates, or

(b) Legally authorized to issue such policies or bonds in the State in which the motor carrier has its principal place of business or domicile, and is willing to designate a person upon whom process, issued by or under the authority of any court having jurisdiction of the subject matter, may be served in any proceeding at law or equity brought in any State in which the motor carrier operates; or

(c) Legally authorized to issue such policies or bonds in any State of the United States and eligible as an excess or surplus lines insurer in any State in which business is written, and is willing to designate a person upon whom process, issued by or under the authority of any court having jurisdiction of the subject matter, may be served in any proceeding at law or equity brought in any State in which the motor carrier operates.

(d) A Canadian insurance company legally authorized to issue a policy of insurance in the Province or Territory of Canada in which the Canadian motor carrier has its principal place of business or domicile, and that is willing to designate a person upon whom process, issued by or under the authority of any court having jurisdiction over the subject matter, may be served in any proceeding at law or equity brought in any State in which the motor carrier operates.

§387.37 Fiduciaries.

The coverage of fiduciaries shall attach at the moment of succession of such fiduciaries.

§387.39 Forms.

Endorsements for policies of insurance (Form MCS-90B) and surety bonds (Form MCS-82B) must be in the form prescribed by the FMCSA and approved by the OMB. Endorsements to policies of insurance and surety bonds shall specify that coverage thereunder will remain in effect continuously until terminated, as required in §387.31 of this subpart. The continuous coverage requirement does not apply to Mexican motor carriers insured under §387.31(b)(3) of this subpart. The endorsement and surety bond shall be issued in the exact name of the motor carrier. The Forms MCS-82B and MCS-90B are available from the FMCSA website at *http://www.fmcsa.dot.gov/mission/forms.*

§387.41 Violation and penalty.

(a) Any person (except an employee who acts without knowledge) who knowingly violates the rules of this subpart shall be liable to the United States for a civil penalty as stated in part 386, appendix B, of this chapter, and if any such violation is a continuing one, each day of violation will constitute a separate offense. The amount of any such penalty shall be assessed by the Administrator or his/her designee, by written notice.

(b) In determining the amount of such penalty, the Administrator or his/her designee shall take into account the nature, circumstances, extent, the gravity of the violation committed and, with respect to the person found to have committed such violation, the degree of culpability, any history of prior violations, the ability to pay, and any effect on ability to continue to do business, and such other matters as justice may require.

§387.43 Electronic filing of surety bonds, trust fund agreements, certificates of insurance and cancellations. [Suspended]

(a) Insurers of for-hire motor carriers of passengers that are registered with FMCSA on September 30, 2016, must file certificates of insurance, surety bonds, and other securities and agreements with FMCSA by December 31, 2016. Insurers of all other exempt for-hire motor carriers of passengers must file certificates of insurance, surety bonds, and other securities and agreements with FMCSA at the time of the application for registration. These filings must be made electronically in accordance with the requirements and procedures set forth at §387.323.

(b) This section does not apply to motor carriers excepted under §387.31(b)(3).

Subpart C—Surety Bonds and Policies of Insurance for Motor Carriers and Property Brokers

§387.301T Surety bond, certificate of insurance, or other securities.

(a) **Public liability.** (1) No common or contract carrier or foreign (Mexican) motor private carrier or foreign motor carrier transporting exempt commodities subject to Subtitle IV, part B, chapter 135 of title 49 of the U.S. Code shall engage in interstate or foreign commerce, and no certificate or permit shall be issued to such a carrier or remain in force unless and until there shall have been filed with and accepted by the FMCSA surety bonds, certificates of insurance, proof of qualifications as self-insurer, or other securities or agreements, in the amounts prescribed in §387.303T, conditioned to pay any final judgment recovered against such motor carrier for bodily injuries to or the death of any person resulting from the negligent operation, maintenance or use of motor vehicles in transportation subject to Subtitle IV, part B, chapter 135 of title 49 of the U.S. Code, or for loss of or damage to property of others, or, in the case of motor carriers of property operating freight vehicles described in §387.303T(b)(2), for environmental restoration.

(2) Motor Carriers of property which are subject to the conditions set forth in paragraph (a)(1) of this section and transport the commodities described in §387.303T(b)(2), are required to obtain security in the minimum limits prescribed in §387.303T(b)(2).

(b) **Household goods motor carriers-cargo insurance.** No household goods motor carrier subject to subtitle IV, part B, chapter 135 of title 49 of the U.S. Code shall engage in interstate or foreign commerce, nor shall any certificate be issued to such a household goods motor carrier or remain in force unless and until there shall have been filed with and accepted by the FMCSA, a surety bond, certificate of insurance, proof of qualifications as a self-insurer, or other securities or agreements in the amounts prescribed in §387.303T, conditioned upon such carrier making compensation to individual shippers for all property belonging to individual shippers and coming into the possession of such carrier in connection with its transportation service. The terms "household goods motor carrier" and "individual shipper" are defined in §375.103 of this subchapter.

(c) **Continuing compliance required.** Such security as is accepted by the FMCSA in accordance with the requirements of section 13906 of title 49 of the U.S. Code, shall remain in effect at all times.

§387.301 Surety bond, certificate of insurance, or other securities. [Suspended]

(a) **Public liability.** (1) No common or contract carrier or foreign (Mexican) motor private carrier or foreign motor carrier transporting exempt commodities subject to Subtitle IV, part B, chapter 135 of Title 49 of the United States Code shall engage in interstate or foreign commerce, and no certificate or permit shall be issued to such a carrier or remain in force unless and until there shall have been filed with and accepted by the FMCSA surety bonds, and certificates of insurance, proof of qualifications as self-insurer, or other securities or agreements, in the amounts prescribed in §387.303, conditioned to pay any final judgment recovered against such motor carrier for bodily injuries to or the death of any person resulting from the negligent operation, maintenance or use of motor vehicles in transportation subject to Subtitle IV, part B, Chapter 135 of Title 49 of the United States Code, or for loss of or damage to property of others, or, in the case of motor carriers of property operating freight vehicles described in §387.303(b)(2) of this part, for environmental restoration.

(2) Motor Carriers of property which are subject to the conditions set forth in paragraph (a)(1) of this section and transport the commodities described in §387.303(b)(2), are required to obtain security in the minimum limits prescribed in §387.303(b)(2).

(b) **Household goods motor carriers-cargo insurance.** No household goods motor carrier subject to subtitle IV, part B, chapter 135 of title 49 of the U.S. Code shall engage in interstate or foreign commerce, nor shall any certificate be issued to such a household goods motor carrier or remain in force unless and until there shall have been filed with and accepted by the FMCSA, a surety bond, certificate of insurance, proof of qualifications as a self-insurer, or other securities or agreements in the amounts prescribed in §387.303, conditioned upon such carrier making compensation to individual shippers for all property belonging to individual shippers and coming into the possession of such carrier in connection with its transportation service. The terms "household goods motor carrier" and "individual shipper" are defined in §375.103 of this subchapter.

(c) **Continuing compliance required.** Such security as is accepted by the FMCSA in accordance with the requirements of Section 13906 of Title 49 of the United States Code shall remain in effect at all times.

§387.303T Security for the protection of the public: Minimum limits.

(a) **Definitions.** (1) **Primary security** means public liability coverage provided by the insurance or surety company responsible for the first dollar of coverage.

(2) **Excess security** means public liability coverage above the primary security, or above any additional underlying security, up to and including the required minimum limits set forth in paragraph (b)(2) of this section.

(b)(1) Motor carriers subject to §387.301T(a)(1) are required to have security for the required minimum limits as follows:

(i) **Small freight vehicles.**

Kind of equipment	Transportation provided	Minimum limits
Fleet including only vehicles under 10,001 pounds (4,536 kilograms) GVWR............	Property (non-hazardous)	$300,000

(ii) **Passenger carriers.**

Passenger Carriers: Kind of Equipment

Vehicle seating capacity	Minimum limits
(A) Any vehicle with a seating capacity of 16 passengers or more (including the driver)....	$5,000,000
(B) Any vehicle designed or used to transport 15 passengers or less (including the driver) for compensation	1,500,000

(2) Motor carriers subject to §387.301T(a)(2) are required to have security for the required minimum limits as follows:

Kind of equipment	Commodity transported	Minimum limits
(i) Freight vehicles of 10,001 pounds (4,536 kilograms) or more GVWR	Property (non-hazardous)	$750,000
(ii) Freight vehicles of 10,001 (4,536 kilograms) pounds or more GVWR	Hazardous substances, as defined in §171.8 of this title, transported in cargo tanks, portable tanks, or hopper-type vehicles with capacities in excess of 3,500 water gallons, or in bulk explosives Division 1,1, 1.2 and 1.3 materials. Division 2.3, Hazard Zone A material; in bulk Division 2.1 or 2.2; or highway route controlled quantities of a Class 7 material, as defined in §173.403 of this title	5,000,000
(iii) Freight vehicles of 10,001 pounds (4,536 kilograms) or more GVWR ...	Oil listed in §172.101 of this title; hazardous waste, hazardous materials and hazardous substances defined in §171.8 of this title and listed in §172.101 of this title, but not mentioned in paragraph (b)(2)(ii) or paragraph (b)(2)(iv) of this section	1,000,000

Kind of equipment	Commodity transported	Minimum limits
(iv) Freight vehicles under 10,001 pounds (4,536 kilograms) GVWR............	Any quantity of Division 1.1, 1.2, or 1.3 material; any quantity of a Division 2.3, Hazard Zone A, or Division 6.1, Packing Group I, Hazard Zone A material; or highway route controlled quantities of Class 7 material as defined in §173.455 of this title	5,000,000

(3) Motor carriers subject to the minimum limits governed by this section, which are also subject to Department of Transportation limits requirements, are at no time required to have security for more than the required minimum limits established by the Secretary of Transportation in the applicable provisions of this part.

(4) **Foreign motor carriers and foreign motor private carriers.** Foreign motor carriers and foreign motor private carriers (Mexican), subject to the requirements of 49 U.S.C. 13902(c) and 49 CFR part 368 regarding obtaining certificates of registration from the FMCSA, must meet our minimum financial responsibility requirements by obtaining insurance coverage, in the required amounts, for periods of 24 hours or longer, from insurance or surety companies, that meet the requirements of §387.315. These carriers must have available for inspection, in each vehicle operating in the United States, copies of the following documents:

(i) The certificate of registration;

(ii) The required insurance endorsement (Form MCS-90); and

(iii) An insurance identification card, binder, or other document issued by an authorized insurer which specifies both the effective date and the expiration date of the insurance coverage.

(5) Notwithstanding the provisions of §387.301T(a)(1), the filing of evidence of insurance is not required as a condition to the issuance of a certificate of registration. Further, the reference to continuous coverage at §387.313T(a)(6) and the reference to cancellation notice at §387.313T(d) are not applicable to these carriers.

(c) **Household goods motor carriers: Cargo liability.** Security required to compensate individual shippers for loss or damage to property belonging to them and coming into the possession of household goods motor carriers in connection with their transportation service:

(1) For loss of or damage to household goods carried on any one motor vehicle—$5,000; and

(2) For loss of or damage to or aggregate of losses or damages of or to household goods occurring at any one time and place—$10,000.

§387.303 Security for the protection of the public: minimum limits. [Suspended]

(a) **Definitions**: (1) "Primary security" means public liability coverage provided by the insurance or surety company responsible for the first dollar of coverage.

(2) "Excess security" means public liability coverage above the primary security, or above any additional underlying security, up to and including the required minimum limits set forth in paragraph (b)(2) of this section.

(b)(1) Motor carriers subject to §387.301(a)(1) are required to have security for the required minimum limits as follows:

(i) **Small freight vehicles:**

Kind of equipment	Transportation provided	Minimum limits
Fleet including only vehicles under 10,001 pounds (4,536 kilograms) GVWR	Property (non-hazardous)........	$300,000

(ii) **Passenger carriers.**

Passenger Carriers: Kind of Equipment

Vehicle seating capacity	Minimum limits
(A) Any vehicle with a seating capacity of 16 passengers or more (including the driver)..........	$5,000,000
(B) Any vehicle designed or used to transport 15 passengers or less (including the driver) for compensation	1,500,000

(2) Motor carriers subject to §387.301(a)(2) are required to have security for the required minimum limits as follows:

Kind of equipment	Commodity transported	Minimum limits
(i) Freight vehicles of 10,001 pounds (4,536 kilograms) or more GVWR.	Property (non-hazardous)........	$750,000
(ii) Freight vehicles of 10,001 (4,536 kilograms) pounds or more GVWR.	Hazardous substances, as defined in §171.8 of this title, transported in cargo tanks, portable tanks, or hopper-type vehicles with capacities in excess of 3,500 water gallons, or in bulk explosives Division 1,1, 1.2 and 1.3 materials. Division 2.3, Hazard Zone A material; in bulk Division 2.1 or 2.2; or highway route controlled quantities of a Class 7 material, as defined in §173.403 of this title.	5,000,000
(iii) Freight vehicles of 10,001 pounds (4,536 kilograms) or more GVWR	Oil listed in §172.101 of this title; hazardous waste, hazardous materials and hazardous substances defined in §171.8 of this title and listed in §172.101 of this title, but not mentioned in paragraph (b)(2)(ii) or paragraph (b)(2)(iv) of this section	1,000,000
(iv) Freight vehicles under 10,001 pounds (4,536 kilograms) GVWR.	Any quantity of Division 1.1, 1.2, or 1.3 material; any quantity of a Division 2.3, Hazard Zone A, or Division 6.1, Packing Group I, Hazard Zone A material; or highway route controlled quantities of Class 7 material as defined in §173.455 of this title.	5,000,000

(3) Motor carriers subject to the minimum limits governed by this section, which are also subject to Department of Transportation limits requirements, are at no time required to have security for more than the required minimum limits established by the Secretary of Transportation in the applicable provisions of 49 CFR Part 387—Minimum Levels of Financial Responsibility for Motor Carriers.

(4) **Foreign motor carriers and foreign motor private carriers**. Foreign motor carriers and foreign motor private carriers (Mexican), subject to the requirements of 49 U.S.C. 13902(c) and 49 CFR part 368 regarding obtaining certificates of registration from the FMCSA, must meet our minimum financial responsibility requirements by obtaining insurance coverage, in the required amounts, for periods of 24 hours or longer, from insurance or surety companies, that meet the requirements of 49 CFR 387.315. These carriers must have available for inspection, in each vehicle operating in the United States, copies of the following documents:

(i) The certificate of registration;

(ii) The required insurance endorsement (Form MCS-90); and

(iii) An insurance identification card, binder, or other document issued by an authorized insurer which specifies both the effective date and the expiration date of the insurance coverage.

(5) Notwithstanding the provisions of §387.301(a)(1), the filing of evidence of insurance is not required as a condition to the issuance of a certificate of registration. Further, the reference to continuous coverage at §387.313(a)(6) and the reference to cancellation notice at §387.313(d) are not applicable to these carriers.

(c) **Household goods motor carriers: Cargo liability**. Security required to compensate individual shippers for loss or damage to property belonging to them and coming into the possession of household goods motor carriers in connection with their transportation service;

(1) For loss of or damage to household goods carried on any one motor vehicle—$5,000,

(2) For loss of or damage to or aggregate of losses or damages of or to household goods occurring at any one time and place—$10,000.

§387.305 Combination vehicles.

The following combinations will be regarded as one motor vehicle for purposes of this part, (a) a tractor and trailer or semi-trailer when the tractor is engaged solely in drawing the trailer or semi-trailer, and (b) a truck and trailer when both together bear a single load.

§387.307 Property broker surety bond or trust fund.

(a) **Security**. A broker must have a surety bond or trust fund in effect for $75,000. The FMCSA will not issue a broker license until a surety bond or trust fund for the full limits of liability prescribed herein is in effect. The broker license shall remain valid or effective only as long as a surety bond or trust fund remains in effect and shall ensure the financial responsibility of the broker.

(b) **Evidence of security**. Evidence of a surety bond must be filed using the FMCSA's prescribed Form BMC-84. Evidence of a trust fund with a financial institution must be filed using the FMCSA's prescribed Form BMC 85. The surety bond or the trust fund shall ensure the financial responsibility of the broker by providing for payments to shippers or motor carriers if the broker fails to carry out its contracts, agreements, or arrangements for the supplying of transportation by authorized motor carriers.

(c) **Financial Institution**. When used in this section and in forms prescribed under this section, where not otherwise distinctly expressed or manifestly incompatible with the intent thereof, shall mean—Each agent, agency, branch or office within the United States of any person, as defined by the ICC Termination Act, doing business in one or more of the capacities listed below:

(1) An insured bank (as defined in section 3(h) of the Federal Deposit Insurance Act (12 U.S.C. 1813(h));

(2) A commercial bank or trust company;

(3) An agency or branch of a foreign bank in the United States;

(4) An insured depository institution (as defined in section 3(c)(2) of the Federal Deposit Insurance Act (12 U.S.C. 1813(c)(2));

(5) A thrift institution (savings bank, building and loan association, credit union, industrial bank or other);

(6) An insurance company;

(7) A loan or finance company; or

(8) A person subject to supervision by any State or Federal bank supervisory authority.

(d) **Forms and Procedures—**

(1) **Forms for broker surety bonds and trust agreements**. Form BMC-84 broker surety bond will be filed with the FMCSA for the full security limits under paragraph (a) of this section; or Form BMC-85 broker trust fund agreement will be filed with the FMCSA for the full security limits under paragraph (a) of this section.

(2) **Broker surety bonds and trust fund agreements in effect continuously**. Surety bonds and trust fund agreements shall specify that coverage thereunder will remain in effect continuously until terminated as herein provided.

(i) **Cancellation notice**. The surety bond and the trust fund agreement may be cancelled as only upon 30 days' written notice to the FMCSA, on prescribed Form BMC 36, by the principal or surety for the surety bond, and on prescribed Form BMC 85, by the trustor/broker or trustee for the trust fund agreement. The notice period commences upon the actual receipt of the notice at the FMCSA's Washington, DC office.

(ii) **Termination by replacement**. Broker surety bonds or trust fund agreements which have been accepted by the FMCSA under these rules may be replaced by other surety bonds or trust fund agreements, and the liability of the retiring surety or trustee under such surety bond or trust fund agreements shall be considered as having terminated as of the effective date of the replacement surety bond or trust fund agreement. However, such termination shall not affect the liability of the surety or the trustee hereunder for the payment of any damages arising as the result of contracts, agreements or arrangements made by the broker for the supplying of transportation prior to the date such termination becomes effective.

(3) **Filing and copies**. Broker surety bonds and trust fund agreements must be filed with the FMCSA in duplicate.

§387.309 Qualifications as a self-insurer and other securities or agreements.

(a) **As a self-insurer**. The FMCSA will consider and will approve, subject to appropriate and reasonable conditions, the application of a motor carrier to qualify as a self-insurer, if the carrier furnishes a true and accurate statement of its financial condition and other evidence that establishes to the satisfaction of the FMCSA the ability of the motor carrier to satisfy its obligation for bodily injury liability, property damage liability, or cargo liability. Application Guidelines: In addition to filing Form BMC 40, applicants for authority to self-insure against bodily injury and property damage claims should submit evidence that will allow the FMCSA to determine:

(1) The adequacy of the tangible net worth of the motor carrier in relation to the size of operations and the extent of its request for self-insurance authority. Applicant should demonstrate that it will maintain a net worth that will ensure that it will be able to meet its statutory obligations to the public to indemnify all claimants in the event of loss.

(2) The existence of a sound self-insurance program. Applicant should demonstrate that is has established, and will maintain, an insurance program that will protect the public against all claims to the same extent as the minimum security limits applicable to applicant under §387.303 of this part. Such a program may include, but not be limited to, one or more of the following: irrevocable letters of credit; irrevocable trust funds; reserves; sinking funds; third party financial guarantees, parent company or affiliate sureties; excess insurance coverage; or other similar arrangements.

(3) The existence of an adequate safety program. Applicant must submit evidence of a current "satisfactory" safety rating by the United States Department of Transportation. Non-rated carriers need only certify that they have not been rated. Applications by carriers with a less than satisfactory rating will be summarily denied. Any self-insurance authority granted by the FMCSA will automatically expire 30 days after a carrier receives a less than satisfactory rating from DOT.

(4) Additional information. Applicant must submit such additional information to support its application as the FMCSA may require.

(b) **Other securities or agreements**. The commission also will consider applications for approval of other securities or agreements and will approve any such application if satisfied that the security or agreement offered will afford the security for the protection of the public contemplated by 49 U.S.C. 13906.

§387.311 Bonds and certificates of insurance.

(a) **Public liability**. Each Form BMC 82 surety bond filed with the FMCSA must be for the full limits of liability required under §387.303(b)(1). Form MCS-82 surety bonds and other forms of similar import prescribed by the Department of Transportation, may be aggregated to comply with the minimum security limits required under §387.303(b)(1) or §387.303(b)(2). Each Form BMC 91 certificate of insurance filed with the FMCSA will always represent the full security minimum limits required for the particular carrier, while it remains in force, under §§387.303(b)(1) or 387.303(b)(2), whichever is applicable. Any previously executed Form BMC 91 filed before the current revision which is left on file with the FMCSA after the effective date of this regulation, and not canceled within 30 days of that date will be deemed to certify the same coverage limits as would the filing of a revised Form BMC 91. Each Form BMC 91X certificate of insurance filed with the FMCSA will represent the full security limits under §§387.303(b)(1) or 387.303(b)(2) or the specific security limits of coverage as indicated on the face of the form. If the filing reflects aggregation, the certificate must show clearly whether the insurance is primary or, if excess coverage, the amount of underlying coverage as well as amount of the maximum limits of coverage. *Each Form BMC 91MX certificate of insurance filed with the FMCSA will represent the security limits of coverage as indicated on the face of the form. The Form BMC 91MX must show clearly whether the insurance is primary or, if excess coverage, the amount of underlying coverage as well as amount of the maximum limits of coverage.

*Note: Aggregation to meet the requirement of §387.303(b)(1) will not be allowed until the completion of our rulemaking in Ex Parte No. MC-5 (Sub-No. 2), *Motor Carrier and Freight Forwarder Insurance Procedures and Minimum Amounts of Liability.*

(b) **Cargo liability**. Each Form BMC 83 surety bond filed with the FMCSA must be for the full limits of liability required under §387.303(c). Each Form BMC 34 certificate of insurance filed with the FMCSA will represent the full security limits under §387.303(c) or the specific limits of coverage as indicated on the face of the form. If the filing reflects aggregation, the certificate must show clearly whether the insurance is primary or, if excess coverage, the amount of underlying coverage as well as amount of the maximum limits of coverage.

(c) Each policy of insurance in connection with certificate of insurance which is filed with the FMCSA, the shall be amended by attachment of the appropriate endorsement prescribed by the FMCSA and the certificate of insurance filed must accurately reflect that endorsement.

§387.313T Forms and procedures.

(a) **Forms for endorsements, certificates of insurance and others—** (1) **In form prescribed.** Endorsements for policies of insurance and surety bonds, certificates of insurance, applications to qualify as a self-insurer, or for approval of other securities or agreements, and notices of cancellation must be in the form prescribed and approved by the FMCSA.

(2) **Aggregation of insurance.** (i) When insurance is provided by more than one insurer in order to aggregate security limits for carriers operating only freight vehicles under 10,000 pounds Gross Vehicle Weight Rating, as defined in §387.303T(b)(1), a separate *Form BMC 90,* with the specific amounts of underlying and limits of coverage shown thereon or appended thereto, and *Form BMC 91X* certificate is required of each insurer.

**Note: See Note for Rule 387.311. Also, it should be noted that DOT is considering prescribing adaptations of the *Form MCS 90* endorsement and the *Form MCS 82* surety bond for use by passenger carriers and Rules §§387.311 and 387.313T have been written sufficiently broad to provide for this contingency when new forms are prescribed by that Agency.

(ii) For aggregation of insurance for all other carriers to cover security limits under §387.303T(b)(1) or (2), a separate Department of Transportation prescribed form endorsement and *Form BMC 91X* certificate is required of each insurer. When insurance is provided by more than one insurer to aggregate coverage for security limits under §387.303T(c) a separate *Form BMC 32* endorsement and *Form BMC 34* certificate of insurance is required for each insurer.

(iii) For aggregation of insurance for foreign motor private carriers of nonhazardous commodities to cover security limits under §387.303T(b)(4), a separate *Form BMC 90* with the specific amounts of underlying and limits of coverage shown thereon or appended thereto, or Department of Transportation prescribed form endorsement, and *Form BMC 91MX* certificate is required for each insurer.

(3) **Use of certificates and endorsements in BMC Series.** Form BMC 91 certificates of insurance will be filed with the FMCSA for the full security limits under §387.303T(b)(1) or (2).

(i) **Form BMC 91X** certificate of insurance will be filed to represent full coverage or any level of aggregation for the security limits under §387.303T(b)(1) or (2).

(ii) **Form BMC 90** endorsement will be used with each filing of *Form BMC 91* or *Form 91X* certificate with the FMCSA which certifies to coverage not governed by the requirements of the Department of Transportation. *Form BMC 32* endorsement and *Form BMC 34* certificate of insurance and *Form BMC 83* surety bonds are used for the limits of cargo liability under §387.303T(c).

(iii) **Form BMC 91MX** certificate of insurance will be filed to represent any level of aggregation for the security limits under §387.303T(b)(4).

(4) **Use of endorsements in MCS Series.** When Security limits certified under §387.303T(b)(1) or (b)(2) involves coverage also required by the Department of Transportation a Form MCS endorsement prescribed by the Department of Transportation such as, and including, the Form MCS 90 endorsement is required.

(5) **Surety bonds.** When surety bonds are used rather than certificates of insurance, Form BMC 82 is required for the security limits under §387.303T(b)(1) not subject to regulation by the Department of Transportation, and Form MCS 82, or any form of similar import prescribed by the Department of Transportation, is used for the security limits subject also to minimum coverage requirements of the Department of Transportation.

(6) **Surety bonds and certificates in effect continuously.** Surety bonds and certificates of insurance shall specify that coverage thereunder will remain in effect continuously until terminated as herein provided, except:

(i) When filed expressly to fill prior gaps or lapses in coverage or to cover grants of emergency temporary authority of unusually short duration and the filing clearly so indicates; or

(ii) In special or unusual circumstances, when special permission is obtained for filing certificates of insurance or surety bonds on terms meeting other particular needs of the situation.

(b) **Filing and copies.** Certificates of insurance, surety bonds, and notices of cancellation must be filed with the FMCSA.

(c) **Name of insured.** Certificates of insurance and surety bonds shall be issued in the full and correct name of the individual, partnership, corporation or other person to whom the certificate, permit, or license is, or is to be, issued. In the case of a partnership, all partners shall be named.

(d) **Cancellation notice.** Except as provided in paragraph (e) of this section, surety bonds, certificates of insurance and other securities or agreements shall not be cancelled or withdrawn until 30 days after written notice has been submitted to the FMCSA at its offices in Washington, DC, on the prescribed form (*Form BMC-35,* Notice of Cancellation Motor Carrier Policies of Insurance under 49 U.S.C. 13906, and *BMC-36,* Notice of Cancellation Motor Carrier and Broker Surety Bonds, as appropriate) by the insurance company, surety or sureties, motor carrier, broker or other party thereto, as the case may be, which period of thirty (30) days shall commence to run from the date such notice on the prescribed form is actually received by the FMCSA.

(e) **Termination by replacement.** Certificates of insurance or surety bonds which have been accepted by the FMCSA under these rules may be replaced by other certificates of insurance, surety bonds or other security, and the liability of the retiring insurer or surety under such certificates of insurance or surety bonds shall be considered as having terminated as of the effective date of the replacement certificate of insurance, surety bond or other security, provided the said replacement certificate, bond or other security is acceptable to the FMCSA under the rules and regulations in this part.

§387.313 Forms and procedures. [Suspended]

(a) **Forms for endorsements, certificates of insurance, and others**.

(1) **In form prescribed**. Endorsements for policies of insurance and surety bonds, certificates of insurance, applications to qualify as a self-insurer, or for approval of other securities or agreements, and notices of cancellation must be in the form prescribed and approved by the FMCSA.

(2) **Aggregation of Insurance**. **When insurance is provided by more than one insurer in order to aggregate security limits for carriers operating only freight vehicles under 10,000 pounds Gross Vehicle Weight Rating, as defined in §387.303(b)(1), a separate Form BMC 90, with the specific amounts of underlying and limits of coverage shown thereon or appended thereto, and Form BMC 91X certificate is required of each insurer.

For aggregation of insurance for all other carriers to cover security limits under §387.303(b)(1) or (b)(2), a separate Department of Transportation prescribed form endorsement and *Form BMC 91X* certificate is required of each insurer.

When insurance is provided by more than one insurer to aggregate coverage for security limits under §387.303(c) a separate Form BMC 32 endorsement and Form BMC 34 certificate of insurance is required for each insurer.

For aggregation of insurance for foreign motor private carriers of nonhazardous commodities to cover security limits under §387.303(b)(4), a separate Form BMC 90 with the specific amounts of underlying and limits of coverage shown thereon or appended thereto, or Department of Transportation prescribed form endorsement, and Form BMC 91MX certificate is required for each insurer.

**NOTE: See NOTE for Rule 387.311. Also, it should be noted that DOT is considering prescribing adaptions of the Form MCS 90 endorsement and the Form MCS 82 surety bond for use by passenger carriers and Rules §§387.311 and 387.313 have been written sufficiently broad to provide for this contingency when new forms are prescribed by that Agency.

(3) **Use of Certificates and Endorsements in BMC Series.—Form BMC 91** certificates of insurance will be filed with the FMCSA for the full security limits under §387.303 (b)(1) or (b)(2).

Form BMC 91X certificate of insurance will be filed to represent full coverage or any level of aggregation for the security limits under §387.303 (b)(1) or (b)(2).

Form BMC 90 endorsement will be used with each filing of Form BMC 91 or Form BMC 91X certificate with the FMCSA which certifies to coverage not governed by the requirements of the Department of Transportation.

Form BMC 32 endorsement and *Form BMC 34* certificate of insurance and *Form BMC 83* surety bonds are used for the limits of cargo liability under §387.303(c).

Form BMC 91MX certificate of insurance will be filed to represent any level of aggregation for the security limits under §387.303(b)(4).

(4) **Use of Endorsements in MCS Series**. When Security limits certified under §387.303 (b)(1) or (b)(2) involves coverage also required by the Department of Transportation a *Form MCS endorsement prescribed by the Department of Transportation such as*, and including, the *Form MCS 90* endorsement is required.

(5) **Surety bonds**. When surety bonds are used rather than certificates of insurance, *Form BMC 82* is required for the security limits under §387.303(b)(1) not subject to regulation by the Department of Transportation, and *Form MCS 82*, or any form of similar import prescribed by the Department of Transportation, is used for the security limits subject also to minimum coverage requirements of the Department of Transportation.

(6) **Surety bonds and certificates in effect continuously**. Surety bonds and certificates of insurance shall specify that coverage thereunder will remain in effect continuously until terminated as herein provided, except:

(i) when filed expressly to fill prior gaps or lapses in coverage or to cover grants of emergency temporary authority of unusually short duration and the filing clearly so indicates, or

(ii) in special or unusual circumstances, when special permission is obtained for filing certificates of insurance or surety bonds on terms meeting other particular needs of the situation.

(b) **Filing and copies.** Certificates of insurance, surety bonds, and notices of cancellation must be filed with the FMCSA at *http://www.fmcsa.dot.gov*.

(c) **Name of insured**. Certificates of insurance and surety bonds shall be issued in the full and correct name of the individual, partnership, corporation or other person to whom the certificate, permit, or license is, or is to be, issued. In the case of a partnership all partners shall be named.

(d) **Cancellation notice**. Except as provided in paragraph (e) of this section, surety bonds, certificates of insurance, and other securities or agreements shall not be cancelled or withdrawn until 30 days after written notice has been submitted to *http://www.fmcsa.dot.gov* on the prescribed form (Form BMC-35, Notice of Cancellation Motor Carrier Policies of Insurance under 49 U.S.C. 13906, and BMC-36, Notice of Cancellation Motor Carrier and Broker Surety Bonds, as appropriate) by the insurance company, surety or sureties, motor carrier, broker or other party thereto, as the case may be, which period of thirty (30) days shall commence to run from the date such notice on the prescribed form is filed with FMCSA at *http://www.fmcsa.dot.gov*.

(e) **Termination by replacement**. Certificates of insurance or surety bonds which have been accepted by the FMCSA under these rules may be replaced by other certificates of insurance, surety bonds or other security, and the liability of the retiring insurer or surety under such certificates of insurance or surety bonds shall be considered as having terminated as of the effective date of the replacement certificate of insurance, surety bond or other security, provided the said replacement certificate, bond or other security is acceptable to the FMCSA under the rules and regulations in this part.

§387.315 Insurance and surety companies.

A certificate of insurance or surety bond will not be accepted by the FMCSA unless issued by an insurance or surety company that is authorized (licensed or admitted) to issue bonds or underlying insurance policies:

(a) In each State in which the motor carrier is authorized by the FMCSA to operate, or

(b) In the State in which the motor carrier has its principal place of business or domicile, and will designate in writing upon request by the FMCSA, a person upon whom process, issued by or under the authority of a court of competent jurisdiction, may be served in any proceeding at law or equity brought in any State in which the carrier operates, or

(c) In any State, and is eligible as an excess or surplus lines insurer in any State in which business is written, and will make the designation of process agent described in paragraph (b) of this section.

(d) In the Province or Territory of Canada in which a Canadian motor carrier has its principal place of business or domicile, and will designate in writing upon request by FMCSA, a person upon whom process, issued by or under the authority of a court of competent jurisdiction, may be served in any proceeding at law or equity brought in any State in which the carrier operates.

§387.317 Refusal to accept, or revocation by the FMCSA of surety bonds, etc.

The FMCSA may, at any time, refuse to accept or may revoke its acceptance of any surety bond, certificate of insurance, qualifications as a self-insurer, or other securities or agreements if, in its judgment such security does not comply with these sections or for any reason fails to provide satisfactory or adequate protection for the public. Revocation of acceptance of any certificate of insurance, surety bond or other security shall not relieve the motor carrier from compliance with §387.301(c).

§387.319 Fiduciaries.

(a) **Definitions**. The terms "insured" and "principal" as used in a certificate of insurance, surety bond, and notice of cancellation, filed by or for a motor carrier, include the motor carrier and its fiduciary as the moment of succession. The term "fiduciary" means any person authorized by law to collect and preserve property of incapacitated, financially disabled, bankrupt, or deceased holders of operating rights, and assignees of such holders.

(b) Insurance coverage in behalf of fiduciaries to apply concurrently. The coverage furnished under the provisions of this section on behalf of fiduciaries shall not apply subsequent to the effective date of other insurance, or other security, filed with and approved by the FMCSA in behalf of such fiduciaries. After the coverage provided in this section shall have been in effect thirty (30) days, it may be cancelled or withdrawn within the succeeding period of thirty (30) days by the insurer, the insured, the surety, or the principal upon ten (10) days' notice in writing to the FMCSA at its office in Washington, D.C., which period of ten (10) days shall commence to run from the date such notice is actually received by the FMCSA. After such coverage has been in effect for a total of sixty (60) days, it may be cancelled or withdrawn only in accordance with §1043.7.

§387.321 Operations in foreign commerce.

No motor carrier may operate in the United States in the course of transportation between places in a foreign country or between a place in one foreign country and a place in another foreign country unless and until there shall have been filed with and accepted by the FMCSA a certificate of insurance, surety bond, proof of qualifications as a self-insurer, or other securities or agreements in the amount prescribed in §387.303(b), conditioned to pay any final judgment recovered against such motor carrier for bodily injuries to or the death of any person resulting from the negligent operation, maintenance, or use of motor vehicles in transportation between places in a foreign country or between a place in one foreign country and a place in another foreign country, insofar as such transportation takes place in the United States, or for loss of or damage to property of others. The security for the protection of the public required by this section shall be maintained in effect at all times and shall be subject to the provisions of §§387.309 through 387.319. The requirements of §387.315(a) shall be satisfied if the insurance or surety company, in addition to having been approved by the FMCSA, is legally authorized to issue policies or surety bonds in at least one of the States in the United States, or one of the Provinces in Canada, and has filed with the FMCSA the name and address of a person upon whom legal process may be served in each State in or through which the motor carrier operates. Such designation may from time to time be changed by like designation similarly filed, but shall be maintained during the effectiveness of any certificate of insurance or surety bond issued by the company, and thereafter with respect to any claims arising during the effectiveness of such certificate or bond. The term "motor carrier" as used in this section shall not include private carriers or carriers operating under the partial exemption from regulation in 49 U.S.C. 13503 and 13506.

§387.323T Electronic filing of surety bonds, trust fund agreements, certificates of insurance and cancellations.

(a) Insurers may, at their option and in accordance with the requirements and procedures set forth in paragraphs (a) through (d) of this section, file forms BMC 34, BMC 35, BMC 36, BMC 82, BMC 83, BMC 84, BMC 85, BMC 91, and BMC 91X electronically, in lieu of using the prescribed printed forms.

(b) Each insurer must obtain authorization to file electronically by registering with the FMCSA. An individual account number and password for computer access will be issued to each registered insurer.

(c) Filings may be transmitted online via the internet at: *https://li-public.fmcsa.dot.gov* or via American Standard Code Information Interchange (ASCII). All ASCII transmission must be in fixed format, *i.e.,* all records must have the same number of fields and same length. The record layouts for ASCII electronic transactions are described in the following table:

Electronic Insurance Filing Transactions

Field name	Number of positions	Description	Required F = filing C = cancel B = both	Start field	End field
Record type..	1 Numeric	1 = Filing, 2 = Cancellation	B	1	1
Insurer number.......	8 Text	FMCSA Assigned Insurer Number (Home Office) With Suffix (Issuing Office), If Different, *e.g.,* 12345-01	B	2	9
Filing type....	1 Numeric	1 = BI&PD, 2 = Cargo, 3 = Bond, 4 = Trust Fund	B	10	10
FMCSA docket number.......	8 Text	FMCSA Assigned MC or FF Number, *e.g.,* MC000045	B	11	18
Insured legal name.........	120 Text	Legal Name	B	19	138
Insured d/b/a name.........	60 Text	Doing Business As Name If Different From Legal Name	B	139	198
Insured address	35 Text	Either street or mailing address	B	199	233
Insured city...	30 Text		B	234	263
Insured state .	2 Text		B	264	265

Electronic Insurance Filing Transactions, Continued

Field name	Number of positions	Description	Required F = filing C = cancel B = both	Start field	End field
Insured zip code..........	9 Numeric	(Do not include dash if using 9 digit code)	B	266	274
Insured country	2 Text	(Will default to U.S.)	B	275	276
Form code ...	10 Text	BMC-91, BMC-91X, BMC-34, BMC-35, etc	B	277	286
Full, primary or excess coverage	1 Text	If BMC-91X, P or E = indicator of primary or excess policy; 1 = Full under §387.303T(b)(1); 2 = Full under §387.303T(b)(2)	F	287	287
Limit of liability........	5 Numeric	$ in Thousands	F	288	292
Underlying limit of liability........	5 Numeric	$ in Thousands (will default to $000 if Primary)	F	293	297
Effective date	8 Text	MM/DD/YY Format for both Filing or Cancellation	B	298	305
Policy number.......	25 Text	Surety companies may enter bond number	B	306	330

(d) All registered insurers agree to furnish upon request to the FMCSA a duplicate original of any policy (or policies) and all endorsements, surety bond, trust fund agreement, or other filing.

§387.323 Electronic filing of surety bonds, trust fund agreements, certificates of insurance and cancellations. [Suspended]

(a) Insurers must electronically file forms BMC 34, BMC 35, BMC 36, BMC 82, BMC 83, BMC 84, BMC 85, BMC 91, and BMC 91X in accordance with the requirements and procedures set forth in paragraphs (b) through (d) of this section.

(b) Each insurer must obtain authorization to file electronically by registering with the FMCSA. An individual account number and password for computer access will be issued to each registered insurer.

(c) Filings may be transmitted online via the internet at: *https://li-public.fmcsa.dot.gov.*

(d) All registered insurers agree to furnish upon request to the FMCSA a copy of any policy (or policies) and all certificates of insurance, endorsements, surety bonds, trust fund agreements, proof of qualification to self-insure or other insurance filings.

Subpart D—Surety Bonds and Policies of Insurance for Freight Forwarders

§387.401 Definitions.

(a) **Freight forwarder** means a person holding itself out to the general public (other than as an express, pipeline, rail. sleeping car, motor, or water carrier) to provide transportation of property for compensation in interstate commerce, and in the ordinary course of its business:

(1) Performs or provides for assembling, consolidating, break-bulk, and distribution of shipments; and

(2) Assumes responsibility for transportation from place of receipt to destination; and

(3) Uses for any part of the transportation a carrier subject to FMCSA jurisdiction.

(b) **Household goods freight forwarder** (HHGFF) means a freight forwarder of household goods, unaccompanied baggage, or used automobiles.

(c) **Motor vehicle** means any vehicle, machine, tractor, trailer, or semitrailer propelled or drawn by mechanical power and used to transport property, but does not include any vehicle, locomotive, or car operated exclusively on a rail or rails. The following combinations will be regarded as one motor vehicle:

(1) A tractor that draws a trailer or semitrailer; and

(2) A truck and trailer bearing a single load.

§387.403T General requirements.

(a) **Cargo.** A household goods freight forwarder may not operate until it has filed with FMCSA an appropriate surety bond, certificate of insurance, qualifications as a self-insurer, or other securities or agreements, in the amounts prescribed in §387.405, for loss of or damage to household goods.

(b) **Public liability.** A HHGFF may not perform transfer, collection, and delivery service until it has filed with the FMCSA an appropriate surety bond, certificate of insurance, qualifications as a self-insurer, or other securities or agreements, in the amounts prescribed at §387.405, conditioned to pay any final judgment recovered against such HHGFF for bodily injury to or the death of any person, or loss of or damage to property (except cargo) of others, or, in the case of freight vehicles described at §387.303T(b)(2), for environmental restoration, resulting from the negligent operation, maintenance, or use of motor vehicles operated by or under its control in performing such service.

(c) **Surety bond or trust fund.** A freight forwarder must have a surety bond or trust fund in effect. The FMCSA will not issue a freight forwarder license until a surety bond or trust fund for the full limit of liability prescribed in §387.405 is in effect. The freight forwarder license shall remain valid or effective only as long as a surety bond or trust fund remains in effect and shall ensure the financial responsibility of the freight forwarder. The requirements applicable to property broker surety bonds and trust funds in §387.307 shall apply to the surety bond or trust fund required by this paragraph (c).

§387.403 General requirements. [Suspended]

(a) **Cargo**. A household goods freight forwarder may not operate until it has filed with FMCSA an appropriate surety bond, certificate of insurance, qualifications as a self-insurer, or other securities or agreements, in the amounts prescribed at §387.405, for loss of or damage to household goods.

(b) **Public liability**. A freight forwarder may not perform transfer, collection, or delivery service until it has filed with the FMCSA an appropriate surety bond, certificate of insurance, qualifications as a self-insurer, or other securities or agreements, in the amounts prescribed at §387.405, conditioned to pay any final judgment recovered against such freight forwarder for bodily injury to or the death of any person, or loss of or damage to property (except cargo) of others, or, in the case of freight vehicles described at §387.303(b)(2), for environmental restoration, resulting from the negligent operation, maintenance, or use of motor vehicles operated by or under its control in performing such service.

(c) **Surety bond or trust fund**. A freight forwarder must have a surety bond or trust fund in effect. The FMCSA will not issue a freight forwarder license until a surety bond or trust fund for the full limit of liability prescribed in §387.405 is in effect. The freight forwarder license shall remain valid or effective only as long as a surety bond or trust fund remains in effect and ensures the financial responsibility of the freight forwarder. The requirements applicable to property broker surety bonds and trust funds in §387.307 shall apply to the surety bond or trust fund required by this paragraph.

§387.405 Limits of liability.

The minimum amounts for cargo and public liability security are identical to those prescribed for motor carriers at 49 CFR 387.303. The minimum amount for the surety bond or trust fund is identical to that prescribed for brokers at 49 CFR 387.307.

§387.407 Surety bonds and certificates of insurance.

(a) The limits of liability under §387.405 may be provided by aggregation under the procedures at 49 CFR part 387, subpart C.

(b) Each policy of insurance used in connection with a certificate of insurance filed with the FMCSA shall be amended by attachment of the appropriate endorsement prescribed by the FMCSA (or the Department of Transportation, where applicable).

§387.409 Insurance and surety companies.

A certificate of insurance or surety bond will not be accepted by the FMCSA unless issued by an insurance or surety company that is authorized (licensed or admitted) to issue bonds or underlying insurance policies:

(a) In each State in which the freight forwarder is authorized by the FMCSA to perform service, or

(b) In the State in which the freight forwarder has its principal place of business or domicile, and will designate in writing upon request by the FMCSA, a person upon whom process, issued by or under the authority of a court of competent jurisdiction, may be served in any proceeding at law or equity brought in any State in which the freight forwarder performs service; or

(c) In any State, and is eligible as an excess or surplus lines insurer in any State in which business is written, and will make the designation of process agent prescribed in paragraph (b) of this section.

(d) In the Province or Territory of Canada in which a Canadian freight forwarder has its principal place of business or domicile, and will designate in writing upon request by FMCSA, a person upon whom process, issued by or under the authority of a court of competent jurisdiction, may be served in any proceeding at law or equity brought in any State in which the freight forwarder operates.

§387.411 Qualifications as a self-insurer and other securities or agreements.

(a) **Self-insurer**. The FMCSA will approve the application of a freight forwarder to qualify as a self-insurer if it is able to meet its obligations for bodily-injury, property-damage, and cargo liability without adversely affecting its business.

(b) **Other securities and agreements**. The FMCSA will grant applications for approval of other securities and agreements if the public will be protected as contemplated by 49 U.S.C. 13906(c).

§387.413T Forms and procedures.

(a) **Forms.** Endorsements for policies of insurance, surety bonds, certificates of insurance, applications to qualify as a self-insurer or for approval of other securities or agreements, and notices of cancellation must be in the form prescribed at subpart C of this part.

(b) **Procedure.** Certificates of insurance, surety bonds, and notices of cancellation must be filed with the FMCSA.

(c) **Names.** Certificates of insurance and surety bonds shall be issued in the full name (including any trade name) of the individual, partnership (all partners named), corporation, or other person holding or to be issued the permit.

(d) **Cancellation.** Except as provided in paragraph (e) of this section, certificates of insurance, surety bonds, and other securities and agreements shall not be cancelled or withdrawn until 30 days after the FMCSA receives written notice from the insurance company, surety, freight forwarder, or other party, as the case may be.

(e) **Termination by replacement.** Certificates of insurance or surety bonds may be replaced by other certificates of insurance, surety bonds, or other security, and the liability of the retiring insurer or surety shall be considered as having terminated as of the replacement's effective date, if acceptable to the FMCSA.

§387.413 Forms and procedures. [Suspended]

(a) **Forms**. Endorsements for policies of insurance, surety bonds, certificates of insurance, applications to qualify as a self-insurer or for approval of other securities or agreements and notices of cancellation must be in the form prescribed at 49 CFR part 387, subpart C.

(b) **Procedure**. Certificates of insurance, surety bonds, and notices of cancellation must be electronically filed with the FMCSA.

(c) **Names**. Certificates of insurance and surety bonds shall be issued in the full name (including any trade name) of the individual, partnership (all partners named), corporation, or other person holding or to be issued the permit.

(d) **Cancellation**. Except as provided in paragraph (e) of this section, certificates of insurance, surety bonds and other securities and agreements shall not be cancelled or withdrawn until 30 days after the FMCSA receives written notice from the insurance company, surety, freight forwarder, or other party, as the case may be.

(e) **Termination by replacement**. Certificates of insurance or surety bonds may be replaced by other certificates of insurance, surety bonds or other security, and the liability of the retiring insurer or surety shall be considered as having terminated as of the replacement's effective date, if acceptable to the FMCSA.

§387.415 Acceptance and revocation by the FMCSA.

The FMCSA may at any time refuse to accept or may revoke its acceptance of any surety bond, certificate of insurance, qualifications as a self-insurer, or other security or agreement that does not comply with these rules or fails to provide adequate public protection.

§387.417 Fiduciaries.

(a) **Interpretations**. The terms "insured" and "principal" as used in a certificate of insurance, surety bond, and notice of cancellation, filed by or for a freight forwarder, include the freight forwarder and its fiduciary (as defined at 49 CFR 387.319(a)) as of the moment of succession.

(b) **Span of security coverage**. The coverage furnished for a fiduciary shall not apply after the effective date of other insurance or security, filed with and accepted by the FMCSA for such fiduciary. After the coverage shall have been in effect 30 days, it may be cancelled or withdrawn within the succeeding 30 days by the insurer, the insured, the surety, or the principal 10 days after the FMCSA receives written notice. After such coverage has been in effect 60 days, it may be cancelled or withdrawn only in accordance with §387.413(d).

§387.419T Electronic filing of surety bonds, certificates of insurance and cancellations.

Insurers may, at their option and in accordance with the requirements and procedures set forth at §387.323T, file certificates of insurance, surety bonds, and other securities and agreements electronically.

§387.419 Electronic filing of surety bonds, certificates of insurance and cancellations. [Suspended]

Insurers must electronically file certificates of insurance, surety bonds, and other securities and agreements and notices of cancellation in accordance with the requirements and procedures set forth at §387.323.

PART 390—FEDERAL MOTOR CARRIER SAFETY REGULATIONS; GENERAL

Subpart A—General Applicability and Definitions

Subpart B—General Requirements and Information

Subpart C—Requirements and Information for Intermodal Equipment Providers and for Motor Carriers Operating Intermodal Equipment

Authority: 49 U.S.C. 113, 504, 508, 31132, 31133, 31134, 31136, 31137, 31144, 31149, 31151, 31502; sec. 114, Pub. L. 103-311, 108 Stat. 1673, 1677; secs. 212 and 217, Pub. L. 106-159, 113 Stat. 1748, 1766, 1767; sec. 229, Pub. L. 106-159 (as added and transferred by sec. 4115 and amended by secs. 4130-4132, Pub. L. 109-59, 119 Stat. 1144, 1726, 1743, 1744), 113 Stat. 1748, 1773; sec. 4136, Pub. L. 109-59, 119 Stat. 1144, 1745; secs. 32101(d) and 32934, Pub. L. 112-141, 126 Stat. 405, 778, 830; sec. 2, Pub. L. 113-125, 128 Stat. 1388; secs. 5403, 5518, and 5524, Pub. L. 114-94, 129 Stat. 1312, 1548, 1558, 1560; sec. 2, Pub. L. 115-105, 131 Stat. 2263; and 49 CFR 1.81, 1.81a, 1.87.

Subpart A—General Applicability and Definitions

§390.1 Purpose.

This part establishes general applicability, definitions, general requirements and information as they pertain to persons subject to this chapter.

§390.3T General applicability.

(a)(1) The rules in this subchapter are applicable to all employers, employees, and commercial motor vehicles that transport property or passengers in interstate commerce.

(2) The rules in 49 CFR 386.12(c) and 390.6 prohibiting the coercion of drivers of commercial motor vehicles operating in interstate commerce:

(i) To violate certain safety regulations are applicable to all motor carriers, shippers, receivers, and transportation intermediaries; and

(ii) To violate certain commercial regulations are applicable to all operators of commercial motor vehicles.

(b) The rules in part 383 of this chapter, Commercial Driver's License Standards; Requirements and Penalties, are applicable to every person who operates a commercial motor vehicle, as defined in §383.5 of this subchapter, in interstate or intrastate commerce and to all employers of such persons.

(c) The rules in part 387 of this chapter, Minimum Levels of Financial Responsibility for Motor Carriers, are applicable to motor carriers as provided in §387.3 or §387.27 of this subchapter.

(d) **Additional requirements.** Nothing in this subchapter shall be construed to prohibit an employer from requiring and enforcing more stringent requirements relating to safety of operation and employee safety and health.

(e) **Knowledge of and compliance with the regulations.** (1) Every employer shall be knowledgeable of and comply with all regulations contained in this subchapter which are applicable to that motor carrier's operations.

(2) Every driver and employee shall be instructed regarding, and shall comply with, all applicable regulations contained in this subchapter.

(3) All motor vehicle equipment and accessories required by this subchapter shall be maintained in compliance with all applicable performance and design criteria set forth in this subchapter.

(f) **Exceptions.** Unless otherwise specifically provided, the rules in this subchapter do not apply to—

(1) All school bus operations as defined in §390.5T, except for §§391.15(e) and (f), 392.15, 392.80, and 392.82 of this chapter;

(2) Transportation performed by the Federal government, a State, or any political subdivision of a State, or an agency established under a compact between States that has been approved by the Congress of the United States;

(3) The occasional transportation of personal property by individuals not for compensation nor in the furtherance of a commercial enterprise;

(4) The transportation of human corpses or sick and injured persons;

(5) The operation of fire trucks and rescue vehicles while involved in emergency and related operations;

(6) The operation of commercial motor vehicles designed or used to transport between 9 and 15 passengers (including the driver), not for direct compensation, provided the vehicle does not otherwise meet the definition of a commercial motor vehicle, except that motor carriers and drivers operating such vehicles are required to comply with §§390.15, 390.19T, 390.21T(a) and (b)(2), 391.15(e) and (f), 392.80 and 392.82 of this chapter.

(7) Either a driver of a commercial motor vehicle used primarily in the transportation of propane winter heating fuel or a driver of a motor vehicle used to respond to a pipeline emergency, if such regulations would prevent the driver from responding to an emergency condition requiring immediate response as defined in §390.5T.

(g) **Motor carriers that transport hazardous materials in intrastate commerce.** The rules in the following provisions of this subchapter apply to motor carriers that transport hazardous materials in intrastate commerce and to the motor vehicles that transport hazardous materials in intrastate commerce:

(1) Part 385, subparts A and E, of this chapter for carriers subject to the requirements of §385.403 of this chapter.

(2) Part 386 of this chapter, Rules of practice for motor carrier, broker, freight forwarder, and hazardous materials proceedings.

(3) Part 387 of this chapter, Minimum Levels of Financial Responsibility for Motor Carriers, to the extent provided in §387.3 of this chapter.

(4) Section 390.19T, Motor carrier identification report, and §390.21T, Marking of CMVs, for carriers subject to the requirements of §385.403 of this chapter. Intrastate motor carriers operating prior to January 1, 2005, are excepted from §390.19T(a)(1).

(h) **Intermodal equipment providers.** The rules in the following provisions of this subchapter apply to intermodal equipment providers:

(1) Subpart F, Intermodal Equipment Providers, of part 385 of this chapter, Safety Fitness Procedures.

(2) Part 386 of this chapter, Rules of Practice for Motor Carrier, Intermodal Equipment Provider, Broker, Freight Forwarder, and Hazardous Materials Proceedings.

(3) This part, Federal Motor Carrier Safety Regulations; General, except §390.15(b) concerning accident registers.

(4) Part 393 of this chapter, Parts and Accessories Necessary for Safe Operation.

(5) Part 396 of this chapter, Inspection, Repair, and Maintenance.

§390.3 General applicability. [Suspended]

(a) The rules in subchapter B of this chapter are applicable to all employers, employees, and commercial motor vehicles that transport property or passengers in interstate commerce.

(b) The rules in part 383 of this chapter, Commercial Driver's License Standards; Requirements and Penalties, are applicable to every person who operates a commercial motor vehicle, as defined in §383.5 of this subchapter, in interstate or intrastate commerce and to all employers of such persons.

(c) The rules in part 387 of this chapter, Minimum Levels of Financial Responsibility for Motor Carriers, are applicable to motor carriers as provided in §§387.3 or 387.27 of this chapter.

(d) **Additional requirements**. Nothing in subchapter B of this chapter shall be construed to prohibit an employer from requiring and enforcing more stringent requirements relating to safety of operation and employee safety and health.

(e) **Knowledge of and compliance with the regulations**. (1) Every employer shall be knowledgeable of and comply with all regulations contained in this subchapter that are applicable to that motor carrier's operations.

(2) Every driver and employee involved in motor carrier operations shall be instructed regarding, and shall comply with, all applicable regulations contained in this subchapter.

(3) All motor vehicle equipment and accessories required by this chapter shall be maintained in compliance with all applicable performance and design criteria set forth in this subchapter.

(f) **Exceptions**. Unless otherwise specifically provided, the rules in this subchapter do not apply to—

(1) All school bus operations as defined in §390.5, except for §§391.15(e) and (f), 392.15, 392.80, and 392.82 of this chapter;

(2) Transportation performed by the Federal government, a State, or any political subdivision of a State, or an agency established under a compact between States that has been approved by the Congress of the United States;

(3) The occasional transportation of personal property by individuals not for compensation and not in the furtherance of a commercial enterprise;

(4) The transportation of human corpses or sick and injured persons;

(5) The operation of fire trucks and rescue vehicles while involved in emergency and related operations;

(6) The operation of commercial motor vehicles designed or used to transport between 9 and 15 passengers (including the driver), not for direct compensation, provided the vehicle does not otherwise meet the definition of a commercial motor vehicle, except for the provisions of §§391.15(e) and (f), 392.80, and 392.82, and except that motor carriers operating such vehicles are required to comply with §§390.15, 390.21(a) and (b)(2), 390.201 and 390.205.

(7) Either a driver of a commercial motor vehicle used primarily in the transportation of propane winter heating fuel or a driver of a motor vehicle used to respond to a pipeline emergency, if such regulations would prevent the driver from responding to an emergency condition requiring immediate response as defined in §390.5.

(g) **Motor carriers that transport hazardous materials in intrastate commerce**. The rules in the following provisions of this subchapter apply to motor carriers that transport hazardous materials in intrastate commerce and to the motor vehicles that transport hazardous materials in intrastate commerce:

(1) Part 385, subparts A and E, for carriers subject to the requirements of §385.403 of this subchapter.

(2) Part 386, Rules of Practice for Motor Carrier, Intermodal Equipment Provider, Broker, Freight Forwarder, and Hazardous Materials Proceedings, of this subchapter.

(3) Part 387, Minimum Levels of Financial Responsibility for Motor Carriers, to the extent provided in §387.3 of this subchapter.

(4) Subpart E of this part, Unified Registration System, and §390.21, Marking of CMVs, for carriers subject to the requirements of §385.403 of this subchapter. Intrastate motor carriers operating prior to January 1, 2005, are excepted from §390.201.

(h) **Intermodal equipment providers**. The rules in the following provisions of this subchapter apply to intermodal equipment providers:

(1) Subpart F, Intermodal Equipment Providers, of Part 385, Safety Fitness Procedures.

(2) Part 386, Rules of Practice for Motor Carrier, Intermodal Equipment Provider, Broker, Freight Forwarder, and Hazardous Materials Proceedings.

(3) Part 390, Federal Motor Carrier Safety Regulations; General, except §390.15(b) concerning accident registers.

(4) Part 393, Parts and Accessories Necessary for Safe Operation.

(5) Part 396, Inspection, Repair, and Maintenance.

(i) **Brokers**. The rules in the following provisions of this subchapter apply to brokers that are required to register with the Agency pursuant to 49 U.S.C. chapter 139.

(1) Part 371, Brokers of Property.

(2) Part 386, Rules of Practice for Motor Carrier, Intermodal Equipment Provider, Broker, Freight Forwarder, and Hazardous Materials Proceedings.

(3) Part 387, Minimum Levels of Financial Responsibility for Motor Carriers, to the extent provided in subpart C of that part.

(4) Section 390.6, prohibiting the coercion of drivers of commercial motor vehicles operating in interstate commerce to violate certain safety regulations, and subpart E of this part, Unified Registration System.

(j) **Freight forwarders**. The rules in the following provisions of this subchapter apply to freight forwarders that are required to register with the Agency pursuant to 49 U.S.C. chapter 139.

(1) Part 386, Rules of Practice for Motor Carrier, Intermodal Equipment Provider, Broker, Freight Forwarder, and Hazardous Materials Proceedings.

(2) Part 387, Minimum Levels of Financial Responsibility for Motor Carriers, to the extent provided in subpart D of that part.

(3) Section 390.6, prohibiting the coercion of drivers of commercial motor vehicles operating in interstate commerce to violate certain safety regulations, and subpart E of this part, Unified Registration System.

(k) **Cargo tank facilities**. The rules in subpart E of this part, Unified Registration System, apply to each cargo tank and cargo tank motor vehicle manufacturer, assembler, repairer, inspector, tester, and design certifying engineer that is subject to registration requirements under 49 CFR 107.502 and 49 U.S.C. 5108.

(l) **Shippers, receivers, consignees, and transportation intermediaries.** The rules in 49 CFR 386.12(c) and 390.6 prohibiting the coercion of drivers of commercial motor vehicles operating in interstate commerce to violate certain safety regulations are applicable to shippers, receivers, and transportation intermediaries.

§390.4 Delegations and redelegations of authority of FMCSA employees to perform assigned actions or duties.

(a) **General.** FMCSA may apply the guidelines and procedures of this section to delegate or redelegate the authority of FMCSA employees to perform assigned actions or duties under this chapter.

(b) **FMCSA Administrator authority to delegate and redelegate.** (1) The FMCSA Administrator is authorized to delegate and redelegate authority and authorize successive redelegations.

(2) The FMCSA Administrator retains concurrent authority to exercise or redelegate any authority that he or she has delegated to an employee in regulation, directive, or memorandum.

(c) **Redelegations by FMCSA employees.** Unless specifically prohibited by law, and in consultation with the FMCSA Office of the Chief Counsel, an FMCSA employee with delegated authority is authorized to—

(1) Redelegate that authority to another FMCSA employee, as appropriate; and

(2) Maintain concurrent authority to exercise or redelegate the authority he or she has delegated to another FMCSA employee.

(d) **Exercise of delegated authority in special circumstances.** In consultation with the FMCSA Office of the Chief Counsel, if the FMCSA employee to whom a regulation assigns the authority to perform an action or a duty is unavailable or otherwise unable to perform such action or duty (*e.g.,* due to a conflict of interest or a vacancy in the position), a supervisor of the FMCSA employee may exercise that authority or redelegate such authority to another FMCSA employee, as appropriate.

(e) **Format of delegations and redelegations.** Delegations and redelegations authorized under this section must be in writing and may be made by regulation, directive, or memorandum.

(f) **Actions or duties performed under delegated or redelegated authority.** Each action or duty performed by any FMCSA employee pursuant to authority delegated or redelegated to him or her in accordance with this section, whether directly or by redelegation, shall be a valid exercise of that authority, notwithstanding any regulation that provides that such action or duty shall be performed by another FMCSA employee.

§390.5T Definitions.

Unless specifically defined elsewhere, in this subchapter:

Accident means—

(1) Except as provided in paragraph (2) of this definition, an occurrence involving a commercial motor vehicle operating on a highway in interstate or intrastate commerce which results in:

(i) A fatality;

(ii) Bodily injury to a person who, as a result of the injury, immediately receives medical treatment away from the scene of the accident; or

(iii) One or more motor vehicles incurring disabling damage as a result of the accident, requiring the motor vehicle(s) to be transported away from the scene by a tow truck or other motor vehicle.

(2) The term accident does not include:

(i) An occurrence involving only boarding and alighting from a stationary motor vehicle; or

(ii) An occurrence involving only the loading or unloading of cargo.

Alcohol concentration (AC) means the concentration of alcohol in a person's blood or breath. When expressed as a percentage it means grams of alcohol per 100 milliliters of blood or grams of alcohol per 210 liters of breath.

Assistant Administrator means the Assistant Administrator of the Federal Motor Carrier Safety Administration or an authorized delegee.

Bus means any motor vehicle designed, constructed, and/or used for the transportation of passengers, including taxicabs.

Business district means the territory contiguous to and including a highway when within any 600 feet along such highway there are buildings in use for business or industrial purposes, including but not limited to hotels, banks, or office buildings which occupy at least 300 feet of frontage on one side or 300 feet collectively on both sides of the highway.

Certified VA medical examiner means a qualified VA examiner who has fulfilled the requirements for and is listed on the National Registry of Certified Medical Examiners.

Charter transportation of passengers means transportation, using a bus, of a group of persons who pursuant to a common purpose, under a single contract, at a fixed charge for the motor vehicle, have acquired the exclusive use of the motor vehicle to travel together under an itinerary either specified in advance or modified after having left the place of origin.

Coerce or **Coercion** means either—

(1) A threat by a motor carrier, shipper, receiver, or transportation intermediary, or their respective agents, officers or representatives, to withhold business, employment or work opportunities from, or to take or permit any adverse employment action against, a driver in order to induce the driver to operate a commercial motor vehicle under conditions which the driver stated would require him or her to violate one or more of the regulations, which the driver identified at least generally, that are codified at 49 CFR parts 171 through 173, 177 through 180, 380 through 383, or 390 through 399, or §385.415 or §385.421T of this chapter, or the actual withholding of business, employment, or work opportunities or the actual taking or permitting of any adverse employment action to punish a driver for having refused to engage in such operation of a commercial motor vehicle; or

(2) A threat by a motor carrier, or its agents, officers or representatives, to withhold business, employment or work opportunities or to take or permit any adverse employment action against a driver in order to induce the driver to operate a commercial motor vehicle under conditions which the driver stated would require a violation of one or more of the regulations, which the driver identified at least generally, that are codified at 49 CFR parts 356, 360, or 365 through 379, or the actual withholding of business, employment or work opportunities or the actual taking or permitting of any adverse employment action to punish a driver for refusing to engage in such operation of a commercial motor vehicle.

Commercial motor vehicle means any self-propelled or towed motor vehicle used on a highway in interstate commerce to transport passengers or property when the vehicle—

(1) Has a gross vehicle weight rating or gross combination weight rating, or gross vehicle weight or gross combination weight, of 4,536 kg (10,001 pounds) or more, whichever is greater; or

(2) Is designed or used to transport more than 8 passengers (including the driver) for compensation; or

(3) Is designed or used to transport more than 15 passengers, including the driver, and is not used to transport passengers for compensation; or

(4) Is used in transporting material found by the Secretary of Transportation to be hazardous under 49 U.S.C. 5103 and transported in a quantity requiring placarding under regulations prescribed by the Secretary under 49 CFR, subtitle B, chapter I, subchapter C.

Conviction means an unvacated adjudication of guilt, or a determination that a person has violated or failed to comply with the law in a court of original jurisdiction or by an authorized administrative tribunal, an unvacated forfeiture of bail or collateral deposited to secure the person's appearance in court, a plea of guilty or nolo contendere accepted by the court, the payment of a fine or court cost, or violation of a condition of release without bail, regardless of whether or not the penalty is rebated, suspended, or probated.

Covered farm vehicle means—

(1) A straight truck or articulated vehicle—

(i) Registered in a State with a license plate or other designation issued by the State of registration that allows law enforcement officials to identify it as a farm vehicle;

(ii) Operated by the owner or operator of a farm or ranch, or an employee or family member of an owner or operator of a farm or ranch;

(iii) Used to transport agricultural commodities, livestock, machinery or supplies to or from a farm or ranch; and

(iv) Not used in for-hire motor carrier operations; however, for-hire motor carrier operations do not include the operation of a vehicle meeting the requirements of paragraphs (1)(i) through (iii) of this definition by a tenant pursuant to a crop share farm lease agreement to transport the landlord's portion of the crops under that agreement.

(2) Meeting the requirements of paragraphs (1)(i) through (iv) of this definition:

(i) With a gross vehicle weight rating or gross combination weight rating, or gross vehicle weight or gross combination weight, whichever is greater, of 26,001 pounds or less may utilize the exemptions in §390.39 anywhere in the United States; or

(ii) With a gross vehicle weight rating or gross combination weight rating, or gross vehicle weight or gross combination weight, whichever is greater, of more than 26,001 pounds may utilize the exemptions in §390.39 anywhere in the State of registration or across State lines within 150 air miles of the farm or ranch with respect to which the vehicle is being operated.

Crash. See accident.

Direct assistance means transportation and other relief services provided by a motor carrier or its driver(s) incident to the immediate restoration of essential services (such as, electricity, medical care, sewer, water, telecommunications, and telecommunication transmissions) or essential supplies (such as, food and fuel). It does not include transportation related to long-term rehabilitation of damaged physical infrastructure or routine commercial deliveries after the initial threat to life and property has passed.

Direct compensation means payment made to the motor carrier by the passengers or a person acting on behalf of the passengers for the transportation services provided, and not included in a total package charge or other assessment for highway transportation services.

Disabling damage means damage which precludes departure of a motor vehicle from the scene of the accident in its usual manner in daylight after simple repairs.

(1) *Inclusions.* Damage to motor vehicles that could have been driven, but would have been further damaged if so driven.

(2) *Exclusions.* (i) Damage which can be remedied temporarily at the scene of the accident without special tools or parts.

(ii) Tire disablement without other damage even if no spare tire is available.

(iii) Headlamp or taillight damage.

(iv) Damage to turn signals, horn, or windshield wipers which makes them inoperative.

Driveaway-towaway operation means an operation in which an empty or unladen motor vehicle with one or more sets of wheels on the surface of the roadway is being transported:

(1) Between vehicle manufacturer's facilities;

(2) Between a vehicle manufacturer and a dealership or purchaser;

(3) Between a dealership, or other entity selling or leasing the vehicle, and a purchaser or lessee;

(4) To a motor carrier's terminal or repair facility for the repair of disabling damage (as defined in this section) following a crash; or

(5) To a motor carrier's terminal or repair facility for repairs associated with the failure of a vehicle component or system; or

(6) By means of a saddle-mount or tow-bar.

Driver means any person who operates any commercial motor vehicle.

Driving a commercial motor vehicle while under the influence of alcohol means committing any one or more of the following acts in a CMV: Driving a CMV while the person's alcohol concentration is 0.04 or more; driving under the influence of alcohol, as prescribed by State law; or refusal to undergo such testing as is required by any State or jurisdiction in the enforcement of Table 1 to §383.51 or §392.5(a)(2) of this subchapter.

Electronic device includes, but is not limited to, a cellular telephone; personal digital assistant; pager; computer; or any other device used to input, write, send, receive, or read text.

Electronic signature means a method of signing an electronic communication that identifies and authenticates a particular person as the source of the electronic communication and indicates such person's approval of the information contained in the electronic communication, in accordance with the Government Paperwork Elimination Act (Pub. L. 105-277, Title XVII, Secs. 1701-1710, 44 U.S.C. 3504 note, 112 Stat. 2681-749).

Emergency means any hurricane, tornado, storm (*e.g.* thunderstorm, snowstorm, icestorm, blizzard, sandstorm, etc.), high water, wind-driven water, tidal wave, tsunami, earthquake, volcanic eruption, mud slide, drought, forest fire, explosion, blackout, or other occurrence, natural or man-made, which interrupts the delivery of essential services (such as, electricity, medical care, sewer, water, telecommunications, and telecommunication transmissions) or essential supplies (such as, food and fuel) or otherwise immediately threatens human life or public welfare, provided such hurricane, tornado, or other event results in:

(1) A declaration of an emergency by the President of the United States, the Governor of a State, or their authorized representatives having authority to declare emergencies; by FMCSA; or by other Federal, State, or local government officials having authority to declare emergencies; or

(2) A request by a police officer for tow trucks to move wrecked or disabled motor vehicles.

Emergency condition requiring immediate response means any condition that, if left unattended, is reasonably likely to result in immediate serious bodily harm, death, or substantial damage to property. In the case of transportation of propane winter heating fuel, such conditions shall include (but are not limited to) the detection of gas odor, the activation of carbon monoxide alarms, the detection of carbon monoxide poisoning, and any real or suspected damage to a propane gas system following a severe storm or flooding. An "emergency condition requiring immediate response" does not include requests to refill empty gas tanks. In the case of a pipeline emergency, such conditions include (but are not limited to) indication of an abnormal pressure event, leak, release or rupture.

Emergency relief means an operation in which a motor carrier or driver of a commercial motor vehicle is providing direct assistance to supplement State and local efforts and capabilities to save lives or property or to protect public health and safety as a result of an emergency as defined in this section.

Employee means any individual, other than an employer, who is employed by an employer and who in the course of his or her employment directly affects commercial motor vehicle safety. Such term includes a driver of a commercial motor vehicle (including an independent contractor while in the course of operating a commercial motor vehicle), a mechanic, and a freight handler. Such term does not include an employee of the United States, any State, any political subdivision of a State, or any agency established under a compact between States and approved by the Congress of the United States who is acting within the course of such employment.

Employer means any person engaged in a business affecting interstate commerce who owns or leases a commercial motor vehicle in connection with that business, or assigns employees to operate it, but such terms does not include the United States, any State, any political subdivision of a State, or an agency established under a compact between States approved by the Congress of the United States.

Exempt intracity zone means the geographic area of a municipality or the commercial zone of that municipality described in appendix A to part 372 of this chapter. The term "exempt intracity zone" does not include any municipality or commercial zone in the State of Hawaii. For purposes of §391.62 of this chapter, a driver may be considered to operate a commercial motor vehicle wholly within an exempt intracity zone notwithstanding any common control, management, or arrangement for a continuous carriage or shipment to or from a point without such zone.

Exempt motor carrier means a person engaged in transportation exempt from economic regulation by the Federal Motor Carrier Safety Administration (FMCSA) under 49 U.S.C. 13506. "Exempt motor carriers" are subject to the safety regulations set forth in this subchapter.

Farm vehicle driver means a person who drives only a commercial motor vehicle that is—

(1) Controlled and operated by a farmer as a private motor carrier of property;

(2) Being used to transport either—

(i) Agricultural products; or

(ii) Farm machinery, farm supplies, or both, to or from a farm;

(3) Not being used in the operation of a for-hire motor carrier;

(4) Not carrying hazardous materials of a type or quantity that requires the commercial motor vehicle to be placarded in accordance with §177.823 of this subtitle; and

(5) Being used within 150 air-miles of the farmer's farm.

Farmer means any person who operates a farm or is directly involved in the cultivation of land, crops, or livestock which—

(1) Are owned by that person; or

(2) Are under the direct control of that person.

Fatality means any injury which results in the death of a person at the time of the motor vehicle accident or within 30 days of the accident.

Federal Motor Carrier Safety Administrator means the chief executive of the Federal Motor Carrier Safety Administration, an agency within the Department of Transportation.

Field Administrator means the head of an FMCSA Service Center who has been delegated authority to initiate compliance and enforcement actions on behalf of FMCSA or an authorized delegee.

For-hire motor carrier means a person engaged in the transportation of goods or passengers for compensation.

Gross combination weight rating (GCWR) is the greater of:

(1) A value specified by the manufacturer of the power unit, if such value is displayed on the Federal Motor Vehicle Safety Standard (FMVSS) certification label required by the National Highway Traffic Safety Administration; or

(2) The sum of the gross vehicle weight ratings (GVWRs) or the gross vehicle weights (GVWs) of the power unit and the towed unit(s), or any combination thereof, that produces the highest value. Exception: The GCWR of the power unit will not be used to define a commercial motor vehicle when the power unit is not towing another vehicle.

Gross vehicle weight rating (GVWR) means the value specified by the manufacturer as the loaded weight of a single motor vehicle.

Hazardous material means a substance or material which has been determined by the Secretary of Transportation to be capable of posing an unreasonable risk to health, safety, and property when transported in commerce, and which has been so designated.

Hazardous substance means a material, and its mixtures or solutions, that is identified in the appendix to §172.101 of this title, List of Hazardous Substances and Reportable Quantities, of this title when offered for transportation in one package, or in one transport motor vehicle if not packaged, and when the quantity of the material therein equals or exceeds the reportable quantity (RQ). This definition does not apply to petroleum products that are lubricants or fuels, or to mixtures or solutions of hazardous substances if in a concentration less than that shown in the table in §171.8 of this title, based on the reportable quantity (RQ) specified for the materials listed in the appendix to §172.101 of this title.

Hazardous waste means any material that is subject to the hazardous waste manifest requirements of the EPA specified in 40 CFR part 262 or would be subject to these requirements absent an interim authorization to a State under 40 CFR part 123, subpart F.

Highway means any road, street, or way, whether on public or private property, open to public travel. "Open to public travel" means that the road section is available, except during scheduled periods, extreme weather or emergency conditions, passable by four-wheel standard passenger cars, and open to

PART 390

the general public for use without restrictive gates, prohibitive signs, or regulation other than restrictions based on size, weight, or class of registration. Toll plazas of public toll roads are not considered restrictive gates.

Interchange means—

(1) The act of providing intermodal equipment to a motor carrier pursuant to an intermodal equipment interchange agreement for the purpose of transporting the equipment for loading or unloading by any person or repositioning the equipment for the benefit of the equipment provider, but it does not include the leasing of equipment to a motor carrier for primary use in the motor carrier's freight hauling operations; or

(2) The act of providing a passenger-carrying commercial motor vehicle by one motor carrier of passengers to another such carrier, at a point which both carriers are authorized to serve, with which to continue a through movement.

(3) For property-carrying vehicles, see §376.2 of this subchapter.

Intermodal equipment means trailing equipment that is used in the intermodal transportation of containers over public highways in interstate commerce, including trailers and chassis.

Intermodal equipment interchange agreement means the Uniform Intermodal Interchange and Facilities Access Agreement (UIIFA) or any other written document executed by an intermodal equipment provider or its agent and a motor carrier or its agent, the primary purpose of which is to establish the responsibilities and liabilities of both parties with respect to the interchange of the intermodal equipment.

Intermodal equipment provider means any person that interchanges intermodal equipment with a motor carrier pursuant to a written interchange agreement or has a contractual responsibility for the maintenance of the intermodal equipment.

Interstate commerce means trade, traffic, or transportation in the United States—

(1) Between a place in a State and a place outside of such State (including a place outside of the United States);

(2) Between two places in a State through another State or a place outside of the United States; or

(3) Between two places in a State as part of trade, traffic, or transportation originating or terminating outside the State or the United States.

Intrastate commerce means any trade, traffic, or transportation in any State which is not described in the term "interstate commerce."

Lease, as used in subpart G of this part, means a contract or agreement in which a motor carrier of passengers grants the use of a passenger-carrying commercial motor vehicle, with or without the driver, to another motor carrier, for a specified period for the transportation of passengers, whether or not compensation for such use is specified or required, when one or more of the motor carriers of passengers is not authorized to operate in interstate commerce pursuant to 49 U.S.C. 13901-13902. The term *lease* includes an interchange, as defined in this section, or other agreement granting the use of a passenger-carrying commercial motor vehicle, with or without the driver, for a specified period, whether or not compensation for such use is specified or required. For a definition of *lease* in the context of property-carrying vehicles, see §376.2 of this subchapter.

Lessee, as used in subpart G of this part, means the motor carrier obtaining the use of a passenger-carrying commercial motor vehicle, with or without the driver, from another motor carrier, through a *lease* as defined in this section. The term *lessee* includes a motor carrier obtaining the use of a passenger-carrying commercial motor vehicle, with or without the driver, from another motor carrier under an interchange or other agreement, whether or not compensation for such use is specified. For a definition of *lessee* in the context of property-carrying vehicles, see subpart G of this subchapter.

Lessor, as used in subpart G of this part, means the motor carrier granting the use of a passenger-carrying commercial motor vehicle, with or without the driver, to another motor carrier, through a *lease* as defined in this section. The term *lessor* includes a motor carrier granting the use of a passenger-carrying commercial motor vehicle, with or without the driver, to another motor carrier under an interchange or other agreement, whether or not compensation for such use is specified. For a definition of *lessor* in the context of property-carrying vehicles, see §376.2 of this subchapter.

Medical examiner means an individual certified by FMCSA and listed on the National Registry of Certified Medical Examiners in accordance with subpart D of this part.

Medical variance means a driver has received one of the following from FMCSA that allows the driver to be issued a medical certificate:

(1) An exemption letter permitting operation of a commercial motor vehicle pursuant to part 381, subpart C, of this chapter or §391.64 of this chapter;

(2) A skill performance evaluation certificate permitting operation of a commercial motor vehicle pursuant to §391.49 of this chapter.

Mobile telephone means a mobile communication device that falls under or uses any commercial mobile radio service, as defined in regulations of the Federal Communications Commission, 47 CFR 20.3. It does not include two-way or Citizens Band Radio services.

Motor carrier means a for-hire motor carrier or a private motor carrier. The term includes a motor carrier's agents, officers and representatives as well as employees responsible for hiring, supervising, training, assigning, or dispatching of drivers and employees concerned with the installation, inspection, and maintenance of motor vehicle equipment and/or accessories. For purposes of this subchapter, this definition includes the terms employer, and exempt motor carrier.

Motor vehicle means any vehicle, machine, tractor, trailer, or semitrailer propelled or drawn by mechanical power and used upon the highways in the transportation of passengers or property, or any combination thereof determined by the Federal Motor Carrier Safety Administration, but does not include any vehicle, locomotive, or car operated exclusively on a rail or rails, or a trolley bus operated by electric power derived from a fixed overhead wire, furnishing local passenger transportation similar to street-railway service.

Motor vehicle record means the report of the driving status and history of a driver generated from the driver record, provided to users, such as, drivers or employers, and subject to the provisions of the Driver Privacy Protection Act, 18 U.S.C. 2721-2725.

Multiple-employer driver means a driver, who in any period of 7 consecutive days, is employed or used as a driver by more than one motor carrier.

Operating authority means the registration required by 49 U.S.C. 13902, 49 CFR part 365, 49 CFR part 368, and 49 CFR 392.9a.

Operator. See driver.

Other terms. Any other term used in this subchapter is used in its commonly accepted meaning, except where such other term has been defined elsewhere in this subchapter. In that event, the definition therein given shall apply.

Out-of-service order means a declaration by an authorized enforcement officer of a Federal, State, Canadian, Mexican, or local jurisdiction that a driver, a commercial motor vehicle, or a motor carrier operation is out of service pursuant to 49 CFR 386.72, 392.5, 392.9a, 395.13, or 396.9, or compatible laws, or the North American Standard Out-of-Service Criteria.

Person means any individual, partnership, association, corporation, business trust, or any other organized group of individuals.

Previous employer means any DOT regulated person who employed the driver in the preceding 3 years, including any possible current employer.

Principal place of business means the single location designated by the motor carrier, normally its headquarters, for purposes of identification under this subchapter. The motor carrier must make records required by parts 382, 387, 390, 391, 395, 396, and 397 of this subchapter available for inspection at this location within 48 hours (Saturdays, Sundays, and Federal holidays excluded) after a request has been made by a special agent or authorized representative of the Federal Motor Carrier Safety Administration.

Private motor carrier means a person who provides transportation of property or passengers, by commercial motor vehicle, and is not a for-hire motor carrier.

Private motor carrier of passengers (business) means a private motor carrier engaged in the interstate transportation of passengers which is provided in the furtherance of a commercial enterprise and is not available to the public at large.

Private motor carrier of passengers (nonbusiness) means private motor carrier involved in the interstate transportation of passengers that does not otherwise meet the definition of a private motor carrier of passengers (business).

Qualified VA examiner means an advanced practice nurse, doctor of chiropractic, doctor of medicine, doctor of osteopathy, physician assistant, or other medical professional who is employed in the Department of Veterans Affairs; is licensed, certified, or registered in a State to perform physical examinations; is familiar with the standards for, and physical requirements of, an operator certified pursuant to 49 U.S.C. 31149; and has never, with respect to such section, been found to have acted fraudulently, including by fraudulently awarding a medical certificate.

Radar detector means any device or mechanism to detect the emission of radio microwaves, laser beams or any other future speed measurement technology employed by enforcement personnel to measure the speed of commercial motor vehicles upon public roads and highways for enforcement purposes. Excluded from this definition are radar detection devices that meet both of the following requirements:

(1) Transported outside the driver's compartment of the commercial motor vehicle. For this purpose, the driver's compartment of a passenger-carrying CMV shall include all space designed to accommodate both the driver and the passengers; and

(2) Completely inaccessible to, inoperable by, and imperceptible to the driver while operating the commercial motor vehicle.

Receiver or consignee means a person who takes delivery from a motor carrier or driver of a commercial motor vehicle of property transported in interstate commerce or hazardous materials transported in interstate or intrastate commerce.

Regional Director of Motor Carriers means the Field Administrator, Federal Motor Carrier Safety Administration, for a given geographical area of the United States.

Residential district means the territory adjacent to and including a highway which is not a business district and for a distance of 300 feet or more along the highway is primarily improved with residences.

School bus means a passenger motor vehicle which is designed or used to carry more than 10 passengers in addition to the driver, and which the Secretary determines is likely to be significantly used for the purpose of transporting preprimary, primary, or secondary school students to such schools from home or from such schools to home.

School bus operation means the use of a school bus to transport only school children and/or school personnel from home to school and from school to home.

Secretary means the Secretary of Transportation.

Shipper means a person who tenders property to a motor carrier or driver of a commercial motor vehicle for transportation in interstate commerce, or who tenders hazardous materials to a motor carrier or driver of a commercial motor vehicle for transportation in interstate or intrastate commerce.

Single-employer driver means a driver who, in any period of 7 consecutive days, is employed or used as a driver solely by a single motor carrier. This term includes a driver who operates a commercial motor vehicle on an intermittent, casual, or occasional basis.

Special agent. See appendix B to this subchapter—Special agents.

State means a State of the United States and the District of Columbia and includes a political subdivision of a State.

Texting means manually entering alphanumeric text into, or reading text from, an electronic device.

(1) This action includes, but is not limited to, short message service, emailing, instant messaging, a command or request to access a World Wide Web page, pressing more than a single button to initiate or terminate a voice communication using a mobile telephone, or engaging in any other form of electronic text retrieval or entry, for present or future communication.

(2) Texting does not include:

(i) Inputting, selecting, or reading information on a global positioning system or navigation system; or

(ii) Pressing a single button to initiate or terminate a voice communication using a mobile telephone; or

(iii) Using a device capable of performing multiple functions (*e.g.*, fleet management systems, dispatching devices, smart phones, citizens band radios, music players, etc.) for a purpose that is not otherwise prohibited in this subchapter.

Trailer includes:

(1) Full trailer means any motor vehicle other than a pole trailer which is designed to be drawn by another motor vehicle and so constructed that no part of its weight, except for the towing device, rests upon the self-propelled towing motor vehicle. A semitrailer equipped with an auxiliary front axle (converter dolly) shall be considered a full trailer.

(2) Pole trailer means any motor vehicle which is designed to be drawn by another motor vehicle and attached to the towing motor vehicle by means of a "reach" or "pole," or by being "boomed" or otherwise secured to the towing motor vehicle, for transporting long or irregularly shaped loads such as poles, pipes, or structural members, which generally are capable of sustaining themselves as beams between the supporting connections.

(3) Semitrailer means any motor vehicle, other than a pole trailer, which is designed to be drawn by another motor vehicle and is constructed so that some part of its weight rests upon the self-propelled towing motor vehicle.

Transportation intermediary means a person who arranges the transportation of property or passengers by commercial motor vehicle in interstate commerce, or who arranges the transportation of hazardous materials by commercial motor vehicle in interstate or intrastate commerce, including but not limited to brokers and freight forwarders.

Truck means any self-propelled commercial motor vehicle except a truck tractor, designed and/or used for the transportation of property.

Truck tractor means a self-propelled commercial motor vehicle designed and/or used primarily for drawing other vehicles.

Use a hand-held mobile telephone means:

(1) Using at least one hand to hold a mobile telephone to conduct a voice communication;

(2) Dialing or answering a mobile telephone by pressing more than a single button; or

(3) Reaching for a mobile telephone in a manner that requires a driver to maneuver so that he or she is no longer in a seated driving position, restrained by a seat belt that is installed in accordance with 49 CFR 393.93 and adjusted in accordance with the vehicle manufacturer's instructions.

United States means the 50 States and the District of Columbia.

Veteran operator means an operator of a commercial motor vehicle who is a veteran enrolled in the health care system established under 38 U.S.C. 1705(a).

Written or in writing means printed, handwritten, or typewritten either on paper or other tangible medium, or by any method of electronic documentation that meets the requirements of 49 CFR 390.32.

§390.5 Definitions. [Suspended]

Unless specifically defined elsewhere, in this subchapter:

Accident means—

(1) Except as provided in paragraph (2) of this definition, an occurrence involving a commercial motor vehicle operating on a highway in interstate or intrastate commerce which results in:

(i) A fatality;

(ii) Bodily injury to a person who, as a result of the injury, immediately receives medical treatment away from the scene of the accident; or

(iii) One or more motor vehicles incurring disabling damage as a result of the accident, requiring the motor vehicle(s) to be transported away from the scene by a tow truck or other motor vehicle.

(2) The term accident does not include:

(i) An occurrence involving only boarding and alighting from a stationary motor vehicle; or

(ii) An occurrence involving only the loading or unloading of cargo.

Alcohol concentration (AC) means the concentration of alcohol in a person's blood or breath. When expressed as a percentage it means grams of alcohol per 100 milliliters of blood or grams of alcohol per 210 liters of breath.

Assistant Administrator means the Assistant Administrator of the Federal Motor Carrier Safety Administration or an authorized delegee.

Bus means any motor vehicle designed, constructed, and/or used for the transportation of passengers, including taxicabs.

Business district means the territory contiguous to and including a highway when within any 600 feet along such highway there are buildings in use for business or industrial purposes, including but not limited to hotels, banks, or office buildings which occupy at least 300 feet of frontage on one side or 300 feet collectively on both sides of the highway.

Certified VA medical examiner means a qualified VA examiner who has fulfilled the requirements for and is listed on the National Registry of Certified Medical Examiners.

Charter transportation of passengers means transportation, using a bus, of a group of persons who pursuant to a common purpose, under a single contract, at a fixed charge for the motor vehicle, have acquired the exclusive use of the motor vehicle to travel together under an itinerary either specified in advance or modified after having left the place of origin.

Coerce or **Coercion** means either—

(1) A threat by a motor carrier, shipper, receiver, or transportation intermediary, or their respective agents, officers or representatives, to withhold business, employment or work opportunities from, or to take or permit any adverse employment action against, a driver in order to induce the driver to operate a commercial motor vehicle under conditions which the driver stated would require him or her to violate one or more of the regulations, which the driver identified at least generally, that are codified at 49 CFR parts 171-173, 177-180, 380-383, or 390-399, or §§385.415 or 385.421, or the actual withholding of business, employment, or work opportunities or the actual taking or permitting of any adverse employment action to punish a driver for having refused to engage in such operation of a commercial motor vehicle; or

(2) A threat by a motor carrier, or its agents, officers or representatives, to withhold business, employment or work opportunities or to take or permit any adverse employment action against a driver in order to induce the driver to operate a commercial motor vehicle under conditions which the driver stated would require a violation of one or more of the regulations, which the driver identified at least generally, that are codified at 49 CFR parts 356, 360, or 365-379, or the actual withholding of business, employment or work opportunities or the actual taking or permitting of any adverse employment action to punish a driver for refusing to engage in such operation of a commercial motor vehicle.

Commercial motor vehicle means any self-propelled or towed motor vehicle used on a highway in interstate commerce to transport passengers or property when the vehicle—

(1) Has a gross vehicle weight rating or gross combination weight rating, or gross vehicle weight or gross combination weight, of 4,536 kg (10,001 pounds) or more, whichever is greater; or

(2) Is designed or used to transport more than 8 passengers (including the driver) for compensation; or

(3) Is designed or used to transport more than 15 passengers, including the driver, and is not used to transport passengers for compensation; or

(4) Is used in transporting material found by the Secretary of Transportation to be hazardous under 49 U.S.C. 5103 and transported in a quantity requiring placarding under regulations prescribed by the Secretary under 49 CFR, subtitle B, chapter I, subchapter C.

Conviction means an unvacated adjudication of guilt, or a determination that a person has violated or failed to comply with the law in a court of original jurisdiction or by an authorized administrative tribunal, an unvacated forfeiture of bail or collateral deposited to secure the person's appearance in court, a plea of guilty or nolo contendere accepted by the court, the payment of a fine or court cost, or violation of a condition of release without bail, regardless of whether or not the penalty is rebated, suspended, or probated.

Covered farm vehicle —

(1) Means a straight truck or articulated vehicle—

(i) Registered in a State with a license plate or other designation issued by the State of registration that allows law enforcement officials to identify it as a farm vehicle;

(ii) Operated by the owner or operator of a farm or ranch, or an employee or family member of an owner or operator of a farm or ranch;

(iii) Used to transport agricultural commodities, livestock, machinery or supplies to or from a farm or ranch; and

(iv) Not used in for-hire motor carrier operations; however, for-hire motor carrier operations do not include the operation of a vehicle meeting the requirements of paragraphs (1)(i) through (iii) of this definition by a tenant pursuant to a crop share farm lease agreement to transport the landlord's portion of the crops under that agreement.

(2) Meeting the requirements of paragraphs (1)(i) through (iv) of this definition:

(i) With a gross vehicle weight rating or gross combination weight rating, or gross vehicle weight or gross combination weight, whichever is greater, of 26,001 pounds or less may utilize the exemptions in §390.39 anywhere in the United States; or

(ii) With a gross vehicle weight rating or gross combination weight rating, or gross vehicle weight or gross combination weight, whichever is greater, of more than 26,001 pounds may utilize the exemptions in §390.39 anywhere in the State of registration or across State lines within 150 air miles of the farm or ranch with respect to which the vehicle is being operated.

Crash —See accident.

Direct Assistance means transportation and other relief services provided by a motor carrier or its driver(s) incident to the immediate restoration of essential services (such as, electricity, medical care, sewer, water, telecommunications, and telecommunication transmissions) or essential supplies (such as, food and fuel). It does not include transportation related to long-term rehabilitation of damaged physical infrastructure or routine commercial deliveries after the initial threat to life and property has passed.

Direct compensation means payment made to the motor carrier by the passengers or a person acting on behalf of the passengers for the transportation services provided, and not included in a total package charge or other assessment for highway transportation services.

Disabling damage means damage which precludes departure of a motor vehicle from the scene of the accident in its usual manner in daylight after simple repairs.

(1) *Inclusions.* Damage to motor vehicles that could have been driven, but would have been further damaged if so driven.

(2) *Exclusions.*

(i) Damage which can be remedied temporarily at the scene of the accident without special tools or parts.

(ii) Tire disablement without other damage even if no spare tire is available.

(iii) Headlamp or taillight damage.

(iv) Damage to turn signals, horn, or windshield wipers which makes them inoperative.

Driveaway-towaway operation means an operation in which an empty or unladen motor vehicle with one or more sets of wheels on the surface of the roadway is being transported:

(1) Between vehicle manufacturer's facilities;

(2) Between a vehicle manufacturer and a dealership or purchaser;

(3) Between a dealership, or other entity selling or leasing the vehicle, and a purchaser or lessee;

(4) To a motor carrier's terminal or repair facility for the repair of disabling damage (as defined in §390.5) following a crash; or

(5) To a motor carrier's terminal or repair facility for repairs associated with the failure of a vehicle component or system; or

(6) By means of a saddle-mount or tow-bar.

Driver means any person who operates any commercial motor vehicle.

Driving a commercial motor vehicle while under the influence of alcohol means committing any one or more of the following acts in a CMV: Driving a CMV while the person's alcohol concentration is 0.04 or more; driving under the influence of alcohol, as prescribed by State law; or refusal to undergo such testing as is required by any State or jurisdiction in the enforcement of Table 1 to §383.51 or §392.5(a)(2) of this subchapter.

Electronic device includes, but is not limited to, a cellular telephone; personal digital assistant; pager; computer; or any other device used to input, write, send, receive, or read text.

Electronic signature means a method of signing an electronic communication that identifies and authenticates a particular person as the source of the electronic communication and indicates such person's approval of the information contained in the electronic communication, in accordance with the Government Paperwork Elimination Act (Pub. L. 105-277, Title XVII, Secs. 1701-1710, 44 U.S.C. 3504 note, 112 Stat. 2681-749).

Emergency means any hurricane, tornado, storm (*e.g.* thunderstorm, snowstorm, icestorm, blizzard, sandstorm, etc.), high water, wind-driven water, tidal wave, tsunami, earthquake, volcanic eruption, mud slide, drought, forest fire, explosion, blackout, or other occurrence, natural or man-made, which interrupts the delivery of essential services (such as, electricity, medical care, sewer, water, telecommunications, and telecommunication transmissions) or essential supplies (such as, food and fuel) or otherwise immediately threatens human life or public welfare, provided such hurricane, tornado, or other event results in:

(1) A declaration of an emergency by the President of the United States, the Governor of a State, or their authorized representatives having authority to declare emergencies; by FMCSA; or by other Federal, State, or local government officials having authority to declare emergencies; or

(2) A request by a police officer for tow trucks to move wrecked or disabled motor vehicles.

Emergency condition requiring immediate response means any condition that, if left unattended, is reasonably likely to result in immediate serious bodily harm, death, or substantial damage to property. In the case of transportation of propane winter heating fuel, such conditions shall include (but are not limited to) the detection of gas odor, the activation of carbon monoxide alarms, the detection of carbon monoxide poisoning, and any real or suspected damage to a propane gas system following a severe storm or flooding. An "emergency condition requiring immediate response" does not include requests to refill empty gas tanks. In the case of a pipeline emergency, such conditions include (but are not limited to) indication of an abnormal pressure event, leak, release or rupture.

Emergency relief means an operation in which a motor carrier or driver of a commercial motor vehicle is providing direct assistance to supplement State and local efforts and capabilities to save lives or property or to protect public health and safety as a result of an emergency as defined in this section.

Employee means any individual, other than an employer, who is employed by an employer and who in the course of his or her employment directly affects commercial motor vehicle safety. Such term includes a driver of a commercial motor vehicle (including an independent contractor while in the course of operating a commercial motor vehicle), a mechanic, and a freight handler. Such term does not include an employee of the United States, any State, any political subdivision of a State, or any agency established under a compact between States and approved by the Congress of the United States who is acting within the course of such employment.

Employer means any person engaged in a business affecting interstate commerce who owns or leases a commercial motor vehicle in connection with that business, or assigns employees to operate it, but such term does not include the United States, any state, any political subdivision of a State, or an agency established under a compact between States approved by the Congress of the United States.

Exempt intracity zone means the geographic area of a municipality or the commercial zone of that municipality described in appendix A to part 372 of this chapter. The term "exempt intracity zone" does not include any municipality or commercial zone in the State of Hawaii. For purposes of §391.62 of this chapter, a driver may be considered to operate a commercial motor vehicle wholly within an exempt intracity zone notwithstanding any common control, management, or arrangement for a continuous carriage or shipment to or from a point without such zone.

Farm vehicle driver means a person who drives only a commercial motor vehicle that is—

(1) Controlled and operated by a farmer as a private motor carrier of property;

(2) Being used to transport either—

(i) Agricultural products, or

(ii) Farm machinery, farm supplies, or both, to or from a farm;

(3) Not being used in the operation of a for-hire motor carrier;

(4) Not carrying hazardous materials of a type or quantity that requires the commercial motor vehicle to be placarded in accordance with §177.823 of this subtitle; and

(5) Being used within 150 air-miles of the farmer's farm.

Farmer means any person who operates a farm or is directly involved in the cultivation of land, crops, or livestock which—

(1) Are owned by that person; or

(2) Are under the direct control of that person.

Fatality means any injury which results in the death of a person at the time of the motor vehicle accident or within 30 days of the accident.

Federal Motor Carrier Safety Administrator means the chief executive of the Federal Motor Carrier Safety Administration, an agency within the Department of Transportation.

Field Administrator means the head of an FMCSA Service Center who has been delegated authority to initiate compliance and enforcement actions on behalf of FMCSA or an authorized delegee.

For-hire motor carrier means a person engaged in the transportation of goods or passengers for compensation.

Gross combination weight rating (GCWR) is the greater of:

(1) A value specified by the manufacturer of the power unit, if such value is displayed on the Federal Motor Vehicle Safety Standard (FMVSS) certification label required by the National Highway Traffic Safety Administration, or

(2) The sum of the gross vehicle weight ratings (GVWRs) or the gross vehicle weights (GVWs) of the power unit and the towed unit(s), or any combination thereof, that produces the highest value. Exception: The GCWR of the power unit will not be used to define a commercial motor vehicle when the power unit is not towing another vehicle.

Gross vehicle weight rating (GVWR) means the value specified by the manufacturer as the loaded weight of a single motor vehicle.

Hazardous material means a substance or material which has been determined by the Secretary of Transportation to be capable of posing an unreasonable risk to health, safety, and property when transported in commerce, and which has been so designated.

Hazardous substance means a material, and its mixtures or solutions, that is identified in the appendix to §172.101, List of Hazardous Substances and Reportable Quantities, of this title when offered for transportation in one package, or in one transport motor vehicle if not packaged, and when the quantity of the material therein equals or exceeds the reportable quantity (RQ). This definition does not apply to petroleum products that are lubricants or fuels, or to mixtures or solutions of hazardous substances if in a concentration less than that shown in the table in §171.8 of this title, based on the reportable quantity (RQ) specified for the materials listed in the appendix to §172.101.

Hazardous waste means any material that is subject to the hazardous waste manifest requirements of the EPA specified in 40 CFR Part 262 or would be subject to these requirements absent an interim authorization to a State under 40 CFR Part 123, Subpart F.

Highway means any road, street, or way, whether on public or private property, open to public travel. "Open to public travel" means that the road section is available, except during scheduled periods, extreme weather or emergency conditions, passable by four-wheel standard passenger cars, and open to the general public for use without restrictive gates, prohibitive signs, or regulation other than restrictions based on size, weight, or class of registration. Toll plazas of public toll roads are not considered restrictive gates.

Interchange means—

(1) The act of providing intermodal equipment to a motor carrier pursuant to an intermodal equipment interchange agreement for the purpose of transporting the equipment for loading or unloading by any person or repositioning the equipment for the benefit of the equipment provider, but it does not include the leasing of equipment to a motor carrier for primary use in the motor carrier's freight hauling operations; or

(2) The act of providing a passenger-carrying commercial motor vehicle by one motor carrier of passengers to another such carrier, at a point which both carriers are authorized to serve, with which to continue a through movement.

(3) For property-carrying vehicles, see §376.2 of this subchapter.

Intermodal equipment means trailing equipment that is used in the intermodal transportation of containers over public highways in interstate commerce, including trailers and chassis.

Intermodal equipment interchange agreement means the Uniform Intermodal Interchange and Facilities Access Agreement (UIIFA) or any other written document executed by an intermodal equipment provider or its agent and a motor carrier or its agent, the primary purpose of which is to establish the responsibilities and liabilities of both parties with respect to the interchange of the intermodal equipment.

Intermodal equipment provider means any person that interchanges intermodal equipment with a motor carrier pursuant to a written interchange agreement or has a contractual responsibility for the maintenance of the intermodal equipment.

Interstate commerce means trade, traffic, or transportation in the United States—

(1) Between a place in a State and a place outside of such State (including a place outside of the United States);

(2) Between two places in a State through another State or a place outside of the United States; or

(3) Between two places in a State as part of trade, traffic, or transportation originating or terminating outside the State or the United States.

Intrastate commerce means any trade, traffic, or transportation in any State which is not described in the term "interstate commerce."

Lease, as used in subpart G of this part, means a contract or agreement in which a motor carrier of passengers grants the use of a passenger-carrying commercial motor vehicle to another motor carrier, with or without a driver, for a specified period for the transportation of passengers, whether or not compensation for such use is specified or required, when one or more of the motor carriers of passengers is not authorized to operate in interstate commerce pursuant to 49 U.S.C. 13901-13902. The term *lease* includes an interchange, as defined in this section, or other agreement granting the use of a passenger-carrying commercial motor vehicle for a specified period, with or without a driver, whether or not compensation for such use is specified or required. For a definition of *lease* in the context of property-carrying vehicles, see §376.2 of this subchapter.

Lessee, as used in subpart G of this part, means the motor carrier obtaining the use of a passenger-carrying commercial motor vehicle, with or without the driver, from another motor carrier, through a *lease* as defined in this section. The term *lessee* includes a motor carrier obtaining the use of a passenger-carrying commercial motor vehicle from another motor carrier under an interchange or other agreement, with or without a driver, whether or not compensation for such use is specified. For a definition of *lessee* in the context of property-carrying vehicles, see §376.2 of this subchapter.

Lessor, as used in subpart G of this part, means the motor carrier granting the use of a passenger-carrying commercial motor vehicle, with or without the driver, to another motor carrier, through a *lease* as defined in this section. The term *lessor* includes a motor carrier granting the use of a passenger-carrying commercial motor vehicle, with or without the driver, to another motor carrier under an interchange or other agreement, whether or not compensation for such use is specified. For a definition of *lessor* in the context of property-carrying vehicles, see §376.2 of this subchapter.

Medical examiner means an individual certified by FMCSA and listed on the National Registry of Certified Medical Examiners in accordance with subpart D of this part.

Medical variance means a driver has received one of the following from FMCSA that allows the driver to be issued a medical certificate:

(1) An exemption letter permitting operation of a commercial motor vehicle pursuant to part 381, subpart C, of this chapter or §391.64 of this chapter;

(2) A skill performance evaluation certificate permitting operation of a commercial motor vehicle pursuant to §391.49 of this chapter.

Mobile telephone means a mobile communication device that falls under or uses any commercial mobile radio service, as defined in regulations of the Federal Communications Commission, 47 CFR 20.3. It does not include two-way or Citizens Band Radio services.

Motor carrier means a for-hire motor carrier or a private motor carrier. The term includes a motor carrier's agents, officers and representatives as well as employees responsible for hiring, supervising, training, assigning, or dispatching of drivers and employees concerned with the installation, inspection, and maintenance of motor vehicle equipment and/or accessories. For purposes of subchapter B, this definition includes the terms **employer** and **exempt motor carrier**.

Motor vehicle means any vehicle, machine, tractor, trailer, or semitrailer propelled or drawn by mechanical power and used upon the highways in the transportation of passengers or property, or any combination thereof determined by the Federal Motor Carrier Safety Administration, but does not include any vehicle, locomotive, or car operated exclusively on a rail or rails, or a trolley bus operated by electric power derived from a fixed overhead wire, furnishing local passenger transportation similar to street-railway service.

Motor vehicle record means the report of the driving status and history of a driver generated from the driver record, provided to users, such as, drivers or employers, and subject to the provisions of the Driver Privacy Protection Act, 18 U.S.C. 2721–2725.

Multiple-employer driver means a driver, who in any period of 7 consecutive days, is employed or used as a driver by more than one motor carrier.

Operating authority means the registration required by 49 U.S.C. 13902, 49 CFR part 365, 49 CFR part 368, and 49 CFR 392.9a.

Operator—See driver.

Other terms—Any other term used in this subchapter is used in its commonly accepted meaning, except where such other term has been defined elsewhere in this subchapter. In that event, the definition therein given shall apply.

PART 390

Out-of-service order means a declaration by an authorized enforcement officer of a Federal, State, Canadian, Mexican, or local jurisdiction that a driver, a commercial motor vehicle, or a motor carrier operation is out of service pursuant to 49 CFR 386.72, 392.5, 392.9a, 395.13, or 396.9, or compatible laws, or the North American Standard Out-of-Service Criteria.

Person means any individual, partnership, association, corporation, business trust, or any other organized group of individuals.

Previous employer means any DOT regulated person who employed the driver in the preceding 3 years, including any possible current employer.

Principal place of business means the single location designated by the motor carrier, normally its headquarters, for purposes of identification under this subchapter. The motor carrier must make records required by parts 382, 387, 390, 391, 395, 396, and 397 of this subchapter available for inspection at this location within 48 hours (Saturdays, Sundays, and Federal holidays excluded) after a request has been made by a special agent or authorized representative of the Federal Motor Carrier Safety Administration.

Private motor carrier means a person who provides transportation of property or passengers, by commercial motor vehicle, and is not a for-hire motor carrier.

Private motor carrier of passengers (business) means a private motor carrier engaged in the interstate transportation of passengers which is provided in the furtherance of a commercial enterprise and is not available to the public at large.

Private motor carrier of passengers (nonbusiness) means private motor carrier involved in the interstate transportation of passengers that does not otherwise meet the definition of a private motor carrier of passengers (business).

Qualified VA examiner means an advanced practice nurse, doctor of chiropractic, doctor of medicine, doctor of osteopathy, physician assistant, or other medical professional who is employed in the Department of Veterans Affairs; is licensed, certified, or registered in a State to perform physical examinations; is familiar with the standards for, and physical requirements of, an operator certified pursuant to 49 U.S.C. 31149; and has never, with respect to such section, been found to have acted fraudulently, including by fraudulently awarding a medical certificate.

Radar detector means any device or mechanism to detect the emission of radio microwaves, laser beams or any other future speed measurement technology employed by enforcement personnel to measure the speed of commercial motor vehicles upon public roads and highways for enforcement purposes. Excluded from this definition are radar detection devices that meet both of the following requirements:

(1) Transported outside the driver's compartment of the commercial motor vehicle. For this purpose, the *driver's compartment* of a passenger-carrying CMV shall include all space designed to accommodate both the driver and the passengers; and

(2) Completely inaccessible to, inoperable by, and imperceptible to the driver while operating the commercial motor vehicle.

Receiver or **consignee** means a person who takes delivery from a motor carrier or driver of a commercial motor vehicle of property transported in interstate commerce or hazardous materials transported in interstate or intrastate commerce.

Regional Director of Motor Carriers means the Regional Field Administrator, for a given geographical area of the United States.

Residential district means the territory adjacent to and including a highway which is not a business district and for a distance of 300 feet or more along the highway is primarily improved with residences.

School bus means a passenger motor vehicle which is designed or used to carry more than 10 passengers in addition to the driver, and which the Secretary determines is likely to be significantly used for the purpose of transporting preprimary, primary, or secondary school students to such schools from home or from such schools to home.

School bus operation means the use of a school bus to transport only school children and/or school personnel from home to school and from school to home.

Secretary means the Secretary of Transportation.

Shipper means a person who tenders property to a motor carrier or driver of a commercial motor vehicle for transportation in interstate commerce, or who tenders hazardous materials to a motor carrier or driver of a commercial motor vehicle for transportation in interstate or intrastate commerce.

Single-employer driver means a driver who, in any period of 7 consecutive days, is employed or used as a driver solely by a single motor carrier. This term includes a driver who operates a commercial motor vehicle on an intermittent, casual, or occasional basis.

Special agent See Appendix B to Subchapter B—Special agents.

State means a State of the United States and the District of Columbia and includes a political subdivision of a State.

Texting means manually entering alphanumeric text into, or reading text from, an electronic device.

(1) This action includes, but is not limited to, short message service, emailing, instant messaging, a command or request to access a World Wide Web page, pressing more than a single button to initiate or terminate a voice communication using a mobile telephone, or engaging in any other form of electronic text retrieval or entry, for present or future communication.

(2) Texting does not include:

(i) Inputting, selecting, or reading information on a global positioning system or navigation system; or

(ii) Pressing a single button to initiate or terminate a voice communication using a mobile telephone; or

(iii) Using a device capable of performing multiple functions (*e.g.*, fleet management systems, dispatching devices, smart phones, citizens band radios, music players, *etc.*) for a purpose that is not otherwise prohibited in this subchapter.

Trailer includes:

(1) **Full trailer** means any motor vehicle other than a pole trailer which is designed to be drawn by another motor vehicle and so constructed that no part of its weight, except for the towing device, rests upon the self-propelled towing motor vehicle. A semitrailer equipped with an auxiliary front axle (converter dolly) shall be considered a full trailer.

(2) **Pole trailer** means any motor vehicle which is designed to be drawn by another motor vehicle and attached to the towing motor vehicle by means of a "reach" or "pole," or by being "boomed" or otherwise secured to the towing motor vehicle, for transporting long or irregularly shaped loads such as poles,

pipes, or structural members, which generally are capable of sustaining themselves as beams between the supporting connections.

(3) **Semitrailer** means any motor vehicle, other than a pole trailer, which is designed to be drawn by another motor vehicle and is constructed so that some part of its weight rests upon the self-propelled towing motor vehicle.

Transportation intermediary means a person who arranges the transportation of property or passengers by commercial motor vehicle in interstate commerce, or who arranges the transportation of hazardous materials by commercial motor vehicle in interstate or intrastate commerce, including but not limited to brokers and freight forwarders.

Truck means any self-propelled commercial motor vehicle except a truck tractor, designed and/or used for the transportation of property.

Truck tractor means a self-propelled commercial motor vehicle designed and/or used primarily for drawing other vehicles.

United States means the 50 States and the District of Columbia.

Use a hand-held mobile telephone means:

(1) Using at least one hand to hold a mobile telephone to conduct a voice communication;

(2) Dialing or answering a mobile telephone by pressing more than a single button, or

(3) Reaching for a mobile telephone in a manner that requires a driver to maneuver so that he or she is no longer in a seated driving position, restrained by a seat belt that is installed in accordance with 49 CFR 393.93 and adjusted in accordance with the vehicle manufacturer's instructions.

Veteran operator means an operator of a commercial motor vehicle who is a veteran enrolled in the health care system established under 38 U.S.C. 1705(a).

Written or in writing means printed, handwritten, or typewritten either on paper or other tangible medium, or by any method of electronic documentation that meets the requirements of 49 CFR 390.32.

§390.6 Coercion prohibited.

(a) **Prohibition**. (1) A motor carrier, shipper, receiver, or transportation intermediary, including their respective agents, officers, or representatives, may not coerce a driver of a commercial motor vehicle to operate such vehicle in violation of 49 CFR parts 171-173, 177-180, 380-383 or 390-399, or §§385.415 or 385.421;

(2) A motor carrier or its agents, officers, or representatives, may not coerce a driver of a commercial motor vehicle to operate such vehicle in violation of 49 CFR parts 356, 360, or 365-379.

(b) **Complaint process**. (1) A driver who believes he or she was coerced to violate a regulation described in paragraph (a)(1) or (2) of this section may file a written complaint under §386.12(c) of this subchapter.

(2) A complaint under paragraph (b)(1) of this section shall describe the action that the driver claims constitutes coercion and identify the regulation the driver was coerced to violate.

(3) A complaint under paragraph (b)(1) of this section may include any supporting evidence that will assist the Division Administrator in determining the merits of the complaint.

§390.7 Rules of construction.

(a) In Part 325 of Subchapter A and in this subchapter, unless the context requires otherwise:

(1) Words imparting the singular include the plural;

(2) Words imparting the plural include the singular;

(3) Words imparting the present tense include the future tense.

(b) In this subchapter the word—

(1) **Officer** includes any person authorized by law to perform the duties of the office;

(2) **Shall** is used in an imperative sense;

(3) **Must** is used in an imperative sense;

(4) **Should** is used in a recommendatory sense;

(5) **May** is used in a permissive sense; and

(6) **Includes** is used as a word of inclusion, not limitation.

§390.8 Separation of functions.

(a) An Agency employee who has taken an active part in investigating, prosecuting, advocating, or making an initial Agency determination in a proceeding under §380.723, §382.717, §390.115, §390.135, or §391.47 of this chapter or section 5.4 to appendix A to subpart B of part 395 of this chapter may not, in that case or a factually-related case, advise or assist the Agency official authorized to issue a final decision in the applicable proceeding.

(b) Nothing in this section shall preclude the Agency official authorized to issue a final decision or anyone advising that Agency official from taking part in a determination to launch an investigation or issue a complaint, or similar preliminary decision.

Subpart B—General Requirements and Information

§390.9 State and local laws, effect on.

Except as otherwise specifically indicated, Subchapter B of this chapter is not intended to preclude States or subdivisions thereof from establishing or enforcing State or local laws relating to safety, the compliance with which would not prevent full compliance with these regulations by the person subject thereto.

§390.11 Motor carrier to require observance of driver regulations.

Whenever in Part 325 of Subchapter A or in this subchapter a duty is prescribed for a driver or a prohibition is imposed upon the driver, it shall be the duty of the motor carrier to require observance of such duty or prohibition. If the motor carrier is a driver, the driver shall likewise be bound.

§390.13 Aiding or abetting violations.

No person shall aid, abet, encourage, or require a motor carrier or its employees to violate the rules of this chapter.

§390.15 Assistance in investigations and special studies.

(a) Each motor carrier and intermodal equipment provider must do the following:

(1) Make all records and information pertaining to an accident available to an authorized representative or special agent of the Federal Motor Carrier Safety

Administration, an authorized State or local enforcement agency representative, or authorized third party representative within such time as the request or investigation may specify.

(2) Give an authorized representative all reasonable assistance in the investigation of any accident, including providing a full, true, and correct response to any question of the inquiry.

(b) Motor carriers must maintain an accident register for 3 years after the date of each accident. Information placed in the accident register must contain at least the following:

(1) A list of accidents as defined at §390.5 of this chapter containing for each accident:

(i) Date of accident.

(ii) City or town, or most near, where the accident occurred and the State where the accident occurred.

(iii) Driver Name.

(iv) Number of injuries.

(v) Number of fatalities.

(vi) Whether hazardous materials, other than fuel spilled from the fuel tanks of motor vehicle involved in the accident, were released.

(2) Copies of all accident reports required by State or other governmental entities or insurers.

(Approved by the Office of Management and Budget under control number 2126-0009)

§390.16 [Reserved]

§390.17 Additional equipment and accessories.

Nothing in this subchapter shall be construed to prohibit the use of additional equipment and accessories, not inconsistent with or prohibited by this subchapter, provided such equipment and accessories do not decrease the safety of operation of the commercial motor vehicles on which they are used.

§390.19T Motor carrier, hazardous material safety permit applicant/ holder, and intermodal equipment provider identification reports.

(a) **Applicability.** Each motor carrier and intermodal equipment provider must file Form MCS-150, Form MCS-150B or Form MCS-150C with FMCSA as follows:

(1) A U.S.-, Canada-, Mexico-, or non-North America-domiciled motor carrier conducting operations in interstate commerce must file a Motor Carrier Identification Report, Form MCS-150.

(2) A motor carrier conducting operations in intrastate commerce and requiring a Safety Permit under 49 CFR part 385, subpart E, must file the Combined Motor Carrier Identification Report and HM Permit Application, Form MCS-150B.

(3) Each intermodal equipment provider that offers intermodal equipment for transportation in interstate commerce must file an Intermodal Equipment Provider Identification Report, Form MCS-150C.

(b) **Filing schedule.** Each motor carrier or intermodal equipment provider must file the appropriate form under paragraph (a) of this section at the following times:

(1) Before it begins operations; and

(2) Every 24 months, according to the following schedule:

USDOT No. ending in	Must file by last day of
1.	January.
2.	February.
3.	March.
4.	April.
5.	May.
6.	June.
7.	July.
8.	August.
9.	September.
0.	October.

(3) If the next-to-last digit of its USDOT Number is odd, the motor carrier or intermodal equipment provider shall file its update in every odd-numbered calendar year. If the next-to-last digit of the USDOT Number is even, the motor carrier or intermodal equipment provider shall file its update in every even-numbered calendar year.

(4) A person that fails to complete biennial updates to the information pursuant to paragraph (b)(2) of this section is subject to the penalties prescribed in 49 U.S.C. 521(b)(2)(B) or 49 U.S.C. 14901(a), as appropriate, and deactivation of its USDOT Number.

(c) **Availability of forms.** The forms described under paragraph (a) of this section and complete instructions are available from the FMCSA Web site at *http://www.fmcsa.dot.gov* (Keyword "MCS-150," or "MCS-150B," or "MCS-150C"); from all FMCSA Service Centers and Division offices nationwide; or by calling 1-800-832-5660.

(d) **Where to file.** The required form under paragraph (a) of this section must be filed with the FMCSA Office of Registration and Safety Information. The form may be filed electronically according to the instructions at the Agency's Web site, or it may be sent to Federal Motor Carrier Safety Administration, Office of Registration and Safety Information (MC-RS), 1200 New Jersey Avenue SE., Washington, DC 20590.

(e) **Special instructions for for-hire motor carriers.** A for-hire motor carrier should submit the Form MCS-150, or Form MCS-150B, along with its application for operating authority (Form OP-1, OP-1(MX), OP-1(NNA) or OP-2), to the appropriate address referenced on that form, or may submit it electronically or by mail separately to the address mentioned in paragraph (d) of this section.

(f) Only the legal name or a single trade name of the motor carrier or intermodal equipment provider may be used on the forms under paragraph (a) of this section (Form MCS-150, MCS-150B, or MCS-150C).

(g) A motor carrier or intermodal equipment provider that fails to file the form required under paragraph (a) of this section, or furnishes misleading information or makes false statements upon the form, is subject to the penalties prescribed in 49 U.S.C. 521(b)(2)(B).

(h)(1) Upon receipt and processing of the form described in paragraph (a) of this section, FMCSA will issue the motor carrier or intermodal equipment provider an identification number (USDOT Number).

(2) The following applicants must additionally pass a pre-authorization safety audit as described below before being issued a USDOT Number:

(i) A Mexico-domiciled motor carrier seeking to provide transportation of property or passengers in interstate commerce between Mexico and points in the United States beyond the municipalities and commercial zones along the United States-Mexico international border must pass the pre-authorization safety audit under §365.507T of this subchapter. The Agency will not issue a USDOT Number until expiration of the protest period provided in §365.115 of this subchapter or—if a protest is received—after FMCSA denies or rejects the protest.

(ii) A non-North America-domiciled motor carrier seeking to provide transportation of property or passengers in interstate commerce within the United States must pass the pre-authorization safety audit under §385.607T(c) of this subchapter. The Agency will not issue a USDOT Number until expiration of the protest period provided in §365.115 of this subchapter or—if a protest is received—after FMCSA denies or rejects the protest.

(3) The motor carrier must display the number on each self-propelled CMV, as defined in §390.5T, along with the additional information required by §390.21T.

(4) The intermodal equipment provider must identify each unit of interchanged intermodal equipment by its assigned USDOT number.

(i) A motor carrier that registers its vehicles in a State that participates in the Performance and Registration Information Systems Management (PRISM) program (authorized under section 4004 of the Transportation Equity Act for the 21st Century [Public Law 105-178, 112 Stat. 107]) is exempt from the requirements of this section, provided it files all the required information with the appropriate State office.

§390.19 Motor carrier identification reports for certain Mexico-domiciled motor carriers. [Suspended]

(a) **Applicability**. A Mexico-domiciled motor carrier requesting authority to provide transportation of property or passengers in interstate commerce between Mexico and points in the United States beyond the municipalities and commercial zones along the United States-Mexico international border must file Form MCS-150 with FMCSA as follows:

(b) **Filing schedule**. Each motor carrier must file the appropriate form under paragraph (a) of this section at the following times:

(1) Before it begins operations; and

(2) Every 24 months, according to the following schedule:

USDOT No. ending in	Must file by last day of
1	January.
2	February.
3	March.
4	April.
5	May.
6	June.
7	July.
8	August.
9	September.
0	October.

(3) If the next-to-last digit of its USDOT Number is odd, the motor carrier shall file its update in every odd-numbered calendar year. If the next-to-last digit of the USDOT Number is even, the motor carrier shall file its update in every even-numbered calendar year.

(4) A person that fails to complete biennial updates to the information pursuant to paragraph (b)(2) of this section is subject to the penalties prescribed in 49 U.S.C. 521(b)(2)(B) or 49 U.S.C. 14901(a), as appropriate, and deactivation of its USDOT Number.

(c) **Availability of forms**. The Form MCS-150 and complete instructions are available from the FMCSA Web site at *http://www.fmcsa.dot.gov/urs;* from all FMCSA Service Centers and Division offices nationwide; or by calling 1-800-832-5660.

(d) **Where to file**. The Form MCS-150 must be filed with the FMCSA Office of Registration and Safety Information. The form may be filed electronically according to the instructions at the Agency's Web site, or it may be sent to Federal Motor Carrier Safety Administration, Office of Registration and Safety Information, MC-RS 1200 New Jersey Avenue SE., Washington, DC 20590.

(e) **Special instructions**. A motor carrier should submit the Form MCS-150 along with its application for operating authority (OP-1(MX)), to the appropriate address referenced on that form, or may submit it electronically or by mail separately to the address mentioned in paragraph (d) of this section.

(f) Only the legal name or a single trade name of the motor carrier may be used on the Form MCS-150.

(g)(1) A motor carrier that fails to file the Form MCS-150 or furnishes misleading information or makes false statements upon the form, is subject to the penalties prescribed in 49 U.S.C. 521(b)(2)(B).

(2) A motor carrier that fails to update the Form MCS-150 as required in paragraph (b) will have its USDOT Number deactivated and will be prohibited from conducting transportation.

(h)(1) Upon receipt and processing of the form described in paragraph (a) of this section, FMCSA will issue the motor carrier or intermodal equipment provider an identification number (USDOT Number).

(2) A Mexico-domiciled motor carrier seeking to provide transportation of property or passengers in interstate commerce between Mexico and points in the United States beyond the municipalities and commercial zones along the United States-Mexico international border must pass the pre-authorization safety audit under §365.507 of this subchapter. The Agency will not issue a USDOT Number until expiration of the protest period provided in §365.115 of this chapter or—if a protest is received–after FMCSA denies or rejects the protest.

(3) The motor carrier must display the USDOT Number on each self-propelled CMV, as defined in §390.5, along with the additional information required by §390.21.

§390.21T Marking of self-propelled CMVs and intermodal equipment.

(a) **General**. Every self-propelled CMV subject to this subchapter must be marked as specified in paragraphs (b), (c), and (d) of this section, and each unit of intermodal equipment interchanged or offered for interchange to a motor carrier by an intermodal equipment provider subject to this subchapter must be marked as specified in paragraph (g) of this section.

(b) **Nature of marking**. The marking must display the following information:

(1) The legal name or a single trade name of the motor carrier operating the self-propelled CMV, as listed on the motor carrier identification report (Form MCS-150) and submitted in accordance with §390.19T.

(2) The identification number issued by FMCSA to the motor carrier or intermodal equipment provider, preceded by the letters "USDOT."

(3) If the name of any person other than the operating carrier appears on the CMV, the name of the operating carrier must be followed by the information required by paragraphs (b)(1) and (2) of this section, and be preceded by the words "operated by."

(4) Other identifying information may be displayed on the vehicle if it is not inconsistent with the information required by this paragraph (b).

(c) **Size, shape, location, and color of marking**. The marking must—

(1) Appear on both sides of the self-propelled CMV;

(2) Be in letters that contrast sharply in color with the background on which the letters are placed;

(3) Be readily legible, during daylight hours, from a distance of 50 feet (15.24 meters) while the CMV is stationary; and

(4) Be kept and maintained in a manner that retains the legibility required by paragraph (c)(3) of this section.

(d) **Construction and durability**. The marking may be painted on the CMV or may consist of a removable device, if that device meets the identification and legibility requirements of paragraph (c) of this section, and such marking must be maintained as required by paragraph (c)(4) of this section.

(e) **Rented CMVs and leased passenger-carrying CMVs.** A motor carrier operating a self-propelled CMV under a rental agreement or a passenger-carrying CMV under a lease, when the rental agreement or lease has a term not in excess of 30 calendar days, meets the requirements of this section if:

(1) The CMV is marked in accordance with the provisions of paragraphs (b) through (d) of this section; or

(2) Except as provided in paragraph (e)(2)(v) of this section, the CMV is marked as set forth in paragraph (e)(2)(i) through (iv) of this section:

(i) The legal name or a single trade name of the lessor is displayed in accordance with paragraphs (c) and (d) of this section.

(ii) The lessor's identification number preceded by the letters "USDOT" is displayed in accordance with paragraphs (c) and (d) of this section; and

(iii) The rental agreement or lease as applicable entered into by the lessor and the renting motor carrier or lessee conspicuously contains the following information:

(A) The name and complete physical address of the principal place of business of the renting motor carrier or lessee;

(B) The identification number issued to the renting motor carrier or lessee by FMCSA, preceded by the letters "USDOT," if the motor carrier has been issued such a number. In lieu of the identification number required in this paragraph, the following information may be shown in a rental agreement:

(*1*) Whether the motor carrier is engaged in "interstate" or "intrastate" commerce; and

(*2*) Whether the renting motor carrier or lessee is transporting hazardous materials in the rented or leased CMV;

(C) The sentence: "This lessor cooperates with all Federal, State, and local law enforcement officials nationwide to provide the identity of customers who operate this rental or leased CMV"; and

(iv) The rental agreement or lease as applicable entered into by the lessor and the renting motor carrier or lessee is carried on the rental CMV or leased passenger-carrying CMV during the full term of the rental agreement or lease. See the property-carrying leasing regulations at 49 CFR part 376 and the passenger-carrying leasing regulations at subpart G of this part for information that should be included in all leasing documents.

(v) *Exception.* (A) A passenger-carrying CMV operating under the 48-hour emergency exception pursuant to §390.403(a)(2) of this part does not need to comply with paragraphs (e)(2)(iii) and (iv) of this section, provided the lessor and lessee comply with the requirements of §390.403(a)(2).

(B) A motor carrier operating a self-propelled CMV under a lease subject to subpart G of this part (§§390.401 and 390.403) must begin complying with this paragraph (e) on January 1, 2021.

(f) **Driveaway services**. In driveaway services, a removable device may be affixed on both sides or at the rear of a single driven vehicle. In a combination driveaway operation, the device may be affixed on both sides of any one unit or at the rear of the last unit. The removable device must display the legal name or a single trade name of the motor carrier and the motor carrier's USDOT number.

(g) **Intermodal equipment**. (1) The requirements for marking intermodal equipment apply to each intermodal equipment provider, as defined in §390.5T, that interchanges or offers for interchange intermodal equipment to a motor carrier.

(2) Each unit of intermodal equipment interchanged or offered for interchange to a motor carrier by an intermodal equipment provider subject to this subchapter must identify the intermodal equipment provider.

(3) The intermodal equipment provider must be identified by its legal name or a single trade name and the identification number issued by FMCSA, preceded by the letters "USDOT."

(4) The intermodal equipment must be identified as follows, using any one of the following methods:

(i) The identification marking must appear on the curb side of the item of equipment. It must be in letters that contrast sharply in color with the background on which the letters are placed. The letters must be readily legible, during daylight hours, from a distance of 50 feet (15.24 meters) while the CMV is stationary; and be kept and maintained in a manner that retains this legibility; or

(ii) The identification marking must appear on a label placed upon the curb side of the item of equipment. The label must be readily visible and legible to an inspection official during daylight hours when the vehicle is stationary. The label must be a color that contrasts sharply with the background on which it is placed, and the letters must also contrast sharply in color with the background of the label. The label must be kept and maintained in a manner that retains this legibility; or

(iii) The USDOT number of the intermodal equipment provider must appear on the interchange agreement so that it is clearly identifiable to an inspection official. The interchange agreement must include additional information to identify the specific item of intermodal equipment (such as the Vehicle Identification Number (VIN) and 4-character Standard Carrier Alpha Code (SCAC) code and 6-digit unique identifying number); or

(iv) The identification marking must be shown on a document placed in a weathertight compartment affixed to the frame of the item of intermodal equipment. The color of the letters used in the document must contrast sharply in color with the background of the document. The document must include additional information to identify the specific item of intermodal equipment (such as the VIN and 4-character SCAC code and 6-digit unique identifying number).

(v) The USDOT number of the intermodal equipment provider is maintained in a database that is available via real-time internet and telephonic access. The database must:

(A) Identify the name and USDOT number of the intermodal equipment provider responsible for the intermodal equipment, in response to an inquiry that includes:

(*i*) SCAC plus trailing digits; or

(*ii*) License plate number and State of license; or

(*iii*) VIN of the item of intermodal equipment.

(B) Offer read-only access for inquiries on individual items of intermodal equipment, without requiring advance user registration, a password, or a usage fee.

§390.21 Marking of self-propelled CMVs and intermodal equipment. [Suspended]

(a) **General**. Every self-propelled CMV subject to subchapter B of this chapter must be marked as specified in paragraphs (b), (c), and (d) of this section, and each unit of intermodal equipment interchanged or offered for interchange to a motor carrier by an intermodal equipment provider subject to subchapter B of this chapter must be marked as specified in paragraph (g) of this section.

(b) **Nature of marking**. The marking must display the following information:

(1) The legal name or a single trade name of the motor carrier operating the self-propelled CMV, as listed on the Form MCSA-1, the URS online application, or the motor carrier identification report (Form MCS-150) and submitted in accordance with §390.201 or §390.19, as appropriate.

(2) The identification number issued by FMCSA to the motor carrier or intermodal equipment provider, preceded by the letters "USDOT."

(3) If the name of any person other than the operating carrier appears on the CMV, the name of the operating carrier must be followed by the information required by paragraphs (b)(1), and (2) of this section, and be preceded by the words "operated by."

(4) Other identifying information may be displayed on the vehicle if it is not inconsistent with the information required by this paragraph.

(c) **Size, shape, location, and color of marking**. The marking must—

(1) Appear on both sides of the self-propelled CMV;

(2) Be in letters that contrast sharply in color with the background on which the letters are placed;

(3) Be readily legible, during daylight hours, from a distance of 50 feet (15.24 meters) while the CMV is stationary; and

(4) Be kept and maintained in a manner that retains the legibility required by paragraph (c)(3) of this section.

(d) **Construction and durability**. The marking may be painted on the CMV or may consist of a removable device, if that device meets the identification and legibility requirements of paragraph (c) of this section, and such marking must be maintained as required by paragraph (c)(4) of this section.

§390.21

(e) **Rented CMVs and leased passenger-carrying CMVs.** A motor carrier operating a self-propelled CMV under a rental agreement or a passenger-carrying CMV under a lease, when the rental agreement or lease has a term not in excess of 30 calendar days, meets the requirements of this section if:

(1) The CMV is marked in accordance with the provisions of paragraphs (b) through (d) of this section; or

(2) Except as provided in paragraph (e)(2)(v) of this section, the CMV is marked as set forth in paragraph (e)(2)(i) through (iv) of this section:

(i) The legal name or a single trade name of the lessor is displayed in accordance with paragraphs (c) and (d) of this section.

(ii) The lessor's identification number preceded by the letters "USDOT" is displayed in accordance with paragraphs (c) and (d) of this section; and

(iii) The rental agreement or lease as applicable entered into by the lessor and the renting motor carrier or lessee conspicuously contains the following information:

(A) The name and complete physical address of the principal place of business of the renting motor carrier or lessee;

(B) The identification number issued to the renting motor carrier or lessee by FMCSA, preceded by the letters "USDOT," if the motor carrier has been issued such a number. In lieu of the identification number required in this paragraph, the following information may be shown in a rental agreement:

(1) Whether the motor carrier is engaged in "interstate" or "intrastate" commerce; and

(2) Whether the renting motor carrier is transporting hazardous materials in the rented CMV;

(C) The sentence: "This lessor cooperates with all Federal, State, and local law enforcement officials nationwide to provide the identity of customers who operate this rental CMV"; and

(iv) The rental agreement or lease as applicable entered into by the lessor and the renting motor carrier or lessee is carried on the rental CMV or leased passenger-carrying CMV during the full term of the rental agreement or lease. See the property-carrying leasing regulations at 49 CFR part 376 and the passenger-carrying leasing regulations at subpart G of this part for information that should be included in all leasing documents.

(v) *Exception.* (A) The passenger-carrying CMV operating under the 48-hour emergency exception pursuant to §390.403(a)(2) of this part does not need to comply with paragraphs (e)(2)(iii) and (iv) of this section, provided the lessor and lessee comply with the requirements of §390.403(a)(2).

(B) A motor carrier operating a self-propelled CMV under a lease subject to subpart G of this part (§§390.401 and 390.403) must begin complying with this paragraph (e) on January 1, 2021.

(f) **Driveaway services.** In driveaway services, a removable device may be affixed on both sides or at the rear of a single driven vehicle. In a combination driveaway operation, the device may be affixed on both sides of any one unit or at the rear of the last unit. The removable device must display the legal name or a single trade name of the motor carrier and the motor carrier's USDOT number.

(g) **Intermodal equipment.** (1) The requirements for marking intermodal equipment apply to each intermodal equipment provider, as defined in §390.5, that interchanges or offers for interchange intermodal equipment to a motor carrier.

PART 390

-339-

(2) Each unit of intermodal equipment interchanged or offered for interchange to a motor carrier by an intermodal equipment provider subject to subchapter B of this chapter must identify the intermodal equipment provider.

(3) The intermodal equipment provider must be identified by its legal name or a single trade name and the identification number issued by FMCSA, preceded by the letters "USDOT."

(4) The intermodal equipment must be identified as follows, using any one of the following methods:

(i) The identification marking must appear on the curb side of the item of equipment. It must be in letters that contrast sharply in color with the background on which the letters are placed. The letters must be readily legible, during daylight hours, from a distance of 50 feet (15.24 meters) while the CMV is stationary; and be kept and maintained in a manner that retains this legibility; or

(ii) The identification marking must appear on a label placed upon the curb side of the item of equipment. The label must be readily visible and legible to an inspection official during daylight hours when the vehicle is stationary. The label must be a color that contrasts sharply with the background on which it is placed, and the letters must also contrast sharply in color with the background of the label. The label must be kept and maintained in a manner that retains this legibility; or

(iii) The USDOT number of the intermodal equipment provider must appear on the interchange agreement so that it is clearly identifiable to an inspection official. The interchange agreement must include additional information to identify the specific item of intermodal equipment (such as the Vehicle Identification Number (VIN) and 4-character Standard Carrier Alpha Code (SCAC) and 6-digit unique identifying number); or

(iv) The identification marking must be shown on a document placed in a weathertight compartment affixed to the frame of the item of intermodal equipment. The color of the letters used in the document must contrast sharply in color with the background of the document. The document must include additional information to identify the specific item of intermodal equipment (such as the VIN and 4-character SCAC code and 6-digit unique identifying number).

(v) The USDOT number of the intermodal equipment provider is maintained in a database that is available via real-time internet and telephonic access. The database must:

(A) Identify the name and USDOT number of the intermodal equipment provider responsible for the intermodal equipment, in response to an inquiry that includes:

(i) SCAC plus trailing digits, or

(ii) License plate number and State of license, or

(iii) VIN of the item of intermodal equipment.

(B) Offer read-only access for inquiries on individual items of intermodal equipment, without requiring advance user registration, a password, or a usage fee.

§390.23 Relief from regulations.

(a) Parts 390 through 399 of this chapter shall not apply to any motor carrier or driver operating a commercial motor vehicle to provide emergency relief during an emergency, subject to the following time limits:

(1) **Regional emergencies**.

(i) The exemption provided by paragraph (a)(1) of this section is effective only when:

(A) An emergency has been declared by the President of the United States, the Governor of a State, or their authorized representatives having authority to declare emergencies; or

(B) FMCSA has declared that a regional emergency exists which justifies an exemption from parts 390 through 399 of this chapter.

(ii)(A) Except as provided in paragraph (a)(1)(ii)(B) of this section and §390.25, the exemption shall not exceed the duration of the motor carrier's or driver's direct assistance in providing emergency relief, or 30 days from the date of the initial declaration of the emergency or the exemption from the regulations by FMCSA, whichever is less.

(B) If a Governor who declares an emergency caused by a shortage of residential heating fuel (namely heating oil, natural gas, and propane), subsequently determines at the end of the 30-day period immediately following the declaration that the emergency shortage has not ended, and extends the declaration of an emergency for up to 2 additional 30-day periods, this exemption shall remain in effect up to the end of such additional periods, not to exceed 60 additional days, for a motor carrier or driver providing residential heating fuel in the geographic area designated by the Governor's declaration of emergency.

(2) **Local emergencies**.

(i) The exemption provided by paragraph (a)(2) of this section is effective only when:

(A) An emergency has been declared by a Federal, State, or local government official having authority to declare an emergency; or

(B) FMCSA has declared that a local emergency exists which justifies an exemption from parts 390 through 399 of this chapter.

(ii) This exemption shall not exceed the duration of the motor carrier's or driver's direct assistance in providing emergency relief, or 5 days from the date of the initial declaration of the emergency or the exemption from the regulations by FMCSA, whichever is less.

(3) **Tow Trucks responding to emergencies**.

(i) The exemption provided by paragraph (a)(3) of this section is effective only when a request has been made by a Federal, State or local police officer for tow trucks to move wrecked or disabled motor vehicles.

(ii) This exemption shall not exceed the length of the motor carrier's or driver's direct assistance in providing emergency relief, or 24 hours from the time of the initial request for assistance by the Federal, State or local police officer, whichever is less.

(b) Upon termination of direct assistance to the regional or local emergency relief effort, the motor carrier or driver is subject to the requirements of parts 390 through 399 of this chapter, with the following exception: A driver may return empty to the motor carrier's terminal or the driver's normal work reporting location without complying with parts 390 through 399 of this chapter. However, a driver who informs the motor carrier that he or she needs immediate rest must be permitted at least 10 consecutive hours off duty before the driver is required to return to such terminal or location. Having returned to the terminal or other location, the driver must be relieved of all duty and responsibilities. Direct assistance terminates when a driver or commercial motor vehicle is used in interstate commerce to transport cargo not destined for the emergency relief effort, or when the motor carrier dispatches such driver or commercial motor vehicle to another location to begin operations in commerce.

(c) When the driver has been relieved of all duty and responsibilities upon termination of direct assistance to a regional or local emergency relief effort, no motor carrier shall permit or require any driver used by it to drive nor shall any such driver drive in commerce until the driver has met the requirements of §§395.3(a) and (c) and 395.5(a) of this chapter.

§390.25 Extension of relief from regulations—emergencies.

FMCSA may extend the 30-day time period of the exemption contained in §390.23(a)(1), but not the 5-day time period contained in §390.23(a)(2) or the 24-hour period contained in §390.23(a)(3). Any motor carrier or driver seeking to extend the 30-day limit shall obtain approval from FMCSA in the region in which the motor carrier's principal place of business is located before the expiration of the 30-day period. The motor carrier or driver shall give full details of the additional relief requested. FMCSA shall determine if such relief is necessary taking into account both the severity of the ongoing emergency and the nature of the relief services to be provided by the carrier or driver. If FMCSA approves an extension of the exemption, he or she shall establish a new time limit and place on the motor carrier or driver any other restrictions deemed necessary.

§390.27 Locations of motor carrier safety service centers.

Service center	Territory included	Location of office
Eastern........	Connecticut, Delaware, District of Columbia, Maine, Maryland, Massachusetts, New Hampshire, New Jersey, New York, Pennsylvania, Puerto Rico, Rhode Island, United States Virgin Islands, Vermont, Virginia, West Virginia	31 Hopkins Plaza, Suite 800, Baltimore, Maryland 21201.
Midwestern...	Illinois, Indiana, Iowa, Kansas, Michigan, Minnesota, Missouri, Nebraska, Ohio, Wisconsin	4749 Lincoln Mall Drive, Suite 300A, Matteson, Illinois 60443.
Southern	Alabama, Arkansas, Florida, Georgia, Kentucky, Louisiana, Mississippi, North Carolina, Oklahoma, South Carolina, Tennessee	1800 Century Boulevard, Suite 1700, Atlanta, Georgia 30345-3220.
Western	Alaska, American Samoa, Arizona, California, Colorado, Guam, Hawaii, Idaho, Mariana Islands, Montana, Nevada, New Mexico, North Dakota, Oregon, South Dakota, Texas, Utah, Washington, Wyoming	12600 West Colfax Avenue, Suite B-300, Lakewood, Colorado 80215.

Note 1: Canadian carriers—for information regarding proper service center, contact an FMCSA division (State) office in Alaska, Maine, Michigan, Montana, New York, North Dakota, Vermont, or Washington.

Note 2: Mexican carriers are handled through the four southern border divisions and the Western Service Center. For information regarding the proper service center, contact an FMCSA division (State) office in Arizona, California, New Mexico, or Texas.

§390.29 Location of records or documents.

(a) A motor carrier with multiple offices or terminals may maintain the records and documents required by this subchapter at its principal place of business, a regional office, or driver work-reporting location unless otherwise specified in this subchapter.

(b) All records and documents required by this subchapter which are maintained at a regional office or driver work-reporting location shall be made available for inspection upon request by a special agent or authorized representative of the Federal Motor Carrier Safety Administration at the motor carrier's principal place of business or other location specified by the agent or representative within 48 hours after a request is made. Saturdays, Sundays, and Federal holidays are excluded from the computation of the 48-hour period of time.

§390.31 Copies of records and documents.

All records and documents required to be maintained under this subchapter must be maintained for the periods specified. Except as otherwise provided, copies that are legible and accurately reflect the information required to be contained in the record or document may be maintained in lieu of originals.

§390.32 Electronic documents and signatures.

(a) **Applicability.** This section applies to documents that entities or individuals are required to retain, regardless of whether FMCSA subsequently requires them to be produced or displayed to FMCSA staff or other parties entitled to access. This section does not apply to documents that must be submitted directly to FMCSA.

(b) **Electronic records or documents.** Any person or entity required to generate, maintain, or exchange documents to satisfy requirements in chapter III of subtitle B of title 49, Code of Federal Regulations (49 CFR 300-399) may use electronic methods to satisfy those requirements.

(c) **Electronic signatures.** (1) Any person or entity required to sign or certify a document to satisfy the requirements of chapter III of subtitle B of title 49, Code of Federal Regulations (49 CFR parts 300-399) may use an electronic signature, as defined in §390.5T of this part.

(2) An electronic signature may be made using any available technology that otherwise satisfies FMCSA's requirements.

(d) **Requirements.** Any person or entity may use documents signed, certified, generated, maintained, or exchanged using electronic methods if the documents accurately reflect the information otherwise required to be contained in them. Records, documents or signatures generated, maintained, or exchanged using electronic methods do not satisfy the requirements of this section if they are not capable of being retained, are not used for the purpose for which they were created, or cannot be accurately reproduced within required timeframes for reference by any party entitled to access. Records or documents generated electronically do not satisfy the requirements of this section if they do not include proof of consent to use electronically generated records or documents, as required by 15 U.S.C. 7001(c).

§390.33 Commercial motor vehicles used for purposes other than defined.

Whenever a commercial motor vehicle of one type is used to perform the functions normally performed by a commercial motor vehicle of another type, the requirements of this subchapter and Part 325 of Subchapter A shall apply to the commercial motor vehicle and to its operation in the same manner as though the commercial motor vehicle were actually a commercial motor vehicle of the latter type.

Example: If a commercial motor vehicle other than a bus is used to perform the functions normally performed by a bus, the regulations pertaining to buses and to the transportation of passengers shall apply to that commercial motor vehicle.

§390.35 Certificates, reports, and records: falsification, reproduction, or alteration.

No motor carrier, its agents, officers, representatives, or employees shall make or cause to make—

(a) A fraudulent or intentionally false statement on any application, certificate, report, or record required by Part 325 of subchapter A or this subchapter;

(b) A fraudulent or intentionally false entry on any application, certificate, report, or record required to be used, completed, or retained, to comply with any requirement of this subchapter or Part 325 of Subchapter A; or

(c) A reproduction, for fraudulent purposes, of any application, certificate, report, or record required by this subchapter or Part 325 of Subchapter A.

§390.36 Harassment of drivers prohibited.

(a) **Harass or harassment defined.** As used in this section, harass or harassment means an action by a motor carrier toward a driver employed by the motor carrier (including an independent contractor while in the course of operating a commercial motor vehicle on behalf of the motor carrier) involving the use of information available to the motor carrier through an ELD, as defined in §395.2 of this chapter, or through other technology used in combination with and not separable from the ELD, that the motor carrier knew, or should have known, would result in the driver violating §392.3 or part 395 of this subchapter.

(b) **Prohibition against harassment.** (1) No motor carrier may harass a driver.

(2) Nothing in paragraph (b)(1) of this section shall be construed to prevent a motor carrier from using technology allowed under this subchapter to monitor productivity of a driver provided that such monitoring does not result in harassment.

(c) **Complaint process.** A driver who believes he or she was the subject of harassment by a motor carrier may file a written complaint under §386.12(b) of this subchapter.

§390.37 Violation and penalty.

Any person who violates the rules set forth in this subchapter or Part 325 of Subchapter A may be subject to civil or criminal penalties.

§390.38 Exemptions for pipeline welding trucks.

(a) **Federal requirements**. A pipeline welding truck, as defined in paragraph (b) of this section, including the individuals operating such vehicle and the employer of such individual, is exempt from the following:

(1) Any requirement relating to registration as a motor carrier, including the requirement to obtain and display a Department of Transportation number, in 49 CFR part 365 or 390.

(2) Any requirement relating to driver qualifications in 49 CFR part 391.

(3) Any requirement relating to driving of commercial motor vehicles in 49 CFR part 392.

(4) Any requirement relating to parts and accessories and inspection, repair, and maintenance of commercial motor vehicles in 49 CFR parts 393 and 396.

(5) Any requirement relating to hours of service of drivers, including maximum driving and on duty time, found in 49 CFR part 395.

(b) **Definition**. "Pipeline welding truck" means a motor vehicle that is travelling in the State in which the vehicle is registered or another State, is owned by a welder, is a pick-up style truck, is equipped with a welding rig that is used in the construction or maintenance of pipelines, and has a gross vehicle weight and combination weight rating and weight of 15,000 pounds or less.

§390.39 Exemptions for "covered farm vehicles."

(a) **Federal requirements**. A covered farm vehicle, as defined in §390.5, including the individual operating that vehicle, is exempt from the following:

(1) Any requirement relating to commercial driver's licenses in 49 CFR Part 383 or controlled substances and alcohol use and testing in 49 CFR Part 382;

(2) Any requirement in 49 CFR Part 391, Subpart E, Physical Qualifications and Examinations.

(3) Any requirement in 49 CFR Part 395, Hours of Service of Drivers.

(4) Any requirement in 49 CFR Part 396, Inspection, Repair, and Maintenance.

(b) **State requirements**—(1) **In general**. Federal transportation funding to a State may not be terminated, limited, or otherwise interfered with as a result of the State exempting a covered farm vehicle, including the individual operating that vehicle, from—

(i) A requirement described in paragraph (a) of this section; or

(ii) Any other minimum standard provided by a State relating to the operation of that vehicle.

(2) **Exception**.—Paragraph (b)(1) of this section does not apply with respect to a covered farm vehicle transporting hazardous materials that require a placard.

(c) **Other exemptions and exceptions**.—The exemptions in paragraphs (a) and (b) of this section are in addition to, not in place of, the agricultural exemptions and exceptions in §§383.3(d)(1), 383.3(e), 383.3(f), 391.2(a), 391.2(b), 391.2(c), 391.67, 395.1(e)(1), 395.1(e)(2), 395.1(h), 395.1(i), and 395.1(k) of this chapter. Motor carriers and drivers may utilize any combination of these exemptions and exceptions, providing they comply fully with each separate exemption and exception.

Subpart C—Requirements and Information for Intermodal Equipment Providers and for Motor Carriers Operating Intermodal Equipment

§390.40T What responsibilities do intermodal equipment providers have under the Federal Motor Carrier Safety Regulations (49 CFR parts 350–399)?

An intermodal equipment provider must—

(a) Identify its operations to the FMCSA by filing the Form MCS-150C required by §390.19T.

(b) Mark its intermodal equipment with the USDOT number as required by §390.21T before tendering the equipment to a motor carrier.

(c) Systematically inspect, repair, and maintain, or cause to be systematically inspected, repaired, and maintained, in a manner consistent with §396.3(a)(1) of this chapter, as applicable, all intermodal equipment intended for interchange with a motor carrier.

(d) Provide intermodal equipment intended for interchange that is in safe and proper operating condition.

(e) Maintain a system of driver vehicle inspection reports submitted to the intermodal equipment provider as required by §396.11 of this chapter.

(f) Maintain a system of inspection, repair, and maintenance records as required by §396.3(b)(3) of this chapter for equipment intended for interchange with a motor carrier.

(g) Periodically inspect equipment intended for interchange, as required under §396.17 of this chapter.

(h) At facilities at which the intermodal equipment provider makes intermodal equipment available for interchange, have procedures in place, and provide sufficient space, for drivers to perform a pre-trip inspection of tendered intermodal equipment.

(i) At facilities at which the intermodal equipment provider makes intermodal equipment available for interchange, develop and implement procedures to repair any equipment damage, defects, or deficiencies identified as part of a pre-trip inspection, or replace the equipment, prior to the driver's departure. The repairs or replacement must be made after being notified by a driver of such damage, defects, or deficiencies.

(j) Refrain from placing intermodal equipment in service on the public highways if that equipment has been found to pose an imminent hazard, as defined in §386.72(b)(3) of this chapter.

§390.40 What responsibilities do intermodal equipment providers have under the Federal Motor Carrier Safety Regulations (49 CFR parts 350–399)? [Suspended]

An intermodal equipment provider must—

(a) Identify its operations to the FMCSA by filing the Form MCSA-1 required by §390.201

(b) Mark its intermodal equipment with the USDOT number as required by §390.21 before tendering the equipment to a motor carrier.

(c) Systematically inspect, repair, and maintain, or cause to be systematically inspected, repaired, and maintained, in a manner consistent with §396.3(a)(1), as applicable, all intermodal equipment intended for interchange with a motor carrier.

(d) Provide intermodal equipment intended for interchange that is in safe and proper operating condition.

(e) Maintain a system of driver vehicle inspection reports submitted to the intermodal equipment provider as required by §396.11 of this chapter.

(f) Maintain a system of inspection, repair, and maintenance records as required by §396.3(b)(3) of this chapter for equipment intended for interchange with a motor carrier.

(g) Periodically inspect equipment intended for interchange, as required under §396.17 of this chapter.

(h) At facilities at which the intermodal equipment provider makes intermodal equipment available for interchange, have procedures in place, and provide sufficient space, for drivers to perform a pre-trip inspection of tendered intermodal equipment.

(i) At facilities at which the intermodal equipment provider makes intermodal equipment available for interchange, develop and implement procedures to repair any equipment damage, defects, or deficiencies identified as part of a pre-trip inspection, or replace the equipment, prior to the driver's departure. The repairs or replacement must be made after being notified by a driver of such damage, defects, or deficiencies.

(j) Refrain from placing intermodal equipment in service on the public highways if that equipment has been found to pose an imminent hazard, as defined in §386.72(b)(3) of this chapter.

§390.42 What are the responsibilities of drivers and motor carriers operating intermodal equipment?

(a) Before operating intermodal equipment over the road, the driver accepting the equipment must inspect the equipment components listed in §392.7(b) of this subchapter and be satisfied they are in good working order.

(b) A driver or motor carrier transporting intermodal equipment must report to the intermodal equipment provider, or its designated agent, any known damage, defects, or deficiencies in the intermodal equipment at the time the equipment is returned to the provider or the provider's designated agent. The report must include, at a minimum, the items in §396.11(b)(1) of this chapter.

§390.44 What are the procedures to correct the safety record of a motor carrier or an intermodal equipment provider?

(a) **An intermodal equipment provider or its agent** may electronically file questions or concerns at *http://dataqs.fmcsa.dot.gov* about Federal and State data that reference the provider. This includes safety violations alleging that the components, parts, or accessories of intermodal chassis or trailers listed in §392.7(b) of this chapter were not in good working order when inspected at roadside. An intermodal equipment provider should not be held responsible for such violations because a motor carrier indicated pursuant to §392.7(b) that these components, parts, or accessories had no safety defects at the time of the pre-trip inspection.

(b) A motor carrier or its agent may electronically file questions or concerns at *http://dataqs.fmcsa.dot.gov* about Federal and State data that reference the motor carrier. This includes safety violations alleging that any components, parts, or accessories of intermodal chassis or trailers, except those listed in §392.7(b) of this chapter, were not in good working order when inspected at roadside. Such violations will not be used by FMCSA in making a safety fitness determination of a motor carrier (unless there is evidence that the driver or motor carrier caused or substantially contributed to the violations) because the driver could not readily detect these violations during a pre-trip inspection performed in accordance with §392.7(b).

(c) An intermodal equipment provider, or its agent, may request FMCSA to investigate a motor carrier believed to be in noncompliance with responsibilities under 49 U.S.C. 31151 or the implementing regulations in this subchapter regarding interchange of intermodal equipment by contacting the appropriate FMCSA Field Office.

(d) A motor carrier or its agent may request FMCSA to investigate an intermodal equipment provider believed to be in noncompliance with responsibilities under 49 U.S.C. 31151 or the implementing regulations in this subchapter regarding interchange of intermodal equipment by contacting the appropriate FMCSA Field Office.

§390.46 Are State and local laws and regulations on the inspection, repair, and maintenance of intermodal equipment preempted by the Federal Motor Carrier Safety Regulations?

(a) **General**. As provided by 49 U.S.C. 31151(d), a law, regulation, order, or other requirement of a State, a political subdivision of a State, or a tribal organization relating to the inspection, repair, and maintenance of intermodal equipment is preempted if such law, regulation, order, or other requirement exceeds or is inconsistent with a requirement imposed by the Federal Motor Carrier Safety Regulations.

(b) **Pre-existing State requirements**— (1) **In general**. Pursuant to 49 U.S.C. 31151(e)(1), unless otherwise provided in paragraph (b)(2) of this section, a State requirement for the periodic inspection of intermodal chassis by intermodal equipment providers that was in effect on January 1, 2005, shall remain in effect only until June 17, 2009.

(2) **Nonpreemption determinations**— (i) **In general**. Pursuant to 49 U.S.C. 31151(e)(2), and notwithstanding paragraph (a) of this section, a State requirement described in paragraph (b)(1) of this section is not preempted if the Administrator determines that the State requirement is as effective as the FMCSA final rule and does not unduly burden interstate commerce.

(ii) **Application required**. Paragraph (b)(2)(i) of this section applies to a State requirement only if the State applies to the Administrator for a determination with respect to the requirement before the effective date of the final rule (June 17, 2009). The Administrator will make a determination with respect to any such application within 6 months after the date on which the Administrator receives the application.

(iii) **Amended State requirements**. If a State amends a regulation for which it previously received a nonpreemption determination from the Administrator under paragraph (b)(2)(i) of this section, it must apply for a determination of nonpreemption for the amended regulation. Any amendment to a State requirement not preempted under this subsection because of a determination by the Administrator may not take effect unless it is submitted to the Agency before the effective date of the amendment, and the Administrator determines that the amendment would not cause the State requirement to be less effective than the FMCSA final rule on "Requirements for Intermodal Equipment Providers and Motor Carriers and Drivers Operating Intermodal Equipment" and would not unduly burden interstate commerce.

Subpart D—National Registry of Certified Medical Examiners

§390.101 Scope.

(a) The rules in this subpart establish the minimum qualifications for FMCSA certification of a medical examiner and for listing the examiner on FMCSA's National Registry of Certified Medical Examiners. The National Registry of Certified Medical Examiners is designed to improve highway safety and operator health by requiring that medical examiners be trained and certified to determine effectively whether an operator meets FMCSA physical qualification standards under part 391 of this chapter. One component of the National Registry is the registry itself, which is a national database of names and contact information for medical examiners who are certified by FMCSA to perform medical examinations of operators.

(b) A qualified VA examiner, as defined in either §390.5 or §390.5T, may be listed on the National Registry of Certified Medical Examiners by satisfying the requirements for medical examiner certification set forth in either §390.103 or §390.123.

Medical examiner certification requirements

§390.103 Eligibility requirements for medical examiner certification.

(a) To receive medical examiner certification from FMCSA, a person must:

(1) Be licensed, certified, or registered in accordance with applicable State laws and regulations to perform physical examinations. The applicant must be an advanced practice nurse, doctor of chiropractic, doctor of medicine, doctor of osteopathy, physician assistant, or other medical professional authorized by applicable State laws and regulations to perform physical examinations.

(2) Register on the National Registry website and receive a National Registry number before taking the training that meets the requirements of §390.105.

(3) Complete a training program that meets the requirements of §390.105.

(4) Pass the medical examiner certification test provided by FMCSA and administered by a testing organization that meets the requirements of §390.107 and that has electronically forwarded to FMCSA the applicant's completed test information no more than 3 years after completion of the training program required by paragraph (a)(3) of this section.

(b) If a person has medical examiner certification from FMCSA, then to renew such certification the medical examiner must remain qualified under paragraph (a)(1) of this section and complete additional testing and training as required by §390.111(a)(5).

§390.105 Medical examiner training programs.

An applicant for medical examiner certification must complete a training program that:

(a) Is conducted by a training provider that:

(1) Is accredited by a nationally recognized medical profession accrediting organization to provide continuing education units; and

(2) Meets the following administrative requirements:

(i) Provides training participants with proof of participation.

(ii) Provides FMCSA point of contact information to training participants.

(b) Provides training to medical examiners on the following topics:

(1) Background, rationale, mission, and goals of the FMCSA medical examiner's role in reducing crashes, injuries, and fatalities involving commercial motor vehicles.

(2) Familiarization with the responsibilities and work environment of commercial motor vehicle operation.

(3) Identification of the operator and obtaining, reviewing, and documenting operator medical history, including prescription and over-the-counter medications.

(4) Performing, reviewing, and documenting the operator's medical examination.

(5) Performing, obtaining, and documenting additional diagnostic tests or medical opinion from a medical specialist or treating physician.

(6) Informing and educating the operator about medications and non-disqualifying medical conditions that require remedial care.

(7) Determining operator certification outcome and period for which certification should be valid.

(8) FMCSA reporting and documentation requirements.

Guidance on the core curriculum specifications for use by training providers is available from FMCSA.

§390.107 Medical examiner certification testing.

An applicant for medical examiner certification or recertification must apply, in accordance with the minimum specifications for application elements established by FMCSA, to a testing organization that meets the following criteria:

(a) The testing organization has documented policies and procedures that:

(1) Use secure protocols to access, process, store, and transmit all test items, test forms, test data, and candidate information and ensure access by authorized personnel only.

(2) Ensure testing environments are reasonably comfortable and have minimal distractions.

(3) Prevent to the greatest extent practicable the opportunity for a test taker to attain a passing score by fraudulent means.

(4) Ensure that test center staff who interact with and proctor examinees or provide technical support have completed formal training, demonstrate competency, and are monitored periodically for quality assurance in testing procedures.

(5) Accommodate testing of individuals with disabilities or impairments to minimize the effect of the disabilities or impairments while maintaining the security of the test and data.

(b) Testing organizations that offer testing of examinees not at locations that are operated and staffed by the organizations but by means of remote, computer-based systems must, in addition to the requirements of paragraph (a) of this section, ensure that such systems:

(1) Provide a means to authenticate the identity of the person taking the test.

(2) Provide a means for the testing organization to monitor the activity of the person taking the test.

(3) Do not allow the person taking the test to reproduce or record the contents of the test by any means.

(c) The testing organization has submitted its documented policies and procedures as defined in paragraph (a) of this section and, if applicable, paragraph (b) of this section to FMCSA and agreed to future reviews by FMCSA to ensure compliance with the criteria listed in this section.

(d) The testing organization administers only the currently authorized version of the medical examiner certification test developed and furnished by FMCSA.

§390.109 Issuance of the FMCSA medical examiner certification credential.

Upon compliance with the requirements of §390.103(a) or (b), FMCSA will issue to a medical examiner applicant an FMCSA medical examiner certification credential and will add the medical examiner's name to the National Registry of Certified Medical Examiners. The certification credential will expire 10 years after the date of its issuance.

§390.111 Requirements for continued listing on the National Registry of Certified Medical Examiners.

(a) To continue to be listed on the National Registry of Certified Medical Examiners, each medical examiner must:

(1) Continue to meet the requirements of §§390.103 through 390.115 and the applicable requirements of part 391 of this chapter.

(2) Report to FMCSA any changes in the registration information submitted under §390.103(a)(2) within 30 days of the change.

(3) Continue to be licensed, certified, or registered, and authorized to perform physical examinations, in accordance with the applicable laws and regulations of each State in which the medical examiner performs examinations.

(4) Maintain documentation of State licensure, registration, or certification to perform physical examinations for each State in which the examiner performs examinations and maintain documentation of and completion of all training required by this section and §390.105. The medical examiner must make this documentation available to an authorized representative of FMCSA or an authorized representative of Federal, State, or local government. The medical examiner must provide this documentation within 48 hours of the request for investigations and within 10 days of the request for regular audits of eligibility.

(5) Maintain medical examiner certification by completing training and testing according to the following schedule:

(i) No sooner than 4 years and no later than 5 years after the date of issuance of the medical examiner certification credential, complete periodic training as specified by FMCSA.

(ii) No sooner than 9 years and no later than 10 years after the date of issuance of the medical examiner certification credential:

(A) Complete periodic training as specified by FMCSA; and

(B) Pass the test required by §390.103(a)(4).

(b) FMCSA will issue a new medical examiner certification credential valid for 10 years to a medical examiner who complies with paragraphs (a)(1) through (4) of this section and who successfully completes the training and testing as required by paragraphs (a)(5)(i) and (ii) of this section.

§390.113 Reasons for removal from the National Registry of Certified Medical Examiners.

FMCSA may remove a medical examiner from the National Registry of Certified Medical Examiners when a medical examiner fails to meet or maintain the qualifications established by §§390.103 through 390.115, the requirements of other regulations applicable to the medical examiner, or otherwise does not meet the requirements of 49 U.S.C. 31149. The reasons for removal may include, but are not limited to:

(a) The medical examiner fails to comply with the requirements for continued listing on the National Registry of Certified Medical Examiners, as described in §390.111.

(b) FMCSA finds that there are errors, omissions, or other indications of improper certification by the medical examiner of an operator in either the completed Medical Examination Reports or the medical examiner's certificates.

(c) The FMCSA determines the medical examiner issued a medical examiner's certificate to an operator of a commercial motor vehicle who failed to meet the applicable standards at the time of the examination.

(d) The medical examiner fails to comply with the examination requirements in §391.43 of this chapter.

(e) The medical examiner falsely claims to have completed training in physical and medical examination standards as required by §§390.103 through 390.115.

§390.115 Procedure for removal from the National Registry of Certified Medical Examiners.

(a) **Voluntary removal**. To be voluntarily removed from the National Registry of Certified Medical Examiners, a medical examiner must submit a request to FMCSA, ATTN: Removal from National Registry of Certified Medical Examiners, 1200 New Jersey Ave. SE, Washington, DC 20590. Except as provided in paragraph (b) of this section, FMCSA will accept the request and the removal will become effective immediately. On and after the date of issuance of a notice of proposed removal from the National Registry of Certified Medical Examiners, as described in paragraph (b) of this section, however, FMCSA will not approve the medical examiner's request for voluntary removal from the National Registry of Certified Medical Examiners.

(b) **Notice of proposed removal**. Except as provided by paragraphs (a) and (e) of this section, FMCSA initiates the process for removal of a medical examiner from the National Registry of Certified Medical Examiners by issuing a written notice of proposed removal to the medical examiner, stating the reasons that removal is proposed under §390.113 and any corrective actions necessary for the medical examiner to remain listed on the National Registry of Certified Medical Examiners.

(c) **Response to notice of proposed removal and corrective action**. A medical examiner who has received a notice of proposed removal from the National Registry of Certified Medical Examiners must submit any written response to FMCSA no later than 30 days after the date of issuance of the notice of proposed removal. The response must indicate either that the medical examiner believes FMCSA has relied on erroneous reasons, in whole or in part, in proposing removal from the National Registry of Certified Medical Examiners, as described in paragraph (c)(1) of this section, or that the medical examiner will comply and take any corrective action specified in the notice of proposed removal, as described in paragraph (c)(2) of this section.

(1) **Opposing a notice of proposed removal**. If the medical examiner believes FMCSA has relied on an erroneous reason, in whole or in part, in proposing removal from the National Registry of Certified Medical Examiners, the medical examiner must explain the basis for his or her belief that FMCSA relied on an erroneous reason in proposing the removal. FMCSA will review the explanation.

(i) If FMCSA finds it has wholly relied on an erroneous reason for proposing removal from the National Registry of Certified Medical Examiners, FMCSA will withdraw the notice of proposed removal and notify the medical examiner in writing of the determination. If FMCSA finds it has partly relied on an erroneous reason for proposing removal from the National Registry of Certified Medical Examiners, FMCSA will modify the notice of proposed removal and notify the medical examiner in writing of the determination. No later than 60 days after the date FMCSA modifies a notice of proposed removal, the medical examiner must comply with §§390.103 through 390.115 and correct any deficiencies identified in the modified notice of proposed removal as described in paragraph (c)(2) of this section.

(ii) If FMCSA finds it has not relied on an erroneous reason in proposing removal, FMCSA will affirm the notice of proposed removal and notify the medical examiner in writing of the determination. No later than 60 days after the date FMCSA affirms the notice of proposed removal, the medical examiner must comply with §§390.103 through 390.115 and correct the deficiencies identified in the notice of proposed removal as described in paragraph (c)(2) of this section.

(iii) If the medical examiner does not submit a written response within 30 days of the date of issuance of a notice of proposed removal, the removal becomes effective and the medical examiner is immediately removed from the National Registry of Certified Medical Examiners.

(2) **Compliance and corrective action**. (i) The medical examiner must comply with §§390.103 through 390.115 and complete the corrective actions specified in the notice of proposed removal no later than 60 days after either the date of issuance of the notice of proposed removal or the date FMCSA affirms or modifies the notice of proposed removal, whichever is later. The medical examiner must provide documentation of compliance and completion of the corrective actions to FMCSA. FMCSA may conduct any investigations and request any documentation necessary to verify that the medical examiner has complied with §§390.103 through 390.115 and completed the required corrective action(s). FMCSA will notify the medical examiner in writing whether he or she has met the requirements to continue to be listed on the National Registry of Certified Medical Examiners.

(ii) If the medical examiner fails to complete the proposed corrective action(s) within the 60-day period, the removal becomes effective and the medical examiner is immediately removed from the National Registry of Certified Medical Examiners. FMCSA will notify the person in writing that he or she has been removed from the National Registry of Certified Medical Examiners.

(3) At any time before a notice of proposed removal from the National Registry of Certified Medical Examiners becomes final, the recipient of the notice of proposed removal and FMCSA may resolve the matter by mutual agreement.

(d) **Request for administrative review**. If a person has been removed from the National Registry of Certified Medical Examiners under paragraph (c)(1)(iii), (c)(2)(ii), or (e) of this section, that person may request an administrative review no later than 30 days after the date the removal becomes effective. The request must be submitted in writing to FMCSA, ATTN: National Registry of Certified Medical Examiners—Request for Administrative Review, 1200 New Jersey Ave. SE, Washington, DC 20590. The request must explain the error(s) committed in removing the medical examiner from the National Registry of Certified Medical Examiners, and include a list of all factual, legal, and procedural issues in dispute, and any supporting information or documents.

(1) **Additional procedures for administrative review**. FMCSA may ask the person to submit additional data or attend a conference to discuss the removal. If the person does not provide the information requested, or does not attend the scheduled conference, FMCSA may dismiss the request for administrative review.

(2) **Decision on administrative review**. FMCSA will complete the administrative review and notify the person in writing of the decision. The decision constitutes final Agency action. If FMCSA decides the removal was not valid, FMCSA will reinstate the person and reissue a certification credential to expire on the expiration date of the certificate that was invalidated under paragraph (g) of this section. The reinstated medical examiner must:

(i) Continue to meet the requirements of §§390.103 through 390.115 and the applicable requirements of part 391 of this chapter.

(ii) Report to FMCSA any changes in the registration information submitted under §390.103(a)(2) within 30 days of the reinstatement.

(iii) Be licensed, certified, or registered in accordance with applicable State laws and regulations to perform physical examinations.

(iv) Maintain documentation of State licensure, registration, or certification to perform physical examinations for each State in which the examiner performs examinations and maintains documentation of completion of all training required by §§390.105 and 390.111 of this part. The medical examiner must also make this documentation available to an authorized representative of FMCSA or an authorized representative of Federal, State, or local government. The medical examiner must provide this documentation within 48 hours of the request for investigations and within 10 days of the request for regular audits of eligibility.

(v) Complete periodic training as required by FMCSA.

(e) **Emergency removal**. In cases of either willfulness or in which public health, interest, or safety requires, the provisions of paragraph (b) of this section are not applicable and FMCSA may immediately remove a medical examiner from the National Registry of Certified Medical Examiners and invalidate the certification credential issued under §390.109. A person who has been removed under the provisions of this paragraph may request an administrative review of that decision as described under paragraph (d) of this section.

(f) **Reinstatement on the National Registry of Certified Medical Examiners**. No sooner than 30 days after the date of removal from the National Registry of Certified Medical Examiners, a person who has been voluntarily or involuntarily removed may apply to FMCSA to be reinstated. The person must:

(1) Continue to meet the requirements of §§390.103 through 390.115 and the applicable requirements of part 391 of this chapter.

(2) Report to FMCSA any changes in the registration information submitted under §390.103(a)(2).

(3) Be licensed, certified, or registered in accordance with applicable State laws and regulations to perform physical examinations.

(4) Maintain documentation of State licensure, registration, or certification to perform physical examinations for each State in which the person performs examinations and maintains documentation of completion of all training required by §§390.105 and 390.111. The medical examiner must also make this documentation available to an authorized representative of FMCSA or an authorized representative of Federal, State, or local government. The person must provide this documentation within 48 hours of the request for investigations and within 10 days of the request for regular audits of eligibility.

(5) Complete training and testing as required by FMCSA.

(6) In the case of a person who has been involuntarily removed, provide documentation showing completion of any corrective actions required in the notice of proposed removal.

(g) **Effect of final decision by FMCSA**. If a person is removed from the National Registry of Certified Medical Examiners under paragraph (c) or (e) of this section, the certification credential issued under §390.109 is no longer valid. However, the removed person's information remains publicly available for 3 years, with an indication that the person is no longer listed on the National Registry of Certified Medical Examiners as of the date of removal.

Medical examiner certification requirements for qualified Department of Veterans Affairs examiners

§390.123 Medical examiner certification for qualified Department of Veterans Affairs examiners.

(a) For a qualified VA examiner to receive medical examiner certification from FMCSA under §§390.123 through 390.135, a person must:

(1) Be an advanced practice nurse, doctor of chiropractic, doctor of medicine, doctor of osteopathy, physician assistant, or other medical professional employed in the Department of Veterans Affairs;

(2) Be licensed, certified, or registered in a State to perform physical examinations;

(3) Register on the National Registry website and receive a National Registry number before taking the training that meets the requirements of §390.125;

(4) Be familiar with FMCSA's standards for, and physical requirements of, a commercial motor vehicle operator requiring medical certification, by completing the training program that meets the requirements of §390.125;

(5) Pass the medical examiner certification test provided by FMCSA, administered in accordance with §390.127, and has had his or her test information forwarded to FMCSA; and

(6) Never have been found to have acted fraudulently with respect to any certification of a commercial motor vehicle operator, including by fraudulently awarding a medical certificate.

(b) If a person becomes a certified VA medical examiner under §§390.123 through 390.135, then to renew such certification the certified VA medical examiner must remain qualified under paragraphs (a)(1) and (2) of this section and complete additional testing and training as required by §390.131(a)(5).

§390.125 Qualified VA examiner certification training.

A qualified VA examiner applying for certification under §§390.123 through 390.135 must complete training developed and provided by FMCSA and delivered through a web-based training system operated by the Department of Veterans Affairs.

§390.127 Qualified VA examiner certification testing.

To receive medical examiner certification from FMCSA under §§390.123 through 390.135, a qualified VA examiner must pass the medical examiner certification test developed and provided by FMCSA and administered through a web-based system operated by the Department of Veterans Affairs.

§390.129 Issuance of the FMCSA medical examiner certification credential.

Upon compliance with the requirements of §390.123(a) or (b), FMCSA will issue to a qualified VA examiner or certified VA medical examiner, as applicable, an FMCSA medical examiner certification credential and will add the certified VA medical examiner's name to the National Registry of Certified Medical Examiners. The certification credential will expire 10 years after the date of its issuance.

§390.131 Requirements for continued listing of a certified VA medical examiner on the National Registry of Certified Medical Examiners.

(a) To continue to be listed on the National Registry of Certified Medical Examiners, each certified VA medical examiner must:

(1) Continue to meet the requirements of §§390.123 through 390.135 and the applicable requirements of part 391 of this chapter.

(2) Report to FMCSA any changes in the registration information submitted under §390.123(a)(3) within 30 days of the change.

(3) Continue to be licensed, certified, or registered, and authorized to perform physical examinations, in accordance with the laws and regulations of a State.

(4) Maintain documentation of licensure, registration, or certification in a State to perform physical examinations and maintain documentation of and completion of all training required by this section and §390.125. The certified VA medical examiner must make this documentation available to an authorized representative of FMCSA or an authorized representative of Federal, State, or local government. The certified VA medical examiner must provide this documentation within 48 hours of the request for investigations and within 10 days of the request for regular audits of eligibility.

(5) Maintain medical examiner certification by completing training and testing according to the following schedule:

(i) No sooner than 4 years and no later than 5 years after the date of issuance of the medical examiner certification credential, complete periodic training as specified by FMCSA.

(ii) No sooner than 9 years and no later than 10 years after the date of issuance of the medical examiner certification credential:

(A) Complete periodic training as specified by FMCSA; and

(B) Pass the test required by §390.123(a)(5).

(b) FMCSA will issue a new medical examiner certification credential valid for 10 years to a certified VA medical examiner who complies with paragraphs (a)(1) through (4) of this section and who successfully completes the training and testing as required by paragraphs (a)(5)(i) and (ii) of this section.

(c) A certified VA medical examiner must report to FMCSA within 30 days that he or she is no longer employed in the Department of Veterans Affairs. Any certified VA medical examiner who is no longer employed in the Department of Veterans Affairs, but would like to remain listed on the National Registry, must, within 30 days of leaving employment in the Department of Veterans Affairs, meet the requirements of §390.111. In particular, he or she must be licensed, certified, or registered, and authorized to perform physical examinations, in accordance with the applicable laws and regulations of each State in which the medical examiner performs examinations. The previously certified VA medical examiner's medical license(s) must be verified and accepted by FMCSA prior to conducting any physical examination of a commercial motor vehicle operator or issuing any medical examiner's certificates.

§390.133 Reasons for removal of a certified VA medical examiner from the National Registry of Certified Medical Examiners.

FMCSA may remove a certified VA medical examiner from the National Registry of Certified Medical Examiners when a certified VA medical examiner fails to meet or maintain the qualifications established by §§390.123 through 390.135, the requirements of other regulations applicable to the certified VA medical examiner, or otherwise does not meet the requirements of 49 U.S.C. 31149. The reasons for removal may include, but are not limited to:

(a) The certified VA medical examiner fails to comply with the requirements for continued listing on the National Registry of Certified Medical Examiners, as described in §390.131.

(b) FMCSA finds that there are errors, omissions, or other indications of improper certification by the certified VA medical examiner of an operator in either the completed Medical Examination Reports or the medical examiner's certificates.

(c) The FMCSA determines the certified VA medical examiner issued a medical examiner's certificate to an operator of a commercial motor vehicle who failed to meet the applicable standards at the time of the examination.

(d) The certified VA medical examiner fails to comply with the examination requirements in §391.43 of this chapter.

(e) The certified VA medical examiner falsely claims to have completed training in physical and medical examination standards as required by §§390.123 through 390.135.

§390.135 Procedure for removal of a certified VA medical examiner from the National Registry of Certified Medical Examiners.

(a) **Voluntary removal**. To be voluntarily removed from the National Registry of Certified Medical Examiners, a certified VA medical examiner must submit a request to FMCSA, ATTN: Removal from National Registry of Certified Medical Examiners., 1200 New Jersey Ave. SE, Washington, DC 20590. Except as provided in paragraph (b) of this section, FMCSA will accept the request and the removal will become effective immediately. On and after the date of issuance of a notice of proposed removal from the National Registry of Certified Medical Examiners, as described in paragraph (b) of this section, however, FMCSA will not approve the certified VA medical examiner's request for voluntary removal from the National Registry of Certified Medical Examiners.

(b) **Notice of proposed removal**. Except as provided by paragraphs (a) and (e) of this section, FMCSA initiates the process for removal of a certified VA medical examiner from the National Registry of Certified Medical Examiners by issuing a written notice of proposed removal to the certified VA medical examiner, stating the reasons that removal is proposed under §390.133 and any corrective actions necessary for the certified VA medical examiner to remain listed on the National Registry of Certified Medical Examiners.

(c) **Response to notice of proposed removal and corrective action**. A certified VA medical examiner who has received a notice of proposed removal from the National Registry of Certified Medical Examiners must submit any written response to FMCSA no later than 30 days after the date of issuance of the notice of proposed removal. The response must indicate either that the certified VA medical examiner believes FMCSA has relied on erroneous reasons, in whole or in part, in proposing removal from the National Registry of Certified Medical Examiners, as described in paragraph (c)(1) of this section, or that the certified VA medical examiner will comply and take any corrective action specified in the notice of proposed removal, as described in paragraph (c)(2) of this section.

(1) *Opposing a notice of proposed removal.* If the certified VA medical examiner believes FMCSA has relied on an erroneous reason, in whole or in part, in proposing removal from the National Registry of Certified Medical Examiners, the certified VA medical examiner must explain the basis for his or her belief that FMCSA relied on an erroneous reason in proposing the removal. FMCSA will review the explanation.

(i) If FMCSA finds it has wholly relied on an erroneous reason for proposing removal from the National Registry of Certified Medical Examiners, FMCSA will withdraw the notice of proposed removal and notify the certified VA medical examiner in writing of the determination. If FMCSA finds it has partly relied on an erroneous reason for proposing removal from the National Registry of Certified Medical Examiners, FMCSA will modify the notice of proposed removal and notify the certified VA medical examiner in writing of the determination. No later than 60 days after the date FMCSA modifies a notice of proposed removal, the certified VA medical examiner must comply with §§390.123 through 390.135 and correct any deficiencies identified in the modified notice of proposed removal as described in paragraph (c)(2) of this section.

(ii) If FMCSA finds it has not relied on an erroneous reason in proposing removal, FMCSA will affirm the notice of proposed removal and notify the certified VA medical examiner in writing of the determination. No later than 60 days after the date FMCSA affirms the notice of proposed removal, the certified VA medical examiner must comply with §§390.123 through 390.135 and correct the deficiencies identified in the notice of proposed removal as described in paragraph (c)(2) of this section.

(iii) If the certified VA medical examiner does not submit a written response within 30 days of the date of issuance of a notice of proposed removal, the removal becomes effective and the certified VA medical examiner is immediately removed from the National Registry of Certified Medical Examiners.

(2) *Compliance and corrective action.* (i) The certified VA medical examiner must comply with §§390.123 through 390.135 and complete the corrective actions specified in the notice of proposed removal no later than 60 days after either the date of issuance of the notice of proposed removal or the date FMCSA affirms or modifies the notice of proposed removal, whichever is later. The certified VA medical examiner must provide documentation of compliance and completion of the corrective actions to FMCSA. FMCSA may conduct any investigations and request any documentation necessary to verify that the certified VA medical examiner has complied with §§390.123 through 390.135 and completed the required corrective action(s). FMCSA will notify the certified VA medical examiner in writing whether he or she has met the requirements to continue to be listed on the National Registry of Certified Medical Examiners.

(ii) If the certified VA medical examiner fails to complete the proposed corrective action(s) within the 60-day period, the removal becomes effective and the certified VA medical examiner is immediately removed from the National Registry of Certified Medical Examiners. FMCSA will notify the person in writing that he or she has been removed from the National Registry of Certified Medical Examiners.

(3) At any time before a notice of proposed removal from the National Registry of Certified Medical Examiners becomes final, the recipient of the notice of proposed removal and FMCSA may resolve the matter by mutual agreement.

(d) **Request for administrative review**. If a person has been removed from the National Registry of Certified Medical Examiners under paragraph (c)(1)(iii), (c)(2)(ii), or (e) of this section, that person may request an administrative review no later than 30 days after the date the removal becomes effective. The request must be submitted in writing to FMCSA, ATTN: National Registry of Certified Medical Examiners—Request for Administrative Review, 1200 New Jersey Ave. SE, Washington, DC 20590. The request must explain the error(s) committed in removing the certified VA medical examiner from the National Registry of Certified Medical Examiners, and include a list of all factual, legal, and procedural issues in dispute, and any supporting information or documents.

(1) *Additional procedures for administrative review.* FMCSA may ask the person to submit additional data or attend a conference to discuss the removal. If the person does not provide the information requested, or does not attend the scheduled conference, FMCSA may dismiss the request for administrative review.

(2) *Decision on administrative review.* FMCSA will complete the administrative review and notify the person in writing of the decision. The decision constitutes final Agency action. If FMCSA decides the removal was not valid, FMCSA will reinstate the person and reissue a certification credential to expire on the expiration date of the certificate that was invalidated under paragraph (g) of this section. The reinstated certified VA medical examiner must:

(i) Continue to meet the requirements of §§390.123 through 390.135 and the applicable requirements of part 391 of this chapter.

(ii) Report to FMCSA any changes in the registration information submitted under §390.123(a)(3) within 30 days of the reinstatement.

(iii) Be licensed, certified, or registered in accordance with applicable State laws and regulations to perform physical examinations.

(iv) Maintain documentation of licensure, registration, or certification in a State to perform physical examinations and maintain documentation of and completion of all training required by §§390.125 and 390.131 of this part. The certified VA medical examiner must make this documentation available to an authorized representative of FMCSA or an authorized representative of Federal, State, or local government. The certified VA medical examiner must provide this documentation within 48 hours of the request for investigations and within 10 days of the request for regular audits of eligibility.

(v) Complete periodic training as required by FMCSA.

(e) **Emergency removal**. In cases of either willfulness or in which public health, interest, or safety requires, the provisions of paragraph (b) of this section are not applicable and FMCSA may immediately remove a certified VA medical examiner from the National Registry of Certified Medical Examiners and invalidate the certification credential issued under §390.129. A person who has been removed under the provisions of this paragraph may request an administrative review of that decision as described under paragraph (d) of this section.

(f) **Reinstatement on the National Registry of Certified Medical Examiners**. No sooner than 30 days after the date of removal from the National Registry of Certified Medical Examiners, a person who has been voluntarily or involuntarily removed may apply to FMCSA to be reinstated. The person must:

(1) Continue to meet the requirements of §§390.123 through 390.135 and the applicable requirements of part 391 of this chapter.

(2) Report to FMCSA any changes in the registration information submitted under §390.123(a)(3).

(3) Be licensed, certified, or registered in accordance with applicable State laws and regulations to perform physical examinations.

(4) Maintain documentation of licensure, registration, or certification in a State to perform physical examinations and maintain documentation of and completion of all training required by §§390.125 and 390.131. The certified VA medical examiner must make this documentation available to an authorized representative of FMCSA or an authorized representative of Federal, State, or local government. The certified VA medical examiner must provide this documentation within 48 hours of the request for investigations and within 10 days of the request for regular audits of eligibility.

(5) Complete training and testing as required by FMCSA.

(6) In the case of a person who has been involuntarily removed, provide documentation showing completion of any corrective actions required in the notice of proposed removal.

(g) **Effect of final decision by FMCSA.** If a person is removed from the National Registry of Certified Medical Examiners under paragraph (c) or (e) of this section, the certification credential issued under §390.129 is no longer valid. However, the removed person's information remains publicly available for 3 years, with an indication that the person is no longer listed on the National Registry of Certified Medical Examiners as of the date of removal.

Subpart E—URS Online Application

§390.200T USDOT Registration.

(a) **Purpose.** This section establishes who must register with FMCSA using the Form MCSA-1, the URS online application, beginning January 14, 2017.

(b) **Applicability.** Notwithstanding any other provisions of this part or 49 CFR 385.305T(b)(2), a new applicant private motor carrier or new applicant exempt for-hire motor carrier subject to the requirements of this subchapter must file Form MCSA-1 with FMCSA to identify its operations with the Federal Motor Carrier Safety Administration for safety oversight. Form MCSA-1 is the URS online application, and both the application and its instructions are available from the FMCSA Web site at *http://www.fmcsa.dot.gov/urs*.

(c) **Definition.** For purposes of this section, a "new applicant" is an entity applying for operating authority registration and a USDOT number who does not at the time of application have an active registration or USDOT, Motor Carrier (MC), Mexican owned or controlled (MX), or Freight Forwarder (FF) number, and who has never had an active registration or USDOT, MC, MX, or FF number.

Subpart E—[Suspended]

§390.201 USDOT Registration. [Suspended]

(a) **Purpose**. This section establishes who must register with FMCSA under the Unified Registration System, the filing schedule, and general information pertaining to persons subject to the Unified Registration System registration requirements.

(b) **Applicability**. (1) Except as provided in paragraph (g) of this section, each motor carrier (including a private motor carrier, an exempt for-hire motor carrier, a non-exempt for-hire motor carrier, and a motor carrier of passengers that participates in a through ticketing arrangement with one or more interstate for-hire motor carriers of passengers), intermodal equipment provider, broker and freight forwarder subject to the requirements of this subchapter must file Form MCSA-1, the URS online application, with FMCSA to:

(i) Identify its operations with the Federal Motor Carrier Safety Administration for safety oversight, as applicable;

(ii) Obtain operating authority required under 49 U.S.C. chapter 139, as applicable; and

(iii) Obtain a hazardous materials safety permit as required under 49 U.S.C. 5109, as applicable.

(2) A cargo tank and cargo tank motor vehicle manufacturer, assembler, repairer, inspector, tester, and design certifying engineer that is subject to registration requirements under 49 CFR 107.502 and 49 U.S.C. 5108 must satisfy those requirements by electronically filing Form MCSA-1 with FMCSA.

(c) **General**. (1)(i) A person that fails to file Form MCSA-1, the URS online application, pursuant to paragraph (d)(1) of this section is subject to the penalties prescribed in 49 U.S.C. 521(b)(2)(B) or 49 U.S.C. 14901(a), as appropriate.

(ii) A person that fails to complete biennial updates to the information pursuant to paragraph (d)(2) of this section is subject to the penalties prescribed in 49 U.S.C. 521(b)(2)(B) or 49 U.S.C. 14901(a), as appropriate, and deactivation of its USDOT Number.

(iii) A person that furnishes misleading information or makes false statements upon Form MCSA-1, the URS online application, is subject to the penalties prescribed in 49 U.S.C. 521(b)(2)(B), 49 U.S.C. 14901(a) or 49 U.S.C. 14907, as appropriate.

(2) Upon receipt and processing of Form MCSA-1, the URS online application, FMCSA will issue the applicant an inactive identification number (USDOT Number). FMCSA will activate the USDOT Number after completion of applicable administrative filings pursuant to §390.205(a), unless the applicant is subject to §390.205(b). An applicant may not begin operations nor mark a commercial motor vehicle with the USDOT Number until after the date of the Agency's written notice that the USDOT Number has been activated.

(3) The motor carrier must display a valid USDOT Number on each self-propelled CMV, as defined in §390.5, along with the additional information required by §390.21.

(d) **Filing schedule**. Each person listed under §390.201(b) must electronically file Form MCSA-1, the URS online application, at the following times:

(1) Before it begins operations; and

(2) Every 24 months as prescribed in paragraph (d)(3) of this section.

(3)(i) Persons assigned a USDOT Number must file an updated Form MCSA-1, the URS online application, every 24 months, according to the following schedule:

USDOT No. ending in . . .	Must file by last day of . . .
1	January.
2	February.
3	March.
4	April.
5	May.
6	June.

USDOT No. ending in . . .	Must file by last day of . . .
7	July.
8	August.
9	September.
0	October.

(ii) If the next-to-last digit of its USDOT Number is odd, the person must file its update in every odd-numbered calendar year. If the next-to-last digit of the USDOT Number is even, the person must file its update in every even-numbered calendar year.

(4) **When there is a change in legal name, form of business, or address**. A registered entity must notify the Agency of a change in legal name, form of business, or address within 30 days of the change by filing an updated Form MCSA-1, the URS online application, reflecting the revised information. Notification of a change in legal name, form of business, or address does not relieve a registered entity from the requirement to file an updated Form MCSA-1 every 24 months in accordance with paragraph (d)(3) of this section.

(5) **When there is a transfer of operating authority**. (i) Both a person who obtains operating authority through a transfer, as defined in part 365, subpart D of this subchapter (transferee), and the person transferring its operating authority (transferor), must each notify the Agency of the transfer within 30 days of consummation of the transfer by filing:

(A) An updated Form MCSA-1, the URS online application, for the transferor, and for the transferee, if the transferee had an existing USDOT Number at the time of the transfer; or

(B) A new Form MCSA-1, the URS online application, if the transferee did not have an existing USDOT Number at the time of the transfer.

(C) A copy of the operating authority that is being transferred.

(ii) Notification of a transfer of operating authority does not relieve a registered entity from the requirement to file an updated Form MCSA-1, the URS online application, every 24 months in accordance with paragraph (d)(3) of this section.

(e) **Availability of form**. Form MCSA-1, the URS online application is available, including complete instructions, from the FMCSA Web site at *http://www.fmcsa.dot.gov/urs*.

(f) **Where to file**. Persons subject to the registration requirements under this subpart must electronically file Form MCSA-1, the URS online application, on the FMCSA Web site at *http://www.fmcsa.dot.gov/urs*.

(g) **Exception**. The rules in this subpart do not govern the application by a Mexico-domiciled motor carrier to provide transportation of property or passengers in interstate commerce between Mexico and points in the United States beyond the municipalities and commercial zones along the United States-Mexico international border. The applicable procedures governing transportation by Mexico-domiciled motor carriers are provided in §390.19.

§390.203 PRISM State registration/biennial updates. [Suspended]

(a) A motor carrier that registers its vehicles in a State that participates in the Performance and Registration Information Systems Management (PRISM) program (authorized under section 4004 of the Transportation Equity Act for the 21st Century [Public Law 105-178, 112 Stat. 107]) alternatively may satisfy the requirements set forth in §390.201 by electronically filing all the required USDOT registration and biennial update information with the State according to its policies and procedures, provided the State has integrated the USDOT registration /update capability into its vehicle registration program.

(b) If the State procedures do not allow a motor carrier to file the Form MCSA-1, the URS online application, or to submit updates within the period specified in §390.201(d)(2), a motor carrier must complete such filings directly with FMCSA.

(c) A for-hire motor carrier, unless providing transportation exempt from the commercial registration requirements of 49 U.S.C. chapter 139, must obtain operating authority as prescribed under §390.201(b) and part 365 of this subchapter before operating in interstate commerce.

§390.205 Special requirements for registration. [Suspended]

(a)(1) **General**. A person applying to operate as a motor carrier, broker, or freight forwarder under this subpart must make the additional filings described in paragraphs (a)(2) and (a)(3) of this section as a condition for registration under this subpart within 90 days of the date on which the application is filed:

(2) **Evidence of financial responsibility**. (i) A person that registers to conduct operations in interstate commerce as a for-hire motor carrier, a broker, or a freight forwarder must file evidence of financial responsibility as required under part 387, subparts C and D of this subchapter.

(ii) A person that registers to transport hazardous materials as defined in 49 CFR 171.8 (or any quantity of a material listed as a select agent or toxin in 42 CFR part 73) in interstate commerce must file evidence of financial responsibility as required under part 387, subpart C of this subchapter.

(3) **Designation of agent for service of process**. All motor carriers (both private and for-hire), brokers and freight forwarders required to register under this subpart must designate an agent for service of process (a person upon whom court or Agency process may be served) following the rules in part 366 of this subchapter:

(b) If an application is subject to a protest period, the Agency will not activate a USDOT Number until expiration of the protest period provided in §365.115 of this subchapter or—if a protest is received—after FMCSA denies or rejects the protest, as applicable.

§390.207 Other governing regulations. [Suspended]

(a) **Motor carriers**. (1) A motor carrier granted registration under this part must successfully complete the applicable New Entrant Safety Assurance Program as described in paragraphs (a)(1)(i) through (a)(1)(iii) of this section as a condition for permanent registration:

(i) A U.S.- or Canada-domiciled motor carrier is subject to the new entrant safety assurance program under part 385, subpart D, of this subchapter.

(ii) A Mexico-domiciled motor carrier is subject to the safety monitoring program under part 385, subpart B of this subchapter.

(iii) A Non-North America-domiciled motor carrier is subject to the safety monitoring program under part 385, subpart I of this subchapter.

(2) Only the legal name or a single trade name of the motor carrier may be used on the Form MCSA-1, the URS online application.

(b) **Brokers, freight forwarders and non-exempt for-hire motor carriers**. (1) A broker or freight forwarder must obtain operating authority pursuant to part 365 of this chapter as a condition for obtaining USDOT Registration.

(2) A motor carrier registering to engage in transportation that is not exempt from economic regulation by FMCSA must obtain operating authority pursuant to part 365 of this subchapter as a condition for obtaining USDOT Registration.

(c) **Intermodal equipment providers**. An intermodal equipment provider is subject to the requirements of subpart C of this part.

(1) Only the legal name or a single trade name of the intermodal equipment provider may be used on the Form MCSA-1, the URS online application.

(2) The intermodal equipment provider must identify each unit of interchanged intermodal equipment by its assigned USDOT Number.

(d) **Hazardous materials safety permit applicants**. A person who applies for a hazardous materials safety permit is subject to the requirements of part 385, subpart E, of this subchapter.

(e) **Cargo tank facilities**. A cargo tank facility is subject to the requirements of 49 CFR part 107, subpart F, 49 CFR part 172, subpart H, and 49 CFR part 180.

§390.209 Pre-authorization safety audit. [Suspended]

A non-North America-domiciled motor carrier seeking to provide transportation of property or passengers in interstate commerce within the United States must pass the pre-authorization safety audit under §385.607(c) of this subchapter as a condition for receiving registration under this part.

Subpart F—[Reserved]

Subpart G—Lease and Interchange of Passenger-Carrying Commercial Motor Vehicles

§390.401 Applicability.

(a) **General.** Beginning on January 1, 2021, and except as provided in paragraphs (b)(1) and (2) of this section, this subpart applies to the following actions, irrespective of duration, or the presence or absence of compensation, by motor carriers operating commercial motor vehicles to transport passengers:

(1) The lease of passenger-carrying commercial motor vehicles; and

(2) The interchange of passenger-carrying commercial motor vehicles between motor carriers.

(b) **Exceptions** — (1) *Contracts and agreements between motor carriers of passengers with active passenger carrier operating authority registrations*. This subpart does not apply to contracts and agreements between motor carriers of passengers that have active passenger carrier operating authority registrations with the Federal Motor Carrier Safety Administration when one such motor carrier acquires transportation service(s) from another such motor carrier(s).

(2) *Financial leases*. This subpart does not apply to a contract (however designated, *e.g.,* lease, closed-end lease, hire purchase, lease purchase, purchase agreement, installment plan, demonstration or loaner vehicle, etc.) between a motor carrier and a bank or similar financial organization or a manufacturer or dealer of passenger-carrying commercial motor vehicles allowing the motor carrier to use the passenger-carrying commercial motor vehicle.

(c) **Penalties.** If the use of a passenger-carrying commercial motor vehicle is conferred on one motor carrier subject to this subpart by another such motor carrier without a lease or interchange agreement, or pursuant to a lease or interchange agreement that fails to meet all applicable requirements of subpart G, both motor carriers shall be subject to a civil penalty.

§390.403 Lease and interchange requirements.

Beginning on January 1, 2021, and except as provided in §390.401(b) of this section, a motor carrier may transport passengers in a leased or interchanged commercial motor vehicle only under the following conditions:

(a) **In general**—(1) *Lease or agreement required.* There shall be in effect either:

(i) A lease granting the use of the passenger-carrying commercial motor vehicle and meeting the conditions of paragraphs (b) and (c) of this section. The provisions of the lease shall be adhered to and performed by the lessee; or

(ii) An agreement meeting the conditions of paragraphs (b) and (c) of this section and governing the interchange of passenger-carrying commercial motor vehicles between motor carriers of passengers conducting service on a route or series of routes. The provisions of the interchange agreement shall be adhered to and performed by the lessee.

(2) *Exception.* When an event occurs (*e.g.,* a crash, the vehicle is disabled) that requires a motor carrier of passengers immediately to obtain a replacement vehicle from another motor carrier of passengers, the two carriers may postpone the writing of the lease or written agreement for the replacement vehicle for up to 48 hours after the time the lessee takes exclusive possession and control of the replacement vehicle. However, during that 48-hour period, until the lease or agreement is written and provided to the driver, the driver must carry, and produce upon demand of an enforcement official, a document signed and dated by the lessee's driver or available company official stating: "[Carrier A, USDOT number, telephone number] has leased this vehicle to [Carrier B, USDOT number, telephone number] pursuant to 49 CFR 390.403(a)(2)."

(b) **Contents of the lease.** The lease or interchange agreement required by paragraph (a) of this section shall contain:

(1) *Vehicle identification information.* The name of the vehicle manufacturer, the year of manufacture, and at least the last 6 digits of the Vehicle Identification Number (VIN) of each passenger-carrying commercial motor vehicle transferred between motor carriers pursuant to the lease or interchange agreement.

(2) *Parties.* The legal name, USDOT number, and telephone number of the motor carrier providing passenger transportation in a commercial motor vehicle (lessee) and the legal name, USDOT number, and telephone number of the motor carrier providing the equipment (lessor), and signatures of both parties or their authorized representatives.

(3) *Specific duration.* The time and date when, and the location where, the lease or interchange agreement begins and ends.

(4) *Exclusive possession and responsibilities.* (i) A clear statement that the motor carrier obtaining the passenger-carrying commercial motor vehicle (the lessee) has exclusive possession, control, and use of the passenger-carrying commercial motor vehicle for the duration of the agreement, and assumes complete responsibility for operation of the vehicle and compliance with all applicable Federal regulations for the duration of the agreement.

(ii) In the event of a sublease between motor carriers, all of the requirements of this section shall apply to a sublease.

(c) **Copies of the lease.** A copy shall be on the passenger-carrying commercial motor vehicle during the period of the lease or interchange agreement, and both the lessee and lessor shall retain a copy of the lease or interchange agreement for 1 year after the expiration date.

PART 391—QUALIFICATIONS OF DRIVERS AND LONGER COMBINATION VEHICLE (LCV) DRIVER INSTRUCTORS

Subpart A—General

Authority: 49 U.S.C. 504, 508, 31133, 31136, 31149, 31502; sec. 4007(b), Pub. L. 102-240, 105 Stat. 1914, 2152; sec. 114, Pub. L. 103-311, 108 Stat. 1673, 1677; sec. 215, Pub. L. 106-159, 113 Stat. 1748, 1767; sec. 32934, Pub. L. 112-141, 126 Stat. 405, 830; secs. 5403 and 5524, Pub. L. 114-94, 129 Stat. 1312, 1548, 1560; sec. 2, Pub. L. 115-105, 131 Stat. 2263; and 49 CFR 1.87.

Subpart A—General

§391.1 Scope of the rules in this part; additional qualifications; duties of carrier-drivers.

(a) The rules in this part establish minimum qualifications for persons who drive commercial motor vehicles as, for, or on behalf of motor carriers. The rules in this part also establish minimum duties of motor carriers with respect to the qualifications of their drivers.

(b) An individual who meets the definition of both a motor carrier and a driver employed by that motor carrier must comply with both the rules in this part that apply to motor carriers and the rules in this part that apply to drivers.

§391.2 General exceptions.

(a) **Farm custom operation**. The rules in this part, except for §391.15(e) and (f), do not apply to a driver who drives a commercial motor vehicle controlled and operated by a person engaged in custom-harvesting operations, if the commercial motor vehicle is used to—

(1) Transport farm machinery, supplies, or both, to or from a farm for custom-harvesting operations on a farm; or

(2) Transport custom-harvested crops to storage or market.

(b) **Apiarian industries**. The rules in this part, except for §391.15(e) and (f), do not apply to a driver who is operating a commercial motor vehicle controlled and operated by a beekeeper engaged in the seasonal transportation of bees.

(c) **Certain farm vehicle drivers**. The rules in this part, except for §391.15(e) and (f), do not apply to a farm vehicle driver except a farm vehicle driver who drives an articulated (combination) commercial motor vehicle, as defined in §390.5 of this chapter. For limited exemptions for farm vehicle drivers of articulated commercial motor vehicles, see §391.67.

(d) **Covered farm vehicles**. The rules in part 391, Subpart E—Physical Qualifications and Examinations—do not apply to drivers of "covered farm vehicles," as defined in 49 CFR 390.5.

(e) **Pipeline welding trucks**. The rules in this part do not apply to drivers of "pipeline welding trucks" as defined in 49 CFR 390.38(b).

Subpart B—Qualification and Disqualification of Drivers

§391.11 General qualifications of drivers.

(a) A person shall not drive a commercial motor vehicle unless he/she is qualified to drive a commercial motor vehicle. Except as provided in §391.63, a motor carrier shall not require or permit a person to drive a commercial motor vehicle unless that person is qualified to drive a commercial motor vehicle.

(b) Except as provided in subpart G of this part, a person is qualified to drive a motor vehicle if he/she—

PART 391

(1) Is at least 21 years old;

(2) Can read and speak the English language sufficiently to converse with the general public, to understand highway traffic signs and signals in the English language, to respond to official inquiries, and to make entries on reports and records;

(3) Can, by reason of experience, training, or both, safely operate the type of commercial motor vehicle he/she drives;

(4) Is physically qualified to drive a commercial motor vehicle in accordance with subpart E—Physical Qualifications and Examinations of this part;

(5) Has a currently valid commercial motor vehicle operator's license issued only by one State or jurisdiction.

(6) Has prepared and furnished the motor carrier that employs him/her with the list of violations or the certificate as required by §391.27;

(7) Is not disqualified to drive a commercial motor vehicle under the rules in §391.15; and

(8) Has successfully completed a driver's road test and has been issued a certificate of driver's road test in accordance with §391.31, or has presented an operator's license or a certificate of road test which the motor carrier that employs him/her has accepted as equivalent to a road test in accordance with §391.33.

§391.13 Responsibilities of drivers.

In order to comply with the requirements of §§392.9(a) and 383.111(a)(16) of this subchapter, a motor carrier shall not require or permit a person to drive a commercial motor vehicle unless the person—

(a) Can, by reason of experience, training, or both, determine whether the cargo he/she transports (including baggage in a passenger-carrying commercial motor vehicle) has been properly located, distributed, and secured in or on the commercial motor vehicle he/she drives;

(b) Is familiar with methods and procedures for securing cargo in or on the commercial motor vehicle he/she drives.

§391.15 Disqualification of drivers.

(a) **General**. A driver who is disqualified shall not drive a commercial motor vehicle. A motor carrier shall not require or permit a driver who is disqualified to drive a commercial motor vehicle.

(b) **Disqualification for loss of driving privileges**. (1) A driver is disqualified for the duration of the driver's loss of his/her privilege to operate a commercial motor vehicle on public highways, either temporarily or permanently, by reason of the revocation, suspension, withdrawal, or denial of an operator's license, permit, or privilege, until that operator's license, permit, or privilege is restored by the authority that revoked, suspended, withdrew, or denied it.

(2) A driver who receives a notice that his/her license, permit, or privilege to operate a commercial motor vehicle has been revoked, suspended, or withdrawn shall notify the motor carrier that employs him/her of the contents of the notice before the end of the business day following the day the driver received it.

(c) **Disqualification for criminal and other offenses**.

(1) **General rule**. A driver who is convicted of (or forfeits bond or collateral upon a charge of) a disqualifying offense specified in paragraph (c)(2) of this section is disqualified for the period of time specified in paragraph (c)(3) of this section, if—

(i) The offense was committed during on-duty time as defined in §395.2 of this subchapter or as otherwise specified; and

(ii) The driver is employed by a motor carrier or is engaged in activities that are in furtherance of a commercial enterprise in interstate, intrastate, or foreign commerce.

(2) **Disqualifying offenses**. The following offenses are disqualifying offenses:

(i) Driving a commercial motor vehicle while under the influence of alcohol. This shall include:

(A) Driving a commercial motor vehicle while the person's alcohol concentration is 0.04 percent or more;

(B) Driving under the influence of alcohol, as prescribed by State law; or

(C) Refusal to undergo such testing as is required by any State or jurisdiction in the enforcement of §391.15(c)(2)(i)(A) or (B), or §392.5(a)(2).

(ii) Driving a commercial motor vehicle under the influence of a 21 CFR 1308.11 *Schedule I* identified controlled substance, an amphetamine, a narcotic drug, a formulation of an amphetamine or a derivative of a narcotic drug;

(iii) Transportation, possession, or unlawful use of a 21 CFR 1308.11 *Schedule I* identified controlled substance, amphetamines, narcotic drugs, formulations of an amphetamine, or derivatives of narcotic drugs while the driver is on duty as the term on-duty time is defined in §395.2 of this subchapter;

(iv) Leaving the scene of an accident while operating a commercial motor vehicle; or

(v) A felony involving the use of a commercial motor vehicle.

(3) **Duration of disqualification—** (i) **First offenders**. A driver is disqualified for 1 year after the date of conviction or forfeiture of bond or collateral if, during the 3 years preceding that date, the driver was not convicted of, or did not forfeit bond or collateral upon a charge of an offense that would disqualify the driver under the rules of this section. **Exemption.** The period of disqualification is 6 months if the conviction or forfeiture of bond or collateral solely concerned the transportation or possession of substances named in paragraph (c)(2)(iii) of this section.

(ii) **Subsequent offenders.** A driver is disqualified for 3 years after the date of his/her conviction or forfeiture of bond or collateral if, during the 3 years preceding that date, he/she was convicted of, or forfeited bond or collateral upon a charge of, an offense that would disqualify him/her under the rules in this section.

(d) **Disqualification for violation of out-of-service orders**.

(1) **General rule.** A driver who is convicted of violating an out-of-service order is disqualified for the period of time specified in paragraph (d)(2) of this section.

(2) **Duration of disqualification** for violation of out-of-service orders.

(i) **First violation.** A driver is disqualified for not less than 90 days nor more than one year if the driver is convicted of a first violation of an out-of-service order.

(ii) **Second violation.** A driver is disqualified for not less than one year nor more than five years if, during any 10-year period, the driver is convicted of two violations of out-of-service orders in separate incidents.

(iii) **Third or subsequent violation.** A driver is disqualified for not less than three years nor more than five years if, during any 10-year period, the driver is convicted of three or more violations of out-of-service orders in separate incidents.

(iv) **Special rule for hazardous materials and passenger offenses.** A driver is disqualified for a period of not less than 180 days nor more than two years if the driver is convicted of a first violation of an out-of-service order while transporting hazardous materials required to be placarded under the Hazardous Materials Transportation Act (49 U.S.C. 5101 *et seq.*), or while operating commercial motor vehicles designed to transport more than 15 passengers, including the driver. A driver is disqualified for a period of not less than three years nor more than five years if, during any 10-year period, the driver is convicted of any subsequent violations of out-of-service orders, in separate incidents, while transporting hazardous materials required to be placarded under the Hazardous Materials Transportation Act, or while operating commercial motor vehicles designed to transport more than 15 passengers, including the driver.

(e) **Disqualification for violation of prohibition of texting while driving a commercial motor vehicle—**

(1) **General rule.** A driver who is convicted of violating the prohibition of texting in §392.80(a) of this chapter is disqualified for the period of time specified in paragraph (e)(2) of this section.

(2) **Duration.** Disqualification for violation of prohibition of texting while driving a commercial motor vehicle—

(i) **Second violation.** A driver is disqualified for 60 days if the driver is convicted of two violations of §392.80(a) of this chapter in separate incidents during any 3-year period.

(ii) **Third or subsequent violation.** A driver is disqualified for 120 days if the driver is convicted of three or more violations of §392.80(a) of this chapter in separate incidents during any 3-year period.

(f) **Disqualification for violation of a restriction on using a hand-held mobile telephone while driving a commercial motor vehicle—**

(1) **General rule.** A driver who is convicted of violating the restriction on using a hand-held mobile telephone in §392.82(a) of this chapter is disqualified from driving a commercial motor vehicle for the period of time specified in paragraph (f)(2) of this section.

(2) **Duration.** Disqualification for violation of a restriction on using a hand-held mobile telephone while driving a commercial motor vehicle—

(i) **Second violation.** A driver is disqualified for 60 days if the driver is convicted of two violations of §392.82(a) of this chapter in separate incidents committed during any 3-year period.

(ii) **Third or subsequent violation.** A driver is disqualified for 120 days if the driver is convicted of three or more violations of §392.82(a) of this chapter in separate incidents committed during any 3-year period.

Subpart C—Background and Character

§391.21 Application for employment.

(a) Except as provided in Subpart G of this part, a person shall not drive a commercial motor vehicle unless he/she has completed and furnished the motor carrier that employs him/her with an application for employment that meets the requirements of paragraph (b) of this section.

(b) The application for employment shall be made on a form furnished by the motor carrier. Each application form must be completed by the applicant, must be signed by him/her, and must contain the following information:

(1) The name and address of the employing motor carrier;

(2) The applicant's name, address, date of birth, and social security number;

(3) The addresses at which the applicant has resided during the 3 years preceding the date on which the application is submitted;

(4) The date on which the application is submitted;

(5) The issuing State, number, and expiration date of each unexpired commercial motor vehicle operator's license or permit that has been issued to the applicant;

(6) The nature and extent of the applicant's experience in the operation of motor vehicles, including the type of equipment (such as buses, trucks, truck tractors, semitrailers, full trailers, and pole trailers) which he/she has operated;

(7) A list of all motor vehicle accidents in which the applicant was involved during the 3 years preceding the date the application is submitted, specifying the date and nature of each accident and any fatalities or personal injuries it caused;

(8) A list of all violations of motor vehicle laws or ordinances (other than violations involving only parking) of which the applicant was convicted or forfeited bond or collateral during the 3 years preceding the date the application is submitted;

(9) A statement setting forth in detail the facts and circumstances of any denial, revocation, or suspension of any license, permit, or privilege to operate a motor vehicle that has been issued to the applicant, or a statement that no such denial, revocation, or suspension has occurred;

(10)(i) A list of the names and addresses of the applicant's employers during the 3 years preceding the date the application is submitted,

(ii) The dates he or she was employed by that employer,

(iii) The reason for leaving the employ of that employer,

(iv) After October 29, 2004, whether the (A) Applicant was subject to the FMCSRs while employed by that previous employer,

(B) Job was designated as a safety sensitive function in any DOT regulated mode subject to alcohol and controlled substances testing requirements as required by 49 CFR part 40;

(11) For those drivers applying to operate a commercial motor vehicle as defined by Part 383 of this subchapter, a list of the names and addresses of the applicant's employers during the 7-year period preceding the 3 years contained in paragraph (b)(10) of this section for which the applicant was an operator of a commercial motor vehicle, together with the dates of employment and the reasons for leaving such employment; and

(12) The following certification and signature line, which must appear at the end of the application form and be signed by the applicant:

This certifies that this application was completed by me, and that all entries on it and information in it are true and complete to the best of my knowledge.

_____   _____
(Date)   (Applicant's signature)

(c) A motor carrier may require an applicant to provide information in addition to the information required by paragraph (b) of this section on the application form.

(d) Before an application is submitted, the motor carrier must inform the applicant that the information he/she provides in accordance with paragraph (b)(10) of this section may be used, and the applicant's previous employers will be contacted, for the purpose of investigating the applicant's safety performance history information as required by paragraphs (d) and (e) of §391.23. The prospective employer must also notify the driver in writing of his/her due process rights as specified in §391.23(i) regarding information received as a result of these investigations.

§391.23 Investigation and inquiries.

(a) Except as provided in Subpart G of this part, each motor carrier shall make the following investigations and inquiries with respect to each driver it employs, other than a person who has been a regularly employed driver of the motor carrier for a continuous period which began before January 1, 1971:

(1) An inquiry, within 30 days of the date the driver's employment begins, to each State where the driver held or holds a motor vehicle operator's license or permit during the preceding 3 years to obtain that driver's motor vehicle record.

(2) An investigation of the driver's safety performance history with Department of Transportation regulated employers during the preceding three years.

(b) A copy of the motor vehicle record(s) obtained in response to the inquiry or inquiries to each State required by paragraph (a)(1) of this section must be placed in the driver qualification file within 30 days of the date the driver's employment begins and be retained in compliance with §391.51. If no motor vehicle record is received from the State or States required to submit this response, the motor carrier must document a good faith effort to obtain such information, and certify that no record exists for that driver in that State or States. The inquiry to the State driver licensing agency or agencies must be made in the form and manner each agency prescribes.

(c)(1) Replies to the investigations of the driver's safety performance history required by paragraph (a)(2) of this section, or documentation of good faith efforts to obtain the investigation data, must be placed in the driver investigation history file, after October 29, 2004, within 30 days of the date the driver's employment begins. Any period of time required to exercise the driver's due process rights to review the information received, request a previous employer to correct or include a rebuttal, is separate and apart from this 30-day requirement to document investigation of the driver safety performance history data.

(2) The investigation may consist of personal interviews, telephone interviews, letters, or any other method for investigating that the carrier deems appropriate. Each motor carrier must make a written record with respect to each previous employer contacted, or good faith efforts to do so. The record must include the previous employer's name and address, the date the previous employer was contacted, or the attempts made, and the information received about the driver from the previous employer. Failures to contact a previous employer, or of them to provide the required safety performance history information, must be documented. The record must be maintained pursuant to §391.53.

(3) Prospective employers should report failures of previous employers to respond to an investigation to the FMCSA and use the complaint procedures specified at §386.12 of this subchapter. Keep a copy of the reports in the driver investigation history file as part of documenting a good faith effort to obtain the required information.

(4) **Exception.** For drivers with no previous employment experience working for a DOT-regulated employer during the preceding three years, documentation that no investigation was possible must be placed in the driver investigation history file, after October 29, 2004, within the required 30 days of the date the driver's employment begins.

(d) The prospective motor carrier must investigate, at a minimum, the information listed in this paragraph from all previous employers of the applicant that employed the driver to operate a CMV within the previous three years. The investigation request must contain specific contact information on where the previous motor carrier employers should send the information requested.

(1) General driver identification and employment verification information.

(2) The data elements as specified in §390.15(b)(1) of this chapter for accidents involving the driver that occurred in the three-year period preceding the date of the employment application.

(i) Any accidents as defined by §390.5 of this chapter.

(ii) Any accidents the previous employer may wish to provide that are retained pursuant to §390.15(b)(2), or pursuant to the employer's internal policies for retaining more detailed minor accident information.

(e) In addition to the investigations required by paragraph (d) of this section, the prospective motor carrier employers must investigate the information listed below in this paragraph from all previous DOT regulated employers that employed the driver within the previous three years from the date of the employment application, in a safety-sensitive function that required alcohol and controlled substance testing specified by 49 CFR part 40.

(1) Whether, within the previous three years, the driver had violated the alcohol and controlled substances prohibitions under subpart B of part 382 of this chapter, or 49 CFR part 40.

(2) Whether the driver failed to undertake or complete a rehabilitation program prescribed by a substance abuse professional (SAP) pursuant to §382.605 of this chapter, or 49 CFR part 40, subpart O. If the previous employer does not know this information (e.g., an employer that terminated an employee who tested positive on a drug test), the prospective motor carrier must obtain documentation of the driver's successful completion of the SAP's referral directly from the driver.

(3) For a driver who had successfully completed a SAP's rehabilitation referral, and remained in the employ of the referring employer, information on whether the driver had the following testing violations subsequent to completion of a §382.605 or 49 CFR part 40, subpart O referral:

(i) Alcohol tests with a result of 0.04 or higher alcohol concentration;

(ii) Verified positive drug tests;

(iii) Refusals to be tested (including verified adulterated or substituted drug test results).

(4) As of January 6, 2023, employers subject to §382.701(a) of this chapter must use the Drug and Alcohol Clearinghouse to comply with the requirements of this section with respect to FMCSA-regulated employers.

(i) **Exceptions**. (A) If an applicant who is subject to follow-up testing has not successfully completed all follow-up tests, the employer must request the applicant's follow-up testing plan directly from the previous employer in accordance with §40.25(b)(5) of this title.

(B) If an applicant was subject to an alcohol and controlled substance testing program under the requirements of a DOT mode other than FMCSA, the employer must request alcohol and controlled substances information required under this section directly from those employers regulated by a DOT mode other than FMCSA.

(ii) [Reserved]

(f)(1) A prospective motor carrier employer must provide to the previous employer the driver's consent meeting the requirements of §40.321(b) of this title for the release of the information in paragraph (e) of this section. If the driver refuses to provide this consent, the prospective motor carrier employer must not permit the driver to operate a commercial motor vehicle for that motor carrier.

(2) If a driver refuses to grant consent for the prospective motor carrier employer to query the Drug and Alcohol Clearinghouse in accordance with paragraph (e)(4) of this section, the prospective motor carrier employer must not permit the driver to operate a commercial motor vehicle.

(g) After October 29, 2004, previous employers must:

(1) Respond to each request for the DOT defined information in paragraphs (d) and (e) of this section within 30 days after the request is received. If there is no safety performance history information to report for that driver, previous motor carrier employers are nonetheless required to send a response confirming the non-existence of any such data, including the driver identification information and dates of employment.

(2) Take all precautions reasonably necessary to ensure the accuracy of the records.

(3) Provide specific contact information in case a driver chooses to contact the previous employer regarding correction or rebuttal of the data.

(4) Keep a record of each request and the response for one year, including the date, the party to whom it was released, and a summary identifying what was provided.

(5) **Exception.** Until May 1, 2006, carriers need only provide information for accidents that occurred after April 29, 2003.

(h) The release of information under this section may take any form that reasonably ensures confidentiality, including letter, facsimile, or e-mail. The previous employer and its agents and insurers must take all precautions reasonably necessary to protect the driver safety performance history records from disclosure to any person not directly involved in forwarding the records, except the previous employer's insurer, except that the previous employer may not provide any alcohol or controlled substances information to the previous employer's insurer.

(i)(1) The prospective employer must expressly notify drivers with Department of Transportation regulated employment during the preceding three years—via the application form or other written document prior to any hiring decision—that he or she has the following rights regarding the investigative information that will be provided to the prospective employer pursuant to paragraphs (d) and (e) of this section:

(i) The right to review information provided by previous employers;

(ii) The right to have errors in the information corrected by the previous employer and for that previous employer to re-send the corrected information to the prospective employer;

(iii) The right to have a rebuttal statement attached to the alleged erroneous information, if the previous employer and the driver cannot agree on the accuracy of the information.

(2) Drivers who have previous Department of Transportation regulated employment history in the preceding three years, and wish to review previous employer-provided investigative information must submit a written request to the prospective employer, which may be done at any time, including when applying, or as late as 30 days after being employed or being notified of denial of

employment. The prospective employer must provide this information to the applicant within five (5) business days of receiving the written request. If the prospective employer has not yet received the requested information from the previous employer(s), then the five-business days deadline will begin when the prospective employer receives the requested safety performance history information. If the driver has not arranged to pick up or receive the requested records within thirty (30) days of the prospective employer making them available, the prospective motor carrier may consider the driver to have waived his/her request to review the records.

(j)(1) Drivers wishing to request correction of erroneous information in records received pursuant to paragraph (i) of this section must send the request for the correction to the previous employer that provided the records to the prospective employer.

(2) After October 29, 2004, the previous employer must either correct and forward the information to the prospective motor carrier employer, or notify the driver within 15 days of receiving a driver's request to correct the data that it does not agree to correct the data. If the previous employer corrects and forwards the data as requested, that employer must also retain the corrected information as part of the driver's safety performance history record and provide it to subsequent prospective employers when requests for this information are received. If the previous employer corrects the data and forwards it to the prospective motor carrier employer, there is no need to notify the driver.

(3) Drivers wishing to rebut information in records received pursuant to paragraph (i) of this section must send the rebuttal to the previous employer with instructions to include the rebuttal in that driver's safety performance history.

(4) After October 29, 2004, within five business days of receiving a rebuttal from a driver, the previous employer must:

(i) Forward a copy of the rebuttal to the prospective motor carrier employer;

(ii) Append the rebuttal to the driver's information in the carrier's appropriate file, to be included as part of the response for any subsequent investigating prospective employers for the duration of the three-year data retention requirement.

(5) The driver may submit a rebuttal initially without a request for correction, or subsequent to a request for correction.

(6) The driver may report failures of previous employers to correct information or include the driver's rebuttal as part of the safety performance information, to the FMCSA following procedures specified at §386.12.

(k)(1) The prospective motor carrier employer must use the information described in paragraphs (d) and (e) of this section only as part of deciding whether to hire the driver.

(2) The prospective motor carrier employer, its agents and insurers must take all precautions reasonably necessary to protect the records from disclosure to any person not directly involved in deciding whether to hire the driver. The prospective motor carrier employer may not provide any alcohol or controlled substances information to the prospective motor carrier employer's insurer.

(l)(1) No action or proceeding for defamation, invasion of privacy, or interference with a contract that is based on the furnishing or use of information in accordance with this section may be brought against—

(i) A motor carrier investigating the information, described in paragraphs (d) and (e) of this section, of an individual under consideration for employment as a commercial motor vehicle driver,

(ii) A person who has provided such information; or

(iii) The agents or insurers of a person described in paragraph (l)(1)(i) or (ii) of this section, except insurers are not granted a limitation on liability for any alcohol and controlled substance information.

(2) The protections in paragraph (l)(1) of this section do not apply to persons who knowingly furnish false information, or who are not in compliance with the procedures specified for these investigations.

(m)(1) The motor carrier must obtain an original or copy of the medical examiner's certificate issued in accordance with §391.43, and any medical variance on which the certification is based, and, beginning on or after May 21, 2014, verify the driver was certified by a medical examiner listed on the National Registry of Certified Medical Examiners as of the date of issuance of the medical examiner's certificate, and place the records in the driver qualification file, before allowing the driver to operate a CMV.

(2) **Exception**. For drivers required to have a commercial driver's license under part 383 of this chapter:

(i) Beginning January 30, 2015, using the CDLIS motor vehicle record obtained from the current licensing State, the motor carrier must verify and document in the driver qualification file the following information before allowing the driver to operate a CMV:

(A) The type of operation the driver self-certified that he or she will perform in accordance with §383.71(b)(1) of this chapter.

(B)*(1)* Beginning on May 21, 2014, and through June 22, 2025, that the driver was certified by a medical examiner listed on the National Registry of Certified Medical Examiners as of the date of medical examiner's certificate issuance.

(2) If the driver has certified under paragraph (m)(2)(i)(A) of this section that he or she expects to operate in interstate commerce, that the driver has a valid medical examiner's certificate and any required medical variances.

(C) **Exception**. Beginning on January 30, 2015, and through June 22, 2025, if the driver provided the motor carrier with a copy of the current medical examiner's certificate that was submitted to the State in accordance with §383.73(b)(5) of this chapter, the motor carrier may use a copy of that medical examiner's certificate as proof of the driver's medical certification for up to 15 days after the date it was issued.

(ii) Until January 30, 2015, if a driver operating in non-excepted, interstate commerce has no medical certification status information on the CDLIS MVR obtained from the current State driver licensing agency, the employing motor carrier may accept a medical examiner's certificate issued to that driver, and place a copy of it in the driver qualification file before allowing the driver to operate a CMV in interstate commerce.

(3) **Exception**. For drivers required to have a commercial learner's permit under part 383 of this chapter:

(i) Beginning July 8, 2015, using the CDLIS motor vehicle record obtained from the current licensing State, the motor carrier must verify and document in the driver qualification file the following information before allowing the driver to operate a CMV:

(A) The type of operation the driver self-certified that he or she will perform in accordance with §383.71(b)(1) and (g) of this chapter.

(B)*(1)* Through June 22, 2025, that the driver was certified by a medical examiner listed on the National Registry of Certified Medical Examiners as of the date of medical examiner's certificate issuance.

(2) If the driver has a commercial learner's permit and has certified under paragraph (m)(3)(i)(A) of this section that he or she expects to operate in interstate commerce, that the driver has a valid medical examiner's certificate and any required medical variances.

(C) Through June 22, 2025, if the driver provided the motor carrier with a copy of the current medical examiner's certificate that was submitted to the State in accordance with §383.73(a)(2)(vii) of this chapter, the motor carrier may use a copy of that medical examiner's certificate as proof of the driver's medical certification for up to 15 days after the date it was issued.

(ii) Until July 8, 2015, if a driver operating in non-excepted, interstate commerce has no medical certification status information on the CDLIS MVR obtained from the current State driver licensing agency, the employing motor carrier may accept a medical examiner's certificate issued to that driver, and place a copy of it in the driver qualification file before allowing the driver to operate a CMV in interstate commerce.

(4) In the event of a conflict between the medical certification information provided electronically by FMCSA and a paper copy of the medical examiner's certificate, the medical certification information provided electronically by FMCSA shall control.

(Approved by the Office of Management and Budget under control number 2126-0004)

§391.25 Annual inquiry and review of driving record.

(a) Except as provided in subpart G of this part, each motor carrier shall, at least once every 12 months, make an inquiry to obtain the motor vehicle record of each driver it employs, covering at least the preceding 12 months, to the appropriate agency of every State in which the driver held a commercial motor vehicle operator's license or permit during the time period.

(b) Except as provided in subpart G of this part, each motor carrier shall, at least once every 12 months, review the motor vehicle record of each driver it employs to determine whether that driver meets minimum requirements for safe driving or is disqualified to drive a commercial motor vehicle pursuant to §391.15.

(1) The motor carrier must consider any evidence that the driver has violated any applicable Federal Motor Carrier Safety Regulations in this subchapter or Hazardous Materials Regulations (49 CFR chapter I, subchapter C).

(2) The motor carrier must consider the driver's accident record and any evidence that the driver has violated laws governing the operation of motor vehicles, and must give great weight to violations, such as speeding, reckless driving, and operating while under the influence of alcohol or drugs, that indicate that the driver has exhibited a disregard for the safety of the public.

(c) **Recordkeeping.** (1) A copy of the motor vehicle record required by paragraph (a) of this section shall be maintained in the driver's qualification file.

(2) A note, including the name of the person who performed the review of the driving record required by paragraph (b) of this section and the date of such review, shall be maintained in the driver's qualification file.

§391.27 Record of violations.

(a) Except as provided in Subpart G of this part, each motor carrier shall, at least once every 12 months, require each driver it employs to prepare and furnish it with a list of all violations of motor vehicle traffic laws and ordinances (other than violations involving only parking) of which the driver has been convicted or on account of which he/she has forfeited bond or collateral during the preceding 12 months.

(b) Each driver shall furnish the list required in accordance with paragraph (a) of this section. If the driver has not been convicted of, or forfeited bond or collateral on account of, any violation which must be listed he/she shall so certify.

(c) The form of the driver's list or certification shall be prescribed by the motor carrier. The following form may be used to comply with this section:

Driver's Certification

I certify that the following is a true and complete list of traffic violations (other than parking violations) for which I have been convicted or forfeited bond or collateral during the past 12 months.

Date of conviction	Offense
_____	_____
_____	_____
_____	_____

Location	Type of motor vehicle operated
_____	_____
_____	_____
_____	_____

If no violations are listed above, I certify that I have not been convicted or forfeited bond or collateral on account of any violation required to be listed during the past 12 months.

(Date of certification)	(Driver's signature)
	(Motor carrier's name)
	(Motor carrier's address)
(Reviewed by: Signature)	(Title)

(d) The motor carrier shall retain the list or certificate required by this section, or a copy of it, in its files as part of the driver's qualification file.

(e) Drivers who have provided information required by §383.31 of this subchapter need not repeat that information in the annual list of violations required by this section.

Subpart D—Tests

§391.31 Road test.

(a) Except as provided in subpart G, a person shall not drive a commercial motor vehicle unless he/she has first successfully completed a road test and has been issued a certificate of driver's road test in accordance with this section.

(b) The road test shall be given by the motor carrier or a person designated by it. However, a driver who is a motor carrier must be given the test by a person other than himself/herself. The test shall be given by a person who is competent to evaluate and determine whether the person who takes the test has demonstrated that he/she is capable of operating the commercial motor vehicle, and associated equipment, that the motor carrier intends to assign him/her.

(c) The road test must be of sufficient duration to enable the person who gives it to evaluate the skill of the person who takes it at handling the commercial motor vehicle and associated equipment, that the motor carrier intends to assign to him/her. As a minimum, the person who takes the test must be tested, while operating the type of commercial motor vehicle the motor carrier intends to assign him/her, on his/her skill at performing each of the following operations:

(1) The pretrip inspection required by §392.7 of this subchapter;

(2) Coupling and uncoupling of combination units, if the equipment he/she may drive includes combination units;

(3) Placing the commercial motor vehicle in operation;

(4) Use of the commercial motor vehicle's controls and emergency equipment;

(5) Operating the commercial motor vehicle in traffic and while passing other motor vehicles;

(6) Turning the commercial motor vehicle;

(7) Braking, and slowing the commercial motor vehicle by means other than braking; and

(8) Backing and parking the commercial motor vehicle.

(d) The motor carrier shall provide a road test form on which the person who gives the test shall rate the performance of the person who takes it at each operation or activity which is a part of the test. After he/she completes the form, the person who gave the test shall sign it.

(e) If the road test is successfully completed, the person who gave it shall complete a certificate of driver's road test in substantially the form prescribed in paragraph (f) of this section.

(f) The form for the certificate of driver's road test is substantially as follows:

CERTIFICATION OF ROAD TEST

Driver's name _____

Social Security No. _____

Operator's or Chauffeur's License No. _____

State _____

Type of power unit _____

Type of trailer(s) _____

If passenger carrier, type of bus _____

This is to certify that the above-named driver was given a road test under my supervision on _____ 20 _____ consisting of approximately _____ miles of driving.

It is my considered opinion that this driver possesses sufficient driving skill to operate safely the type of commercial motor vehicle listed above.

_____   _____
(Signature of examiner)   (Title)

_____
(Organization and address of examiner)

(g) A copy of the certificate required by paragraph (e) of this section shall be given to the person who was examined. The motor carrier shall retain in the driver qualification file of the person who was examined—

(1) The original of the signed road test form required by paragraph (d) of this section; and

(2) The original, or a copy of, the certificate required by paragraph (e) of this section.

§391.33 Equivalent of road test.

(a) In place of, and as equivalent to, the road test required by §391.31, a person who seeks to drive a commercial motor vehicle may present, and a motor carrier may accept—

(1) A valid Commercial Driver's License as defined in §383.5 of this subchapter, but not including double/triple trailer or tank vehicle endorsements, which has been issued to him/her to operate specific categories of commercial motor vehicles and which, under the laws of that State, licenses him/her after successful completion of a road test in a commercial motor vehicle of the type the motor carrier intends to assign to him/her; or

(2) A copy of a valid certificate of driver's road test issued to him/her pursuant to §391.31 within the preceding 3 years.

(b) If a driver presents, and a motor carrier accepts, a license or certificate as equivalent to the road test, the motor carrier shall retain a legible copy of the license or certificate in its files as part of the driver's qualification file.

(c) A motor carrier may require any person who presents a license or certificate as equivalent to the road test to take a road test or any other test of his/her driving skill as a condition to his/her employment as a driver.

Subpart E—Physical Qualifications and Examinations

§391.41 Physical qualifications for drivers.

(a)(1)(i) A person subject to this part must not operate a commercial motor vehicle unless he or she is medically certified as physically qualified to do so, and, except as provided in paragraph (a)(2) of this section, when on-duty has on his or her person the original, or a copy, of a current medical examiner's certificate that he or she is physically qualified to drive a commercial motor vehicle. NOTE: Effective December 29, 1991, and as amended on January 19, 2017, the FMCSA Administrator determined that the Licencia Federal de Conductor issued by the United Mexican States is recognized as proof of medical fitness to drive a CMV. The United States and Canada entered into a Reciprocity Agreement, effective March 30, 1999, recognizing that a Canadian commercial driver's license is proof of medical fitness to drive a CMV. Therefore, Canadian and Mexican CMV drivers are not required to have in their possession a medical examiner's certificate if the driver has been issued, and possesses, a valid commercial driver license issued by the United Mexican States, or a Canadian Province or Territory, and whose license and medical status, including any waiver or exemption, can be electronically verified. Drivers from any of the countries who have received a medical authorization that deviates from the mutually accepted compatible medical standards of the resident country are not qualified to drive a CMV in the other countries. For example, Canadian drivers who do not meet the medical fitness provisions of the Canadian National Safety Code for Motor Carriers but are issued a waiver by one of the Canadian Provinces or Territories, are not qualified to drive a CMV in the United States. In addition, U.S. drivers who received a medical variance from FMCSA are not qualified to drive a CMV in Canada.

(ii) A person who qualifies for the medical examiner's certificate by virtue of having obtained a medical variance from FMCSA, in the form of an exemption letter or a skill performance evaluation certificate, must have on his or her person a copy of the variance documentation when on-duty.

(2) **CDL exception**. (i)(A) Beginning on January 30, 2015 and through June 22, 2025, a driver required to have a commercial driver's license under part 383 of this chapter, and who submitted a current medical examiner's certificate to the State in accordance with 49 CFR 383.71(h) documenting that he or she meets the physical qualification requirements of this part, no longer needs to carry on his or her person the medical examiner's certificate specified at §391.43(h), or a copy, for more than 15 days after the date it was issued as valid proof of medical certification.

(B) On or after June 23, 2025, a driver required to have a commercial driver's license or a commercial learner's permit under 49 CFR part 383, and who has a current medical examiner's certificate documenting that he or she meets the physical qualification requirements of this part, no longer needs to carry on his or her person the medical examiner's certificate specified at §391.43(h).

(ii) Beginning on July 8, 2015, and through June 22, 2025, a driver required to have a commercial learner's permit under part 383 of this chapter, and who submitted a current medical examiner's certificate to the State in accordance with §383.71(h) of this chapter documenting that he or she meets the physical qualification requirements of this part, no longer needs to carry on his or her person the medical examiner's certificate specified at §391.43(h), or a copy for more than 15 days after the date it was issued as valid proof of medical certification.

(iii) A CDL or CLP holder required by §383.71(h) of this chapter to obtain a medical examiner's certificate, who obtained such by virtue of having obtained a medical variance from FMCSA, must continue to have in his or her possession the original or copy of that medical variance documentation at all times when on-duty.

(iv) In the event of a conflict between the medical certification information provided electronically by FMCSA and a paper copy of the medical examiner's certificate, the medical certification information provided electronically by FMCSA shall control.

(3) A person is physically qualified to drive a commercial motor vehicle if:

(i) That person meets the physical qualification standards in paragraph (b) of this section and has complied with the medical examination requirements in §391.43; or

(ii) That person obtained from FMCSA a medical variance from the physical qualification standards in paragraph (b) of this section and has complied with the medical examination requirement in §391.43.

(b) A person is physically qualified to drive a commercial motor vehicle if that person—

(1) Has no loss of a foot, a leg, a hand, or an arm, or has been granted a skill performance evaluation certificate pursuant to §391.49;

(2) Has no impairment of:

(i) A hand or finger which interferes with prehension or power grasping; or

(ii) An arm, foot, or leg which interferes with the ability to perform normal tasks associated with operating a commercial motor vehicle; or any other significant limb defect or limitation which interferes with the ability to perform normal tasks associated with operating a commercial motor vehicle; or has been granted a skill performance evaluation certificate pursuant to §391.49;

(3) Has no established medical history or clinical diagnosis of diabetes mellitus currently treated with insulin for control, unless the person meets the requirements in §391.46;

(4) Has no current clinical diagnosis of myocardial infarction, angina pectoris, coronary insufficiency, thrombosis, or any other cardiovascular disease of a variety known to be accompanied by syncope, dyspnea, collapse, or congestive cardiac failure;

(5) Has no established medical history or clinical diagnosis of a respiratory dysfunction likely to interfere with his/her ability to control and drive a commercial motor vehicle safely;

(6) Has no current clinical diagnosis of high blood pressure likely to interfere with his/her ability to operate a commercial motor vehicle safely;

(7) Has no established medical history or clinical diagnosis of rheumatic, arthritic, orthopedic, muscular, neuromuscular, or vascular disease which interferes with his/her ability to control and operate a commercial motor vehicle safely;

(8) Has no established medical history or clinical diagnosis of epilepsy or any other condition which is likely to cause loss of consciousness or any loss of ability to control a commercial motor vehicle;

(9) Has no mental, nervous, organic, or functional disease or psychiatric disorder likely to interfere with his/her ability to drive a commercial motor vehicle safely;

(10) Has distant visual acuity of at least 20/40 (Snellen) in each eye without corrective lenses or visual acuity separately corrected to 20/40 (Snellen) or better with corrective lenses, distant binocular acuity of at least 20/40 (Snellen) in both eyes with or without corrective lenses, field of vision of at least 70° in the horizontal meridian in each eye, and the ability to recognize the colors of traffic signals and devices showing standard red, green, and amber;

(11) First perceives a forced whispered voice in the better ear at not less than 5 feet with or without the use of a hearing aid or, if tested by use of an audiometric device, does not have an average hearing loss in the better ear greater than 40 decibels at 500 Hz, 1,000 Hz, and 2,000 Hz with or without a hearing aid when the audiometric device is calibrated to American National Standard (formerly ASA Standard) Z24.5—1951;

(12)(i) Does not use any drug or substance identified in 21 CFR 1308.11 Schedule I, an amphetamine, a narcotic, or other habit-forming drug; or

(ii) Does not use any non-Schedule I drug or substance that is identified in the other Schedules in 21 CFR part 1308 except when the use is prescribed by a licensed medical practitioner, as defined in §382.107 of this chapter, who is familiar with the driver's medical history and has advised the driver that the substance will not adversely affect the driver's ability to safely operate a commercial motor vehicle; and

(13) Has no current clinical diagnosis of alcoholism.

§391.43 Medical examination; certificate of physical examination.

(a) Except as provided by paragraph (b) of this section, the medical examination must be performed by a medical examiner listed on the National Registry of Certified Medical Examiners under subpart D of part 390 of this chapter.

(b) Exceptions:

(1) A licensed optometrist may perform so much of the medical examination as pertains to visual acuity, field of vision, and the ability to recognize colors as specified in paragraph (10) of §391.41(b).

(2) A certified VA medical examiner must only perform medical examinations of veteran operators.

(c) Medical examiners shall:

(1) Be knowledgeable of the specific physical and mental demands associated with operating a commercial motor vehicle and the requirements of this subpart, including the medical advisory criteria prepared by the FMCSA as guidelines to aid the medical examiner in making the qualification determination; and

(2) Be proficient in the use of and use the medical protocols necessary to adequately perform the medical examination required by this section.

(d) Any driver authorized to operate a commercial motor vehicle within an exempt intra city zone pursuant to §391.62 of this part shall furnish the examining medical examiner with a copy of the medical findings that led to the issuance of the first certificate of medical examination which allowed the driver to operate a commercial motor vehicle wholly within an exempt intra city zone.

(e) Any driver operating under a limited exemption authorized by §391.64 shall furnish the medical examiner with a copy of the annual medical findings of the ophthalmologist or optometrist, as required under §391.64. If the medical examiner finds the driver qualified under the limited exemption in §391.64, such fact shall be noted on the Medical Examiner's Certificate.

(f) The medical examination shall be performed, and its results shall be recorded on the Medical Examination Report Form, MCSA-5875, set out in this paragraph (f):

1632

Form MCSA-5875

OMB No: 2126-0006

Public Burden Statement
A Federal agency may not conduct or sponsor, and a person is not required to respond to, nor shall a person be subject to a penalty for failure to comply with a collection of information subject to the requirements of the Paperwork Reduction Act unless that collection of information displays a currently valid OMB Control Number. The OMB Control Number for this information collection is 2126-0006. Public reporting for this collection of information is estimated to be approximately 20 minutes per response, including the time for reviewing instructions, gathering the data needed, and completing and reviewing the collection of information. All responses to this collection of information are mandatory. Send comments regarding this burden estimate or any other aspect of this collection of information, including suggestions for reducing this burden to: Information Collection Clearance Office, Federal Motor Carrier Safety Administration, MC-RRA, 1200 New Jersey Avenue, SE, Washington, D.C. 20590.

U.S. Department of Transportation
Federal Motor Carrier
Safety Administration

Medical Examination Report Form
(for Commercial Driver Medical Certification)

MEDICAL RECORD #

_____
(or sticker)

SECTION 1. Driver Information *(to be filled out by the driver)*

PERSONAL INFORMATION

Last Name: _____ First Name: _____ Middle Initial: ____ Date of Birth: _____ Age: ____

Street Address: _____ City: _____ State/Province: ____ Zip Code: ____

Driver's License Number: _____ Issuing State/Province: _____ Phone: ____

E-Mail *(optional)*: _____ CLP/CDL Applicant/Holder*: ○ Yes ○ No

Driver ID Verified By**: _____

Has your USDOT/FMCSA medical certificate ever been denied or issued for less than 2 years? ○ Yes ○ No ○ Not Sure

*CLP/CDL Applicant/Holder: See instructions for definitions.   **Driver ID Verified By: Re-set what type of photo ID was used to verify the identity of the driver, e.g., CDL, driver's license, passport.

DRIVER HEALTH HISTORY

Have you ever had surgery? If "yes," please list and explain below.   ○ Yes ○ No ○ Not Sure

Are you currently taking medications *(prescription, over-the-counter, herbal remedies, diet supplements)*?   ○ Yes ○ No ○ Not Sure
If "yes," please describe below.

(Attach additional sheets if necessary)

This document contains sensitive information and is for official use only. Improper handling of this information could negatively affect individuals. Handle and secure this information appropriately to prevent inadvertent disclosure by keeping the documents under the control of authorized persons. Properly dispose of this document when no longer required to be maintained by regulatory requirements.

Rev 6/11/20

Page 1

1633

Form MCSA-5875   OMB No: 2126-0006

Last Name:	First Name:	DOB:	Exam Date:

DRIVER HEALTH HISTORY (continued)

Do you have or have you ever had:	Yes	No	Not Sure		Yes	No	Not Sure
1. Head/brain injuries or illnesses (e.g., concussion)	○	○	○	16. Dizziness, headaches, numbness, tingling, or memory loss	○	○	○
2. Seizures/epilepsy	○	○	○	17. Unexplained weight loss	○	○	○
3. Eye problems (except glasses or contacts)	○	○	○	18. Stroke, mini-stroke (TIA), paralysis, or weakness	○	○	○
4. Ear and/or hearing problems	○	○	○	19. Missing or limited use of arm, hand, finger, leg, foot, toe	○	○	○
5. Heart disease, heart attack, bypass, or other heart problems	○	○	○	20. Neck or back problems	○	○	○
6. Pacemaker, stents, implantable devices, or other heart procedures	○	○	○	21. Bone, muscle, joint, or nerve problems	○	○	○
7. High blood pressure	○	○	○	22. Blood clots or bleeding problems	○	○	○
8. High cholesterol	○	○	○	23. Cancer	○	○	○
9. Chronic (long-term) cough, shortness of breath, or other breathing problems	○	○	○	24. Chronic (long-term) infection or other chronic diseases	○	○	○
10. Lung disease (e.g., asthma)	○	○	○	25. Sleep disorders, pauses in breathing while asleep, daytime sleepiness, loud snoring	○	○	○
11. Kidney problems, kidney stones, or pain/problems with urination	○	○	○	26. Have you ever had a sleep test (e.g., sleep apnea)?	○	○	○
				27. Have you ever spent a night in the hospital?	○	○	○
12. Stomach, liver, or digestive problems	○	○	○	28. Have you ever had a broken bone?	○	○	○
13. Diabetes or blood sugar problems	○	○	○	29. Have you ever used or do you now use tobacco?	○	○	○
Insulin used	○	○	○	30. Do you currently drink alcohol?	○	○	○
14. Anxiety, depression, nervousness, other mental health problems	○	○	○	31. Have you used an illegal substance within the past two years?	○	○	○
15. Fainting or passing out	○	○	○	32. Have you ever failed a drug test or been dependent on an illegal substance?	○	○	○

Other health condition(s) not described above: ○ Yes   ○ No   ○ Not Sure

Did you answer "yes" to any of questions 1-32? If so, please comment further on those health conditions below: ○ Yes   ○ No   ○ Not Sure

(Attach additional sheets if necessary)

CMV DRIVER'S SIGNATURE

I certify that the above information is accurate and complete. I understand that inaccurate, false or missing information may invalidate the examination and my Medical Examiner's Certificate, that submission of fraudulent or intentionally false information is a violation of 49 CFR 390.35, and that submission of fraudulent or intentionally false information may subject me to civil or criminal penalties under 49 CFR 390.37 and 49 CFR 386 Appendices A and B.

Driver's Signature: _____   Date: _____

SECTION 2. Examination Report *(to be filled out by the medical examiner)*

DRIVER HEALTH HISTORY REVIEW

Review and discuss pertinent driver answers and any available medical records. Comment on the driver's responses to the "health history" questions that may affect the driver's safe operation of a commercial motor vehicle (CMV).

(Attach additional sheets if necessary)

Page 2

1634

Form MCSA-5875   OMB No: 2126-0006

| Last Name: | First Name: | DOB: | Exam Date: |

TESTING

Pulse Rate: _____ Pulse rhythm regular: ○ Yes ○ No   Height: _____ feet _____ inches Weight: _____ pounds

Blood Pressure	Systolic	Diastolic
Sitting		
Second reading (optional)		

Urinalysis	Sp. Gr.	Protein	Blood	Sugar
Urinalysis is required. Numerical readings must be recorded.				

Other testing if indicated

Protein, blood, or sugar in the urine may be an indication for further testing to rule out any underlying medical problem.

Vision

Standard is at least 20/40 acuity (Snellen) in each eye with or without correction. At least 70° field of vision in horizontal meridian measured in each eye. The use of corrective lenses should be noted on the Medical Examiner's Certificate.

Acuity	Uncorrected	Corrected	Horizontal Field of Vision
Right Eye:	20/____	20/____	Right Eye: ____ degrees
Left Eye:	20/____	20/____	Left Eye: ____ degrees
Both Eyes:	20/____	20/____	

	Yes	No
Applicant can recognize and distinguish among traffic control signals and devices showing red, green, and amber colors	○	○
Monocular vision	○	○
Referred to ophthalmologist or optometrist?	○	○
Received documentation from ophthalmologist or optometrist?	○	○

Hearing

Standard: Must first perceive whispered voice at not less than 5 feet OR average hearing loss of less than or equal to 40 dB, in better ear (with or without hearing aid).

Check if hearing aid used for test: ☐ Right Ear ☐ Left Ear ☐ Neither

Whisper Test Results   Right Ear   Left Ear
Record distance *(in feet)* from driver at which a forced
whispered voice can first be heard   _____   _____

OR

Audiometric Test Results

Right Ear:			Left Ear:		
500 Hz	1000 Hz	2000 Hz	500 Hz	1000 Hz	2000 Hz
_____	_____	_____	_____	_____	_____

Average (right): _____   Average (left): _____

PHYSICAL EXAMINATION

The presence of a certain condition may not necessarily disqualify a driver, particularly if the condition is controlled adequately, is not likely to worsen, or is readily amenable to treatment. Even if a condition does not disqualify a driver, the Medical Examiner may consider deferring the driver temporarily. Also, the driver should be advised to take the necessary steps to correct the condition as soon as possible, particularly if neglecting the condition could result in a more serious illness that might affect driving.

Check the body systems for abnormalities.

Body System	Normal	Abnormal	Body System	Normal	Abnormal
1. General	○	○	8. Abdomen	○	○
2. Skin	○	○	9. Genito-urinary system including hernias	○	○
3. Eyes	○	○	10. Back/spine	○	○
4. Ears	○	○	11. Extremities/joints	○	○
5. Mouth/throat	○	○	12. Neurological system including reflexes	○	○
6. Cardiovascular	○	○	13. Gait	○	○
7. Lungs/chest	○	○	14. Vascular system	○	○

Discuss any abnormal answers in detail in the space below and indicate whether it would affect the driver's ability to operate a CMV. Enter applicable item number before each comment.

(Attach additional sheets if necessary)

Page 3

Form MCSA-5875
OMB No.: 2126-0006

| Last Name: | First Name: | DOB: | Exam Date: |

Please complete only one of the following (Federal or State) Medical Examiner Determination sections:

MEDICAL EXAMINER DETERMINATION (Federal)

Use this section for examinations performed in accordance with the Federal Motor Carrier Safety Regulations (49 CFR 391.41-391.49):

○ Does not meet standards *(specify reason)*:

○ Meets standards in 49 CFR 391.41; qualifies for 2-year certificate

○ Meets standards, but periodic monitoring required *(specify reason)*:

    Driver qualified for: ○ 3 months ○ 6 months ○ 1 year ○ other *(specify)*:

    ☐ Wearing corrective lenses ☐ Wearing hearing aid ☐ Accompanied by a waiver/exemption *(specify type)*:

    ☐ Accompanied by a Skill Performance Evaluation (SPE) Certificate ☐ Qualified by operation of 49 CFR 391.64 (Federal)

    ☐ Driving within an exempt intracity zone *(see 49 CFR 391.62)* (Federal)

○ Determination pending *(specify reason)*:

    ☐ Return to medical exam office for follow-up on *(must be 45 days or less)*:

    ☐ Medical Examination Report amended *(specify reason)*:

        (if amended) Medical Examiner's Signature: Date:

○ Incomplete examination *(specify reason)*:

> **If the driver meets the standards outlined in 49 CFR 391.41, then complete a Medical Examiner's Certificate as stated in 49 CFR 391.43(h), as appropriate.**

I have performed this evaluation for certification. I have personally reviewed all available records and recorded information pertaining to this evaluation, and attest that, to the best of my knowledge, I believe it to be true and correct.

Medical Examiner's Signature:

Medical Examiner's Name *(please print or type)*:

Medical Examiner's Address: City: State: Zip Code:

Medical Examiner's Telephone Number: Date Certificate Signed:

Medical Examiner's State License, Certificate, or Registration Number: Issuing State:

☐ MD ☐ DO ☐ Physician Assistant ☐ Chiropractor ☐ Advanced Practice Nurse

☐ Other Practitioner *(specify)*:

National Registry Number: | Medical Examiner's Certificate Expiration Date: |

1636

Form MCSA-5875   OMB No: 2126-0006

Last Name:	First Name:	DOB:	Exam Date:

MEDICAL EXAMINER DETERMINATION (State)

Use this section for examinations performed in accordance with the Federal Motor Carrier Safety Regulations (49 CFR 391.41-391.49) with any applicable State variances (which will only be valid for intrastate operations):

○ Does not meet standards in 49 CFR 391.41 with any applicable State variances *(specify reason)*: _____

○ Meets standards in 49 CFR 391.41 with any applicable State variances

○ Meets standards, but periodic monitoring required *(specify reason)*: _____

　Driver qualified for: ○ 3 months ○ 6 months ○ 1 year ○ other *(specify)* _____

　☐ Wearing corrective lenses　☐ Wearing hearing aid　☐ Accompanied by a waiver/exemption *(specify type)*

　☐ Accompanied by a Skill Performance Evaluation (SPE) Certificate　☐ Grandfathered from State requirements *(State)*

> **If the driver meets the standards outlined in 49 CFR 391.41, with applicable State variances, then complete a Medical Examiner's Certificate, as appropriate.**

I have performed this evaluation for certification. I have personally reviewed all available records and recorded information pertaining to this evaluation, and attest that, to the best of my knowledge, I believe it to be true and correct.

Medical Examiner's Signature: _____

Medical Examiner's Name *(please print or type)*: _____

Medical Examiner's Address: _____ City: _____ State: ____ Zip Code: ____

Medical Examiner's Telephone Number: _____ Date Certificate Signed: _____

Medical Examiner's State License, Certificate, or Registration Number: _____ Issuing State: ____

☐ MD ☐ DO ☐ Physician Assistant ☐ Chiropractor ☐ Advanced Practice Nurse

☐ Other Practitioner *(specify)*: _____

National Registry Number: _____ | Medical Examiner's Certificate Expiration Date: [_____]

Page 5

§391.43

Instructions for Completing the Medical Examination Report Form (MCSA-5875)

I. Step-By-Step Instructions

Driver:

Section 1: Driver Information

- **Personal Information:** Please complete this section using your name as written on your driver's license, your current address and phone number, your date of birth, age, driver's license number and issuing state.

  - **CLP/CDL Applicant/Holder:** Check "yes" if you are a commercial learner's permit (**CLP**) or commercial driver's license (**CDL**) holder, or are applying for a CLP or CDL. CDL means a license issued by a State or the District of Columbia which authorizes the individual to operate a class of a commercial motor vehicle (**CMV**). A CMV that requires a CDL is one that: (1) has a gross combination weight rating or gross combination weight of 26,001 pounds or more inclusive of a towed unit with a gross vehicle weight rating (**GVWR**) or gross vehicle weight (**GVW**) of more than 10,000 pounds; or (2) has a GVWR or GVW of 26,001 pounds or more; or (3) is designed to transport 16 or more passengers, including the driver; or (4) is used to transport either hazardous materials requiring hazardous materials placards on the vehicle or any quantity of a select agent or toxin.

  - **Driver ID Verified By:** The Medical Examiner/staff completes this item and notes the type of photo ID used to verify the driver's identity such as, commercial driver's license, driver's license, or passport, etc.

  - **Has your USDOT/FMCSA medical certificate ever been denied or issued for less than two years?** Please check the correct box "yes" or "no" and if you aren't sure check the "not sure" box.

- **Driver Health History:**

  - **Have you ever had surgery:** Please check "yes" if you have ever had surgery and provide a written explanation of the details (type of surgery, date of surgery, etc.)

  - **Are you currently taking medications (prescription, over-the-counter, herbal remedies, diet supplements):** Please check "yes" if you are taking any diet supplements, herbal remedies, or prescription or over the counter medications. In the box below the question, indicate the name of the medication and the dosage.

  - **#1-32:** Please complete this section by checking the "yes" box to indicate that you have, or have ever had, the health condition listed or the "No" box if you have not. Check the "not sure" box if you are unsure.

  - **Other Health Conditions not described above:** If you have, or have had, any other health conditions not listed in the section above, check "Yes" and in the box provided and list those condition(s).

  - **Any yes answers to questions #1-32 above:** If you have answered "yes" to any of the questions in the Driver Health History section above, please explain your answers further in the box below the question. For example, if you answered "yes" to question #5 regarding heart disease, heart attack, bypass, or other heart problem, indicate which type of heart condition. If you checked "yes" to question #23 regarding cancer, indicate the type of cancer. Please add any information that will be helpful to the Medical Examiner.

- **CMV Driver Signature and Date:** Please read the certification statement, sign and date it, indicating that the information you provided in Section 1 is accurate and complete.

PART 391

Instructions MCSA-5875

Medical Examiner:

Section 2: Examination Report

- **Driver Health History Review:** Review answers provided by the driver in the driver health history section and discuss any "yes" and "not sure" responses. In addition, be sure to compare the medication list to the health history responses ensuring that the medication list matches the medical conditions noted. Explore with the driver any answers that seem unclear. Record any information that the driver omitted. As the Medical Examiner conducting the driver's physical examination you are required to complete the entire medical examination even if you detect a medical condition that you consider disqualifying, such as deafness. Medical Examiners are expected to determine the driver's physical qualification for operating a commercial vehicle safely. Thus, if you find a disqualifying condition for which a driver may receive a Federal Motor Carrier Safety Administration medical exemption, please record that on the driver's Medical Examiner's Certificate, Form MCSA-5876, as well as on the Medical Examination Report Form, MCSA-5875.

- **Testing:**

  - **Pulse rate and rhythm, height, and weight:** record these as indicated on the form.

  - **Blood Pressure:** record the blood pressure (systolic and diastolic) of the driver being examined. A second reading is optional and should be recorded if found to be necessary.

  - **Urinalysis:** record the numerical readings for the specific gravity, protein, blood and sugar.

  - **Vision:** The current vision standard is provided on the form. When other than the Snellen chart is used, give test results in Snellen-comparable values. When recording distance vision, use 20 feet as normal. Record the vision acuity results and indicate if the driver can recognize and distinguish among traffic control signals and devices showing red, green, and amber colors; has monocular vision; has been referred to an ophthalmologist or optometrist; and if documentation has been received from an ophthalmologist or optometrist.

  - **Hearing:** The current hearing standard is provided on the form. Hearing can be tested using either a whisper test or audiometric test. Record the test results in the corresponding section for the test used.

- **Physical Examination:** Check the body systems for abnormalities and indicate normal or abnormal for each body system listed. Discuss any abnormal answers in detail in the space provided and indicate whether it would affect the driver's ability to safely operate a commercial motor vehicle.

In this next section, you will be completing either the Federal or State determination, not both.

- **Medical Examiner Determination (Federal):** Use this section for examinations performed in accordance with the FMCSRs (49 CFR 391.41-391.49). Complete the medical examiner determination section completely. When determining a driver's physical qualification, please note that English language proficiency (49 CFR part 391.11: General qualifications of drivers) is not factored into that determination.

  - **Does not meet standards:** Select this option when a driver is determined to be not qualified and provide an explanation of why the driver does not meet the standards in 49 CFR 391.41.

  - **Meets standards in 49 CFR 391.41; qualifies for 2-year certification:** Select this option when a driver is determined to be qualified and will be issued a 2-year Medical Examiner's Certificate.

Instructions MCSA-5875

Meets standards, but periodic monitoring is required: Select this option when a driver is determined to be qualified but needs periodic monitoring and provide an explanation of why periodic monitoring is required. Select the corresponding time frame that the driver is qualified for, and if selecting "other" specify the time frame.

— **Determination that driver meets standards:** Select all categories that apply to the driver's certification (e.g., wearing corrective lenses, accompanied by a waiver/exemption, driving within an exempt intracity zone, etc.).

Determination pending: Select this option when more information is needed to make a qualification decision and specify a date, on or before the 45 day expiration date, for the driver to return to the medical exam office for follow-up. This will allow for a delay of the qualification decision for as many as 45 days. If the disposition of the pending examination is not updated via the National Registry on or before the 45 day expiration date, FMCSA will notify the examining medical examiner and the driver in writing that the examination is no longer valid and that the driver is required to be re-examined.

— **MER amended:** A Medical Examination Report Form (MER), MCSA-5875, may only be amended while in determination pending status for situations where new information (e.g., test results, etc.) has been received or there has been a change in the driver's medical status since the initial examination, but prior to a final qualification determination. Select this option when a Medical Examination Report Form, MCSA-5875, is being amended; provide the reason for the amendment, sign and date. In addition, initial and date any changes made on the Medical Examination Report Form, MCSA-5875. A Medical Examination Report Form, MCSA-5875, cannot be amended after an examination has been in determination pending status for more than 45 days or after a final qualification determination has been made. The driver is required to obtain a new physical examination and a new Medical Examination Report Form, MCSA-5875, should be completed.

Incomplete examination: Select this when the physical examination is not completed for any reason (e.g., driver decides they do not want to continue with the examination and leaves) other than situations outlined under determination pending.

Medical Examiner information, signature and date: Provide your name, address, phone number, occupation, license, certificate, or registration number and issuing state, national registry number, signature and date.

Medical Examiner's Certificate Expiration Date: Enter the date the **driver's** Medical Examiner's Certificate (MEC) expires.

- **Medical Examiner Determination (State):** Use this section for examinations performed in accordance with the FMCSRs (49 CFR 391.41-391.49) with any applicable State variances (which will only be valid for intrastate operations). Complete the medical examiner determination section completely.

Does not meet standards in 49 CFR 391.41 with any applicable State variances: Select this option when a driver is determined to be not qualified and provide an explanation of why the driver does not meet the standards in 49 CFR 391.41 with any applicable State variances.

Meets standards in 49 CFR 391.41 with any applicable State variances: Select this option when a driver is determined to be qualified and will be issued a 2-year Medical Examiner's Certificate.

PART 391

Page 8

1640

Instructions MCSA-5875

> **Meets standards, but periodic monitoring is required:** Select this option when a driver is determined to be qualified but needs periodic monitoring and provide an explanation of why periodic monitoring is required. Select the corresponding time frame that the driver is qualified for, and if selecting "other" specify the time frame.

> — **Determination that driver meets standards:** Select all categories that apply to the driver's certification (e.g., wearing corrective lenses, accompanied by a waiver/exemption, etc.).

> **Medical Examiner information, signature and date:** Provide your name, address, phone number, occupation, license, certificate, or registration number and issuing state, national registry number, signature and date.

> **Medical Examiner's Certificate Expiration Date:** Enter the date the **driver's** Medical Examiner's Certificate (MEC) expires.

II. If updating an existing exam, you must resubmit the new exam results, via the Medical Examination Results Form, MCSA-5850, to the National Registry, and the most recent dated exam will take precedence.

III. To obtain additional information regarding this form go to the Medical Program's page on the Federal Motor Carrier Safety Administration's website at http://www.fmcsa.dot.gov/regulations/medical.

Page 9

(g) Upon completion of the medical examination required by this subpart:

(1) The medical examiner must date and sign the Medical Examination Report and provide his or her full name, office address, and telephone number on the Report.

(2)(i) Before June 23, 2025, if the medical examiner finds that the person examined is physically qualified to operate a commercial motor vehicle in accordance with §391.41(b), he or she must complete a certificate in the form prescribed in paragraph (h) of this section and furnish the original to the person who was examined. The examiner must provide a copy to a prospective or current employing motor carrier who requests it.

(ii) On or after June 23, 2025, if the medical examiner identifies that the person examined will not be operating a commercial motor vehicle that requires a commercial driver's license or a commercial learner's permit and finds that the driver is physically qualified to operate a commercial motor vehicle in accordance with §391.41(b), he or she must complete a certificate in the form prescribed in paragraph (h) of this section and furnish the original to the person who was examined. The examiner must provide a copy to a prospective or current employing motor carrier who requests it.

(3) On or after June 23, 2025, if the medical examiner finds that the person examined is not physically qualified to operate a commercial motor vehicle in accordance with §391.41(b), he or she must inform the person examined that he or she is not physically qualified, and that this information will be reported to FMCSA. All medical examiner's certificates previously issued to the person are not valid and no longer satisfy the requirements of §391.41(a).

(4) Beginning December 22, 2015, if the medical examiner finds that the determination of whether the person examined is physically qualified to operate a commercial motor vehicle in accordance with §391.41(b) should be delayed to receive additional information or to conduct further examination in order for the medical examiner to make such determination, he or she must inform the person examined that the additional information must be provided or the further examination completed within 45 days, and that the pending status of the examination will be reported to FMCSA.

(5)(i)(A) Once every calendar month, beginning May 21, 2014 and ending on June 22, 2018, the medical examiner must electronically transmit to FMCSA, via a secure Web account on the National Registry, a completed CMV Driver Medical Examination Results Form, MCSA-5850. The Form must include all information specified for each medical examination conducted during the previous month for any driver who is required to be examined by a medical examiner listed on the National Registry of Certified Medical Examiners.

(B) Beginning June 22, 2018 by midnight (local time) of the next calendar day after the medical examiner completes a medical examination for any driver who is required to be examined by a medical examiner listed on the National Registry of Certified Medical Examiners, the medical examiner must electronically transmit to FMCSA, via a secure FMCSA-designated Web site, a completed CMV Driver Medical Examination Results Form, MCSA-5850. The Form must include all information specified for each medical examination conducted for each driver who is required to be examined by a medical examiner listed on the National Registry of Certified Medical Examiners in accordance with the provisions of this subpart E, and should also include information for each driver who is required by a State to be examined by a medical examiner listed on the National Registry of Certified Medical Examiners in accordance with the provisions of this subpart E and any variances from those provisions adopted by such State.

(ii) Beginning on June 22, 2015, if the medical examiner does not perform a medical examination of any driver who is required to be examined by a medical examiner listed on the National Registry of Certified Medical Examiners during any calendar month, the medical examiner must report that fact to FMCSA, via a secure FMCSA-designated Web site, by the close of business on the last day of such month.

(h) The medical examiner's certificate shall be completed in accordance with the following Form MCSA-5876, Medical Examiner's Certificate:

(i) Each original (paper or electronic) completed Medical Examination Report and a copy or electronic version of each medical examiner's certificate must be retained on file at the office of the medical examiner for at least 3 years from the date of examination. The medical examiner must make all records and information in these files available to an authorized representative of FMCSA or an authorized Federal, State, or local enforcement agency representative, within 48 hours after the request is made.

§391.45 Persons who must be medically examined and certified.

The following persons must be medically examined and certified in accordance with §391.43 as physically qualified to operate a commercial motor vehicle:

(a) Any person who has not been medically examined and certified as physically qualified to operate a commercial motor vehicle;

(b) Any driver who has not been medically examined and certified as qualified to operate a commercial motor vehicle during the preceding 24 months, unless the driver is required to be examined and certified in accordance with paragraph (c), (d), (e), (f), or (g) of this section;

(c) Any driver authorized to operate a commercial motor vehicle only within an exempt intra-city zone pursuant to §391.62, if such driver has not been medically examined and certified as qualified to drive in such zone during the preceding 12 months;

(d) Any driver authorized to operate a commercial motor vehicle only by operation of the exemption in §391.64, if such driver has not been medically examined and certified as qualified to drive during the preceding 12 months;

(e) Any driver who has diabetes mellitus treated with insulin for control and who has obtained a medical examiner's certificate under the standards in §391.46, if such driver's most recent medical examination and certification as qualified to drive did not occur during the preceding 12 months;

(f) Any driver whose ability to perform his or her normal duties has been impaired by a physical or mental injury or disease; and

(g) On or after June 23, 2025, any person found by a medical examiner not to be physically qualified to operate a commercial motor vehicle under the provisions of paragraph (g)(3) of §391.43.

§391.46 Physical qualification standards for an individual with diabetes mellitus treated with insulin for control.

(a) **Diabetes mellitus treated with insulin**. An individual with diabetes mellitus treated with insulin for control is physically qualified to operate a commercial motor vehicle provided:

(1) The individual otherwise meets the physical qualification standards in §391.41 or has an exemption or skill performance evaluation certificate, if required; and

(2) The individual has the evaluation required by paragraph (b) and the medical examination required by paragraph (c) of this section.

(b) **Evaluation by the treating clinician**. Prior to the examination required by §391.45 or the expiration of a medical examiner's certificate, the individual must be evaluated by his or her "treating clinician." For purposes of this section, "treating clinician" means a healthcare professional who manages, and prescribes insulin for, the treatment of the individual's diabetes mellitus as authorized by the healthcare professional's State licensing authority.

(1) During the evaluation of the individual, the treating clinician must complete the Insulin-Treated Diabetes Mellitus Assessment Form, MCSA-5870.

(2) Upon completion of the Insulin-Treated Diabetes Mellitus Assessment Form, MCSA-5870, the treating clinician must sign and date the Form and provide his or her full name, office address, and telephone number on the Form.

(c) **Medical examiner's examination**. At least annually, but no later than 45 days after the treating clinician signs and dates the Insulin-Treated Diabetes Mellitus Assessment Form, MCSA-5870, an individual with diabetes mellitus treated with insulin for control must be medically examined and certified by a medical examiner as physically qualified in accordance with §391.43 and as free of complications from diabetes mellitus that might impair his or her ability to operate a commercial motor vehicle safely.

(1) The medical examiner must receive a completed Insulin-Treated Diabetes Mellitus Assessment Form, MCSA-5870, signed and dated by the individual's

PART 391

treating clinician for each required examination. This Form shall be treated and retained as part of the Medical Examination Report Form, MCSA-5875.

(2) The medical examiner must determine whether the individual meets the physical qualification standards in §391.41 to operate a commercial motor vehicle. In making that determination, the medical examiner must consider the information in the Insulin-Treated Diabetes Mellitus Assessment Form, MCSA-5870, signed by the treating clinician and, utilizing independent medical judgment, apply the following qualification standards in determining whether the individual with diabetes mellitus treated with insulin for control may be certified as physically qualified to operate a commercial motor vehicle.

(i) The individual is not physically qualified to operate a commercial motor vehicle if he or she is not maintaining a stable insulin regimen and not properly controlling his or her diabetes mellitus.

(ii) The individual is not physically qualified on a permanent basis to operate a commercial motor vehicle if he or she has either severe non-proliferative diabetic retinopathy or proliferative diabetic retinopathy.

(iii) The individual is not physically qualified to operate a commercial motor vehicle up to the maximum 12-month period under §391.45(e) until he or she provides the treating clinician with at least the preceding 3 months of electronic blood glucose self-monitoring records while being treated with insulin that are generated in accordance with paragraph (d) of this section.

(iv) The individual who does not provide the treating clinician with at least the preceding 3 months of electronic blood glucose self-monitoring records while being treated with insulin that are generated in accordance with paragraph (d) of this section is not physically qualified to operate a commercial motor vehicle for more than 3 months. If 3 months of compliant electronic blood glucose self-monitoring records are then provided by the individual to the treating clinician and the treating clinician completes a new Insulin-Treated Diabetes Mellitus Assessment Form, MCSA-5870, the medical examiner may issue a medical examiner's certificate that is valid for up to the maximum 12-month period allowed by §391.45(e) and paragraph (c)(2)(iii) of this section.

(d) **Blood glucose self-monitoring records**. Individuals with diabetes mellitus treated with insulin for control must self-monitor blood glucose in accordance with the specific treatment plan prescribed by the treating clinician. Such individuals must maintain blood glucose records measured with an electronic glucometer that stores all readings, that records the date and time of readings, and from which data can be electronically downloaded. A printout of the electronic blood glucose records or the glucometer must be provided to the treating clinician at the time of any of the evaluations required by this section.

(e) **Severe hypoglycemic episodes**. (1) An individual with diabetes mellitus treated with insulin for control who experiences a severe hypoglycemic episode after being certified as physically qualified to operate a commercial motor vehicle is prohibited from operating a commercial motor vehicle, and must report such occurrence to and be evaluated by a treating clinician as soon as is reasonably practicable. A severe hypoglycemic episode is one that requires the assistance of others, or results in loss of consciousness, seizure, or coma. The prohibition on operating a commercial motor vehicle continues until a treating clinician:

(i) Has determined that the cause of the severe hypoglycemic episode has been addressed;

(ii) Has determined that the individual is maintaining a stable insulin regimen and proper control of his or her diabetes mellitus; and

(iii) Completes a new Insulin-Treated Diabetes Mellitus Assessment Form, MCSA-5870.

(2) The individual must retain the Form and provide it to the medical examiner at the individual's next medical examination.

§391.47 Resolution of conflicts of medical evaluation.

(a) **Applications**. Applications for determination of a driver's medical qualifications under standards in this part will only be accepted if they conform to the requirements of this section.

(b) **Content**. Applications will be accepted for consideration only if the following conditions are met.

(1) The application must contain the name and address of the driver, motor carrier, and all physicians involved in the proceeding.

(2) The applicant must submit proof that there is a disagreement between the physician for the driver and the physician for the motor carrier concerning the driver's qualifications.

(3) The applicant must submit a copy of an opinion and report including results of all tests of an impartial medical specialist in the field in which the medical conflict arose. The specialist should be one agreed to by the motor carrier and the driver.

(i) In cases where the driver refuses to agree on a specialist and the applicant is the motor carrier the applicant must submit a statement of his/her agreement to submit the matter to an impartial medical specialist in the field, proof that he/she has requested the driver to submit to the medical specialist, and the response, if any, of the driver to his/her request.

(ii) In cases where the motor carrier refuses to agree on a medical specialist, the driver must submit an opinion and test results of an impartial medical specialist, proof that he/she has requested the motor carrier to agree to submit the matter to the medical specialist and the response, if any, of the motor carrier to his/her request.

(4) The applicant must include a statement explaining in detail why the decision of the medical specialist identified in paragraph (b)(3) of this section is unacceptable.

(5) The applicant must submit proof that the medical specialist mentioned in paragraph (b)(3) of this section was provided, prior to his/her determination, the medical history of the driver and an agreed-upon statement of the work the driver performs.

(6) The applicant must submit the medical history and statement of work provided to the medical specialist under paragraph (b)(5) of this section.

(7) The applicant must submit all medical records and statements of the physicians who have given opinions on the driver's qualifications.

(8) The applicant must submit a description and a copy of all written and documentary evidence upon which the party making application relies in the form set out in 49 CFR §386.37.

(9) The application must be accompanied by a statement of the driver that he/she intends to drive in interstate commerce not subject to the commercial zone exemption or a statement of the carrier that he/she has used or intends to use the driver for such work.

(10) The applicant must submit three copies of the application and all records.

(c) **Information**. FMCSA (MC-PS) may request further information from the applicant if he/she determines that a decision cannot be made on the evidence submitted. If the applicant fails to submit the information requested, FMCSA may refuse to issue a determination.

(d)(1) **Action**. Upon receiving a satisfactory application FMCSA (MC-PS) shall notify the parties (the driver, motor carrier, or any other interested party) that the application has been accepted and that a determination will be made. A copy of all evidence received shall be attached to the notice.

(2) **Reply**. Any party may submit a reply to the notification within 15 days after service. Such reply must be accompanied by all evidence the party wants FMCSA (MC-PS) to consider in making his/her determination. Evidence submitted should include all medical records and test results upon which the party relies.

(3) **Parties**. A party for the purposes of this section includes the motor carrier and the driver, or anyone else submitting an application.

(e) **Petitions to review, burden of proof**. The driver or motor carrier may petition to review FMCSA's determination. Such petition must be submitted in accordance with §386.13(a) of this chapter. The burden of proof in such a proceeding is on the petitioner.

(f) **Status of driver**. Once an application is submitted to FMCSA (MC-PS), the driver shall be deemed disqualified until such time as FMCSA (MC-PS) makes a determination, or until FMCSA (MC-PS) orders otherwise.

§391.49 Alternative physical qualification standards for the loss or impairment of limbs.

(a) A person who is not physically qualified to drive under §391.41(b)(1) or (b)(2) and who is otherwise qualified to drive a commercial motor vehicle, may drive a commercial motor vehicle if FMCSA has granted a Skill Performance Evaluation (SPE) Certificate to that person.

(b)(1) **Application.** A letter of application for an SPE certificate may be submitted jointly by the person (driver applicant) who seeks an SPE certificate and by the motor carrier that will employ the driver applicant, if the application is accepted.

(2) **Application address.** The application must be addressed to the SPE Certificate Program at the applicable FMCSA service center for the State in which the co-applicant motor carrier's principal place of business is located. The address of each, and the States serviced, are listed in §390.27 of this chapter.

(3) **Exception.** A letter of application for an SPE certificate may be submitted unilaterally by a driver applicant. The application must be addressed to the field service center, FMCSA, for the State in which the driver has legal residence. The driver applicant must comply with all the requirements of paragraph (c) of this section except those in (c)(1)(i) and (iii). The driver applicant shall respond to the requirements of paragraphs (c)(2)(i) to (v) of this section, if the information is known.

(c) A letter of application for an SPE certificate shall contain:

(1) Identification of the applicant(s):

(i) Name and complete address of the motor carrier co-applicant;

(ii) Name and complete address of the driver applicant;

(iii) The U.S. DOT Motor Carrier Identification Number, if known; and

(iv) A description of the driver applicant's limb impairment for which SPE certificate is requested.

(2) Description of the type of operation the driver will be employed to perform:

(i) State(s) in which the driver will operate for the motor carrier co-applicant (if more than 10 States, designate general geographic area only);

(ii) Average period of time the driver will be driving and/or on duty, per day;

(iii) Type of commodities or cargo to be transported;

(iv) Type of driver operation (*i.e.*, sleeper team, relay, owner operator, etc.); and

(v) Number of years experience operating the type of commercial motor vehicle(s) requested in the letter of application and total years of experience operating all types of commercial motor vehicles.

(3) Description of the commercial motor vehicle(s) the driver applicant intends to drive:

(i) Truck, truck tractor, or bus make, model, and year (if known);

(ii) Drive train;

(A) Transmission type (automatic or manual—if manual, designate number of forward speeds);

(B) Auxiliary transmission (if any) and number of forward speeds; and

(C) Rear axle (designate single speed, 2 speed, or 3 speed)

(iii) Type of brake system;

(iv) Steering, manual or power assisted;

(v) Description of type of trailer(s) (i.e., van, flatbed, cargo tank, drop frame, lowboy, or pole);

(vi) Number of semitrailers or full trailers to be towed at one time;

(vii) For commercial motor vehicles designed to transport passengers, indicate the seating capacity of commercial motor vehicle; and

(viii) Description of any modification(s) made to the commercial motor vehicle for the driver applicant; attach photograph(s) where applicable.

(4) Otherwise qualified:

(i) The co-applicant motor carrier must certify that the driver applicant is otherwise qualified under the regulations of this part;

(ii) In the case of a unilateral application, the driver applicant must certify that he/she is otherwise qualified under the regulations of this part.

(5) Signature of applicant(s):

(i) Driver applicant's signature and date signed;

(ii) Motor carrier official's signature (if application has a co-applicant), title, and date signed. Depending upon the motor carrier's organizational structure (corporation, partnership, or proprietorship), the signer of the application shall be an officer, partner, or the proprietor.

(d) The letter of application for an SPE certificate shall be accompanied by:

(1) A copy of the Medical Examination Report Form, MCSA-5875, documenting the results of the medical examination performed pursuant to §391.43;

(2) A copy of the Medical Examiner's Certificate, Form MCSA-5876, completed pursuant to §391.43(h);

(3) A medical evaluation summary completed by either a board qualified or board certified physiatrist (doctor of physical medicine) or orthopedic surgeon. The co-applicant motor carrier or the driver applicant shall provide the physiatrist or orthopedic surgeon with a description of the job-related tasks the driver applicant will be required to perform;

(i) The medical evaluation summary for a driver applicant disqualified under §391.41(b)(1) shall include:

(A) An assessment of the functional capabilities of the driver as they relate to the ability of the driver to perform normal tasks associated with operating a commercial motor vehicle; and

(B) A statement by the examiner that the applicant is capable of demonstrating precision prehension (*e.g.*, manipulating knobs and switches) and power grasp prehension (*e.g.*, holding and maneuvering the steering wheel) with each upper limb separately. This requirement does not apply to an individual who was granted a waiver, absent a prosthetic device, prior to the publication of this amendment.

(ii) The medical evaluation summary for a driver applicant disqualified under §391.41(b)(2) shall include:

(A) An explanation as to how and why the impairment interferes with the ability of the applicant to perform normal tasks associated with operating a commercial motor vehicle;

(B) An assessment and medical opinion of whether the condition will likely remain medically stable over the lifetime of the driver applicant; and

(C) A statement by the examiner that the applicant is capable of demonstrating precision prehension (*e.g.*, manipulating knobs and switches) and power grasp prehension (*e.g.*, holding and maneuvering the steering wheel) with each upper limb separately. This requirement does not apply to an individual who was granted an SPE certificate, absent an orthotic device, prior to the publication of this amendment.

(4) A description of the driver applicant's prosthetic or orthotic device worn, if any;

(5) Road test:

(i) A copy of the driver applicant's road test administered by the motor carrier co-applicant and the certificate issued pursuant to §391.31(b) through (g);

(ii) A unilateral applicant shall be responsible for having a road test administered by a motor carrier or a person who is competent to administer the test and evaluate its results.

(6) Application for employment:

(i) A copy of the driver applicant's application for employment completed pursuant to §391.21; or

(ii) A unilateral applicant shall be responsible for submitting a copy of the last commercial driving position's employment application he/she held. If not previously employed as a commercial driver, so state.

(7) A copy of the driver applicant's SPE certificate of certain physical defects issued by the individual State(s), where applicable; and

(8) A copy of the driver applicant's State Motor Vehicle Driving Record for the past 3 years from each State in which a motor vehicle driver's license or permit has been obtained.

(e) A motor carrier that employs a driver with an SPE certificate agrees to:

(1) File promptly (within 30 days of the involved incident) with the SPE Certificate Program, FMCSA service center, such documents and information as may be required about driving activities, accidents, arrests, license suspensions, revocations, or withdrawals, and convictions which involve the driver applicant. This paragraph (e)(1) applies whether the driver SPE certificate is a unilateral one or has a co-applicant motor carrier;

(i) A motor carrier who is a co-applicant must file the required documents with the SPE Certificate Program, FMCSA service center, for the State in which the carrier's principal place of business is located; or

(ii) A motor carrier who employs a driver who has been issued a unilateral SPE certificate must file the required documents with the SPE Certificate Program, FMCSA service center, for the State in which the driver has legal residence.

(2) Evaluate the driver with a road test using the trailer the motor carrier intends the driver to transport or, in lieu of, accept a certificate of a trailer road test from another motor carrier if the trailer type(s) is similar, or accept the trailer road test done during the Skill Performance Evaluation if it is a similar trailer type(s) to that of the prospective motor carrier. Job tasks, as stated in paragraph (e)(3) of this section, are not evaluated in the Skill Performance Evaluation;

(3) Evaluate the driver for those nondriving safety related job tasks associated with whatever type of trailer(s) will be used and any other nondriving safety related or job related tasks unique to the operations of the employing motor carrier; and

(4) Use the driver to operate the type of commercial motor vehicle defined in the SPE certificate only when the driver is in compliance with the conditions and limitations of the SPE certificate.

(f) The driver shall supply each employing motor carrier with a copy of the SPE certificate.

(g) FMCSA may require the driver applicant to demonstrate his or her ability to safely operate the commercial motor vehicle(s) the driver intends to drive to an agent of FMCSA. The SPE certificate form will identify the power unit (bus, truck, truck tractor) for which the SPE certificate has been granted. The SPE certificate forms will also identify the trailer type used in the Skill Performance Evaluation; however, the SPE certificate is not limited to that specific trailer type. A driver may use the SPE certificate with other trailer types if a successful trailer road test is completed in accordance with paragraph (e)(2) of this section. Job tasks, as stated in paragraph (e)(3) of this section, are not evaluated during the Skill Performance Evaluation.

(h) FMCSA may deny the application for SPE certificate or may grant it totally or in part and issue the SPE certificate subject to such terms, conditions, and limitations as deemed consistent with the public interest. The SPE certificate is valid for a period not to exceed 2 years from date of issue, and may be renewed 30 days prior to the expiration date.

(i) The SPE certificate renewal application shall be submitted to the SPE Certificate Program, FMCSA service center, for the State in which the driver has legal residence, if the SPE certificate was issued unilaterally. If the SPE certificate has a co-applicant, then the renewal application is submitted to the SPE Certificate Program, FMCSA service center, for the State in which the co-applicant motor carrier's principal place of business is located. The SPE certificate renewal application shall contain the following:

(1) Name and complete address of motor carrier currently employing the applicant;

(2) Name and complete address of the driver;

(3) Effective date of the current SPE certificate;

(4) Expiration date of the current SPE certificate;

(5) Total miles driven under the current SPE certificate;

(6) Number of accidents incurred while driving under the current SPE certificate, including date of the accident(s), number of fatalities, number of injuries, and the estimated dollar amount of property damage;

(7) A current Medical Examination Report Form, MCSA-5875;

(8) A medical evaluation summary pursuant to paragraph (d)(3) of this section, if an unstable medical condition exists. All handicapped conditions classified under §391.41(b)(1) are considered unstable. Refer to paragraph (d)(3)(ii) of this section for the condition under §391.41(b)(2) which may be considered medically stable.

(9) A copy of driver's current State motor vehicle driving record for the period of time the current SPE certificate has been in effect;

(10) Notification of any change in the type of tractor the driver will operate;

(11) Driver's signature and date signed; and

(12) Motor carrier coapplicant's signature and date signed.

(j)(1) Upon granting an SPE certificate, FMCSA will notify the driver applicant and co-applicant motor carrier (if applicable) by letter. The terms, conditions, and limitations of the SPE certificate will be set forth. A motor carrier shall maintain a copy of the SPE certificate in its driver qualification file. A copy of the SPE certificate shall be retained in the motor carrier's file for a period of 3 years after the driver's employment is terminated. The driver applicant shall have the SPE certificate (or a legible copy) in his/her possession whenever on duty.

(2) Upon successful completion of the skill performance evaluation, FMCSA must notify the driver by letter and enclose an SPE certificate substantially in the following form:

Skill Performance Evaluation Certificate

Name of Issuing Agency: _____

Agency Address: _____

Telephone Number: ( ) _____

Issued Under 49 CFR 391.49, subchapter B of the Federal Motor Carrier Safety Regulations

Driver's Name: _____

Effective Date: _____

SSN: _____

DOB: _____

Expiration Date: _____

Address: _____

_____

_____

Driver Disability: _____

Check One: _____

New _____

Renewal

Driver's License: _____

      (State)   (Number)

In accordance with 49 CFR 391.49, subchapter B of the Federal Motor Carrier Safety Regulations (FMCSRs), the driver application for a skill performance evaluation (SPE) certificate is hereby granted authorizing the above-named driver to operate in interstate or foreign commerce under the provisions set forth below. This certificate is granted for the period shown above, not to exceed 2 years, subject to periodic review as may be found necessary. This certificate may be renewed upon submission of a renewal application. Continuation of this certificate is dependent upon strict adherence by the above-named driver to the provisions set forth below and compliance with the FMCSRs. Any failure to comply with provisions herein may be cause for cancellation.

CONDITIONS: As a condition of this certificate, reports of all accidents, arrests, suspensions, revocations, withdrawals of driver licenses or permits, and convictions involving the above-named driver shall be reported in writing to the Issuing Agency by the EMPLOYING MOTOR CARRIER within 30 days after occurrence.

LIMITATIONS:

1. Vehicle Type (power unit):* _____
2. Vehicle modification(s): _____
3. Prosthetic or Orthotic device(s) (Required to be Worn While Driving): ____
4. Additional Provision(s): _____

NOTICE: To all MOTOR CARRIERS employing a driver with an SPE certificate. This certificate is granted for the operation of the *power unit only*. It is the responsibility of the employing motor carrier to evaluate the driver with a road test using the trailer type(s) the motor carrier intends the driver to transport, or in lieu of, accept the trailer road test done during the SPE if it is a similar trailer type(s) to that of the prospective motor carrier. Also, it is the responsibility of the employing motor carrier to evaluate the driver for those non-driving safety-related job tasks associated with the type of trailer(s) utilized, as well as, any other non-driving safety-related or job-related tasks unique to the operations of the employing motor carrier.

The SPE of the above-named driver was given by an SPE Evaluator. It was successfully completed utilizing the above-named power unit and _____ (trailer, if applicable)

The tractor or truck had a _____ transmission.

Please read the *NOTICE* paragraph above.

Name: _____
Signature: _____
Title: _____
Date: _____

(k) FMCSA may revoke an SPE certificate after the person to whom it was issued is given notice of the proposed revocation and has been allowed a reasonable opportunity to appeal.

(l) Falsifying information in the letter of application, the renewal application, or falsifying information required by this section by either the applicant or motor carrier is prohibited.

Subpart F—Files and Records

§391.51 General requirements for driver qualification files.

(a) Each motor carrier shall maintain a driver qualification file for each driver it employs. A driver's qualification file may be combined with his/her personnel file.

(b) The qualification file for a driver must include:

(1) The driver's application for employment completed in accordance with §391.21;

(2) A copy of the motor vehicle record received from each State pursuant to §391.23(a)(1);

(3) The certificate of driver's road test issued to the driver pursuant to §391.31(e), or a copy of the license or certificate which the motor carrier accepted as equivalent to the driver's road test pursuant to §391.33;

(4) The motor vehicle record received from each State driver licensing agency to the annual driver record inquiry required by §391.25(a);

(5) A note relating to the annual review of the driver's driving record as required by §391.25(c)(2);

(6) A list or certificate relating to violations of motor vehicle laws and ordinances required by §391.27;

(7)(i) The medical examiner's certificate as required by §391.43(g) or a legible copy of the certificate.

(ii) For CDL holders, beginning January 30, 2012, if the CDLIS motor vehicle record contains medical certification status information, the motor carrier employer must meet this requirement by obtaining the CDLIS motor vehicle record defined at §384.105 of this chapter. That record must be obtained from the current licensing State and placed in the driver qualification file. After January 30, 2015, a non-excepted, interstate CDL holder without medical certification status information on the CDLIS motor vehicle record is designated "not-certified" to operate a CMV in interstate commerce. After January 30, 2015, and through June 22, 2025, a motor carrier may use a copy of the driver's current medical examiner's certificate that was submitted to the State for up to 15 days from the date it was issued as proof of medical certification.

(iii) If that driver obtained the medical certification based on having obtained a medical variance from FMCSA, the motor carrier must also include a copy of the medical variance documentation in the driver qualification file in accordance with §391.51(b)(8);

(8) A Skill Performance Evaluation Certificate issued by FMCSA in accordance with §391.49; or the Medical Exemption document issued by a Federal medical program in accordance with part 381 of this chapter; and

(9)(i) For drivers not required to have a CDL, a note relating to verification of medical examiner listing on the National Registry of Certified Medical Examiners required by §391.23(m)(1).

(ii) Through June 22, 2025, for drivers required to have a CDL, a note relating to verification of medical examiner listing on the National Registry of Certified Medical Examiners required by §391.23(m)(2).

(c) Except as provided in paragraph (d) of this section, each driver's qualification file shall be retained for as long as a driver is employed by that motor carrier and for three years thereafter.

(d) The following records may be removed from a driver's qualification file three years after the date of execution:

(1) The motor vehicle record received from each State driver licensing agency to the annual driver record inquiry required by §391.25(a);

(2) The note relating to the annual review of the driver's driving record as required by §391.25(c)(2);

(3) The list or certificate relating to violations of motor vehicle laws and ordinances required by §391.27;

(4) The medical examiner's certificate required by §391.43(g), a legible copy of the certificate, or for CDL drivers any CDLIS MVR obtained as required by §391.51(b)(7)(ii);

(5) Any medical variance issued by FMCSA, including a Skill Performance Evaluation Certificate issued in accordance with §391.49; or the Medical Exemption letter issued by a Federal medical program in accordance with part 381 of this chapter; and

(6) The note relating to verification of medical examiner listing on the National Registry of Certified Medical Examiners required by §391.23(m).

(Approved by the Office of Management and Budget under control number 2126-004)

§391.53 Driver investigation history file.

(a) Each motor carrier must maintain records relating to the investigation into the safety performance history of a new or prospective driver pursuant to §391.23(d) and (e). This file must be maintained in a secure location with controlled access.

(1) The motor carrier must ensure that access to this data is limited to those who are involved in the hiring decision or who control access to the data. In addition, the motor carrier's insurer may have access to the data, except the alcohol and controlled substances data.

(2) This data must only be used for the hiring decision.

(b) The file must include:

(1) A copy of the driver's written authorization for the motor carrier to seek information about a driver's alcohol and controlled substances history as required under §391.23(f)(1).

(2) A copy of the response(s) received for investigations required by paragraphs (d) and (e) of §391.23 from each previous employer, or documentation of good faith efforts to contact them. The record must include the previous employer's name and address, the date the previous employer was contacted, and the information received about the driver from the previous employer. Failures to contact a previous employer, or of them to provide the required safety performance history information, must be documented.

(c) The safety performance histories received from previous employers for a driver who is hired must be retained for as long as the driver is employed by that motor carrier and for three years thereafter.

(d) A motor carrier must make all records and information in this file available to an authorized representative or special agent of the Federal Motor Carrier Safety Administration, an authorized State or local enforcement agency representative, or an authorized third party, upon request or as part of any inquiry within the time period specified by the requesting representative.

(Approved by the Office of Management and Budget under control number 2126-004)

§391.55 LCV Driver-instructor qualification files.

(a) Each motor carrier must maintain a qualification file for each LCV driver instructor it employs or uses. The LCV driver-instructor qualification file may be combined with his/her personnel file.

(b) The LCV driver-instructor qualification file must include the information in paragraphs (b)(1) and(b)(2) of this section for a skills instructor or the information in paragraph (b)(1) of this section for a classroom instructor, as follows:

(1) Evidence that the instructor has met the requirements of 49 CFR 380.301 or 380.303;

(2) A copy of the individual's currently valid CDL with the appropriate endorsements.

Subpart G—Limited Exemptions

§391.61 Drivers who were regularly employed before January 1, 1971.

The provisions of §§391.21 (relating to applications for employment), §391.23 (relating to investigations and inquiries), and 391.31 (relating to road tests) do not apply to a driver who has been a single-employer driver (as defined in §390.5 of this subchapter) of a motor carrier for a continuous period which began before January 1, 1971, as long as he/she continues to be a single-employer driver of that motor carrier.

§391.62 Limited exemptions for intra-city zone drivers.

The provisions of §§391.11(b)(1) and 391.41(b)(1) through (b)(11) do not apply to a person who:

(a) Was otherwise qualified to operate and operated a commercial motor vehicle in a municipality or exempt intracity zone thereof throughout the one-year period ending November 18, 1988;

(b) Meets all the other requirements of this section;

(c) Operates wholly within the exempt intra-city zone (as defined in 49 CFR 390.5);

(d) Does not operate a vehicle used in the transportation of hazardous materials in a quantity requiring placarding under regulations issued by the Secretary under 49 U.S.C. chapter 51.; and

(e) Has a medical or physical condition which:

(1) Would have prevented such person from operating a commercial motor vehicle under the Federal Motor Carrier Safety Regulations contained in this subchapter;

(2) Existed on July 1, 1988, or at the time of the first required physical examination after that date; and

(3) The examining physician has determined this condition has not substantially worsened since July 1, 1988, or at the time of the first required physical examination after that date.

§391.63 Multiple-employer drivers.

(a) If a motor carrier employs a person as a multiple-employer driver (as defined in §390.5 of this subchapter) the motor carrier shall comply with all requirements of this part, except that the motor carrier need not—

(1) Require the person to furnish an application for employment in accordance with §391.21;

(2) Make the investigations and inquiries specified in §391.23 with respect to that person;

(3) Perform the annual driving record inquiry required by §391.25(a);

(4) Perform the annual review of the person's driving record required by §391.25(b); or

(5) Require the person to finish a record of violations or a certificate in accordance with §391.27.

(b) Before a motor carrier permits a multiple-employer driver to drive a commercial motor vehicle, the motor carrier must obtain his/her name, his/her social security number, and the identification number, type and issuing State of his/her commercial motor vehicle operator's license. The motor carrier must maintain this information for 3 years after employment of the multiple-employer driver ceases.

§391.64 Grandfathering for certain drivers who participated in a vision waiver study program.

(a) [Reserved]

(b) The provisions of §391.41(b)(10) do not apply to a driver who was a participant in good standing on March 31, 1996, in a waiver study program concerning the operation of commercial motor vehicles by drivers with visual impairment in one eye; provided:

(1) The driver is physically examined every year, including an examination by an ophthalmologist or optometrist attesting to the fact that the driver:

(i) Is otherwise qualified under §391.41; and

(ii) Continues to measure at least 20/40 (Snellen) in the better eye.

(2) The driver provides a copy of the ophthalmologist or optometrist report to the medical examiner at the time of the annual medical examination.

(3) The driver provides a copy of the annual medical certification to the employer for retention in the driver's qualification file and retains a copy of the certification on his/her person while driving for presentation to a duly authorized federal, state or local enforcement official.

§391.65 Drivers furnished by other motor carriers.

(a) A motor carrier may employ a driver who is not a single-employer driver, as defined in §390.5, of that motor carrier without complying with the generally applicable driver qualification file requirements in this part, if—

(1) The driver is a single-employer driver for another motor carrier; and

(2) That other motor carrier certifies that the driver is fully qualified to drive a commercial motor vehicle in a written statement which—

(i) Is signed and dated by an officer or authorized employee of the motor carrier that employs the single-employer driver;

(ii) Contains the driver's name and signature;

(iii) Certifies that the driver has been employed as a single-employer driver.

(iv) Certifies that the driver is fully qualified to drive a commercial motor vehicle under the rules in Part 391 of the Federal Motor Carrier Safety Regulations;

(v) States the expiration date of the driver's medical examiner's certificate;

(vi) Specifies an expiration date for the certificate, which shall be not longer than 2 years or, if earlier, the expiration date of the driver's current medical examiner's certificate; and

(vii) Is substantially in accordance with the following form:

(Name of driver)	(SS No.)

_____
(Signature of driver)

I certify that the above named driver, as defined in §390.5, is a single-employer driver driving a commercial motor vehicle operated by the below named carrier and is fully qualified under part 391, Federal Motor Carrier Safety Regulations. His/her current medical examiner's certificate expires on _____

(Date)

This certificate expires _____

(Date not later than expiration date of medical certificate)

Issued on _____

(Date)

§391.67

Issued by _____

(Name of Carrier)

_____

(Address)

_____   _____

(Signature)   (Title)

(b) A motor carrier that obtains a certificate in accordance with paragraph (a)(2) of this section shall:

(1) Contact the motor carrier which certified the driver's qualifications under this section to verify the validity of the certificate. This contact may be made in person, by telephone, or by letter.

(2) Retain a copy of that certificate in its files for three years.

(c) A motor carrier which certifies a driver's qualifications under this section shall be responsible for the accuracy of the certificate. The certificate is no longer valid if the driver leaves the employment of the motor carrier which issued the certificate or is no longer qualified under the rules in this part.

§391.67 Farm vehicle drivers of articulated commercial motor vehicles.

The following rules in this part do not apply to a farm vehicle driver (as defined in §390.5 of this subchapter) who is 18 years of age or older and who drives an articulated commercial motor vehicle:

(a) Section 391.11(b)(1), (b)(6), and (b)(8) (relating to general qualifications of drivers);

(b) Subpart C (relating to disclosure of, investigation into, and inquiries about the background, character, and driving record of drivers);

(c) Subpart D (relating to road tests); and

(d) Subpart F (relating to maintenance of files and records).

§391.68 Private motor carrier of passengers (nonbusiness).

The following rules in this part do not apply to a private motor carrier of passengers (nonbusiness) and its drivers:

(a) Section 391.11(b)(1), (b)(6), and (b)(8), (relating to general qualifications of drivers);

(b) Subpart C (relating to disclosure of, investigation into, and inquiries about the background, character, and driving record of, drivers);

(c) So much of §§391.41 and 391.45 as require a driver to be medically examined and to have a medical examiner's certificate on his/her person; and

(d) Subpart F (relating to maintenance of files and records).

§391.69 Private motor carrier of passengers (business).

The provisions of §391.21 (relating to applications for employment), §391.23 (relating to investigations and inquiries), and §391.31 (relating to road tests) do not apply to a driver who was a single-employer driver (as defined in §390.5 of this subchapter) of a private motor carrier of passengers (business) as of July 1, 1994, so long as the driver continues to be a single-employer driver of that motor carrier.

§391.71 [Reserved.]

Appendix A to Part 391—Medical Advisory Criteria

I. Introduction

This appendix contains the Agency's guidelines in the form of Medical Advisory Criteria to help medical examiners assess a driver's physical qualification. These guidelines are strictly advisory and were established after consultation with physicians, States, and industry representatives, and, in some areas, after consideration of recommendations from the Federal Motor Carrier Safety Administration's Medical Review Board and Medical Expert Panels.

II. Interpretation of Medical Standards

Since the issuance of the regulations for physical qualifications of commercial motor vehicle drivers, the Federal Motor Carrier Safety Administration has published recommendations called Advisory Criteria to help medical examiners in determining whether a driver meets the physical qualifications for commercial driving. These recommendations have been condensed to provide information to medical examiners that is directly relevant to the physical examination and is not already included in the Medical Examination Report Form.

A. Loss of Limb: §391.41(b)(1)

A person is physically qualified to drive a commercial motor vehicle if that person: Has no loss of a foot, leg, hand or an arm, or has been granted a Skills Performance Evaluation certificate pursuant to §391.49.

B. Limb Impairment: §391.41(b)(2)

1. A person is physically qualified to drive a commercial motor vehicle if that person: Has no impairment of:

(i) A hand or finger which interferes with prehension or power grasping; or

(ii) An arm, foot, or leg which interferes with the ability to perform normal tasks associated with operating a commercial motor vehicle; or

(iii) Any other significant limb defect or limitation which interferes with the ability to perform normal tasks associated with operating a commercial motor vehicle; or

(iv) Has been granted a Skills Performance Evaluation certificate pursuant to §391.49.

2. A person who suffers loss of a foot, leg, hand or arm or whose limb impairment in any way interferes with the safe performance of normal tasks associated with operating a commercial motor vehicle is subject to the Skills Performance Evaluation Certificate Program pursuant to §391.49, assuming the person is otherwise qualified.

3. With the advancement of technology, medical aids and equipment modifications have been developed to compensate for certain disabilities. The Skills Performance Evaluation Certificate Program (formerly the Limb Waiver Program) was designed to allow persons with the loss of a foot or limb or with functional impairment to qualify under the Federal Motor Carrier Safety Regulations by use of prosthetic devices or equipment modifications which enable them to safely operate a commercial motor vehicle. Since there are no medical aids equivalent to the original body or limb, certain risks are still present, and thus restrictions may be included on individual Skills Performance Evaluation certificates when a State Director for the Federal Motor Carrier Safety Administration determines they are necessary to be consistent with safety and public interest.

PART 391

4. If the driver is found otherwise medically qualified (§391.41(b)(3) through (13)), the medical examiner must check on the Medical Examiner's Certificate that the driver is qualified only if accompanied by a Skills Performance Evaluation certificate. The driver and the employing motor carrier are subject to appropriate penalty if the driver operates a motor vehicle in interstate or foreign commerce without a current Skill Performance Evaluation certificate for his/her physical disability.

C. [Reserved]

D. Cardiovascular Condition: §391.41(b)(4)

1. A person is physically qualified to drive a commercial motor vehicle if that person: Has no current clinical diagnosis of myocardial infarction, angina pectoris, coronary insufficiency, thrombosis or any other cardiovascular disease of a variety known to be accompanied by syncope, dyspnea, collapse or congestive cardiac failure.

2. The term "has no current clinical diagnosis of" is specifically designed to encompass: "a clinical diagnosis of" a current cardiovascular condition, or a cardiovascular condition which has not fully stabilized regardless of the time limit. The term "known to be accompanied by" is designed to include a clinical diagnosis of a cardiovascular disease which is accompanied by symptoms of syncope, dyspnea, collapse or congestive cardiac failure; and/or which is s likely to cause syncope, dyspnea, collapse or congestive cardiac failure.

3. It is the intent of the Federal Motor Carrier Safety Regulations to render unqualified, a driver who has a current cardiovascular disease which is accompanied by and/or likely to cause symptoms of syncope, dyspnea, collapse, or congestive cardiac failure. However, the subjective decision of whether the nature and severity of an individual's condition will likely cause symptoms of cardiovascular insufficiency is on an individual basis and qualification rests with the medical examiner and the motor carrier. In those cases where there is an occurrence of cardiovascular insufficiency (myocardial infarction, thrombosis, etc.), it is suggested before a driver is certified that he or she have a normal resting and stress electrocardiogram, no residual complications and no physical limitations, and is taking no medication likely to interfere with safe driving.

4. Coronary artery bypass surgery and pacemaker implantation are remedial procedures and thus, not medically disqualifying. Implantable cardioverter defibrillators are disqualifying due to risk of syncope. Coumadin is a medical treatment which can improve the health and safety of the driver and should not, by its use, medically disqualify the commercial motor vehicle driver. The emphasis should be on the underlying medical condition(s) which require treatment and the general health of the driver. The Federal Motor Carrier Safety Administration should be contacted at (202) 366-4001 for additional recommendations regarding the physical qualification of drivers on coumadin.

E. Respiratory Dysfunction: §391.41(b)(5)

1. A person is physically qualified to drive a commercial motor vehicle if that person: Has no established medical history or clinical diagnosis of a respiratory dysfunction likely to interfere with ability to control and drive a commercial motor vehicle safely.

2. Since a driver must be alert at all times, any change in his or her mental state is in direct conflict with highway safety. Even the slightest impairment in

respiratory function under emergency conditions (when greater oxygen supply is necessary for performance) may be detrimental to safe driving.

3. There are many conditions that interfere with oxygen exchange and may result in incapacitation, including emphysema, chronic asthma, carcinoma, tuberculosis, chronic bronchitis and sleep apnea. If the medical examiner detects a respiratory dysfunction, that in any way is likely to interfere with the driver's ability to safely control and drive a commercial motor vehicle, the driver must be referred to a specialist for further evaluation and therapy. Anticoagulation therapy for deep vein thrombosis and/or pulmonary thromboembolism is not medically disqualifying once optimum dose is achieved, provided lower extremity venous examinations remain normal and the treating physician gives a favorable recommendation.

F. Hypertension: §391.41(b)(6)

1. A person is physically qualified to drive a commercial motor vehicle if that person: Has no current clinical diagnosis of high blood pressure likely to interfere with ability to operate a commercial motor vehicle safely.

2. Hypertension alone is unlikely to cause sudden collapse; however, the likelihood increases when target organ damage, particularly cerebral vascular disease, is present. This regulatory criteria is based on the Federal Motor Carrier Safety Administration's Cardiovascular Advisory Guidelines for the Examination of commercial motor vehicle Drivers, which used the Sixth Report of the Joint National Committee on Detection, Evaluation, and Treatment of High Blood Pressure (1997).

3. Stage 1 hypertension corresponds to a systolic blood pressure of 140-159 mmHg and/or a diastolic blood pressure of 90-99 mmHg. The driver with a blood pressure in this range is at low risk for hypertension-related acute incapacitation and may be medically certified to drive for a one-year period. Certification examinations should be done annually thereafter and should be at or less than 140/90. If less than 160/100, certification may be extended one time for 3 months.

4. A blood pressure of 160-179 systolic and/or 100-109 diastolic is considered Stage 2 hypertension, and the driver is not necessarily unqualified during evaluation and institution of treatment. The driver is given a one-time certification of three months to reduce his or her blood pressure to less than or equal to 140/90. A blood pressure in this range is an absolute indication for antihypertensive drug therapy. Provided treatment is well tolerated and the driver demonstrates a blood pressure value of 140/90 or less, he or she may be certified for one year from date of the initial exam. The driver is certified annually thereafter.

5. A blood pressure at or greater than 180 (systolic) and 110 (diastolic) is considered Stage 3, high risk for an acute blood pressure-related event. The driver may not be qualified, even temporarily, until reduced to 140/90 or less and treatment is well tolerated. The driver may be certified for 6 months and biannually (every 6 months) thereafter if at recheck blood pressure is 140/90 or less.

6. Annual recertification is recommended if the medical examiner does not know the severity of hypertension prior to treatment. An elevated blood pressure finding should be confirmed by at least two subsequent measurements on different days.

7. Treatment includes nonpharmacologic and pharmacologic modalities as well as counseling to reduce other risk factors. Most antihypertensive medications also have side effects, the importance of which must be judged on an individual basis. Individuals must be alerted to the hazards of these medications while driving. Side effects of somnolence or syncope are particularly undesirable in commercial motor vehicle drivers.

8. Secondary hypertension is based on the above stages. Evaluation is warranted if patient is persistently hypertensive on maximal or near-maximal doses of 2-3 pharmacologic agents. Some causes of secondary hypertension may be amenable to surgical intervention or specific pharmacologic disease.

G. Rheumatic, Arthritic, Orthopedic, Muscular, Neuromuscular or Vascular Disease: §391.41(b)(7)

1. A person is physically qualified to drive a commercial motor vehicle if that person: Has no established medical history or clinical diagnosis of rheumatic, arthritic, orthopedic, muscular, neuromuscular or vascular disease which interferes with the ability to control and operate a commercial motor vehicle safely.

2. Certain diseases are known to have acute episodes of transient muscle weakness, poor muscular coordination (ataxia), abnormal sensations (paresthesia), decreased muscular tone (hypotonia), visual disturbances and pain which may be suddenly incapacitating. With each recurring episode, these symptoms may become more pronounced and remain for longer periods of time. Other diseases have more insidious onsets and display symptoms of muscle wasting (atrophy), swelling and paresthesia which may not suddenly incapacitate a person but may restrict his/her movements and eventually interfere with the ability to safely operate a motor vehicle. In many instances these diseases are degenerative in nature or may result in deterioration of the involved area.

3. Once the individual has been diagnosed as having a rheumatic, arthritic, orthopedic, muscular, neuromuscular or vascular disease, then he/she has an established history of that disease. The physician, when examining an individual, should consider the following: The nature and severity of the individual's condition (such as sensory loss or loss of strength); the degree of limitation present (such as range of motion); the likelihood of progressive limitation (not always present initially but may manifest itself over time); and the likelihood of sudden incapacitation. If severe functional impairment exists, the driver does not qualify. In cases where more frequent monitoring is required, a certificate for a shorter period of time may be issued.

H. Epilepsy: §391.41(b)(8)

1. A person is physically qualified to drive a commercial motor vehicle if that person: Has no established medical history or clinical diagnosis of epilepsy or any other condition which is likely to cause loss of consciousness or any loss of ability to control a motor vehicle.

2. Epilepsy is a chronic functional disease characterized by seizures or episodes that occur without warning, resulting in loss of voluntary control which may lead to loss of consciousness and/or seizures. Therefore, the following drivers cannot be qualified:

(i) A driver who has a medical history of epilepsy;

(ii) A driver who has a current clinical diagnosis of epilepsy; or

(ii) A driver who is taking antiseizure medication.

3. If an individual has had a sudden episode of a nonepileptic seizure or loss of consciousness of unknown cause which did not require antiseizure medication, the decision as to whether that person's condition will likely cause loss of consciousness or loss of ability to control a motor vehicle is made on an individual basis by the medical examiner in consultation with the treating physician. Before certification is considered, it is suggested that a 6 month waiting period elapse from the time of the episode. Following the waiting period, it is suggested that the individual have a complete neurological examination. If the results of the examination are negative and antiseizure medication is not required, then the driver may be qualified.

4. In those individual cases where a driver has a seizure or an episode of loss of consciousness that resulted from a known medical condition (*e.g.*, drug reaction, high temperature, acute infectious disease, dehydration or acute metabolic disturbance), certification should be deferred until the driver has fully recovered from that condition and has no existing residual complications, and not taking antiseizure medication.

5. Drivers with a history of epilepsy/seizures off antiseizure medication and seizure-free for 10 years may be qualified to drive a commercial motor vehicle in interstate commerce. Interstate drivers with a history of a single unprovoked seizure may be qualified to drive a commercial motor vehicle in interstate commerce if seizure-free and off antiseizure medication for a 5-year period or more.

I. Mental Disorders: §391.41(b)(9)

1. A person is physically qualified to drive a commercial motor vehicle if that person: Has no mental, nervous, organic or functional disease or psychiatric disorder likely to interfere with ability to drive a motor vehicle safely.

2. Emotional or adjustment problems contribute directly to an individual's level of memory, reasoning, attention, and judgment. These problems often underlie physical disorders. A variety of functional disorders can cause drowsiness, dizziness, confusion, weakness or paralysis that may lead to incoordination, inattention, loss of functional control and susceptibility to accidents while driving. Physical fatigue, headache, impaired coordination, recurring physical ailments and chronic "nagging" pain may be present to such a degree that certification for commercial driving is inadvisable. Somatic and psychosomatic complaints should be thoroughly examined when determining an individual's overall fitness to drive. Disorders of a periodically incapacitating nature, even in the early stages of development, may warrant disqualification.

3. Many bus and truck drivers have documented that "nervous trouble" related to neurotic, personality, or emotional or adjustment problems is responsible for a significant fraction of their preventable accidents. The degree to which an individual is able to appreciate, evaluate and adequately respond to environmental strain and emotional stress is critical when assessing an individual's mental alertness and flexibility to cope with the stresses of commercial motor vehicle driving.

4. When examining the driver, it should be kept in mind that individuals who live under chronic emotional upsets may have deeply ingrained maladaptive or erratic behavior patterns. Excessively antagonistic, instinctive, impulsive, openly aggressive, paranoid or severely depressed behavior greatly interfere with the driver's ability to drive safely. Those individuals who are

highly susceptible to frequent states of emotional instability (schizophrenia, affective psychoses, paranoia, anxiety or depressive neuroses) may warrant disqualification. Careful consideration should be given to the side effects and interactions of medications in the overall qualification determination.

J. Vision: §391.41(b)(10)

1. A person is physically qualified to drive a commercial motor vehicle if that person: Has distant visual acuity of at least 20/40 (Snellen) in each eye with or without corrective lenses or visual acuity separately corrected to 20/40 (Snellen) or better with corrective lenses, distant binocular acuity of at least 20/40 (Snellen) in both eyes with or without corrective lenses, field of vision of at least 70 degrees in the horizontal meridian in each eye, and the ability to recognize the colors of traffic signals and devices showing standard red, green, and amber.

2. The term "ability to recognize the colors of" is interpreted to mean if a person can recognize and distinguish among traffic control signals and devices showing standard red, green and amber, he or she meets the minimum standard, even though he or she may have some type of color perception deficiency. If certain color perception tests are administered, (such as Ishihara, Pseudoisochromatic, Yarn) and doubtful findings are discovered, a controlled test using signal red, green and amber may be employed to determine the driver's ability to recognize these colors.

3. Contact lenses are permissible if there is sufficient evidence to indicate that the driver has good tolerance and is well adapted to their use. Use of a contact lens in one eye for distance visual acuity and another lens in the other eye for near vision is not acceptable, nor telescopic lenses acceptable for the driving of commercial motor vehicles.

4. If an individual meets the criteria by the use of glasses or contact lenses, the following statement shall appear on the Medical Examiner's Certificate: "Qualified only if wearing corrective lenses." commercial motor vehicle drivers who do not meet the Federal vision standard may call (202) 366-4001 for an application for a vision exemption.

K. Hearing: §391.41(b)(11)

1. A person is physically qualified to drive a commercial motor vehicle if that person: First perceives a forced whispered voice in the better ear at not less than 5 feet with or without the use of a hearing aid, or, if tested by use of an audiometric device, does not have an average hearing loss in the better ear greater than 40 decibels at 500 Hz, 1,000 Hz, and 2,000 Hz with or without a hearing aid when the audiometric device is calibrated to American National Standard (formerly ADA Standard) Z24.5-1951.

2. Since the prescribed standard under the Federal Motor Carrier Safety Regulations is from the American National Standards Institute, formerly the American Standards Association, it may be necessary to convert the audiometric results from the International Organization for Standardization standard to the American National Standards Institute standard. Instructions are included on the Medical Examination Report Form.

3. If an individual meets the criteria by using a hearing aid, the driver must wear that hearing aid and have it in operation at all times while driving. Also, the driver must be in possession of a spare power source for the hearing aid.

4. For the whispered voice test, the individual should be stationed at least 5 feet from the medical examiner with the ear being tested turned toward the medical examiner. The other ear is covered. Using the breath which remains after a normal expiration, the medical examiner whispers words or random numbers such as 66, 18, 3, etc. The medical examiner should not use only sibilants (s sounding materials). The opposite ear should be tested in the same manner.

5. If the individual fails the whispered voice test, the audiometric test should be administered. If an individual meets the criteria by the use of a hearing aid, the following statement must appear on the Medical Examiner's Certificate "Qualified only when wearing a hearing aid."

L. Drug Use: §391.41(b)(12)

1. A person is physically qualified to drive a commercial motor vehicle if that person does not use any drug or substance identified in 21 CFR 1308.11, an amphetamine, a narcotic, or other habit-forming drug. A driver may use a non-Schedule I drug or substance that is identified in the other Schedules in 21 CFR part 1308 if the substance or drug is prescribed by a licensed medical practitioner who:

(i) Is familiar with the driver's medical history, and assigned duties; and

(ii) Has advised the driver that the prescribed substance or drug will not adversely affect the driver's ability to safely operate a commercial motor vehicle.

2. This exception does not apply to methadone. The intent of the medical certification process is to medically evaluate a driver to ensure that the driver has no medical condition which interferes with the safe performance of driving tasks on a public road. If a driver uses an amphetamine, a narcotic or any other habit-forming drug, it may be cause for the driver to be found medically unqualified. If a driver uses a Schedule I drug or substance, it will be cause for the driver to be found medically unqualified. Motor carriers are encouraged to obtain a practitioner's written statement about the effects on transportation safety of the use of a particular drug.

3. A test for controlled substances is not required as part of this biennial certification process. The Federal Motor Carrier Safety Administration or the driver's employer should be contacted directly for information on controlled substances and alcohol testing under Part 382 of the FMCSRs.

4. The term "uses" is designed to encompass instances of prohibited drug use determined by a physician through established medical means. This may or may not involve body fluid testing. If body fluid testing takes place, positive test results should be confirmed by a second test of greater specificity. The term "habit-forming" is intended to include any drug or medication generally recognized as capable of becoming habitual, and which may impair the user's ability to operate a commercial motor vehicle safely.

5. The driver is medically unqualified for the duration of the prohibited drug(s) use and until a second examination shows the driver is free from the prohibited drug(s) use. Recertification may involve a substance abuse evaluation, the successful completion of a drug rehabilitation program, and a negative drug test result. Additionally, given that the certification period is normally two years, the medical examiner has the option to certify for a period of less than 2 years if this medical examiner determines more frequent monitoring is required.

M. Alcoholism: §391.41(b)(13)

1. A person is physically qualified to drive a commercial motor vehicle if that person: Has no current clinical diagnosis of alcoholism.

2. The term "current clinical diagnosis of" is specifically designed to encompass a current alcoholic illness or those instances where the individual's physical condition has not fully stabilized, regardless of the time element. If an individual shows signs of having an alcohol-use problem, he or she should be referred to a specialist. After counseling and/or treatment, he or she may be considered for certification.

PART 392—DRIVING OF COMMERCIAL MOTOR VEHICLES

Subpart A—General

Subpart B—Driving of Commercial Motor Vehicles

Subpart C —Stopped Commercial Motor Vehicles

Subpart D—Use of Lighted Lamps and Reflectors

Subpart E—License Revocation; Duties of Driver

Subpart F—Fueling Precautions

Subpart G—Prohibited Practices

Authority: 49 U.S.C. 504, 13902, 31136, 31151, 31502; Section 112 of Pub. L. 103-311, 108 Stat. 1673, 1676 (1994), as amended by sec. 32509 of Pub. L. 112-141, 126 Stat. 405-805 (2012); and 49 CFR 1.87.

Subpart A—General

§392.1 Scope of the rules in this part.

(a) Every motor carrier, its officers, agents, representatives, and employees responsible for the management, maintenance, operation, or driving of commercial motor vehicles, or the hiring, supervising, training, assigning, or dispatching of drivers, shall be instructed in and comply with the rules in this part.

(b) The rules in this part do not apply to drivers of "pipeline welding trucks" as defined in 49 CFR 390.38(b).

§392.2 Applicable operating rules.

Every commercial motor vehicle must be operated in accordance with the laws, ordinances, and regulations of the jurisdiction in which it is being operated. However, if a regulation of the Federal Motor Carrier Safety Administration imposes a higher standard of care than that law, ordinance or regulation, the Federal Motor Carrier Safety Administration regulation must be complied with.

§392.3 Ill or fatigued operator.

No driver shall operate a commercial motor vehicle, and a motor carrier shall not require or permit a driver to operate a commercial motor vehicle, while the driver's ability or alertness is so impaired, or so likely to become impaired, through fatigue, illness, or any other cause, as to make it unsafe for him/her to begin or continue to operate the commercial motor vehicle. However, in a case of grave emergency where the hazard to occupants of the commercial motor vehicle or other users of the highway would be increased by compliance with this section, the driver may continue to operate the commercial motor vehicle to the nearest place at which that hazard is removed.

§392.4 Drugs and other substances.

(a) No driver shall be on duty and possess, be under the influence of, or use, any of the following drugs or other substances:

(1) Any 21 CFR 1308.11 *Schedule I* substance;

(2) An amphetamine or any formulation thereof (including, but not limited, to "pep pills," and "bennies");

(3) A narcotic drug or any derivative thereof; or

(4) Any other substance, to a degree which renders the driver incapable of safely operating a motor vehicle.

(b) No motor carrier shall require or permit a driver to violate paragraph (a) of this section.

(c) Paragraphs (a) (2), (3), and (4) do not apply to the possession or use of a substance administered to a driver by or under the instructions of a licensed medical practitioner, as defined in §382.107 of this subchapter, who has advised the driver that the substance will not affect the driver's ability to safely operate a motor vehicle.

(d) As used in this section, "possession" does not include possession of a substance which is manifested and transported as part of a shipment.

§392.5 Alcohol prohibition.

(a) No driver shall—

(1) Use alcohol, as defined in §382.107 of this subchapter, or be under the influence of alcohol, within 4 hours before going on duty or operating, or having physical control of, a commercial motor vehicle; or

(2) Use alcohol, be under the influence of alcohol, or have any measured alcohol concentration or detected presence of alcohol, while on duty, or operating, or in physical control of a commercial motor vehicle; or

(3) Be on duty or operate a commercial motor vehicle while the driver possesses wine of not less than one-half of one per centum of alcohol by volume, beer *as defined in 26 U.S.C. 5052(a), of the Internal Revenue Code of 1954,* or distilled spirits *as defined in section 5002(a)(8), of such Code.* However, this does not apply to possession of wine, beer, or distilled spirits which are:

(i) Manifested and transported as part of a shipment; or

(ii) Possessed or used by bus passengers.

(b) No motor carrier shall require or permit a driver to—

(1) Violate any provision of paragraph (a) of this section; or

(2) Be on duty or operate a commercial motor vehicle if, by the driver's general appearance or conduct or by other substantiating evidence, the driver appears to have used alcohol within the preceding 4 hours.

(c) Any driver who is found to be in violation of the provisions of paragraph (a) or (b) of this section shall be placed out-of-service immediately for a period of 24 hours.

(1) The 24-hour out-of-service period will commence upon issuance of an out-of-service order.

(2) No driver shall violate the terms of an out-of-service order issued under this section.

(d) Any driver who is issued an out-of-service order under this section shall:

(1) Report such issuance to his/her employer within 24 hours; and

(2) Report such issuance to a State official, designated by the State which issued his/her driver's license, within 30 days unless the driver chooses to request a review of the order. In this case, the driver shall report the order to the State official within 30 days of an affirmation of the order by either the Division Administrator or State Director for the geographical area or the Administrator.

(e) Any driver who is subject to an out-of-service order under this section may petition for review of that order by submitting a petition for review in writing within 10 days of the issuance of the order to the Division Administrator or State Director for the geographical area in which the order was issued. The Division Administrator or State Director may affirm or reverse the order. Any driver adversely affected by such order of the Division Administrator or State Director may petition the Administrator for review in accordance with 49 CFR 386.13.

§392.6 Schedules to conform with speed limits.

No motor carrier shall schedule a run nor permit nor require the operation of any commercial motor vehicle between points in such period of time as would necessitate the commercial vehicle being operated at speeds greater than those prescribed by the jurisdictions in or through which the commercial motor vehicle is being operated.

§392.7 Equipment, inspection, and use.

(a) No commercial motor vehicle shall be driven unless the driver is satisfied that the following parts and accessories are in good working order, nor shall any driver fail to use or make use of such parts and accessories when and as needed:

Service brakes, including trailer brake connections.

Parking (hand) brake.

Steering mechanism.

Lighting devices and reflectors.

Tires.

Horn.

Windshield wiper or wipers.

Rear-vision mirror or mirrors.

Coupling devices.

Wheels and rims.

Emergency equipment.

(b) Drivers preparing to transport intermodal equipment must make an inspection of the following components, and must be satisfied they are in good working order before the equipment is operated over the road. Drivers who operate the equipment over the road shall be deemed to have confirmed the following components were in good working order when the driver accepted the equipment:

—Service brake components that are readily visible to a driver performing as thorough a visual inspection as possible without physically going under the vehicle, and trailer brake connections

—Lighting devices, lamps, markers, and conspicuity marking material

—Wheels, rims, lugs, tires

—Air line connections, hoses, and couplers

—King pin upper coupling device

—Rails or support frames

—Tie down bolsters

—Locking pins, clevises, clamps, or hooks

—Sliders or sliding frame lock

§392.8 Emergency equipment, inspection, and use.

No commercial motor vehicle shall be driven unless the driver thereof is satisfied that the emergency equipment required by §393.95 of this subchapter is in place and ready for use; nor shall any driver fail to use or make use of such equipment when and as needed.

§392.9 Inspection of cargo, cargo securement devices and systems.

(a) **General**. A driver may not operate a commercial motor vehicle and a motor carrier may not require or permit a driver to operate a commercial motor vehicle unless—

(1) The commercial motor vehicle's cargo is properly distributed and adequately secured as specified in §§393.100 through 393.136 of this subchapter.

(2) The commercial motor vehicle's tailgate, tailboard, doors, tarpaulins, spare tire and other equipment used in its operation, and the means of fastening the commercial motor vehicle's cargo, are secured; and

(3) The commercial motor vehicle's cargo or any other object does not obscure the driver's view ahead or to the right or left sides (except for drivers of self-steer dollies), interfere with the free movement of his/her arms or legs, prevent his/her free and ready access to accessories required for emergencies, or prevent the free and ready exit of any person from the commercial motor vehicle's cab or driver's compartment.

(b) **Drivers of trucks and truck tractors**. Except as provided in paragraph (b)(4) of this section, the driver of a truck or truck tractor must—

(1) Assure himself/herself that the provisions of paragraph (a) of this section have been complied with before he/she drives that commercial motor vehicle;

(2) Inspect the cargo and the devices used to secure the cargo within the first 50 miles after beginning a trip and cause any adjustments to be made to the cargo or load securement devices as necessary, including adding more securement devices, to ensure that cargo cannot shift on or within, or fall from the commercial motor vehicle; and

(3) Reexamine the commercial motor vehicle's cargo and its load securement devices during the course of transportation and make any necessary adjustment to the cargo or load securement devices, including adding more securement devices, to ensure that cargo cannot shift on or within, or fall from, the commercial motor vehicle. Reexamination and any necessary adjustments must be made whenever—

(i) The driver makes a change of his/her duty status; or

(ii) The commercial motor vehicle has been driven for 3 hours; or

(iii) The commercial motor vehicle has been driven for 150 miles, whichever occurs first.

(4) The rules in this paragraph (b) do not apply to the driver of a sealed commercial motor vehicle who has been ordered not to open it to inspect its cargo or to the driver of a commercial motor vehicle that has been loaded in a manner that makes inspection of its cargo impracticable.

§392.9a Operating authority.

(a) **Operating authority required**. A motor vehicle providing transportation requiring operating authority must not be operated—

(1) Without the required operating authority or

(2) Beyond the scope of the operating authority granted.

(b) **Penalties**. Every motor carrier providing transportation requiring operating authority shall be ordered out of service if it is determined that the motor carrier is operating a vehicle in violation of paragraph (a) of this section. In addition, the motor carrier may be subject to penalties in accordance with 49 U.S.C. 14901.

(c) **Administrative Review**. Upon issuance of the out-of-service order under paragraph (b) of this section, the driver shall comply immediately with such order. Opportunity for review shall be provided in accordance with 5 U.S.C. 554 not later than 10 days after issuance of such order.

§392.9b Prohibited transportation.

(a) **Safety registration required.** A commercial motor vehicle providing transportation in interstate commerce must not be operated without a safety registration and an active USDOT Number.

(b) **Penalties**. If it is determined that the motor carrier responsible for the operation of such a vehicle is operating in violation of paragraph (a) of this section, it may be subject to penalties in accordance with 49 U.S.C. 521.

Subpart B—Driving of Vehicles

§392.10 Railroad grade crossings; stopping required.

(a) Except as provided in paragraph (b) of this section, the driver of a commercial motor vehicle specified in paragraphs (1) through (6) of this section shall not cross a railroad track or tracks at grade unless he/she first: Stops the commercial motor vehicle within 50 feet of, and not closer than 15 feet to, the tracks; thereafter listens and looks in each direction along the tracks for an approaching train; and ascertains that no train is approaching. When it is safe to do so, the driver may drive the commercial motor vehicle across the tracks in a gear that permits the commercial motor vehicle to complete the crossing without a change of gears. The driver must not shift gears while crossing the tracks.

(1) Every bus transporting passengers,

(2) Every commercial motor vehicle transporting any quantity of a Division 2.3 chlorine.

(3) Every commercial motor vehicle which, in accordance with the regulations of the Department of Transportation, is required to be marked or placarded with one of the following classifications:

(i) Division 1.1

(ii) Division 1.2, or Division 1.3

(iii) Division 2.3 Poison gas

(iv) Division 4.3

(v) Class 7

(vi) Class 3 Flammable

(vii) Division 5.1

(viii) Division 2.2

(ix) Division 2.3 Chlorine

(x) Division 6.1 Poison

(xi) Division 2.2 Oxygen

(xii) Division 2.1

(xiii) Class 3 Combustible liquid

(xiv) Division 4.1

(xv) Division 5.1

(xvi) Division 5.2

(xvii) Class 8

(xviii) Division 1.4

(4) Every cargo tank motor vehicle, whether loaded or empty, used for the transportation of any hazardous material as defined in the Hazardous Materials Regulations of the Department of Transportation, Parts 107 through 180 of this title.

(5) Every cargo tank motor vehicle transporting a commodity which at the time of loading has a temperature above its flashpoint as determined by §173.120 of this title.

(6) Every cargo tank motor vehicle, whether loaded or empty, transporting any commodity under exemption in accordance with the provisions of Subpart B of Part 107 of this title.

(b) A stop need not be made at:

(1) A streetcar crossing, or railroad tracks used exclusively for industrial switching purposes, within a business district, as defined in §390.5 of this chapter.

(2) A railroad grade crossing when a police officer or crossing flagman directs traffic to proceed.

(3) A railroad grade crossing controlled by a functioning highway traffic signal transmitting a green indication which, under local law, permits the commercial motor vehicle to proceed across the railroad tracks without slowing or stopping.

(4) An abandoned railroad grade crossing which is marked with a sign indicating that the rail line is abandoned.

(5) An industrial or spur line railroad grade crossing marked with a sign reading "Exempt." Such "Exempt" signs shall be erected only by or with the consent of the appropriate State or local authority.

§392.11 Railroad grade crossings; slowing down required.

Every commercial motor vehicle other than those listed in §392.10 shall, upon approaching a railroad grade crossing, be driven at a rate of speed which will permit said commercial motor vehicle to be stopped before reaching the nearest rail of such crossing and shall not be driven upon or over such crossing until due caution has been taken to ascertain that the course is clear.

§392.12 Highway-rail crossings; safe clearance.

No driver of a commercial motor vehicle shall drive onto a highway-rail grade crossing without having sufficient space to drive completely through the crossing without stopping.

§392.13 [Reserved]

§392.14 Hazardous conditions; extreme caution.

Extreme caution in the operation of a commercial motor vehicle shall be exercised when hazardous conditions, such as those caused by snow, ice, sleet, fog, mist, rain, dust, or smoke, adversely affect visibility or traction. Speed shall be reduced when such conditions exist. If conditions become sufficiently dangerous, the operation of the commercial motor vehicle shall be discontinued and shall not be resumed until the commercial motor vehicle can be safely operated. Whenever compliance with the foregoing provisions of this rule increases hazard to passengers, the commercial motor vehicle may be operated to the nearest point at which the safety of passengers is assured.

§392.15 Prohibited driving status.

No driver, who holds a commercial learner's permit or a commercial driver's license, shall operate a commercial motor vehicle if prohibited by §382.501(a) of this subchapter.

§392.16 Use of seat belts.

(a) **Drivers.** No driver shall operate a commercial motor vehicle, and a motor carrier shall not require or permit a driver to operate a commercial motor vehicle, that has a seat belt assembly installed at the driver's seat unless the driver is properly restrained by the seat belt assembly.

(b) **Passengers.** No driver shall operate a property-carrying commercial motor vehicle, and a motor carrier shall not require or permit a driver to operate a property-carrying commercial motor vehicle, that has seat belt assemblies installed at the seats for other occupants of the vehicle unless all other occupants are properly restrained by such seat belt assemblies.

§392.18

§392.18 [Reserved.]

Subpart C—Stopped Vehicles

§§392.20–392.21 [Reserved.]

§392.22 Emergency signals; stopped commercial motor vehicles.

(a) **Hazard warning signal flashers**. Whenever a commercial motor vehicle is stopped upon the traveled portion of a highway or the shoulder of a highway for any cause other than necessary traffic stops, the driver of the stopped commercial motor vehicle shall immediately activate the vehicular hazard warning signal flashers and continue the flashing until the driver places the warning devices required by paragraph (b) of this section. The flashing signals shall be used during the time the warning devices are picked up for storage before movement of the commercial motor vehicle. The flashing lights may be used at other times while a commercial motor vehicle is stopped in addition to, but not in lieu of, the warning devices required by paragraph (b) of this section.

(b) **Placement of warning devices**—

(1) **General rule.** Except as provided in paragraph (b)(2) of this section, whenever a commercial motor vehicle is stopped upon the traveled portion or the shoulder of a highway for any cause other than necessary traffic stops, the driver shall, as soon as possible, but in any event within 10 minutes, place the warning devices required by §393.95 of this subchapter, in the following manner:

(i) One on the traffic side of and 4 paces (approximately 3 meters or 10 feet) from the stopped commercial motor vehicle in the direction of approaching traffic;

(ii) One at 40 paces (approximately 30 meters or 100 feet) from the stopped commercial motor vehicle in the center of the traffic lane or shoulder occupied by the commercial motor vehicle and in the direction of approaching traffic; and

(iii) One at 40 paces (approximately 30 meters or 100 feet) from the stopped commercial motor vehicle in the center of the traffic lane or shoulder occupied by the commercial motor vehicle and in the direction away from approaching traffic.

(2) **Special rules**— (i)**Fusees and liquid-burning flares.** The driver of a commercial motor vehicle equipped with only fusees or liquid-burning flares shall place a lighted fusee or liquid-burning flare at each of the locations specified in paragraph (b)(1) of this section. There shall be at least one lighted fusee or liquid-burning flare at each of the prescribed locations, as long as the commercial motor vehicle is stopped. Before the stopped commercial motor vehicle is moved, the driver shall extinguish and remove each fusee or liquid-burning flare.

(ii) **Daylight hours.** Except as provided in paragraph (b)(2)(iii) of this section, during the period lighted lamps are not required, three bidirectional reflective triangles, or three lighted fusees or liquid-burning flares shall be placed as specified in paragraph (b)(1) of this section within a time of 10 minutes. In the event the driver elects to use only fusees or liquid-burning flares in lieu of bidirectional reflective triangles or red flags, the driver must ensure that at least one fusee or liquid-burning flare remains lighted at each of the prescribed locations as long as the commercial motor vehicle is stopped or parked.

(iii) **Business or residential districts.** The placement of warning devices is not required within the business or residential district of a municipality, except during the time lighted lamps are required and when street or highway lighting is insufficient to make a commercial motor vehicle clearly discernable at a distance of 500 feet to persons on the highway.

(iv) **Hills, curves, and obstructions.** If a commercial motor vehicle is stopped within 500 feet of a curve, crest of a hill, or other obstruction to view, the driver shall place the warning signal required by paragraph (b)(1) of this section in the direction of the obstruction to view a distance of 100 feet to 500 feet from the stopped commercial motor vehicle so as to afford ample warning to other users of the highway.

(v) **Divided or one-way roads.** If a commercial motor vehicle is stopped upon the traveled portion or the shoulder of a divided or one-way highway, the driver shall place the warning devices required by paragraph (b)(1) of this section, one warning device at a distance of 200 feet and one warning device at a distance of 100 feet in a direction toward approaching traffic in the center of the lane or shoulder occupied by the commercial motor vehicle. He/she shall place one warning device at the traffic side of the commercial motor vehicle within 10 feet of the rear of the commercial motor vehicle.

(vi) **Leaking, flammable material.** If gasoline or any other flammable liquid, or combustible liquid or gas seeps or leaks from a fuel container or a commercial motor vehicle stopped upon a highway, no emergency warning signal producing a flame shall be lighted or placed except at such a distance from any such liquid or gas as will assure the prevention of a fire or explosion.

§392.24 Emergency signals; flame-producing.

No driver shall attach or permit any person to attach a lighted fusee or other flame-producing emergency signal to any part of a commercial motor vehicle.

§392.25 Flame producing devices.

No driver shall use or permit the use of any flame-producing emergency signal for protecting any commercial motor vehicle transporting Division 1.1, Division 1.2, or Division 1.3 explosives; any cargo tank motor vehicle used for the transportation of any Class 3 or Division 2.1, whether loaded or empty; or any commercial motor vehicle using compressed gas as a motor fuel. In lieu thereof, emergency reflective triangles, red electric lanterns, or red emergency reflectors shall be used, the placement of which shall be in the same manner as prescribed in §392.22(b).

Subpart D—Use of Lighted Lamps and Reflectors

§§392.30–392.32 [Reserved.]

§392.33 Obscured lamps or reflective devices/material.

(a) No commercial motor vehicle shall be driven when any of the lamps or reflective devices/material required by subpart B of part 393 of this title are obscured by the tailboard, or by any part of the load or its covering, by dirt, or other added vehicle or work equipment or otherwise.

(b) **Exception.** The conspicuity treatments on the front end protection devices of the trailer may be obscured by part of the load being transported.

PART 392

Subpart E—License Revocation: Duties of Driver

§§392.40–392.42 [Reserved.]

Subpart F—Fueling Precautions

§392.50 Ignition of fuel; prevention.

No driver or any employee of a motor carrier shall:

(a) Fuel a commercial motor vehicle with the engine running, except when it is necessary to run the engine to fuel the commercial motor vehicle;

(b) Smoke or expose any open flame in the vicinity of a commercial motor vehicle being fueled;

(c) Fuel a commercial motor vehicle unless the nozzle of the fuel hose is continuously in contact with the intake pipe of the fuel tank;

(d) Permit, insofar as practicable, any other person to engage in such activities as would be likely to result in fire or explosion.

§392.51 Reserve fuel; materials of trade.

Small amounts of fuel for the operation or maintenance of a commercial motor vehicle (including its auxiliary equipment) may be designated as materials of trade (see 49 CFR 171.8).

(a) The aggregate gross weight of all materials of trade on a motor vehicle may not exceed 200 kg (440 pounds).

(b) Packaging for gasoline must be made of metal or plastic and conform to requirements of 49 CFR Parts 171, 172, 173, and 178 or requirements of the Occupational Safety and Health Administration contained in 29 CFR 1910.106.

(c) For Packing Group II (including gasoline), Packing Group III (including aviation fuel and fuel oil), or ORM-D, the material is limited to 30 kg (66 pounds) or 30 L (8 gallons).

(d) For diesel fuel, the capacity of the package is limited to 450 L (119 gallons).

(e) A Division 2.1 material in a cylinder is limited to a gross weight of 100 kg (220 pounds). (A Division 2.1 material is a flammable gas, including liquefied petroleum gas, butane, propane, liquefied natural gas, and methane).

§392.52 [Reserved.]

Subpart G—Prohibited Practices

§392.60 Unauthorized persons not to be transported.

(a) Unless specifically authorized in writing to do so by the motor carrier under whose authority the commercial motor vehicle is being operated, no driver shall transport any person or permit any person to be transported on any commercial motor vehicle other than a bus. When such authorization is issued, it shall state the name of the person to be transported, the points where the transportation is to begin and end, and the date upon which such authority expires. No written authorization, however, shall be necessary for the transportation of:

(1) Employees or other persons assigned to a commercial motor vehicle by a motor carrier;

(2) Any person transported when aid is being rendered in case of an accident or other emergency;

(3) An attendant delegated to care for livestock.

(b) This section shall not apply to the operation of commercial motor vehicles controlled and operated by any farmer and used in the transportation of agricultural commodities or products thereof from his/her farm or in the transportation of supplies to his/her farm.

§392.61 [Reserved.]

§392.62 Safe operation, buses.

No person shall drive a bus and a motor carrier shall not require or permit a person to drive a bus unless—

(a) All standees on the bus are rearward of the standee line or other means prescribed in §393.90 of this subchapter;

(b) All aisle seats in the bus conform to the requirements of §393.91 of this subchapter; and

(c) Baggage or freight on the bus is stowed and secured in a manner which assures—

(1) Unrestricted freedom of movement to the driver and his proper operation of the bus;

(2) Unobstructed access to all exits by any occupant of the bus; and

(3) Protection of occupants of the bus against injury resulting from the falling or displacement of articles transported in the bus.

§392.63 Towing or pushing loaded buses.

No disabled bus with passengers aboard shall be towed or pushed; nor shall any person use or permit to be used a bus with passengers aboard for the purpose of towing or pushing any disabled motor vehicle, except in such circumstances where the hazard to passengers would be increased by observance of the foregoing provisions of this section, and then only in traveling to the nearest point where the safety of the passengers is assured.

§392.64 Riding within closed commercial motor vehicles without proper exits.

No person shall ride within the closed body of any commercial motor vehicle unless there are means on the inside thereof of obtaining exit. Said means shall be in such condition as to permit ready operation by the occupant.

§392.65 [Reserved.]

§392.66 Carbon monoxide; use of commercial motor vehicle when detected.

(a) No person shall dispatch or drive any commercial motor vehicle or permit any passengers thereon, when the following conditions are known to exist, until such conditions have been remedied or repaired:

(1) Where an occupant has been affected by carbon monoxide;

(2) Where carbon monoxide has been detected in the interior of the commercial motor vehicle;

(3) When a mechanical condition of the commercial motor vehicle is discovered which would be likely to produce a hazard to the occupants by reason of carbon monoxide.

(b) [Reserved]

§392.67 Heater, flame-producing; on commercial motor vehicle in motion.

No open flame heater used in the loading or unloading of the commodity transported shall be in operation while the commercial motor vehicle is in motion.

§§392.68–392.69 [Reserved.]

§392.71 Radar detectors; use and/or possession.

(a) No driver shall use a radar detector in a commercial motor vehicle, or operate a commercial motor vehicle that is equipped with or contains any radar detector.

(b) No motor carrier shall require or permit a driver to violate paragraph (a) of this section.

Subpart H—Limiting the Use of Electronic Devices

§392.80 Prohibition against texting.

(a) **Prohibition.** No driver shall engage in texting while driving.

(b) **Motor Carriers**. No motor carrier shall allow or require its drivers to engage in texting while driving.

(c) **Definition**. For the purpose of this section only, *driving* means operating a commercial motor vehicle, with the motor running, including while temporarily stationary because of traffic, a traffic control device, or other momentary delays. Driving does not include operating a commercial motor vehicle with or without the motor running when the driver moved the vehicle to the side of, or off, a highway, as defined in 49 CFR 390.5, and halted in a location where the vehicle can safely remain stationary.

(d) **Emergency exception**. Texting while driving is permissible by drivers of a commercial motor vehicle when necessary to communicate with law enforcement officials or other emergency services.

§392.82 Using a hand-held mobile telephone.

(a)(1) No driver shall use a hand-held mobile telephone while driving a CMV.

(2) No motor carrier shall allow or require its drivers to use a hand-held mobile telephone while driving a CMV.

(b) **Definitions**. For the purpose of this section only, *driving* means operating a commercial motor vehicle on a highway, including while temporarily stationary because of traffic, a traffic control device, or other momentary delays. Driving does not include operating a commercial motor vehicle when the driver has moved the vehicle to the side of, or off, a highway and has halted in a location where the vehicle can safely remain stationary.

(c) **Emergency exception.** Using a hand-held mobile telephone is permissible by drivers of a CMV when necessary to communicate with law enforcement officials or other emergency services.

PART 393—PARTS AND ACCESSORIES NECESSARY FOR SAFE OPERATION

Subpart A—General

Subpart B—Lamps, Reflective Devices, and Electrical Wiring

Subpart C—Brakes

Subpart D—Glazing and Window Construction

Subpart E—Fuel Systems

393.65 All fuel systems.
393.67 Liquid fuel tanks.
393.68 Compressed natural gas fuel containers.
393.69 Liquefied petroleum gas systems.

Subpart F—Coupling Devices and Towing Methods

393.70 Coupling devices and towing methods, except for drive-away-towaway operations.
393.71 Coupling devices and towing methods, driveaway-tow-away operations.

Subpart G—Miscellaneous Parts and Accessories

393.75 Tires.
393.76 Sleeper berths.
393.77 Heaters.
393.78 Windshield wiping and washing systems.
393.79 Windshield defrosting and defogging systems.
393.80 Rear-vision mirrors.
393.81 Horn.
393.82 Speedometer.
393.83 Exhaust systems.
393.84 Floors.
393.85 [Reserved]
393.86 Rear impact guards and rear end protection.
393.87 Warning flags on projecting loads.
393.88 Television receivers.
393.89 Buses, driveshaft protection.
393.90 Buses, standee line or bar.
393.91 Buses, aisle seats prohibited.
393.92 [Reserved]
393.93 Seats, seat belt assemblies and seat belt assembly anchorages.
393.94 Interior noise levels in power units.

Subpart H—Emergency Equipment

393.95 Emergency equipment on all power units.

Subpart I—Protection Against Shifting and Falling Cargo

393.100 Which types of commercial motor vehicles are subject to the cargo securement standards of this subpart, and what general requirements apply?
393.102 What are the minimum performance criteria for cargo securement devices and systems?
393.104 What standards must cargo securement devices and systems meet in order to satisfy the requirements of this subpart?
393.106 What are the general requirements for securing articles of cargo?
393.108 How is the working load limit of a tiedown, or the load restraining value of a friction mat, determined?
393.110 What else do I have to do to determine the minimum number of tiedowns?
393.112 Must a tiedown be adjustable?
393.114 What are the requirements for front end structures used as part of a cargo securement system?

PART 393

Authority: 49 U.S.C. 31136, 31151, 31502; sec. 1041(b), Pub. L. 102-240, 105 Stat. 1914, 1993; secs. 5301 and 5524, Pub. L. 114-94, 129 Stat. 1312, 1543, 1560; and 49 CFR 1.87.

Subpart A—General

§393.1 Scope of the rules in this part.

(a) The rules in this part establish minimum standards for commercial motor vehicles as defined in §390.5 of this title. Only motor vehicles (as defined in §390.5) and combinations of motor vehicles which meet the definition of a commercial motor vehicle are subject to the requirements of this part. All requirements that refer to motor vehicles with a GVWR below 4,536 kg (10,001 pounds) are applicable only when the motor vehicle or combination of motor vehicles meets the definition of a commercial motor vehicle.

(b)(1) Every motor carrier and its employees must be knowledgeable of and comply with the requirements and specifications of this part.

(2) Every intermodal equipment provider and its employees or agents responsible for the inspection, repair, and maintenance of intermodal equipment interchanged to motor carriers must be knowledgeable of and comply with the applicable requirements and specifications of this part.

(c) No motor carrier may operate a commercial motor vehicle, or cause or permit such vehicle to be operated, unless it is equipped in accordance with the requirements and specifications of this part.

(d) No intermodal equipment provider may operate intermodal equipment, or cause or permit such equipment to be operated, unless it is equipped in accordance with the requirements and specifications of this part.

(e) The rules in this part do not apply to "pipeline welding trucks" as defined in 49 CFR 390.38(b).

§393.3 Additional equipment and accessories.

The use of additional equipment or accessories in a manner that decreases the safety of operation of a commercial motor vehicle in interstate commerce is prohibited. Nothing contained in this subchapter shall be construed to prohibit the use of additional equipment and accessories, not inconsistent with or prohibited by this subchapter, provided such equipment and accessories do not decrease the safety of operation of the motor vehicles on which they are used.

§393.5 Definitions.

As used in this part, the following words and terms are construed to mean:

Aggregate working load limit. The summation of the working load limits or restraining capacity of all devices used to secure an article of cargo on a vehicle.

Agricultural commodity trailer. A trailer that is designed to transport bulk agricultural commodities in off road harvesting sites and to a processing plant or storage location, as evidenced by skeletal construction that accommodates harvest containers, a maximum length of 28 feet, and an arrangement of air control lines and reservoirs that minimizes damage in field operations.

Air brake system. A system, including an air-over-hydraulic brake subsystem, that uses air as a medium for transmitting pressure or force from the driver control to the service brake, but does not include a system that uses compressed air or vacuum only to assist the driver in applying muscular force to hydraulic or mechanical components.

Air-over-hydraulic brake subsystem. A subsystem of the air brake system that uses compressed air to transmit a force from the driver control to a hydraulic brake system to actuate the service brakes.

Anchor point. Part of the structure, fitting or attachment on a vehicle or article of cargo to which a tiedown is attached.

Antilock Brake System or ABS. Means a portion of a service brake system that automatically controls the degree of rotational wheel slip during braking by:

(1) Sensing the rate of angular rotation of the wheels;

(2) Transmitting signals regarding the rate of wheel angular rotation to one or more controlling devices which interpret those signals and generate responsive controlling output signals; and

(3) Transmitting those controlling signals to one or more modulators which adjust brake actuating forces in response to those signals.

Article of cargo. A unit of cargo, other than a liquid, gas, or aggregate that lacks physical structure (e.g., grain, gravel, etc.) including articles grouped together so that they can be handled as a single unit or unitized by wrapping, strapping, banding or edge protection device(s).

Auxiliary driving lamp. A lighting device mounted to provide illumination forward of the vehicle which supplements the upper beam of a standard headlighting system. It is not intended for use alone or with the lower beam of a standard headlamp system.

Bell pipe concrete. Pipe whose flanged end is of larger diameter than its barrel.

Blocking. A structure, device or another substantial article placed against or around an article of cargo to prevent horizontal movement of the article of cargo.

Boat trailer. A trailer designed with cradle-type mountings to transport a boat and configured to permit launching of the boat from the rear of the trailer.

Bracing. A structure, device, or another substantial article placed against an article of cargo to prevent it from tipping, that may also prevent it from shifting.

Brake. An energy conversion mechanism used to stop, or hold a vehicle stationary.

Brake power assist unit. A device installed in a hydraulic brake system that reduces the operator effort required to actuate the system, but which if inoperative does not prevent the operator from braking the vehicle by a continued application of muscular force on the service brake control.

Brake power unit. A device installed in a brake system that provides the energy required to actuate the brakes, either directly or indirectly through an auxiliary device, with the operator action consisting only of modulating the energy application level.

Brake tubing/hose. Metallic brake tubing, nonmetallic brake tubing and brake hose are conduits or lines used in a brake system to transmit or contain the medium (fluid or vacuum) used to apply the motor vehicle's brakes.

Chassis. The load-supporting frame of a commercial motor vehicle, exclusive of any appurtenances which might be added to accommodate cargo.

Clearance lamps. Lamps that provide light to the front or rear, mounted on the permanent structure of the vehicle, such that they indicate the overall width of the vehicle.

Container chassis trailer. A semitrailer of skeleton construction limited to a bottom frame, one or more axles, specially built and fitted with locking devices for the transport of intermodal cargo containers, so that when the chassis and container are assembled, the units serve the same function as an over the road trailer.

Converter dolly. A motor vehicle consisting of a chassis equipped with one or more axles, a fifth wheel and/or equivalent mechanism, and drawbar, the attachment of which converts a semitrailer to a full trailer.

Crib-type log trailer. Means a trailer equipped with stakes, bunks, a front-end structure, and a rear structure to restrain logs. The stakes prevent movement of the logs from side to side on the vehicle while the front-end and rear structures prevent movement of the logs from front to back on the vehicle.

Curb weight. The weight of a motor vehicle with standard equipment, maximum capacity of fuel, oil, and coolant; and, if so equipped, air conditioning and additional weight of optional engine. Curb weight does not include the driver.

Dunnage. All loose materials used to support and protect cargo.

Dunnage bag. An inflatable bag intended to fill otherwise empty space between articles of cargo, or between articles of cargo and the wall of the vehicle.

Edge protector. A device placed on the exposed edge of an article to distribute tiedown forces over a larger area of cargo than the tiedown itself, to protect the tie-down and/or cargo from damage, and to allow the tiedown to slide freely when being tensioned.

Electric brake system. A system that uses electric current to actuate the service brake.

Emergency brake. A mechanism designed to stop a motor vehicle after a failure of the service brake system.

Emergency brake system. A mechanism designed to stop a vehicle after a single failure occurs in the service brake system of a part designed to contain compressed air or brake fluid or vacuum (except failure of a common valve, manifold brake fluid housing or brake chamber housing).

Fifth wheel. A device mounted on a truck tractor or similar towing vehicle (e.g., converter dolly) which interfaces with and couples to the upper coupler assembly of a semitrailer.

Frame vehicle. A vehicle with skeletal structure fitted with one or more bunk units for transporting logs. A bunk unit consists of U-shaped front and rear bunks that together cradle logs. The bunks are welded, gusseted or otherwise firmly fastened to the vehicle's main beams, and are an integral part of the vehicle.

Friction mat. A device placed between the deck of a vehicle and article of cargo, or between articles of cargo, intended to provide greater friction than exists naturally between these surfaces.

Front fog lamp. A lighting device whose beam provides downward illumination forward of the vehicle and close to the ground, and is to be used only under conditions of rain, snow, dust, smoke or fog. A pair of fog lamps may be used alone, with parking, tail, side, marker, clearance and identification lamps, or with a lower beam headlamp at the driver's discretion in accordance with state and local use law.

Fuel tank fitting. Any removable device affixed to an opening in the fuel tank with the exception of the filler cap.

g. The acceleration due to gravity, 32.2 ft/sec ^{2} (9.81 m/sec ^{2}).

Grommet. A device that serves as a support and protection to that which passes through it.

Hazard warning signal. Lamps that flash simultaneously to the front and rear, on both the right and left sides of a commercial motor vehicle, to indicate to an approaching driver the presence of a vehicular hazard.

Head lamps. Lamps used to provide general illumination ahead of a motor vehicle.

Heater. Any device or assembly of devices or appliances used to heat the interior of any motor vehicle. This includes a catalytic heater which must meet the requirements of §177.834(l)(2) of this title when Class 3 (flammable liquid) or Division 2.1 (flammable gas) is transported.

Heavy hauler trailer. A trailer which has one or more of the following characteristics, but which is not a container chassis trailer:

(1) Its brake lines are designed to adapt to separation or extension of the vehicle frame; or

(2) Its body consists only of a platform whose primary cargo-carrying surface is not more than 1,016 mm (40 inches) above the ground in an unloaded condition, except that it may include sides that are designed to be easily removable and a permanent "front-end structure" as that term is used in §393.106 of this title.

Hook-lift container. A specialized container, primarily used to contain and transport materials in the waste, recycling, construction/demolition and scrap industries, which is used in conjunction with specialized vehicles, in which the container is loaded and unloaded onto a tilt frame body by an articulating hook-arm.

Hydraulic brake system. A system that uses hydraulic fluid as a medium for transmitting force from a service brake control to the service brake, and that may incorporate a brake power assist unit, or a brake power unit.

Identification lamps. Lamps used to identify certain types of commercial motor vehicles.

Integral securement system. A system on certain roll-on/roll-off containers and hook-lift containers and their related transport vehicles in which compatible front and rear hold down devices are mated to provide securement of the complete vehicle and its articles of cargo.

Lamp. A device used to produce artificial light.

Length of a manufactured home. The largest exterior length in the traveling mode, including any projections which contain interior space. Length does not include bay windows, roof projections, overhangs, or eaves under which there is no interior space, nor does it include drawbars, couplings or hitches.

License plate lamp. A lamp used to illuminate the license plate on the rear of a motor vehicle.

Longwood. Means all logs, including utility poles, that are not shortwood, i.e., that are over 4.9 m (16 feet) long. Such logs are usually described as long logs or treelength.

Low chassis vehicle. (1) A trailer or semitrailer manufactured on or after January 26, 1998, having a chassis which extends behind the rearmost point of the rearmost tires and which has a lower rear surface that meets the guard width, height, and rear surface requirements of §571.224 in effect on the date of manufacture, or a subsequent edition.

(2) A motor vehicle, not described by paragraph (1) of this definition, having a chassis which extends behind the rearmost point of the rearmost tires and which has a lower rear surface that meets the guard configuration requirements of §393.86(b)(1).

Major tread groove is the space between two adjacent tread ribs or lugs on a tire that contains a tread wear indicator or wear bar. (In most cases, the locations of tread wear indicators are designated on the upper sidewall/shoulder of the tire on original tread tires.)

Manufactured home. Means a structure, transportable in one or more sections, which in the traveling mode, is eight body feet or more in width or forty body feet or more in length, or, when erected on site, is three hundred twenty or more square feet, and which is built on a permanent chassis and designed to be used as a dwelling with or without a permanent foundation when connected to the required utilities, and includes the plumbing, heating, air-conditioning, and electrical systems contained therein. Calculations used to determine the number of square feet in a structure will be based on the structure's exterior dimensions measured at the largest horizontal projections when erected on site. These dimensions will include all expandable rooms, cabinets, and other projections containing interior space, but do not include bay windows. This term includes all structures which meet the above requirements except the size requirements and with respect to which the manufacturer voluntarily files a certification pursuant to 24 CFR 3282.13 and complies with the standards set forth in 24 CFR part 3280.

Metal coil. Means an article of cargo comprised of elements, mixtures, compounds, or alloys commonly known as metal, metal foil, metal leaf, forged metal, stamped metal, metal wire, metal rod, or metal chain that are packaged as a roll, coil, spool, wind, or wrap, including plastic or rubber coated electrical wire and communications cable.

Multi-piece windshield. A windshield consisting of two or more windshield glazing surface areas.

Parking brake system. A mechanism designed to prevent the movement of a stationary motor vehicle.

Play. Any free movement of components.

Pulpwood trailer. A trailer or semitrailer that is designed exclusively for harvesting logs or pulpwood and constructed with a skeletal frame with no means for attachment of a solid bed, body, or container.

Rail vehicle. A vehicle whose skeletal structure is fitted with stakes at the front and rear to contain logs loaded crosswise.

Rear extremity. The rearmost point on a motor vehicle that falls above a horizontal plane located 560 mm (22 inches) above the ground and below a horizontal plane located 1,900 mm (75 inches) above the ground when the motor vehicle is stopped on level ground; unloaded; its fuel tanks are full; the tires (and air suspension, if so equipped) are inflated in accordance with the manufacturer's recommendations; and the motor vehicle's cargo doors, tailgate, or other permanent structures are positioned as they normally are when the vehicle is in motion. Nonstructural protrusions such as taillamps, rubber bumpers, hinges and latches are excluded from the determination of the rearmost point.

Reflective material. A material conforming to Federal Specification L S 300, "Sheeting and Tape, Reflective; Non exposed Lens, Adhesive Backing," (September 7, 1965) meeting the performance standard in either Table 1 or Table 1A of SAE Standard J594f, "Reflex Reflectors" (January, 1977).

Reflex reflector. A device which is used on a vehicle to give an indication to an approaching driver by reflected light from the lamps on the approaching vehicle.

Road construction controlled horizontal discharge trailer means a trailer or semitrailer that is equipped with a mechanical drive and a conveyor to deliver asphalt and other road building materials, in a controlled horizontal manner, into a lay down machine or paving equipment for road construction and paving operations.

Saddle-mount. A device, designed and constructed as to be readily demountable, used in driveaway-towaway operations to perform the functions of a conventional fifth wheel:

(1) Upper-half. "Upper-half" of a "saddle-mount" means that part of the device which is securely attached to the towed vehicle and maintains a fixed position relative thereto, but does not include the "king-pin;"

(2) Lower-half. "Lower-half" of a "saddle-mount" means that part of the device which is securely attached to the towing vehicle and maintains a fixed position relative thereto but does not include the "king-pin;" and

(3) King pin. "King-pin" means that device which is used to connect the "upper-half" to the "lower-half" in such manner as to permit relative movement in a horizontal plane between the towed and towing vehicles.

Service brake system. A primary brake system used for slowing and stopping a vehicle.

Shoring bar. A device placed transversely between the walls of a vehicle and cargo to prevent cargo from tipping or shifting.

Shortwood. All logs typically up to 4.9 m (16 feet) long. Such logs are often described as cut-up logs, cut-to-length logs, bolts or pulpwood. Shortwood may be loaded lengthwise or crosswise, though that loaded crosswise is usually no more than 2.6 m (102 inches) long.

Side extremity. The outermost point on a side of the motor vehicle that is above a horizontal plane located 560 mm (22 inches) above the ground, below a horizontal plane located 1,900 mm (75 inches) above the ground, and between a transverse vertical plane tangent to the rear extremity of the vehicle and a transverse vertical plane located 305 mm (12 inches) forward of that plane when the vehicle is unloaded; its fuel tanks are full; and the tires (and air suspension, if so equipped) are inflated in accordance with the manufacturer's recommendations. Non-structural protrusions such as taillights, hinges and latches are excluded from the determination of the outermost point.

Side marker lamp (Intermediate). A lamp mounted on the side, on the permanent structure of the motor vehicle that provides light to the side to indicate the approximate middle of the vehicle, when the motor vehicle is 9.14 meters (30 feet) or more in length.

Side marker lamps. Lamps mounted on the side, on the permanent structure of the motor vehicle as near as practicable to the front and rear of the vehicle, that provide light to the side to indicate the overall length of the motor vehicle.

Sided vehicle. A vehicle whose cargo compartment is enclosed on all four sides by walls of sufficient strength to contain articles of cargo, where the walls may include latched openings for loading and unloading, and includes vans, dump bodies, and a sided intermodal container carried by a vehicle.

Special purpose vehicle. (1) A trailer or semitrailer manufactured on or after January 26, 1998, having work-performing equipment that, while the motor vehicle is in transit, resides in or moves through the area that could be occupied by the horizontal member of the rear impact guard, as defined by the guard width, height and rear surface requirements of §571.224 (paragraphs S5.1.1 through S5.1.3), in effect on the date of manufacture, or a subsequent edition.

(2) A motor vehicle, not described by paragraph (1) of this definition, having work-performing equipment that, while the motor vehicle is in transit, resides in or moves through the area that could be occupied by the horizontal member of the rear impact guard, as defined by the guard width, height and rear surface requirements of §393.86(b)(1).

Split service brake system. A brake system consisting of two or more subsystems actuated by a single control designed so that a leakage-type failure of a pressure component in a single subsystem (except structural failure of a housing that is common to two or more subsystems) shall not impair the operation of any other subsystem.

Steering wheel lash. The condition in which the steering wheel may be turned through some part of a revolution without associated movement of the front wheels.

Stop lamps. Lamps shown to the rear of a motor vehicle to indicate that the service brake system is engaged.

Surge brake. A self-contained, permanently closed hydraulic brake system for trailers that relies on inertial forces, developed in response to the braking action of the towing vehicle, applied to a hydraulic device mounted on or connected to the tongue of the trailer, to slow down or stop the towed vehicle.

Tail lamps. Lamps used to designate the rear of a motor vehicle.

Tiedown. A combination of securing devices which forms an assembly that attaches articles of cargo to, or restrains articles of cargo on, a vehicle or trailer, and is attached to anchor point(s).

Tow bar. A strut or column-like device temporarily attached between the rear of a towing vehicle and the front of the vehicle being towed.

Tractor-pole trailer. A combination vehicle that carries logs lengthwise so that they form the body of the vehicle. The logs are supported by a bunk located on the rear of the tractor, and another bunk on the skeletal trailer. The tractor bunk may rotate about a vertical axis, and the trailer may have a fixed, scoping, or cabled reach, or other mechanical freedom, to allow it to turn.

Trailer kingpin. A pin (with a flange on its lower end) which extends vertically from the front of the underside of a semitrailer and which locks into a fifth wheel.

Turn signals. Lamps used to indicate a change in direction by emitting a flashing light on the side of a motor vehicle towards which a turn will be made.

Upper coupler assembly. A structure consisting of an upper coupler plate, king pin and supporting framework which interfaces with and couples to a fifth wheel.

Upper coupler plate. A plate structure through which the king pin neck and collar extend. The bottom surface of the plate contacts the fifth wheel when coupled.

Vacuum brake system. A system that uses a vacuum and atmospheric pressure for transmitting a force from the driver control to the service brake, not including a system that uses vacuum only to assist the driver in applying muscular force to hydraulic or mechanical components.

Vehicle safety technology. Vehicle safety technology includes a fleet-related incident management system, performance or behavior management system, speed management system, lane departure warning system, forward collision warning or mitigation system, active cruise control system, and transponder.

Void filler. Material used to fill a space between articles of cargo and the structure of the vehicle that has sufficient strength to prevent movement of the articles of cargo.

Well. The depression formed between two cylindrical articles of cargo when they are laid with their eyes horizontal and parallel against each other.

Wheels back vehicle. (1) A trailer or semitrailer manufactured on or after January 26, 1998, whose rearmost axle is permanently fixed and is located such that the rearmost surface of the tires (of the size recommended by the vehicle manufacturer for the rear axle) is not more than 305 mm (12 inches) forward of the transverse vertical plane tangent to the rear extremity of the vehicle.

(2) A motor vehicle, not described by paragraph (1) of this definition, whose rearmost axle is permanently fixed and is located such that the rearmost surface of the tires (of the size recommended by the vehicle manufacturer for the rear axle) is not more than 610 mm (24 inches) forward of the transverse vertical plane tangent to the rear extremity of the vehicle.

Width of a manufactured home. The largest exterior width in the traveling mode, including any projections which contain interior space. Width does not include bay windows, roof projections, overhangs, or eaves under which there is no interior space.

Windshield. The principal forward facing glazed surface provided for forward vision in operating a motor vehicle.

Working load limit (WLL). The maximum load that may be applied to a component of a cargo securement system during normal service, usually assigned by the manufacturer of the component.

§393.7 Matter incorporated by reference.

(a) **Incorporation by reference**. Part 393 includes references to certain matter or materials, as listed in paragraph (b) of this section. The text of the materials is not included in the regulations contained in part 393. The materials are hereby made a part of the regulations in part 393. The Director of the Federal Register has approved the materials incorporated by reference in accordance with 5 U.S.C. 552(a) and 1 CFR part 51. For materials subject to change, only the specific version approved by the Director of the Federal Register and specified in the regulation are incorporated. Material is incorporated as it exists on the date of the approval and a notice of any change in these materials will be published in the *Federal Register*.

(b) **Matter or materials referenced in part 393**. The matter or materials listed in this paragraph are incorporated by reference in the corresponding sections noted.

(1) Auxiliary Upper Beam Lamps, Society of Automotive Engineers (SAE) J581, July 2004, incorporation by reference approved for §393.24(b).

(2) Front Fog Lamp, SAE J583, August 2004, incorporation by reference approved for §393.24(b).

(3) Stop Lamps for Use on Motor Vehicles Less Than 2032 mm in Overall Width, SAE J586, March 2000, incorporation by reference approved for §393.25(c).

(4) Stop Lamps and Front- and Rear-Turn Signal Lamps for Use on Motor Vehicles 2032 mm or more in Overall Width, SAE J2261, January 2002, incorporated by reference approved for §393.25(c).

(5) Tail Lamps (Rear Position Lamps) for Use on Motor Vehicles Less Than 2032 mm in Overall Width, SAE J585, March 2000, incorporation by reference approved for §393.25(c).

(6) Tail Lamps (Rear Position Lamps) for Use on Vehicles 2032 mm or More in Overall Width, SAE J2040, March 2002, incorporation by reference approved for §393.25(c).

(7) Turn Signal Lamps for Use on Motor Vehicles Less Than 2032 mm in Overall Width, SAE J588, March 2000, incorporation by reference approved for §393.25(c).

(8) Sidemarker Lamps for Use on Road Vehicles Less Than 2032 mm in Overall Width, SAE J592, August 2000, incorporation by reference approved for §393.25(c).

(9) Directional Flashing Optical Warning Devices for Authorized Emergency, Maintenance, and Service Vehicles, SAE J595, January 2005, incorporation by reference approved for §393.25(e).

(10) Optical Warning Devices for Authorized Emergency, Maintenance, and Service Vehicles, SAE J845, May 1997, incorporation by reference approved for §393.25(e).

(11) Gaseous Discharge Warning Lamp for Authorized Emergency, Maintenance, and Service Vehicles, SAE J1318, May 1998, incorporation by reference approved for §393.25(e).

(12) Reflex Reflectors, SAE J594, December 2003, incorporation by reference approved for §393.26(c).

(13) Standard Specification for Retroreflective Sheeting for Traffic Control, American Society of Testing and Materials, ASTM D 4956-04, 2004, incorporation by reference approved for §393.26(c).

(14) Automobile, Truck, Truck-Tractor, Trailer, and Motor Coach Wiring, SAE J1292, October 1981, incorporated by reference approved for §393.28.

(15) Highway Emergency Signals, Fourth Edition, Underwriters Laboratories, Inc., UL No. 912, July 30, 1979 (with an amendment dated November 9, 1981), incorporation by reference approved for §393.95(j).

(16) American National Standard for Safety Glazing Materials for Glazing Motor Vehicles and Motor Vehicle Equipment Operating on Land Highways-Safety Standard, SAE Z26.1-1996, August 1997, incorporation by reference approved for §393.62(d).

(17) Specification for Sound Level Meters, American National Standards Institute, S1.4-1983, incorporation by reference approved for §393.94(c).

(18) Standard Specification for Strapping, Flat Steel and Seals, American Society for Testing and Materials (ASTM), D3953-97, February 1998, incorporation by reference approved for §393.104(e).

(19) Welded Steel Chain Specifications, National Association of Chain Manufacturers, September 28, 2005, incorporation by reference approved for §393.104(e).

(20) Recommended Standard Specification for Synthetic Web Tiedowns, Web Sling and Tiedown Association, WSTDA-T1, 1998, incorporation by reference approved for §393.104(e).

(21) Wire Rope Users Manual, 2nd Edition, Wire Rope Technical Board November 1985, incorporation by reference approved for §393.104(e).

(22) Cordage Institute rope standards approved for incorporation into §393.104(e):

(i) PETRS-2, Polyester Fiber Rope, 3-Strand and 8-Strand Constructions, January 1993;

(ii) PPRS-2, Polypropylene Fiber Rope, 3-Strand and 8-Strand Constructions, August 1992;

(iii) CRS-1, Polyester/Polypropylene Composite Rope Specifications, Three-Strand and Eight-Strand Standard Construction, May 1979;

(iv) NRS-1, Nylon Rope Specifications, Three-Strand and Eight-Strand Standard Construction, May 1979; and

(v) C-1, Double Braided Nylon Rope Specifications DBN, January 1984.

(c) **Availability**. The materials incorporated by reference are available as follows:

(1) Standards of the Underwriters Laboratories, Inc. Information and copies may be obtained by writing to: Underwriters Laboratories, Inc., 333 Pfingsten Road, Northbrook, Illinois 60062.

(2) Specifications of the American Society for Testing and Materials. Information and copies may be obtained by writing to: American Society for Testing and Materials, 100 Barr Harbor Drive, West Conshohocken, Pennsylvania 19428-2959.

(3) Specifications of the National Association of Chain Manufacturers. Information and copies may be obtained by writing to: National Association of Chain Manufacturers, P.O. Box 22681, Lehigh Valley, Pennsylvania 18002-2681.

(4) Specifications of the Web Sling and Tiedown Association. Information and copies may be obtained by writing to: Web Sling and Tiedown Association, Inc., 5024-R Campbell Boulevard, Baltimore, Maryland 21236-5974.

(5) Manuals of the Wire Rope Technical Board. Information and copies may be obtained by writing to: Wire Rope Technical Committee, P.O. Box 849, Stevensville, Maryland 21666.

(6) Standards of the Cordage Institute. Information and copies may be obtained by writing to: Cordage Institute, 350 Lincoln Street, 115, Hingham, Massachusetts 02043.

(7) Standards of the Society of Automotive Engineers (SAE). Information and copies may be obtained by writing to: Society of Automotive Engineers, Inc., 400 Commonwealth Drive, Warrendale, Pennsylvania 15096.

(8) Standards of the American National Standards Institute (ANSI). Information and copies may be obtained by writing to: American National Standards Institute, 25 West 43rd Street, New York, New York 10036.

(9) [Reserved].

(10) All of the materials incorporated by reference are available for inspection at:

(i) The Federal Motor Carrier Safety Administration, Office of Bus and Truck Standards and Operations (MC-PS), 1200 New Jersey Ave., SE., Washington, DC 20590-0001; and

(ii) The Office of the Federal Register, 800 North Capitol Street, NW, Suite 700, Washington, DC.

Subpart B—Lamps, Reflective Devices and Electrical Wiring

§393.9 Lamps operable, prohibition of obstructions of lamps and reflectors.

(a) All lamps required by this subpart shall be capable of being operated at all times. This paragraph shall not be construed to require that any auxiliary or additional lamp be capable of operating at all times.

(b) Lamps and reflective devices/material required by this subpart must not be obscured by the tailboard, or by any part of the load, or its covering by dirt, or other added vehicle or work equipment, or otherwise. Exception: The conspicuity treatments on the front end protection devices may be obscured by part of the load being transported.

§393.11 Lamps and reflective devices.

(a)(1) **Lamps and reflex reflectors**. Table 1 specifies the requirements for lamps, reflective devices and associated equipment by the type of commercial motor vehicle. The diagrams in this section illustrate the position of the lamps, reflective devices and associated equipment specified in Table 1. All commercial motor vehicles manufactured on or after December 25, 1968, must, at a minimum, meet the applicable requirements of 49 CFR 571.108 (FMVSS No. 108) in effect at the time of manufacture of the vehicle. Commercial motor vehicles manufactured before December 25, 1968, must, at a minimum, meet the requirements of subpart B of part 393 in effect at the time of manufacture.

(2) **Exceptions:** Pole trailers and trailer converter dollies must meet the part 393 requirements for lamps, reflective devices and electrical equipment in effect

at the time of manufacture. Trailers which are equipped with conspicuity material which meets the requirements of §393.11(b) are not required to be equipped with the reflex reflectors listed in Table 1 if—

(i) The conspicuity material is placed at the locations where reflex reflectors are required by Table 1; and

(ii) The conspicuity material when installed on the motor vehicle meets the visibility requirements for the reflex reflectors.

(b) **Conspicuity Systems**. Each trailer of 2,032 mm (80 inches) or more overall width, and with a GVWR over 4,536 kg (10,000 pounds), manufactured on or after December 1, 1993, except pole trailers and trailers designed exclusively for living or office use, shall be equipped with either retroreflective sheeting that meets the requirements of FMVSS No. 108 (S5.7.1), reflex reflectors that meet the requirements FMVSS No. 108 (S5.7.2), or a combination of retroreflective sheeting and reflex reflectors that meet the requirements of FMVSS No. 108 (S5.7.3). The conspicuity system shall be installed and located as specified in FMVSS No. 108 [S5.7.1.4 (for retroreflective sheeting), S5.7.2.2 (for reflex reflectors), S5.7.3 (for a combination of sheeting and reflectors)] and have certification and markings as required by S5.7.1.5 (for retroreflective tape) and S5.7.2.3 (for reflex reflectors).

(c) **Prohibition on the use of amber stop lamps and tail lamps**. No commercial motor vehicle may be equipped with an amber stop lamp, a tail lamp, or other lamp which is optically combined with an amber stop lamp or tail lamp.

Table 1 of §393.11—Required lamps and reflectors on commercial motor vehicles

Item on the vehicle	Quantity	Color	Location	Position	Height above the road surface in millimeters (mm) (with English units in parenthesis) measured from the center of the lamp at curb weight	Vehicles for which the devices are required
Headlamps	2	White	Front	On the front at the same height, with an equal number at each side of the vertical center line as far apart as practicable.	Not less than 559 mm (22 inches) nor more than 1,372 mm (54 inches).	A, B, C
Turn signal (front). See footnotes #2 and 12.	2	Amber	At or near the front.	One on each side of the vertical centerline at the same height and as far apart as practicable.	Not less than 381 mm (15 inches) nor more than 2,108 mm (83 inches).	A, B, C
Identification lamps (front). See footnote #1.	3	Amber	Front	As close as practicable to the top of the vehicle, at the same height, and as close as practicable to the vertical centerline of the vehicle (or the vertical centerline of the cab where different from the centerline of the vehicle) with lamp centers spaced not less than 152 mm (6 inches) or more than 305 mm (12 inches) apart. Alternatively, the front lamps may be located as close as practicable to the top of the cab.	All three on the same level as close as practicable to the top of the motor vehicle.	B, C
Tail lamps. See footnotes #5 and 11.	2	Red	Rear	One lamp on each side of the vertical centerline at the same height and as far apart as practicable.	Both on the same level between 381 mm (15 inches) and 1,829 mm (72 inches).	A, B, C, D, E, F, G, H

Table 1 of §393.11—Required lamps and reflectors on commercial motor vehicles, Continued

Item on the vehicle	Quantity	Color	Location	Position	Height above the road surface in millimeters (mm) (with English units in parenthesis) measured from the center of the lamp at curb weight	Vehicles for which the devices are required
Stop lamps. See footnotes #5 and 13.	2	Red	Rear	One lamp on each side of the vertical centerline at the same height and as far apart as practicable.	Both on the same level between 381 mm (15 inches) and 1,829 mm (72 inches).	A, B, C, D, E, F, G
Clearance lamps. See footnotes #8, 9, 10, 15 & 17.	2	Amber	One on each side of the front of the vehicle.	One on each side of the vertical centerline to indicate overall width.	Both on the same level as high as practicable.	B, C, D, G, H
Clearance lamps. See footnotes #8, 9, 10, 15 & 17.	2	Red	One on each side of the rear of the vehicle.	One on each side of the vertical centerline to indicate overall width.	Both on the same level as high as practicable.	B, D, G, H
Reflex reflector, intermediate (side).	2	Amber	One on each side.	At or near the midpoint between the front and rear side marker lamps, if the length of the vehicle is more than 9,144 mm (30 feet).	Between 381 mm (15 inches) and 1,524 (60 inches).	A, B, D, F, G
Reflex reflector (rear). See footnotes #5, 6, and 8.	2	Red	Rear	One on each side of the vertical centerline, as far apart as practicable and at the same height.	Both on the same level, between 381 mm (15 inches) and 1,524 mm (60 inches).	A, B, C, D, E, F, G
Reflex reflector (rear side).	2	Red	One on each side (rear).	As far to the rear as practicable.	Both on the same level, between 381 mm (15 inches) and 1,524 mm (60 inches).	A, B, D, F, G

Table 1 of §393.11—Required lamps and reflectors on commercial motor vehicles, Continued

Item on the vehicle	Quantity	Color	Location	Position	Height above the road surface in millimeters (mm) (with English units in parenthesis) measured from the center of the lamp at curb weight	Vehicles for which the devices are required
Reflex reflector (front side). See footnote #16.	2	Amber	One on each side (front).	As far to the front as practicable.	Between 381 mm (15 inches) and 1,524 mm (60 inches).	A, B, C, D, F, G
License plate lamp (rear). See footnote #11.	1	White	At rear license plate to illuminate the plate from the top or sides.		No requirements	A, B, C, D, F, G
Side marker lamp (front). See footnote #16.	2	Amber	One on each side.	As far to the front as practicable.	Not less than 381 mm (15 inches).	A, B, C, D, F
Side marker lamp intermediate.	2	Amber	One on each side.	At or near the midpoint between the front and rear side marker lamps, if the length of the vehicle is more than 9,144 mm (30 feet).	Not less than 381 mm (15 inches).	A, B, D, F, G
Side marker lamp (rear). See footnotes #4 and 8.	2	Red	One on each side.	As far to the rear as practicable.	Not less than 381 mm (15 inches), and on the rear of trailers not more than 1,524 mm (60 inches).	A, B, D, F, G
Turn signal (rear). See footnotes #5 and 12.	2	Amber or red	Rear	One lamp on each side of the vertical centerline as far apart as practicable.	Both on the same level, between 381 mm (15 inches) and 2,108 mm (83 inches).	A, B, C, D, E, F, G

Table 1 of §393.11—Required lamps and reflectors on commercial motor vehicles, Continued

Item on the vehicle	Quantity	Color	Location	Position	Height above the road surface in millimeters (mm) (with English units in parenthesis) measured from the center of the lamp at curb weight	Vehicles for which the devices are required
Identification lamp (rear). See footnotes #3, 7, and 15.	3	Red	Rear	One as close as practicable to the vertical centerline. One on each side with lamp centers spaced not less than 152 mm (6 inches) or more than 305 mm (12 inches) apart.	All three on the same level as practicable to the top of the vehicle.	B, D, G
Vehicular hazard warning signal flasher lamps. See footnotes #5 and 12.	2	Amber	Front	One lamp on each side of the vertical centerline, as far apart as practicable.	Both on the same level, between 381 mm (15 inches) and 2,108 mm (83 inches).	A, B, C
Vehicular hazard warning signal flasher lamps. See footnotes #5 and 12.	2	Amber or red	Rear	One lamp on each side of the vertical centerline, as far apart as practicable.	Both on the same level, between 381 mm (15 inches) and 2,108 mm (83 inches).	A, B, C, D, E, F, G
Backup lamp. See footnote #14.	1 or 2	White	Rear	Rear	No requirement	A, B, C
Parking lamp	2	Amber or white	Front	One lamp on each side of the vertical centerline, as far apart as practicable.	Both on the same level, between 381 mm (15 inches) and 2,108 mm (83 inches).	A

Legend: Types of commercial motor vehicles shown in the last column of Table 1.
A. Buses and trucks less than 2,032 mm (80 inches) in overall width.
B. Buses and trucks 2,032 mm (80 inches) or more in overall width.
C. Truck tractors.
D. Semitrailers and full trailers 2,032 mm (80 inches) or more in overall width except converter dollies.

E. Converter dolly.
F. Semitrailers and full trailers less than 2,032 mm (80 inches) in overall width.
G. Pole trailers.
H. Projecting loads.
Note: Lamps and reflectors may be combined as permitted by §393.22 and S5.4 of 49 CFR 571.108, Equipment combinations.

Footnote—1 Identification lamps may be mounted on the vertical centerline of the cab where different from the centerline of the vehicle, except where the cab is not more than 42 inches wide at the front roofline, then a single lamp at the center of the cab shall be deemed to comply with the requirements for identification lamps. No part of the identification lamps or their mountings may extend below the top of the vehicle windshield.

Footnote—2 Unless the turn signals on the front are so constructed (double—faced) and located as to be visible to passing drivers, two turn signals are required on the rear of the truck tractor, one at each side as far apart as practicable.

Footnote—3 The identification lamps need not be visible or lighted if obscured by a vehicle in the same combination.

Footnote—4 Any semitrailer or full trailer manufactured on or after March 1, 1979, shall be equipped with rear side—marker lamps at a height of not less than 381 mm (15 inches), and on the rear of trailers not more than 1,524 mm (60 inches) above the road surface, as measured from the center of the lamp on the vehicle at curb weight.

Footnote—5 Each converter dolly, when towed singly by another vehicle and not as part of a full trailer, shall be equipped with one stop lamp, one tail lamp, and two reflectors (one on each side of the vertical centerline, as far apart as practicable) on the rear. Each converter dolly shall be equipped with rear turn signals and vehicular hazard warning signal flasher lamps when towed singly by another vehicle and not as part of a full trailer, if the converter dolly obscures the turn signals at the rear of the towing vehicle.

Footnote—6 Pole trailers shall be equipped with two reflex reflectors on the rear, one on each side of the vertical centerline as far apart as practicable, to indicate the extreme width of the trailer.

Footnote—7 Pole trailers, when towed by motor vehicles with rear identification lamps meeting the requirements of §393.11 and mounted at a height greater than the load being transported on the pole trailer, are not required to have rear identification lamps.

Footnote—8 Pole trailers shall have on the rearmost support for the load: (1) two front clearance lamps, one on each side of the vehicle, both on the same level and as high as practicable to indicate the overall width of the pole trailer; (2) two rear clearance lamps, one on each side of the vehicle, both on the same level and as high as practicable to indicate the overall width of the pole trailer; (3) two rear side marker lamps, one on each side of the vehicle, both on the same level, not less than 375 mm (15 inches) above the road surface; (4) two rear reflex reflectors, one on each side, both on the same level, not less than 375 mm (15 inches) above the road surface to indicate maximum width of the pole trailer; and (5) one red reflector on each side of the rearmost support for the load. Lamps and reflectors may be combined as allowed in §393.22.

Footnote—9 Any motor vehicle transporting a load which extends more than 102 mm (4 inches) beyond the overall width of the motor vehicle shall be equipped with the following lamps in addition to other required lamps when operated during the hours when headlamps are required to be used.

(1) The foremost edge of that portion of the load which projects beyond the side of the vehicle shall be marked (at its outermost extremity) with an amber lamp visible from the front and side.

(2) The rearmost edge of that portion of the load which projects beyond the side of the vehicle shall be marked (at its outermost extremity) with a red lamp visible from the rear and side.

(3) If the projecting load does not measure more than 914 mm (3 feet) from front to rear, it shall be marked with an amber lamp visible from the front, both sides, and rear, except that if the projection is located at or near the rear it shall be marked by a red lamp visible from front, side, and rear.

Footnote—10 Projections beyond rear of motor vehicles. Motor vehicles transporting loads which extend more than 1,219 mm (4 feet) beyond the rear of the motor vehicle, or which have tailboards or tailgates extending more than 1,219 mm (4 feet) beyond the body, shall have these projections marked as follows when the vehicle is operated during the hours when headlamps are required to be used:

(1) On each side of the projecting load, one red side marker lamp, visible from the side, located so as to indicate maximum overhang.

(2) On the rear of the projecting load, two red lamps, visible from the rear, one at each side; and two red reflectors visible from the rear, one at each side, located so as to indicate maximum width.

Footnote—11 To be illuminated when headlamps are illuminated. No rear license plate lamp is required on vehicles that do not display a rear license plate.

Footnote—12 Every bus, truck, and truck tractor shall be equipped with a signaling system that, in addition to signaling turning movements, shall have a switch or combination of switches that will cause the two front turn signals and the two rear signals to flash simultaneously as a vehicular traffic signal warning, required by §392.22(a). The system shall be capable of flashing simultaneously with the ignition of the vehicle on or off.

Footnote—13 To be actuated upon application of service brakes.

Footnote—14 Backup lamp required to operate when bus, truck, or truck tractor is in reverse.

Footnote—15

(1) For the purposes of §393.11, the term "overall width" refers to the nominal design dimension of the widest part of the vehicle, exclusive of the signal lamps, marker lamps, outside rearview mirrors, flexible fender extensions, and mud flaps.

(2) Clearance lamps may be mounted at a location other than on the front and rear if necessary to indicate the overall width of a vehicle, or for protection from damage during normal operation of the vehicle.

(3) On a trailer, the front clearance lamps may be mounted at a height below the extreme height if mounting at the extreme height results in the lamps failing to mark the overall width of the trailer.

(4) On a truck tractor, clearance lamps mounted on the cab may be located to indicate the width of the cab, rather than the width of the vehicle.

(5) When the rear identification lamps are mounted at the extreme height of a vehicle, rear clearance lamps are not required to be located as close as practicable to the top of the vehicle.

Footnote—16 A trailer subject to this part that is less than 1829 mm (6 feet) in overall length, including the trailer tongue, need not be equipped with front side marker lamps and front side reflex reflectors.

Footnote—17 A boat trailer subject to this part whose overall width is 2032 mm (80 inches) or more need not be equipped with both front and rear clearance lamps provided an amber (front) and red (rear) clearance lamp is located at or near the midpoint on each side so as to indicate its extreme width.

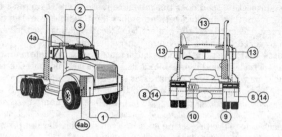

Figure 1 Truck Illustration for § 393.11

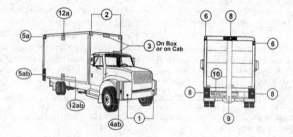

Figure 2 Straight Truck Illustration for § 393.11

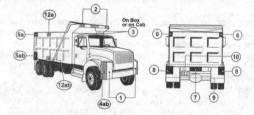

Figure 3 Straight Truck illustration for § 393.11

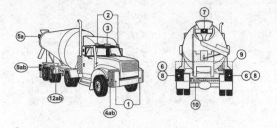

Figure 4 Straight Truck Illustration for § 393.11

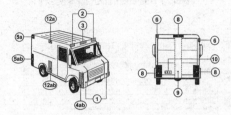

Figure 5 Straight Truck Illustration for § 393.11

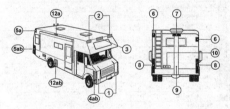

Figure 6 Straight Truck Illustration for § 393.11

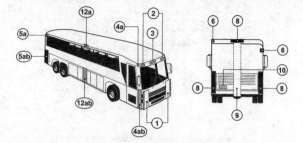

Figure 7 Bus Illustration for § 393.11

LEGEND FOR FIGURES 1 THROUGH 7 - 49 CFR 393.11
TRUCK & BUS VEHICLE ILLUSTRATIONS
(DOES NOT APPLY TO FIGURES 8 THROUGH 18 FOR TRAILERS)

Area	Equipment
	Headlamps - Lower Beam
	Headlamps - Upper Beam
1	Parking Lamps - Attention: *Required only on vehicles less than 2032mm wide*
	Front Turn Signal/Hazard Warning Lamps
2	Front Clearance Lamps - Attention: *Required for vehicles 2032mm wide or wider*
3	Front Identification Lamps (ID)
4a	Front Side Marker Lamps
4ab	Front Side Reflex Reflectors
5a	Rear Side Marker Lamps - *Not required on Truck Tractors*
5b	Rear Side Reflex Reflectors - *Not required on Truck Tractors*
6	Rear Clearance Lamps Attention: *Required for vehicles 2032mm wide or wider, but not required on Truck Tractors*
7	Rear Identification Lamps (ID) Attention: *Required for vehicles 2032mm wide or wider, but not required on Truck Tractors*
	Tail Lamps
8	Stop Lamps
	Rear Turn Signal/Hazard Warning Lamps
	Rear Reflex Reflectors
9	Backup Lamp
10	License Plate Lamp
11	Center High Mounted Stop Lamp Attention: *Required for vehicles less than 2032mm wide and 4536kg*

ADDITIONAL EQUIPMENT FOR SPECIFIC TRUCKS AND BUS VEHICLES

Area	Equipment
12a	Intermediate Side Marker Lamps
12b	Intermediate Side Reflex Reflectors

TRUCK TRACTORS

	DESCRIPTION
Area	Conspicuity Treatment
13	Rear Upper Body Marking
14	Rear Marking

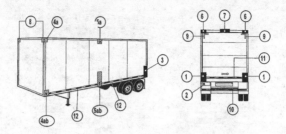

Figure 8 Semi Trailer Illustration for § 393.11

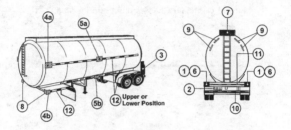

Figure 9 Semi Trailer Illustration for § 393.11

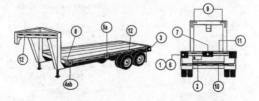

Figure 10 Semi Trailer Illustration for § 393.11

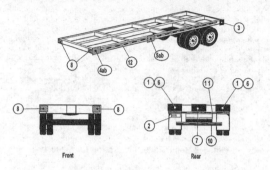

Front   Rear

Figure 11 Container Chassis Illustration for § 393.11

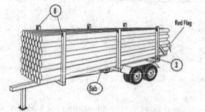

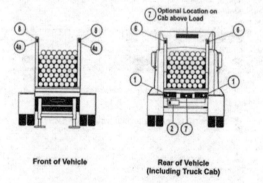

Front of Vehicle   Rear of Vehicle
                                    (Including Truck Cab)

Figure 12 Pole Trailer Illustration for § 393.11

Side View of Dolly   **Rear**

Figure 13 Converter Dolly Illustration for § 393.11

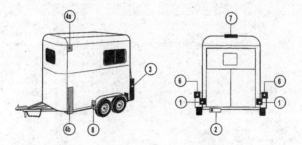

Figure 14 Semi Trailer Illustration for § 393.11

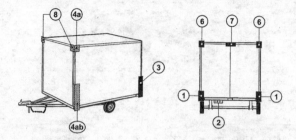

Figure 15 Semi Trailer Illustration for § 393.11

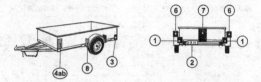

Figure 16 Semi Trailer Illustration for § 393.11

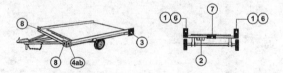

Figure 17 Semi Trailer Illustration for § 393.11

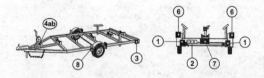

Figure 18 Semi Trailer Illustration for § 393.11

LEGEND FOR FIGURES 8 THROUGH 18 - 49 CFR 393.11
TRAILER ILLUSTRATIONS

(DOES NOT APPLY TO FIGURES 1 THROUGH 7 FOR TRUCKS & BUSES)

Area	Equipment
1	Tail Lamps
	Stop Lamps
	Rear Turn Signal Lamps
	Rear Reflex Reflectors
2	License Plate Lamp (s)
3	Rear Side Marker Lamps
	Rear Side Reflex Reflectors
4a	Front Side Marker Lamps
4b	Front Side Reflex Reflectors

ADDITIONAL EQUIPMENT FOR TRAILERS EXCEEDING THE FOLLOWING PARAMETERS

LENGTH 9.1 m (30 ft.) OR LONGER

Area	Equipment
5a	Intermediate Side Marker Lamps
5b	Intermediate Side Reflex Reflectors

WIDTH 2.032 m (80 in.) OR WIDER

Area	Equipment
6	Rear Clearance Lamps
7	Rear Identification Lamps
8	Front Clearance Lamps

WIDTH 2.032 m (80 in.) OR WIDER AND GVWR 4,536 kg (10,000 lb.) OR MORE

Area	DESCRIPTION
	Conspicuity Treatment
9	Rear Upper Body Marking
10	Bumper Bar Marking
11	Rear Lower Body Marking
12	Side Marking

§393.13 Retroreflective sheeting and reflex reflectors, requirements for semitrailers and trailers manufactured before December 1, 1993.

(a) **Applicability**. All trailers and semitrailers manufactured prior to December 1, 1993, which have an overall width of 2,032 mm (80 inches) or more and a gross vehicle weight rating of 4,536 kg (10,001 pounds) or more, except trailers that are manufactured exclusively for use as offices or dwellings, pole trailers (as defined in §390.5 of this subchapter), and trailers transported in a driveaway-towaway operation, must be equipped with retroreflective sheeting or an array of reflex reflectors that meet the requirements of this section. Motor carriers operating trailers, other than container chassis (as defined in

§393.5), have until June 1, 2001, to comply with the requirements of this section. Motor carriers operating container chassis have until December 1, 2001, to comply with the requirements of this section.

(b) **Retroreflective sheeting and reflex reflectors**. Motor carriers are encouraged to retrofit their trailers with a conspicuity system that meets all of the requirements applicable to trailers manufactured on or after December 1, 1993, including the use of retroreflective sheeting or reflex reflectors in a red and white pattern (see Federal Motor Vehicle Safety Standard No. 108 (49 CFR 571.108), S5.7, Conspicuity systems). Motor carriers which do not retrofit their trailers to meet the requirements of FMVSS No. 108, for example by using an alternative color pattern, must comply with the remainder of this paragraph and with paragraph (c) or (d) of this section. Retroreflective sheeting or reflex reflectors in colors or color combinations other than red and white may be used on the sides or lower rear area of the semitrailer or trailer until June 1, 2009. The alternate color or color combination must be uniform along the sides and lower rear area of the trailer. The retroreflective sheeting or reflex reflectors on the upper rear area of the trailer must be white and conform to the requirements of FMVSS No. 108 (S5.7). Red retroreflective sheeting or reflex reflectors shall not be used along the sides of the trailer unless it is used as part of a red and white pattern. Retroreflective sheeting shall have a width of at least 50 mm (2 inches).

(c) **Locations for retroreflective sheeting**.

(1) **Sides.** Retroreflective sheeting shall be applied to each side of the trailer or semitrailer. Each strip of retroreflective sheeting shall be positioned as horizontally as practicable, beginning and ending as close to the front and rear as practicable. The strip need not be continuous but the sum of the length of all of the segments shall be at least half of the length of the trailer and the spaces between the segments of the strip shall be distributed as evenly as practicable. The centerline for each strip of retroreflective sheeting shall be between 375 mm (15 inches) and 1,525 mm (60 inches) above the road surface when measured with the trailer empty or unladen, or as close as practicable to this area. If necessary to clear rivet heads or other similar obstructions, 50 mm (2 inches) wide retroreflective sheeting may be separated into two 25 mm (1 inch) wide strips of the same length and color, separated by a space of not more than 25 mm (1 inch).

(2) **Lower rear area.** The rear of each trailer and semitrailer must be equipped with retroreflective sheeting. Each strip of retroreflective sheeting shall be positioned as horizontally as practicable, extending across the full width of the trailer, beginning and ending as close to the extreme edges as practicable. The centerline for each of the strips of retroreflective sheeting shall be between 375 mm (15 inches) and 1,525 mm (60 inches) above the road surface when measured with the trailer empty or unladen, or as close as practicable to this area.

(3) **Upper rear area.** Two pairs of white strips of retroreflective sheeting, each pair consisting of strips 300 mm (12 inches) long, must be positioned horizontally and vertically on the right and left upper corners of the rear of the body of each trailer and semitrailer, as close as practicable to the top of the trailer and as far apart as practicable. If the perimeter of the body, as viewed from the rear, is not square or rectangular, the strips may be applied along the perimeter, as close as practicable to the uppermost and outermost areas of the rear of the body on the left and right sides.

(d) **Locations for reflex reflectors**.

(1) **Sides.** Reflex reflectors shall be applied to each side of the trailer or semi-trailer. Each array of reflex reflectors shall be positioned as horizontally as practicable, beginning and ending as close to the front and rear as practicable. The array need not be continuous but the sum of the length of all of the array segments shall be at least half of the length of the trailer and the spaces between the segments of the strip shall be distributed as evenly as practicable. The centerline for each array of reflex reflectors shall be between 375 mm (15 inches) and 1,525 mm (60 inches) above the road surface when measured with the trailer empty or unladen, or as close as practicable to this area. The center of each reflector shall not be more than 100 mm (4 inches) from the center of each adjacent reflector in the segment of the array. If reflex reflectors are arranged in an alternating color pattern, the length of reflectors of the first color shall be as close as practicable to the length of the reflectors of the second color.

(2) **Lower rear area.** The rear of each trailer and semitrailer must be equipped with reflex reflectors. Each array of reflex reflectors shall be positioned as horizontally as practicable, extending across the full width of the trailer, beginning and ending as close to the extreme edges as practicable. The centerline for each array of reflex reflectors shall be between 375 mm (15 inches) and 1,525 mm (60 inches) above the road surface when measured with the trailer empty or unladen, or as close as practicable to this area. The center of each reflector shall not be more than 100 mm (4 inches) from the center of each adjacent reflector in the segment of the array.

(3) **Upper rear area.** Two pairs of white reflex reflector arrays, each pair at least 300 mm (12 inches) long, must be positioned horizontally and vertically on the right and left upper corners of the rear of the body of each trailer and semitrailer, as close as practicable to the top of the trailer and as far apart as practicable. If the perimeter of the body, as viewed from the rear, is not square or rectangular, the arrays may be applied along the perimeter, as close as practicable to the uppermost and outermost areas of the rear of the body on the left and right sides. The center of each reflector shall not be more than 100 mm (4 inches) from the center of each adjacent reflector in the segment of the array.

§393.17 Lamps and reflectors—combinations in driveaway-towaway operation.

A combination of motor vehicles engaged in driveaway-tow-away operation must be equipped with operative lamps and reflectors conforming to the rules in this section.

(a) The towing vehicle must be equipped as follows:

(1) On the front, there must be at least two headlamps, an equal number at each side, two turn signals, one at each side, and two clearance lamps, one at each side.

(2) On each side, there must be at least one side-marker lamp, located near the front of the vehicle.

(3) On the rear, there must be at least two tail lamps, one at each side, and two stop lamps, one at each side.

(b) Except as provided in paragraph (c) of this section, the rearmost towed vehicle of the combination (including the towed vehicles of a tow-bar combination, the towed vehicle of a single saddle-mount combination, and the rearmost towed vehicle of a double or triple saddle-mount combination) or, in the case of a vehicle full-mounted on a saddle-mount vehicle, either the full-mounted vehicle or the rearmost saddle-mounted vehicle must be equipped as follows:

(1) On each side, there must be at least one side-marker lamp, located near the rear of the vehicle.

(2) On the rear, there must be at least two tail lamps, two stop lamps, two turn signals, two clearance lamps, and two reflectors, one of each type at each side. In addition, if any vehicle in the combination is 80 inches or more in overall width, there must be three identification lamps on the rear.

(c) If the towed vehicle in a combination is a mobile structure trailer, it must be equipped in accordance with the following lighting devices. For the purposes of this part, "mobile structure trailer" means a trailer that has a roof and walls, is at least 10 feet wide, and can be used off road for dwelling or commercial purposes.

(1) When the vehicle is operated in accordance with the terms of a special permit prohibiting operation during the times when lighted lamps are required, it must have on the rear—

(i) Two stop lamps, one on each side of the vertical centerline, at the same height, and as far apart as practicable;

(ii) Two tail lamps, one on each side of the vertical centerline, at the same height, and as far apart as practicable;

(iii) Two red reflex reflectors, one on each side of the vertical centerline, at the same height, and as far apart as practicable; and

(iv) Two turn signal lamps, one on each side of the vertical centerline, at the same height, and as far apart as practicable.

(2) At all other times, the vehicle must be equipped as specified in paragraph (b) of this section.

(d) An intermediate towed vehicle in a combination consisting of more than two vehicles (including the first saddle-mounted vehicle of a double saddle-mount combination and the first and second saddle-mount vehicles of a triple saddle-mount combination) must have one side-marker lamp on each side, located near the rear of the vehicle.

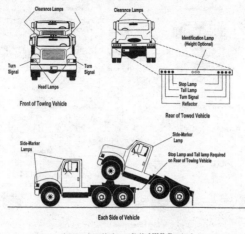

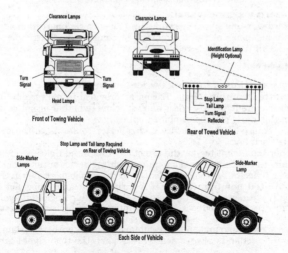

Figure 19 Single-Saddle-Mount Diagram to Illustrate § 393.17

Figure 20 Double-Saddle-Mount Diagram to Illustrate § 393.17

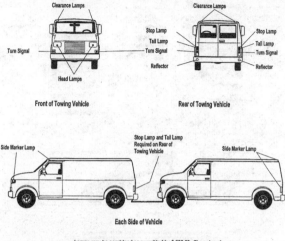

Front of Towing Vehicle · Rear of Towing Vehicle

Each Side of Vehicle

Lamps may be combined as permitted by § 393.22. The color of exterior lighting devices and reflectors shall conform to requirements of § 393.11

Figure 21 Tow-bar Diagram to Illustrate § 393.17

§393.19 Hazard warning signals.

The hazard warning signal operating unit on each commercial motor vehicle shall operate independently of the ignition or equivalent switch, and when activated, cause all turn signals required by §393.11 to flash simultaneously.

§393.20 [Reserved]

§393.22 Combination of lighting devices and reflectors.

(a) **Permitted combinations**. Except as provided in paragraph (b) of this section, two or more lighting devices and reflectors (whether or not required by the rules in this part) may be combined optically if—

(1) Each required lighting device and reflector conforms to the applicable rules in this Part; and

(2) Neither the mounting nor the use of a nonrequired lighting device or reflector impairs the effectiveness of a required lighting device or reflector or causes that device or reflector to be inconsistent with the applicable rules in this Part.

(b) **Prohibited combinations**. (1) A turn signal lamp must not be combined optically with either a head lamp or other lighting device or combination of lighting devices that produces a greater intensity of light than the turn signal lamp;

(2) A turn signal lamp must not be combined optically with a stop lamp unless the stop lamp function is always deactivated when the turn signal function is activated;

(3) A clearance lamp must not be combined optically with a tail lamp or identification lamp.

§393.23 Power supply for lamps.

All required lamps must be powered by the electrical system of the motor vehicle with the exception of battery powered lamps used on projecting loads.

§393.24 Requirement for head lamps, auxiliary driving lamps and front fog lamps.

(a) **Headlamps**. Every bus, truck and truck tractor shall be equipped with headlamps as required by §393.11(a). The head-lamps shall provide an upper and lower beam distribution of light, selectable at the driver's will and be steady-burning. The headlamps shall be marked in accordance with FMVSS No. 108. Auxiliary driving lamps and/or front fog lamps may not be used to satisfy the requirements of this paragraph.

(b) **Auxiliary driving lamps and front fog lamps**. Commercial motor vehicles may be equipped with auxiliary driving lamps and/or front fog lamps for use in conjunction with, but not in lieu of the required headlamps. Auxiliary driving lamps shall meet SAE Standard J581 Auxiliary Upper Beam Lamps, July 2004, and front fog lamps shall meet SAE Standard J583 Front Fog Lamp, August 2004. (See §393.7 for information on the incorporation by reference and availability of these documents.)

(c) **Mounting**. Headlamps shall be mounted and aimable in accordance with FMVSS No. 108. Auxiliary driving lamps and front fog lamps shall be mounted so that the beams are aimable and the mounting shall prevent the aim of the lighting device from being disturbed while the vehicle is operating on public roads.

(d) **Aiming**. Headlamps, auxiliary driving lamps and front fog lamps shall be aimed to meet the aiming specifications in FMVSS No. 108 (49 CFR 571.108), SAE J581, and SAE J583, respectively.

§393.25 Requirements for lamps other than head lamps.

(a) **Mounting**. All lamps shall be securely mounted on a rigid part of the vehicle. Temporary lamps must be securely mounted to the load and are not required to be mounted to a permanent part of the vehicle.

(b) **Visibility**. Each lamp shall be located so that it meets the visibility requirements specified by FMVSS No. 108 in effect at the time of manufacture of the vehicle. Vehicles which were not subject to FMVSS No. 108 at the time of manufacture shall have each lamp located so that it meets the visibility requirements specified in the SAE standards listed in paragraph (c) of this section. If motor vehicle equipment (e.g., mirrors, snow plows, wrecker booms, backhoes, and winches) prevents compliance with this paragraph by any required lamp, an auxiliary lamp or device meeting the requirements of this paragraph shall be provided. This shall not be construed to apply to lamps on one unit which are obscured by another unit of a combination of vehicles.

(c) **Specifications**. All required lamps (except marker lamps on projecting loads, lamps which are temporarily attached to vehicles transported in driveaway-towaway operations, and lamps on converter dollies and pole trailers) on vehicles manufactured on or after December 25, 1968, shall, at a minimum, meet the applicable requirements of FMVSS No. 108 in effect on the date of manufacture of the vehicle. Marker lamps on projecting loads, all lamps which are temporarily attached to vehicles transported in driveaway-towaway operations, and all lamps on converter dollies and pole trailers must meet the following applicable SAE standards: J586-Stop Lamps for Use on Motor Vehicles Less Than 2032 mm in Overall Width, March 2000; J2261 Stop Lamps and Front- and Rear-Turn Signal Lamps for Use on Motor Vehicles 2032 mm or More in Overall Width, January 2002; J585-Tail Lamps (Rear Position Lamps) for Use on Motor Vehicles Less Than 2032 mm in Overall Width, March 2000; J588-Turn Signal Lamps for Use on Motor Vehicles Less Than 2032 mm in Overall Width, March 2000; J2040-Tail Lamps (Rear Position Lamps) for Use on Vehicles 2032 mm or More in Overall Width, March 2002; J592-Sidemarker Lamps for Use on Road Vehicles Less Than 2032 mm in Overall Width, August 2000. (See §393.7 for information on the incorporation by reference and availability of these documents.)

(d) **(Reserved)**

(e) **Lamps to be steady-burning**. All exterior lamps (both required lamps and any additional lamps) shall be steady-burning with the exception of turn signal lamps; hazard warning signal lamps; school bus warning lamps; amber warning lamps or flashing warning lamps on tow trucks and commercial motor vehicles transporting oversized loads; and warning lamps on emergency and service vehicles authorized by State or local authorities. Lamps combined into the same shell or housing with a turn signal are not required to be steady burning while the turn signal is in use. Amber warning lamps must meet SAE J845-Optical Warning Devices for Authorized Emergency, Maintenance and Service Vehicles, May 1997. Amber flashing warning lamps must meet SAE J595-Directional Flashing Optical Warning Devices for Authorized Emergency, Maintenance and Service Vehicles, January 2005. Amber gaseous discharge warning lamps must meet SAE J1318 Gaseous Discharge Warning Lamp for Authorized Emergency, Maintenance, and Service Vehicles, May 1998. (See §393.7(b) for information on the incorporation by reference and availability of these documents.)

(f) **Stop lamp operation**. The stop lamps on each vehicle shall be activated upon application of the service brakes. The stop lamps are not required to be activated when the emergency feature of the trailer brakes is used or when the stop lamp is optically combined with the turn signal and the turn signal is in use.

§393.26 Requirements for reflex reflectors.

(a) **Mounting**. Reflex reflectors shall be mounted at the locations required by §393.11. In the case of motor vehicles so constructed that requirement for a 381 mm (15-inch) minimum height above the road surface is not practical, the reflectors shall be mounted as close as practicable to the required mounting height range. All permanent reflex reflectors shall be securely mounted on a rigid part of the vehicle. Temporary reflectors on projecting loads must be securely mounted to the load and are not required to be permanently mounted to a part of the vehicle. Temporary reflex reflectors on vehicles transported in drive-away-towaway operations must be firmly attached.

(b) **Specifications**. All required reflex reflectors (except reflex reflectors on projecting loads, vehicles transported in a driveaway-towaway operation, converter dollies and pole trailers) on vehicles manufactured on or after December 25, 1968, shall meet the applicable requirements of FMVSS No. 108 in effect on the date of manufacture of the vehicle. Reflex reflectors on projecting loads, vehicles transported in a driveaway-tow-away operation, and all reflex reflectors on converter dollies and pole trailers must conform to SAE J594-Reflex Reflectors, December 2003.

(c) **Substitute material for side reflex reflectors**. Reflective material conforming to ASTM D 4956-04, Standard Specification for Retroreflective Sheeting for Traffic Control, may be used in lieu of reflex reflectors if the material as used on the vehicle, meets the performance standards in either Table I of SAE J594 or Table IA of SAE J594-Reflex Reflectors, December 2003. (See §393.7(b) for information on the incorporation by reference and availability of these documents.)

(d) **Use of additional retroreflective surfaces**. Additional retroreflective surfaces may be used in conjunction with, but not in lieu of the reflex reflectors required in subpart B of part 393, and the substitute material for side reflex reflectors allowed by paragraph (c) of this section, provided:

(1) Designs do not resemble traffic control signs, lights, or devices, except that straight edge striping resembling a barricade pattern may be used.

(2) Designs do not tend to distort the length and/or width of the motor vehicle.

(3) Such surfaces shall be at least 3 inches from any required lamp or reflector unless of the same color as such lamp or reflector.

(4) No red color shall be used on the front of any motor vehicle, except for display of markings or placards required by §177.823 of this title.

(5) Retroreflective license plates required by State or local authorities may be used.

§393.27 [Reserved]

§393.28 Wiring systems.

Electrical wiring shall be installed and maintained to conform to SAE J1292-Automobile, Truck, Truck-Tractor, Trailer, and Motor Coach Wiring, October 1981, except the jumper cable plug and receptacle need not conform to SAE J560. The reference to SAE J1292 shall not be construed to require circuit protection on trailers. (See §393.7(b) for information on the incorporation by reference and availability of this document.)

§393.29 [Reserved]

§393.30 Battery installation.

Every storage battery on every vehicle, unless located in the engine compartment, shall be covered by a fixed part of the motor vehicle or protected by a removable cover or enclosure. Removable covers, or enclosures shall be substantial and shall be securely latched or fastened. The storage battery compartment and adjacent metal parts which might corrode by reason of battery leakage shall be painted or coated with an acid-resisting paint or coating and shall have openings to provide ample battery ventilation and drainage. Whenever the cable to the starting motor passes through a metal compartment, the cable shall be protected against grounding by an acid and waterproof insulating bushing. Wherever a battery and a fuel tank are both placed under the driver's seat, they shall be partitioned from each other, and each compartment shall be provided with an independent cover, ventilation, and drainage.

§§393.31–393.33 [Reserved]

Subpart C—Brakes

§393.40 Required brake systems.

(a) Each commercial motor vehicle must have brakes adequate to stop and hold the vehicle or combination of motor vehicles. Each commercial motor vehicle must meet the applicable service, parking, and emergency brake system requirements provided in this section.

(b) **Service brakes**. (1) **Hydraulic brake systems.** Motor vehicles equipped with hydraulic brake systems and manufactured on or after September 2, 1983, must, at a minimum, have a service brake system that meets the requirements of FMVSS No. 105 in effect on the date of manufacture. Motor vehicles which were not subject to FMVSS No. 105 on the date of manufacture must have a service brake system that meets the applicable requirements of §§393.42, 393.48, 393.49, 393.51, and 393.52 of this subpart.

(2) **Air brake systems.** Buses, trucks and truck-tractors equipped with air brake systems and manufactured on or after March 1, 1975, and trailers manufactured on or after January 1, 1975, must, at a minimum, have a service brake system that meets the requirements of FMVSS No. 121 in effect on the date of manufacture. Motor vehicles which were not subject to FMVSS No. 121 on the date of manufacture must have a service brake system that meets the applicable requirements of §§393.42, 393.48, 393.49, 393.51, and 393.52 of this subpart.

(3) **Vacuum brake systems.** Motor vehicles equipped with vacuum brake systems must have a service brake system that meets the applicable requirements of §§393.42, 393.48, 393.49, 393.51, and 393.52 of this subpart.

(4) **Electric brake systems.** Motor vehicles equipped with electric brake systems must have a service brake system that meets the applicable requirements of §§393.42, 393.48, 393.49, 393.51, and 393.52 of this subpart.

(5) **Surge brake systems.** Motor vehicles equipped with surge brake systems must have a service brake system that meets the applicable requirements of §§393.42, 393.48, 393.49, and 393.52 of this subpart.

(c) **Parking brakes**. Each commercial motor vehicle must be equipped with a parking brake system that meets the applicable requirements of §393.41.

(d) **Emergency brakes—partial failure of service brakes**.

(1) **Hydraulic brake systems.** Motor vehicles manufactured on or after September 2, 1983, and equipped with a split service brake system must, at a minimum, meet the partial failure requirements of FMVSS No. 105 in effect on the date of manufacture.

(2) **Air brake systems.** Buses, trucks and truck tractors manufactured on or after March 1, 1975, and trailers manufactured on or after January 1, 1975, must be equipped with an emergency brake system which, at a minimum, meets the requirements of FMVSS No. 121 in effect on the date of manufacture.

(3) **Vehicles not subject to FMVSS Nos. 105 and 121 on the date of manufacture.** Buses, trucks and truck tractors not subject to FMVSS Nos. 105 or 121 on the date of manufacture must meet the requirements of §393.40(e). Trailers not subject to FMVSS No. 121 at the time of manufacture must meet the requirements of §393.43.

(e) **Emergency brakes, vehicles manufactured on or after July 1, 1973**. (1) A bus, truck, truck tractor, or a combination of motor vehicles manufactured on or after July 1, 1973, and not covered under paragraphs (d)(1) or (d)(2) of this section, must have an emergency brake system which consists of emergency features of the service brake system or an emergency system separate from the service brake system. The emergency brake system must meet the applicable requirements of §§393.43 and 393.52.

(2) A control by which the driver applies the emergency brake system must be located so that the driver can operate it from the normal seating position while restrained by any seat belts with which the vehicle is equipped. The emergency brake control may be combined with either the service brake control or the parking brake control. However, all three controls may not be combined.

(f) **Interconnected systems**. (1) If the brake systems required by §393.40(a) are interconnected in any way, they must be designed, constructed, and maintained so that in the event of a failure of any part of the operating mechanism of one or more of the systems (except the service brake actuation pedal or valve), the motor vehicle will have operative brakes and, for vehicles manufactured on or after July 1, 1973, be capable of meeting the requirements of §393.52(b).

(2) A motor vehicle to which the requirements of FMVSS No. 105 (S5.1.2), dealing with partial failure of the service brake, applied at the time of manufacture meets the requirements of §393.40(f)(1) if the motor vehicle is maintained in conformity with FMVSS No. 105 and the motor vehicle is capable of meeting the requirements of §393.52(b), except in the case of a structural failure of the brake master cylinder body.

(3) A bus is considered to meet the requirements of §393.40(f)(1) if it meets the requirements of §393.44 and §393.52(b).

§393.41 Parking brake system.

(a) **Hydraulic-braked vehicles manufactured on or after September 2, 1983**. Each truck and bus (other than a school bus) with a GVWR of 4,536 kg (10,000 pounds) or less which is subject to this part and school buses with a GVWR greater than 4,536 kg (10,000 pounds) shall be equipped with a parking brake system as required by FMVSS No. 571.105 (S5.2) in effect at the time of manufacture. The parking brake shall be capable of holding the vehicle or combination of vehicles stationary under any condition of loading in which it is found on a public road (free of ice and snow). Hydraulic-braked vehicles which were not subject to the parking brake requirements of FMVSS No. 571.105 (S5.2) must be equipped with a parking brake system that meets the requirements of paragraph (c) of this section.

(b) **Air-braked power units manufactured on or after March 1, 1975, and air-braked trailers manufactured on or after January 1, 1975**. Each air-braked bus, truck and truck tractor manufactured on and after March 1, 1975, and each air-braked trailer except an agricultural commodity trailer, converter dolly, heavy hauler trailer or pulpwood trailer, shall be equipped with a parking brake system as required by FMVSS No. 121 (S5.6) in effect at the time of manufacture. The parking brake shall be capable of holding the vehicle or combination of vehicles stationary under any condition of loading in which it is found on a public road (free of ice and snow). An agricultural commodity trailer, heavy hauler or pulpwood trailer shall carry sufficient chocking blocks to prevent movement when parked.

(c) **Vehicles not subject to FMVSS Nos. 105 and 121 on the date of manufacture**. (1) Each singly driven motor vehicle not subject to parking brake requirements of FMVSS Nos. 105 or 121 at the time of manufacturer, and every combination of motor vehicles must be equipped with a parking brake system adequate to hold the vehicle or combination on any grade on which it is operated, under any condition of loading in which it is found on a public road (free of ice and snow).

(2) The parking brake system shall, at all times, be capable of being applied by either the driver's muscular effort or by spring action. If other energy is used to apply the parking brake, there must be an accumulation of that energy isolated from any common source and used exclusively for the operation of the parking brake.

Exception: This paragraph shall not be applicable to air-applied, mechanically-held parking brake systems which meet the parking brake requirements of FMVSS No. 121 (S5.6).

(3) The parking brake system shall be held in the applied position by energy other than fluid pressure, air pressure, or electric energy. The parking brake system shall not be capable of being released unless adequate energy is available to immediately reapply the parking brake with the required effectiveness.

§393.42 Brakes required on all wheels.

(a) Every commercial motor vehicle shall be equipped with brakes acting on all wheels. This requirement also applies to certain motor vehicles being towed in a driveaway-towaway operation, as follows:

(1) Any motor vehicle towed by means of a tow-bar when another motor vehicle is full-mounted on the towed vehicle; and

(2) Any saddlemount configuration with a fullmount.

(b) **Exception**.

(1) Trucks or truck tractors having three or more axles and manufactured before July 25, 1980, are not required to have brakes on the front wheels. However, these vehicles must meet the requirements of §393.52.

(2) Motor vehicles being towed in a driveaway-towaway operation (including the last truck of triple saddle-mount combinations (see §393.71(a)(3)) are not required to have operative brakes provided the combination of vehicles meets the requirements of §393.52.

(3) Any semitrailer or pole trailer (laden or unladen) with a gross weight of 1,361 kg (3,000 pounds) or less which is subject to this part is not required to be equipped with brakes if the axle weight of the towed vehicle does not exceed 40 percent of the sum of the axle weights of the towing vehicle.

(4) Any full trailer or four-wheel pole trailer (laden or unladen) with a gross weight of 1,361 kg (3,000 pounds) or less which is subject to this part is not required to be equipped with brakes if the sum of the axle weights of the towed vehicle does not exceed 40 percent of the sum of the axle weights of the towing vehicle.

(5) Brakes are not required on the steering axle of a three-axle dolly which is steered by a co-driver.

(6) Loaded housemoving dollies, specialized trailers and dollies used to transport industrial furnaces, reactors, and similar motor vehicles are not required to be equipped with brakes, provided the speed at which the combination of vehicles will be operated does not exceed 32 km/hour (20 mph) and brakes on the combination of vehicles are capable of stopping the combination within 12.2 meters (40 feet) from the speed at which the vehicle is being operated or 32 km/hour (20 mph), whichever is less.

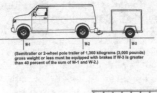

(Semitrailer or 2-wheel pole trailer of 1,360 kilograms (3,000 pounds) gross weight or less must be equipped with brakes if W-3 is greater than 40 percent of the sum of W-1 and W-2.)

(Full trailer or 4-wheel pole trailer of 1,360 kilograms (3,000 pounds) gross weight or less must be equipped with brakes if the sum of W-3 and W-4 is greater than 40 percent of the sum of W-1 and W-2.)

Figure 22-Illustrations of Brake Requirements for Light-Duty Trailers in §393.42

§393.43 Breakaway and emergency braking.

(a) **Towing vehicle protection system**. Every motor vehicle, if used to tow a trailer equipped with brakes, shall be equipped with a means for providing that in the case of a breakaway of the trailer, the service brakes on the towing vehicle will be capable of stopping the towing vehicle. For air braked towing units, the tractor protection valve or similar device shall operate automatically when the air pressure on the towing vehicle is between 138 kPa and 310 kPa (20 psi and 45 psi).

(b) **Emergency brake requirements, air brakes**. Every truck or truck tractor equipped with air brakes, when used for towing other vehicles equipped with air brakes, shall be equipped with two means of activating the emergency features of the trailer brakes. One of these means shall operate automatically in the event of reduction of the towing vehicle air supply to a fixed pressure which shall not be lower than 20 pounds per square inch nor higher than 45 pounds per square inch. The other means shall be a manually controlled device readily operable by a person seated in the driving seat. Its emergency position or method of operation shall be clearly indicated. In no instance may the manual means be so arranged as to permit its use to prevent operation of the automatic means. The automatic and manual means required by this section may be, but are not required to be, separate.

(c) **Emergency brake requirements, vacuum brakes**. Every truck tractor and truck when used for towing other vehicles equipped with vacuum brakes, shall have, in addition to the single control required by §393.49 to operate all brakes of the combination, a second manual control device which can be used to operate the brakes on the towed vehicles in emergencies. Such second control shall be independent of brake air, hydraulic, and other pressure, and independent of other controls, unless the braking system be so arranged that failure of the pressure on which the second control depends will cause the towed vehicle brakes to be applied automatically. The second control is not required by this rule to provide modulated or graduated braking.

(d) **Breakaway braking requirements for trailers**. Every trailer required to be equipped with brakes shall have brakes which apply automatically and immediately upon breakaway from the towing vehicle. With the exception of trailers having three or more axles, all brakes with which the trailer is required to be equipped must be applied upon breakaway from the towing vehicle. The brakes must remain in the applied position for at least 15 minutes.

(e) **Emergency valves**. Air brake systems installed on towed vehicles shall be so designed, by the use of "no-bleed-back" relay emergency valves or equivalent devices, that the supply reservoir used to provide air for brakes shall be safeguarded against backflow of air to the towing vehicle upon reduction of the towing vehicle air pressure.

(f) **Exception**. The requirements of paragraphs (b), (c) and (d) of this section shall not be applicable to commercial motor vehicles being transported in driveaway-towaway operations.

§393.44 Front brake lines, protection.

On every bus, if equipped with air brakes, the braking system shall be so constructed that in the event any brake line to any of the front wheels is broken, the driver can apply the brakes on the rear wheels despite such breakage. The means used to apply the brakes may be located forward of the driver's seat as long as it can be operated manually by the driver when the driver is properly restrained by any seat belt assembly provided for use. Every bus shall meet this requirement or comply with the regulations in effect at the time of its manufacture.

§393.45 Brake tubing and hoses; hose assemblies and end fittings.

(a) **General construction requirements for tubing and hoses, assemblies, and end fittings**. All brake tubing and hoses, brake hose assemblies, and brake hose end fittings must meet the applicable requirements of FMVSS No. 106 (49 CFR 571.106).

(b) **Brake tubing and hose installation**. Brake tubing and hose must—

(1) Be long and flexible enough to accommodate without damage all normal motions of the parts to which it is attached;

(2) Be secured against chaffing, kinking, or other mechanical damage; and

(3) Be installed in a manner that prevents it from contacting the vehicle's exhaust system or any other source of high temperatures.

(c) **Nonmetallic brake tubing**. Coiled nonmetallic brake tubing may be used for connections between towed and towing motor vehicles or between the frame of a towed vehicle and the unsprung subframe of an adjustable axle of the motor vehicle if—

(1) The coiled tubing has a straight segment (pigtail) at each end that is at least 51 mm (2 inches) in length and is encased in a spring guard or similar device which prevents the tubing from kinking at the fitting at which it is attached to the vehicle; and

(2) The spring guard or similar device has at least 51 mm (2 inches) of closed coils or similar surface at its interface with the fitting and extends at least 38 mm (1 ½ inches) into the coiled segment of the tubing from its straight segment.

(d) **Brake tubing and hose connections**. All connections for air, vacuum, or hydraulic braking systems shall be installed so as to ensure an attachment free of leaks, constrictions or other conditions which would adversely affect the performance of the brake system.

§393.46 [Reserved]

§393.47 Brake actuators, slack adjusters, linings/pads, and drums/rotors.

(a) **General requirements** . Brake components must be constructed, installed and maintained to prevent excessive fading and grabbing. The means of attachment and physical characteristics must provide for safe and reliable stopping of the commercial motor vehicle.

(b) **Brake chambers** . The service brake chambers and spring brake chambers on each end of an axle must be the same size.

(c) **Slack adjusters** . The effective length of the slack adjuster on each end of an axle must be the same.

(d) **Linings and pads** . The thickness of the brake linings or pads shall meet the applicable requirements of this paragraph—

(1) **Steering axle brakes.** The brake lining/pad thickness on the steering axle of a truck, truck-tractor or bus shall not be less than 4.8 mm (3/16 inch) at the shoe center for a shoe with a continuous strip of lining; less than 6.4 mm (1/4 inch) at the shoe center for a shoe with two pads; or worn to the wear indicator if the lining is so marked, for air drum brakes. The steering axle brake lining/pad thickness shall not be less than 3.2 mm (1/8 inch) for air disc brakes, or 1.6 mm (1/16 inch) or less for hydraulic disc, drum and electric brakes.

(2) **Non-steering axle brakes.** An air braked commercial motor vehicle shall not be operated with brake lining/pad thickness less than 6.4 mm (1/4 inch) or to the wear indicator if the lining is so marked (measured at the shoe center for drum brakes); or less than 3.2 mm (1/8 inch) for disc brakes. Hydraulic or electric braked commercial motor vehicles shall not be operated with a lining/pad thickness less than 1.6 mm (1/16 inch) (measured at the shoe center) for disc or drum brakes.

(e) **Clamp, Bendix DD–3, bolt-type, and rotochamber brake actuator readjustment limits** . (1) The pushrod stroke must not be greater than the values specified in the following tables:

Clamp-type brake chambers

Type	Outside diameter	Brake readjustment limit: standard stroke chamber	Brake readjustment limit: long stroke chamber
6	4 1/2 in. (114 mm)	1 1/4 in. (31.8 mm).	
9	5 1/4 in. (133 mm)	1 3/8 in. (34.9 mm).	
12	5 11/16 in. (145 mm)	1 3/8 in. (34.9 mm)	1 3/4 in. (44.5 mm).
16	6 3/8 in. (162 mm)	1 3/4 in. (44.5 mm)	2 in. (50.8 mm).
20	6 25/32 in. (172 mm)	1 3/4 in. (44.5 mm)	2 in. (50.8 mm). 2 1/2 in. (63.5 mm). [1]
24	7 7/32 in. (184 mm)	1 3/4 in. (44.5 mm)	2 in. (50.8 mm). 2 1/2 in. (63.5 mm). [2]
30	8 3/32 in. (206 mm)	2 in. (50.8 mm)	2 1/2 in. (63.5 mm).
36	9 in. (229 mm)	2 1/2 in. (63.5 mm)	

[1] For type 20 chambers with a 3-inch (76 mm) rated stroke.

[2] For type 24 chambers with a 3-inch (76 mm) rated stroke.

Bendix DD–3 brake chambers

Type	Outside diameter	Brake readjustment limit
30	8 ⅛ in. (206 mm)	2 ¼ in. (57.2 mm).

Bolt-type brake chambers

Type	Outside diameter	Brake readjustment limit
A	6 ¹⁵/₁₆ in. (176 mm)	1 ⅜ in. (34.9 mm).
B	9 ³/₁₆ in. (234 mm)	1 ¾ in. (44.5 mm).
C	8 ¹/₁₆ in. (205 mm)	1 ¾ in. (44.5 mm)
D	5 ¼ in. (133 mm)	1 ¼ in. (31.8 mm).
E	6 ³/₁₆ in. (157 mm)	1 ⅜ in. (34.9 mm).
F	11 in. (279 mm)	2 ¼ in. (57.2 mm).
G	9 ⅞ in. (251 mm)	2 in. (50.8 mm).

Rotochamber-type brake chambers

Type	Outside diameter	Brake readjustment limit
9	4 ⁹/₃₂ in. (109 mm)	1 ½ in. (38.1 mm).
12	4 ¹³/₁₆ in. (122 mm)	1 ½ in. (38.1 mm).
16	5 ¹³/₃₂ in. (138 mm)	2 in. (50.8 mm).
20	5 ¹⁵/₁₆ in. (151 mm)	2 in. (50.8 mm).
24	6 ¹³/₃₂ in. (163 mm)	2 in. (50.8 mm).
30	7 ¹/₁₆ in. (180 mm)	2 ¼ in. (57.2 mm).
36	7 ⅝ in. (194 mm)	2 ¾ in. (69.9 mm).
50	8 ⅞ in. (226 mm)	3 in. (76.2 mm).

(2) For actuator types not listed in these tables, the pushrod stroke must not be greater than 80 percent of the rated stroke marked on the actuator by the actuator manufacturer, or greater than the readjustment limit marked on the actuator by the actuator manufacturer.

(f) **Wedge Brake Adjustment**. The movement of the scribe mark on the lining shall not exceed 1.6 mm (¹/₁₆ inch).

(g) **Drums and rotors**. The thickness of the drums or rotors shall not be less than the limits established by the brake drum or rotor manufacturer.

§393.48 Brakes to be operative.

(a) **General rule**. Except as provided in paragraphs (b), (c), and (d) of this section, all brakes with which a motor vehicle is equipped must at all times be capable of operating.

(b) **Devices to reduce or remove front-wheel braking effort**. A commercial motor vehicle may be equipped with a device to reduce the front wheel braking effort (or in the case of a three-axle truck or truck tractor manufactured before March 1, 1975, a device to remove the front-wheel braking effort) if that device meets the applicable requirements of paragraphs (b)(1) and (2) of this section.

(1) **Manually operated devices.** Manually operated devices to reduce or remove front-wheel braking effort may only be used on buses, trucks, and truck tractors manufactured before March 1, 1975. Such devices must not be used unless the vehicle is being operated under adverse conditions such as wet, snowy, or icy roads.

(2) **Automatic devices.** Automatic devices must not reduce the front-wheel braking force by more than 50 percent of the braking force available when the automatic device is disconnected (regardless of whether or not an antilock system failure has occurred on any axle). The device must not be operable by the driver except upon application of the control that activates the braking system. The device must not be operable when the brake control application pressure exceeds 85 psig (for vehicles equipped with air brakes) or 85 percent of the maximum system pressure (for vehicles which are not equipped with air brakes).

(c) **Exception**. Paragraph (a) of this section does not apply to—

(1) A towed vehicle with disabling damage as defined in §390.5;

(2) A vehicle which is towed in a driveaway-towaway operation and is included in the exemption to the requirement for brakes on all wheels, §393.42(b);

(3) Unladen converter dollies with a gross weight of 1,361 kg (3,000 lbs) or less, and manufactured prior to March 1, 1998;

(4) The steering axle of a three-axle dolly which is steered by a co-driver;

(5) Loaded house moving dollies, specialized trailers and dollies used to transport industrial furnaces, reactors, and similar motor vehicles provided the speed at which the combination of vehicles will be operated does not exceed 32 km/hour (20 mph) and brakes on the combination of vehicles are capable of stopping the combination within 12.2 meters (40 feet) from the speed at which the vehicle is being operated or 32 km/hour (20 mph), whichever is less.

(6) **Raised lift axles.** Brakes on lift axles need not be capable of being operated while the lift axle is raised. However, brakes on lift axles must be capable of being applied whenever the lift axle is lowered and the tires contact the roadway.

(d) **Surge brakes**. (1) Surge brakes are allowed on:

(i) Any trailer with a gross vehicle weight rating (GVWR) of 12,000 pounds or less, when its GVWR does not exceed 1.75 times the GVWR of the towing vehicle; and

(ii) Any trailer with a GVWR greater than 12,000 pounds, but less than 20,001 pounds, when its GVWR does not exceed 1.25 times the GVWR of the towing vehicle.

(2) The gross vehicle weight (GVW) of a trailer equipped with surge brakes may be used instead of its GVWR to calculate compliance with the weight ratios specified in paragraph (d)(1) of this section when the trailer manufacturer's GVWR label is missing.

(3) The GVW of a trailer equipped with surge brakes must be used to calculate compliance with the weight ratios specified in paragraph (d)(1) of this section when the trailer's GVW exceeds its GVWR.

(4) The surge brakes must meet the requirements of §393.40.

§393.49 Control valves for brakes.

(a) **General rule**. Except as provided in paragraphs (b) and (c) of this section, every motor vehicle manufactured after June 30, 1953, which is equipped with power brakes, must have the braking system so arranged that one application valve must when activated cause all of the service brakes on the motor vehicle or combination motor vehicle to operate. This requirement must not be construed to prohibit motor vehicles from being equipped with an additional valve to be used to operate the brakes on a trailer or trailers or as required for buses in §393.44.

(b) **Driveaway-towaway exception**. This section is not applicable to driveaway-towaway operations unless the brakes on such operations are designed to be operated by a single valve.

(c) **Surge brake exception**. This requirement is not applicable to trailers equipped with surge brakes that satisfy the conditions specified in §393.48(d).

§393.50 Reservoirs required.

(a) **Reservoir capacity for air-braked power units manufactured on or after March 1, 1975, and air-braked trailers manufactured on or after January 1, 1975**. Buses, trucks, and truck-tractors manufactured on or after March 1, 1975, and air-braked trailers manufactured on or after January 1, 1975, must meet the reservoir requirements of FMVSS No. 121, S5.1.2, in effect on the date of manufacture.

(b) **Reservoir capacity for air-braked vehicles not subject to FMVSS No. 121 on the date of manufacture and all vacuum braked vehicles**. Each motor vehicle using air or vacuum braking must have either reserve capacity, or a reservoir, that would enable the driver to make a full service brake application with the engine stopped without depleting the air pressure or vacuum below 70 percent of that indicated by the air or vacuum gauge immediately before the brake application is made. For the purposes of this paragraph, a full service brake application means depressing the brake pedal or treadle valve to the limit of its travel.

(c) **Safeguarding of air and vacuum**. Each service reservoir system on a motor vehicle shall be protected against a loss of air pressure or vacuum due to a failure or leakage in the system between the service reservoir and the source of air pressure or vacuum, by check valves or equivalent devices whose proper functioning can be checked without disconnecting any air or vacuum line, or fitting.

(d) **Drain valves for air braked vehicles**. Each reservoir must have a condensate drain valve that can be manually operated. Automatic condensate drain valves may be used provided (1) they may be operated manually, or (2) a manual means of draining the reservoirs is retained.

§393.51 Warning signals, air pressure and vacuum gauges.

(a) **General rule**. Every bus, truck and truck tractor, except as provided in paragraph (f), must be equipped with a signal that provides a warning to the driver when a failure occurs in the vehicle's service brake system. The warning signal must meet the applicable requirements of paragraphs (b), (c), (d) or (e) of this section.

(b) **Hydraulic brakes**. Vehicles manufactured on or after September 1, 1975, must meet the brake system indicator lamp requirements of FMVSS No. 571.105 (S5.3) applicable to the vehicle on the date of manufacture. Vehicles manufactured on or after July 1, 1973 but before September 1, 1975, or to which FMVSS No. 571.105 was not applicable on the date of manufacture, must have a warning signal which operates before or upon application of the brakes in the event of a hydraulic-type complete failure of a partial system. The signal must be either visible within the driver's forward field of view or audible. The signal must be continuous. (Note: FMVSS No. 105 was applicable to trucks and buses from September 1, 1975 to October 12, 1976, and from September 1, 1983, to the present. FMVSS No. 105 was not applicable to trucks and buses manufactured between October 12, 1976, and September 1, 1983. Motor carriers have the option of equipping those vehicles to meet either the indicator lamp requirements of FMVSS No. 105, or the indicator lamp requirements specified in this paragraph for vehicles which were not subject to FMVSS No. 105 on the date of manufacture.)

(c) **Air brakes.** A commercial motor vehicle (regardless of the date of manufacture) equipped with service brakes activated by compressed air (air brakes) or a commercial motor vehicle towing a vehicle with service brakes activated by compressed air (air brakes) must be equipped with a pressure gauge and a warning signal. Trucks, truck tractors, and buses manufactured on or after March 1, 1975, must, at a minimum, have a pressure gauge and a warning signal which meets the requirements of FMVSS No. 121 (S5.1.4 for the pressure gauge and S5.1.5 for the warning signal) applicable to the vehicle on the date of manufacture of the vehicle. Power units to which FMVSS No. 571.121 was not applicable on the date of manufacture of the vehicle must be equipped with—

(1) A pressure gauge, visible to a person seated in the normal driving position, which indicates the air pressure (in kilopascals (kPa) or pounds per square inch (psi)) available for braking; and

(2) A warning signal that is audible or visible to a person in the normal driving position and provides a continuous warning to the driver whenever the air pressure in the service reservoir system is at 379 kPa (55 psi) and below, or one-half of the compressor governor cutout pressure, whichever is less.

(d) **Vacuum brakes.** A commercial motor vehicle (regardless of the date it was manufactured) having service brakes activated by vacuum or a vehicle towing a vehicle having service brakes activated by vacuum must be equipped with—

(1) A vacuum gauge, visible to a person seated in the normal driving position, which indicates the vacuum (in millimeters or inches of mercury) available for braking; and

(2) A warning signal that is audible or visible to a person in the normal driving position and provides a continuous warning to the driver whenever the vacuum in the vehicle's supply reservoir is less than 203 mm (8 inches) of mercury.

(e) **Hydraulic brakes applied or assisted by air or vacuum.** Each vehicle equipped with hydraulically activated service brakes which are applied or assisted by compressed air or vacuum, and to which FMVSS No. 105 was not applicable on the date of manufacture, must be equipped with a warning signal that conforms to paragraph (b) of this section for the hydraulic portion of the system; paragraph (c) of this section for the air assist/air applied portion; or paragraph (d) of this section for the vacuum assist/vacuum applied portion. This paragraph shall not be construed as requiring air pressure gauges or vacuum gauges, only warning signals.

(f) **Exceptions.** The rules in paragraphs (c), (d) and (e) of this section do not apply to property carrying commercial motor vehicles which have less than three axles and (1) were manufactured before July 1, 1973, and (2) have a manufacturer's gross vehicle weight rating less than 4,536 kg (10,001 pounds).

§393.52 Brake performance.

(a) Upon application of its service brakes, a motor vehicle or combination of motor vehicles must under any condition of loading in which it is found on a public highway, be capable of—

(1) Developing a braking force at least equal to the percentage of its gross weight specified in the table in paragraph (d) of this section;

(2) Decelerating to a stop from 20 miles per hour at not less than the rate specified in the table in paragraph (d) of this section; and

(3) Stopping from 20 miles per hour in a distance, measured from the point at which movement of the service brake pedal or control begins, that is not greater than the distance specified in the table in paragraph (d) of this section; or, for motor vehicles or motor vehicle combinations that have a GVWR or GVW greater than 4,536 kg (10,000 pounds),

(4) Developing only the braking force specified in paragraph (a)(1) of this section and the stopping distance specified in paragraph (a)(3) of this section, if braking force is measured by a performance-based brake tester which meets the requirements of functional specifications for performance-based brake testers for commercial motor vehicles, where braking force is the sum of the braking force at each wheel of the vehicle or vehicle combination as a percentage of gross vehicle or combination weight.

(b) Upon application of its emergency brake system and with no other brake system applied, a motor vehicle or combination of motor vehicles must, under any condition of loading in which it is found on a public highway, be capable of stopping from 20 miles per hour in a distance, measured from the point at which movement of the emergency brake control begins, that is not greater than the distance specified in the table in paragraph (d) of this section.

(c) Conformity to the stopping-distance requirements of paragraphs (a) and (b) of this section shall be determined under the following conditions:

(1) Any test must be made with the vehicle on a hard surface that is substantially level, dry, smooth, and free of loose material.

(2) The vehicle must be in the center of a 12-foot-wide lane when the test begins and must not deviate from that lane during the test.

(d) Vehicle brake performance table:

Type of motor vehicle	Service brake systems			Emergency brake systems
	Braking force as a percentage of gross vehicle or combination weight	Deceleration in feet per second per second	Application and braking distance in feet from initial speed of 20 m.p.h.	Application and braking distance in feet from initial speed of 20 m.p.h.
A. *Passenger-carrying vehicles.*				
(1) Vehicles with a seating capacity of 10 persons or less, including driver, and built on a passenger car chassis	65.2	21	20	54
(2) Vehicles with a seating capacity of more than 10 persons, including driver, and built on a passenger car chassis; vehicles built on a truck or bus chassis and having a manufacturer's GVWR of 10,000 pounds or less	52.8	17	25	66
(3) All other passenger-carrying vehicles	43.5	14	35	85
B. *Property-carrying vehicles.*				
(1) Single unit vehicles having a manufacturer's GVWR of 10,000 pounds or less	52.8	17	25	66
(2) Single unit vehicles having a manufacturer's GVWR of more than 10,000 pounds, except truck tractors. Combinations of a 2-axle towing vehicle and trailer having a GVWR of 3,000 pounds or less. All combinations of 2 or less vehicles in drive-away or tow-away operation	43.5	14	35	85
(3) All other property-carrying vehicles and combinations of property-carrying vehicles	43.5	14	40	90

Notes: (a) There is a definite mathematical relationship between the figures in columns 2 and 3. If the decelerations set forth in column 3 are divided by 32.2 feet per-second per-second, the figures in column 2 will be obtained. (For example, 21 divided by 32.2 equals 65.2 percent.) Column 2 is included in the tabulation because certain brake testing devices utilize this factor.

(b) The decelerations specified in column 3 are an indication of the effectiveness of the basic brakes, and as measured in practical brake testing are the maximum decelerations attained at some time during the stop. These decelerations as measured in brake tests cannot be used to compute the values in column 4 because the deceleration is not sustained at the same rate over the entire period of the stop. The deceleration increases from zero to a maximum during a period of brake system application and brake-force buildup. Also, other factors may cause the deceleration to decrease after reaching a maximum. The added distance that results because maximum deceleration is not sustained is included in the figures in column 4 but is not indicated by the usual brake-testing devices for checking deceleration.

(c) The distances in column 4 and the decelerations in column 3 are not directly related. "Brake-system application and braking distance in feet" (column 4) is a definite measure of the overall effectiveness of the braking system, being the distance traveled between the point at which the driver starts to move the braking controls and the point at which the vehicle comes to rest. It includes distance traveled while the brakes are being applied and distance traveled while the brakes are retarding the vehicle.

(d) The distance traveled during the period of brake-system application and brake-force buildup varies with vehicle type, being negligible for many passenger cars and greatest for combinations of commercial vehicles. This fact accounts for the variation from 20 to 40 feet in the values in column 4 for the various classes of vehicles.

(e) The terms "GVWR" and "GVW" refer to the manufacturer's gross vehicle rating and the actual gross vehicle weight, respectively.

§393.53 Automatic brake adjusters and brake adjustment indicators.

(a) **Automatic brake adjusters (hydraulic brake systems)**. Each commercial motor vehicle manufactured on or after October 20, 1993, and equipped with a hydraulic brake system, shall meet the automatic brake adjustment system requirements of Federal Motor Vehicle Safety Standard No. 105 (49 CFR 571.105, S5.1) applicable to the vehicle at the time it was manufactured.

(b) **Automatic brake adjusters (air brake systems)**. Each commercial motor vehicle manufactured on or after October 20, 1994, and equipped with an air brake system must meet the automatic brake adjustment system requirements of Federal Motor Vehicle Safety Standard No. 121 (49 CFR 571.121, S5.1.8 or S5.2.2) applicable to the vehicle at the time it was manufactured.

(c) **Brake adjustment indicator (air brake systems)**. On each commercial motor vehicle manufactured on or after October 20, 1994, and equipped with an air brake system which contains an external automatic adjustment mechanism and an exposed pushrod, the condition of service brake underadjustment must be displayed by a brake adjustment indicator conforming to the requirements of Federal Motor Vehicle Safety Standard No. 121 (49 CFR 571.121, S5.1.8 or S5.2.2) applicable to the vehicle at the time it was manufactured.

§393.55 Antilock brake systems.

(a) **Hydraulic brake systems**. Each truck and bus manufactured on or after March 1, 1999 (except trucks and buses engaged in driveaway-towaway operations), and equipped with a hydraulic brake system, shall be equipped with an antilock brake system that meets the requirements of Federal Motor Vehicle Safety Standard (FMVSS) No. 105 (49 CFR 571.105, S5.5).

(b) **ABS malfunction indicators for hydraulic braked vehicles**. Each hydraulic braked vehicle subject to the requirements of paragraph (a) of this section shall be equipped with an ABS malfunction indicator system that meets the requirements of FMVSS No. 105 (49 CFR 571.105, S5.3).

(c) **Air brake systems**. (1) Each truck tractor manufactured on or after March 1, 1997 (except truck tractors engaged in drive-away-towaway operations), shall be equipped with an antilock brake system that meets the requirements of FMVSS No. 121 (49 CFR 571.121, S5.1.6.1(b)).

(2) Each air braked commercial motor vehicle other than a truck tractor, manufactured on or after March 1, 1998 (except commercial motor vehicles engaged in driveaway-towaway operations), shall be equipped with an antilock brake system that meets the requirements of FMVSS No. 121 (49 CFR 571.121, S5.1.6.1(a) for trucks and buses, S5.2.3 for semitrailers, converter dollies and full trailers).

(d) **ABS malfunction circuits and signals for air braked vehicles**.

(1) Each truck tractor manufactured on or after March 1, 1997, and each single-unit air braked vehicle manufactured on or after March 1, 1998, subject to the requirements of paragraph (c) of this section, shall be equipped with an electrical circuit that is capable of signaling a malfunction that affects the generation or transmission of response or control signals to the vehicle's antilock brake system (49 CFR 571.121, S5.1.6.2(a)).

(2) Each truck tractor manufactured on or after March 1, 2001, and each single-unit vehicle that is equipped to tow another air-braked vehicle, subject to the requirements of paragraph (c) of this section, shall be equipped with an electrical circuit that is capable of transmitting a malfunction signal from the antilock brake system(s) on the towed vehicle(s) to the trailer ABS malfunction lamp in the cab of the towing vehicle, and shall have the means for connection of the electrical circuit to the towed vehicle. The ABS malfunction circuit and signal shall meet the requirements of FMVSS No. 121 (49 CFR 571.121, S5.1.6.2(b)).

(3) Each semitrailer, trailer converter dolly, and full trailer manufactured on or after March 1, 2001, and subject to the requirements of paragraph (c)(2) of this section, shall be equipped with an electrical circuit that is capable of signaling a malfunction in the trailer's antilock brake system, and shall have the means for connection of this ABS malfunction circuit to the towing vehicle. In addition, each trailer manufactured on or after March 1, 2001, subject to the requirements of paragraph (c)(2) of this section, that is designed to tow another air-brake equipped trailer shall be capable of transmitting a malfunction signal from the antilock brake system(s) of the trailer(s) it tows to the vehicle in front of the trailer. The ABS malfunction circuit and signal shall meet the requirements of FMVSS No. 121 (49 CFR 571.121, S5.2.3.2).

(e) **Exterior ABS malfunction indicator lamps for trailers**. Each trailer (including a trailer converter dolly) manufactured on or after March 1, 1998, and subject to the requirements of paragraph (c)(2) of this section, shall be equipped with an ABS malfunction indicator lamp which meets the requirements of FMVSS No. 121 (49 CFR 571.121, S5.2.3.3).

Subpart D—Glazing and Window Construction

§393.60 Glazing in specified openings.

(a) **Glazing material**. Glazing material used in windshields, windows, and doors on a motor vehicle manufactured on or after December 25, 1968, shall at a minimum meet the requirements of Federal Motor Vehicle Safety Standard

(FMVSS) No. 205 in effect on the date of manufacture of the motor vehicle. The glazing material shall be marked in accordance with FMVSS No. 205 (49 CFR 571.205, S6).

(b) **Windshields required**. Each bus, truck and truck-tractor shall be equipped with a windshield. Each windshield or portion of a multi-piece windshield shall be mounted using the full periphery of the glazing material.

(c) **Windshield condition**. With the exception of the conditions listed in paragraphs (c)(1), (c)(2), and (c)(3) of this section, each windshield shall be free of discoloration or damage in the area extending upward from the height of the top of the steering wheel (excluding a 51 mm (2 inch) border at the top of the windshield) and extending from a 25 mm (1 inch) border at each side of the windshield or windshield panel.

Exceptions:

(1) Coloring or tinting which meets the requirements of paragraph (d) of this section;

(2) Any crack that is not intersected by any other cracks;

(3) Any damaged area which can be covered by a disc 19 mm (¾ inch) in diameter if not closer than 76 mm (3 inches) to any other similarly damaged area.

(d) **Coloring or tinting of windshields and windows**. Coloring or tinting of windshields and the windows to the immediate right and left of the driver is allowed, provided the parallel luminous transmittance through the colored or tinted glazing is not less than 70 percent of the light at normal incidence in those portions of the windshield or windows which are marked as having a parallel luminous transmittance of not less than 70 percent. The transmittance restriction does not apply to other windows on the commercial motor vehicle.

(e) **Prohibition on obstructions to the driver's field of view—(1) Devices mounted on the interior of the windshield**. (i) Antennas, and similar devices must not be mounted more than 152 mm (6 inches) below the upper edge of the windshield. These devices must be located outside the area swept by the windshield wipers, and outside the driver's sight lines to the road and highway signs and signals.

(ii) Paragraph (e)(1)(i) of this section does not apply to vehicle safety technologies, as defined in §393.5, that are mounted on the interior of a windshield. Devices with vehicle safety technologies must be mounted outside the driver's sight lines to the road and to highway signs and signals, and:

(A) Not more than 100 mm (4 inches) below the upper edge of the area swept by the windshield wipers; or

(B) Not more than 175 mm (7 inches) above the lower edge of the area swept by the windshield wipers.

(2) **Decals and stickers mounted on the windshield.** Commercial Vehicle Safety Alliance (CVSA) inspection decals, and stickers and/or decals required under Federal or State laws may be placed at the bottom or sides of the windshield provided such decals or stickers do not extend more than 115 mm (4¹/₂ inches) from the bottom of the windshield and are located outside the area swept by the windshield wipers, and outside the driver's sight lines to the road and highway signs or signals.

§393.61 Truck and truck tractor window construction.

Each truck and truck tractor (except trucks engaged in armored car service) shall have at least one window on each side of the driver's compartment. Each window must have a minimum area of 1,290 cm^2 (200 in^2) formed by a rectangle 33 cm by 45 cm (13 inches by 17 ¾ inches). The maximum radius of the corner arcs shall not exceed 152 mm (6 inches). The long axis of the rectangle shall not make an angle of more than 45 degrees with the surface on which the unladen vehicle stands. If the cab is designed with a folding door or doors or with clear openings where doors or windows are customarily located, no windows shall be required in those locations.

§393.62 Emergency exits for buses.

(a) **Buses manufactured on or after September 1, 1994**. Each bus with a GVWR of 4,536 kg (10,000 pounds) or less must meet the emergency exit requirements of FMVSS No. 217 (S5.2.2.3) in effect on the date of manufacture. Each bus with a GVWR of more than 4,536 kg (10,000 pounds) must have emergency exits which meet the applicable emergency exit requirements of FMVSS No. 217 (S5.2.2 or S5.2.3) in effect on the date of manufacture.

(b) **Buses manufactured on or after September 1, 1973, but before September 1, 1994**. (1) Each bus (including a school bus used in interstate commerce for non-school bus operations) with a GVWR of more than 4,536 kg (10,000 lbs) must meet the requirements of FMVSS No. 217, S5.2.2 in effect on the date of manufacture.

(2) Each bus (including a school bus used in interstate commerce for non-school bus operations) with a GVWR of 4,536 kg (10,000 lbs) or less must meet the requirements of FMVSS No. 217, S5.2.2.3 in effect on the date of manufacture.

(c) **Buses manufactured before September 1, 1973**. For each seated passenger space provided, inclusive of the driver there shall be at least 432 cm^2 (67 square inches) of glazing if such glazing is not contained in a push-out window; or, at least 432 cm^2 (67 square inches) of free opening resulting from opening of a push-out type window. No area shall be included in this minimum prescribed area unless it will provide an unobstructed opening of at least 1,290 cm^2 (200 in^2) formed by a rectangle 33 cm by 45 cm (13 inches by 17 ¾ inches). The maximum radius of the corner arcs shall not exceed 152 mm (6 inches). The long axis of the rectangle shall not make an angle of more than 45 degrees with the surface on which the unladen vehicle stands. The area shall be measured either by removal of the glazing if not of the push-out type, or of the movable sash if of the push-out type. The exit must comply with paragraph (d) of this section. Each side of the bus must have at least 40 percent of emergency exit space required by this paragraph.

(d) **Laminated safety glass/push-out window requirements for buses manufactured before September 1, 1973**. Emergency exit space used to satisfy the requirements of paragraph (c) of this section must have laminated safety glass or push-out windows designed and maintained to yield outward to provide a free opening.

(1) **Safety glass.** Laminated safety glass must meet Test No. 25, Egress, of American National Standard for Safety Glazing Materials for Glazing Motor Vehicles and Motor Vehicle Equipment Operating on Land Highways-Safety Standards ANSI/SAE Z26. 1/96, August 1997. (See §393.7(b) for information on incorporation by reference and availability of this document.)

(2) **Push-out windows.** Each push-out window shall be releasable by operating no more than two mechanisms and allow manual release of the exit by a single occupant. For mechanisms which require rotary or straight (parallel to the undisturbed exit surface) motions to operate the exit, no more than 89 Newtons (20 pounds) of force shall be required to release the exit. For exits which require a straight motion perpendicular to the undisturbed exit surface, no more than 267 Newtons (60 pounds) shall be required to release the exit.

(e) **Emergency exit identification.** Each bus and each school bus used in interstate commerce for non-school bus operations, manufactured on or after September 1, 1973, shall meet the applicable emergency exit identification or marking requirements of FMVSS No. 217, S5.5, in effect on the date of manufacture. The emergency exits and doors on all buses (including school buses used in interstate commerce for non-school bus operations) must be marked "Emergency Exit" or "Emergency Door" followed by concise operating instructions describing each motion necessary to unlatch or open the exit located within 152 mm (6 inches) of the release mechanism.

(f) **Exception for the transportation of prisoners.** The requirements of this section do not apply to buses used exclusively for the transportation of prisoners.

§393.63 [Reserved]

Subpart E—Fuel Systems

§393.65 All fuel systems.

(a) **Application of the rules in this section.** The rules in this section apply to systems for containing and supplying fuel for the operation of motor vehicles or for the operation of auxiliary equipment installed on, or used in connection with, motor vehicles.

(b) **Location.** Each fuel system must be located on the motor vehicle so that—

(1) No part of the system extends beyond the widest part of the vehicle;

(2) No part of a fuel tank is forward of the front axle of a power unit;

(3) Fuel spilled vertically from a fuel tank while it is being filled will not contact any part of the exhaust or electrical systems of the vehicle, except the fuel level indicator assembly;

(4) Fill pipe openings are located outside the vehicle's passenger compartment and its cargo compartment;

(5) A fuel line does not extend between a towed vehicle and the vehicle that is towing it while the combination of vehicles is in motion; and

(6) No part of the fuel system of a bus manufactured on or after January 1, 1973, is located within or above the passenger compartment.

(c) **Fuel tank installation.** Each fuel tank must be securely attached to the motor vehicle in a workmanlike manner.

(d) **Gravity or syphon feed prohibited.** A fuel system must not supply fuel by gravity or syphon feed directly to the carburetor or injector.

(e) **Selection control valve location.** If a fuel system includes a selection control valve which is operable by the driver to regulate the flow of fuel from two or more fuel tanks, the valve must be installed so that either—

(1) The driver may operate it while watching the roadway and without leaving his driving position; or

(2) The driver must stop the vehicle and leave his seat in order to operate the valve.

(f) **Fuel lines**. A fuel line which is not completely enclosed in a protective housing must not extend more than 2 inches below the fuel tank or its sump. Diesel fuel crossover, return, and withdrawal lines which extend below the bottom of the tank or sump must be protected against damage from impact. Every fuel line must be—

(1) Long enough and flexible enough to accommodate normal movements of the parts to which it is attached without incurring damage; and

(2) Secured against chafing, kinking, or other causes of mechanical damage.

(g) **Excess flow valve**. When pressure devices are used to force fuel from a fuel tank, a device which prevents the flow of fuel from the fuel tank if the fuel feed line is broken must be installed in the fuel system.

§393.67 Liquid fuel tanks.

(a) **Application of the rules in this section**. The rules in this section apply to tanks containing or supplying fuel for the operation of commercial motor vehicles or for the operation of auxiliary equipment installed on, or used in connection with commercial motor vehicles.

(1) A liquid fuel tank manufactured on or after January 1, 1973, and a side-mounted gasoline tank must conform to all the rules in this section.

(2) A diesel fuel tank manufactured before January 1, 1973, and mounted on a bus must conform to the rules in paragraphs (c)(7)(ii) and (d)(2) of this section.

(3) A diesel fuel tank manufactured before January 1, 1973, and mounted on a vehicle other than bus must conform to the rules in paragraph (c)(7)(ii) of this section.

(4) A gasoline tank, other than a side-mounted gasoline tank, manufactured before January 1, 1973, and mounted on a bus must conform to the rules in paragraphs (c)(1) through (10) and (d)(2) of this section.

(5) A gasoline tank, other than a side-mounted gasoline tank, manufactured before January 1, 1973, and mounted on a vehicle other than a bus must conform to the rules in paragraphs (c)(1) through (10), inclusive, of this section.

(6) **Private motor carrier of passengers.** Motor carriers engaged in the private transportation of passengers may continue to operate a commercial motor vehicle which was not subject to this section or 49 CFR 571.301 at the time of its manufacture, provided the fuel tank of such vehicle is maintained to the original manufacturer's standards.

(7) Motor vehicles that meet the fuel system integrity requirements of 49 CFR 571.301 are exempt from the requirements of this subpart, as they apply to the vehicle's fueling system.

(b) **Definitions**. As used in this section—

(1) The term "liquid fuel tank" means a fuel tank designed to contain a fuel that is liquid at normal atmospheric pressures and temperatures.

(2) A "side-mounted" fuel tank is a liquid fuel tank which—

(i) If mounted on a truck tractor, extends outboard of the vehicle frame and outside of the plan view outline of the cab; or

(ii) If mounted on a truck, extends outboard of a line parallel to the longitudinal centerline of the truck and tangent to the outboard side of a front tire in a straight ahead position. In determining whether a fuel tank on a truck or truck tractor is side-mounted, the fill pipe is not considered a part of the tank.

(c) **Construction of liquid fuel tanks—**

(1) **Joints.** Joints of a fuel tank body must be closed by arc-, gas-, seam-, or spot-welding, by brazing, by silver soldering, or by techniques which provide heat resistance and mechanical securement at least equal to those specifically named. Joints must not be closed solely by crimping or by soldering with a lead-based or other soft solder.

(2) **Fittings.** The fuel tank body must have flanges or spuds suitable for the installation of all fittings.

(3) **Threads.** The threads of all fittings must be Dryseal American Standard Taper Pipe Thread or Dryseal SAE Short Taper Pipe Thread, specified in Society of Automotive Engineers Standard J476, as contained in the 1971 edition of the "SAE Handbook", except that straight (non-tapered) threads may be used on fittings having integral flanges and using gaskets for sealing. At least four full threads must be in engagement in each fitting.

(4) **Drains and bottom fittings.**

(i) Drains or other bottom fittings must not extend more than ¾ of an inch below the lowest part of the fuel tank or sump.

(ii) Drains or other bottom fittings must be protected against damage from impact.

(iii) If a fuel tank has drains the drain fittings must permit substantially complete drainage of the tank.

(iv) Drains or other bottom fittings must be installed in a flange or spud designed to accommodate it.

(5) **Fuel withdrawal fittings.** Except for diesel fuel tanks, the fittings through which fuel is withdrawn from a fuel tank must be located above the normal level of fuel in the tank when the tank is full.

(6) [Reserved]

(7) **Fill pipe.** (i) Each fill pipe must be designed and constructed to minimize the risk of fuel spillage during fueling operations and when the vehicle is involved in a crash.

(ii) For diesel-fueled vehicles, the fill pipe and vents of a fuel tank having a capacity of more than 94.75 L (25 gallons) of fuel must permit filling the tank with fuel at a rate of at least 75.8 L/m (20 gallons per minute) without fuel spillage.

(iii) For gasoline- and methanol-fueled vehicles with a GVWR of 3,744 kg (8,500 pounds) or less, the vehicle must permit filling the tank with fuel dispensed at the applicable fill rate required by the regulations of the Environmental Protection Agency under 40 CFR 80.22.

(iv) For gasoline- and methanol-fueled vehicles with a GVWR of 14,000 pounds (6,400 kg) or less, the vehicle must comply with the applicable fuel-spitback prevention and onboard refueling vapor recovery regulations of the Environmental Protection Agency under 40 CFR part 86.

(v) Each fill pipe must be fitted with a cap that can be fastened securely over the opening in the fill pipe. Screw threads or a bayonet-type point are methods of conforming to the requirements of paragraph (c) of this section.

(8) **Safety venting system.** A liquid fuel tank with a capacity of more than 25 gallons of fuel must have a venting system which, in the event the tank is subjected to fire, will prevent internal tank pressure from rupturing the tank's body, seams, or bottom opening (if any).

(9) **Pressure resistance.** The body and fittings of a liquid fuel tank with a capacity of more than 25 gallons of fuel must be capable of withstanding an

internal hydrostatic pressure equal to 150 percent of the maximum internal pressure reached in the tank during the safety venting system test specified in paragraph (d)(1) of this section.

(10) **Air vent.** Each fuel tank must be equipped with a non-spill air vent (such as a ball check). The air vent may be combined with the fill-pipe cap or safety vent, or it may be a separate unit installed on the fuel tank.

(11) **Markings.** If the body of the fuel tank is readily visible when the tank is installed on the vehicle, the tank must be plainly marked with its liquid capacity. The tank must also be plainly marked with a warning against filling it to more than 95 percent of its liquid capacity.

(12) **Overfill restriction.** A liquid fuel tank manufactured on or after January 1, 1973, must be designed and constructed so that—

(i) The tank cannot be filled, in a normal filling operation, with a quantity of fuel that exceeds 95 percent of the tank's liquid capacity; and

(ii) When the tank is filled, normal expansion of the fuel will not cause fuel spillage.

(d) **Liquid fuel tank tests**. Each liquid fuel tank must be capable of passing the tests specified in paragraphs (d)(1) and (2) of this section. The specified tests are a measure of performance only. Alternative procedures which assure that equipment meets the required performance standards may be used.

(1) **Safety venting system test—**

(i) **Procedure.** Fill the tank three-fourths full with fuel, seal the fuel feed outlet, and invert the tank. When the fuel temperature is between 50°F. and 80°F., apply an enveloping flame to the tank so that the temperature of the fuel rises at a rate of not less than 6°F. and not more than 8°F. per minute.

(ii) **Required performance.** The safety venting system required by paragraph (c)(8) of this section must activate before the internal pressure in the tank exceeds 50 pounds per square inch, gauge, and the internal pressure must not thereafter exceed the pressure at which the system activated by more than five pounds per square inch despite any further increase in the temperature of the fuel.

(2) **Leakage test—**

(i) **Procedure.** Fill the tank to capacity with fuel having a temperature between 50 °F. and 80 °F. With the fill-pipe cap installed, turn the tank through an angle of 150° in any direction about any axis from its normal position.

(ii) **Required performance.** Neither the tank nor any fitting may leak more than a total of one ounce by weight of fuel per minute in any position the tank assumes during the test.

(e) **Side-mounted liquid fuel tank tests**. Each side-mounted liquid fuel tank must be capable of passing the tests specified in paragraphs (e)(1) and (2) of this section and the test specified in paragraphs (d)(1) and (2) of this section. The specified tests are a measure of performance only. Alternative procedures which assure that equipment meets the required performance criteria may be used.

(1) **Drop test—**

(i) **Procedure.** Fill the tank with a quantity of water having a weight equal to the weight of the maximum fuel load of the tank and drop the tank 30 feet onto an unyielding surface so that it lands squarely on one corner.

(ii) **Required performance.** Neither the tank nor any fitting may leak more than a total of 1 ounce by weight of water per minute.

(2) **Fill-pipe test—**

(i) **Procedure.** Fill the tank with a quantity of water having a weight equal to the weight of the maximum fuel load of the tank and drop the tank 10 feet onto an unyielding surface so that it lands squarely on its fill-pipe.

(ii) **Required performance.** Neither the tank nor any fitting may leak more than a total of 1 ounce by weight of water per minute.

(f) **Certification and markings.** Each liquid fuel tank shall be legibly and permanently marked by the manufacturer with the following minimum information:

(1) The month and year of manufacture.

(2) The manufacturer's name on tanks manufactured on and after July 1, 1989, and means of identifying the facility at which the tank was manufactured, and

(3) A certificate that it conforms to the rules in this section applicable to the tank. The certificate must be in the form set forth in either of the following:

(i) If a tank conforms to all rules in this section pertaining to side-mounted fuel tanks: "Meets all FMCSA sidemounted tank requirements."

(ii) If a tank conforms to all rules in this section pertaining to tanks which are not side-mounted fuel tanks: "Meets all FMCSA requirements for non-side-mounted fuel tanks."

(iii) The form of certificate specified in paragraph (f)(3) (i) or (ii) of this section may be used on a liquid fuel tank manufactured before July 11, 1973, but it is not mandatory for liquid fuel tanks manufactured before March 7, 1989. The form of certification manufactured on or before March 7, 1989, must meet the requirements in effect at the time of manufacture.

(4) **Exception.** The following previously exempted vehicles are not required to carry the certification and marking specified in paragraphs (f)(1) through (3) of this section:

(i) Ford vehicles with GVWR over 10,000 pounds identified as follows: The vehicle identification numbers (VINs) contain A, K, L, M, N, W, or X in the fourth position.

(ii) GM G-Vans (Chevrolet Express and GMC Savanna) and full-sized C/K trucks (Chevrolet Silverado and GMC Sierra) with GVWR over 10,000 pounds identified as follows: The VINs contain either a "J" or a "K" in the fourth position. In addition, the seventh position of the VINs on the G-Van will contain a "1."

§393.68 Compressed natural gas fuel containers.

(a) **Applicability.** The rules in this section apply to compressed natural gas (CNG) fuel containers used for supplying fuel for the operation of commercial motor vehicles or for the operation of auxiliary equipment installed on, or used in connection with commercial motor vehicles.

(b) **CNG containers manufactured on or after March 26, 1995.** Any motor vehicle manufactured on or after March 26, 1995, and equipped with a CNG fuel tank must meet the CNG container requirements of FMVSS No. 304 (49 CFR 571.304) in effect at the time of manufacture of the vehicle.

(c) **Labeling.** Each CNG fuel container shall be permanently labeled in accordance with the requirements of FMVSS No. 304, S7.4.

§393.69 Liquefied petroleum gas systems.

(a) A fuel system that uses liquefied petroleum gas as a fuel for the operation of a motor vehicle or for the operation of auxiliary equipment installed on, or used in connection with, a motor vehicle must conform to the "Standards for the Storage and Handling of Liquefied Petroleum Gases" of the National Fire Protection Association, Battery March Park, Quincy, MA 02269, as follows:

(1) A fuel system installed before December 31, 1962, must conform to the 1951 edition of the Standards.

(2) A fuel system installed on or after December 31, 1962, and before January 1, 1973, must conform to Division IV of the June 1959 edition of the Standards.

(3) A fuel system installed on or after January 1, 1973, and providing fuel for propulsion of the motor vehicle must conform to Division IV of the 1969 edition of the Standards.

(4) A fuel system installed on or after January 1, 1973, and providing fuel for the operation of auxiliary equipment must conform to Division VII of the 1969 edition of the Standards.

(b) When the rules in this section require a fuel system to conform to a specific edition of the Standards, the fuel system may conform to the applicable provisions in a later edition of the Standards specified in this section.

(c) The tank of a fuel system must be marked to indicate that the system conforms to the Standards.

Subpart F—Coupling Devices and Towing Methods

§393.70 Coupling devices and towing methods, except for driveaway-towaway operations.

(a) **Tracking**. When two or more vehicles are operated in combination, the coupling devices connecting the vehicles shall be designed, constructed, and installed, and the vehicles shall be designed and constructed, so that when the combination is operated in a straight line on a level, smooth, paved surface, the path of the towed vehicle will not deviate more than 3 inches to either side of the path of the vehicle that tows it.

(b) **Fifth wheel assemblies**—(1) **Mounting**—(i) **Lower half**. The lower half of a fifth wheel mounted on a truck tractor or converter dolly must be secured to the frame of that vehicle with properly designed brackets, mounting plates or angles and properly tightened bolts of adequate size and grade, or devices that provide equivalent security. The installation shall not cause cracking, warping, or deformation of the frame. The installation must include a device for positively preventing the lower half of the fifth wheel from shifting on the frame to which it is attached.

(ii) **Upper half**. The upper half of a fifth wheel must be fastened to the motor vehicle with at least the same security required for the installation of the lower half on a truck tractor or converter dolly.

(2) **Locking**. Every fifth wheel assembly must have a locking mechanism. The locking mechanism, and any adapter used in conjunction with it, must prevent separation of the upper and lower halves of the fifth wheel assembly unless a positive manual release is activated. The release may be located so that the driver can operate it from the cab. If a motor vehicle has a fifth wheel designed and constructed to be readily separable, the fifth wheel locking devices shall apply automatically on coupling.

(3) **Location**. The lower half of a fifth wheel shall be located so that, regardless of the condition of loading, the relationship between the kingpin and the rear axle or axles of the towing motor vehicle will properly distribute the gross weight of both the towed and towing vehicles on the axles of those vehicles, will not

unduly interfere with the steering, braking, and other maneuvering of the towing vehicle, and will not otherwise contribute to unsafe operation of the vehicles comprising the combination. The upper half of a fifth wheel shall be located so that the weight of the vehicles is properly distributed on their axles and the combination of vehicles will operate safely during normal operation.

(c) **Towing of full trailers**. A full trailer must be equipped with a tow-bar and a means of attaching the tow-bar to the towing and towed vehicles. The tow-bar and the means of attaching it must—

(1) Be structurally adequate for the weight being drawn;

(2) Be properly and securely mounted;

(3) Provide for adequate articulation at the connection without excessive slack at that location; and

(4) Be provided with a locking device that prevents accidental separation of the towed and towing vehicles. The mounting of the trailer hitch (pintle hook or equivalent mechanism) on the towing vehicle must include reinforcement or bracing of the frame sufficient to produce strength and rigidity of the frame to prevent its undue distortion.

(d) **Safety devices in case of tow-bar failure or disconnection**. Every full trailer and every converter dolly used to convert a semitrailer to a full trailer must be coupled to the frame, or an extension of the frame, of the motor vehicle which tows it with one or more safety devices to prevent the towed vehicle from breaking loose in the event the tow-bar fails or becomes disconnected. The safety device must meet the following requirements:

(1) The safety device must not be attached to the pintle hook or any other device on the towing vehicle to which the tow-bar is attached. However, if the pintle hook or other device was manufactured prior to July 1, 1973, the safety device may be attached to the towing vehicle at a place on a pintle hook forging or casting if that place is independent of the pintle hook.

(2) The safety device must have no more slack than is necessary to permit the vehicles to be turned properly.

(3) The safety device, and the means of attaching it to the vehicles, must have an ultimate strength of not less than the gross weight of the vehicle or vehicles being towed.

(4) The safety device must be connected to the towed and towing vehicles and to the tow-bar in a manner which prevents the tow-bar from dropping to the ground in the event it fails or becomes disconnected.

(5) Except as provided in paragraph (d) (6) of this section, if the safety device consists of safety chains or cables, the towed vehicle must be equipped with either two safety chains or cables or with a bridle arrangement of a single chain or cable attached to its frame or axle at two points as far apart as the configuration of the frame or axle permits. The safety chains or cables shall be either two separate pieces, each equipped with a hook or other means for attachment to the towing vehicle, or a single piece leading along each side of the tow-bar from the two points of attachment on the towed vehicle and arranged into a bridle with a single means of attachment to be connected to the towing vehicle. When a single length of cable is used, a thimble and twin-base cable clamps shall be used to form the forward bridle eye. The hook or other means of attachment to the towing vehicle shall be secured to the chains or cables in a fixed position.

(6) If the towed vehicle is a converter dolly with a solid tongue and without a hinged tow-bar or other swivel between the fifth wheel mounting and the attachment point of the tongue eye or other hitch device—

(i) Safety chains or cables, when used as the safety device for that vehicle, may consist of either two chains or cables or a single chain or cable used alone;

(ii) A single safety device, including a single chain or cable used alone as the safety device, must be in line with the centerline of the trailer tongue; and

(iii) The device may be attached to the converter dolly at any point to the rear of the attachment point of the tongue eye or other hitch device.

(7) Safety devices other than safety chains or cables must provide strength, security of attachment, and directional stability equal to, or greater than, safety chains or cables installed in accordance with paragraphs (d)(5) and (6) of this section.

(8)(i) When two safety devices, including two safety chains or cables, are used and are attached to the towing vehicle at separate points, the points of attachment on the towing vehicle shall be located equally distant from, and on opposite sides of, the longitudinal centerline of the towing vehicle.

(ii) Where two chains or cables are attached to the same point on the towing vehicle, and where a bridle or a single chain or cable is used, the point of attachment must be on the longitudinal centerline or within 152 mm (6 inches) to the right of the longitudinal centerline of the towing vehicle.

(iii) A single safety device, other than a chain or cable, must also be attached to the towing vehicle at a point on the longitudinal centerline or within 152 mm (6 inches) to the right of the longitudinal centerline of the towing vehicle.

§393.71 Coupling devices and towing methods, driveaway-towaway operations.

(a) **Number in combination**. (1) No more than three saddle-mounts may be used in any combination.

(2) No more than one tow-bar or ball-and-socket type coupling device may be used in any combination.

(3) When motor vehicles are towed by means of triple saddle-mounts, all but the final towed vehicle must have brakes acting on all wheels in contact with the roadway.

(b) **Carrying vehicles on towing vehicle**. (1) When adequately and securely attached by means equivalent in security to that provided in paragraph (j)(2) of this section, a motor vehicle or motor vehicles may be full-mounted on the structure of a towing vehicle engaged in any driveaway-towaway operation.

(2) No motor vehicle or motor vehicles may be full-mounted on a towing vehicle unless the relationship of such full-mounted vehicles to the rear axle or axles results in proper distribution of the total gross weight of the vehicles and does not unduly interfere with the steering, braking, or maneuvering of the towing vehicle, or otherwise contribute to the unsafe operation of the vehicles comprising the combination.

(3) Saddle-mounted vehicles must be arranged such that the gross weight of the vehicles is properly distributed to prevent undue interference with the steering, braking, or maneuvering of the combination of vehicles.

(c) **Carrying vehicles on towed vehicles**. (1) When adequately and securely attached by means equivalent in security to that provided in paragraph (j)(2) of this section, a motor vehicle or motor vehicles may be full-mounted on the structure of towed vehicles engaged in any driveaway-towaway operation.

(2) No motor vehicle shall be full-mounted on a motor vehicle towed by means of a tow-bar unless the towed vehicle is equipped with brakes and is provided with means for effective application of brakes acting on all wheels and is towed on its own wheels.

(3) No motor vehicle or motor vehicles shall be full-mounted on a motor vehicle towed by means of a saddle-mount unless the centerline of the kingpin or equivalent means of attachment of such towed vehicle shall be so located on the towing vehicle that the relationship to the rear axle or axles results in proper distribution of the total gross weight of the vehicles and does not unduly interfere with the steering, braking, or maneuvering of the towing vehicle or otherwise contribute to the unsafe operation of vehicles comprising the combination; and unless a perpendicular to the ground from the center of gravity of the full-mounted vehicles lies forward of the centerline of the rear axle of the saddle-mounted vehicle.

(4) If a motor vehicle towed by means of a saddle-mount has any vehicle full-mounted on it, the saddle-mounted vehicle must at all times while so loaded have effective brakes acting on all wheels in contact with the roadway.

(d) **Bumper tow-bars on heavy vehicles prohibited** . Tow-bars of the type which depend upon the bumpers as a means of transmitting forces between the vehicles shall not be used to tow a motor vehicle weighing more than 5,000 pounds.

(e) **Front wheels of saddle-mounted vehicles restrained** . A motor vehicle towed by means of a saddle-mount shall have the motion of the front wheels restrained if under any condition of turning of such wheels they will project beyond the widest part of either the towed or towing vehicle.

(f) **Vehicles to be towed in forward position** . Unless the steering mechanism is adequately locked in a straight forward position, all motor vehicles towed by means of a saddle-mount shall be towed with the front end mounted on the towing vehicle.

(g) **Means required for towing** . No motor vehicles or combination of motor vehicles shall be towed in driveaway-towaway operations by means other than a tow-bar, ball-and-socket type coupling device, saddle-mount connections which meet the requirements of this section, or in the case of a semitrailer equipped with an upper coupler assembly, a fifth-wheel meeting the requirements of §393.70 .

(h) **Requirements for tow-bars** . Tow-bars shall comply with the following requirements:

(1) **Tow-bars, structural adequacy and mounting.** Every tow-bar shall be structurally adequate and properly installed and maintained. To ensure that it is structurally adequate, it must, at least, meet the requirements of the following table:

Gross weight of towed vehicle (pounds) [1]	Longitudinal strength in tension and compression [2]		Strength as a beam (in any direction concentrated load at center) [2,3]
	All towbars	New towbars acquired and used by a motor carrier after Sept. 30, 1948	
	Pounds	Pounds	Pounds
Less than 5,000	3,000	6,500	3,000
5,000 and over			
Less than 10,000	6,000	([1])	([1])

Gross weight of towed vehicle (pounds) [1]	Longitudinal strength in tension and compression [2]		Strength as a beam (in any direction concentrated load at center) [2,3]
	All towbars	New towbars acquired and used by a motor carrier after Sept. 30, 1948	
10,000 and over			
Less than 15,000	9,000	([1])	([1])

[1] The required strength of tow-bars for towed vehicles of 15,000 pounds and over gross weight and of new tow-bars acquired and used after Sept. 30, 1948, for towed vehicles of 5,000 pounds and over gross weight shall be computed by means of the following formulae: Longitudinal strength = gross weight of towed vehicle x 1.3. Strength as a beam = gross weight of towed vehicle x 0.6.

[2] In testing, the whole unit shall be tested with all clamps, joints, and pins so mounted and fastened as to approximate conditions of actual operation.

[3] This test shall be applicable only to tow-bars which are, in normal operation, subjected to a bending movement such as tow-bars for house trailers.

(2) **Tow-bars, jointed.** The tow-bar shall be so constructed as to freely permit motion in both horizontal and vertical planes between the towed and towing vehicles. The means used to provide the motion shall be such as to prohibit the transmission of stresses under normal operation between the towed and towing vehicles, except along the longitudinal axis of the tongue or tongues.

(3) **Tow-bar fastenings.** The means used to transmit the stresses to the chassis or frames of the towed and towing vehicles may be either temporary structures or bumpers or other integral parts of the vehicles: Provided, however, that the means used shall be so constructed, installed, and maintained that, when tested as an assembly, failure in such members shall not occur when the weakest new tow-bar which is permissible under paragraph (h)(1) of this section is subjected to the tests given therein.

(4) **Means of adjusting length.** On tow-bars, adjustable as to length, the means used to make such adjustment shall fit tightly and not result in any slackness or permit the tow-bar to bend. With the tow-bar supported rigidly at both ends and with a load of 50 pounds at the center, the sag, measured at the center, in any direction shall not exceed 0.25 inch under any condition of adjustment as to length.

(5) **Method of clamping.** Adequate means shall be provided for securely fastening the tow-bar to the towed and towing vehicles.

(6) **Tow-bar connection to steering mechanism.** The tow-bar shall be provided with suitable means of attachment to and actuation of the steering mechanism, if any, of the towed vehicle. The attachment shall provide for sufficient angularity of movement of the front wheels of the towed vehicle so that it may follow substantially in the path of the towing vehicle without cramping the tow-bar. The tow-bar shall be provided with suitable joints to permit such movement.

(7) **Tracking**. The tow-bar shall be so designed, constructed, maintained, and mounted as to cause the towed vehicle to follow substantially in the path of the towing vehicle. Tow-bars of such design or in such condition as to permit the

towed vehicle to deviate more than 3 inches to either side of the path of a towing vehicle moving in a straight line as measured from the center of the towing vehicle are prohibited.

(8) **Passenger car-trailer type couplings.** Trailer couplings used for driveaway-towaway operations of passenger car trailers shall conform to Society of Automotive Engineers Standard No. J684c, "Trailer Couplings and Hitches—Automotive Type," July 1970. [1]

(9) **Marking tow-bars.** Every tow-bar acquired and used in driveaway-towaway operations by a motor carrier shall be plainly marked with the following certification of the manufacturer thereof (or words of equivalent meaning):

This tow-bar complies with the requirements of the Federal Motor Carrier Safety Administration for (maximum gross weight for which tow-bar is manufactured) vehicles.

Allowable Maximum Gross Weight _____

Manufactured _____

(Month and year)

by _____

(Name of manufacturer)

Tow-bar certification manufactured before March 7, 1989 must meet requirements in effect at the time of manufacture.

(10) **Safety devices in case of tow-bar failure or disconnection.** (i) The towed vehicle shall be connected to the towing vehicle by a safety device to prevent the towed vehicle from breaking loose in the event the tow-bar fails or becomes disconnected. When safety chains or cables are used as the safety device for that vehicle, at least two safety chains or cables meeting the requirements of paragraph (h)(10)(ii) of this section shall be used. The tensile strength of the safety device and the means of attachment to the vehicles shall be at least equivalent to the corresponding longitudinal strength for tow-bars required in the table of paragraph (h)(1) of this section. If safety chains or cables are used as the safety device, the required strength shall be the combined strength of the combination of chains and cables.

(ii) If chains or cables are used as the safety device, they shall be crossed and attached to the vehicles near the points of bumper attachments to the chassis of the vehicles. The length of chain used shall be no more than necessary to permit free turning of the vehicles. The chains shall be attached to the tow-bar at the point of crossing or as close to that point as is practicable.

(iii) A safety device other than safety chains or cables must provide strength, security of attachment, and directional stability equal to, or greater than, that provided by safety chains or cables installed in accordance with paragraph (h)(10)(ii) of this section. A safety device other than safety chains or cables must be designed, constructed, and installed so that, if the tow-bar fails or becomes disconnected, the tow-bar will not drop to the ground.

(i) [Reserved]

(j) **Requirements for upper-half of saddle-mounts**. The upper-half of any saddle-mount shall comply with the following requirements:

(1) **Upper-half connection to towed vehicle.** The upper-half shall be securely attached to the frame or axle of the towed vehicle by means of U-bolts or other means providing at least equivalent security.

---

[1]See footnote 1 to §393.24(c).

(2) **U-bolts or other attachments.** U-bolts used to attach the upper-half to the towed vehicles shall be made of steel rod, free of defects, so shaped as to avoid at any point a radius of less than 1 inch; Provided, however, that a lesser radius may be utilized if the U-bolt is so fabricated as not to cause more than 5 percent reduction in cross-sectional area at points of curvature, in which latter event the minimum radius shall be one-sixteenth inch. U-bolts shall have a diameter not less than required by the following table:

Diameter of U-bolts in inches

Weights in pounds of heaviest towed vehicle	Double or triple saddle-mount			Single saddle-mount [1]
	Front mount	Middle or front mount	Rear mount	
Up to 5,000	0.625	0.5625	0.0500	0.500
5,000 and over	0.6875	0.625	0.5625	0.5625

[1] The total weight of all the vehicles being towed shall govern. If other devices are used to accomplish the same purposes as U-bolts they shall have at least equivalent strength of U-bolts made of mild steel. Cast iron shall not be used for clamps or any other holding devices.

(3) **U-bolts and points of support, location** . The distance between the most widely separated U-bolts shall not be less than 9 inches. The distance between the widely separated points where the upper-half supports the towed vehicle shall not be less than 9 inches, except that saddle-mounts employing ball and socket joints shall employ a device which clamps the axle of the towed vehicle throughout a length of not less than 5 inches.

(4) **Cradle-type upper-halves, specifications.** Upper-halves of the cradle-type using vertical members to restrain the towed vehicle from relative movement in the direction of motion of the vehicles shall be substantially constructed and adequate for the purpose. Such cradle-mounts shall be equipped with at least one bolt or equivalent means to provide against relative vertical movement between the upper-half and the towed vehicle. Bolts, if used, shall be at least one-half inch in diameter. Devices using equivalent means shall have at least equivalent strength. The means used to provide against relative vertical motion between the upper-half and the towed vehicle shall be such as not to permit a relative motion of over one-half inch. The distance between the most widely separated points of support between the upper-half and the towed vehicle shall be at least 9 inches.

(5) **Lateral movement of towed vehicle.** (i) Towed vehicles having a straight axle or an axle having a drop of less than 3 inches, unless the saddle-mount is constructed in accordance with paragraph (m)(2) of this section, shall be securely fastened by means of chains or cables to the upper-half so as to ensure against relative lateral motion between the towed vehicle and the upper-half. The chains or cables shall be at least ³⁄₁₆ -inch diameter and secured by bolts of at least equal diameter.

(ii) Towed vehicles with an axle with a drop of 3 inches or more, or connected by a saddle-mount constructed in accordance with paragraph (m)(2) of this section, need not be restrained by chains or cables provided that the upper-half is so designed as to provide against such relative motion.

(iii) Chains or cables shall not be required if the upper-half is so designed as positively to provide against lateral movement of the axle.

(k) **Requirements for lower half of saddle-mounts** . The lower half of any saddle-mount shall comply with the following requirements:

(1) **U-bolts or other attachments.** U-bolts used to attach the lower half to the towing vehicle shall be made of steel rod, free of defects, so shaped as to avoid at any point a radius of less than 1 inch: Provided, however, That a lesser radius may be utilized if the U-bolt is so fabricated as not to cause more than 5 percent reduction in cross-sectional area at points of curvature, in which latter event the minimum radius shall be one-sixteenth inch. U-bolts shall have a total cross-sectional area not less than as required by the following table:

Total cross-sectional area of U-bolts in square inches

Weight in pounds of heaviest towed vehicle	Double or triple saddle-mount			Single saddle-mount [1]
	Front mount	Middle or front mount	Rear mount	
Up to 5,000....................	1.2	1.0	0.8	0.8
5,000 and over................	1.4	1.2	1.0	1.0

[1] The total weight of all the vehicles being towed shall govern. If other devices are used to accomplish the same purposes as U-bolts they shall have at least equivalent strength of U-bolts made of mild steel. Cast iron shall not be used for clamps or any other holding devices.

(2) **Shifting** . Adequate provision shall be made by design and installation to provide against relative movement between the lower-half and the towing vehicle especially during periods of rapid acceleration and deceleration. To ensure against shifting, designs of the tripod type shall be equipped with adequate and securely fastened hold-back chains or similar devices.

(3) **Swaying.** (i) Adequate provision shall be made by design and installation to provide against swaying or lateral movement of the towed vehicle relative to the towing vehicle. To ensure against swaying, lower-halves designed with cross-members attached to but separable from vertical members shall have such cross-members fastened to the vertical members by at least two bolts on each side. Such bolts shall be of at least equivalent cross-sectional area as those required for U-bolts for the corresponding saddle-mount as given in the table in paragraph (k)(1) of this section. The minimum distance between the most widely separated points of support of the cross-member by the vertical member shall be three inches as measured in a direction parallel to the longitudinal axis of the towing vehicle.

(ii) The lower-half shall have a bearing surface on the frame of the towing vehicle of such dimensions that the pressure exerted by the lower-half upon the frame of the towing vehicle shall not exceed 200 pounds per square inch under any conditions of static loading. Hardwood blocks or blocks of other suitable material, such as hard rubber, aluminum or brakelining, if used between the lower-half and the frame of the towing vehicle shall be at least ½ inch thick, 3 inches wide, and a combined length of 6 inches.

(iii) Under no condition shall the highest point of support of the towed vehicle by the upper-half be more than 24 inches, measured vertically, above the top of the frame of the towing vehicle, measured at the point where the lower-half rests on the towing vehicle.

(4) **Wood blocks**. (i) Hardwood blocks of good quality may be used to build up the height of the front end of the towed vehicle, provided that the total height of such wood blocks shall not exceed 8 inches and not over two separate pieces are placed upon each other to obtain such height; however, hardwood blocks, not over 4 in number, to a total height not to exceed 14 inches, may be used if the total cross-sectional area of the U-bolts used to attach the lower-half of the towing vehicle is at least 50 percent greater than that required by the table contained in paragraph (k)(1) of this section, or, if other devices are used in lieu of U-bolts, they shall provide for as great a resistance to bending as is provided by the larger U-bolts above prescribed.

(ii) Hardwood blocks must be at least 4 inches in width and the surfaces between blocks or block and lower-half or block and upper-half shall be planed and so installed and maintained as to minimize any tendency of the towed vehicle to sway or rock.

(5) **Cross-member, general requirements.** The cross-member, which is that part of the lower-half used to distribute the weight of the towed vehicle equally to each member of the frame of the towing vehicle, if used, shall be structurally adequate and properly installed and maintained adequately to perform this function.

(6) **Cross-member, use of wood.** No materials, other than suitable metals, shall be used as the cross-member, and wood may not be used structurally in any manner that will result in its being subject to tensile stresses. Wood may be used in cross-members if supported throughout its length by suitable metal cross-members.

(7) **Lower-half strength**. The lower-half shall be capable of supporting the loads given in the following table. For the purpose of test, the saddle-mount shall be mounted as normally operated and the load applied through the upper-half:

Minimum test load in pounds

Weight in pounds of heaviest towed vehicle	Double or triple saddle-mount			Single saddle-mount [1]
	Front mount	Middle or front mount	Rear mount	
Up to 5,000.....................	15,000	10,000	5,000	5,000
5,000 and over.................	30,000	20,000	10,000	10,000

[1] The total weight of all the vehicles being towed shall govern.

(l) **Requirements for kingpins of saddle-mounts**. The kingpin of any saddle-mount shall comply with the following requirements:

(1) **Kingpin size.** (i) Kingpins shall be constructed of steel suitable for the purpose, free of defects, and having a diameter not less than required by the following table:

Diameter of solid kingpin in inches

Weight in pounds of heaviest towed vehicle	Double or triple saddle-mount						Single saddle-mount [1]	
	Front mount		Middle or front mount		Rear mount			
	Mild steel	H.T.S. [2]	Mild steel	H.T.S. [2]	Mild steel	H.T.S. [2]	Mild steel	H.T.S.
Up to 5,000	1.125	1.000	1.000	0.875	0.875	0.750	0.875	0.750
5,000 & over	1.500	1.125	1.250	1.000	1.000	0.875	1.000	0.875

[1] The total weight of all the vehicles being towed shall govern.

[2] High tensile steel is steel having a minimum ultimate strength of 65,000 pounds per square inch.

(ii) If a ball and socket joint is used in place of a kingpin, the diameter of the neck of the ball shall be at least equal to the diameter of the corresponding solid kingpin given in the above table. If hollow kingpins are used, the metallic cross-sectional area shall be at least equal to the cross-sectional area of the corresponding solid kingpin.

(2) **Kingpin fit.** If a kingpin bushing is not used, the kingpin shall fit snugly into the upper and lower-halves but shall not bind. Those portions of the upper or lower-halves in moving contact with the kingpin shall be smoothly machined with no rough or sharp edges. The bearing surface thus provided shall not be less in depth than the radius of the kingpin.

(3) **Kingpin bushing on saddle-mounts.** The kingpin of all new saddle-mounts acquired and used shall be snugly enclosed in a bushing at least along such length of the kingpin as may be in moving contact with either the upper or lower-halves. The bearing surface thus provided shall not be less in depth than the radius of the kingpin.

(4) **Kingpin to restrain vertical motion.** The kingpin shall be so designed and installed as to restrain the upper-half from moving in a vertical direction relative to the lower-half.

(m) **Additional requirements for saddle-mounts .** Saddle-mounts shall comply with the following requirements:

(1) **Bearing surface between upper and lower-halves.** The upper and lower-halves shall be so constructed and connected that the bearing surface between the two halves shall not be less than 16 square inches under any conditions of angularity between the towing and towed vehicles: Provided, however, That saddle-mounts using a ball and socket joint shall have a ball of such dimension that the static bearing load shall not exceed 800 pounds per square inch, based on the projected cross-sectional area of the ball: And further provided, That saddle-mounts having the upper-half supported by ball, taper, or roller-bearings shall not have such bearings loaded beyond the limits prescribed for such bearings by the manufacturer thereof. The upper-half shall rest evenly and smoothly upon the lower-half and the contact surfaces shall be lubricated and maintained so that there shall be a minimum of frictional resistance between the parts.

(2) **Saddle-mounts, angularity.** All saddle-mounts acquired and used shall provide for angularity between the towing and towed vehicles due to vertical

curvatures of the highway. Such means shall not depend upon either the looseness or deformation of the parts of either the saddle-mount or the vehicles to provide for such angularity.

(3) **Tracking**. The saddle-mount shall be so designed, constructed, maintained, and installed that the towed vehicle or vehicles will follow substantially in the path of the towing vehicle without swerving. Towed vehicles shall not deviate more than 3 inches to either side of the path of the towing vehicle when moving in a straight line.

(4) **Prevention of frame bending.** Where necessary, provision shall be made to prevent the bending of the frame of the towing vehicle by insertion of suitable blocks inside the frame channel to prevent kinking. The saddle-mount shall not be so located as to cause deformation of the frame by reason of cantilever action.

(5) **Extension of frame.** No saddle-mount shall be located at a point to the rear of the frame of a towing vehicle.

(6) **Nuts, secured.** All nuts used on bolts, U-bolts, kingpins, or in any other part of the saddle-mount shall be secured against accidental disconnection by means of cotter-keys, lock-washers, double nuts, safety nuts, or equivalent means. Parts shall be so designed and installed that nuts shall be fully engaged.

(7) **Inspection of all parts**. The saddle-mount shall be so designed that it may be disassembled and each separate part inspected for worn, bent, cracked, broken, or missing parts.

(8) **Saddle-mounts, marking.** Every new saddle-mount acquired and used in driveaway-towaway operations by a motor carrier shall have the upper-half and the lower-half separately marked with the following certification of the manufacturer thereof (or words of equivalent meaning).

This saddle-mount complies with the requirements of the Federal Motor Carrier Safety Administration for vehicles up to 5,000 pounds (or over 5,000 pounds): Manufactured _____

(Month and year)

by _____

(Name of manufacturer)

(n) Requirements for devices used to connect motor vehicles or parts of motor vehicles together to form one vehicle—

(1) **Front axle attachment.** The front axle of one motor vehicle intended to be coupled with another vehicle or parts of motor vehicles together to form one vehicle shall be attached with U-bolts meeting the requirements of paragraph (j)(2) of this section.

(2) **Rear axle attachment.** The rear axle of one vehicle shall be coupled to the frame of the other vehicle by means of a connecting device which when in place forms a rectangle. The device shall be composed of two pieces, top and bottom. The device shall be made of 4-inch by ½-inch steel bar bent to shape and shall have the corners reinforced with a plate at least 3 inches by ½ inch by 8 inches long. The device shall be bolted together with ¾-inch bolts and at least three shall be used on each side. Wood may be used as spacers to keep the frames apart and it shall be at least 4 inches square.

Subpart G—Miscellaneous Parts and Accessories

§393.75 Tires.

(a) No motor vehicle shall be operated on any tire that (1) has body ply or belt material exposed through the tread or sidewall, (2) has any tread or sidewall separation, (3) is flat or has an audible leak, or (4) has a cut to the extent that the ply or belt material is exposed.

(b) Any tire on the front wheels of a bus, truck, or truck tractor shall have a tread groove pattern depth of at least 4/32 of an inch when measured at any point on a major tread groove. The measurements shall not be made where tie bars, humps, or fillets are located.

(c) Except as provided in paragraph (b) of this section, tires shall have a tread groove pattern depth of at least 2/32 of an inch when measured in a major tread groove. The measurement shall not be made where tie bars, humps or fillets are located.

(d) No bus shall be operated with regrooved, recapped or retreaded tires on the front wheels.

(e) A regrooved tire with a load-carrying capacity equal to or greater than 2,232 kg (4,920 pounds) shall not be used on the front wheels of any truck or truck tractor.

(f) No motor vehicle may be operated with speed-restricted tires labeled with a maximum speed of 55 mph or less in accordance with S6.5(e) of FMVSS No. 119 at speeds that exceed the rated limit of the tire.

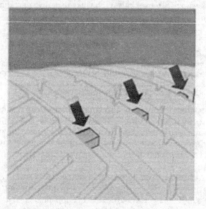

Figure 23—Location of tread wear indicators or wear bars signifying a major tread groove

(g) **Tire loading restrictions (except on manufactured homes)**. No motor vehicle (except manufactured homes, which are governed by paragraph (h) of this section) shall be operated with tires that carry a weight greater than that marked on the side-wall of the tire or, in the absence of such a marking, a weight greater than that specified for the tires in any of the publications of any of the organizations listed in Federal Motor Vehicle Safety Standard No. 119 (49 CFR 571.119, S5.1(b)) unless:

(1) The vehicle is being operated under the terms of a special permit issued by the State; and

(2) The vehicle is being operated at a reduced speed to compensate for the tire loading in excess of the manufacturer's rated capacity for the tire. In no case shall the speed exceed 80 km/hr (50 mph).

(h)(1) **Tire loading restrictions for manufactured homes built before January 1, 2002.** Manufactured homes that are labeled pursuant to 24 CFR 3282.362(c)(2)(i) before January 1, 2002, must not be transported on tires that are loaded more than 18 percent over the load rating marked on the sidewall of the tire or, in the absence of such a marking, more than 18 percent over the load rating specified in any of the publications of any of the organizations listed in FMVSS No. 119 (49 CFR 571.119, S5.1(b)). Manufactured homes labeled before January 1, 2002, transported on tires overloaded by 9 percent or more must not be operated at speeds exceeding 80 km/hr (50 mph).

(2) **Tire loading restrictions for manufactured homes built on or after January 1, 2002.** Manufactured homes that are labeled pursuant to 24 CFR 3282.362(c)(2)(i) on or after January 1, 2002, must not be transported on tires loaded beyond the load rating marked on the sidewall of the tire or, in the absence of such a marking, the load rating specified in any of the publications of any of the organizations listed in FMVSS No. 119 (49 CFR 571.119, S5.1(b)).

(i) **Tire inflation pressure.** (1) No motor vehicle shall be operated on a tire which has a cold inflation pressure less than that specified for the load being carried.

(2) If the inflation pressure of the tire has been increased by heat because of the recent operation of the vehicle, the cold inflation pressure shall be estimated by subtracting the inflation buildup factor shown in Table 1 from the measured inflation pressure.

Table 1—inflation pressure measurement correction for heat

Average speed of vehicle in the previous hour	Minimum inflation pressure buildup	
	Tires with 1,814 kg (4,000 lbs.) maximum load rating or less	Tires with over 1,814 kg (4,000 lbs.) load rating
66–88.5 km/hr (41–55 mph)	34.5 kPa (5 psi)	103.4 kPa (15 psi).

§393.76 Sleeper berths.

(a) **Dimensions**—(1) **Size.** A sleeper berth must be at least the following size:

Date of installation on motor vehicle	Length measured on centerline of longitudinal axis (inches)	Width measured on centerline of transverse axis (inches)	Height measured from highest point of top of mattress (inches)[1]
Before January 1, 1953	72	18	18
After December 31, 1952, and before October 1, 1975....................	75	21	21
After September 30, 1975	75	24	24

[1]In the case of a sleeper berth which utilizes an adjustable mechanical suspension system, the required clearance can be measured when the suspension system is adjusted to the height to which it would settle when occupied by a driver.

(2) **Shape.** A sleeper berth installed on a motor vehicle on or after January 1, 1953 must be of generally rectangular shape, except that the horizontal corners and the roof corners may be rounded to radii not exceeding 10-½ inches.

(3) **Access.** A sleeper berth must be constructed so that an occupant's ready entrance to, and exit from, the sleeper berth is not unduly hindered.

(b) **Location.** (1) A sleeper berth must not be installed in or on a semitrailer or a full trailer other than a house trailer.

(2) A sleeper berth located within the cargo space of a motor vehicle must be securely compartmentalized from the remainder of the cargo space. A sleeper berth installed on or after January 1, 1953 must be located in the cab or immediately adjacent to the cab and must be securely fixed with relation to the cab.

(c) **Exit from the berth.** (1) Except as provided in paragraph (c)(2) of this section, there must be a direct and ready means of exit from a sleeper berth into the driver's seat or compartment. If the sleeper berth was installed on or after January 1, 1963, the exit must be a doorway or opening at least 18 inches high and 36 inches wide. If the sleeper berth was installed before January 1, 1963, the exit must have sufficient area to contain an ellipse having a major axis of 24 inches and a minor axis of 16 inches.

(2) A sleeper berth installed before January 1, 1953 must either:

(i) Conform to the requirements of paragraph (c)(1) of this section; or

(ii) Have at least two exits, each of which is at least 18 inches high and 21 inches wide, located at opposite ends of the vehicle and useable by the occupant without the assistance of any other person.

(d) **Communication with the driver.** A sleeper berth which is not located within the driver's compartment and has no direct entrance into the driver's compartment must be equipped with a means of communication between the occupant and the driver. The means of communication may consist of a telephone, speaker tube, buzzer, pull cord, or other mechanical or electrical device.

(e) **Equipment.** A sleeper berth must be properly equipped for sleeping. Its equipment must include:

(1) Adequate bedclothing and blankets; and

(2) Either:

(i) Springs and a mattress; or

(ii) An innerspring mattress; or

(iii) A cellular rubber or flexible foam mattress at least four inches thick; or

(iv) A mattress filled with a fluid and of sufficient thickness when filled to prevent "bottoming-out" when occupied while the vehicle is in motion.

(f) **Ventilation.** A sleeper berth must have louvers or other means of providing adequate ventilation. A sleeper berth must be reasonably tight against dust and rain.

(g) **Protection against exhaust and fuel leaks and exhaust heat.** A sleeper berth must be located so that leaks in the vehicle's exhaust system or fuel system do not permit fuel, fuel system gases, or exhaust gases to enter the sleeper berth. A sleeper berth must be located so that it will not be overheated or damaged by reason of its proximity to the vehicle's exhaust system.

(h) **Occupant restraint.** A motor vehicle manufactured on or after July 1, 1971, and equipped with a sleeper berth must be equipped with a means of preventing ejection of the occupant of the sleeper berth during deceleration of the vehicle. The restraint system must be designed, installed, and maintained to withstand a minimum total force of 6,000 pounds applied toward the front of the vehicle and parallel to the longitudinal axis of the vehicle.

§393.77 Heaters.

On every motor vehicle, every heater shall comply with the following requirements:

(a) **Prohibited types of heaters**. The installation or use of the following types of heaters is prohibited:

(1) **Exhaust heaters.** Any type of exhaust heater in which the engine exhaust gases are conducted into or through any space occupied by persons or any heater which conducts engine compartment air into any such space.

(2) **Unenclosed flame heaters.** Any type of heater employing a flame which is not fully enclosed, except that such heaters are not prohibited when used for heating the cargo of tank motor vehicles.

(3) **Heaters permitting fuel leakage.** Any type of heater from the burner of which there could be spillage or leakage of fuel upon the tilting or overturning of the vehicle in which it is mounted.

(4) **Heaters permitting air contamination.** Any heater taking air, heated or to be heated, from the engine compartment or from direct contact with any portion of the exhaust system; or any heater taking air in ducts from the outside atmosphere to be conveyed through the engine compartment, unless said ducts are so constructed and installed as to prevent contamination of the air so conveyed by exhaust or engine compartment gases.

(5) **Solid fuel heaters except wood charcoal.** Any stove or other heater employing solid fuel except wood charcoal.

(6) **Portable heaters.** Portable heaters shall not be used in any space occupied by persons except the cargo space of motor vehicles which are being loaded or unloaded.

(b) **Heater specifications**. All heaters shall comply with the following specifications:

(1) **Heating elements, protection.** Every heater shall be so located or protected as to prevent contact therewith by occupants, unless the surface temperature of the protecting grilles or of any exposed portions of the heaters, inclusive of exhaust stacks, pipes, or conduits shall be lower than would cause contact burns. Adequate protection shall be afforded against igniting parts of the vehicle or burning occupants by direct radiation. Wood charcoal heaters shall be enclosed within a metal barrel, drum, or similar protective enclosure which enclosure shall be provided with a securely fastened cover.

(2) **Moving parts, guards.** Effective guards shall be provided for the protection of passengers or occupants against injury by fans, belts, or any other moving parts.

(3) **Heaters, secured.** Every heater and every heater enclosure shall be securely fastened to the vehicle in a substantial manner so as to provide against relative motion within the vehicle during normal usage or in the event the vehicle overturns. Every heater shall be so designed, constructed, and mounted as to minimize the likelihood of disassembly of any of its parts, including exhaust stacks, pipes, or conduits, upon overturn of the vehicle in or on which it is mounted. Wood charcoal heaters shall be secured against relative motion within the enclosure required by paragraph (c)(1) of this section, and the enclosure shall be securely fastened to the motor vehicle.

(4) **Relative motion between fuel tank and heater.** When either in normal operation or in the event of overturn, there is or is likely to be relative motion between the fuel tank for a heater and the heater, or between either of such units

and the fuel lines between them, a suitable means shall be provided at the point of greatest relative motion so as to allow this motion without causing failure of the fuel lines.

(5) **Operating controls to be protected.** On every bus designed to transport more than 15 passengers, including the driver, means shall be provided to prevent unauthorized persons from tampering with the operating controls. Such means may include remote control by the driver; installation of controls at inaccessible places; control of adjustments by key or keys; enclosure of controls in a locked space, locking of controls, or other means of accomplishing this purpose.

(6) **Heater, hoses.** Hoses for all hot water and steam heater systems shall be specifically designed and constructed for that purpose.

(7) **Electrical apparatus.** Every heater employing any electrical apparatus shall be equipped with electrical conductors, switches, connectors, and other electrical parts of ample current-carrying capacity to provide against overheating; any electric motor employed in any heater shall be of adequate size and so located that it will not be overheated; electrical circuits shall be provided with fuses and/or circuit breakers to provide against electrical overloading; and all electrical conductors employed in or leading to any heater shall be secured against dangling, chafing, and rubbing and shall have suitable protection against any other condition likely to produce short or open circuits.

NOTE: Electrical parts certified as proper for use by Underwriters' Laboratories, Inc., shall be deemed to comply with the foregoing requirements.

(8) **Storage battery caps.** If a separate storage battery is located within the personnel or cargo space, such battery shall be securely mounted and equipped with nonspill filler caps.

(9) **Combustion heater exhaust construction.** Every heater employing the combustion of oil, gas, liquefied petroleum gas, or any other combustible material shall be provided with substantial means of conducting the products of combustion to the outside of the vehicle: Provided, however, That this requirement shall not apply to heaters used solely to heat the cargo space of motor vehicles where such motor vehicles or heaters are equipped with means specifically designed and maintained so that the carbon monoxide concentration will never exceed 0.2 percent in the cargo space. The exhaust pipe, stack, or conduit if required shall be sufficiently substantial and so secured as to provide reasonable assurance against leakage or discharge of products of combustion within the vehicle and, if necessary, shall be so insulated as to make unlikely the burning or charring of parts of the vehicle by radiation or by direct contact. The place of discharge of the products of combustion to the atmosphere and the means of discharge of such products shall be such as to minimize the likelihood of their reentry into the vehicle under all operating conditions.

(10) **Combustion chamber construction.** The design and construction of any combustion-type heater except cargo space heaters permitted by the proviso of paragraph (c)(9) of this section and unenclosed flame heaters used for heating cargo of tank motor vehicles shall be such as to provide against the leakage of products of combustion into air to be heated and circulated. The material employed in combustion chambers shall be such as to provide against leakage because of corrosion, oxidation or other deterioration. Joints between combustion chambers and the air chambers with which they are in thermal and mechanical contact shall be so designed and constructed as to prevent leakage between the

chambers and the materials employed in such joints shall have melting points substantially higher than the maximum temperatures likely to be attained at the points of jointure.

(11) **Heater fuel tank location.** Every bus designed to transport more than 15 passengers, including the driver, with heaters of the combustion type shall have fuel tanks therefor located outside of and lower than the passenger space. When necessary, suitable protection shall be afforded by shielding or other means against the puncturing of any such tank or its connections by flying stones or other objects.

(12) **Heater, automatic fuel control.** Gravity or siphon feed shall not be permitted for heaters using liquid fuels. Heaters using liquid fuels shall be equipped with automatic means for shutting off the fuel or for reducing such flow of fuel to the smallest practicable magnitude, in the event of overturn of the vehicle. Heaters using liquefied petroleum gas as fuel shall have the fuel line equipped with automatic means at the source of supply for shutting off the fuel in the event of separation, breakage, or disconnection of any of the fuel lines between the supply source and the heater.

(13) **"Tell-tale" indicators.** Heaters subject to paragraph (b)(14) of this section and not provided with automatic controls shall be provided with "tell-tale" means to indicate to the driver that the heater is properly functioning. The requirement shall not apply to heaters used solely for the cargo space in semitrailers or full trailers.

(14) **Shut-off control.** Automatic means, or manual means if the control is readily accessible to the driver without moving from the driver's seat, shall be provided to shut off the fuel and electrical supply in case of failure of the heater to function for any reason, or in case the heater should function improperly or overheat. This requirement shall not apply to wood charcoal heaters or to heaters used solely to heat the contents of cargo tank motor vehicles, but wood charcoal heaters must be provided with a controlled method of regulating the flow of combustion air.

(15) **Certification required.** Every combustion-type heater, except wood charcoal heaters, the date of manufacture of which is subsequent to December 31, 1952, and every wood charcoal heater, the date of manufacture of which is subsequent to September 1, 1953, shall be marked plainly to indicate the type of service for which such heater is designed and with a certification by the manufacturer that the heater meets the applicable requirements for such use. For example, "Meets I.C.C. Bus Heater Requirements," "Meets I.C.C. Flue-Vented Cargo Space Heater Requirements," and after December 31, 1967, such certification shall read "Meets FMCSA Bus Heater Requirements," "Meets FMCSA Flue-Vented Cargo Space Heater Requirements," etc.

(c) **Exception.** The certification for a catalytic heater which is used in transporting flammable liquid or gas shall be as prescribed under §177.834(l) of this title.

§393.78 Windshield wiping and washing systems.

(a) **Vehicles manufactured on or after December 25, 1968.** Each bus, truck, and truck-tractor manufactured on or after December 25, 1968, must have a windshield wiping system that meets the requirements of FMVSS No. 104 (S4.1) in effect on the date of manufacture. Each of these vehicles must have a windshield washing system that meets the requirements of FMVSS No. 104 (S4.2.2) in effect on the date of manufacture.

(b) **Vehicles manufactured between June 30, 1953, and December 24, 1968**. Each truck, truck-tractor, and bus manufactured between June 30, 1953, and December 24, 1968, shall be equipped with a power-driven windshield wiping system with at least two wiper blades, one on each side of the centerline of the windshield. Motor vehicles which depend upon vacuum to operate the windshield wipers, shall have the wiper system constructed and maintained such that the performance of the wipers will not be adversely affected by a change in the intake manifold pressure.

(c) **Driveaway-towaway operations**. Windshield wiping and washing systems need not be in working condition while a commercial motor vehicle is being towed in a driveaway-tow-away operation.

§393.79 Windshield defrosting and defogging systems.

(a) **Vehicles manufactured on or after December 25, 1968**. Each bus, truck, and truck-tractor manufactured on or after December 25, 1968, must have a windshield defrosting and defogging system that meets the requirements of FMVSS No. 103 in effect on the date of manufacture.

(b) **Vehicles manufactured before December 25, 1968**. Each bus, truck, and truck-tractor shall be equipped with a means for preventing the accumulation of ice, snow, frost, or condensation that could obstruct the driver's view through the windshield while the vehicle is being driven.

§393.80 Rear-vision mirrors.

(a) Every bus, truck, and truck tractor shall be equipped with two rear-vision mirrors, one at each side, firmly attached to the outside of the motor vehicle, and so located as to reflect to the driver a view of the highway to the rear, along both sides of the vehicle. All such regulated rear-vision mirrors and their replacements shall meet, as a minimum, the requirements of FMVSS No. 111 (49 CFR 571.111) in force at the time the vehicle was manufactured.

(b) **Exceptions**. (1) Mirrors installed on a vehicle manufactured prior to January 1, 1981, may be continued in service, provided that if the mirrors are replaced they shall be replaced with mirrors meeting, as a minimum, the requirements of FMVSS No. 111 (49 CFR 571.111) in force at the time the vehicle was manufactured.

(2) Only one outside mirror shall be required, which shall be on the driver's side, on trucks which are so constructed that the driver has a view to the rear by means of an interior mirror.

(3) In driveaway-towaway operations, the driven vehicle shall have at least one mirror furnishing a clear view to the rear.

§393.81 Horn.

Every bus, truck, truck tractor, and every driven motor vehicle in driveaway-towaway operations shall be equipped with a horn and actuating elements which shall be in such condition as to give an adequate and reliable warning signal.

§393.82 Speedometer.

Each bus, truck, and truck-tractor must be equipped with a speedometer indicating vehicle speed in miles per hour and/or kilometers per hour. The speedometer must be accurate to within plus or minus 8 km/hr (5 mph) at a speed of 80 km/hr (50 mph).

§393.83 Exhaust systems.

(a) Every motor vehicle having a device (other than as part of its cargo) capable of expelling harmful combustion fumes shall have a system to direct the discharge of such fumes. No part shall be located where its location would likely result in burning, charring, or damaging the electrical wiring, the fuel supply, or any combustible part of the motor vehicle.

(b) No exhaust system shall discharge to the atmosphere at a location immediately below the fuel tank or the fuel tank filler pipe.

(c) The exhaust system of a bus powered by a gasoline engine shall discharge to the atmosphere at or within 6 inches forward of the rearmost part of the bus.

(d) The exhaust system of a bus using fuels other than gasoline shall discharge to the atmosphere either:

(1) At or within 15 inches forward of the rearmost part of the vehicle; or

(2) To the rear of all doors or windows designed to be open, except windows designed to be opened solely as emergency exits.

(e) The exhaust system of every truck and truck tractor shall discharge to the atmosphere at a location to the rear of the cab or, if the exhaust projects above the cab, at a location near the rear of the cab.

(f) No part of the exhaust system shall be temporarily repaired with wrap or patches.

(g) No part of the exhaust system shall leak or discharge at a point forward of or directly below the driver/sleeper compartment. The exhaust outlet may discharge above the cab/sleeper roofline.

(h) The exhaust system must be securely fastened to the vehicle.

(i) Exhaust systems may use hangers which permit required movement due to expansion and contraction caused by heat of the exhaust and relative motion between engine and chassis of a vehicle.

§393.84 Floors.

The flooring in all motor vehicles shall be substantially constructed, free of unnecessary holes and openings, and shall be maintained so as to minimize the entrance of fumes, exhaust gases, or fire. Floors shall not be permeated with oil or other substances likely to cause injury to persons using the floor as a traction surface.

§393.85 [Reserved]

§393.86 Rear impact guards and rear end protection.

(a)(1) **General requirements for trailers and semitrailers manufactured on or after January 26, 1998**. Each trailer and semitrailer with a gross vehicle weight rating of 4,536 kg (10,000 pounds) or more, and manufactured on or after January 26, 1998, must be equipped with a rear impact guard that meets the requirements of Federal Motor Vehicle Safety Standard No. 223 (49 CFR 571.223) in effect at the time the vehicle was manufactured. When the rear impact guard is installed on the trailer or semitrailer, the vehicle must, at a minimum, meet the requirements of FMVSS No. 224 (49 CFR 571.224) in effect at the time the vehicle was manufactured. The requirements of paragraph (a) of this section do not apply to pole trailers (as defined in §390.5 of this chapter); pulpwood trailers, low chassis vehicles, special purpose vehicles, wheels back vehicles, and road construction controlled horizontal discharge trailers (as defined in §393.5); and trailers towed in driveaway-towaway operations (as defined in §390.5).

(2) **Impact Guard Width.** The outermost surfaces of the horizontal member of the guard must extend to within 100 mm (4 inches) of the side extremities of the vehicle. The outermost surface of the horizontal member shall not extend beyond the side extremity of the vehicle.

(3) **Guard Height.** The vertical distance between the bottom edge of the horizontal member of the guard and the ground shall not exceed 560 mm (22 inches) at any point across the full width of the member. Guards with rounded corners may curve upward within 255 mm (10 inches) of the longitudinal vertical planes that are tangent to the side extremities of the vehicle.

(4) **Guard Rear Surface.** At any height 560 mm (22 inches) or more above the ground, the rearmost surface of the horizontal member of the guard must be within 305 mm (12 inches) of the rear extremity of the vehicle. This paragraph shall not be construed to prohibit the rear surface of the guard from extending beyond the rear extremity of the vehicle. Guards with rounded corners may curve forward within 255 mm (10 inches) of the side extremity.

(5) **Cross-Sectional Vertical Height.** The horizontal member of each guard must have a cross sectional vertical height of at least 100 mm (3.94 inches) at any point across the guard width.

(6) **Certification and labeling requirements for rear impact protection guards.** Each rear impact guard used to satisfy the requirements of paragraph (a)(1) of this section must be permanently marked or labeled as required by FMVSS No. 223 (49 CFR 571.223, S5.3). The label shall be placed on the forward or rearward facing surface of the horizontal member of the guard, provided that the label does not interfere with the retroreflective sheeting required by S5.7.1.4.1(c) of FMVSS No. 108 (49 CFR 571.108), and is readily accessible for visual inspection. The certification label must contain the following information:

(i) The impact guard manufacturer's name and address;

(ii) The statement "Manufactured in _____" (inserting the month and a year that the guard was manufactured); and,

(iii) The letters "DOT", constituting a certification by the guard manufacturer that the guard conforms to all requirements of FMVSS No. 223.

(b)(1) **Requirements for motor vehicles manufactured after December 31, 1952 (except trailers or semitrailers manufactured on or after January 26, 1998).** Each motor vehicle manufactured after December 31, 1952, (except truck tractors, pole trailers, pulpwood trailers, road construction controlled horizontal discharge trailers, or vehicles in driveaway-towaway operations) in which the vertical distance between the rear bottom edge of the body (or the chassis assembly if the chassis is the rearmost part of the vehicle) and the ground is greater than 76.2 cm (30 inches) when the motor vehicle is empty, shall be equipped with a rear impact guard(s). The rear impact guard(s) must be installed and maintained in such a manner that:

(i) The vertical distance between the bottom of the guard(s) and the ground does not exceed 76.2 cm (30 inches) when the motor vehicle is empty;

(ii) The maximum lateral distance between the closest points between guards, if more than one is used, does not exceed 61 cm (24 inches);

(iii) The outermost surfaces of the horizontal member of the guard are no more than 45.7 cm (18 inches) from each side extremity of the motor vehicle;

(iv) The impact guard(s) are no more than 61 cm (24 inches) forward of the rear extremity of the motor vehicle.

(2) **Construction and Attachment.** The rear impact guard(s) must be substantially constructed and attached by means of bolts, welding, or other comparable means.

(3) **Vehicle Components and Structures that may be used to satisfy the requirements of paragraph (b) of this section.** Low chassis vehicles, special purpose vehicles, or wheels back vehicles constructed and maintained so that the body, chassis, or other parts of the vehicle provide the rear end protection comparable to impact guard(s) conforming to the requirements of paragraph (b)(1) of this section shall be considered to be in compliance with those requirements.

§393.87 Warning flags on projecting loads.

(a) Any commercial motor vehicle transporting a load which extends beyond the sides by more than 102 mm (4 inches) or more than 1,219 mm (4 feet) beyond the rear must have the extremities of the load marked with red or orange fluorescent warning flags. Each warning flag must be at least 457 mm (18 inches) square.

(b) **Position of flags**. There must be a single flag at the extreme rear if the projecting load is two feet wide or less. Two warning flags are required if the projecting load is wider than two feet. Flags must be located to indicate maximum width of loads which extend beyond the sides and/or rear of the vehicle.

§393.88 Television receivers.

Any motor vehicle equipped with a television viewer, screen or other means of visually receiving a television broadcast shall have the viewer or screen located in the motor vehicle at a point to the rear of the back of the driver's seat if such viewer or screen is in the same compartment as the driver and the viewer or screen shall be so located as not to be visible to the driver, while he/she is driving the motor vehicle. The operating controls for the television receiver shall be so located that the driver cannot operate them without leaving the driver's seat.

§393.89 Buses, driveshaft protection.

Any driveshaft extending lengthways under the floor of the passenger compartment of a bus, shall be protected by means of at least one guard or bracket at that end of the shaft which is provided with a sliding connection (spline or other such device) to prevent the whipping of the shaft in the event of failure thereof or of any of its component parts. A shaft contained within a torque tube shall not require any such device.

§393.90 Buses, standee line or bar.

Except as provided below, every bus which is designed and constructed so as to allow standees, shall be plainly marked with a line of contrasting color at least 2 inches wide or equipped with some other means so as to indicate to any person that he/she is prohibited from occupying a space forward of a perpendicular plane drawn through the rear of the driver's seat and perpendicular to the longitudinal axis of the bus. Every bus shall have clearly posted at or near the front, a sign with letters at least one-half inch high stating that it is a violation of the Federal Motor Carrier Safety Administration's regulations for a bus to be operated with persons occupying the prohibited area. The requirements of this section shall not apply to any bus being transported in driveaway-towaway operation or to any level of the bus other than that level in which the driver is located nor shall they be construed to prohibit any seated person from occupying permanent seats located in the prohibited area provided such seats are so located that persons sitting therein will not interfere with the driver's safe operation of the bus.

§393.91 Buses, aisle seats prohibited.

No bus shall be equipped with aisle seats unless such seats are so designed and installed as to automatically fold and leave a clear aisle when they are unoccupied. No bus shall be operated if any seat therein is not securely fastened to the vehicle.

§393.92 [Reserved]

§393.93 Seats, seat belt assemblies, and seat belt assembly anchorages.

(a) **Buses**— (1) **Buses manufactured on or after January 1, 1965, and before July 1, 1971.** After June 30, 1972, every bus manufactured on or after January 1, 1965, and before July 1, 1971, must be equipped with a Type 1 or Type 2 seat belt assembly that conforms to Federal Motor Vehicle Safety Standard No. 209[1] (§571.209) installed at the driver's seat and seat belt assembly anchorages that conform to the location and geometric requirements of Federal Motor Vehicle Safety Standard No. 210[1] (§571.210) for that seat belt assembly.

(2) **Buses manufactured on or after July 1, 1971.** Every bus manufactured on or after July 1, 1971, must conform to the requirements of Federal Motor Vehicle Safety Standard No. 208[1] (§571.208) (relating to installation of seat belt assemblies) and Federal Motor Vehicle Safety Standard No. 210[1] (§571.210) (relating to installation of seat belt assembly anchorages).

(3) **Buses manufactured on or after January 1, 1972.** Every bus manufactured on or after January 1, 1972, must conform to the requirements of Federal Motor Vehicle Safety Standard No. 207[1] (§571.207) (relating to seating systems).

(b) **Trucks and truck tractors**. (1) **Trucks and truck tractors manufactured on and after January 1, 1965, and before July 1, 1971.** Except as provided in paragraph (d) of this section, after June 30, 1972, every truck and truck tractor manufactured on or after January 1, 1965, and before July 1, 1971, must be equipped with a Type 1 or Type 2 seat belt assembly that conforms to Federal Motor Vehicle Safety Standard No. 209 (§571.209) installed at the driver's seat and at the right front outboard seat, if the vehicle has one, and seat belt assembly anchorages that conform to the location and geometric requirements of Federal Motor Vehicle Safety Standard No. 210 (§571.210) for each seat belt assembly that is required by this subparagraph.

(2) **Trucks and truck tractors manufactured on or after July 1, 1971.** Every truck and truck tractor manufactured on or after July 1, 1971, except a truck or truck tractor being transported in driveaway-towaway operation and having an incomplete vehicle seating and cab configuration, must conform to the requirements of Federal Motor Vehicle Safety Standard No. 208[1] (§571.208) (relating to installation of seat belt assemblies) and Federal Motor Vehicle Safety Standard No. 210[1] (§571.210) (relating to installation of seat belt assembly anchorages).

(3) **Trucks and truck tractors manufactured on or after January 1, 1972.** Every truck and truck tractor manufactured on or after January 1, 1972,

---

[1]Individual copies of Federal Motor Vehicle Safety Standards may be obtained from the National Highway Traffic Safety Administration, 1200 New Jersey Ave., SE., Washington, DC 20590-0001.

except a truck or truck tractor being transported in driveaway-towaway operation and having an incomplete vehicle seating and cab configuration, must conform to the requirements of Federal Motor Vehicle Safety Standard No. 207 [1](§571.207) (relating to seating systems).

(c) **Effective date of standards**. Whenever paragraph (a) or (b) of this section requires conformity to a Federal Motor Vehicle Safety Standard, the vehicle or equipment must conform to the version of the Standard that is in effect on the date the vehicle is manufactured or on the date the vehicle is modified to conform to the requirements of paragraph (a) or (b) of this section, whichever is later.

(d) Trucks and truck tractors manufactured on or after January 1, 1965, and before July 1, 1971, and operated in the State of Hawaii, must comply with the provisions of paragraph (b) of this section on and after January 1, 1976.

§393.94 Interior noise levels in power units.

(a) **Applicability of this section**. The interior noise level requirements apply to all trucks, truck-tractors, and buses.

(b) **General rule**. The interior sound level at the driver's seating position of a motor vehicle must not exceed 90 dB(A) when measured in accordance with paragraph (c) of this section.

(c) **Test procedure**. (1) Park the vehicle at a location so that no large reflecting surfaces, such as other vehicles, signboards, buildings, or hills, are within 50 feet of the driver's seating position.

(2) Close all vehicle doors, windows, and vents. Turn off all power-operated accessories.

(3) Place the driver in his/her normal seated position at the vehicle's controls. Evacuate all occupants except the driver and the person conducting the test.

(4) The sound level meters used to determine compliance with the requirements of this section must meet the American National Standards Institute *"Specification for Sound Level Meters,"* ANSI S1.4-1983. (See §393.7(b) for information on the incorporation by reference and availability of this document.)

(5) Locate the microphone, oriented vertically upward, 6 inches to the right of, in the same plane as, and directly in line with, the driver's right ear.

(6) With the vehicle's transmission in neutral gear, accelerate its engine to either its maximum governed engine speed, if it is equipped with an engine governor, or its speed at its maximum rated horsepower, if it is not equipped with an engine governor. Stabilize the engine at that speed.

(7) Observe the A-weighted sound level reading on the meter for the stabilized engine speed condition. Record that reading, if the reading has not been influenced by extraneous noise sources such as motor vehicles operating on adjacent roadways.

(8) Return the vehicle's engine speed to idle and repeat the procedure specified in paragraphs (c)(6) and (7) of this section until two maximum sound levels within 2 dB of each other are recorded. Numerically average those two maximum sound level readings.

(9) The average obtained in accordance with paragraph (c)(8) of this section is the vehicle's interior sound level at the driver's seating position for the purpose of determining whether the vehicle conforms to the rule in paragraph (b) of this section. However, a 2dB tolerance over the sound level limitation specified in that paragraph is permitted to allow for variations in test conditions and variations in the capabilities of meters.

(10) If the motor vehicle's engine radiator fan drive is equipped with a clutch or similar device that automatically either reduces the rotational speed of the fan or completely disengages the fan from its power source in response to reduced engine cooling loads the vehicle may be parked before testing with its engine running at high idle or any other speed the operator may choose, for sufficient time but not more than 10 minutes, to permit the engine radiator fan to automatically disengage.

Subpart H—Emergency Equipment

§393.95 Emergency equipment on all power units.

Each truck, truck tractor, and bus (except those towed in driveaway-towaway operations) must be equipped as follows:

(a) **Fire Extinguishers**

(1) **Minimum ratings:**

(i) A power unit that is used to transport hazardous materials in a quantity that requires placarding (See §177.823 of this title) must be equipped with a fire extinguisher having an Underwriters' Laboratories rating of 10 B:C or more.

(ii) A power unit that is not used to transport hazardous materials must be equipped with either:

(A) A fire extinguisher having an Underwriters' Laboratories rating of 5 B:C or more; or

(B) Two fire extinguishers, each of which has an Underwriters' Laboratories rating of 4 B:C or more.

(2) **Labeling and marking.** Each fire extinguisher required by this section must be labeled or marked by the manufacturer with its Underwriters' Laboratories rating.

(3) **Visual Indicators.** The fire extinguisher must be designed, constructed, and maintained to permit visual determination of whether it is fully charged.

(4) **Condition, location, and mounting.** The fire extinguisher(s) must be filled and located so that it is readily accessible for use. The extinguisher(s) must be securely mounted to prevent sliding, rolling, or vertical movement relative to the motor vehicle.

(5) **Extinguishing agents.** The fire extinguisher must use an extinguishing agent that does not need protection from freezing. Extinguishing agents must comply with the toxicity provisions of the Environmental Protection Agency's Significant New Alternatives Policy (SNAP) regulations under 40 CFR Part 82, Subpart G.

(6) **Exception.** This paragraph (a) does not apply to the driven unit in a driveaway-towaway operation.

(b) **Spare fuses.** Power units for which fuses are needed to operate any required parts and accessories must have at least one spare fuse for each type/size of fuse needed for those parts and accessories.

(c)–(e) [Reserved]

(f) **Warning devices for stopped vehicles**. Except as provided in paragraph (g) of this section, one of the following options must be used:

(1) Three bidirectional emergency reflective triangles that conform to the requirements of Federal Motor Vehicle Safety Standard No. 125, §571.125 of this title; or

(2) At least 6 fusees or 3 liquid-burning flares. The vehicle must have as many additional fusees or liquid-burning flares as are necessary to satisfy the requirements of §392.22.

(3) Other warning devices may be used in addition to, but not in lieu of, the required warning devices, provided those warning devices do not decrease the effectiveness of the required warning devices.

(g) **Restrictions on the use of flame-producing devices**. Liquid-burning flares, fusees, oil lanterns, or any signal produced by a flame shall not be carried on any commercial motor vehicle transporting Division 1.1, 1.2, 1.3 (explosives) hazardous materials; any cargo tank motor vehicle used for the transportation of Division 2.1 (flammable gas) or Class 3 (flammable liquid) hazardous materials whether loaded or empty; or any commercial motor vehicle using compressed gas as a motor fuel.

(h)–(i) [Reserved]

(j) **Requirements for fusees and liquid-burning flares**. Each fusee shall be capable of burning for 30 minutes, and each liquid-burning flare shall contain enough fuel to burn continuously for at least 60 minutes. Fusees and liquid-burning flares shall conform to the requirements of Underwriters Laboratories, Inc., UL No. 912, Highway Emergency Signals, Fourth Edition, July 30, 1979, (with an amendment dated November 9, 1981). (See §393.7 for information on the incorporation by reference and availability of this document.) Each fusee and liquid-burning flare shall be marked with the UL symbol in accordance with the requirements of UL 912.

(k) **Requirements for red flags**. Red flags shall be not less than 12 inches square, with standards adequate to maintain the flags in an upright position.

Subpart I—Protection Against Shifting and Falling Cargo

§393.100 Which types of commercial motor vehicles are subject to the cargo securement standards of this subpart, and what general requirements apply?

(a) **Applicability**. The rules in this subpart are applicable to trucks, truck tractors, semitrailers, full trailers, and pole trailers.

(b) **Prevention against loss of load**. Each commercial motor vehicle must, when transporting cargo on public roads, be loaded and equipped, and the cargo secured, in accordance with this subpart to prevent the cargo from leaking, spilling, blowing or falling from the motor vehicle.

(c) **Prevention against shifting of load**. Cargo must be contained, immobilized or secured in accordance with this subpart to prevent shifting upon or within the vehicle to such an extent that the vehicle's stability or maneuverability is adversely affected.

§393.102 What are the minimum performance criteria for cargo securement devices and systems?

(a) **Performance criteria—(1) Breaking Strength.** Tiedown assemblies (including chains, wire rope, steel strapping, synthetic webbing, and cordage) and other attachment or fastening devices used to secure articles of cargo to, or in, commercial motor vehicles must be designed, installed, and maintained to ensure that the maximum forces acting on the devices or systems do not exceed the manufacturer's breaking strength rating under the following conditions, applied separately:

(i) 0.8 g deceleration in the forward direction;

(ii) 0.5 g acceleration in the rearward direction; and

(iii) 0.5 g acceleration in a lateral direction.

(2) **Working Load Limit.** Tiedown assemblies (including chains, wire rope, steel strapping, synthetic webbing, and cordage) and other attachment or fastening devices used to secure articles of cargo to, or in, commercial motor vehicles must be designed, installed, and maintained to ensure that the forces acting on the devices or systems do not exceed the working load limit for the devices under the following conditions, applied separately:

(i) 0.435 g deceleration in the forward direction;

(ii) 0.5 g acceleration in the rearward direction; and

(iii) 0.25 g acceleration in a lateral direction.

(b) **Performance criteria for devices to prevent vertical movement of loads that are not contained within the structure of the vehicle**. Securement systems must provide a downward force equivalent to at least 20 percent of the weight of the article of cargo if the article is not fully contained within the structure of the vehicle. If the article is fully contained within the structure of the vehicle, it may be secured in accordance with §393.106(b).

(c) **Equivalent means of securement**. The means of securing articles of cargo are considered to meet the performance requirements of this section if the cargo is:

(1) Immobilized, such so that it cannot shift or tip to the extent that the vehicle's stability or maneuverability is adversely affected; or

(2) Transported in a sided vehicle that has walls of adequate strength, such that each article of cargo within the vehicle is in contact with, or sufficiently close to a wall or other articles, so that it cannot shift or tip to the extent that the vehicle's stability or maneuverability is adversely affected; or

(3) Secured in accordance with the applicable requirements of §§393.104 through 393.136.

§393.104 What standards must cargo securement devices and systems meet in order to satisfy the requirements of this subpart?

(a) **General**. All devices and systems used to secure cargo to or within a vehicle must be capable of meeting the requirements of §393.102.

(b) **Prohibition on the use of damaged securement devices**. All tiedowns, cargo securement systems, parts and components used to secure cargo must be in proper working order when used to perform that function with no damaged or weakened components, such as, but not limited to, cracks or cuts that will adversely affect their performance for cargo securement purposes, including reducing the working load limit.

(c) **Vehicle structures and anchor points**. Vehicle structures, floors, walls, decks, tiedown anchor points, headerboards, bulkheads, stakes, posts, and associated mounting pockets used to contain or secure articles of cargo must be strong enough to meet the performance criteria of §393.102, with no damaged or weakened components, such as, but not limited to, cracks or cuts that will adversely affect their performance for cargo securement purposes, including reducing the working load limit.

(d) **Material for dunnage, chocks, cradles, shoring bars, blocking and bracing**. Material used as dunnage or dunnage bags, chocks, cradles, shoring bars, or used for blocking and bracing, must not have damage or defects which would compromise the effectiveness of the securement system.

(e) **Manufacturing standards for tiedown assemblies**. Tie-down assemblies (including chains, wire rope, steel strapping, synthetic webbing, and cordage) and other attachment or fastening devices used to secure articles of cargo to, or in, commercial motor vehicles must conform to the following applicable standards:

An assembly component of...	Must conform to...
(1) Steel strapping [1], [2]	Standard Specification for Strapping, Flat Steel and Seals, American Society for Testing and Materials (ASTM) D3953-97, February 1998. [4]
(2) Chain	National Association of Chain Manufacturers' Welded Steel Chain Specifications, dated September 28, 2005. [4]
(3) Webbing	Web Sling and Tiedown Association's Recommended Standard Specification for Synthetic Web Tiedowns, WSTDA-T1, 1998. [4]
(4) Wire rope [3]	Wire Rope Technical Board's Wire Rope Users Manual, 2nd Edition, November 1985. [4]
(5) Cordage	Cordage Institute rope standard:
	(i) PETRS-2, Polyester Fiber Rope, three-Strand and eight-Strand Constructions, January 1993; [4]
	(ii) PPRS-2, Polypropylene Fiber Rope, three-Strand and eight-Strand Constructions, August 1992; [4]
	(iii) CRS-1, Polyester/Polypropylene Composite Rope Specifications, three-Strand and eight-Strand Standard Construction, May 1979; [4]
	(iv) NRS-1, Nylon Rope Specifications, three-Strand and eight-Strand Standard Construction, May 1979; [4] and
	(v) C-1, Double Braided Nylon Rope Specifications DBN, January 1984. [4]

[1] Steel strapping not marked by the manufacturer with a working load limit will be considered to have a working load limit equal to one-fourth of the breaking strength listed in ASTM D3953-97.

[2] Steel strapping 25.4 mm (1 inch) or wider must have at least two pairs of crimps in each seal and, when an end-over-end lap joint is formed, must be sealed with at least two seals.

[3] Wire rope which is not marked by the manufacturer with a working load limit shall be considered to have a working load limit equal to one-fourth of the nominal strength listed in the manual.

[4] See §393.7 for information on the incorporation by reference and availability of this document.

(f) **Use of tiedowns**. (1) Tiedowns and securing devices must not contain knots.

(2) If a tiedown is repaired, it must be repaired in accordance with the applicable standards in paragraph (e) of this section, or the manufacturer's instructions.

(3) Each tiedown must be attached and secured in a manner that prevents it from becoming loose, unfastening, opening or releasing while the vehicle is in transit.

(4) Edge protection must be used whenever a tiedown would be subject to abrasion or cutting at the point where it touches an article of cargo. The edge protection must resist abrasion, cutting and crushing.

§393.106 What are the general requirements for securing articles of cargo?

(a) **Applicability**. The rules in this section are applicable to the transportation of all types of articles of cargo, except commodities in bulk that lack structure or fixed shape (e.g., liquids, gases, grain, liquid concrete, sand, gravel, aggregates) and are transported in a tank, hopper, box, or similar device that forms part of the structure of a commercial motor vehicle. The rules in this section apply to the cargo types covered by the commodity-specific rules of §393.116 through §393.136. The commodity-specific rules take precedence over the general requirements of this section when additional requirements are given for a commodity listed in those sections.

(b) **General**. Cargo must be firmly immobilized or secured on or within a vehicle by structures of adequate strength, dunnage or dunnage bags, shoring bars, tiedowns or a combination of these.

(c) **Cargo placement and restraint**. (1) Articles of cargo that are likely to roll must be restrained by chocks, wedges, a cradle or other equivalent means to prevent rolling. The means of preventing rolling must not be capable of becoming unintentionally unfastened or loose while the vehicle is in transit.

(2) Articles or cargo placed beside each other and secured by transverse tiedowns must either:

(i) Be placed in direct contact with each other, or

(ii) Be prevented from shifting towards each other while in transit.

(d) **Aggregate working load limit for tiedowns**. The aggregate working load limit of tiedowns used to secure an article or group of articles against movement must be at least one-half times the weight of the article or group of articles. The aggregate working load limit is the sum of:

(1) One-half the working load limit of each tiedown that goes from an anchor point on the vehicle to an anchor point on an article of cargo;

(2) One-half the working load limit of each tiedown that is attached to an anchor point on the vehicle, passes through, over, or around the article of cargo, and is then attached to an anchor point on the same side of the vehicle.

(3) The working load limit for each tiedown that goes from an anchor point on the vehicle, through, over, or around the article of cargo, and then attaches to another anchor point on the other side of the vehicle.

§393.108 How is the working load limit of a tiedown, or the load restraining value of a friction mat, determined?

(a) The working load limit (WLL) of a tiedown, associated connector or attachment mechanism is the lowest working load limit of any of its components (including tensioner), or the working load limit of the anchor points to which it is attached, whichever is less.

(b) The working load limits of tiedowns may be determined by using either the tiedown manufacturer's markings or by using the tables in this section. The working load limits listed in the tables are to be used when the tiedown material is not marked by the manufacturer with the working load limit. Tiedown materials which are marked by the manufacturer with working load limits that differ from the tables, shall be considered to have a working load limit equal to the value for which they are marked.

(c) Synthetic cordage (e.g., nylon, polypropylene, polyester) which is not marked or labeled to enable identification of its composition or working load limit shall be considered to have a working load limit equal to that for polypropylene fiber rope.

(d) Welded steel chain which is not marked or labeled to enable identification of its grade or working load limit shall be considered to have a working load limit equal to that for grade 30 proof coil chain.

(e)(1) Wire rope which is not marked by the manufacturer with a working load limit shall be considered to have a working load limit equal to one-fourth of the nominal strength listed in the Wire Rope Users Manual.

(2) Wire which is not marked or labeled to enable identification of its construction type shall be considered to have a working load limit equal to that for 6 x 37, fiber core wire rope.

(f) Manila rope which is not marked by the manufacturer with a working load limit shall be considered to have a working load limit based on its diameter as provided in the tables of working load limits.

(g) Friction mats which are not marked or rated by the manufacturer shall be considered to provide resistance to horizontal movement equal to 50 percent of the weight placed on the mat.

Tables to §393.108 [Working load limits (WLL), chain]

Size mm (inches)	WLL in kg (pounds)				
	Grade 30 proof coil	Grade 43 high test	Grade 70 transport	Grade 80 alloy	Grade 100 alloy
1. 7 (¼).............	580 (1,300)	1,180 (2,600)	1,430 (3,150)	1,570 (3,500)	1,950 (4,300)
2. 8 (⁵⁄₁₆)	860 (1,900)	1,770 (3,900)	2,130 (4,700)	2,000 (4,500)	2,600 (5,700)
3. 10 (⅜)	1,200 (2,650)	2,450 (5,400)	2,990 (6,600)	3,200 (7,100)	4,000 (8,800)
4. 11 (⁷⁄₁₆).........	1,680 (3,700)	3,270 (7,200)	3,970 (8,750)		
5. 13 (½)..........	2,030 (4,500)	4,170 (9,200)	5,130 (11,300)	5,400 (12,000)	6,800 (15,000)
6. 16 (⅝)..........	3,130 (6,900)	5,910 (13,000)	7,170 (15,800)	8,200 (18,100)	10,300 (22,600)
Chain Mark Examples					
Example 1	3	4	7	8	10
Example 2	30	43	70	80	100
Example 3	300	430	700	800	1000

Synthetic Webbing

Width mm (inches)	WLL kg (pounds)
45 (1¾)	790 (1,750)
50 (2)	910 (2,000)
75 (3)	1,360 (3,000)
100 (4)	1,810 (4,000)

Wire Rope (6 x 37, Fiber Core)

Width mm (inches)	WLL kg (pounds)
7 (¼)	640 (1,400)
8 (⁵⁄₁₆)	950 (2,100)
10 (⅜)	1,360 (3,000)
11 (⁷⁄₁₆)	1,860 (4,100)
13 (½)	2,400 (5,300)
16 (⅝)	3,770 (8,300)
20 (¾)	4,940 (10,900)
22 (⅞)	7,300 (16,100)
25 (1)	9,480 (20,900)

Manila Rope

Width mm (inches)	WLL kg (pounds)
10 (⅜)	90 (205)
11 (⁷⁄₁₆)	120 (265)
13 (½)	150 (315)
16 (⅝)	210 (465)
20 (¾)	290 (640)
25 (1)	480 (1,050)

Polypropylene Fiber Rope WLL (3-Strand and 8-Strand Constructions)

Width mm (inches)	WLL kg (pounds)
10 (⅜)	180 (400)
11 (⁷⁄₁₆)	240 (525)
13 (½)	280 (625)
16 (⅝)	420 (925)
20 (¾)	580 (1,275)
25 (1)	950 (2,100)

Polyester Fiber Rope WLL (3-Strand and 8-Strand Constructions)

Width mm (inches)	WLL kg (pounds)
10 (⅜)	250 (555)
11 (⁷⁄₁₆)	340 (750)
13 (½)	440 (960)

Polyester Fiber Rope WLL (3-Strand and 8-Strand Constructions)

Width mm (inches)	WLL kg (pounds)
16 (⅝)	680 (1,500)
20 (¾)	850 (1,880)
25 (1)	1,500 (3,300)

Nylon Rope

Width mm (inches)	WLL kg (pounds)
10 (⅜)	130 (278)
11 (⁷⁄₁₆)	190 (410)
13 (½)	240 (525)
16 (⅝)	420 (935)
20 (¾)	640 (1,420)
25 (1)	1,140 (2,520)

Double Braided Nylon Rope

Width mm (inches)	WLL kg (pounds)
10 (⅜)	150 (336)
11 (⁷⁄₁₆)	230 (502)
13 (½)	300 (655)
16 (⅝)	510 (1,130)
20 (¾)	830 (1,840)
25 (1)	1,470 (3,250)

Steel Strapping

Width mm (inches)	WLL kg (pounds)
31.7 x .74 (1¼ x 0.029)	540 (1,190)
31.7 x .79 (1¼ x 0.031)	540 (1,190)
31.7 x .89 (1¼ x 0.035)	540 (1,190)
31.7 x 1.12 (1¼ x 0.044)	770 (1,690)
31.7 x 1.27 (1¼ x 0.05)	770 (1,690)
31.7 x 1.5 (1¼ x 0.057)	870 (1,925)
50.8 x 1.12 (2 x 0.044)	1,200 (2,650)
50.8 x 1.27 (2 x 0.05)	1,200 (2,650)

§393.110 What else do I have to do to determine the minimum number of tiedowns?

(a) When tiedowns are used as part of a cargo securement system, the minimum number of tiedowns required to secure an article or group of articles against movement depends on the length of the article(s) being secured, and the requirements of paragraphs (b) and (c) of this section. These requirements are in addition to the rules under §393.106.

(b) When an article is not blocked or positioned to prevent movement in the forward direction by a headerboard, bulkhead, other cargo that is positioned to prevent movement, or other appropriate blocking devices, it must be secured by at least:

(1) One tiedown for articles 5 feet (1.52 meters) or less in length, and 1,100 pounds (500 kg) or less in weight;

(2) Two tiedowns if the article is:

(i) 5 feet (1.52 meters) or less in length and more than 1,100 pounds (500 kg) in weight; or

(ii) Longer than 5 feet (1.52 meters) but less than or equal to 10 feet (3.04 meters) in length, irrespective of the weight.

(3) Two tiedowns if the article is longer than 10 feet (3.04 meters), and one additional tiedown for every 10 feet (3.04 meters) of article length, or fraction thereof, beyond the first 10 feet (3.04 meters) of length.

(c) If an individual article is blocked, braced, or immobilized to prevent movement in the forward direction by a headerboard, bulkhead, other articles which are adequately secured or by an appropriate blocking or immobilization method, it must be secured by at least one tiedown for every 3.04 meters (10 feet) of article length, or fraction thereof.

(d) Special rule for special purpose vehicles. The rules in this section do not apply to a vehicle transporting one or more articles of cargo such as, but not limited to, machinery or fabricated structural items (e.g., steel or concrete beams, crane booms, girders, and trusses, etc.) which, because of their design, size, shape, or weight, must be fastened by special methods. However, any article of cargo carried on that vehicle must be securely and adequately fastened to the vehicle.

§393.112 Must a tiedown be adjustable?

Each tiedown, or its associated connectors, or its attachment mechanisms must be designed, constructed, and maintained so the driver of an in-transit commercial motor vehicle can tighten them. However, this requirement does not apply to the use of steel strapping.

§393.114 What are the requirements for front end structures used as part of a cargo securement system?

(a) **Applicability**. The rules in this section are applicable to commercial motor vehicles transporting articles of cargo that are in contact with the front end structure of the vehicle. The front end structure on these cargo-carrying vehicles must meet the performance requirements of this section.

(b) **Height and width**. (1) The front end structure must extend either to a height of 4 feet above the floor of the vehicle or to a height at which it blocks forward movement of any item or article of cargo being carried on the vehicle, whichever is lower.

(2) The front end structure must have a width which is at least equal to the width of the vehicle or which blocks forward movement of any article of cargo being transported on the vehicle, whichever is narrower.

(c) **Strength**. The front end structure must be capable of withstanding the following horizontal forward static load:

(1) For a front end structure less than 6 feet in height, a horizontal forward static load equal to one-half (0.5) of the weight of the articles of cargo being transported on the vehicle uniformly distributed over the entire portion of the front end structure that is within 4 feet above the vehicle's floor or that is at or below a height above the vehicle's floor at which it blocks forward movement of any article of the vehicle's cargo, whichever is less; or

(2) For a front end structure 6 feet in height or higher, a horizontal forward static load equal to four-tenths (0.4) of the weight of the articles of cargo being transported on the vehicle uniformly distributed over the entire front end structure.

(d) **Penetration resistance**. The front end structure must be designed, constructed, and maintained so that it is capable of resisting penetration by any article of cargo that contacts it when the vehicle decelerates at a rate of 20 feet per second, per second. The front end structure must have no aperture large enough to permit any article of cargo in contact with the structure to pass through it.

(e) **Substitute devices**. The requirements of this section may be met by the use of devices performing the same functions as a front end structure, if the devices are at least as strong as, and provide protection against shifting articles of cargo at least equal to, a front end structure which conforms to those requirements.

Specific securement requirements by commodity type

§393.116 What are the rules for securing logs?

(a) **Applicability**. The rules in this section are applicable to the transportation of logs with the following exceptions:

(1) Logs that are unitized by banding or other comparable means may be transported in accordance with the general cargo securement rules of §§393.100 through 393.114.

(2) Loads that consist of no more than four processed logs may be transported in accordance with the general cargo securement rules of §§393.100 through 393.114.

(3) Firewood, stumps, log debris and other such short logs must be transported in a vehicle or container enclosed on both sides, front, and rear and of adequate strength to contain them. Longer logs may also be so loaded.

(b) **Components of a securement system**. (1) Logs must be transported on a vehicle designed and built, or adapted, for the transportation of logs. Any such vehicle must be fitted with bunks, bolsters, stakes or standards, or other equivalent means, that cradle the logs and prevent them from rolling.

(2) All vehicle components involved in securement of logs must be designed and built to withstand all anticipated operational forces without failure, accidental release or permanent deformation. Stakes or standards that are not permanently attached to the vehicle must be secured in a manner that prevents unintentional separation from the vehicle in transit.

(3) Tiedowns must be used in combination with the stabilization provided by bunks, stakes, and bolsters to secure the load unless the logs:

(i) are transported in a crib-type log trailer (as defined in 49 CFR 393.5), and

(ii) are loaded in compliance with paragraphs (b)(2) and (c) of this section.

(4) The aggregate working load limit for tiedowns used to secure a stack of logs on a frame vehicle, or a flatbed vehicle equipped with bunks, bolsters, or stakes must be at least one-sixth the weight of the stack of logs.

(c) **Use of securement system**. (1) Logs must be solidly packed, and the outer bottom logs must be in contact with and resting solidly against the bunks, bolsters, stakes or standards.

(2) Each outside log on the side of a stack of logs must touch at least two stakes, bunks, bolsters, or standards. If one end does not actually touch a stake, it must rest on other logs in a stable manner and must extend beyond the stake, bunk, bolster or standard.

(3) The center of the highest outside log on each side or end must be below the top of each stake, bunk or standard.

(4) Each log that is not held in place by contact with other logs or the stakes, bunks, or standards must be held in place by a tie-down. Additional tiedowns or securement devices must be used when the condition of the wood results in such low friction between logs that they are likely to slip upon each other.

(d) **Securement of shortwood logs loaded crosswise on frame, rail and flatbed vehicles**. In addition to the requirements of paragraphs (b) and (c) of this section, each stack of logs loaded crosswise must meet the following rules:

(1) In no case may the end of a log in the lower tier extend more than one-third of the log's total length beyond the nearest supporting structure on the vehicle.

(2) When only one stack of shortwood is loaded crosswise, it must be secured with at least two tiedowns. The tiedowns must attach to the vehicle frame at the front and rear of the load, and must cross the load in this direction.

(3) When two tiedowns are used, they must be positioned at approximately one-third and two-thirds of the length of the logs.

(4) A vehicle that is more than 10 meters (33 feet) long must be equipped with center stakes, or comparable devices, to divide it into sections approximately equal in length. Where a vehicle is so divided, each tiedown must secure the highest log on each side of the center stake, and must be fastened below these logs. It may be fixed at each end and tensioned from the middle, or fixed in the middle and tensioned from each end, or it may pass through a pulley or equivalent device in the middle and be tensioned from one end.

(5) Any structure or stake that is subjected to an upward force when the tiedowns are tensioned must be anchored to resist that force.

(6) If two stacks of shortwood are loaded side-by-side, in addition to meeting the requirements of paragraphs (d)(1) through (d)(5) of this section, they must be loaded so that:

(i) There is no space between the two stacks of logs;

(ii) The outside of each stack is raised at least 2.5 cm (1 in) within 10 cm (4 in) of the end of the logs or the side of the vehicle;

(iii) The highest log is no more than 2.44 m (8 ft) above the deck; and

(iv) At least one tiedown is used lengthwise across each stack of logs.

(e) **Securement of logs loaded lengthwise on flatbed and frame vehicles**. (1) **Shortwood.** In addition to meeting the requirements of paragraphs (b) and (c) of this section, each stack of shortwood loaded lengthwise on a frame vehicle or on a flatbed must be cradled in a bunk unit or contained by stakes and

(i) Secured to the vehicle by at least two tiedowns, or

(ii) If all the logs in any stack are blocked in the front by a front-end structure strong enough to restrain the load, or by another stack of logs, and blocked in the rear by another stack of logs or vehicle end structure, the stack may be secured with one tiedown. If one tiedown is used, it must be positioned about midway between the stakes, or

(iii) Be bound by at least two tiedown-type devices such as wire rope, used as wrappers that encircle the entire load at locations along the load that provide effective securement. If wrappers are being used to bundle the logs together, the wrappers are not required to be attached to the vehicle.

(2) **Longwood.** Longwood must be cradled in two or more bunks and must either:

(i) Be secured to the vehicle by at least two tiedowns at locations that provide effective securement, or

(ii) Be bound by at least two tiedown-type devices, such as wire rope, used as wrappers that encircle the entire load at locations along the load that provide effective securement. If a wrapper(s) is being used to bundle the logs together, the wrapper is not required to be attached to the vehicle.

(f) **Securement of logs transported on pole trailers.** (1) The load must be secured by at least one tiedown at each bunk, or alternatively, by at least two tiedowns used as wrappers that encircle the entire load at locations along the load that provide effective securement.

(2) The front and rear wrappers must be at least 3.04 meters (10 feet) apart.

(3) Large diameter single and double log loads must be immobilized with chock blocks or other equivalent means to prevent shifting.

(4) Large diameter logs that rise above bunks must be secured to the underlying load with at least two additional wrappers.

§393.118 What are the rules for securing dressed lumber or similar building products?

(a) **Applicability.** The rules in this section apply to the transportation of bundles of dressed lumber, packaged lumber, building products such as plywood, gypsum board or other materials of similar shape. Lumber or building products which are not bundled or packaged must be treated as loose items and transported in accordance with §§393.100 through 393.114 of this subpart. For the purpose of this section, "bundle" refers to packages of lumber, building materials or similar products which are unitized for securement as a single article of cargo.

(b) **Positioning of bundles.** Bundles must be placed side by side in direct contact with each other, or a means must be provided to prevent bundles from shifting towards each other.

(c) **Securement of bundles transported using no more than one tier.** Bundles carried on one tier must be secured in accordance with the general provisions of §§393.100 through 393.114.

(d) **Securement of bundles transported using more than one tier.** Bundles carried in more than one tier must be either:

(1) Blocked against lateral movement by stakes on the sides of the vehicle and secured by tiedowns laid out over the top tier, as outlined in the general provisions of §§393.100 through 393.114; or

(2) Restrained from lateral movement by blocking or high friction devices between tiers and secured by tiedowns laid out over the top tier, as outlined in the general provisions of §§393.100 through 393.114; or

(3) Placed directly on top of other bundles or on spacers and secured in accordance with the following:

(i) The length of spacers between bundles must provide support to all pieces in the bottom row of the bundle.

(ii) The width of individual spacers must be equal to or greater than the height.

(iii) If spacers are comprised of layers of material, the layers must be unitized or fastened together in a manner which ensures that the spacer performs as a single piece of material.

(iv) The arrangement of the tiedowns for the bundles must be:

(A) Secured by tiedowns over the top tier of bundles, in accordance with the general provisions of §§393.100 through 393.114 with a minimum of two tiedowns for bundles longer than 1.52 meters (5 ft); and

(B) Secured by tiedowns as follows:

(1) If there are 3 tiers, the middle and top bundles must be secured by tiedowns in accordance with the general provisions of §§393.100 through 393.114; or

(2)(i) If there are more than 3 tiers, then one of the middle bundles and the top bundle must be secured by tiedown devices in accordance with the general provision of §§393.100 through 393.114, and the maximum height for the middle tier that must be secured may not exceed 6 feet above the deck of the trailer; or

(ii) Otherwise, the second tier from the bottom must be secured in accordance with the general provisions of §§393.100 through 393.114; or

(4) Secured by tiedowns over each tier of bundles, in accordance with §§393.100 through 393.114 using a minimum of two tiedowns over each of the top bundles longer than 1.52 meters (5 ft), in all circumstances; or

(e) When loaded in a sided vehicle or container of adequate strength, dressed lumber or similar building products may be secured in accordance with the general provisions of §§393.100 through 393.114.

§393.120 What are the rules for securing metal coils?

(a) **Applicability**. The rules in this section apply to the transportation of one or more metal coils which, individually or grouped together, weigh 2268 kg (5000 pounds) or more. Shipments of metal coils that weigh less than 2268 kg (5000 pounds) may be secured in accordance with the provisions of §§393.100 through 393.114.

(b) **Securement of coils transported with eyes vertical on a flatbed vehicle, in a sided vehicle or in an intermodal container with anchor points**—(1) An individual coil. Each coil must be secured by tiedowns arranged in a manner to prevent the coils from tipping in the forward, rearward, and lateral directions. The restraint system must include the following:

(i) At least one tiedown attached diagonally from the left side of the vehicle or intermodal container (near the forwardmost part of the coil), across the eye of the coil, to the right side of the vehicle or intermodal container (near the rearmost part of the coil);

(ii) At least one tiedown attached diagonally from the right side of the vehicle or intermodal container (near the forwardmost part of the coil), across the eye of the coil, to the left side of the vehicle or intermodal container (near the rearmost part of the coil);

(iii) At least one tiedown attached transversely over the eye of the coil; and

(iv) Either blocking and bracing, friction mats or tiedowns to prevent longitudinal movement in the forward direction.

(2) Coils grouped in rows. When coils are grouped and loaded side by side in a transverse or longitudinal row, then each row of coils must be secured by the following:

(i) At least one tiedown attached to the front of the row of coils, restraining against forward motion, and whenever practicable, making an angle no more than 45 degrees with the floor of the vehicle or intermodal container when viewed from the side of the vehicle or container;

(ii) At least one tiedown attached to the rear of the row of coils, restraining against rearward motion, and whenever practicable, making an angle no more than 45 degrees with the floor of the vehicle or intermodal container when viewed from the side of the vehicle or container;

(iii) At least one tiedown over the top of each coil or transverse row of coils, restraining against vertical motion. Tiedowns going over the top of a coil(s) must be as close as practicable to the eye of the coil and positioned to prevent the tiedown from slipping or becoming unintentionally unfastened while the vehicle is in transit; and

(iv) Tiedowns must be arranged to prevent shifting or tipping in the forward, rearward and lateral directions.

(c) **Securement of coils transported with eyes crosswise on a flatbed vehicle, in a sided vehicle or in an intermodal container with anchor points**—(1) An individual coil. Each coil must be secured by the following:

(i) A means (e.g., timbers, chocks or wedges, a cradle, etc.) to prevent the coil from rolling. The means of preventing rolling must support the coil off the deck, and must not be capable of becoming unintentionally unfastened or loose while the vehicle is in transit. If timbers, chocks or wedges are used, they must be held in place by coil bunks or similar devices to prevent them from coming loose. The use of nailed blocking or cleats as the sole means to secure timbers, chocks or wedges, or a nailed wood cradle, is prohibited;

(ii) At least one tiedown through its eye, restricting against forward motion, and whenever practicable, making an angle no more than 45 degrees with the floor of the vehicle or intermodal container when viewed from the side of the vehicle or container; and

(iii) At least one tiedown through its eye, restricting against rearward motion, and whenever practicable, making an angle no more than 45 degrees with the floor of the vehicle or intermodal container when viewed from the side of the vehicle or container.

(2) Prohibition on crossing of tiedowns when coils are transported with eyes crosswise. Attaching tiedowns diagonally through the eye of a coil to form an X-pattern when viewed from above the vehicle is prohibited.

(d) **Securement of coils transported with eyes lengthwise on a flatbed vehicle, in a sided vehicle or in an intermodal container with anchor points**—(1) An individual coil-option 1. Each coil must be secured by:

(i) A means (e.g., timbers, chocks or wedges, a cradle, etc.) to prevent the coil from rolling. The means of preventing rolling must support the coil off the deck, and must not be capable of becoming unintentionally unfastened or loose while the vehicle is in transit. If timbers, chocks or wedges are used, they must be held in place by coil bunks or similar devices to prevent them from coming loose. The use of nailed blocking or cleats as the sole means to secure timbers, chocks or wedges, or a nailed wood cradle, is prohibited;

(ii) At least one tiedown attached diagonally through its eye from the left side of the vehicle or intermodal container (near the forward-most part of the coil), to the right side of the vehicle or intermodal container (near the rearmost part of the coil), making an angle no more than 45 degrees, whenever practicable, with the floor of the vehicle or intermodal container when viewed from the side of the vehicle or container;

(iii) At least one tiedown attached diagonally through its eye, from the right side of the vehicle or intermodal container (near the forward-most part of the coil), to the left side of the vehicle or intermodal container (near the rearmost part of the coil), making an angle no more than 45 degrees, whenever practicable, with the floor of the vehicle or intermodal container when viewed from the side of the vehicle or container;

(iv) At least one tiedown attached transversely over the top of the coil; and

(v) Either blocking or friction mats to prevent longitudinal movement.

(2) An individual coil-option 2. Each coil must be secured by:

(i) A means (e.g., timbers, chocks or wedges, a cradle, etc.) to prevent the coil from rolling. The means of preventing rolling must support the coil off the deck, and must not be capable of becoming unintentionally unfastened or loose while the vehicle is in transit. If timbers, chocks or wedges are used, they must be held in place by coil bunks or similar devices to prevent them from coming loose. The use of nailed blocking or cleats as the sole means to secure timbers, chocks or wedges, or a nailed wood cradle, is prohibited;

(ii) At least one tiedown attached straight through its eye from the left side of the vehicle or intermodal container (near the forward-most part of the coil), to the left side of the vehicle or intermodal container (near the rearmost part of the coil), and, whenever practicable, making an angle no more than 45 degrees with the floor of the vehicle or intermodal container when viewed from the side of the vehicle or container;

(iii) At least one tiedown attached straight through its eye, from the right side of the vehicle or intermodal container (near the forward-most part of the coil), to the right side of the vehicle or intermodal container (near the rearmost part of the coil), and whenever practicable, making an angle no more than 45 degrees with the floor of the vehicle or intermodal container when viewed from the side of the vehicle or container;

(iv) At least one tiedown attached transversely over the top of the coil; and

(v) Either blocking or friction mats to prevent longitudinal movement.

(3) An individual coil-option 3. Each coil must be secured by:

(i) A means (e.g., timbers, chocks or wedges, a cradle, etc.) to prevent the coil from rolling. The means of preventing rolling must support the coil off the deck, and must not be capable of becoming unintentionally unfastened or loose while the vehicle is in transit. If timbers, chocks or wedges are used, they must be held in place by coil bunks or similar devices to prevent them from coming loose. The use of nailed blocking or cleats as the sole means to secure timbers, chocks or wedges, or a nailed wood cradle, is prohibited;

(ii) At least one tiedown over the top of the coil, located near the forward-most part of the coil;

(iii) At least one tiedown over the top of the coil located near the rearmost part of the coil; and

(iv) Either blocking or friction mats to prevent longitudinal movement.

(4) Rows of coils. Each transverse row of coils having approximately equal outside diameters must be secured with:

(i) A means (e.g., timbers, chocks or wedges, a cradle, etc.) to prevent each coil in the row of coils from rolling. The means of preventing rolling must support each coil off the deck, and must not be capable of becoming unintentionally unfastened or loose while the vehicle is in transit. If timbers, chocks or wedges are used, they must be held in place by coil bunks or similar devices to prevent them from coming loose. The use of nailed blocking or cleats as the sole means to secure timbers, chocks or wedges, or a nailed wood cradle, is prohibited;

(ii) At least one tiedown over the top of each coil or transverse row, located near the forward-most part of the coil;

(iii) At least one tiedown over the top of each coil or transverse row, located near the rearmost part of the coil; and

(iv) Either blocking, bracing or friction mats to prevent longitudinal movement.

(e) **Securement of coils transported in a sided vehicle without anchor points or an intermodal container without anchor points**. Metal coils transported in a vehicle with sides without anchor points or an intermodal container without anchor points must be loaded in a manner to prevent shifting and tipping. The coils may also be secured using a system of blocking and bracing, friction mats, tiedowns, or a combination of these to prevent any horizontal movement and tipping.

§393.122 What are the rules for securing paper rolls?

(a) **Applicability**. The rules in this section apply to shipments of paper rolls which, individually or together, weigh 2268 kg (5000 lb) or more. Shipments of paper rolls that weigh less than 2268 kg (5000 lb), and paper rolls that are unitized on a pallet, may either be secured in accordance with the rules in this section or the requirements of §§393.100 through 393.114.

(b) **Securement of paper rolls transported with eyes vertical in a sided vehicle**. (1) Paper rolls must be placed tightly against the walls of the vehicle, other paper rolls, or other cargo, to prevent movement during transit.

(2) If there are not enough paper rolls in the shipment to reach the walls of the vehicle, lateral movement must be prevented by filling the void, blocking, bracing, tiedowns or friction mats. The paper rolls may also be banded together.

(3) When any void behind a group of paper rolls, including that at the rear of the vehicle, exceeds the diameter of the paper rolls, rearward movement must be prevented by friction mats, blocking, bracing, tiedowns, or banding to other rolls.

(4)(i) If a paper roll is not prevented from tipping or falling sideways or rearwards by vehicle structure or other cargo, and its width is more than 2 times its diameter, it must be prevented from tipping or falling by banding it to other rolls, bracing, or tiedowns.

(ii) If the forwardmost roll(s) in a group of paper rolls has a width greater than 1.75 times its diameter and it is not prevented from tipping or falling forwards by vehicle structure or other cargo, then it must be prevented from tipping or falling forwards by banding it to other rolls, bracing, or tiedowns.

(iii) If the forwardmost roll(s) in a group of paper rolls has a width equal to or less than 1.75 times its diameter, and it is restrained against forward movement by friction mat(s) alone, then banding, bracing, or tiedowns are not required to prevent tipping or falling forwards.

(iv) If a paper roll or the forwardmost roll in a group of paper rolls has a width greater than 1.25 times its diameter, and it is not prevented from tipping or falling forwards by vehicle structure or other cargo, and it is not restrained against forward movement by friction mat(s) alone, then it must be prevented from tipping or falling by banding it to other rolls, bracing or tiedowns.

(5) If paper rolls are banded together, the rolls must be placed tightly against each other to form a stable group. The bands must be applied tightly, and must be secured so that they cannot fall off the rolls or to the deck.

(6) A friction mat used to provide the principal securement for a paper roll must protrude from beneath the roll in the direction in which it is providing that securement.

(c) **Securement of split loads of paper rolls transported with eyes vertical in a sided vehicle**. (1) If a paper roll in a split load is not prevented from forward movement by vehicle structure or other cargo, it must be prevented from forward movement by filling the open space, or by blocking, bracing, tiedowns, friction mats, or some combination of these.

(2) A friction mat used to provide the principal securement for a paper roll must protrude from beneath the roll in the direction in which it is providing that securement.

(d) **Securement of stacked loads of paper rolls transported with eyes vertical in a sided vehicle**. (1) Paper rolls must not be loaded on a layer of paper rolls beneath unless the lower layer extends to the front of the vehicle.

(2) Paper rolls in the second and subsequent layers must be prevented from forward, rearward or lateral movement by means as allowed for the bottom layer, or by use of a blocking roll from a lower layer.

(3) The blocking roll must be at least 38 mm (1.5 in) taller than other rolls, or must be raised at least 38 mm (1.5 in) using dunnage.

(4) A roll in the rearmost row of any layer raised using dunnage may not be secured by friction mats alone.

(e) **Securement of paper rolls transported with eyes crosswise in a sided vehicle**. (1) The paper rolls must be prevented from rolling or shifting longitudinally by contact with vehicle structure or other cargo, by chocks, wedges or blocking and bracing of adequate size, or by tiedowns.

(2) Chocks, wedges or blocking must be held securely in place by some means in addition to friction, so they cannot become unintentionally unfastened or loose while the vehicle is in transit.

(3) The rearmost roll must not be secured using the rear doors of the vehicle or intermodal container, or by blocking held in place by those doors.

(4) If there is more than a total of 203 mm (8 in) of space between the ends of a paper roll, or a row of rolls, and the walls of the vehicle, void fillers, blocking, bracing, friction mats, or tie-downs must be used to prevent the roll from shifting towards either wall.

(f) **Securement of stacked loads of paper rolls transported with eyes crosswise in a sided vehicle**. (1) Rolls must not be loaded in a second layer unless the bottom layer extends to the front of the vehicle.

(2) Rolls must not be loaded in a third or higher layer unless all wells in the layer beneath are filled.

(3) The foremost roll in each upper layer, or any roll with an empty well in front of it, must be secured against forward movement by:

(i) Banding it to other rolls, or

(ii) Blocking against an adequately secured eye-vertical blocking roll resting on the floor of the vehicle which is at least 1.5 times taller than the diameter of the roll being blocked, or

(iii) Placing it in a well formed by two rolls on the lower row whose diameter is equal to or greater than that of the roll on the upper row.

(4) The rearmost roll in each upper layer must be secured by banding it to other rolls if it is located in either of the last two wells formed by the rearmost rolls in the layer below.

(5) Rolls must be secured against lateral movement by the same means allowed for the bottom layer when there is more than a total of 203 mm (8 in) of space between the ends of a paper roll, or a row of rolls, and the walls of the vehicle.

(g) **Securement of paper rolls transported with the eyes lengthwise in a sided vehicle**.

(1) Each roll must be prevented from forward movement by contact with vehicle structure, other cargo, blocking or tie-downs.

(2) Each roll must be prevented from rearward movement by contact with other cargo, blocking, friction mats or tiedowns.

(3) The paper rolls must be prevented from rolling or shifting laterally by contact with the wall of the vehicle or other cargo, or by chocks, wedges or blocking of adequate size.

(4) Chocks, wedges or blocking must be held securely in place by some means in addition to friction, so they cannot become unintentionally unfastened or loose while the vehicle is in transit.

(h) **Securement of stacked loads of paper rolls transported with the eyes lengthwise in a sided vehicle**. (1) Rolls must not be loaded in a higher layer if another roll will fit in the layer beneath.

(2) An upper layer must be formed by placing paper rolls in the wells formed by the rolls beneath.

(3) A roll in an upper layer must be secured against forward and rearward movement by any of the means allowed for the bottom layer, by use of a blocking roll, or by banding to other rolls.

(i) **Securement of paper rolls transported on a flatbed vehicle or in a curtain-sided vehicle**— (1) Paper rolls with eyes vertical or with eyes lengthwise.

(i) The paper rolls must be loaded and secured as described for a sided vehicle, and the entire load must be secured by tie-downs in accordance with the requirements of §§393.100 through 393.114.

(ii) Stacked loads of paper rolls with eyes vertical are prohibited.

(2) Paper rolls with eyes crosswise. (i) The paper rolls must be prevented from rolling or shifting longitudinally by contact with vehicle structure or other cargo, by chocks, wedges or blocking and bracing of adequate size, or by tiedowns.

(ii) Chocks, wedges or blocking must be held securely in place by some means in addition to friction so that they cannot become unintentionally unfastened or loose while the vehicle is in transit.

(iii) Tiedowns must be used in accordance with the requirements of §§393.100 through 393.114 to prevent lateral movement.

§393.124 What are the rules for securing concrete pipe?

(a) **Applicability**. (1) The rules in this section apply to the transportation of concrete pipe on flatbed trailers and vehicles, and lowboy trailers.

(2) Concrete pipe bundled tightly together into a single rigid article that has no tendency to roll, and concrete pipe loaded in a sided vehicle or container must be secured in accordance with the provisions of §§393.100 through 393.114.

(b) **General specifications for tiedowns**. (1) The aggregate working load limit of all tiedowns on any group of pipes must not be less than half the total weight of all the pipes in the group.

(2) A transverse tiedown through a pipe on an upper tier or over longitudinal tiedowns is considered to secure all those pipes beneath on which that tiedown causes pressure.

(c) **Blocking**. (1) Blocking may be one or more pieces placed symmetrically about the center of a pipe.

(2) One piece must extend at least half the distance from the center to each end of the pipe, and two pieces must be placed on the opposite side, one at each end of the pipe.

(3) Blocking must be placed firmly against the pipe, and must be secured to prevent it moving out from under the pipe.

(4) Timber blocking must have minimum dimensions of at least 10 x 15 cm (4 x 6 in).

(d) **Arranging the load**—(1) **Pipe of different diameter**. If pipe of more than one diameter are loaded on a vehicle, groups must be formed that consist of pipe of only one size, and each group must be separately secured.

(2) **Arranging a bottom tier.** The bottom tier must be arranged to cover the full length of the vehicle, or as a partial tier in one group or two groups.

(3) **Arranging an upper tier.** Pipe must be placed only in the wells formed by adjacent pipes in the tier beneath. A third or higher tier must not be started unless all wells in the tier beneath are filled.

(4) **Arranging the top tier.** The top tier must be arranged as a complete tier, a partial tier in one group, or a partial tier in two groups.

(5) **Arranging bell pipe.** (i) Bell pipe must be loaded on at least two longitudinal spacers of sufficient height to ensure that the bell is clear of the deck.

(ii) Bell pipe loaded in one tier must have the bells alternating on opposite sides of the vehicle.

(iii) The ends of consecutive pipe must be staggered, if possible, within the allowable width, otherwise they must be aligned.

(iv) Bell pipe loaded in more than one tier must have the bells of the bottom tier all on the same side of the vehicle.

(v) Pipe in every upper tier must be loaded with bells on the opposite side of the vehicle to the bells of the tier below.

(vi) If the second tier is not complete, pipe in the bottom tier which do not support a pipe above must have their bells alternating on opposite sides of the vehicle.

(e) **Securing pipe with an inside diameter up to 1,143 mm (45 in)**. In addition to the requirements of paragraphs (b), (c) and (d) of this section, the following rules must be satisfied:

(1) **Stabilizing the bottom tier.** (i) The bottom tier must be immobilized longitudinally at each end by blocking, vehicle end structure, stakes, a locked pipe unloader, or other equivalent means.

(ii) Other pipe in the bottom tier may also be held in place by blocks and/or wedges; and

(iii) Every pipe in the bottom tier must also be held firmly in contact with the adjacent pipe by tiedowns though the front and rear pipes:

(A) At least one tiedown through the front pipe of the bottom tier must run aft at an angle not more than 45 degrees with the horizontal, whenever practicable.

(B) At least one tiedown through the rear pipe of the bottom tier must run forward at an angle not more than 45 degrees with the horizontal, whenever practicable.

(2) **Use of tiedowns.** (i) Each pipe may be secured individually with tiedowns through the pipe.

(ii) If each pipe is not secured individually with a tiedown, then:

(A) Either one ½-inch diameter chain or wire rope, or two ⅜ -inch diameter chain or wire rope, must be placed longitudinally over the group of pipes;

(B) One transverse tiedown must be used for every 3.04 m (10 ft) of load length. The transverse tiedowns may be placed through a pipe, or over both longitudinal tiedowns between two pipes on the top tier;

(C) If the first pipe of a group in the top tier is not placed in the first well formed by pipes at the front of the tier beneath, it must be secured by an additional tiedown that runs rearward at an angle not more than 45 degrees to the horizontal, whenever practicable. This tiedown must pass either through the front pipe of the upper tier, or outside it and over both longitudinal tie-downs; and

(D) If the last pipe of a group in the top tier is not placed in the last well formed by pipes at the rear of the tier beneath, it must be secured by an additional tiedown that runs forward at an angle not more than 45 degrees to the horizontal, whenever practicable. This tiedown must pass either through the rear pipe of the upper tier or outside it and over both longitudinal tiedowns.

(f) **Securing large pipe, with an inside diameter over 1143 mm (45 in)**. In addition to the requirements of paragraphs (b), (c) and (d) of this section, the following rules must be satisfied:

(1) The front pipe and the rear pipe must be immobilized by blocking, wedges, vehicle end structure, stakes, locked pipe unloader, or other equivalent means.

(2) Each pipe must be secured by tiedowns through the pipe:

(i) At least one tiedown through each pipe in the front half of the load, which includes the middle one if there is an odd number, and must run rearward at an angle not more than 45 degrees with the horizontal, whenever practicable;

(ii) At least one tiedown through each pipe in the rear half of the load, and must run forward at an angle not more than 45 degrees with the horizontal, whenever practicable, to hold each pipe firmly in contact with adjacent pipe; and

(iii) If the front or rear pipe is not also in contact with vehicle end structure, stakes, a locked pipe unloader, or other equivalent means, at least two tiedowns positioned as described in paragraphs (f)(2)(i) and (ii) of this section, must be used through that pipe.

(3) If only one pipe is transported, or if several pipes are transported without contact between other pipes, the requirements in this paragraph apply to each pipe as a single front and rear article.

§393.126 What are the rules for securing intermodal containers?

(a) **Applicability**. The rules in this section apply to the transportation of intermodal containers. Cargo contained within an intermodal container must be secured in accordance with the provisions of §§393.100 through 393.114 or, if applicable, the commodity specific rules of this part.

(b) **Securement of intermodal containers transported on container chassis vehicle(s)**. (1) All lower corners of the intermodal container must be secured to the container chassis with securement devices or integral locking devices that cannot unintentionally become unfastened while the vehicle is in transit.

(2) The securement devices must restrain the container from moving more than 1.27 cm (½ in) forward, more than 1.27 cm (½ in) aft, more than 1.27 cm (½ in) to the right, more than 1.27 cm (½ in) to the left, or more than 2.54 cm (1 in) vertically.

(3) The front and rear of the container must be secured independently.

(c) **Securement of loaded intermodal containers transported on vehicles other than container chassis vehicle(s).** (1) All lower corners of the intermodal container must rest upon the vehicle, or the corners must be supported by a structure capable of bearing the weight of the container and that support structure must be independently secured to the motor vehicle.

(2) Each container must be secured to the vehicle by:

(i) Chains, wire ropes or integral devices which are fixed to all lower corners; or

(ii) Crossed chains which are fixed to all upper corners; and,

(3) The front and rear of the container must be secured independently. Each chain, wire rope, or integral locking device must be attached to the container in a manner that prevents it from being unintentionally unfastened while the vehicle is in transit.

(d) **Securement of empty intermodal containers transported on vehicles other than container chassis vehicle(s).** Empty intermodal containers transported on vehicles other than container chassis vehicles do not have to have all lower corners of the intermodal container resting upon the vehicle, or have all lower corners supported by a structure capable of bearing the weight of the empty container, provided:

(1) The empty intermodal container is balanced and positioned on the vehicle in a manner such that the container is stable before the addition of tiedowns or other securement equipment; and,

(2) The amount of overhang for the empty container on the trailer does not exceed five feet on either the front or rear of the trailer;

(3) The empty intermodal container must not interfere with the vehicle's maneuverability; and,

(4) The empty intermodal container is secured to prevent lateral, longitudinal, or vertical shifting.

§393.128 What are the rules for securing automobiles, light trucks and vans?

(a) **Applicability.** The rules in this section apply to the transportation of automobiles, light trucks, and vans which individually weigh 4,536 kg. (10,000 lb) or less. Vehicles which individually are heavier than 4,536 kg (10,000 lb) must be secured in accordance with the provisions of §393.130 of this part.

(b) **Securement of automobiles, light trucks, and vans.**

(1) Automobiles, light trucks, and vans must be restrained at both the front and rear to prevent lateral, forward, rearward, and vertical movement using a minimum of two tiedowns.

(2) Tiedowns that are designed to be affixed to the structure of the automobile, light truck, or van must use the mounting points on those vehicles that have been specifically designed for that purpose.

(3) Tiedowns that are designed to fit over or around the wheels of an automobile, light truck, or van must provide restraint in the lateral, longitudinal and vertical directions.

(4) Edge protectors are not required for synthetic webbing at points where the webbing comes in contact with the tires.

§393.130 What are the rules for securing heavy vehicles, equipment and machinery?

(a) **Applicability.** The rules in this section apply to the transportation of heavy vehicles, equipment and machinery which operate on wheels or tracks, such as front end loaders, bulldozers, tractors, and power shovels and which individually weigh 4,536 kg (10,000 lb.) or more. Vehicles, equipment and machinery which is lighter than 4,536 kg (10,000 lb.) may also be secured in accordance with the provisions of this section, with §393.128, or in accordance with the provisions of §§393.100 through 393.114.

(b) **Preparation of equipment being transported.** (1) Accessory equipment, such as hydraulic shovels, must be completely lowered and secured to the vehicle.

(2) Articulated vehicles shall be restrained in a manner that prevents articulation while in transit.

(c) **Securement of heavy vehicles, equipment or machinery with crawler tracks or wheels.** (1) In addition to the requirements of paragraph (b) of this section, heavy equipment or machinery with crawler tracks or wheels must be restrained against movement in the lateral, forward, rearward, and vertical direction using a minimum of four tiedowns.

(2) Each of the tiedowns must be affixed as close as practicable to the front and rear of the vehicle, or mounting points on the vehicle that have been specifically designed for that purpose.

§393.132 What are the rules for securing flattened or crushed vehicles?

(a) **Applicability.** The rules in this section apply to the transportation of vehicles such as automobiles, light trucks, and vans that have been flattened or crushed.

(b) **Prohibition on the use of synthetic webbing.** The use of synthetic webbing to secure flattened or crushed vehicles is prohibited except that such webbing may be used to connect wire rope or chain to anchor points on the commercial motor vehicle. However, the webbing (regardless of whether edge protection is used) must not come into contact with the flattened or crushed cars.

(c) **Securement of flattened or crushed vehicles.** Flattened or crushed vehicles must be transported on vehicles which have:

(1) Containment walls or comparable means on four sides which extend to the full height of the load and which block against movement of the cargo in the forward, rearward and lateral directions; or

(2)(i) Containment walls or comparable means on three sides which extend to the full height of the load and which block against movement of the cargo in the direction for which there is a containment wall or comparable means, and

(ii) A minimum of two tiedowns are required per vehicle stack; or

(3)(i) Containment walls on two sides which extend to the full height of the load and which block against movement of the cargo in the forward and rearward directions, and

(ii) A minimum of three tiedowns are required per vehicle stack; or

(4) A minimum of four tiedowns per vehicle stack.

(5) In addition to the requirements of paragraphs (c)(2), (3), and (4), the following rules must be satisfied:

(i) Vehicles used to transport flattened or crushed vehicles must be equipped with a means to prevent liquids from leaking from the bottom of the vehicle, and loose parts from falling from the bottom and all four sides of the vehicle extending to the full height of the cargo.

(ii) The means used to contain loose parts may consist of structural walls, sides or sideboards, or suitable covering material, alone or in combinations.

(iii) The use of synthetic material for containment of loose parts is permitted.

§393.134 What are the rules for securing roll-on/roll-off or hook lift containers?

(a) **Applicability**. The rules in this section apply to the transportation of roll-on/roll-off or hook lift containers.

(b) **Securement of a roll-on/roll-off and hook lift container**. Each roll-on/roll-off and hook lift container carried on a vehicle which is not equipped with an integral securement system must be:

(1) Blocked against forward movement by the lifting device, stops, a combination of both or other suitable restraint mechanism;

(2) Secured to the front of the vehicle by the lifting device or other suitable restraint against lateral and vertical movement;

(3) Secured to the rear of the vehicle with at least one of the following mechanisms:

(i) One tiedown attached to both the vehicle chassis and the container chassis;

(ii) Two tiedowns installed lengthwise, each securing one side of the container to one of the vehicle's side rails; or

(iii) Two hooks, or an equivalent mechanism, securing both sides of the container to the vehicle chassis at least as effectively as the tiedowns in the two previous items.

(4) The mechanisms used to secure the rear end of a roll-on/roll off or hook lift container must be installed no more than two meters (6 ft 7 in) from the rear of the container.

(5) In the event that one or more of the front stops or lifting devices are missing, damaged or not compatible, additional manually installed tiedowns must be used to secure the container to the vehicle, providing the same level of securement as the missing, damaged or incompatible components.

§393.136 What are the rules for securing large boulders?

(a) **Applicability**. (1) The rules in this section are applicable to the transportation of any large piece of natural, irregularly shaped rock weighing in excess of 5,000 kg (11,000 lb.) or with a volume in excess of 2 cubic-meters on an open vehicle, or in a vehicle whose sides are not designed and rated to contain such cargo.

(2) Pieces of rock weighing more than 100 kg (220 lb.), but less than 5,000 kg (11,000 lb.) must be secured, either in accordance with this section, or in accordance with the provisions of §§393.100 through 393.114, including:

(i) Rock contained within a vehicle which is designed to carry such cargo; or

(ii) Secured individually by tiedowns, provided each piece can be stabilized and adequately secured.

(3) Rock which has been formed or cut to a shape and which provides a stable base for securement must also be secured, either in accordance with the provisions of this section, or in accordance with the provisions of §§393.100 through 393.114.

(b) **General requirements for the positioning of boulders on the vehicle**. (1) Each boulder must be placed with its flattest and/or largest side down.

(2) Each boulder must be supported on at least two pieces of hardwood blocking at least 10 cm x 10 cm (4 inches x 4 inches) side dimensions extending the full width of the boulder.

(3) Hardwood blocking pieces must be placed as symmetrically as possible under the boulder and should support at least three-fourths of the length of the boulder.

(4) If the flattest side of a boulder is rounded or partially rounded, so that the boulder may roll, it must be placed in a crib made of hardwood timber fixed to the deck of the vehicle so that the boulder rests on both the deck and the timber, with at least three well-separated points of contact that prevent its tendency to roll in any direction.

(5) If a boulder is tapered, the narrowest end must point towards the front of the vehicle.

(c) **General tiedown requirements**. (1) Only chain may be used as tiedowns to secure large boulders.

(2) Tiedowns which are in direct contact with the boulder should, where possible, be located in valleys or notches across the top of the boulder, and must be arranged to prevent sliding across the rock surface.

(d) **Securement of a cubic shaped boulder**. In addition to the requirements of paragraphs (b) and (c) of this section, the following rules must be satisfied:

(1) Each boulder must be secured individually with at least two chain tiedowns placed transversely across the vehicle.

(2) The aggregate working load limit of the tiedowns must be at least half the weight of the boulder.

(3) The tiedowns must be placed as closely as possible to the wood blocking used to support the boulder.

(e) **Securement of a non-cubic shaped boulder-with a stable base**. In addition to the requirements of paragraphs (b) and (c) of this section, the following rules must be satisfied:

(1) The boulder must be secured individually with at least two chain tiedowns forming an "X" pattern over the boulder.

(2) The aggregate working load limit of the tiedowns must be at least half the weight of the boulder.

(3) The tiedowns must pass over the center of the boulder and must be attached to each other at the intersection by a shackle or other connecting device.

(f) **Securement of a non-cubic shaped boulder-with an unstable base**. In addition to the requirements of paragraphs (b) and (c) of this section, each boulder must be secured by a combination of chain tiedowns as follows:

(1) One chain must surround the top of the boulder (at a point between one-half and two-thirds of its height). The working load limit of the chain must be at least half the weight of the boulder.

(2) Four chains must be attached to the surrounding chain and the vehicle to form a blocking mechanism which prevents any horizontal movement. Each chain

must have a working load limit of at least one-fourth the weight of the boulder. Whenever practicable, the angle of the chains must not exceed 45 degrees from the horizontal.

Subpart J—Frames, Cab and Body Components, Wheels, Steering, and Suspension Systems.

§393.201 Frames.

(a) The frame or chassis of each commercial motor vehicle shall not be cracked, loose, sagging or broken.

(b) Bolts or brackets securing the cab or the body of the vehicle to the frame must not be loose, broken, or missing.

(c) The frame rail flanges between the axles shall not be bent, cut or notched, except as specified by the manufacturer.

(d) Parts and accessories shall not be welded to the frame or chassis of a commercial motor vehicle except in accordance with the vehicle manufacturer's recommendations. Any welded repair of the frame must also be in accordance with the vehicle manufacturer's recommendations.

(e) No holes shall be drilled in the top or bottom rail flanges, except as specified by the manufacturer.

§393.203 Cab and body components.

(a) The cab compartment doors or door parts used as an entrance or exit shall not be missing or broken. Doors shall not sag so that they cannot be properly opened or closed. No door shall be wired shut or otherwise secured in the closed position so that it cannot be readily opened. Exception: When the vehicle is loaded with pipe or bar stock that blocks the door and the cab has a roof exit.

(b) Bolts or brackets securing the cab or the body of the vehicle to the frame shall not be loose, broken, or missing.

(c) The hood must be securely fastened.

(d) All seats must be securely mounted.

(e) The front bumper must not be missing, loosely attached, or protruding beyond the confines of the vehicle so as to create a hazard.

§393.205 Wheels.

(a) Wheels and rims shall not be cracked or broken.

(b) Stud or bolt holes on the wheels shall not be elongated (out of round).

(c) Nuts or bolts shall not be missing or loose.

§393.207 Suspension systems.

(a) **Axles**. No axle positioning part shall be cracked, broken, loose or missing. All axles must be in proper alignment.

(b) **Adjustable axles**. Adjustable axle assemblies shall not have locking pins missing or disengaged.

(c) **Leaf springs**. No leaf spring shall be cracked, broken, or missing nor shifted out of position.

(d) **Coil springs**. No coil spring shall be cracked or broken.

(e) **Torsion bar**. No torsion bar or torsion bar suspension shall be cracked or broken.

(f) **Air Suspensions**. The air pressure regulator valve shall not allow air into the suspension system until at least 55 psi is in the braking system. The vehicle shall be level (not tilting to the left or right). Air leakage shall not be greater than 3 psi in a 5-minute time period when the vehicle's air pressure gauge shows normal operating pressure.

(g) **Air suspension exhaust controls**. The air suspension exhaust controls must not have the capability to exhaust air from the suspension system of one axle of a two-axle air suspension trailer unless the controls are either located on the trailer, or the power unit and trailer combination are not capable of traveling at a speed greater than 10 miles per hour while the air is exhausted from the suspension system. This paragraph shall not be construed to prohibit—

(1) Devices that could exhaust air from both axle systems simultaneously; or

(2) Lift axles on multi-axle units.

§393.209 Steering wheel systems.

(a) The steering wheel shall be secured and must not have any spokes cracked through or missing.

(b) **Steering wheel lash**. (1) The steering wheel lash shall not exceed the following parameters:

Steering wheel diameter	Manual steering system	Power steering system
406 mm or less (16 inches or less).........................	51 mm (2 inches)	108 mm (4¼ inches)
457 mm (18 inches).............	57 mm (2¼ inches)	121 mm (4¾ inches)
483 mm (19 inches).............	60 mm (2⅜ inches)	127 mm (5 inches)
508 mm (20 inches).............	64 mm (2½ inches)	133 mm (5¼ inches)
533 mm (21 inches).............	67 mm (2⅝ inches)	140 mm (5½ inches)
559 mm (22 inches).............	70 mm (2¾ inches)	146 mm (5¾ inches)

(2) For steering wheel diameters not listed in paragraph (b)(1) of this section the steering wheel lash shall not exceed 14 degrees angular rotation for manual steering systems, and 30 degrees angular rotation for power steering systems.

(c) **Steering column**. The steering column must be securely fastened.

(d) **Steering system**. Universal joints and ball-and-socket joints shall not be worn, faulty or repaired by welding. The steering gear box shall not have loose or missing mounting bolts or cracks in the gear box or mounting brackets. The pitman arm on the steering gear output shaft shall not be loose. Steering wheels shall turn freely through the limit of travel in both directions.

(e) **Power steering systems**. All components of the power system must be in operating condition. No parts shall be loose or broken. Belts shall not be frayed, cracked or slipping. The system shall not leak. The power steering system shall have sufficient fluid in the reservoir.

PART 395—HOURS OF SERVICE OF DRIVERS

Subpart A—General

Authority: 49 U.S.C. 504, 21104(e), 31133, 31136, 31137, 31502; sec. 113, Pub. L. 103-311, 108 Stat. 1673, 1676; sec. 229, Pub. L. 106-159 (as added and transferred by sec. 4115 and amended by secs. 4130-4132, Pub. L. 109-59, 119 Stat. 1144, 1726, 1743, 1744), 113 Stat. 1748, 1773; sec. 4133, Pub. L. 109-59, 119 Stat. 1144, 1744; sec. 32934, Pub. L. 112-141, 126 Stat. 405, 830; sec. 5206(b), Pub. L. 114-94, 129 Stat. 1312, 1537; and 49 CFR 1.87.

Subpart A—General

§395.1 Scope of rules in this part.

(a) **General.** (1) The rules in this part apply to all motor carriers and drivers, except as provided in paragraphs (b) through (x) of this section.

(2) The exceptions from Federal requirements contained in paragraphs (l) and (m) of this section do not preempt State laws and regulations governing the safe operation of commercial motor vehicles.

(b) **Driving conditions.** (1) **Adverse driving conditions.** Except as provided in paragraph (h)(3) of this section, a driver who encounters adverse driving conditions, as defined in §395.2, and cannot, because of those conditions, safely complete the run within the maximum driving time or duty time during which driving is permitted under §395.3(a) or §395.5(a) may drive and be permitted or required to drive a commercial motor vehicle for not more than two additional hours beyond the maximum allowable hours permitted under §395.3(a) or §395.5(a) to complete that run or to reach a place offering safety for the occupants of the commercial motor vehicle and security for the commercial motor vehicle and its cargo.

(2) **Emergency conditions.** In case of any emergency, a driver may complete his/her run without being in violation of the provisions of the regulations in this part, if such run reasonably could have been completed absent the emergency.

(c) **Driver-salesperson**. The provisions of §395.3(b) shall not apply to any driver-salesperson whose total driving time does not exceed 40 hours in any period of 7 consecutive days.

(d) **Oilfield operations**. (1) In the instance of drivers of commercial motor vehicles used exclusively in the transportation of oilfield equipment, including the stringing and picking up of pipe used in pipelines, and servicing of the field operations of the natural gas and oil industry, any period of 8 consecutive days may end with the beginning of any off-duty period of 24 or more successive hours.

(2) In the case of specially trained drivers of commercial motor vehicles that are specially constructed to service oil wells, on-duty time shall not include waiting time at a natural gas or oil well site. Such waiting time shall be recorded as "off duty" for purposes of §§395.8 and 395.15, with remarks or annotations to indicate the specific off-duty periods that are waiting time, or on a separate "waiting time" line on the record of duty status to show that off-duty time is also waiting time. Waiting time shall not be included in calculating the 14-hour period in §395.3(a)(2). Specially trained drivers of such commercial motor vehicles are not eligible to use the provisions of §395.1(e)(1).

(e) **Short-haul operations** — (1) **150 air-mile radius driver.** A driver is exempt from the requirements of §§395.8 and 395.11 if:

(i) The driver operates within a 150 air-mile radius (172.6 statute miles) of the normal work reporting location;

(ii) The driver, except a driver-salesperson, returns to the work reporting location and is released from work within 14 consecutive hours;

(iii)(A) A property-carrying commercial motor vehicle driver has at least 10 consecutive hours off-duty separating each 14 hours on-duty;

(B) A passenger-carrying commercial motor vehicle driver has at least 8 consecutive hours off-duty separating each 14 hours on-duty; and

(iv) The motor carrier that employs the driver maintains and retains for a period of 6 months accurate and true time records showing:

(A) The time the driver reports for duty each day;

(B) The total number of hours the driver is on-duty each day;

(C) The time the driver is released from duty each day; and

(D) The total time for the preceding 7 days in accordance with §395.8(j)(2) for drivers used for the first time or intermittently.

(2) **Operators of property-carrying commercial motor vehicles not requiring a commercial driver's license.** Except as provided in this paragraph, a driver is exempt from the requirements of §§395.3(a)(2), 395.8, and 395.11 and ineligible to use the provisions of §395.1(e)(1), (g), and (o) if:

(i) The driver operates a property-carrying commercial motor vehicle for which a commercial driver's license is not required under part 383 of this subchapter;

(ii) The driver operates within a 150 air-mile radius of the location where the driver reports to and is released from work, *i.e.,* the normal work reporting location;

(iii) The driver returns to the normal work reporting location at the end of each duty tour;

(iv) The driver does not drive:

(A) After the 14th hour after coming on duty on 5 days of any period of 7 consecutive days; and

(B) After the 16th hour after coming on duty on 2 days of any period of 7 consecutive days;

(v) The motor carrier that employs the driver maintains and retains for a period of 6 months accurate and true time records showing:

(A) The time the driver reports for duty each day;

(B) The total number of hours the driver is on duty each day;

(C) The time the driver is released from duty each day;

(D) The total time for the preceding 7 days in accordance with §395.8(j)(2) for drivers used for the first time or intermittently.

(f) **Retail store deliveries.** The provisions of §395.3 (a) and (b) shall not apply with respect to drivers of commercial motor vehicles engaged solely in making local deliveries from retail stores and/or retail catalog businesses to the ultimate consumer, when driving solely within a 100-air mile radius of the driver's work-reporting location, during the period from December 10 to December 25, both inclusive, of each year.

(g) **Sleeper berths**. (1) **Property-carrying commercial motor vehicle**—(i) *General.* A driver who operates a property-carrying commercial motor vehicle equipped with a sleeper berth, as defined in §§395.2, and uses the sleeper berth to obtain the off-duty time required by §395.3(a)(1) must accumulate:

(A) At least 10 consecutive hours off-duty;

(B) At least 10 consecutive hours of sleeper berth time;

(C) A combination of consecutive sleeper berth and off-duty time amounting to at least 10 hours;

(D) A combination of sleeper berth time of at least 7 consecutive hours and up to 3 hours riding in the passenger seat of the vehicle while the vehicle is moving on the highway, either immediately before or after the sleeper berth time, amounting to at least 10 consecutive hours; or

(E) The equivalent of at least 10 consecutive hours off-duty calculated under paragraphs (g)(1)(ii) and (iii) of this section.

(ii) *Sleeper berth.* A driver may accumulate the equivalent of at least 10 consecutive hours off-duty by taking not more than two periods of either sleeper berth time or a combination of off-duty time and sleeper berth time if:

(A) Neither rest period is shorter than 2 consecutive hours;

(B) One rest period is at least 7 consecutive hours in the sleeper berth;

(C) The total of the two periods is at least 10 hours; and

(D) Driving time in the period immediately before and after each rest period, when added together:

(*1*) Does not exceed 11 hours under §395.3(a)(3); and

(*2*) Does not violate the 14-hour duty-period limit under §395.3(a)(2).

(iii) *Calculation*—(A) *In general.* The driving time limit and the 14-hour duty-period limit must be re-calculated from the end of the first of the two periods used to comply with paragraph (g)(1)(i)(E) of this section.

(B) *14-hour period.* The 14-hour driving window for purposes of §395.3(a)(2) does not include qualifying rest periods under paragraph (g)(1)(ii) of this section.

(2) **Specially trained driver of a specially constructed oil well servicing commercial motor vehicle at a natural gas or oil well location.** A specially trained driver who operates a commercial motor vehicle specially constructed to service natural gas or oil wells that is equipped with a sleeper berth, as defined in §§395.2 and 393.76 of this subchapter, or who is off duty at a natural gas or oil well location, may accumulate the equivalent of 10 consecutive hours off duty time by taking a combination of at least 10 consecutive hours of off-duty time, sleeper-berth time, or time in other sleeping accommodations at a natural gas or oil well location; or by taking two periods of rest in a sleeper berth, or other sleeping accommodation at a natural gas or oil well location, providing:

(i) Neither rest period is shorter than 2 hours;

(ii) The driving time in the period immediately before and after each rest period, when added together, does not exceed the limit specified in §395.3(a)(3);

(iii) The driver does not drive after the 14th hour after coming on duty following 10 hours off duty, where the 14th hour is calculated:

(A) by excluding any sleeper berth or other sleeping accommodation period of at least 2 hours which, when added to a subsequent sleeper berth or other sleeping accommodation period, totals at least 10 hours, and

(B) by including all on-duty time, all off-duty time not spent in the sleeper berth or other sleeping accommodations, all such periods of less than 2 hours, and any period not described in paragraph (g)(2)(iii)(A) of this section; and

(iv) The driver may not return to driving subject to the normal limits under §395.3 without taking at least 10 consecutive hours off duty, at least 10 consecutive hours in the sleeper berth or other sleeping accommodations, or a combination of at least 10 consecutive hours off duty, sleeper berth time, or time in other sleeping accommodations.

(3) **Passenger-carrying commercial motor vehicles.** A driver who is driving a passenger-carrying commercial motor vehicle that is equipped with a sleeper berth, as defined in §§395.2 and 393.76 of this subchapter, may accumulate the equivalent of 8 consecutive hours of off-duty time by taking a combination of at least 8 consecutive hours off-duty and sleeper berth time; or by taking two periods of rest in the sleeper berth, providing:

(i) Neither rest period is shorter than two hours;

(ii) The driving time in the period immediately before and after each rest period, when added together, does not exceed 10 hours;

(iii) The on-duty time in the period immediately before and after each rest period, when added together, does not include any driving time after the 15th hour; and

(iv) The driver may not return to driving subject to the normal limits under §395.5 without taking at least 8 consecutive hours off duty, at least 8 consecutive hours in the sleeper berth, or a combination of at least 8 consecutive hours off duty and sleeper berth time.

(h) **State of Alaska**—(1) **Property-carrying commercial motor vehicle**—(i) *In general.* The provisions of §395.3(a) and (b) do not apply to any driver who is driving a commercial motor vehicle in the State of Alaska. A driver who is driving a property-carrying commercial motor vehicle in the State of Alaska must not drive or be required or permitted to drive:

(A) More than 15 hours following 10 consecutive hours off-duty;

(B) After being on-duty for 20 hours or more following 10 consecutive hours off-duty;

(C) After having been on-duty for 70 hours in any period of 7 consecutive days, if the motor carrier for which the driver drives does not operate every day in the week; or

(D) After having been on-duty for 80 hours in any period of 8 consecutive days, if the motor carrier for which the driver drives operates every day in the week.

(ii) *Off-duty periods.* Before driving, a driver who operates a property-carrying commercial motor vehicle equipped with a sleeper berth, as defined in §395.2, and uses the sleeper berth to obtain the required off-duty time in the State of Alaska, must accumulate:

(A) At least 10 consecutive hours off-duty;

(B) At least 10 consecutive hours of sleeper berth time;

(C) A combination of consecutive sleeper berth and off-duty time amounting to at least 10 hours;

(D) A combination of consecutive sleeper berth time and up to 3 hours riding in the passenger seat of the vehicle while the vehicle is moving on a highway, either immediately before or after a period of at least 7, but less than 10, consecutive hours in the sleeper berth; or

(E) The equivalent of at least 10 consecutive hours off-duty calculated under paragraph (h)(1)(iii) of this section.

(iii) *Sleeper berth.* A driver who uses a sleeper berth to comply with the hours of service regulations may accumulate the equivalent of at least 10 consecutive hours off-duty by taking not more than two periods of either sleeper berth time or a combination of off-duty time and sleeper berth time if:

(A) Neither rest period is shorter than 2 consecutive hours;

(B) One rest period is at least 7 consecutive hours in the sleeper berth;

(C) The total of the two periods is at least 10 hours; and

(D) Driving time in the period immediately before and after each rest period, when added together:

(*1*) Does not exceed 15 hours; and

(*2*) Does not violate the 20-hour duty period under paragraph (h)(1)(i)(B) of this section.

(iv) *Calculation*—(A) *In general.* The driving time limit and the 20-hour duty-period limit must be re-calculated from the end of the first of the two periods used to comply with paragraph (h)(1)(ii)(E) of this section.

(B) *20-hour period.* The 20-hour duty period under paragraph (h)(1)(i)(B) does not include off-duty or sleeper berth time.

(2) **Passenger-carrying commercial motor vehicle.** The provisions of §395.5 do not apply to any driver who is driving a passenger-carrying commercial motor vehicle in the State of Alaska. A driver who is driving a passenger-carrying commercial motor vehicle in the State of Alaska must not drive or be required or permitted to drive—

(i) More than 15 hours following 8 consecutive hours off-duty;

(ii) After being on-duty for 20 hours or more following 8 consecutive hours off-duty;

(iii) After having been on-duty for 70 hours in any period of 7 consecutive days, if the motor carrier for which the driver drives does not operate every day in the week; or

(iv) After having been on-duty for 80 hours in any period of 8 consecutive days, if the motor carrier for which the driver drives operates every day in the week.

(3) **Adverse driving conditions.** (i) A driver who is driving a commercial motor vehicle in the State of Alaska and who encounters adverse driving conditions (as defined in §395.2) may drive and be permitted or required to drive a commercial motor vehicle for the period of time needed to complete the run.

(ii) After a property-carrying commercial motor vehicle driver completes the run, that driver must be off-duty for at least 10 consecutive hours before he/she drives again; and

(iii) After a passenger-carrying commercial motor vehicle driver completes the run, that driver must be off-duty for at least 8 consecutive hours before he /she drives again.

(i) **State of Hawaii**. The rules in §395.8 do not apply to a driver who drives a commercial motor vehicle in the State of Hawaii, if the motor carrier who employs the driver maintains and retains for a period of 6 months accurate and true records showing—

(1) The total number of hours the driver is on duty each day; and

(2) The time at which the driver reports for, and is released from, duty each day.

(j) **Travel time**. (1) When a property-carrying commercial motor vehicle driver at the direction of the motor carrier is traveling, but not driving or assuming any other responsibility to the carrier, such time must be counted as on-duty time unless the driver is afforded at least 10 consecutive hours off duty when arriving at destination, in which case he/she must be considered off duty for the entire period.

(2) When a passenger-carrying commercial motor vehicle driver at the direction of the motor carrier is traveling, but not driving or assuming any other responsibility to the carrier, such time must be counted as on-duty time unless the driver is afforded at least 8 consecutive hours off duty when arriving at destination, in which case he/she must be considered off duty for the entire period.

(k) **Agricultural operations**. The provisions of this part shall not apply during planting and harvesting periods, as determined by each State, to drivers transporting

(1) Agricultural commodities from the source of the agricultural commodities to a location within a 150 air-mile radius from the source;

(2) Farm supplies for agricultural purposes from a wholesale or retail distribution point of the farm supplies to a farm or other location where the farm supplies are intended to be used within a 150 air-mile radius from the distribution point; or

(3) Farm supplies for agricultural purposes from a wholesale distribution point of the farm supplies to a retail distribution point of the farm supplies within a 150 air-mile radius from the wholesale distribution point.

(l) **Ground water well drilling operations**. In the instance of a driver of a commercial motor vehicle who is used primarily in the transportation and operations of a ground water well drilling rig, any period of 7 or 8 consecutive days may end with the beginning of any off-duty period of 24 or more successive hours.

(m) **Construction materials and equipment**. In the instance of a driver of a commercial motor vehicle who is used primarily in the transportation of construction materials and equipment, any period of 7 or 8 consecutive days may end with the beginning of any off-duty period of 24 or more successive hours.

(n) **Utility service vehicles**. The provisions of this part shall not apply to a driver of a utility service vehicle as defined in §395.2

(o) **Property-carrying driver**. A property-carrying driver is exempt from the requirements of §395.3(a)(2) if:

(1) The driver has returned to the driver's normal work reporting location and the carrier released the driver from duty at that location for the previous five duty tours the driver has worked;

(2) The driver has returned to the normal work reporting location and the carrier releases the driver from duty within 16 hours after coming on duty following 10 consecutive hours off duty; and

(3) The driver has not taken this exemption within the previous 6 consecutive days, except when the driver has begun a new 7- or 8-consecutive day period with the beginning of any off-duty period of 34 or more consecutive hours as allowed by §395.3(c).

(p) **Commercial motor vehicle transportation to or from a motion picture production site**. A driver of a commercial motor vehicle providing transportation of property or passengers to or from a theatrical or television motion picture production site is exempt from the requirements of §395.3(a) if the driver operates within a 100 air-mile radius of the location where the driver reports to and is released from work, i.e., the normal work-reporting location. With respect to the maximum daily hours of service, such a driver may not drive—

(1) More than 10 hours following 8 consecutive hours off duty;

(2) For any period after having been on duty 15 hours following 8 consecutive hours off duty.

(3) If a driver of a commercial motor vehicle providing transportation of property or passengers to or from a theatrical or television motion picture production site operates beyond a 100 air-mile radius of the normal work reporting location, the driver is subject to §395.3(a), and paragraphs (p)(1) and (2) of this section do not apply.

(q) **Attendance on commercial motor vehicles containing Division 1.1, 1.2, or 1.3 explosives.** Operators who are required by 49 CFR 397.5 to be in attendance on commercial motor vehicles containing Division 1.1, 1.2, or 1.3 explosives are on duty at all times while performing attendance functions or any other work for a motor carrier. Operators of commercial motor vehicles containing Division 1.1, 1.2, or 1.3 explosives subject to the requirements for a 30-minute rest break in §395.3(a)(3)(ii) may use 30 minutes or more of attendance time to meet the requirement for a rest break, providing they perform no other work during the break. Such drivers must record the rest break as on-duty time in their record of duty status with remarks or annotations to indicate the specific on-duty periods that are used to meet the requirement for break.

(r) **Railroad signal employees**. The provisions of this part shall not apply to a signal employee, as defined in §395.2, who operates a commercial motor vehicle, is engaged in installing, repairing, or maintaining signal systems, is employed by a railroad carrier or a contractor or subcontractor to a railroad carrier, while regulated by the Federal Railroad Administration.

(s) **Covered farm vehicles**. The rules in this part do not apply to drivers of "covered farm vehicles," as defined in 49 CFR 390.5.

(t) **Ready-mixed concrete delivery vehicle**. A driver of a ready-mixed concrete delivery vehicle subject to the requirement for a 30-minute rest break in §395.3(a)(3)(ii) may use 30 minutes or more of time spent while waiting with the commercial motor vehicle at a job site or terminal to meet the requirement for the 30-minute rest break, providing the driver performs no other work during the break.

(u) **Transport of commercial bees**. The provisions of §395.3(a)(3)(ii), requiring a 30-minute rest break, do not apply to a driver engaged in the interstate transportation of bees by commercial motor vehicle as long as the bees are on the vehicle.

(v) **Transport of livestock**. The provisions of §395.3(a)(3)(ii), requiring a 30-minute rest break, do not apply to a driver engaged in the interstate transportation of livestock by commercial motor vehicle while the livestock are on the vehicle.

(w) **Hi-rail vehicles**. For the driver of a hi-rail vehicle, the maximum on duty time under §395.3 shall not include time in transportation to or from a duty assignment if such time in transportation—

(1) Does not exceed 2 hours per calendar day or a total of 30 hours per calendar month; and

(2) Is fully and accurately accounted for in records to be maintained by the motor carrier and such records are made available upon request of the Federal Motor Carrier Safety Administration or the Federal Railroad Administration.

(x) **Pipeline welding trucks**. The rules in this part do not apply to drivers of "pipeline welding trucks," as defined in 49 CFR 390.38(b).

§395.2 Definitions.

As used in this part, the following words and terms are construed to mean:

Adverse driving conditions means snow, ice, sleet, fog, or other adverse weather conditions or unusual road or traffic conditions that were not known, or could not reasonably be known, to a driver immediately prior to beginning the duty day or immediately before beginning driving after a qualifying rest break or sleeper berth period, or to a motor carrier immediately prior to dispatching the driver.

Agricultural commodity means:

(1) Any agricultural commodity, non-processed food, feed, fiber, or livestock as defined in this section.

(2) As used in this definition, the term "any agricultural commodity" means horticultural products at risk of perishing, or degrading in quality, during transport by commercial motor vehicle, including plants, sod, flowers, shrubs, ornamentals, seedlings, live trees, and Christmas trees.

Automatic on-board recording device means an electric, electronic, electromechanical, or mechanical device capable of recording driver's duty status information accurately and automatically as required by §395.15. The device must be integrally synchronized with specific operations of the commercial motor vehicle in which it is installed. At a minimum, the device must record engine use, road speed, miles driven, the date, and time of day.

Driver-salesperson means any employee who is employed solely as such by a private carrier of property by commercial motor vehicle, who is engaged both in selling goods, services, or the use of goods, and in delivering by commercial motor vehicle the goods sold or provided or upon which the services are performed, who does so entirely within a radius of 100 miles of the point at which he/she reports for duty, who devotes not more than 50 percent of his/her hours on duty to driving time. The term **selling goods** for purposes of this section shall include in all cases solicitation or obtaining of reorders or new accounts, and may also include other selling or merchandising activities designed to retain the customer or to increase the sale of goods or services, in addition to solicitation or obtaining of reorders or new accounts.

Driving time means all time spent at the driving controls of a commercial motor vehicle in operation.

Eight consecutive days means the period of 8 consecutive days beginning on any day at the time designated by the motor carrier for a 24-hour period.

ELD record means a record of duty status, recorded on an ELD, that reflects the data elements that an ELD must capture.

Electronic logging device (ELD) means a device or technology that automatically records a driver's driving time and facilitates the accurate recording of the driver's hours of service, and that meets the requirements of subpart B of this part.

Farm supplies for agricultural purposes means products directly related to the growing or harvesting of agricultural commodities during the planting and harvesting seasons within each State, as determined by the State, and livestock feed at any time of the year.

Ground water well drilling rig means any vehicle, machine, tractor, trailer, semi-trailer, or specialized mobile equipment propelled or drawn by mechanical power and used on highways to transport water well field operating equipment, including water well drilling and pump service rigs equipped to access ground water.

Hi-rail vehicle means an internal rail flaw detection vehicle equipped with flange hi-rails.

Livestock means livestock as defined in sec. 602 of the Emergency Livestock Feed Assistance Act of 1988 [7 U.S.C. 1471], as amended, insects, and all other living animals cultivated, grown, or raised for commercial purposes, including aquatic animals.

Multiple stops means all stops made in any one village, town, or city may be computed as one.

Non-processed food means food commodities in a raw or natural state and not subjected to significant post-harvest changes to enhance shelf life, such as canning, jarring, freezing, or drying. The term "non-processed food" includes fresh fruits and vegetables, and cereal and oilseed crops which have been minimally processed by cleaning, cooling, trimming, cutting, chopping, shucking, bagging, or packaging to facilitate transport by commercial motor vehicle.

On duty time means all time from the time a driver begins to work or is required to be in readiness to work until the time the driver is relieved from work and all responsibility for performing work. **On-duty time** shall include:

(1) All time at a plant, terminal, facility, or other property of a motor carrier or shipper, or on any public property, waiting to be dispatched, unless the driver has been relieved from duty by the motor carrier;

(2) All time inspecting, servicing, or conditioning any commercial motor vehicle at any time;

(3) All driving time as defined in the term **driving time**;

(4) All time in or on a commercial motor vehicle, other than:

(i) Time spent resting in or on a parked vehicle, except as otherwise provided in §397.5 of this subchapter;

(ii) Time spent resting in a **sleeper berth**; or

(iii) Up to 3 hours riding in the passenger seat of a property-carrying vehicle moving on the highway immediately before or after a period of at least 7 consecutive hours in the sleeper berth;

(5) All time loading or unloading a commercial motor vehicle, supervising, or assisting in the loading or unloading, attending a commercial motor vehicle being loaded or unloaded, remaining in readiness to operate the commercial motor vehicle, or in giving or receiving receipts for shipments loaded or unloaded;

(6) All time repairing, obtaining assistance, or remaining in attendance upon a disabled commercial motor vehicle;

(7) All time spent providing a breath sample or urine specimen, including travel time to and from the collection site, in order to comply with the random, reasonable suspicion, post-crash, or follow-up testing required by part 382 of this subchapter when directed by a motor carrier;

(8) Performing any other work in the capacity, employ, or service of a motor carrier; and

(9) Performing any compensated work for a person who is not a motor carrier.

Ready-mixed concrete delivery vehicle means a vehicle designed to deliver ready-mixed concrete on a daily basis and equipped with a mechanism under which the vehicle's propulsion engine provides the power to operate a mixer drum to agitate and mix the product en route to the delivery site.

Seven consecutive days means the period of 7 consecutive days beginning on any day at the time designated by the motor carrier for a 24-hour period.

Signal employee, as defined in 49 U.S.C. 21101(4), means an individual who is engaged in installing, repairing, or maintaining signal systems.

Sleeper berth means a berth conforming to the requirements of §393.76 of this chapter.

Supporting document means a document, in any medium, generated or received by a motor carrier in the normal course of business as described in §395.11 that can be used, as produced or with additional identifying information, by the motor carrier and enforcement officials to verify the accuracy of a driver's record of duty status.

Transportation of construction materials and equipment means the transportation of construction and pavement materials, construction equipment, and construction maintenance vehicles, by a driver to or from an active construction site (a construction site between mobilization of equipment and materials to the site to the final completion of the construction project) within a 75 air mile radius of the normal work reporting location of the driver, except that a State, upon notice to the Administrator, may establish a different air mile radius limitation for purposes of this definition if such limitation is between 50 and 75 air miles and applies only to movements that take place entirely within the State. This paragraph does not apply to the transportation of material found by the Secretary to be hazardous under 49 U.S.C. 5103 in a quantity requiring placarding under regulations issued to carry out such section.

Twenty-four-hour period means any 24-consecutive-hour period beginning at the time designated by the motor carrier for the terminal from which the driver is normally dispatched.

Utility service vehicle means any commercial motor vehicle:

PART 395

(1) Used in the furtherance of repairing, maintaining, or operating any structures or any other physical facilities necessary for the delivery of public utility services, including the furnishing of electric, gas, water, sanitary sewer, telephone, and television cable or community antenna service;

(2) While engaged in any activity necessarily related to the ultimate delivery of such public utility services to consumers, including travel or movement to, from, upon, or between activity sites (including occasional travel or movement outside the service area necessitated by any utility emergency as determined by the utility provider); and

(3) Except for any occasional emergency use, operated primarily within the service area of a utility's subscribers or consumers, without regard to whether the vehicle is owned, leased, or rented by the utility.

§395.3 Maximum driving time for property-carrying vehicles.

(a) Except as otherwise provided in §395.1, no motor carrier shall permit or require any driver used by it to drive a property-carrying commercial motor vehicle, nor shall any such driver drive a property-carrying commercial motor vehicle, regardless of the number of motor carriers using the driver's services, unless the driver complies with the following requirements:

(1) **Start of work shift.** A driver may not drive without first taking 10 consecutive hours off duty;

(2) **14-hour period.** A driver may not drive after a period of 14 consecutive hours after coming on-duty following 10 consecutive hours off-duty.

(3) **Driving time and interruptions of driving periods**—(i) **Driving time.** A driver may drive a total of 11 hours during the period specified in paragraph (a)(2) of this section.

(ii) **Interruption of driving time.** Except for drivers who qualify for either of the short-haul exceptions in §395.1(e)(1) or (2), driving is not permitted if more than 8 hours of driving time have passed without at least a consecutive 30-minute interruption in driving status. A consecutive 30-minute interruption of driving status may be satisfied either by off-duty, sleeper berth or on-duty not driving time or by a combination of off-duty, sleeper berth and on-duty not driving time.

(b) No motor carrier shall permit or require a driver of a property-carrying commercial motor vehicle to drive, nor shall any driver drive a property-carrying commercial motor vehicle, regardless of the number of motor carriers using the driver's services, for any period after—

(1) Having been on duty 60 hours in any period of 7 consecutive days if the employing motor carrier does not operate commercial motor vehicles every day of the week; or

(2) Having been on duty 70 hours in any period of 8 consecutive days if the employing motor carrier operates commercial motor vehicles every day of the week.

(c)(1) Any period of 7 consecutive days may end with the beginning of an off-duty period of 34 or more consecutive hours.

(2) Any period of 8 consecutive days may end with the beginning of an off-duty period of 34 or more consecutive hours.

§395.5 Maximum driving time for passenger-carrying vehicles.

Subject to the exceptions and exemptions in §395.1:

(a) No motor carrier shall permit or require any driver used by it to drive a passenger-carrying commercial motor vehicle, nor shall any such driver drive a passenger-carrying commercial motor vehicle:

(1) More than 10 hours following 8 consecutive hours off duty; or

(2) For any period after having been on duty 15 hours following 8 consecutive hours off duty.

(b) No motor carrier shall permit or require a driver of a passenger-carrying commercial motor vehicle to drive, nor shall any driver drive a passenger-carrying commercial motor vehicle, regardless of the number of motor carriers using the driver's services, for any period after—

(1) Having been on duty 60 hours in any 7 consecutive days if the employing motor carrier does not operate commercial motor vehicles every day of the week; or

(2) Having been on duty 70 hours in any period of 8 consecutive days if the employing motor carrier operates commercial motor vehicles every day of the week.

§395.7 [Reserved]

§395.8 Driver's record of duty status.

(a)(1) Except for a private motor carrier of passengers (nonbusiness), as defined in §390.5 of this subchapter, a motor carrier subject to the requirements of this part must require each driver used by the motor carrier to record the driver's duty status for each 24-hour period using the method prescribed in paragraphs (a)(1)(i) through (iv) of this section, as applicable.

(i) Subject to paragraphs (a)(1)(ii) and (iii) of this section, a motor carrier operating commercial motor vehicles must install and require each of its drivers to use an ELD to record the driver's duty status in accordance with subpart B of this part no later than December 18, 2017.

(ii) A motor carrier that installs and requires a driver to use an automatic on-board recording device in accordance with §395.15 before December 18, 2017 may continue to use the compliant automatic on-board recording device no later than December 16, 2019.

(iii)(A) A motor carrier may require a driver to record the driver's duty status manually in accordance with this section, rather than require the use of an ELD, if the driver is operating a commercial motor vehicle:

(1) In a manner requiring completion of a record of duty status on not more than 8 days within any 30-day period;

(2) In a driveaway-towaway operation in which the vehicle being driven is part of the shipment being delivered;

(3) In a driveaway-towaway operation in which the vehicle being transported is a motor home or a recreation vehicle trailer; or

(4) That was manufactured before model year 2000, as reflected in the vehicle identification number as shown on the vehicle's registration.

(B) The record of duty status must be recorded in duplicate for each 24-hour period for which recording is required. The duty status shall be recorded on a specified grid, as shown in paragraph (g) of this section. The grid and the requirements of paragraph (d) of this section may be combined with any company form.

PART 395

(iv) Subject to paragraphs (a)(1)(i) through (iii) of this section, until December 18, 2017, a motor carrier operating commercial motor vehicles shall require each of its drivers to record the driver's record of duty status:

(A) Using an ELD that meets the requirements of subpart B of this part;

(B) Using an automatic on-board recording device that meets the requirements of §395.15; or

(C) Manually, recorded on a specified grid as shown in paragraph (g) of this section. The grid and the requirements of paragraph (d) of this section may be combined with any company form. The record of duty status must be recorded in duplicate for each 24-hour period for which recording is required.

(2) A driver operating a commercial motor vehicle must:

(i) Record the driver's duty status using one of the methods under paragraph (a)(1) of this section; and

(ii) Submit the driver's record of duty status to the motor carrier within 13 days of the 24-hour period to which the record pertains.

(b) The duty status shall be recorded as follows:

(1) "Off duty" or "OFF."

(2) "Sleeper berth" or "SB" (only if a sleeper berth used).

(3) "Driving" or "D."

(4) "On-duty not driving" or "ON."

(c) For each change of duty status (e.g., the place of reporting for work, starting to drive, on-duty not driving and where released from work), the name of the city, town or village, with State abbreviation, shall be recorded.

NOTE: If a change of duty status occurs at a location other than a city, town, or village, show one of the following: (1) the highway number and nearest milepost followed by the name of the nearest city, town, or village and State abbreviation, (2) the highway number and the name of the service plaza followed by the name of the nearest city, town, or village and State abbreviation, or (3) the highway numbers of the nearest two intersecting roadways followed by the name of the nearest city, town, or village and State abbreviation.

(d) The following information must be included on the form in addition to the grid:

(1) Date;

(2) Total miles driving today;

(3) Truck or tractor and trailer number;

(4) Name of carrier;

(5) Driver's signature/certification;

(6) 24-hour period starting time (e.g., midnight, 9:00 a.m., noon, 3:00 p.m.);

(7) Main office address;

(8) Remarks;

(9) Name of co-driver;

(10) Total hours (far right edge of grid); and

(11) Shipping document number(s), or name of shipper and commodity.

(e)(1) No driver or motor carrier may make a false report in connection with a duty status.

(2) No driver or motor carrier may disable, deactivate, disengage, jam, or otherwise block or degrade a signal transmission or reception, or reengineer, reprogram, or otherwise tamper with an automatic on-board recording device or ELD so that the device does not accurately record and retain required data.

(3) No driver or motor carrier may permit or require another person to disable, deactivate, disengage, jam, or otherwise block or degrade a signal transmission or reception, or reengineer, reprogram, or otherwise tamper with an

automatic on-board recording device or ELD so that the device does not accurately record and retain required data.

(f) The driver's activities shall be recorded in accordance with the following provisions:

(1) **Entries to be current**. Drivers shall keep their record of duty status current to the time shown for the last change of duty status.

(2) **Entries made by driver only**. All entries relating to a driver's duty status must be legible and made by the driver.

(3) **Date.** The month, day and year for the beginning of each 24-hour period shall be shown on the form containing the driver's duty status record.

(4) **Total miles driving today.** Total mileage driven during the 24-hour period shall be recorded on the form containing the driver's duty status record.

(5) **Commercial motor vehicle identification**. The driver shall show the number assigned by the motor carrier or the license number and licensing state of each commercial motor vehicle operated during each 24-hour period on his/her record of duty status. The driver of an articulated (combination) commercial motor vehicle shall show the number assigned by the motor carrier or the license number and licensing state of each motor vehicle used in each commercial motor vehicle combination operated during that 24-hour period on his/her record of duty status.

(6) **Name of motor carrier.** The name(s) of the motor carrier(s) for which work is performed shall be shown on the form containing the driver's record of duty status. When work is performed for more than one motor carrier during the same 24-hour period, the beginning and finishing time, showing a.m. or p.m., worked for each motor carrier shall be shown after each motor carrier's name. Drivers of leased commercial motor vehicles shall show the name of the motor carrier performing the transportation.

(7) **Signature/certification.** The driver shall certify to the correctness of all entries by signing the form containing the driver's duty status record with his/her legal name or name of record. The driver's signature certifies that all entries required by this section made by the driver are true and correct.

(8) **Time base to be used.**

(i) The driver's duty status record shall be prepared, maintained, and submitted using the time standard in effect at the driver's home terminal, for a 24-hour period beginning with the time specified by the motor carrier for that driver's home terminal.

(ii) The term "7 or 8 consecutive days" means the 7 or 8 consecutive 24-hour periods as designated by the carrier for the driver's home terminal.

(iii) The 24-hour period starting time must be identified on the driver's duty status record. One-hour increments must appear on the graph, be identified, and preprinted. The words "Midnight" and "Noon" must appear above or beside the appropriate one-hour increment.

(9) **Main office address**. The motor carrier's main office address shall be shown on the form containing the driver's duty status record.

(10) **Recording days off duty.** Two or more consecutive 24-hour periods off duty may be recorded on one duty status record.

(11) **Total hours.** The total hours in each duty status: off duty other than in a sleeper berth; off duty in a sleeper berth; driving, and on duty not driving, shall be entered to the right of the grid, the total of such entries shall equal 24 hours.

(12) Shipping document number(s), or name of shipper and commodity shall be shown on the driver's record of duty status.

(g) **Graph grid.** The following graph grid must be incorporated into a motor carrier recordkeeping system which must also contain the information required in paragraph (d) of this section.

Graph Grid - Horizontally

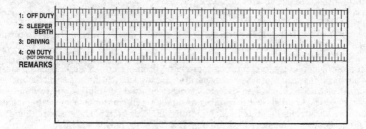

Graph Grid - Vertically

(h) **Graph Grid Preparation**. The graph grid may be used horizontally or vertically and shall be completed as follows:

(1) **Off-duty.** Except for time spent resting in a sleeper berth, a continuous line shall be drawn between the appropriate time markers to record the period(s) of time when the driver is not on duty, is not required to be in readiness to work, or is not under any responsibility for performing work.

(2) **Sleeper berth.** A continuous line shall be drawn between the appropriate time markers to record the period(s) of time off duty resting in a sleeper berth, as defined in §395.2. (If a non-sleeper berth operation, sleeper berth need not be shown on the grid.)

(3) **Driving.** A continuous line shall be drawn between the appropriate time markers to record the period(s) of driving time, as defined in §395.2.

(4) **On duty not driving.** A continuous line shall be drawn between the appropriate time markers to record the period(s) of time on duty not driving specified in §395.2.

(5) **Location—Remarks.** The name of the city, town, or village, with State abbreviation where each change of duty status occurs shall be recorded.

NOTE: If a change of duty status occurs at a location other than a city, town, or village, show one of the following: (1) the highway number and nearest milepost followed by the name of the nearest city, town, or village and State abbreviation, (2) the highway number and the name of the service plaza followed by the name of the nearest city, town, or village and State abbreviation, or (3) the highway numbers of the nearest two intersecting roadways followed by the name of the nearest city, town, or village and State abbreviation.

(i) [Reserved]

(j) **Drivers used by more than one motor carrier**. (1) When the services of a driver are used by more than one motor carrier during any 24-hour period in effect at the driver's home terminal, the driver shall submit a copy of the record of duty status to each motor carrier. The record shall include:

(i) All duty time for the entire 24-hour period;

(ii) The name of each motor carrier served by the driver during that period; and

(iii) The beginning and finishing time, including a.m. or p.m., worked for each carrier.

(2) Motor carriers, when using a driver for the first time or intermittently, shall obtain from the driver a signed statement giving the total time on duty during the immediately preceding 7 days and the time at which the driver was last relieved from duty prior to beginning work for the motor carriers.

(k) **Retention of driver's record of duty status and supporting documents**. (1) A motor carrier shall retain records of duty status and supporting documents required under this part for each of its drivers for a period of not less than 6 months from the date of receipt.

(2) The driver shall retain a copy of each record of duty status for the previous 7 consecutive days which shall be in his/her possession and available for inspection while on duty.

NOTE: Driver's Record of Duty Status.

The graph grid, when incorporated as part of any form used by a motor carrier, must be of sufficient size to be legible.

The following executed specimen grid illustrates how a driver's duty status should be recorded for a trip from Richmond, Virginia, to Newark, New Jersey. The grid reflects the midnight to midnight 24 hour period.

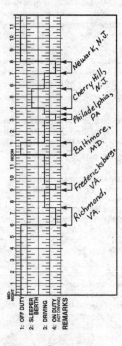

Graph Grid (Midnight to Midnight Operation).

The driver in this instance reported for duty at the motor carrier's terminal. The driver reported for work at 6 a.m., helped load, checked with dispatch, made a pretrip inspection, and performed other duties until 7:30 a.m. when the driver began driving. At 9 a.m. the driver had a minor accident in Fredericksburg, Virginia, and spent one half hour handling details with the local police. The driver arrived at the company's Baltimore, Maryland, terminal at noon and went to lunch while minor repairs were made to the tractor. At 1 p.m. the driver resumed the trip and made a delivery in Philadelphia, Pennsylvania, between 3 p.m. and 3:30 p.m. at which time the driver started driving again. Upon arrival at Cherry Hill, New Jersey, at 4 p.m., the driver entered the sleeper berth for a rest break until 5:45 p.m. at which time the driver resumed driving again. At 7 p.m. the driver arrived at the company's terminal in Newark, New Jersey. Between 7 p.m. and 8 p.m. the driver prepared the required paperwork including completing the driver's record of duty status, driver vehicle inspection report, insurance report for the Fredericksburg, Virginia, accident, checked for the next day's dispatch, etc. At 8 p.m., the driver went off duty.

§395.10 [Reserved]

§395.11 Supporting documents.

(a) **Effective date.** This section takes effect December 18, 2017.

(b) **Submission of supporting documents to motor carrier.** Except drivers for a private motor carrier of passengers (nonbusiness), a driver must submit to the driver's employer the driver's supporting documents within 13 days of either the 24-hour period to which the documents pertain or the day the document comes into the driver's possession, whichever is later.

(c) **Supporting document retention.** (1) Subject to paragraph (d) of this section, a motor carrier must retain each supporting document generated or received in the normal course of business in the following categories for each of its drivers for every 24-hour period to verify on-duty not driving time in accordance with §395.8(k):

(i) Each bill of lading, itinerary, schedule, or equivalent document that indicates the origin and destination of each trip;

(ii) Each dispatch record, trip record, or equivalent document;

(iii) Each expense receipt related to any on-duty not driving time;

(iv) Each electronic mobile communication record, reflecting communications transmitted through a fleet management system; and

(v) Each payroll record, settlement sheet, or equivalent document that indicates payment to a driver.

(2)(i) A supporting document must include each of the following data elements:

(A) On the document or on another document that enables the carrier to link the document to the driver, the driver's name or personal identification number (PIN) or a unit (vehicle) number if the unit number can be associated with the driver operating the unit;

(B) The date, which must be the date at the location where the date is recorded;

(C) The location, which must include the name of the nearest city, town, or village to enable Federal, State, or local enforcement personnel to quickly determine a vehicle's location on a standard map or road atlas; and

(D) Subject to paragraph (c)(2)(ii) of this section, the time, which must be convertible to the local time at the location where it is recorded.

(ii) If a driver has fewer than eight supporting documents containing the four data elements under paragraph (c)(2)(i) of this section for a 24-hour period, a document containing the data elements under paragraphs (c)(2)(i)(A) through (C) of this section is considered a supporting document for purposes of paragraph (d) of this section.

(d) **Maximum number of supporting documents.** (1) Subject to paragraphs (d)(3) and (4) of this section, a motor carrier need not retain more than eight supporting documents for an individual driver's 24-hour period under paragraph (c) of this section.

(2) In applying the limit on the number of documents required under paragraph (d)(1) of this section, each electronic mobile communication record applicable to an individual driver's 24-hour period shall be counted as a single document.

(3) If a motor carrier has more than eight supporting documents for a driver's 24 hour period, the motor carrier must retain the supporting documents containing the earliest and the latest time indications among the eight supporting documents retained.

(4) In addition to other supporting documents required under this section, and notwithstanding the maximum number of documents under paragraph (d)(1) of this section, a motor carrier that requires a driver to complete a paper record of duty status under §395.8(a)(1)(iii) must maintain toll receipts for any period when the driver kept paper records of duty status.

(e) **Link to driver's record of duty status.** A motor carrier must retain supporting documents in such a manner that they may be effectively matched to the corresponding driver's record of duty status.

(f) **Prohibition of destruction.** No motor carrier or driver may obscure, deface, destroy, mutilate, or alter existing information contained in a supporting document.

(g) **Supporting documents at roadside.** (1) Upon request during a roadside inspection, a driver must make available to an authorized Federal, State, or local official for the official's review any supporting document in the driver's possession.

(2) A driver need not produce a supporting document under paragraph (g)(1) of this section in a format other than the format in which the driver possesses it.

(h) **Self-compliance systems.** (1) FMCSA may authorize on a case-by-case basis motor carrier self-compliance systems.

(2) Requests for use of a supporting document self-compliance system may be submitted to FMCSA under the procedures described in 49 CFR part 381, subpart C (Procedures for Applying for Exemptions).

(3) FMCSA will consider requests concerning types of supporting documents retained by a motor carrier under §395.8(k)(1) and the method by which a driver retains a copy of the record of duty status for the previous 7 days and makes it available for inspection while on duty in accordance with §395.8.

§395.12 [Reserved]

§395.13 Drivers ordered out of service.

(a) **Authority to order drivers out of service.** Every special agent of the Federal Motor Carrier Safety Administration (as defined in appendix B to this subchapter) is authorized to order a driver out of service and to notify the motor carrier of that order, upon finding at the time and place of examination that the driver has violated the out-of- service criteria as set forth in paragraph (b) of this section.

(b) **Out of Service criteria**. (1) No driver shall drive after being on duty in excess of the maximum periods permitted by this part.

(2) No driver required to maintain a record of duty status under §395.8 or §395.15 of this part shall fail to have a record of duty status current on the day of examination and for the prior seven consecutive days.

(3) **Exception.** A driver failing only to have possession of a record of duty status current on the day of examination and the prior day, but has completed records of duty status up to that time (previous 6 days), will be given the opportunity to make the duty status record current.

(c) **Responsibilities of motor carriers**. (1) No motor carrier shall:

(i) Require or permit a driver who has been ordered out of service to operate a commercial motor vehicle until that driver may lawfully do so under the rules in this part.

(ii) Require a driver who has been ordered out of service for failure to prepare a record of duty status to operate a commercial motor vehicle until that driver has been off duty for the appropriate number of consecutive hours required by this part and is in compliance with this section. The appropriate consecutive hours off duty may include sleeper berth time.

(2) A motor carrier shall complete the "Motor Carrier Certification of Action Taken" portion of the form "Driver/Vehicle Examination Report" and deliver the

copy of the form either personally or by mail to the Division Administrator or State Director Federal Motor Carrier Safety Administration, at the address specified upon the form within 15 days following the date of examination. If the motor carrier mails the form, delivery is made on the date it is postmarked.

(d) **Responsibilities of the driver**. (1) No driver who has been ordered out of service shall operate a commercial motor vehicle until that driver may lawfully do so under the rules of this part.

(2) No driver who has been ordered out of service, for failing to prepare a record of duty status, shall operate a commercial motor vehicle until the driver has been off duty for the appropriate number of consecutive hours required by this part and is in compliance with this section.

(3) A driver to whom a form has been tendered ordering the driver out of service shall within 24 hours thereafter deliver or mail the copy to a person or place designated by the motor carrier to receive it.

(4) §395.13 does not alter the hazardous materials requirements prescribed in §397.5 pertaining to attendance and surveillance of commercial motor vehicles.

§395.15 Automatic on-board recording devices.

(a) **Authority to use**. (1) A motor carrier that installs and requires a driver to use an automatic on-board recording device in accordance with this section before December 18, 2017 may continue to use the compliant automatic on-board recording device no later than December 16, 2019. Otherwise, the authority to use automatic on-board recording devices under this section ends on December 18, 2017.

(2) In accordance with paragraph (a)(1) of this section, a motor carrier may require a driver to use an automatic on-board recording device to record the driver's hours of service.

(3) Every driver required by a motor carrier to use an automatic on-board recording device shall use such device to record the driver's hours of service.

(b) **Information requirements**. (1) Automatic on-board recording devices shall produce, upon demand, a driver's hours of service chart, electronic display, or printout showing the time and sequence of duty status changes including the drivers' starting time at the beginning of each day.

(2) The device shall provide a means whereby authorized Federal, State, or local officials can immediately check the status of a driver's hours of service. This information may be used in conjunction with records of duty status maintained in other media, for the previous 7 days.

(3) Support systems used in conjunction with on-board recorders at a driver's home terminal or the motor carrier's principal place of business must be capable of providing authorized Federal, State or local officials with summaries of an individual driver's hours of service records, including the information specified in §395.8(d) of this part. The support systems must also provide information concerning on-board system sensor failures and identification of edited data. Such support systems should meet the information interchange requirements of the American National Standard Code for Information Interchange (ANSCII) (EIARS-232/CCITT V.24 port (National Bureau of Standards "Code for Information Interchange," FIPS PUB 1-1)).

(4) The driver shall have in his/her possession records of duty status for the previous 7 consecutive days available for inspection while on duty. These records shall consist of information stored in and retrievable from the automatic on-board recording device, other written records, or any combination thereof.

(5) All copies of other written records of duty status referenced in paragraph (b)(4) of this section must be signed by the driver. The driver's signature certifies that the information contained thereon is true and correct.

(c) **The duty status and additional information shall be recorded as follows**:

(1) "Off duty" or "OFF", or by an identifiable code or character;

(2) "Sleeper berth" or "SB" or by an identifiable code or character (only if the sleeper berth is used);

(3) "Driving" or "D", or by an identifiable code or character; and

(4) "On-duty not driving" or "ON", or by an identifiable code or character;

(5) Date;

(6) Total miles driving today;

(7) Truck or tractor and trailer number;

(8) Name of carrier;

(9) Main office address;

(10) 24-hour period starting time (e.g., midnight, 9:00 a.m., noon, 3:00 p.m.);

(11) Name of co-driver;

(12) Total hours; and

(13) Shipping document number(s), or name of shipper and commodity.

(d) **Location of duty status change**. (1) For each change of duty status (e.g., the place and time of reporting for work, starting to drive, on-duty not driving and where released from work), the name of the city, town, or village, with State abbreviation, shall be recorded.

(2) Motor carriers are permitted to use location codes in lieu of the requirements of paragraph (d)(1) of this section. A list of such codes showing all possible location identifiers shall be carried in the cab of the commercial motor vehicle and available at the motor carrier's principal place of business. Such lists shall be made available to an enforcement official on request.

(e) **Entries made by driver only**. If a driver is required to make written entries relating to the driver's duty status, such entries must be made by the driver and be legible.

(f) **Reconstruction of records of duty status**. Drivers are required to note any failure of automatic on-board recording devices, and to reconstruct the driver's record of duty status for the current day and the past 7 days, less any days for which the drivers have records, and to continue to prepare a written record of all subsequent duty status until the device is again operational.

(g) **On-board information**. Each commercial motor vehicle must have on-board the commercial motor vehicle an information packet containing the following items:

(1) An instruction sheet describing in detail how data may be stored and retrieved from an automatic on-board recording system; and

(2) A supply of blank driver's records of duty status graph-grids sufficient to record the driver's duty status and other related information for the duration of the current trip.

(h) **Submission of driver's record of duty status**. (1) The driver shall submit to the employing motor carrier, each record of the driver's duty status within 13 days following the completion of each record;

(2) The driver shall review and verify that all entries are accurate prior to submission to the employing motor carrier; and

(3) The submission of the record of duty status certifies that all entries made by the driver are true and correct.

(i) **Performance of recorders**. Motor carriers that use automatic on-board recording devices for recording their drivers' records of duty status shall ensure that:

(1) A certificate is obtained from the manufacturer certifying that the design of the automatic on-board recorder has been sufficiently tested to meet the requirements of this section and under the conditions it will be used;

(2) The automatic on-board recording device permits duty status to be updated only when the commercial motor vehicle is at rest, except when registering the time a commercial motor vehicle crosses a State boundary;

(3) The automatic on-board recording device and associated support systems are, to the maximum extent practicable, tamper-proof and do not permit altering of the information collected concerning the driver's hours of service;

(4) The automatic on-board recording device warns the driver visually and/or audibly that the device has ceased to function;

(5) Automatic on-board recording devices with electronic displays shall have the capability of displaying the following:

(i) Driver's total hours of driving today;

(ii) The total hours on duty today;

(iii) Total miles driving today;

(iv) Total hours on duty for the 7 consecutive day period, including today;

(v) Total hours on duty for the prior 8 consecutive day period, including the present day; and

(vi) The sequential changes in duty status and the times the changes occurred for each driver using the device.

(6) The on-board recorder is capable of recording separately each driver's duty status when there is a multiple-driver operation;

(7) The on-board recording device/system identifies sensor failures and edited data;

(8) The on-board recording device is maintained and recalibrated in accordance with the manufacturer's specifications;

(9) The motor carrier's drivers are adequately trained regarding the proper operation of the device; and

(10) The motor carrier must maintain a second copy (back-up copy) of the electronic hours-of-service files, by month, in a different physical location than where the original data is stored.

(j) **Rescission of authority**. (1) The FMCSA may, after notice and opportunity to reply, order any motor carrier or driver to comply with the requirements of §395.8 of this part.

(2) The FMCSA may issue such an order if the FMCSA has determined that—

(i) The motor carrier has been issued conditional or unsatisfactory safety rating by the FMCSA;

(ii) The motor carrier has required or permitted a driver to establish, or the driver has established, a pattern of exceeding the hours of service limitations of this part;

(iii) The motor carrier has required or permitted a driver to fail, or the driver has failed, to accurately and completely record the driver's hours of service as required in this section; or

(iv) The motor carrier or driver has tampered with or otherwise abused the automatic on-board recording device on any commercial motor vehicle.

§395.16 [Reserved]

§395.17

§395.17 [Reserved]

§395.18 [Reserved]

§395.19 [Reserved]

Subpart B—Electronic Logging Devices (ELDs)

§395.20 ELD applicability and scope.

(a) **Scope.** This subpart applies to ELDs used to record a driver's hours of service under §395.8(a).

(b) **Applicability.** An ELD used after December 18, 2017 must meet the requirements of this subpart.

§395.22 Motor carrier responsibilities—In general.

(a) **Registered ELD required.** A motor carrier required to use an ELD must use only an ELD that is listed on the Federal Motor Carrier Safety Administration's registered ELDs list, accessible through the Agency's Web site, *www.fmcsa.dot.gov/devices*.

(b) **User rights management.** (1) This paragraph applies to a motor carrier whose drivers use ELDs and to the motor carrier's support personnel who have been authorized by the motor carrier to access ELD records and make or suggest authorized edits.

(2) A motor carrier must:

(i) Manage ELD accounts, including creating, deactivating, and updating accounts, and ensure that properly authenticated individuals have ELD accounts with appropriate rights;

(ii) Assign a unique ELD username to each user account with the required user identification data;

(iii) Ensure that a driver's license used in the creation of an ELD driver account is valid and corresponds to the driver using the ELD account; and

(iv) Ensure that information entered to create a new account is accurate.

(c) **Driver identification data.** (1) The ELD user account assigned by the motor carrier to a driver requires the following data elements:

(i) A driver's first and last name, as reflected on the driver's license;

(ii) A unique ELD username selected by the motor carrier;

(iii) The driver's valid driver's license number; and

(iv) The State or jurisdiction that issued the driver's license.

(2) The driver's license number or Social Security number must not be used as, or as part of, the username for the account created on an ELD.

(d) **Motor carrier support personnel identification data.** The ELD user account assigned by a motor carrier to support personnel requires the following data elements:

(1) The individual's first and last name, as reflected on a government issued identification; and

(2) A unique ELD username selected by the motor carrier.

(e) **Proper log-in required.** The motor carrier must require that its drivers and support personnel log into the ELD system using their proper identification data.

(f) **Calibration.** A motor carrier must ensure that an ELD is calibrated and maintained in accordance with the provider's specifications.

(g) **Portable ELDs.** If a driver uses a portable ELD, the motor carrier shall ensure that the ELD is mounted in a fixed position during the operation of the commercial motor vehicle and visible to the driver when the driver is seated in the normal driving position.

(h) **In-vehicle information.** A motor carrier must ensure that its drivers possess onboard a commercial motor vehicle an ELD information packet containing the following items:

(1) A user's manual for the driver describing how to operate the ELD;

(2) An instruction sheet for the driver describing the data transfer mechanisms supported by the ELD and step-by-step instructions for the driver to produce and transfer the driver's hours-of-service records to an authorized safety official;

(3) An instruction sheet for the driver describing ELD malfunction reporting requirements and recordkeeping procedures during ELD malfunctions; and

(4) A supply of blank driver's records of duty status graph-grids sufficient to record the driver's duty status and other related information for a minimum of 8 days.

(i) **Record backup and security.** (1) A motor carrier must retain for 6 months a back-up copy of the ELD records on a device separate from that on which the original data are stored.

(2) A motor carrier must retain a driver's ELD records so as to protect a driver's privacy in a manner consistent with sound business practices.

(j) **Record production.** When requested by an authorized safety official, a motor carrier must produce ELD records in an electronic format either at the time of the request or, if the motor carrier has multiple offices or terminals, within the time permitted under §390.29 of this subchapter.

§395.24 Driver responsibilities—In general.

(a) **In general.** A driver must provide the information the ELD requires as prompted by the ELD and required by the motor carrier.

(b) **Driver's duty status.** A driver must input the driver's duty status by selecting among the following categories available on the ELD:

(1) "Off duty" or "OFF" or "1";

(2) "Sleeper berth" or "SB" or "2", to be used only if sleeper berth is used;

(3) "Driving" or "D" or "3"; or

(4) "On-duty not driving" or "ON" or "4".

(c) **Miscellaneous data.** (1) A driver must manually input the following information in the ELD:

(i) Annotations, when applicable;

(ii) Driver's location description, when prompted by the ELD; and

(iii) Output file comment, when directed by an authorized safety officer.

(2) A driver must manually input or verify the following information on the ELD:

(i) Commercial motor vehicle power unit number;

(ii) Trailer number(s), if applicable; and

(iii) Shipping document number, if applicable.

(d) **Driver use of ELD.** On request by an authorized safety official, a driver must produce and transfer from an ELD the driver's hours-of-service records in accordance with the instruction sheet provided by the motor carrier.

§395.26 ELD data automatically recorded.

(a) **In general**. An ELD provides the following functions and automatically records the data elements listed in this section in accordance with the requirements contained in appendix A to subpart B of this part.

(b) **Data automatically recorded**. The ELD automatically records the following data elements:

(1) Date;

(2) Time;

(3) CMV geographic location information;

(4) Engine hours;

(5) Vehicle miles;

(6) Driver or authenticated user identification data;

(7) Vehicle identification data; and

(8) Motor carrier identification data.

(c) **Change of duty status**. When a driver indicates a change of duty status under §395.24(b), the ELD records the data elements in paragraphs (b)(1) through (8) of this section.

(d) **Intermediate recording**. (1) When a commercial motor vehicle is in motion and there has not been a duty status change or another intermediate recording in the previous 1 hour, the ELD automatically records an intermediate recording that includes the data elements in paragraphs (b)(1) through (8) of this section.

(2) If the intermediate recording is created during a period when the driver indicates authorized personal use of a commercial motor vehicle, the data elements in paragraphs (b)(4) and (5) of this section (engine hours and vehicle miles) will be left blank and paragraph (b)(3) of this section (location) will be recorded with a single decimal point resolution (approximately within a 10-mile radius).

(e) **Change in special driving category**. If a driver indicates a change in status under §395.28(a)(2), the ELD records the data elements in paragraphs (b)(1) through (8) of this section.

(f) **Certification of the driver's daily record**. The ELD provides a function for recording the driver's certification of the driver's records for every 24-hour period. When a driver certifies or recertifies the driver's records for a given 24-hour period under §395.30(b)(2), the ELD records the date, time and driver identification data elements in paragraphs (b)(1), (2), and (6) of this section.

(g) **Log in/log out**. When an authorized user logs into or out of an ELD, the ELD records the data elements in paragraphs (b)(1) and (2) and (b)(4) through (8) of this section.

(h) **Engine power up/shut down**. When a commercial motor vehicle's engine is powered up or powered down, the ELD records the data elements in paragraphs (b)(1) through (8) of this section.

(i) **Authorized personal use**. If the record is created during a period when the driver has indicated authorized personal use of a commercial motor vehicle, the data element in paragraph (b)(3) of this section is logged with a single decimal point resolution (approximately within a 10-mile radius).

(j) **Malfunction and data diagnostic event**. When an ELD detects or clears a malfunction or data diagnostic event, the ELD records the data elements in paragraphs (b)(1) and (2) and (b)(4) through (8) of this section.

§395.28 Special driving categories; other driving statuses.

(a) **Special driving categories**—(1) **Motor carrier options**. A motor carrier may configure an ELD to authorize a driver to indicate that the driver is operating a commercial motor vehicle under any of the following special driving categories:

(i) Authorized personal use; and

(ii) Yard moves.

(2) **Driver's responsibilities**. A driver operating a commercial motor vehicle under one of the authorized categories listed in paragraph (a)(1) of this section:

(i) Must select on the ELD the applicable special driving category before the start of the status and deselect when the indicated status ends; and

(ii) When prompted by the ELD, annotate the driver's ELD record describing the driver's activity.

(b) **Drivers exempt from ELD use**. A motor carrier may configure an ELD to designate a driver as exempt from ELD use.

(c) **Other driving statuses**. A driver operating a commercial motor vehicle under any exception under §390.3(f) of this subchapter or §395.1 who is not covered under paragraph (a) or (b) of this section must annotate the driver's ELD record to explain the applicable exemption.

§395.30 ELD record submissions, edits, annotations, and data retention.

(a) **Accurate record keeping**. A driver and the motor carrier must ensure that the driver's ELD records are accurate.

(b) **Review of records and certification by driver**. (1) A driver must review the driver's ELD records, edit and correct inaccurate records, enter any missing information, and certify the accuracy of the information.

(2) Using the certification function of the ELD, the driver must certify the driver's records by affirmatively selecting "Agree" immediately following a statement that reads, "I hereby certify that my data entries and my record of duty status for this 24-hour period are true and correct." The driver must certify the record immediately after the final required entry has been made or corrected for the 24-hour period.

(3) The driver must submit the driver's certified ELD records to the motor carrier in accordance with §395.8(a)(2).

(4) If any edits are necessary after the driver submits the records to the motor carrier, the driver must recertify the record after the edits are made.

(c) **Edits, entries, and annotations**. (1) Subject to the edit limitations of an ELD, a driver may edit, enter missing information, and annotate ELD recorded events. When edits, additions, or annotations are necessary, a driver must use the ELD and respond to the ELD's prompts.

(2) The driver or support personnel must annotate each change or addition to a record.

(3) In the case of team drivers, if there were a mistake resulting in the wrong driver being assigned driving-time hours by the ELD, and if the team drivers were both indicated in each other's records for that period as co-drivers, driving time may be edited and reassigned between the team drivers following the procedure supported by the ELD.

(d) **Motor carrier-proposed edits**. (1) On review of a driver's submitted records, the motor carrier may request edits to a driver's records of duty status

PART 395

to ensure accuracy. A driver must confirm or reject any proposed change, implement the appropriate edits on the driver's record of duty status, and recertify and resubmit the records in order for any motor carrier-proposed changes to take effect.

(2) A motor carrier may not request edits to the driver's electronic records before the records have been submitted by the driver.

(3) Edits requested by any system or by any person other than the driver must require the driver's electronic confirmation or rejection.

(e) **Coercion prohibited**. A motor carrier may not coerce a driver to make a false certification of the driver's data entries or record of duty status.

(f) **Motor carrier data retention requirements**. A motor carrier must not alter or erase, or permit or require alteration or erasure of, the original information collected concerning the driver's hours of service, the source data streams used to provide that information, or information contained in any ELD that uses the original information and HOS source data.

§395.32 Non-authenticated driver logs.

(a) **Tracking non-authenticated operation**. The ELD must associate the non-authenticated operation of a commercial motor vehicle with a single account labeled "Unidentified Driver" as soon as the vehicle is in motion, if no driver has logged into the ELD.

(b) **Driver**. When a driver logs into an ELD, the driver must review any unassigned driving time when prompted by the ELD and must:

(1) Assume any records that belong to the driver under the driver's account; or

(2) Indicate that the records are not attributable to the driver.

(c) **Motor carrier**. (1) A motor carrier must ensure that records of unidentified driving are reviewed and must:

(i) Annotate the record, explaining why the time is unassigned; or

(ii) Assign the record to the appropriate driver to correctly reflect the driver's hours of service.

(2) A motor carrier must retain unidentified driving records for each ELD for a minimum of 6 months from the date of receipt.

(3) During a safety inspection, audit or investigation by an authorized safety official, a motor carrier must make available unidentified driving records from the ELD corresponding to the time period for which ELD records are required.

§395.34 ELD malfunctions and data diagnostic events.

(a) **Recordkeeping during ELD malfunctions**. In case of an ELD malfunction, a driver must do the following:

(1) Note the malfunction of the ELD and provide written notice of the malfunction to the motor carrier within 24 hours;

(2) Reconstruct the record of duty status for the current 24-hour period and the previous 7 consecutive days, and record the records of duty status on graph-grid paper logs that comply with §395.8, unless the driver already possesses the records or the records are retrievable from the ELD; and

(3) Continue to manually prepare a record of duty status in accordance with §395.8 until the ELD is serviced and brought back into compliance with this subpart.

(b) **Inspections during malfunctions**. When a driver is inspected for hours of service compliance during an ELD malfunction, the driver must provide the authorized safety official the driver's records of duty status manually kept as specified under paragraphs (a)(2) and (3) of this section.

(c) **Driver requirements during ELD data diagnostic events**. If an ELD indicates that there is a data inconsistency that generates a data diagnostic event, the driver must follow the motor carrier's and ELD provider's recommendations in resolving the data inconsistency.

(d) **Motor carrier requirements for repair, replacement, or service**. (1) If a motor carrier receives or discovers information concerning the malfunction of an ELD, the motor carrier must take actions to correct the malfunction of the ELD within 8 days of discovery of the condition or a driver's notification to the motor carrier, whichever occurs first.

(2) A motor carrier seeking to extend the period of time permitted for repair, replacement, or service of one or more ELDs shall notify the FMCSA Division Administrator for the State of the motor carrier's principal place of business within 5 days after a driver notifies the motor carrier under paragraph (a)(1) of this section. Each request for an extension under this section must be signed by the motor carrier and must contain:

(i) The name, address, and telephone number of the motor carrier representative who files the request;

(ii) The make, model, and serial number of each ELD;

(iii) The date and location of each ELD malfunction as reported by the driver to the carrier; and

(iv) A concise statement describing actions taken by the motor carrier to make a good faith effort to repair, replace, or service the ELD units, including why the carrier needs additional time beyond the 8 days provided by this section.

(3) If FMCSA determines that the motor carrier is continuing to make a good faith effort to ensure repair, replacement, or service to address the malfunction of each ELD, FMCSA may allow an additional period.

(4) FMCSA will provide written notice to the motor carrier of its determination. The determination may include any conditions that FMCSA considers necessary to ensure hours-of-service compliance. The determination shall constitute a final agency action.

(5) A motor carrier providing a request for extension that meets the requirements of paragraph (d)(2) of this section is deemed in compliance with §395.8(a)(1)(i) and (a)(2) until FMCSA makes an extension determination under this section, provided the motor carrier and driver continue to comply with the other requirements of this section.

§395.36 Driver access to records.

(a) **Records on ELD**. Drivers must be able to access their own ELD records. A motor carrier must not introduce a process that would require a driver to go through the motor carrier to obtain copies of the driver's own ELD records if such records exist on or are automatically retrievable through the ELD operated by the driver.

(b) **Records in motor carrier's possession**. On request, a motor carrier must provide a driver with access to and copies of the driver's own ELD records unavailable under paragraph (a) of this section during the period a motor carrier is required to retain the records under §395.8(k).

§395.38 Incorporation by reference.

(a) **Incorporation by reference**. Certain materials are incorporated by reference in part 395, with the approval of the Director of the Office of the Federal Register under 5 U.S.C. 552(a), and 1 CFR part 51. To enforce any edition other than that specified in this section, the Federal Motor Carrier Safety Administration must publish notice of the change in the *Federal Register*, and the material must be available to the public. All approved material is available for inspection at the Federal Motor Carrier Safety Administration, Office of Analysis, Research and Technology, (800) 832-5660, and is available from the sources listed below. It is also available for inspection at the National Archives and Records Administration (NARA). For information on the availability of this material at NARA, call 202-741-6030 or go to *http://www.archives.gov/federal_register/code_of_federal_regulations/ibr_locations.html*.

(b) **American National Standards Institute (ANSI)**. 11 West 42nd Street, New York, New York 10036, *http://webstore.ansi.org*, (212) 642-4900.

(1) ANSI INCITS 4-1986 (R2012), American National Standard for Information Systems—Coded Character Sets—7-Bit American National Standard Code for Information Interchange (7-Bit ASCII), approved June 14, 2007, IBR in section 4.8.2.1, Appendix A to subpart B.

(2) ANSI INCITS 446-2008 (R2013), American National Standard for Information Technology—Identifying Attributes for Named Physical and Cultural Geographic Features (Except Roads and Highways) of the United States, Territories, Outlying Areas, and Freely Associated Areas, and the Waters of the Same to the Limit of the Twelve-Mile Statutory Zone, approved October 28, 2008, IBR in section 4.4.2, Appendix A to subpart B.

(c) **Bluetooth SIG, Inc.** 5209 Lake Washington Blvd. NE., Suite 350, Kirkland, WA 98033, *https://www.bluetooth.org/Technical/Specifications/adopted.htm*, (425) 691-3535.

(1) Bluetooth SIG, Inc., Specification of the Bluetooth System: Wireless Connections Made Easy, Covered Core Package version 2.1 + EDR, volumes 0 through 4, approved July 26, 2007, IBR in sections 4.9.1, 4.9.2, 4.10.1.4, 4.10.2, Appendix A to subpart B.

(2) [Reserved]

(d) **Institute of Electrical and Electronic Engineers (IEEE) Standards Association**. 445 Hoes Lane, Piscataway, NJ 08854-4141, *http://standards.ieee.org/index.html*, (732) 981-0060.

(1) IEEE Std 1667-2009, IEEE Standard for Authentication in Host Attachments of Transient Storage Devices, approved 11 November 2009, IBR in section 4.10.1.3, Appendix A to subpart B.

(2) [Reserved]

(e) **Internet Engineering Task Force (IETF)**. C/o Association Management Solutions, LLC (AMS) 48377 Freemont Blvd., Suite 117, Freemont, CA 94538, (510) 492-4080.

(1) IETF RFC 3565, Use of the Advanced Encryption Standard (AES) Encryption Algorithm in Cryptographic Message Syntax (CMS), approved July 2003, IBR in section 4.10.1.2, Appendix A to subpart B.

(2) IETF RFC 4056, Use of the RSASSA-PSS Signature Algorithm in Cryptographic Message Syntax (CMS), approved June 2005, IBR in section 4.10.1.2, Appendix A to subpart B.

(3) IETF RFC 5246, The Transport Layer Security (TLS) Protocol Version 1.2, approved August 2008, IBR in section 4.10.1.1, Appendix AA to subpart B.

(4) IETF RFC 5321, Simple Mail Transfer Protocol, approved October 2008, IBR in section 4.10.1.2, Appendix A to subpart B.

(5) IETF RFC 5322, Internet Message Format, approved October 2008, IBR in section 4.10.1.2, Appendix A to subpart B.

(6) IETF RFC 5751, Secure/Multipurpose Internet Mail Extensions (S/MIME) Version 3.2, Message Specification, approved January 2010, IBR in section 4.10.1.2, Appendix A to subpart B.

(7) IETF RFC 7230, Hypertext Transfer Protocol (HTTP/1.1): Message Syntax and Routing, approved June 2014, IBR in section 4.10.1.1, Appendix A to subpart B.

(8) IETF RFC 7231, Hypertext Transfer Protocol (HTTP/1.1): Semantics and Content, approved June 2014, IBR in section 4.10.1.1, Appendix A to subpart B.

(f) **National Institute of Standards and Technology (NIST)**. 100 Bureau Drive, Stop 1070, Gaithersburg, MD 20899-1070, *http://www.nist.gov*, (301) 975-6478.

(1) Federal Information Processing Standards Publication (FIPS PUB) 197, Advanced Encryption Standard (AES), approved November 26, 2001, IBR in sections 4.10.1.2 and 4.10.1.3, Appendix A to subpart B.

(2) SP 800-32, Introduction to Public Key Technology and the Federal PKI Infrastructure, approved February 26, 2001, IBR in section 4.10.1.2, Appendix A to subpart B.

(g) **Universal Serial Bus Implementers Forum (USBIF)**. 3855 SW. 153rd Drive, Beaverton, Oregon 97006, *http://www.usb.org*, (503) 619-0426.

(1) USB Implementers Forum, Inc., Universal Serial Bus Specification, Revision 2.0, approved April 27, 2000, as revised through April 3, 2015, IBR in sections 4.9.1, 4.9.2, 4.10.1.3, and 4.10.2, Appendix A to subpart B.

(2) [Reserved]

(h) **World Wide Web Consortium (W3C)**. 32 Vassar Street, Building 32-G514, Cambridge, MA 02139, *http://www.w3.org*, (617) 253-2613.

(1) W3C Recommendation 27, SOAP Version 1.2 Part 1: Messaging Framework (Second Edition), including errata, approved April 2007, IBR in section 4.10.1.1, Appendix A to subpart B.

(2) [Reserved]

Editor's Note: Appendix A to Subpart B of Part 395, which contains the functional specifications for the manufacture of ELDs, is not included in this pocketbook due to space considerations.

PART 396—INSPECTION, REPAIR, AND MAINTENANCE

Authority: 49 U.S.C. 504, 31133, 31136, 31151, 31502; sec. 32934, Pub. L. 112-141, 126 Stat. 405, 830; sec. 5524, Pub. L. 114-94, 129 Stat. 1312, 1560; and 49 CFR 1.87.

§396.1 Scope.

(a) Every motor carrier, its officers, drivers, agents, representatives, and employees directly concerned with the inspection or maintenance of commercial motor vehicles must be knowledgeable of and comply with the rules of this part.

(b) Every intermodal equipment provider, its officers, agents, representatives, and employees directly concerned with the inspection or maintenance of intermodal equipment interchanged or offered for interchange to motor carriers must be knowledgeable of and comply with the rules of this part.

(c) This part does not apply to "covered farm vehicles," as defined in 49 CFR 390.5, or to the drivers of such vehicles.

(d) The rules in this part do not apply to "pipeline welding trucks" as defined in 49 CFR 390.38(b).

§396.3 Inspection, repair and maintenance.

(a) **General**. Every motor carrier and intermodal equipment provider must systematically inspect, repair, and maintain, or cause to be systematically inspected, repaired, and maintained, all motor vehicles and intermodal equipment subject to its control.

(1) Parts and accessories shall be in safe and proper operating condition at all times. These include those specified in Part 393 of this subchapter and any additional parts and accessories which may affect safety of operation, including but not limited to, frame and frame assemblies, suspension systems, axles and attaching parts, wheels and rims, and steering systems.

(2) Pushout windows, emergency doors, and emergency door marking lights in buses shall be inspected at least every 90 days.

(b) **Required records**. Motor carriers, except for a private motor carrier of passengers (nonbusiness), must maintain, or cause to be maintained, records for each motor vehicle they control for 30 consecutive days. Intermodal equipment providers must maintain or cause to be maintained, records for each unit of intermodal equipment they tender or intend to tender to a motor carrier. These records must include:

(1) An identification of the vehicle including company number, if so marked, make, serial number, year, and tire size. In addition, if the motor vehicle is not owned by the motor carrier, the record shall identify the name of the person furnishing the vehicle;

(2) A means to indicate the nature and due date of the various inspection and maintenance operations to be performed;

(3) A record of inspection, repairs and maintenance indicating their date and nature; and

(4) A record of tests conducted on pushout windows, emergency doors, and emergency door marking lights on buses.

(c) **Record retention**—The records required by this section shall be retained where the vehicle is either housed or maintained for a period of 1 year and for 6 months after the motor vehicle leaves the motor carrier's control.

§396.5 Lubrication.

Every motor carrier shall ensure that each motor vehicle subject to its control is—

(a) properly lubricated; and

(b) free of oil and grease leaks.

§396.7 Unsafe operations forbidden.

(a) **General**—A motor vehicle shall not be operated in such a condition as to likely cause an accident or a breakdown of the vehicle.

(b) **Exemption**—Any motor vehicle discovered to be in an unsafe condition while being operated on the highway may be continued in operation only to the nearest place where repairs can safely be effected. Such operation shall be conducted only if it is less hazardous to the public than to permit the vehicle to remain on the highway.

§396.9 Inspection of motor vehicles and intermodal equipment in operation.

(a) **Personnel authorized to perform inspections**—Every special agent of the FMCSA (as defined in Appendix B to this subchapter) is authorized to enter upon and perform inspections of a motor carrier's vehicles in operation and intermodal equipment in operation.

(b) **Prescribed inspection report**—The Driver Vehicle Examination Report shall be used to record results of motor vehicle inspections and results of intermodal equipment inspections conducted by authorized FMCSA personnel.

(c) **Motor vehicles and intermodal equipment declared "out-of-service."** (1) Authorized personnel shall declare and mark "out-of-service" any motor vehicle or intermodal equipment which by reason of its mechanical condition or loading would likely cause an accident or a breakdown. An "Out-of-Service Vehicle" sticker shall be used to mark vehicles and intermodal equipment "out-of-service."

(2) No motor carrier or intermodal equipment provider shall require or permit any person to operate nor shall any person operate any motor vehicle or intermodal equipment declared and marked "out-of-service" until all repairs required by the "out-of-service notice" have been satisfactorily completed. The term *operate* as used in this section shall include towing the vehicle or intermodal equipment, except that vehicles or intermodal equipment marked "out-of-service" may be towed away by means of a vehicle using a crane or hoist. A vehicle combination consisting of an emergency towing vehicle and an "out-of-service" vehicle shall not be operated unless such combination meets the performance requirements of this subchapter except for those conditions noted on the Driver Vehicle Examination Report.

(3) No person shall remove the "Out-of-Service Vehicle" sticker from any motor vehicle or intermodal equipment prior to completion of all repairs required by the "out-of-service notice."

(d) **Motor carrier or intermodal equipment provider disposition.**

(1) The driver of any motor vehicle, including a motor vehicle transporting intermodal equipment, who receives an inspection report shall deliver a copy to both the motor carrier operating the vehicle and the intermodal equipment provider upon his/her arrival at the next terminal or facility. If the driver is not scheduled to arrive at a terminal or facility of the motor carrier operating the vehicle or at a facility of the intermodal equipment provider within 24 hours, the driver shall immediately mail, fax, or otherwise transmit the report to the motor carrier and intermodal equipment provider.

(2) Motor carriers and intermodal equipment providers shall examine the report. Violations or defects noted thereon shall be corrected in accordance with §396.11(a)(3). Repairs of items of intermodal equipment placed out-of-service are also to be documented in the maintenance records for such equipment.

(3) Within 15 days following the date of the inspection, the motor carrier or intermodal equipment provider shall—

(i) Certify that all violations noted have been corrected by completing the "Signature of Carrier/Intermodal Equipment Provider Official, Title, and Date Signed" portions of the form; and

(ii) Return the completed roadside inspection form to the issuing agency at the address indicated on the form and retain a copy at the motor carrier's principal place of business, at the intermodal equipment provider's principal place of business, or where the vehicle is housed for 12 months from the date of the inspection.

§396.11 Driver vehicle inspection report(s).

(a) **Equipment provided by motor carrier.** (1) **Report required.** Every motor carrier shall require its drivers to report, and every driver shall prepare a report in writing at the completion of each day's work on each vehicle operated, except for intermodal equipment tendered by an intermodal equipment provider. The report shall cover at least the following parts and accessories:

(i) Service brakes including trailer brake connections;

(ii) Parking brake;

(iii) Steering mechanism;

(iv) Lighting devices and reflectors;

(v) Tires;

(vi) Horn;

(vii) Windshield wipers;

(viii) Rear vision mirrors;

(ix) Coupling devices;

(x) Wheels and rims;

(xi) Emergency equipment.

(2) **Report content**. (i) The report must identify the vehicle and list any defect or deficiency discovered by or reported to the driver which would affect the safety of operation of the vehicle or result in its mechanical breakdown. If a driver operates more than one vehicle during the day, a report must be prepared for each vehicle operated. Drivers are not required to prepare a report if no defect or deficiency is discovered by or reported to the driver.

(ii) The driver must sign the report. On two-driver operations, only one driver needs to sign the driver vehicle inspection report, provided both drivers agree as to the defects or deficiencies identified.

(3) **Corrective action**. (i) Prior to requiring or permitting a driver to operate a vehicle, every motor carrier or its agent shall repair any defect or deficiency listed on the driver vehicle inspection report which would be likely to affect the safety of operation of the vehicle.

(ii) Every motor carrier or its agent shall certify on the driver vehicle inspection report which lists any defect or deficiency that the defect or deficiency has been repaired or that repair is unnecessary before the vehicle is operated again.

(4) **Retention period for reports**. Every motor carrier shall maintain the driver vehicle inspection report, the certification of repairs, and the certification of the driver's review for three months from the date the written report was prepared.

(5) **Exceptions**. The rules in this section shall not apply to a private motor carrier of passengers (nonbusiness), a driveaway-towaway operation, or any motor carrier operating only one commercial motor vehicle.

(b) **Equipment provided by intermodal equipment provider**. (1) **Report required.** Every intermodal equipment provider must have a process to receive driver reports of, and each driver or motor carrier transporting intermodal equipment must report to the intermodal equipment provider or its designated agent, any known damage, defects, or deficiencies in the intermodal equipment at the time the equipment is returned to the provider or the provider's designated agent. The report must include, at a minimum, the following parts and accessories:

(i) Brakes;

(ii) Lighting devices, lamps, markers, and conspicuity marking material;

(iii) Wheels, rims, lugs, tires;

(iv) Air line connections, hoses, and couplers;

(v) King pin upper coupling device;

(vi) Rails or support frames;

(vii) Tie down bolsters;

(viii) Locking pins, clevises, clamps, or hooks;

(ix) Sliders or sliding frame lock.

(2) **Report content**. (i) Name of the motor carrier responsible for the operation of the intermodal equipment at the time the damage, defects, or deficiencies were discovered by, or reported to, the driver.

(ii) Motor carrier's USDOT number; intermodal equipment provider's USDOT number, and a unique identifying number for the item of intermodal equipment.

(iii) Date and time the report was submitted.

PART 396

(iv) All damage, defects, or deficiencies of the intermodal equipment reported to the equipment provider and discovered by, or reported to, the motor carrier or its driver which would

(A) Affect the safety of operation of the intermodal equipment, or

(B) Result in its mechanical breakdown while transported on public roads.

(v) The signature of the driver who prepared the report.

(3) **Corrective action**. (i) Prior to allowing or permitting a motor carrier to transport a piece of intermodal equipment for which a motor carrier or driver has submitted a report about damage, defects or deficiencies, each intermodal equipment provider or its agent must repair the reported damage, defects, or deficiencies that are likely to affect the safety of operation of the vehicle.

(ii) Each intermodal equipment provider or its agent must certify on the original driver's report which lists any damage, defects, or deficiencies of the intermodal equipment that the reported damage, defects, or deficiencies have been repaired, or that repair is unnecessary, before the vehicle is operated again.

(4) **Retention period for reports**. Each intermodal equipment provider must maintain all documentation required by this section, including the driver report and the certification of repairs on all intermodal equipment, for a period of three months from the date that a motor carrier or its driver submits the report to the intermodal equipment provider or its agent.

§396.12 Procedures for intermodal equipment providers to accept reports required by §390.42(b) of this chapter.

(a) **System for reports**. Each intermodal equipment provider must establish a system for motor carriers and drivers to report to it any damage, defects, or deficiencies of intermodal equipment discovered by, or reported to, the motor carrier or driver which would—

(1) Affect the safety of operation of the intermodal equipment, or

(2) Result in its mechanical breakdown while transported on public roads.

(b) **Report content**. The system required by paragraph (a) of this section must include documentation of all of the following:

(1) Name of the motor carrier responsible for the operation of the intermodal equipment at the time the damage, defects, or deficiencies were discovered by, or reported to, the driver.

(2) Motor carrier's USDOT number; intermodal equipment provider's USDOT number, and a unique identifying number for the item of intermodal equipment.

(3) Date and time the report was submitted.

(4) All damage, defects, or deficiencies of the intermodal equipment must be reported to the equipment provider by the motor carrier or its driver. If no defect or deficiency in the intermodal equipment is discovered by or reported to the driver, no written report is required.

(5) The signature of the driver who prepared the report.

(c) **Corrective action**. (1) Prior to allowing or permitting a motor carrier to transport a piece of intermodal equipment for which a motor carrier or driver has submitted a report about damage, defects or deficiencies, each intermodal equipment provider or its agent must repair the reported damage, defects, or deficiencies that are likely to affect the safety of operation of the vehicle.

(2) Each intermodal equipment provider or its agent must certify on the original driver's report which lists any damage, defects, or deficiencies of the intermodal equipment that the reported damage, defects, or deficiencies have been repaired, or that repair is unnecessary, before the vehicle is operated again.

(d) **Retention period for reports**. Each intermodal equipment provider must maintain all documentation required by this section, including the driver report and the certification of repairs on all intermodal equipment, for a period of three months from the date that a motor carrier or its driver submits the report to the intermodal equipment provider or its agent.

§396.13 Driver inspection.

Before driving a motor vehicle, the driver shall:

(a) Be satisfied that the motor vehicle is in safe operating condition;

(b) Review the last driver vehicle inspection report if required by §396.11(a)(2)(i); and

(c) Sign the report to acknowledge that the driver has reviewed it and that there is a certification that the required repairs have been performed. The signature requirement does not apply to listed defects on a towed unit which is no longer part of the vehicle combination.

§396.15 Driveaway-towaway operations and inspections.

(a) **General**. Every motor carrier, with respect to motor vehicles engaged in driveaway-towaway operations, shall comply with the requirements of this part. Exception: Maintenance records required by §396.3, the vehicle inspection report required by §396.11, and the periodic inspection required by §396.17 of this part shall not be required for any vehicle which is part of the shipment being delivered.

(b) **Pre-trip inspection**. Before the beginning of any driveaway-towaway operation of motor vehicles in combination, the motor carrier shall make a careful inspection and test to ascertain that:

(1) The tow-bar or saddle-mount connections are properly secured to the towed and towing vehicle;

(2) They function adequately without cramping or binding of any of the parts; and

(3) The towed motor vehicle follows substantially in the path of the towing vehicle without whipping or swerving.

(c) **Post-trip inspection**. Motor carriers shall maintain practices to ensure that following completion of any trip in driveaway-towaway operation of motor vehicles in combination, and before they are used again, the tow-bars and saddle-mounts are disassembled and inspected for worn, bent, cracked, broken, or missing parts. Before reuse, suitable repair or replacement shall be made of any defective parts and the devices shall be properly reassembled.

§396.17 Periodic inspection.

(a) Every commercial motor vehicle must be inspected as required by this section. The inspection must include, at a minimum, the parts and accessories set forth in appendix A to this part. The term *commercial motor vehicle* includes each vehicle in a combination vehicle. For example, for a tractor semitrailer, full trailer combination, the tractor, semitrailer, and the full trailer (including the converter dolly if so equipped) must each be inspected.

(b) Except as provided in §396.23 and this paragraph, motor carriers must inspect or cause to be inspected all motor vehicles subject to their control. Intermodal equipment providers must inspect or cause to be inspected intermodal equipment that is interchanged or intended for interchange to motor carriers in intermodal transportation.

PART 396

(c) A motor carrier must not use a commercial motor vehicle, and an intermodal equipment provider must not tender equipment to a motor carrier for interchange, unless each component identified in appendix A to this part has passed an inspection in accordance with the terms of this section at least once during the preceding 12 months and documentation of such inspection is on the vehicle. The documentation may be:

(1) The inspection report prepared in accordance with §396.21(a), or

(2) Other forms of documentation, based on the inspection report (e.g., sticker or decal), which contains the following information:

(i) The date of inspection;

(ii) Name and address of the motor carrier, intermodal equipment provider, or other entity where the inspection report is maintained;

(iii) Information uniquely identifying the vehicle inspected if not clearly marked on the motor vehicle; and

(iv) A certification that the vehicle has passed an inspection in accordance with §396.17.

(d) A motor carrier may perform the required annual inspection for vehicles under the carrier's control which are not subject to an inspection under §396.23(a)(1). An intermodal equipment provider may perform the required annual inspection for intermodal equipment interchanged or intended for interchange to motor carriers that are not subject to an inspection under §396.23(a)(1).

(e) In lieu of the self-inspection provided for in paragraph (d) of this section, a motor carrier or intermodal equipment provider responsible for the inspection may choose to have a commercial garage, fleet leasing company, truck stop, or other similar commercial business perform the inspection as its agent, provided that business operates and maintains facilities appropriate for commercial vehicle inspections and it employs qualified inspectors, as required by §396.19.

(f) Vehicles passing periodic inspections performed under the auspices of any State government or equivalent jurisdiction in the Canadian Provinces, the Yukon Territory, and Mexico, meeting the minimum standards contained in appendix A to this part, will be considered to have met the requirements of an annual inspection for a period of 12 months commencing from the last day of the month in which the inspection was performed.

(g) It is the responsibility of the motor carrier or intermodal equipment provider to ensure that all parts and accessories on commercial motor vehicles intended for use in interstate commerce for which they are responsible are maintained at, or promptly repaired to, the minimum standards set forth in appendix A to this part.

(h) Failure to perform properly the annual inspection required by this section shall cause the motor carrier or intermodal equipment provider to be subject to the penalty provisions of 49 U.S.C. 521(b).

§396.19 Inspector qualifications.

(a) Motor carriers and intermodal equipment providers must ensure that individuals performing annual inspections under §396.17(d) or (e) are qualified as follows:

(1) Understand the inspection criteria set forth in part 393 and appendix A to this part and can identify defective components;

(2) Are knowledgeable of and have mastered the methods, procedures, tools and equipment used when performing an inspection; and

(3) Are capable of performing an inspection by reason of experience, training, or both as follows:

(i) Successfully completed a Federal- or State-sponsored training program or have a certificate from a State or Canadian Province that qualifies the individuals to perform commercial motor vehicle safety inspections, or

(ii) Have a combination of training or experience totaling at least 1 year. Such training or experience may consist of:

(A) Participation in a commercial motor vehicle manufacturer-sponsored training program or similar commercial training program designed to train students in commercial motor vehicle operation and maintenance;

(B) Experience as a mechanic or inspector in a motor carrier or intermodal equipment maintenance program;

(C) Experience as a mechanic or inspector in commercial motor vehicle maintenance at a commercial garage, fleet leasing company, or similar facility; or

(D) Experience as a commercial motor vehicle inspector for a State, Provincial or Federal government.

(b) Motor carriers and intermodal equipment providers must retain evidence of that individual's qualifications under this section. They must retain this evidence for the period during which that individual is performing annual motor vehicle inspections for the motor carrier or intermodal equipment provider, and for one year thereafter. However, motor carriers and intermodal equipment providers do not have to maintain documentation of inspector qualifications for those inspections performed as part of a State periodic inspection program.

§396.21 Periodic inspection recordkeeping requirements.

(a) The qualified inspector performing the inspection shall prepare a report that:

(1) Identifies the individual performing the inspection;

(2) Identifies the motor carrier operating the vehicle or intermodal equipment provider intending to interchange the vehicle to a motor carrier;

(3) Identifies the date of the inspection;

(4) Identifies the vehicle inspected;

(5) Identifies the vehicle components inspected and describes the results of the inspection, including the identification of those components not meeting the minimum standards set forth in appendix A to this part; and

(6) Certifies the accuracy and completeness of the inspection as complying with all the requirements of this section.

(b)(1) The original or a copy of the inspection report shall be retained by the motor carrier, intermodal equipment provider, or other entity that is responsible for the inspection for a period of fourteen months from the date of the inspection report. The original or a copy of the inspection report must be retained where the vehicle is either housed or maintained.

(2) The original or a copy of the inspection report must be available for inspection upon demand of an authorized Federal, State or local official.

(3) **Exception.** If the motor carrier operating the commercial motor vehicles did not perform the commercial motor vehicle's last annual inspection, or if an intermodal equipment provider did not itself perform the annual inspection on equipment intended for interchange to a motor carrier, the motor carrier or intermodal equipment provider is responsible for obtaining the original or a copy of the last annual inspection report upon demand of an authorized Federal, State, or local official.

§396.23 Equivalent to periodic inspection.

(a)(1) If a commercial motor vehicle is subject to a mandatory inspection program that is determined by the Administrator to be as effective as §396.17, the motor carrier or intermodal equipment provider must meet the requirement of §396.17 through that inspection program. Commercial motor vehicle inspections may be conducted by government personnel, at commercial facilities authorized by a State government or equivalent jurisdiction in the Canadian Provinces, the Yukon Territory, or Mexico, or by the motor carrier or intermodal equipment provider itself under the auspices of a self-inspection program authorized by a State government or equivalent jurisdiction in the Canadian Provinces, the Yukon Territory, or Mexico.

(2) Should FMCSA determine that an inspection program, in whole or in part, is not as effective as §396.17, the motor carrier or intermodal equipment provider must ensure that the periodic inspection required by §396.17 is performed on all commercial motor vehicles under its control in a manner specified in §396.17.

Editor's Note: A vehicle will meet the Federal requirements if inspected under a state mandatory inspection program in Alabama (LPG Board), California, Connecticut (bus inspection program), District of Columbia, Hawaii, Illinois, Louisiana, Maine, Maryland, Massachusetts, Michigan (bus inspection program), Minnesota, New Hampshire, New Jersey, New York, Ohio (church bus inspection program), Pennsylvania, Rhode Island, Texas, Utah, Vermont, Virginia, West Virginia, and Wisconsin (bus inspection program). The Federal Motor Carrier Safety Administration has also determined that all of the Canadian Provinces and the Yukon Territory have periodic inspection programs that are as effective as the Federal requirements. Vehicles displaying a current "NOM-68" inspection decal from Mexico will also be deemed compliant with U.S. Federal inspection standards.

(b) [Reserved]

§396.25 Qualifications of brake inspectors.

(a) Motor carriers and intermodal equipment providers must ensure that all inspections, maintenance, repairs or service to the brakes of its commercial motor vehicles, are performed in compliance with the requirements of this section.

(b) For purposes of this section, *brake inspector* means any employee of a motor carrier or intermodal equipment provider who is responsible for ensuring that all brake inspections, maintenance, service, or repairs to any commercial motor vehicle, subject to the motor carrier's or intermodal equipment provider's control, meet the applicable Federal standards.

(c) No motor carrier or intermodal equipment provider may require or permit any employee who does not meet the minimum brake inspector qualifications of paragraph (d) of this section to be responsible for the inspection, maintenance, service or repairs of any brakes on its commercial motor vehicle.

(d) The motor carrier or intermodal equipment provider must ensure that each brake inspector is qualified as follows:

(1) Understands the brake service or inspection task to be accomplished and can perform that task; and

(2) Is knowledgeable of and has mastered the methods, procedures, tools and equipment used when performing an assigned brake service or inspection task; and

(3) Is capable of performing the assigned brake service or inspection by reason of experience, training, or both as follows:

(i) Has successfully completed an apprenticeship program sponsored by a State, a Canadian Province, a Federal agency or a labor union, or a training program approved by a State, Provincial or Federal agency, or has a certificate from a State or Canadian Province that qualifies the person to perform the assigned brake service or inspection task (including passage of Commercial Driver's License air brake tests in the case of a brake inspection); or

(ii) Has brake-related training or experience or a combination thereof totaling at least one year. Such training or experience may consist of:

(A) Participation in a training program sponsored by a brake or vehicle manufacturer or similar commercial training program designed to train students in brake maintenance or inspection similar to the assigned brake service or inspection tasks; or

(B) Experience performing brake maintenance or inspection similar to the assigned brake service or inspection task in a motor carrier or intermodal equipment provider maintenance program; or

(C) Experience performing brake maintenance or inspection similar to the assigned brake service or inspection task at a commercial garage, fleet leasing company, or similar facility.

(e) No motor carrier or intermodal equipment provider may employ any person as a brake inspector unless the evidence of the inspector's qualifications, required under this section, is maintained by the motor carrier or intermodal equipment provider at its principal place of business, or at the location at which the brake inspector is employed. The evidence must be maintained for the period during which the brake inspector is employed in that capacity and for one year thereafter. However, motor carriers and intermodal equipment providers do not have to maintain evidence of qualifications to inspect air brake systems for such inspections performed by persons who have passed the air brake knowledge and skills test for a Commercial Driver's License.

Appendix A to Part 396—Minimum Periodic Inspection Standards

[Editor's Note: Appendix G to Subchapter B of Chapter III was redesignated as Appendix A to part 396.]

A vehicle does not pass an inspection if it has one of the following defects or deficiencies:

1. **Brake System**.

a. **Service Brakes**.

(1) Absence of braking action on any axle required to have brakes upon application of the service brakes (such as missing brakes or brake shoe(s) failing to move upon application of a wedge. S-cam, cam, or disc brake).

(2) Missing or broken mechanical components including: shoes, lining pads, springs, anchor pins, spiders, cam rollers, push-rods, and air chamber mounting bolts.

(3) Loose brake components including air chambers, spiders, and cam shaft support brackets.

(4) Audible air leak at brake chamber (Example-ruptured diaphragm, loose chamber clamp, etc.).

(5) Readjustment limits.

(a) The maximum pushrod stroke must not be greater than the values given in the tables below and at §393.47(e). Any brake stroke exceeding the readjustment limit will be rejected. Stroke must be measured with engine off and reservoir pressure of 80 to 90 psi with brakes fully applied.

Clamp-type brake chambers

Type	Outside diameter	Brake readjustment limit: standard stroke chamber	Brake readjustment limit: long stroke chamber
6.........	4½ in. (114 mm)	1¼ in. (31.8 mm).	
9	5¼ in. (133 mm)	1⅜ in. (34.9 mm).	
12	5¹¹⁄₁₆ in. (145 mm)	1⅜ in. (34.9 mm)	1¾ in. (44.5 mm).
16........	6⅜ in. (162 mm)	1¾ in. (44.5 mm)...........	2 in. (50.8 mm).
20	6²⁵⁄₃₂ in. (172 mm)	1¾ in. (44.5 mm)...........	2 in. (50.8 mm). 2½ in. (63.5 mm).[1]
24........	7 ⁷⁄₃₂ in. (184 mm)	1¾ in. (44.5 mm)	2 in. (50.8 mm). 2½ in. (63.5 mm).[2]
30........	8³⁄₃₂ in. (206 mm)	2 in. (50.8 mm)	2½ in. (63.5 mm).
36........	9 in. (229 mm)	2 ½ in. (63.5 mm)	

[1] For type 20 chambers with a 3-inch (76 mm) rated stroke.

[2] For type 24 chambers with a 3-inch (76 mm) rated stroke.

Bendix DD–3 brake chambers

Type	Outside diameter	Brake readjustment limit
30	8⅛ in. (206 mm)........................	2¼ in. (57.2 mm).

Bolt-type brake chambers

Type	Outside diameter	Brake readjustment limit
A...........	6¹⁵⁄₁₆ in. (176 mm)	1⅜ in. (34.9 mm).
B	9³⁄₁₆ in. (234 mm)........................	1¾ in. (44.5 mm).
C...........	8¹⁄₁₆ in. (205 mm)........................	1¾ in. (44.5 mm)
D...........	5¼ in. (133 mm).........................	1¼ in. (31.8 mm).
E...........	6³⁄₁₆ in. (157 mm)........................	1⅜ in. (34.9 mm).
F...........	11 in. (279 mm).........................	2¼ in. (57.2 mm).
G	9⅞ in. (251 mm)	2 in. (50.8 mm).

Rotochamber-type brake chambers

Type	Outside diameter	Brake readjustment limit
9	4⁹⁄₃₂ in. (109 mm)........................	1½ in. (38.1 mm).
12	4¹³⁄₁₆ in. (122 mm).......................	1½ in. (38.1 mm).
16...........	5¹³⁄₃₂ in. (138 mm).......................	2 in. (50.8 mm).
20	5¹⁵⁄₁₆ in. (151 mm).......................	2 in. (50.8 mm).

Rotochamber-type brake chambers, Continued

Type	Outside diameter	Brake readjustment limit
24.........	6¹³⁄₃₂ in. (163 mm)	2 in. (50.8 mm).
30.........	7¹⁄₁₆ in. (180 mm)........................	2¼ in. (57.2 mm).
36.........	7⅝ in. (194 mm)........................	2¾ in. (69.9 mm).
50.........	8⅞ in. (226 mm)........................	3 in. (76.2 mm).

(b) For actuator types not listed in these tables, the pushrod stroke must not be greater than 80 percent of the rated stroke marked on the actuator by the actuator manufacturer, or greater than the readjustment limit marked on the actuator by the actuator manufacturer.

(6) Brake linings or pads.

(a) Lining or pad is not firmly attached to the shoe;

(b) Saturated with oil, grease, or brake fluid; or

(c) Non-steering axles: Lining with a thickness less than ¼ inch at the shoe center for air drum brakes, ¹⁄₁₆ inch or less at the shoe center for hydraulic and electric drum brakes, and less than ⅛ inch for air disc brakes.

(d) Steering axles: Lining with a thickness less than ¼ inch at the shoe center for drum brakes, less than ⅛ inch for air disc brakes and ¹⁄₁₆ inch or less for hydraulic disc and electric brakes.

(7) Missing brake on any axle required to have brakes.

(8) Mismatch across any power unit steering axle of:

(a) Air chamber sizes.

(b) Slack adjuster length.

Wedge Brake Data—Movement of the scribe mark on the lining shall not exceed ¹⁄₁₆ inch.

b. **Parking Brake System**. No brakes on the vehicle or combination are applied upon actuation of the parking brake control, including driveline hand controlled parking brakes.

c. **Brake Drum or Rotors**.

(1) With any external crack or cracks that open upon brake application (do not confuse short hairline heat check cracks with flexural cracks).

(2) Any portion of the drum or rotor missing or in danger of falling away.

d. **Brake Hose**.

(1) Hose with any damage extending through the outer reinforcement ply. (Rubber impregnated fabric cover is not a reinforcement ply). (Thermoplastic nylon may have braid reinforcement or color difference between cover and inner tube. Exposure of second color is cause for rejection.

(2) Bulge or swelling when air pressure is applied.

(3) Any audible leaks.

(4) Two hoses improperly joined (such as a splice made by sliding the hose ends over a piece of tubing and clamping the hose to the tube).

(5) Air hose cracked, broken or crimped.

e. **Brake Tubing**.

(1) Any audible leak.

(2) Tubing cracked, damaged by heat, broken or crimped.

f. **Low Pressure Warning Device** missing, inoperative, or does not operate at 55 psi and below, or ½ the governor cut-out pressure, whichever is less.

PART 396

g. **Tractor Protection Valve**. Inoperable or missing tractor protection valve(s) on power unit.

h. **Air Compressor**.

(1) Compressor drive belts in condition of impending or probable failure.

(2) Loose compressor mounting bolts.

(3) Cracked, broken or loose pulley.

(4) Cracked or broken mounting brackets, braces or adapters.

i. **Electric Brakes**.

(1) Absence of braking action on any wheel required to have brakes.

(2) Missing or inoperable breakaway braking device.

j. **Hydraulic Brakes. (Including Power Assist Over Hydraulic and Engine Drive Hydraulic Booster)**.

(1) Master cylinder less than ¼ full.

(2) No pedal reserve with engine running except by pumping pedal.

(3) Power assist unit fails to operate.

(4) Seeping or swelling brake hose(s) under application of pressure.

(5) Missing or inoperative check valve.

(6) Has any visually observed leaking hydraulic fluid in the brake system.

(7) Has hydraulic hose(s) abraded (chafed) through outer cover-to-fabric layer.

(8) Fluid lines or connections leaking restricted, crimped, cracked or broken.

(9) Brake failure or low fluid warning light on and/or inoperative.

k. **Vacuum Systems**. Any vacuum system which:

(1) Has insufficient vacuum reserve to permit one full brake application after engine is shut off.

(2) Has vacuum hose(s) or line(s) restricted, abraded (chafed) through outer cover to cord ply, crimped, cracked, broken or has collapse of vacuum hose(s) when vacuum is applied.

(3) Lacks an operative low-vacuum warning device as required.

l. **Antilock Brake System** [1] [2] [3]

(1) Missing ABS malfunction indicator components (*i.e.*, bulb, wiring, etc.).

(2) ABS malfunction indicator that does not illuminate when power is first applied to the ABS controller (ECU) during initial power up.

(3) ABS malfunction indicator that stays illuminated while power is continuously applied to the ABS controller (ECU).

(4) ABS malfunction indicator lamp on a trailer or dolly does not cycle when electrical power is applied (a) only to the vehicle's constant ABS power circuit, or (b) only to the vehicle's stop lamp circuit.

(5) With its brakes released and its ignition switch in the normal run position, power unit does not provide continuous electrical power to the ABS on any air-braked vehicle it is equipped to tow.

(6) Other missing or inoperative ABS components.

---

[1] Power units manufactured after March 1, 2001, have two ABS malfunction indicators, one for the power unit and one for the units that they tow. Both malfunction indicators are required to be fully functional.

[2] Air-braked vehicles: Subsections (1)-(6) of this section are applicable to tractors with air brakes built on or after March 1, 1997, and all other vehicles with air brakes built on or after March 1, 1998.

[3] Hydraulic-braked vehicles: Subsections (1)-(3) of this section are applicable to vehicles over 10,000 lbs. GVWR with hydraulic brakes built on or after September 1, 1999. Subsection (6) of this section is applicable to vehicles over 10,000 lbs. with hydraulic brakes built on or after March 1, 1999.

m. **Automatic Brake Adjusters**

(1) Failure to maintain a brake within the brake stroke limit specified by the vehicle manufacturer.

(2) Any automatic brake adjuster that has been replaced with a manual adjuster.

(3) Damaged, loose, or missing components.

(4) Any brake that is found to be out of adjustment on initial inspection must be evaluated to determine why the automatic brake adjuster is not functioning properly and the problem must be corrected in order for the vehicle to pass the inspection. It is not acceptable to manually adjust automatic brake adjusters without first correcting the underlying problem. For example, there may be other components within the braking system that are distressed or out of specification (*i.e.,* broken welds, loose mounting hardware, cracked brake drums, worn bushings, etc.) that would require immediate attention.

2. **Coupling Devices**.

a. **Fifth Wheels**.

(1) Mounting to frame.

(a) Any fasteners missing or ineffective.

(b) Any movement between mounting components.

(c) Any mounting angle iron cracked or broken.

(2) Mounting plates and pivot brackets.

(a) Any fasteners missing or ineffective.

(b) Any welds or parent metal cracked.

(c) More than ⅜ inch horizontal movement between pivot bracket pin and bracket.

(d) Pivot bracket pin missing or not secured.

(3) Sliders.

(a) Any latching fasteners missing or ineffective.

(b) Any fore or aft stop missing or not securely attached.

(c) Movement more than ⅜ inch between slider bracket and slider base.

(d) Any slider component cracked in parent metal or weld.

(4) Lower coupler.

(a) Horizontal movement between the upper and lower fifth wheel halves exceeds ½ inch.

(b) Operating handle not in closed or locked position.

(c) Kingpin not properly engaged.

(d) Separation between upper and lower coupler allowing light to show through from side to side.

(e) Cracks in the fifth wheel plate.

Exceptions: Cracks in fifth wheel approach ramps and casting shrinkage cracks in the ribs of the body of a cast fifth wheel.

(f) Locking mechanism parts missing, broken, or deformed to the extent the kingpin is not securely held.

b. **Pintle Hooks**.

(1) Mounting to frame.

(a) Any missing or ineffective fasteners (a fastener is not considered missing if there is an empty hole in the device but no corresponding hole in the frame or vise versa).

(b) Mounting surface cracks extending from point of attachment (e.g., cracks in the frame at mounting bolt holes).

(c) Loose mounting.

(d) Frame crossmember providing pintle hook attachment cracked.

(2) Integrity.

(a) Cracks anywhere in pintle hook assembly.

(b) Any welded repairs to the pintle hook.

(c) Any part of the horn section reduced by more than 20%.

(d) Latch insecure.

c. **Drawbar/Towbar Eye**.

(1) Mounting.

(a) Any cracks in attachment welds.

(b) Any missing or ineffective fasteners.

(2) Integrity.

(a) Any cracks.

(b) Any part of the eye reduced by more than 20%.

d. **Drawbar/Towbar Tongue**.

(1) Slider (power or manual).

(a) Ineffective latching mechanism.

(b) Missing or ineffective stop.

(c) Movement of more than ¼ inch between slider and housing.

(d) Any leaking, air or hydraulic cylinders, hoses, or chambers (other than slight oil weeping normal with hydraulic seals).

(2) Integrity.

(a) Any cracks.

(b) Movement of ¼ inch between subframe and drawbar at point of attachment.

e. **Safety Devices**.

(1) Safety devices missing.

(2) Unattached or incapable of secure attachment.

(3) Chains and hooks.

(a) Worn to the extent of a measurable reduction in link cross section.

(b) Improper repairs including welding, wire, small bolts, rope and tape.

(4) Cable.

(a) Kinked or broken cable strands.

(b) Improper clamps or clamping.

f. **Saddle-Mounts**.

(1) Method of attachment.

(a) Any missing or ineffective fasteners.

(b) Loose mountings.

(c) Any cracks or breaks in a stress or load bearing member.

(d) Horizontal movement between upper and lower saddle-mount halves exceeds ¼ inch.

3. **Exhaust System**.

a. Any exhaust system determined to be leaking at a point forward of or directly below the driver/sleeper compartment.

b. A bus exhaust system leaking or discharging to the atmosphere:

(1) **Gasoline powered**—excess of 6 inches forward of the rearmost part of the bus.

(2) **Other than gasoline powered**—in excess of 15 inches forward of the rearmost part of the bus.

(3) **Other than gasoline powered**—forward of a door or window designed to be opened. (Exception: emergency exits).

c. No part of the exhaust system of any motor vehicle shall be so located as would be likely to result in burning, charring, or damaging the electrical wiring, the fuel supply, or any combustible part of the motor vehicle.

4. **Fuel System**.

a. A fuel system with a visible leak at any point.

b. A fuel tank filler cap missing.

c. A fuel tank not securely attached to the motor vehicle by reason of loose, broken or missing mounting bolts or brackets (some fuel tanks use springs or rubber bushings to permit movement).

5. **Lighting Devices**.

All lighting devices and reflectors required by part 393 shall be operable.

6. **Safe loading**.

a. Part(s) of vehicle or condition of loading such that the spare tire or any part of the load or dunnage can fall onto the roadway.

b. Protection Against Shifting Cargo—Any vehicle without a front-end structure or equivalent device as required.

c. Container securement devices on intermodal equipment—All devices used to secure an intermodal container to a chassis, including rails or support frames, tiedown bolsters, locking pins, clevises, clamps, and hooks that are cracked, broken, loose, or missing.

7. **Steering Mechanism**

a. **Steering Wheel Free Play** (on vehicles equipped with power steering the engine must be running).

Steering wheel diameter	Manual steering system	Power steering system
16"	2"	4 ½"
18"	2 ¼"	4 ¾"
20"	2 ½"	5 ¼"
22"	2 ¾"	5 ¾"

b. **Steering Column**.

(1) Any absence or looseness of U-bolt(s) or positioning part(s).

(2) Worn, faulty or obviously repair welded universal joint(s).

(3) Steering wheel not properly secured.

c. **Front Axle Beam and All Steering Components Other Than Steering Column**.

(1) Any crack(s).

(2) Any obvious welded repair(s).

d. **Steering Gear Box**.

(1) Any mounting bolt(s) loose or missing.

(2) Any crack(s) in gear box or mounting brackets.

e. **Pitman Arm**. Any looseness of the pitman arm on the steering gear output shaft.

f. **Power Steering**. Auxiliary power assist cylinder loose.

g. **Ball and Socket Joints**.

(1) Any movement under steering load of a stud nut.

(2) Any motion, other than rotational, between any linkage member and it's attachment point of more than ¼ inch.

h. **Tie Rods and Drag Links**.

(1) Loose clamp(s) or clamp bolt(s) on tie rods or drag links.

(2) Any looseness in any threaded joint.

i. **Nuts**. Nut(s) loose or missing on tie rods pitman arm, drag link, steering arm or tie rod arm.

j. **Steering System**. Any modification or other condition that interferes with free movement of any steering component.

8. **Suspension**.

a. Any U-bolt(s), spring hanger(s), or other axle positioning part(s) cracked, broken, loose or missing resulting in shifting of an axle from its normal position. (After a turn, lateral axle displacement is normal with some suspensions. Forward or rearward operation in a straight line will cause the axle to return to alignment.)

b. **Spring Assembly**.

(1) Any leaves in a leaf spring assembly broken or missing.

(2) Any broken main leaf in a leaf spring assembly. (Includes assembly with more than one main spring).

(3) Coil spring broken.

(4) Rubber spring missing.

(5) One or more leaves displaced in a manner that could result in contact with a tire, rim, brake drum or frame.

(6) Broken torsion bar spring in a torsion bar suspension.

(7) Deflated air suspension, i.e., system failure, leak, etc.

c. **Torque, Radius or Tracking Components**.

Any part of a torque, radius or tracking component assembly or any part used for attaching the same to the vehicle frame or axle that is cracked, loose, broken or missing. (Does not apply to loose bushings in torque or track rods.)

9. **Frame**.

a. **Frame Members**.

(1) Any cracked, broken, loose, or sagging frame member.

(2) Any loose or missing fasteners including fasteners attaching functional component such as engine, transmission, steering gear, suspension, body parts, and fifth wheel.

b. **Tire and Wheel Clearance**. Any condition, including loading, that causes the body or frame to be in contact with a tire or any part of the wheel assemblies.

c. (1) **Adjustable Axle Assemblies (Sliding Subframes)**. Adjustable axle assembly with locking pins missing or not engaged.

10. **Tires**.

a. **Any tire on any steering axle of a power unit**.

(1) With less than $\frac{4}{32}$ inch tread when measured at any point on a major tread groove.

(2) Has body ply or belt material exposed through the tread or sidewall.

(3) Has any tread or sidewall separation.

(4) Has a cut where the ply or belt material is exposed.

(5) Labeled "Not for Highway Use" or displaying other marking which would exclude use on steering axle.

(6) A tube-type radial tire without radial tube stem markings. These markings include a red band around the tube stem, the word "radial" embossed in metal stems, or the word "radial" molded in rubber stems.

(7) Mixing bias and radial tires on the same axle.

(8) Tire flap protrudes through valve slot in rim and touches stem.

(9) Regrooved tire except motor vehicles used solely in urban or suburban service (see exception in §393.75(e).

(10) Boot, blowout patch or other ply repair.

(11) Weight carried exceeds tire load limit. This includes overloaded tire resulting from low air pressure.

(12) Tire is flat or has noticeable (e.g., can be heard or felt) leak.

(13) Any bus equipped with recapped or retreaded tire(s).

(14) So mounted or inflated that it comes in contact with any part of the vehicle.

b. **All tires other than those found on the steering axle of a power unit**.

(1) Weight carried exceeds tire load limit. This includes overloaded tire resulting from low air pressure.

(2) Tire is flat or has noticeable (e.g., can be heard or felt) leak.

(3) Has body ply or belt material exposed through the tread or sidewall.

(4) Has any tread or sidewall separation.

(5) Has a cut where ply or belt material is exposed.

(6) So mounted or inflated that it comes in contact with any part of the vehicle. (This includes a tire that contacts its mate.)

(7) Is marked "Not for highway use" or otherwise marked and having like meaning.

(8) With less than $\frac{2}{32}$ inch tread when measured at any point on a major tread groove.

c. Installation of **speed-restricted tires** unless specifically designated by motor carrier.

11. **Wheels and Rims**.

a. **Lock or Side Ring**. Bent, broken, cracked, improperly seated, sprung or mismatched ring(s).

b. **Wheels and Rims**. Cracked or broken or has elongated bolt holes.

c. **Fasteners (both spoke and disc wheels)**. Any loose, missing, broken, cracked, stripped or otherwise ineffective fasteners.

d. **Welds**.

(1) Any cracks in welds attaching disc wheel disc to rim.

(2) Any crack in welds attaching tubeless demountable rim to adapter.

(3) Any welded repair on aluminum wheel(s) on a steering axle.

(4) Any welded repair other than disc to rim attachment on steel disc wheel(s) mounted on the steering axle.

12. **Windshield Glazing**.

(Not including a 2 inch border at the top, a 1 inch border at each side and the area below the topmost portion of the steering wheel.) Any crack, discoloration or vision reducing matter except: (1) coloring or tinting applied at time of manufacture; (2) any crack not over $\frac{1}{4}$ inch wide, if not intersected by any other crack; (3) any damaged area not more than $\frac{3}{4}$ inch in diameter, if not closer than 3 inches to any other such damaged area; (4) labels, stickers, decalcomania, etc. (see §393.60 for exceptions).

13. **Windshield Wipers**.

Any power unit that has an inoperative wiper, or missing or damaged parts that render it ineffective.

14. **Motorcoach Seats**

a. Any passenger seat that is not securely fastened to the vehicle structure.

PART 396

b. [Reserved]

15. **Rear Impact Guard**

a. **Trailers and semitrailers with a GVWR of 4,536 kg (10,001 lbs.) or more, manufactured on or after January 26, 1998 (see exceptions in §393.86(a)(1)).**

1. Missing guard.

2. Guard is not securely attached to trailer, including broken or missing fasteners, any welds or parent metal cracked, or other damage that compromises secure attachment of the guard.

3. Guard horizontal member does not extend to within 100 mm (4 inches) of each, or extends beyond either, side extremity of the vehicle.

4. Guard horizontal member is more than 560 mm (22 inches) above the ground.

5. Guard horizontal member is more than 305 mm (12 inches) forward of the rear extremity of the vehicle.

6. Guard horizontal member does not have a cross sectional vertical height of at least 100 mm (4 inches) across its entire width.

b. **Commercial motor vehicles manufactured after December 31, 1952 (except trailers and semitrailers manufactured on or after January 26, 1998) (see exceptions in §393.86(b)(1) and §393.86(b)(3)).**

1. Missing guard.

2. Guard is not securely attached to trailer by bolts, welding, or other comparable means.

3. Guard horizontal member is more than 762 mm (30 inches) above the ground.

4. Guard horizontal member does not extend to within 457 mm (18 inches) of each side extremity of the vehicle.

5. Guard horizontal member is more than 610 mm (24 inches) forward of the rear extremity of the vehicle.

PART 397—TRANSPORTATION OF HAZARDOUS MATERIALS; DRIVING AND PARKING RULES

Subpart A—General

Subpart B—Reserved

Subpart C—Routing of Non-Radioactive Hazardous Materials

Subpart D—Routing of Class 7 (Radioactive) Materials

Subpart E—Preemption Procedures

Authority: 49 U.S.C. 322; 49 CFR 1.87. Subpart A also issued under 49 U.S.C. 5103, 31136, 31502, and 49 CFR 1.97. Subparts C, D, and E also issued under 49 U.S.C. 5112, 5125.

Subpart A—General

§397.1 Application of the rules in this part.

(a) The rules in this part apply to each motor carrier engaged in the transportation of hazardous materials by a motor vehicle which must be marked or placarded in accordance with §177.823 of this title and to—

(1) Each officer or employee of the motor carrier who performs supervisory duties related to the transportation of hazardous materials; and

(2) Each person who operates or who is in charge of a motor vehicle containing hazardous materials.

(b) Each person designated in paragraph (a) of this section must know and obey the rules in this part.

§397.2 Compliance with Federal motor carrier safety regulations.

A motor carrier or other person to whom this part is applicable must comply with the rules in Part 390 through 397, inclusive, of this subchapter when he/she is transporting hazardous materials by a motor vehicle which must be marked or placarded in accordance with §177.823 of this title.

§397.3 State and local laws, ordinances and regulations.

Every motor vehicle containing hazardous materials must be driven and parked in compliance with the laws, ordinances, and regulations of the jurisdiction in which it is being operated, unless they are at variance with specific regulations of the Department of Transportation which are applicable to the operation of that vehicle and which impose a more stringent obligation or restraint.

§397.5 Attendance and surveillance of motor vehicles.

(a) Except as provided in paragraph (b) of this section, a motor vehicle which contains a Division 1.1, 1.2, or 1.3 (explosive) material must be attended at all times by its driver or a qualified representative of the motor carrier that operates it.

(b) The rules in paragraph (a) of this section do not apply to a motor vehicle which contains Division 1.1, 1.2, or 1.3 material if all the following conditions exist—

(1) The vehicle is located on the property of a motor carrier, on the property of a shipper or consignee of the explosives, in a safe haven, or, in the case of a vehicle containing 50 pounds or less of a Division 1.1, 1.2, or 1.3 material, on a construction or survey site; and

(2) The lawful bailee of the explosives is aware of the nature of the explosives the vehicle contains and has been instructed in the procedures which must be followed in emergencies; and

(3) The vehicle is within the bailee's unobstructed field of view or is located in a safe haven.

(c) A motor vehicle which contains hazardous materials other than Division 1.1, 1.2, or 1.3, materials, and which is located on a public street or highway, or the shoulder of a public highway, must be attended by its driver. However, the vehicle need not be attended while its driver is performing duties which are incident and necessary to the driver's duties as the operator of the vehicle.

(d) For purposes of this section—

(1) A motor vehicle is attended when the person in charge of the vehicle is on the vehicle, awake, and not in a sleeper berth, or is within 100 feet of the vehicle and has it within his/her unobstructed field of view.

(2) A qualified representative of a motor carrier is a person who—

(i) Has been designated by the carrier to attend the vehicle;

(ii) Is aware of the nature of the hazardous materials contained in the vehicle he/she attends;

(iii) Has been instructed in the procedures he/she must follow in emergencies; and

(iv) Is authorized to move the vehicle and has the means and ability to do so.

(3) A safe haven is an area specifically approved in writing by local, State, or Federal governmental authorities for the parking of unattended vehicles containing Division 1.1, 1.2, or 1.3 materials.

(e) The rules in this section do not relieve the driver from any obligation imposed by law relating to the placing of warning devices when a motor vehicle is stopped on a public street or highway.

§397.7 Parking.

(a) A motor vehicle which contains Division 1.1, 1.2, or 1.3 materials must not be parked under any of the following circumstances—

(1) On or within 5 feet of the traveled portion of a public street or highway;

(2) On private property (including premises of a fueling or eating facility) without the knowledge and consent of the person who is in charge of the property and who is aware of the nature of the hazardous materials the vehicle contains; or

(3) Within 300 feet of a bridge, tunnel, dwelling, or place where people work, congregate, or assemble, except for brief periods when the necessities of operation require the vehicle to be parked and make it impracticable to park the vehicle in any other place.

(b) A motor vehicle which contains hazardous materials other than Division 1.1, 1.2, or 1.3 materials must not be parked on or within five feet of the traveled portion of public street or highway except for brief periods when the necessities of operation require the vehicle to be parked and make it impracticable to park the vehicle in any other place.

§397.9 [Removed and Reserved]

§397.11 Fires.

(a) A motor vehicle containing hazardous materials must not be operated near an open fire unless its driver has first taken precautions to ascertain that the vehicle can safely pass the fire without stopping.

(b) A motor vehicle containing hazardous materials must not be parked within 300 feet of an open fire.

§397.13 Smoking.

No person may smoke or carry a lighted cigarette, cigar, or pipe on or within 25 feet of—

(a) A motor vehicle which contains Class 1 materials, Class 5 materials, or flammable materials classified as Division 2.1, Class 3, Divisions 4.1 and 4.2; or

(b) An empty tank motor vehicle which has been used to transport Class 3, flammable materials or Division 2.1 flammable gases, which, when so used, was required to be marked or placarded in accordance with the rules in §177.823 of this title.

§397.15 Fueling.

When a motor vehicle which contains hazardous materials is being fueled—

(a) Its engine must not be operating; and

(b) A person must be in control of the fueling process at the point where the fuel tank is filled.

§397.17 Tires.

(a) A driver must examine each tire on a motor vehicle at the beginning of each trip and each time the vehicle is parked.

(b) If, as the result of an examination pursuant to paragraph (a) of this section, or otherwise, a tire is found to be flat, leaking, or improperly inflated, the driver must cause the tire to be repaired, replaced, or properly inflated before the vehicle is driven. However, the vehicle may be driven to the nearest safe place to perform the required repair, replacement, or inflation.

(c) If, as the result of an examination pursuant to paragraph (a) of this section, or otherwise, a tire is found to be overheated, the driver shall immediately cause the overheated tire to be removed and placed at a safe distance from the vehicle. The driver shall not operate the vehicle until the cause of the overheating is corrected.

(d) Compliance with the rules in this section does not relieve a driver from the duty to comply with the rules in §§397.5 and 397.7.

§397.19 Instructions and documents.

(a) A motor carrier that transports Division 1.1, 1.2, or 1.3 (explosive) materials must furnish the driver of each motor vehicle in which the explosives are transported with the following documents:

(1) A copy of the rules in this part;

(2) [Reserved]

(3) A document containing instructions on procedures to be followed in the event of accident or delay. The documents must include the names and telephone numbers of persons (including representatives of carriers or shippers) to be contacted, the nature of the explosives being transported, and the precautions to be taken in emergencies such as fires, accidents, or leakages.

(b) A driver who receives documents in accordance with paragraph (a) of this section must sign a receipt for them. The motor carrier shall maintain the receipt for a period of one year from the date of signature.

(c) A driver of a motor vehicle which contains Division 1.1, 1.2, or 1.3 materials must be in possession of, be familiar with, and be in compliance with

(1) The documents specified in paragraph (a) of this section;

(2) The documents specified in §177.817 of this title; and

(3) The written route plan specified in §397.67.

Subpart B—[Reserved]

Subpart C—Routing of Non-Radioactive Hazardous Materials

§397.61 Purpose and scope.

This subpart contains routing requirements and procedures that States and Indian tribes are required to follow if they establish, maintain, or enforce routing designations over which a non-radioactive hazardous material (NRHM) in a quantity which requires placarding may or may not be transported by a motor vehicle. It also provides regulations for motor carriers transporting placarded or marked NRHM and procedures for dispute resolutions regarding NRHM routing designations.

§397.63 Applicability.

The provisions of this subpart apply to any State or Indian tribe that establishes, maintains, or enforces any routing designations over which NRHM may or may not be transported by motor vehicle. They also apply to any motor carrier that transports or causes to be transported placarded or marked NRHM in commerce.

§397.65 Definitions.

For purposes of this subpart, the following definitions apply:

Administrator. The Federal Motor Carrier Safety Administrator, who is the chief executive of the Federal Motor Carrier Safety Administration, an agency within the United States Department of Transportation, or his/her designate.

Commerce. Any trade, traffic, or transportation in the United States which:

(1) is between a place under the jurisdiction of a State or Indian tribe and any place outside of such jurisdiction; or

(2) is solely within a place under the jurisdiction of a State or Indian tribe but which affects trade, traffic, or transportation described in subparagraph (a).

FMCSA. The Federal Motor Carrier Safety Administration, an agency within the Department of Transportation.

Hazardous material. A substance or material, including a hazardous substance, which has been determined by the Secretary of Transportation to be capable of posing an unreasonable risk to health, safety, or property when transported in commerce, and which has been so designated.

Indian tribe. Has the same meaning as contained in section 4 of the Indian Self-Determination and Education Act, 25 U.S.C. 450b.

Motor carrier. A for-hire motor carrier or a private motor carrier of property. The term includes a motor carrier's agents, officers and representatives as well as employees responsible for hiring, supervising, training, assigning, or dispatching of drivers.

Motor vehicle. Any vehicle, machine, tractor, trailer, or semitrailer propelled or drawn by mechanical power and used upon the highways in the transportation of passengers or property, or any combination thereof.

NRHM. A non-radioactive hazardous material transported by motor vehicle in types and quantities which require placarding, pursuant to Table 1 or 2 of 49 CFR 172.504.

Political subdivision. A municipality, public agency or other instrumentality of one or more States, or a public corporation, board, or commission established under the laws of one or more States.

Radioactive material. As defined in 49 CFR 173.403, radioactive material means any material containing radionuclides where both the activity concentration and the total activity in the consignment exceed the values of the table in 49 CFR 173.436 or values derived according to the instructions in 49 CFR 173.433.

Routing agency. The State highway agency or other State agency designated by the Governor of that State, or an agency designated by an Indian tribe, to supervise, coordinate, and approve the NRHM routing designations for that State or Indian tribe.

Routing designations. Any regulation, limitation, restriction, curfew, time of travel restriction, lane restriction, routing ban, port-of-entry designation, or route weight restriction, applicable to the highway transportation of NRHM over a specific highway route or portion of a route.

Secretary. The Secretary of Transportation.

State. A State of the United States, the District of Columbia, the Commonwealth of Puerto Rico, the Commonwealth of the Northern Mariana Islands, the Virgin Islands, American Samoa or Guam.

§397.67 Motor carrier responsibility for routing.

(a) A motor carrier transporting NRHM shall comply with NRHM routing designations of a State or Indian tribe pursuant to this subpart.

(b) A motor carrier carrying hazardous materials required to be placarded or marked in accordance with 49 CFR 177.823 and not subject to NRHM routing designations pursuant to this subpart, shall operate the vehicle over routes which do not go through or near heavily populated areas, places where crowds are assembled, tunnels, narrow streets, or alleys, except where the motor carrier determines that:

(1) There is no practicable alternative;

(2) A reasonable deviation is necessary to reach terminals, points of loading and unloading, facilities for food, fuel, repairs, rest, or a safe haven; or

(3) A reasonable deviation is required by emergency conditions, such as a detour that has been established by a highway authority, or a situation exists where a law enforcement official requires the driver to take an alternative route.

(c) Operating convenience is not a basis for determining whether it is practicable to operate a motor vehicle in accordance with paragraph (b) of this section.

(d) Before a motor carrier requires or permits a motor vehicle containing explosives in Class 1, Divisions 1.1, 1.2, or 1.3, as defined in 49 CFR 173.50 and 173.53 respectively, to be operated, the carrier or its agent shall prepare a written route plan that complies with this section and shall furnish a copy to the driver. However, the driver may prepare the written plan as agent for the motor carrier when the trip begins at a location other than the carrier's terminal.

§397.69 Highway routing designations; preemption.

(a) Any State or Indian tribe that establishes or modifies a highway routing designation over which NRHM may or may not be transported on or after November 14, 1994, and maintains or enforces such designation, shall comply with the highway routing standards set forth in §397.71 of this subpart. For purposes of this subpart, any highway routing designation affecting the highway transportation of NRHM, made by a political subdivision of a State is considered as one made by that State, and all requirements of this subpart apply.

(b) Except as provided in §§397.75 and 397.219, an NRHM route designation made in violation of paragraph (a) of this section is preempted pursuant to 49 U.S.C. 5125(c).

(c) A highway routing designation established by a State, political subdivision, or Indian tribe before November 14, 1994 is subject to preemption in accordance with the preemption standards in paragraphs (a)(1) and (a)(2) of §397.203.

(d) A State, political subdivision, or Indian tribe may petition for a waiver of preemption in accordance with §397.213 of this part.

§397.71 Federal standards.

(a) A State or Indian tribe shall comply with the Federal standards under paragraph (b) of this section when establishing, maintaining or enforcing specific NRHM routing designations over which NRHM may or may not be transported.

(b) The Federal standards are as follows:

(1) **Enhancement of public safety**. The State or Indian tribe shall make a finding, supported by the record to be developed in accordance with paragraphs (b)(2)(ii) and (b)(3)(iv) of this section, that any NRHM routing designation enhances public safety in the areas subject to its jurisdiction and in other areas which are directly affected by such highway routing designation. In making such a finding, the State or Indian tribe shall consider:

(i) The factors listed in paragraph (b)(9) of this section; and

(ii) The DOT "Guidelines for Applying Criteria to Designate Routes for Transporting Hazardous Materials," DOT/RSPA/OHMT-89-02, July 1989 [1] or its most current version; or an equivalent routing analysis which adequately considers overall risk to the public.

(2) **Public participation**. Prior to the establishment of any NRHM routing designation, the State or Indian tribe shall undertake the following actions to ensure participation by the public in the routing process:

(i) The State or Indian tribe shall provide the public with notice of any proposed NRHM routing designation and a 30-day period in which to comment. At any time during this period or following review of the comments received, the State or Indian tribe shall decide whether to hold a public hearing on the proposed NRHM route designation. The public shall be given 30 days prior notice of the public hearing which shall be conducted as described in paragraph (b)(2)(ii) of this section. Notice for both the comment period and the public hearing, if one is held, shall be given by publication in at least two newspapers of general circulation in the affected area or areas and shall contain a complete description of the proposed routing designation, together with the date, time, and location of any public hearings. Notice for both the comment period and any public hearing may also be published in the official register of the State.

(ii) If it is determined that a public hearing is necessary, the State or Indian tribe shall hold at least one public hearing on the record during which the public will be afforded the opportunity to present its views and any information or data related to the proposed NRHM routing designation. The State shall make available to the public, upon payment of prescribed costs, copies of the transcript of the hearing, which shall include all exhibits and documents presented during the hearing or submitted for the record.

[1] This document may be obtained from Federal Motor Carrier Safety Administration, Office of Enforcement and Compliance (MC-EC), 1200 New Jersey Ave., SE., Washington, DC 20590-0001.

(3) **Consultation with others**. Prior to the establishment of any NRHM routing designation, the State or Indian tribe shall provide notice to, and consult with, officials of affected political subdivisions, States and Indian tribes, and any other affected parties. Such actions shall include the following:

(i) At least 60 days prior to establishing a routing designation, the State or Indian tribe shall provide notice, in writing, of the proposed routing designation to officials responsible for highway routing in all other affected States or Indian tribes. A copy of this notice may also be sent to all affected political subdivisions. This notice shall request approval, in writing, by those States or Indian tribes, of the proposed routing designations. If no response is received within 60 days from the day of receipt of the notification of the proposed routing designation, the routing designation shall be considered approved by the affected State or Indian tribe.

(ii) The manner in which consultation under this paragraph is conducted is left to the discretion of the State or Indian tribe.

(iii) The State or Indian tribe shall attempt to resolve any concern or disagreement expressed by any consulted official related to the proposed routing designation.

(iv) The State or Indian tribe shall keep a record of the names and addresses of the officials notified pursuant to this section and of any consultation or meeting conducted with these officials or their representatives. Such record shall describe any concern or disagreement expressed by the officials and any action undertaken to resolve such disagreement or address any concern.

(4) **Through routing**. In establishing any NRHM routing designation, the State or Indian tribe shall ensure through highway routing for the transportation of NRHM between adjacent areas. The term "through highway routing" as used in this paragraph means that the routing designation must ensure continuity of movement so as to not impede or unnecessarily delay the transportation of NRHM. The State or Indian tribe shall utilize the procedures established in paragraphs (b)(2) and (b)(3) of this section in meeting these requirements. In addition, the State or Indian tribe shall make a finding, supported by a risk analysis conducted in accordance with paragraph (b)(1) of this section, that the routing designation enhances public safety. If the risk analysis shows—

(i) That the current routing presents at least 50 percent more risk to the public than the deviation under the proposed routing designation, then the proposed routing designation may go into effect.

(ii) That the current routing presents a greater risk but less than 50 percent more risk to the public than the deviation under the proposed routing restriction, then the proposed routing restriction made by a State or Indian tribe shall only go into effect if it does not force a deviation of more than 25 miles or result in an increase of more than 25 percent of that part of a trip affected by the deviation, whichever is shorter, from the most direct route through a jurisdiction as compared to the intended deviation.

(iii) That the current route has the same or less risk to the public than the deviation resulting from the proposed routing designation, then the routing designation shall not be allowed.

(5) **Agreement of other States; burden on commerce**. Any NRHM routing designation which affects another State or Indian tribe shall be established, maintained, or enforced only if:

(i) It does not unreasonably burden commerce, and

(ii) It is agreed to by the affected State or Indian tribe within 60 days of receipt of the notice sent pursuant to paragraph (b)(3)(i) of this section, or it is approved by the Administrator pursuant to §397.75.

(6) **Timeliness**. The establishment of an NRHM routing designation by any State or Indian tribe shall be completed within 18 months of the notice given in either paragraph (b)(2) or (b)(3) of this section, whichever occurs first.

(7) **Reasonable routes to terminals and other facilities**. In establishing or providing for reasonable access to and from designated routes, the State or Indian tribe shall use the shortest practicable route considering the factors listed in paragraph (b)(9) of this section. In establishing any NRHM routing designation, the State or Indian tribe shall provide reasonable access for motor vehicles transporting NRHM to reach:

(i) Terminals,

(ii) Points of loading, unloading, pickup and delivery, and

(iii) Facilities for food, fuel, repairs, rest, and safe havens.

(8) **Responsibility for local compliance**. The States shall be responsible for ensuring that all of their political subdivisions comply with the provisions of this subpart. The States shall be responsible for resolving all disputes between such political subdivisions within their jurisdictions. If a State or any political subdivision thereof, or an Indian tribe chooses to establish, maintain, or enforce any NRHM routing designation, the Governor, or Indian tribe, shall designate a routing agency for the State or Indian tribe, respectively. The routing agency shall ensure that all NRHM routing designations within its jurisdiction comply with the Federal standards in this section. The State or Indian tribe shall comply with the public information and reporting requirements contained in §397.73.

(9) **Factors to consider**. In establishing any NRHM routing designation, the State or Indian tribe shall consider the following factors:

(i) **Population density**. The population potentially exposed to an NRHM release shall be estimated from the density of the residents, employees, motorists, and other persons in the area, using United States census tract maps or other reasonable means for determining the population within a potential impact zone along a designated highway route. The impact zone is the potential range of effects in the event of a release. Special populations such as schools, hospitals, prisons, and senior citizen homes shall, among other things, be considered when determining the potential risk to the populations along a highway routing. Consideration shall be given to the amount of time during which an area will experience a heavy population density.

(ii) **Type of highway**. The characteristics of each alternative NRHM highway routing designation shall be compared. Vehicle weight and size limits, underpass and bridge clearances, roadway geometrics, number of lanes, degree of access control, and median and shoulder structures are examples of characteristics which a State or Indian tribe shall consider.

(iii) **Types and quantities of NRHM**. An examination shall be made of the type and quantity of NRHM normally transported along highway routes which are included in a proposed NRHM routing designation, and consideration shall be given to the relative impact zone and risks of each type and quantity.

(iv) **Emergency response capabilities**. In consultation with the proper fire, law enforcement, and highway safety agencies, consideration shall be given to the emergency response capabilities which may be needed as a result of an NRHM routing designation. The analysis of the emergency response capabilities shall be based upon the proximity of the emergency response facilities and their capabilities to contain and suppress NRHM releases within the impact zones.

(v) **Results of consultation with affected persons**. Consideration shall be given to the comments and concerns of all affected persons and entities provided during public hearings and consultations conducted in accordance with this section.

(vi) **Exposure and other risk factors**. States and Indian tribes shall define the exposure and risk factors associated with any NRHM routing designations. The distance to sensitive areas shall be considered. Sensitive areas include, but are not limited to, homes and commercial buildings; special populations in hospitals, schools, handicapped facilities, prisons and stadiums; water sources such as streams and lakes; and natural areas such as parks, wetlands, and wildlife reserves.

(vii) **Terrain considerations**. Topography along and adjacent to the proposed NRHM routing designation that may affect the potential severity of an accident, the dispersion of the NRHM upon release and the control and clean up of NRHM if released shall be considered.

(viii) **Continuity of routes**. Adjacent jurisdictions shall be consulted to ensure routing continuity for NRHM across common borders. Deviations from the most direct route shall be minimized.

(ix) **Alternative routes**. Consideration shall be given to the alternative routes to, or resulting from, any NRHM route designation. Alternative routes shall be examined, reviewed, or evaluated to the extent necessary to demonstrate that the most probable alternative routing resulting from a routing designation is safer than the current routing.

(x) **Effects on commerce**. Any NRHM routing designation made in accordance with this subpart shall not create an unreasonable burden upon interstate or intrastate commerce.

(xi) **Delays in transportation**. No NRHM routing designations may create unnecessary delays in the transportation of NRHM.

(xii) **Climatic conditions**. Weather conditions unique to a highway route such as snow, wind, ice, fog, or other climatic conditions that could affect the safety of a route, the dispersion of the NRHM upon release, or increase the difficulty of controlling it and cleaning it up shall be given appropriate consideration.

(xiii) **Congestion and accident history**. Traffic conditions unique to a highway routing such as: traffic congestion; accident experience with motor vehicles, traffic considerations that could affect the potential for an accident, exposure of the public to any release, ability to perform emergency response operations, or the temporary closing of a highway for cleaning up any release shall be given appropriate consideration.

§397.73 Public information and reporting requirements.

(a) **Public information**. Information on NRHM routing designations must be made available by the States and Indian tribes to the public in the form of maps, lists, road signs or some combination thereof. If road signs are used, those signs and their placements must comply with the provisions of the

Manual on Uniform Traffic Control Devices for Streets and Highways, published by the Federal Highway Administration (FHWA), particularly the Hazardous Cargo signs identified as R14-2 and R14-3 shown in Section 2B-62 of that Manual. This publication may be accessed free of charge on the Internet at *http://mutcd.fhwa.dot.gov/*.

(b) **Reporting and publishing requirements**. (1) Each State or Indian tribe, through its routing agency, shall provide information identifying all NRHM routing designations that exist within its jurisdiction:

(i) Electronically, by email to *HMRouting@dot.gov*; or

(ii) By mail to the Federal Motor Carrier Safety Administration, Office of Enforcement and Compliance (MC-EC), 1200 New Jersey Ave. SE, Washington, DC 20590-0001.

(2) States and Indian tribes shall also submit to FMCSA the current name of the State or Indian tribal agency responsible for NHRM highway routing designations. The State or Indian tribe shall include descriptions of these routing designations, along with the dates they were established. Information on any subsequent changes or new NRHM routing designations shall be furnished within 60 days after establishment to the FMCSA.

(3)(i) FMCSA will consolidate information on the NRHM routing designations, make it available on its website, *https://www.fmcsa.dot.gov/regulations/hazardous-materials/national-hazardous-materials-route-registry,* and publish it annually in whole or as updates in the *Federal Register*.

(ii) Each State or Indian tribe may also publish this information in its official register of State or tribal regulations.

(c) A State or Tribally-designated route is effective only after it is published in the National Hazardous Materials Route Registry on FMCSA's website at *https://www.fmcsa.dot.gov/regulations/hazardous-materials/national-hazardous-materials-route-registry.*

§397.75 Dispute resolution.

(a) **Petition**. One or more States or Indian tribes may petition the Administrator to resolve a dispute relating to an agreement on a proposed NRHM routing designation. In resolving a dispute under these provisions, the Administrator will provide the greatest level of safety possible without unreasonably burdening commerce, and ensure compliance with the Federal standards established at §397.71 of this subpart.

(b) **Filing**. Each petition for dispute resolution filed under this section must:

(1) Be submitted to the Administrator, Federal Motor Carrier Safety Administration, 1200 New Jersey Ave., SE., Washington, DC 20590-0001. Attention: Office of the Chief Counsel (MC-CC).

(2) Identify the State or Indian tribe filing the petition and any other State, political subdivision, or Indian tribe whose NRHM routing designation is the subject of the dispute.

(3) Contain a certification that the petitioner has complied with the notification requirements of paragraph (c) of this section, and include a list of the names and addresses of each State, political subdivision, or Indian tribe official who was notified of the filing of the petition.

(4) Clearly set forth the dispute for which resolution is sought, including a complete description of any disputed NRHM routing designation and an explanation of how the disputed routing designation affects the petitioner or how it

impedes through highway routing. If the routing designation being disputed results in alternative routing, then a comparative risk analysis for the designated route and the resulting alternative routing shall be provided.

(5) Describe any actions taken by the State or Indian tribe to resolve the dispute.

(6) Explain the reasons why the petitioner believes that the Administrator should intervene in resolving the dispute.

(7) Describe any proposed actions that the Administrator should take to resolve the dispute and how these actions would provide the greatest level of highway safety without unreasonably burdening commerce and would ensure compliance with the Federal standards established in this subpart.

(c) **Notice**. (1) Any State or Indian tribe that files a petition for dispute resolution under this subpart shall mail a copy of the petition to any affected State, political subdivision, or Indian tribe, accompanied by a statement that the State, political subdivision, or Indian tribe may submit comments regarding the petition to the Administrator within 45 days.

(2) By serving notice on any other State, political subdivision, or Indian tribe determined by the Administrator to be possibly affected by the issues in dispute or the resolution sought, or by publication in the *Federal Register*, the Administrator may afford those persons an opportunity to file written comments on the petition.

(3) Any affected State, political subdivision, or Indian tribe submitting written comments to the Administrator with respect to a petition filed under this section shall send a copy of the comments to the petitioner and certify to the Administrator as to having complied with this requirement. The Administrator may notify other persons participating in the proceeding of the comments and provide an opportunity for those other persons to respond.

(d) **Court actions**. After a petition for dispute resolution is filed in accordance with this section, no court action may be brought with respect to the subject matter of such dispute until a final decision has been issued by the Administrator or until the last day of the one-year period beginning on the day the Administrator receives the petition, whichever occurs first.

(e) **Hearings; alternative dispute resolution**. Upon receipt of a petition filed pursuant to paragraph (a) of this section, the Administrator may schedule a hearing to attempt to resolve the dispute and, if a hearing is scheduled, will notify all parties to the dispute of the date, time, and place of the hearing. During the hearing the parties may offer any information pertinent to the resolution of the dispute. If an agreement is reached, it may be stipulated by the parties, in writing, and, if the Administrator agrees, made part of the decision in paragraph (f) of this section. If no agreement is reached, the Administrator may take the matter under consideration and announce his or her decision in accordance with paragraph (f) of this section. Nothing in this section shall be construed as prohibiting the parties from settling the dispute or seeking other methods of alternative dispute resolution prior to the final decision by the Administrator.

(f) **Decision**. The Administrator will issue a decision based on the petition, the written comments submitted by the parties, the record of the hearing, and any other information in the record. The decision will include a written statement setting forth the relevant facts and the legal basis for the decision.

(g) **Record**. The Administrator will serve a copy of the decision upon the petitioner and any other party who participated in the proceedings. A copy of each decision will be placed on file in the public docket. The Administrator may publish the decision or notice of the decision in the *Federal Register*.

§397.77 Judicial review of dispute decision.

Any State or Indian tribe adversely affected by the Administrator's decision under §397.75 of this subpart may seek review by the appropriate district court of the United States under such proceeding only by filing a petition with such court within 90 days after such decision becomes final.

Subpart D—Routing of Class 7 (Radioactive) Materials

§397.101 Requirements for motor carriers and drivers.

(a) Except as provided in paragraph (b) of this section or in circumstances when there is only one practicable highway route available, considering operating necessity and safety, a carrier or any person operating a motor vehicle that contains a Class 7 (radioactive) material, as defined in 49 CFR 172.403, for which placarding is required under 49 CFR part 172 shall:

(1) Ensure that the motor vehicle is operated on routes that minimize radiological risk;

(2) Consider available information on accident rates, transit time, population density and activities, and the time of day and the day of week during which transportation will occur to determine the level of radiological risk; and

(3) Tell the driver which route to take and that the motor vehicle contains Class 7 (radioactive) materials.

(b) Except as otherwise permitted in this paragraph and in paragraph (f) of this section, a carrier or any person operating a motor vehicle containing a highway route controlled quantity of Class 7 (radioactive) materials, as defined in 49 CFR 173.403, shall operate the motor vehicle only over preferred routes.

(1) For purposes of this subpart, a preferred route is an Interstate System highway for which an alternative route is not designated by a State routing agency; a State-designated route selected by a State routing agency pursuant to §397.103; or both of the above.

(2) The motor carrier or the person operating a motor vehicle containing a highway route controlled quantity of Class 7 (radioactive) materials, as defined in 49 CFR 173.403, shall select routes to reduce time in transit over the preferred route segment of the trip. An Interstate System bypass or Interstate System beltway around a city, when available, shall be used in place of a preferred route through a city, unless a State routing agency has designated an alternative route.

(c) A motor vehicle may be operated over a route, other than a preferred route, only under the following conditions:

(1) The deviation from the preferred route is necessary to pick up or deliver a highway route controlled quantity of Class 7 (radioactive) materials, to make necessary rest, fuel or motor vehicle repair stops, or because emergency conditions make continued use of the preferred route unsafe or impossible;

(2) For pickup and delivery not over preferred routes, the route selected must be the shortest-distance route from the pickup location to the nearest preferred route entry location, and the shortest-distance route to the delivery location from the nearest preferred route exit location. Deviation from the shortest-distance pickup or delivery route is authorized if such deviation:

(i) Is based upon the criteria in paragraph (a) of this section to minimize the radiological risk; and

(ii) Does not exceed the shortest-distance pickup or delivery route by more than 25 miles and does not exceed 5 times the length of the shortest-distance pickup or delivery route.

(iii) Deviations from preferred routes, or pickup or delivery routes other than preferred routes, which are necessary for rest, fuel, or motor vehicle repair stops or because of emergency conditions, shall be made in accordance with the criteria in paragraph (a) of this section to minimize radiological risk, unless due to emergency conditions, time does not permit use of those criteria.

(d) A carrier (or a designated agent) who operates a motor vehicle which contains a package of highway route controlled quantity of Class 7 (radioactive) materials, as defined in 49 CFR 173.403, shall prepare a written route plan and supply a copy before departure to the motor vehicle driver and a copy to the shipper (before departure for exclusive use shipments, as defined in 49 CFR 173.403, or within fifteen working days following departure for all other shipments). Any variation between the route plan and routes actually used, and the reason for it, shall be reported in an amendment to the route plan delivered to the shipper as soon as practicable but within 30 days following the deviation. The route plan shall contain:

(1) A statement of the origin and destination points, a route selected in compliance with this section, all planned stops, and estimated departure and arrival times; and

(2) Telephone numbers which will access emergency assistance in each State to be entered.

(e) No person may transport a package of highway route controlled quantity of Class 7 (radioactive) materials on a public highway unless:

(1) The driver has received within the two preceding years, written training on:

(i) Requirements in 49 CFR parts 172, 173, and 177 pertaining to the Class 7 (radioactive) materials transported;

(ii) The properties and hazards of the Class 7 (radioactive) materials being transported; and

(iii) Procedures to be followed in case of an accident or other emergency.

(2) The driver has in his or her immediate possession a certificate of training as evidence of training required by this section, and a copy is placed in his or her qualification file (see §391.51 of this subchapter), showing:

(i) The driver's name and operator's license number;

(ii) The dates training was provided;

(iii) The name and address of the person providing the training;

(iv) That the driver has been trained in the hazards and characteristics of highway route controlled quantity of Class 7 (radioactive) materials; and

(v) A statement by the person providing the training that information on the certificate is accurate.

(3) The driver has in his or her immediate possession the route plan required by paragraph (d) of this section and operates the motor vehicle in accordance with the route plan.

(f) A person may transport irradiated reactor fuel only in compliance with a plan if required under 49 CFR 173.22(c) that will ensure the physical security of the material. Variation for security purposes from the requirements of this section is permitted so far as necessary to meet the requirements imposed under such a plan, or otherwise imposed by the U.S. Nuclear Regulatory Commission in 10 CFR part 73.

§397.103 Requirements for State routing designations.

(a) The State routing agency, as defined in §397.201(c), shall select routes to minimize radiological risk using "Guidelines for Selecting Preferred Highway Routes for Highway Route Controlled Quantity Shipments of Radioactive Materials," or an equivalent routing analysis which adequately considers overall risk to the public. Designations must be preceded by substantive consultation with affected local jurisdictions and with any other affected States to ensure consideration of all impacts and continuity of designated routes.

(b) State routing agencies may designate preferred routes as an alternative to, or in addition to, one or more Interstate System highways, including interstate system bypasses, or Interstate System beltways.

(c) A State-designated route is effective when—

(1) The State gives written notice to the Federal Motor Carrier Safety Administration:

(i) By email to *HMRouting@dot.gov;* or

(ii) By certified mail, return receipt requested, to the Federal Motor Carrier Safety Administration, Office of Enforcement and Compliance (MC-EC), 1200 New Jersey Ave., SE., Washington, DC 20590-0001. Attention: National Hazardous Materials Route Registry.

(2) Receipt thereof is acknowledged in writing by the FMCSA.

(3) The route is published in the National Hazardous Materials Route Registry on FMCSA's website at *https://www.fmcsa.dot.gov/regulations/hazardous-materials/national-hazardous-materials-route-registry*.

(d) A list of State-designated preferred routes and a copy of the "Guidelines for Selecting Preferred Highway Routes for Highway Route Controlled Quantity Shipments of Radioactive Materials" are available upon request to Federal Motor Carrier Safety Administration, Office of Enforcement and Compliance (MC-EC), 1200 New Jersey Ave. SE, Washington, DC 20590-0001, or by email to *HMRouting@dot.gov*.

Subpart E—Preemption Procedures

§397.201 Purpose and scope of the procedures.

(a) This subpart prescribes procedures by which:

(1) Any person, including a State, political subdivision thereof, or Indian tribe, directly affected by any highway routing designation for hazardous materials may apply to the Administrator for a determination as to whether that highway routing designation is preempted under 49 U.S.C. §5125, or §397.69 or §397.203 of this part; and

(2) A State, political subdivision thereof, or Indian tribe may apply to the Administrator for a waiver of preemption with respect to any highway routing designation that the State, political subdivision thereof, or Indian tribe acknowledges to be preempted by 49 U.S.C. §5125, or §397.69 or §397.203 of this part, or that has been determined by a court of competent jurisdiction to be so preempted.

(b) Unless otherwise ordered by the Administrator, an application for a preemption determination which includes an application for a waiver of preemption will be treated and processed solely as an application for a preemption determination.

(c) For purposes of this subpart:

Act means 49 U.S.C. §5101 *et seq.*, formerly known as the Hazardous Materials Transportation Act.

Administrator means the Federal Motor Carrier Safety Administrator, who is the chief executive of the Federal Motor Carrier Safety Administration, an agency of the United States Department of Transportation, or his/her designate.

Hazardous material means a substance or material, including a hazardous substance, which has been determined by the Secretary of Transportation to be capable of posing an unreasonable risk to health, safety, or property, when transported in commerce, and which has been so designated.

Indian tribe has the same meaning as contained in §4 of the Indian Self-Determination and Education Act, 25 U.S.C. 450b.

Person means an individual, firm, copartnership, corporation, company, association, joint-stock association, including any trustee, receiver, assignee, or similar representative thereof, or government, Indian tribe, or agency or instrumentality of any government or Indian tribe when it offers hazardous materials for transportation in commerce or transports hazardous materials in furtherance of a commercial enterprise, but such term does not include the United States Postal Service.

Political subdivision includes a municipality; a public agency or other instrumentality of one or more States, or a public corporation, board, or commission established under the laws of one or more States.

Routing agency means the State highway agency or other State agency designated by the Governor of a State, or an agency designated by an Indian tribe, to supervise, coordinate, and approve the highway routing designations for that State or Indian tribe. Any highway routing designation made by a political subdivision of a State shall be considered a designation made by that State.

Routing designation includes any regulation, limitation, restriction, curfew, time of travel restriction, lane restriction, routing ban, port-of-entry designation, or route weight restriction applicable to the highway transportation of hazardous materials over a specific highway route or portion of a route.

State means a State of the United States, the District of Columbia, the Commonwealth of Puerto Rico, the Commonwealth of the Northern Mariana Islands, the Virgin Islands, American Samoa, Guam, or any other territory of possession of the United States designated by the Secretary.

§397.203 Standards for determining preemption.

(a) Any highway routing designation established, maintained, or enforced by a State, political subdivision thereof, or Indian tribe is preempted if—

(1) Compliance with both the highway routing designation and any requirement under the Act or of a regulation issued under the Act is not possible;

(2) The highway routing designation as applied or enforced creates an obstacle to the accomplishment and execution of the Act or the regulations issued under the Act; or

(3) The highway routing designation is preempted pursuant to §397.69(b) of this part.

(b) [Reserved]

§397.205 Preemption application.

(a) Any person, including a State, political subdivision thereof, or Indian tribe directly affected by any highway routing designation of another State, political subdivision, or Indian tribe, may apply to the Administrator for a determination of whether that highway routing designation is preempted by the Act or §397.203 of this subpart. The Administrator shall publish notice of the application in the *Federal Register*.

(b) Each application filed under this section for a determination must:

(1) Be submitted to the Administrator, Federal Motor Carrier Safety Administration, 1200 New Jersey Ave., SE., Washington, DC 20590-0001. Attention: Office of the Chief Counsel, Enforcement and Litigation Division (MC-CCE).

(2) Set forth a detailed description of the highway routing designation of the State, political subdivision thereof, or Indian tribe for which the determination is sought;

(3) If applicable, specify the provisions of the Act or the regulations issued under the Act under which the applicant seeks preemption of the highway routing designation of the State, political subdivision thereof, or Indian tribe;

(4) Explain why the applicant believes the highway routing designation of the State, political subdivision thereof, or Indian tribe should or should not be preempted under the standards of §397.203; and

(5) State how the applicant is affected by the highway routing designation of the State, political subdivision thereof, or Indian tribe.

(c) The filing of an application for a determination under this section does not constitute grounds for noncompliance with any requirement of the Act or any regulation issued under the Act.

(d) Once the Administrator has published notice in the *Federal Register* of an application received under paragraph (a) of this section, no applicant for such determination may seek relief with respect to the same or substantially the same issue in any court until final action has been taken on the application or until 180 days after filing of the application, whichever occurs first. Nothing in this section shall be construed as prohibiting any person, including a State, political subdivision thereof, or Indian tribe, directly affected by any highway routing designation from seeking a determination of preemption in any court of competent jurisdiction in lieu of applying to the Administrator under paragraph (a) of this section.

§397.207 Preemption notice.

(a) If the applicant is other than a State, political subdivision thereof, or Indian tribe, the applicant shall mail a copy of the application to the State, political subdivision thereof, or Indian tribe concerned, accompanied by a statement that comments may be submitted regarding the application to the Administrator within 45 days. The application filed with the Administrator must include a certification that the applicant has complied with this paragraph and must include the names and addresses of each official to whom a copy of the application was sent.

(b) The Administrator may afford interested persons an opportunity to file written comments on the application by serving notice on any persons readily identifiable by the Administrator as persons who will be affected by the ruling sought or by publication in the *Federal Register*.

(c) Each person submitting written comments to the Administrator with respect to an application filed under this section shall send a copy of the comments to the applicant and certify to the Administrator that he or she has complied with this requirement. The Administrator may notify other persons participating in the proceeding of the comments and provide an opportunity for those other persons to respond.

§397.209 Preemption processing.

(a) The Administrator may initiate an investigation of any statement in an application and utilize in his or her evaluation any relevant facts obtained by that investigation. The Administrator may solicit and accept submissions from third persons relevant to an application and will provide the applicant an opportunity to respond to all third person submissions. In evaluating an application, the Administrator may consider any other source of information. The Administrator may convene a hearing or conference, if a hearing or conference will advance the evaluation of the application.

(b) The Administrator may dismiss the application without prejudice if:

(1) He or she determines that there is insufficient information upon which to base a determination; or

(2) He or she requests additional information from the applicant and it is not submitted.

§397.211 Preemption determination.

(a) Upon consideration of the application and other relevant information received, the Administrator issued a determination.

(b) Notwithstanding that an application for a determination has not been filed under §397.205, the Administrator, on his or her own initiative, may issue a determination as to whether a particular highway routing designation of a State, political subdivision thereof, or Indian tribe is preempted under the Act or the regulations issued under the Act.

(c) The determination includes a written statement setting forth the relevant facts and the legal basis for the determination, and provides that any person aggrieved thereby may file a petition for reconsideration within 20 days in accordance with §397.223.

(d) Unless the determination is issued pursuant to paragraph (b) of this section, the Administrator serves a copy of the determination upon the applicant. In all preemption determinations, the Administrator serves a copy of the determination upon any other person who participated in the proceeding or who is readily identifiable by the Administrator as affected by the determination. A copy of each determination is placed on file in the public docket. The Administrator may publish the determination or notice of the determination in the *Federal Register*.

(e) If no petition for reconsideration is filed within 20 days in accordance with §397.223, a determination issued under this section constitutes the final agency decision as to whether a particular highway routing designation of a State, political subdivision thereof, or Indian tribe is preempted under the Act and regulations issued thereunder. The fact that a determination has not been issued under this section with respect to a particular highway routing designation of a State, political subdivision thereof, or Indian tribe carries no implication as to whether the requirement is preempted under the Act or regulations issued thereunder.

§397.213 Waiver of preemption application.

(a) Any State, political subdivision thereof, or Indian tribe may apply to the Administrator for a waiver of preemption with respect to any highway routing designation that the State, political subdivision thereof, or Indian tribe acknowledges to be preempted by the Act, §397.203 of this subpart, or a court of competent jurisdiction. The Administrator may waive preemption with respect to such requirement upon a determination that such requirement—

(1) Affords an equal or greater level of protection to the public than is afforded by the requirements of the Act or regulations issued under the Act, and

(2) Does not unreasonably burden commerce.

(b) Each application filed under this section for a waiver of preemption determination must:

(1) Be submitted to the Administrator, Federal Motor Carrier Safety Administration, 1200 New Jersey Ave., SE., Washington, DC 20590-0001. Attention: Office of the Chief Counsel, Enforcement and Litigation Division (MC-CCE).

(2) Set forth a detailed description of the highway routing designation of the State, political subdivision thereof, or Indian tribe for which the determination is being sought;

(3) Include a copy of any relevant court order or determination issued pursuant to §397.211;

(4) Contain an express acknowledgment by the applicant that the highway routing designation of the State, political subdivision thereof, or Indian tribe is preempted under the Act or the regulations issued under the Act, unless it has been so determined by a court of competent jurisdiction or in a determination issued under this subpart;

(5) Specify each provision of the Act or the regulations issued under the Act that preempts the highway routing designation of the State, political subdivision thereof, or Indian tribe;

(6) State why the applicant believes that the highway routing designation of the State, political subdivision thereof, or Indian tribe affords an equal or greater level of protection to the public than is afforded by the requirements of the Act or the regulations issued under the Act;

(7) State why the applicant believes that the highway routing designation of the State, political subdivision thereof, or Indian tribe does not unreasonably burden commerce; and

(8) Specify what steps the State, political subdivision thereof, or Indian tribe is taking to administer and enforce effectively the preempted requirement.

§397.215 Waiver notice.

(a) The applicant State, political subdivision thereof, or Indian tribe shall mail a copy of the application and any subsequent amendments or other documents relating to the application to each person whom the applicant reasonably ascertains will be affected by the determination sought. The copy of the application must be accompanied by a statement that the person may submit comments regarding the application to the Administrator within 45 days. The application filed with the Administrator must include a certification that the application complies with this paragraph and must include the names and addresses of each person to whom the application was sent.

(b) Notwithstanding the provisions of paragraph (a) of this section, if the State, political subdivision thereof, or Indian tribe determines that compliance with paragraph (a) of this section would be impracticable, the applicant shall:

(1) Comply with the requirements of paragraph (a) of this section with regard to those persons whom it is reasonable and practicable to notify; and

(2) Include with the application filed with the Administrator a description of the persons or class or classes of persons to whom notice was not sent.

(c) The Administrator may require the applicant to provide notice in addition to that required by paragraphs (a) and (b) of this section, or may determine that

PART 397

the notice required by paragraph (a) of this section is not impracticable, or that notice should be published in the *Federal Register*.

(d) The Administrator may serve notice on any other persons readily identifiable by the Administrator as persons who will be affected by the determination sought and may afford those persons an opportunity to file written comments on the application.

(e) Any person submitting written comments to the Administrator with respect to an application filed under this section shall send a copy of the comments to the applicant. The person shall certify to the Administrator that he or she has complied with the requirements of this paragraph. The Administrator may notify other persons participating in the proceeding of the comments and provide an opportunity for those persons to respond.

§397.217 Waiver processing.

(a) The Administrator may initiate an investigation of any statement in an application and utilize any relevant facts obtained by that investigation. The Administrator may solicit and accept submissions from third persons relevant to an application and will provide the applicant an opportunity to respond to all third person submissions. In evaluating an application, the Administrator may convene a hearing or conference, if a hearing or conference will advance the evaluation of the application.

(b) The Administrator may dismiss the application without prejudice if:

(1) He or she determines that there is insufficient information upon which to base a determination;

(2) Upon his or her request, additional information is not submitted by the applicant; or

(3) The applicant fails to provide the notice required by this subpart.

(c) Except as provided in this subpart, the Administrator will only consider an application for a waiver of preemption determination if:

(1) The applicant expressly acknowledges in its application that the highway routing designation of the State, political subdivision thereof, or Indian tribe for which the determination is sought is preempted by the Act or the regulations thereunder; or

(2) The highway routing designation of the State, political subdivision thereof, or Indian tribe has been determined by a court of competent jurisdiction or in a determination issued pursuant to §397.211 to be preempted by the Act or the regulations issued thereunder.

(d) When the Administrator has received all substantive information necessary to process an application for a waiver of preemption determination, notice of that fact will be served upon the applicant. Additional notice to all other persons who received notice of the proceeding may be served by publishing a notice in the *Federal Register*.

§397.219 Waiver determination and order.

(a) Upon consideration of the application and other relevant information received or obtained during the proceeding, the Administrator issued an order setting forth his or her determination.

(b) The Administrator may issue a waiver of preemption order only if he or she finds that the requirement of the State, political subdivision thereof, or Indian tribe affords the public a level of safety at least equal to that afforded by the requirements of the Act and the regulations issued under the Act and does not unreasonably burden commerce. In determining whether the requirement of the State, political subdivision thereof, or Indian tribe unreasonably burdens commerce, the Administrator may consider the following factors:

(1) The extent to which increased costs and impairment of efficiency result from the highway routing designation of the State, political subdivision thereof, or Indian tribe;

(2) Whether the highway routing designation of the State, political subdivision thereof, or Indian tribe has a rational basis;

(3) Whether the highway routing designation of the State, political subdivision thereof, or Indian tribe achieves its stated purpose; and

(4) Whether there is need for uniformity with regard to the subject concerned and if so, whether the highway routing designation of the State, political subdivision thereof, or Indian tribe competes or conflicts with those of other States, political subdivisions thereof, or Indian tribes.

(c) The order includes a written statement setting forth the relevant facts and the legal basis for the determination, and provides that any person aggrieved by the order may file a petition for reconsideration in accordance with §397.223.

(d) The Administrator serves a copy of the order upon the applicant, any other person who participated in the proceeding and upon any other person readily identifiable by the Administrator as one who may be affected by the order. A copy of each order is placed on file in the public docket. The Administrator may publish the order or notice of the order in the *Federal Register*.

(e) If no petition for reconsideration is filed within 20 days in accordance with §397.223, an order issued under this section constitutes the final agency decision regarding whether a particular requirement of a State, political subdivision thereof, or Indian tribe is preempted under the Act or any regulations issued thereunder, or whether preemption is waived.

§397.221 Timeliness.

If the Administrator fails to take action on the application within 90 days of serving the notice required by §397.217(d), the applicant may treat the application as having been denied in all respects.

§397.223 Petition for reconsideration.

(a) Any person aggrieved by an order issued under §397.211 or §397.219 may file a petition for reconsideration with the Administrator. The petition must be filed within 20 days of service of the determination or order issued under the above sections.

(b) The petition must contain a concise statement of the basis for seeking reconsideration, including any specific factual or legal errors, or material information not previously available.

(c) The petitioner shall mail a copy of the petition to each person who participated, either as an applicant or routing, in the waiver of preemption proceeding, accompanied by a statement that the person may submit comments concerning the petition to the Administrator within 20 days. The petition filed with the Administrator must contain a certification that the petitioner has complied with this paragraph and include the names and addresses of all persons to whom a copy of the petition was sent.

(d) The Administrator's decision under this section constitutes the final agency decision. If no petition for reconsideration is filed under this section, then the determination issued under §397.211 or §397.219 becomes the final agency decision at the end of the 20 day period.

§397.225 Judicial review.

A party to a proceeding under §397.205(a), §397.213(a), or §397.223(a) may seek review by the appropriate district court of the United States of the decision of the Administrator under such proceeding only by filing a petition with such court within 60 days after the final agency decision.

PART 399—EMPLOYEE SAFETY AND HEALTH STANDARDS

Subparts A through K [Reserved]
Subpart L—Step, handhold, and deck requirements for commercial motor vehicles

Authority: 49 U.S.C. 31502; and 49 CFR 1.87.

Subparts A—K [Reserved]

Subpart L—Step, Handhold, and Deck Requirements for Commercial Motor Vehicles

§399.201 Purpose and scope.

This subpart prescribes step, handhold, and deck requirements on commercial motor vehicles. These requirements are intended to enhance the safety of motor carrier employees.

§399.203 Applicability.

This subpart applies to all trucks and truck-tractors, having a high profile cab-over-engine (COE) configuration, for entrance, egress and back of cab access, manufactured on and after September 1, 1982.

§399.205 Definitions.

Cab-over-engine (COE) —A truck or truck-tractor having all, or the front portion, of the engine under the cab.

COE - High profile —A COE having the door sill step above the height of the front tires.

Deck plate —A horizontal surface designed to provide a person with stable footing for the performance of work such as the connection and disconnection of air and electrical lines, gaining access to permanently-mounted equipment or machinery or for similar needs.

Door sill step —Any step normally protected from the elements by the cab door when closed.

Effective peripheral grip —Any shaped surface, free of sharp edges, in which a full grasp can be made to secure a handhold by a person.

Fingertip grasp —A handhold surface which provides a person contact restricted to finger segments 1 and/or 2 only; or which limits wrap-around closure of finger segment 1 with the palm of the hand to 90 degrees as shown in Illustration I.

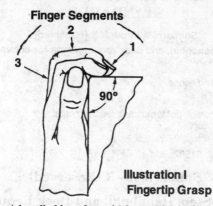

Finger Segments

90°

**Illustration I
Fingertip Grasp**

Full grasp —A handhold surface which provides a person contact with finger segments 2 and 3 and which provides space for finger segment 1 to wrap around toward the palm of the hand beyond the 90-degree surface restriction shown in Illustration I. The handhold need not require contact between fingers and thumb. For example, the hand position shown in Illustration II qualifies as full grasp.

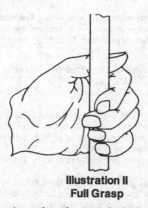

**Illustration II
Full Grasp**

Ground —The flat horizontal surface on which the tires of a motor vehicle rest.

Handhold —That which qualifies as providing full grasp if a person is able to find a hand position on the handhold which allows more than fingertip grasp.

Handprint —The surface area contacted by the hand when grasping a handhold. The size of this area is the width of the hand across the metacarpal and half the circumference of the handhold. The hand breadth of the typical person is 88.9 millimeters (3.5 inches).

Person —Any individual within the 5th percentile female adult through the 95th percentile male adult of anthropometric measures as described by the 1962 Health Examination Survey, "Weight, Height and Selected Body Dimensions of Adults, United States 1960–1962" which is incorporated by reference. It is Public Health Service publication No. 1000-Series 11-No. 8 and is for sale from the U.S. Department of Commerce, National Technical Information Service, 5285 Port Royal Road, Spring-field, Virginia 22161. When ordering use NTIS Accession No. PB 267174. It is also available for inspection at the Office of the Federal Register Library, Room 8301, 1100 L Street, NW, Washington, D.C. 20408. This incorporation by reference was approved by the Director of the Federal Register on July 17, 1979. These materials are incorporated as they exist on the date of the approval and a notice of any change in these materials will be published in the *Federal Register*.

Slip resistant material —Any material designed to minimize the accumulation of grease, ice, mud and other debris and afford protection from accidental slipping.

§399.207 Truck and truck-tractor access requirements.

(a) **General rule**. Any person entering or exiting the cab or accessing the rear portion of a high profile COE truck or truck-tractor shall be afforded sufficient steps and handholds, and/or deck plates to allow the user to have at least 3 limbs in contact with the truck or truck-tractor at any time. This rule applies to intermediate positions as well as transition between intermediate positions. To allow for changes in climbing sequence, the step design shall include, as a minimum, one intermediate step of sufficient size to accommodate two feet. **Exception**. If air and electrical connections necessary to couple or uncouple a truck-tractor from a trailer are accessible from the ground, no step, handholds, or deck plates are required to permit access to the rear of the cab.

(b) **Performance requirements**. All high profile COE trucks or truck-tractors shall be equipped on each side of the vehicle where a seat is located, with a sufficient number of steps and handholds to conform with the requirements of paragraph (a) of this section and shall meet the performance requirements:

(1) **Vertical height**. All measurements of vertical height shall be made from ground level with the vehicle at unladen weight.

(2) **Distance between steps**. The distance between steps, up to and including the door sill step, shall provide any person a stable resting position which can be sustained without body motion and by exerting no more arm force than 35 percent of the person's body weight per grasp during all stages of entry and exit. This criterion applies to intermediate positions as well as transition between intermediate positions above ground level.

(i) When the ground provides the person foot support during entry or is the final step in the sequence during exit, and the step is 508 millimeters (20 inches) or more above ground, the stable resting position shall be achievable by the person using both hands to grasp the handhold(s) and requiring no more arm force than 35 percent of body weight per grasp.

(ii) The vertical height of the first step shall be no more than 609 millimeters (24 inches) from ground level.

(3) **Construction**. Each step or deck plate shall be of a slip resistant design which minimizes the accumulation of foreign material. Wherever practicable, a self-cleaning material should be used.

(4) **Foot accommodation**. Step depth or clearance and step width necessary to accommodate a climbing person are defined by using a minimum 127 millimeter (5 inch) diameter disc as shown in Illustration III.

(i) **Single foot accommodation**. The disc shall fit on a tread rung, or in a step recess, with no exterior overhang.

(ii) **Two-foot accommodations**. Two discs shall fit on a tread rung, or in a step recess, with no exterior overhang.

Single - foot Accommodation

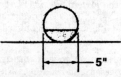

Two - foot Accommodation

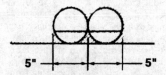

Illustration III
Foot Accommodation

NOTE: The 127 millimeter (5 inch) disc is only intended to test for a minimum depth and width requirement. The step need not retain the disc at rest.

(5) **Step strength**. Each step must withstand a vertical static load of at least 204 kilograms (450 pounds) uniformly distributed over any 127 millimeter (5 inch) increment of step width.

(6) **Handhold location**. A handhold must be located within the reach of any person entering or exiting the vehicle.

(7) **Exterior mounting specifications for handholds**. Each handhold, affixed to the exterior of the vehicle, shall have at least 38 millimeters (1.5 inches) clearance between the handhold and the surface to which it is mounted for the distance between its mounting points.

(8) **Handhold size and shape**. Each handhold shall be free of sharp edges (minimum 1 millimeter [0.04 inch] radius) and have an effective peripheral grip length that permits full grasp by any person.

(9) **Handhold strength**. Each handhold shall withstand a horizontal static load of at least 114 kilograms (250 pounds) uniformly distributed over the area of a hand print and applied away from the mounting surface.

(10) **Deck plates**. Deck plates shall be on the rear of a truck-tractor as necessary to couple or uncouple air and/or electrical connections.

(11) **Deck plate strength**. Each deck plate shall be capable of withstanding the vertical static load of a least 205 kilograms (450 pounds) uniformly distributed over a 127 millimeter (5 inch) diameter disc.

§399.209 Test procedures.

(a) The force exerted on a handhold will be measured using a handheld spring scale or force transducer which can be attached to the vehicle and is free to rotate into alignment with a person's hand position.

(b) Hand grasp will be evaluated by observing the handgrip of any individual who conforms with the definition of "person" appearing in §399.205 of this subpart.

§399.211 Maintenance.

All steps, handholds, and/or deck plates required by this subpart shall be adequately maintained to serve their intended function.

SUBJECT INDEX

This subject index is designed to help you quickly locate information in the Federal Motor Carrier Safety Regulations Pocketbook.

SUBJECT, REGULATION NO.   **PAGE**

A

C

E

F

G

H

I

L

P

Q

R

S

<h2 style="text-align:center">T</h2>

NOTES

NOTES